# THE NATIONAL

# HANDBOOK

for members and visitors

March 2002 to February 2003

The National Trust is a registered charity
and is independent of government

## ❧ THE NATIONAL TRUST

Chairman: Charles Nunneley · Director-General: Fiona Reynolds

For enquiries please write to:
The National Trust, PO Box 39, Bromley, Kent BR1 3XL,
telephone 0870 458 4000 or email **enquiries@thenationaltrust.org.uk**
Registered Charity No. 205846

Information about the National Trust and its work,
including places to visit, can be viewed on the Internet at
**www.nationaltrust.org.uk**

© 2002 The National Trust
ISBN 0 7078 0312 8
Editor: Liz Dittner
Assistant to the Editor: Antonia Harrison
Production: Lorna Simmonds
Managing Editor: Margaret Willes
Designed by Pardoe Blacker Ltd, Lingfield, Surrey (2806)
Maps: ©Maps in Minutes™ 2001.©Crown Copyright, Ordnance Survey & Ordnance Survey Northern Ireland 2001
Permit No. NI 1675 & ©Government of Ireland, Ordnance Survey Ireland.
Print managed by Centurion Press Ltd
Printed by Clays Ltd, Bungay

The quotation from *Beowulf* on page 22 is taken from D. Wright's translation, published by Panther Books, 1957.

Illustrations by: Terry Aldos, Norman Charlton, F. N. Colwell, L. R. Dawson, Brian Delf, Brin Edwards, Claude Page,
David Peacock, Neil Rutherford, Sarah Sole, Eric Thomas, Soun Vannithone, Margaret Wetherbee

*Front cover:* Close-up of the larder at Petworth House (NTPL/Andreas von Einsiedel).
*Inside front cover:* The Plant Shop at Anglesey Abbey (NTPL/David Levenson).
*Title page:* Nymans Garden (NTPL/Stephen Robson).
*This page:* The Vyne (NTPL/Andrea Jones).
*Contents page:* clockwise from above: Lanhydrock (NTPL/Andreas von Einsiedel); Lindisfarne Castle
(NTPL/Joe Cornish); Golden Cap Estate (NTPL/David Noton).
*Back cover:* Sutton Hoo on a winter's morning (NTPL/Joe Cornish).

# Contents

| | |
|---|---|
| Area Maps | 4 |
| Introduction | 4 |
| How to use this Handbook | 25 |
| National Trust Membership | 26 |
| Making the most of your visits | 30 |
| Conservation and Access | 36 |

**Places to visit**

| | |
|---|---|
| South West | 38 |
| South and South East | 113 |
| London | 175 |
| East of England | 186 |
| East Midlands | 216 |
| West Midlands | 237 |
| North West | 263 |
| Yorkshire | 292 |
| North East | 308 |
| Wales | 322 |
| Northern Ireland | 343 |
| | |
| National Trust Books | 360 |
| Holidays with the National Trust | 361 |
| Making contact | 362 |
| About the National Trust | 364 |
| Property index by county | 366 |
| Property index by name | 372 |

4 · INTRODUCTION

## Area Maps

The key opposite shows how England, Wales and Northern Ireland are divided into 11 areas for the purposes of this Handbook and displayed on seven maps. The maps show those properties which have individual entries as well as those which are mentioned briefly in the area introduction. Please note that the map for London is incorporated within that covering the South East.

In order to help with general orientation, the maps show main roads and population centres. However, the plotting of each site serves only as a guide to its location. Please note that some countryside properties, eg. those in the Lake District, cover many thousands of hectares. In such cases the symbol is placed centrally as an indication of general location.

## Your safety

We endeavour to provide a safe and healthy environment for visitors to our properties as far as is reasonably practicable, and to ensure that the work of our staff, volunteers and contractors does not in any way jeopardise the health and safety of visitors. You can help us by observing all notices and signs relating to this subject during your visit, by following any instructions and advice given by Trust staff, by ensuring that children are properly supervised at all times and by wearing appropriate clothing and footwear at countryside properties and in gardens.

At all our properties the responsibility for the safety of visitors should be seen as one that is shared between the Trust and the individual visitor. The Trust takes reasonable measures to minimise risks in ways that are compatible with our conservation objectives – but not necessarily to eliminate all risks. This is especially the case at our coastal and countryside properties. As the landscape becomes more remote, the balance of responsibility between the landowner and the visitor changes. There will be fewer safety measures and warning signs, and visitors will need to rely more on their own skills, knowledge, equipment and preparation. You can help to ensure your own safety by:

- taking note of weather conditions and forecasts and being properly equipped for changes in the weather;
- making sure you are properly prepared, equipped and clothed for the terrain and the activity in which you are participating;
- giving notice of your intended route and estimated time of return;
- making sure you have the necessary skills and fitness for the location and activity, and being aware of your own limitations.

**Car parks:** please note that visitors use car parks at National Trust properties entirely at their own risk, and are advised to secure their cars and not to leave any valuable items in their car during their visit.

INTRODUCTION · 5

**KEY:**

| | | | | |
|---|---|---|---|---|
| Map 1 | South West | Map 4 | West Midlands |
| Map 2 | South and South East | Map 5 | Yorkshire |
| | London | | North West |
| Map 3 | East of England | Map 6 | North West |
| | East Midlands | | North East |
| Map 4 | Wales | Map 7 | Northern Ireland |

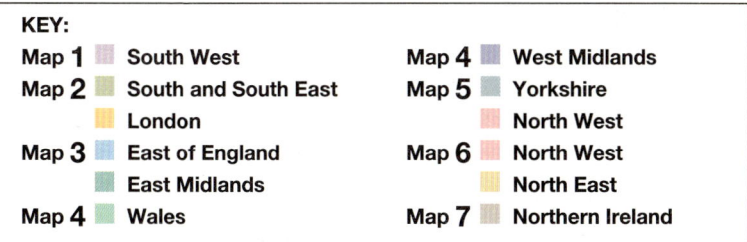

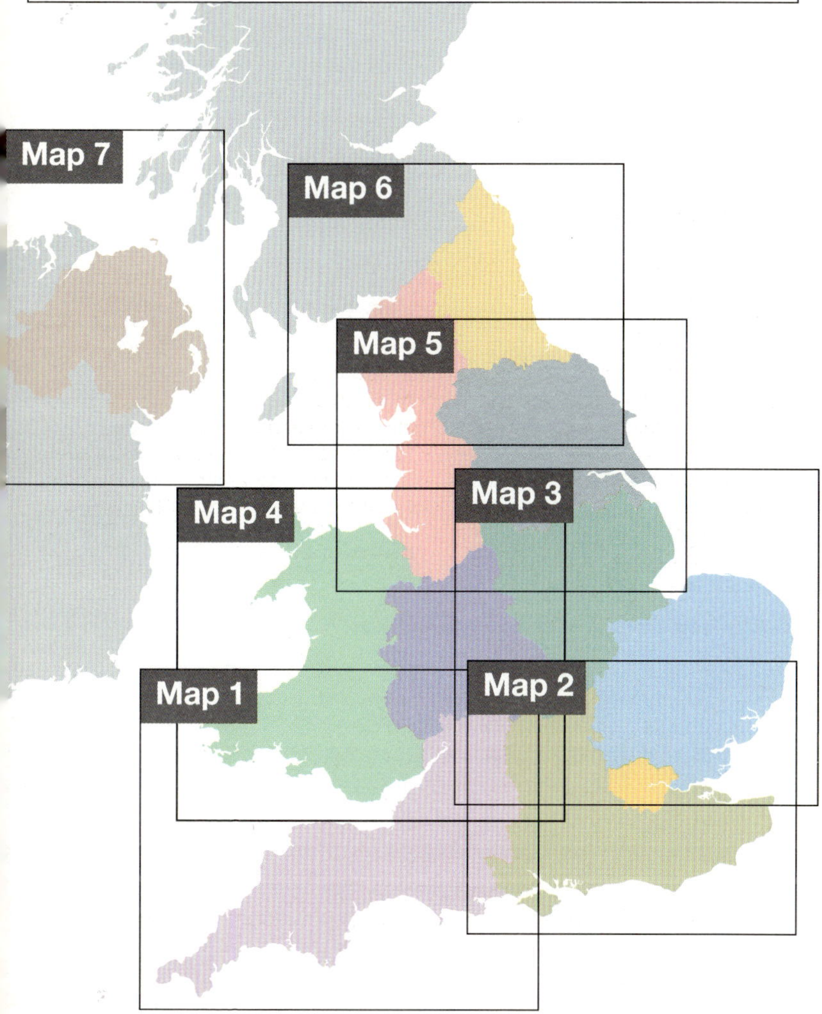

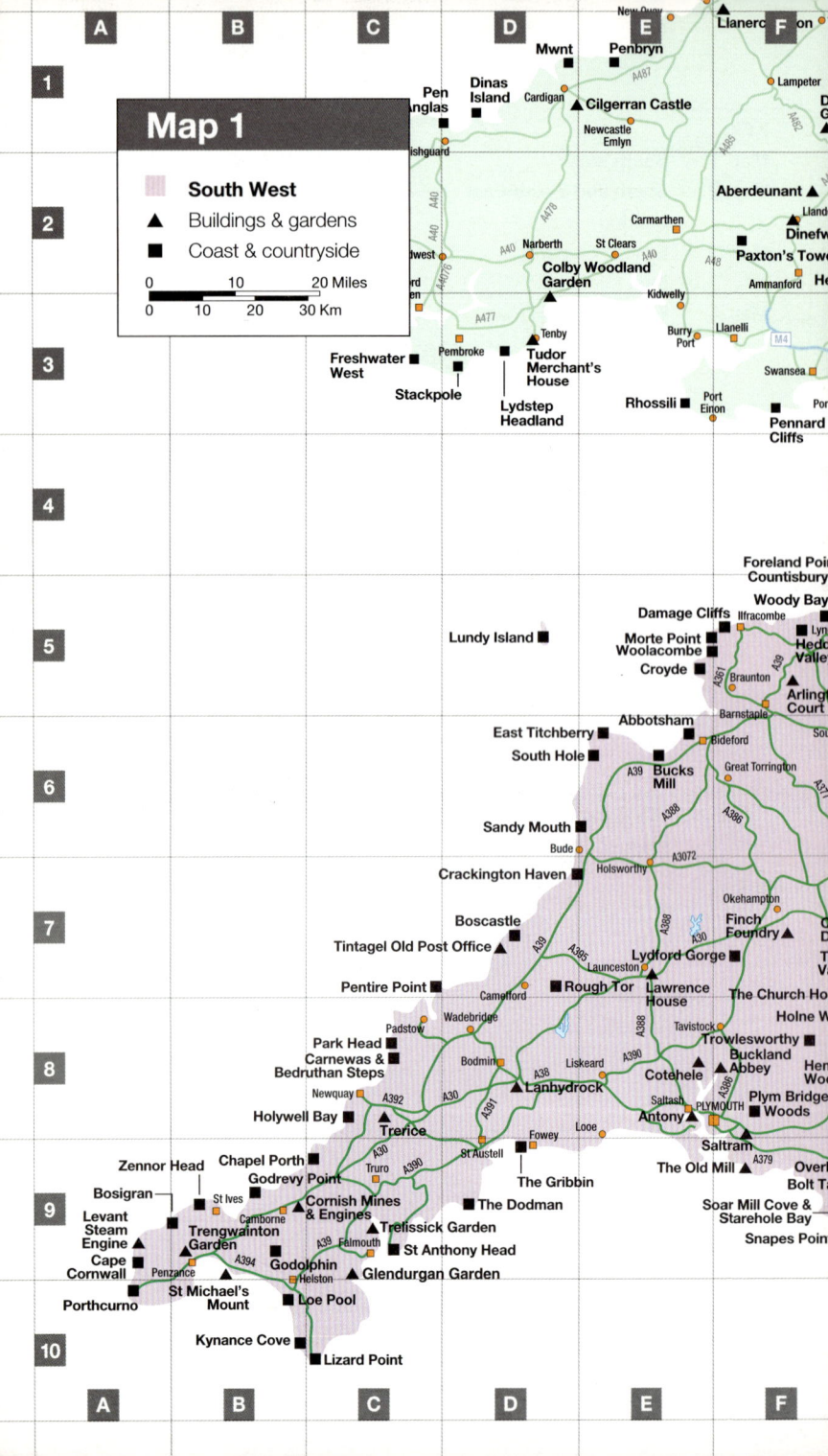

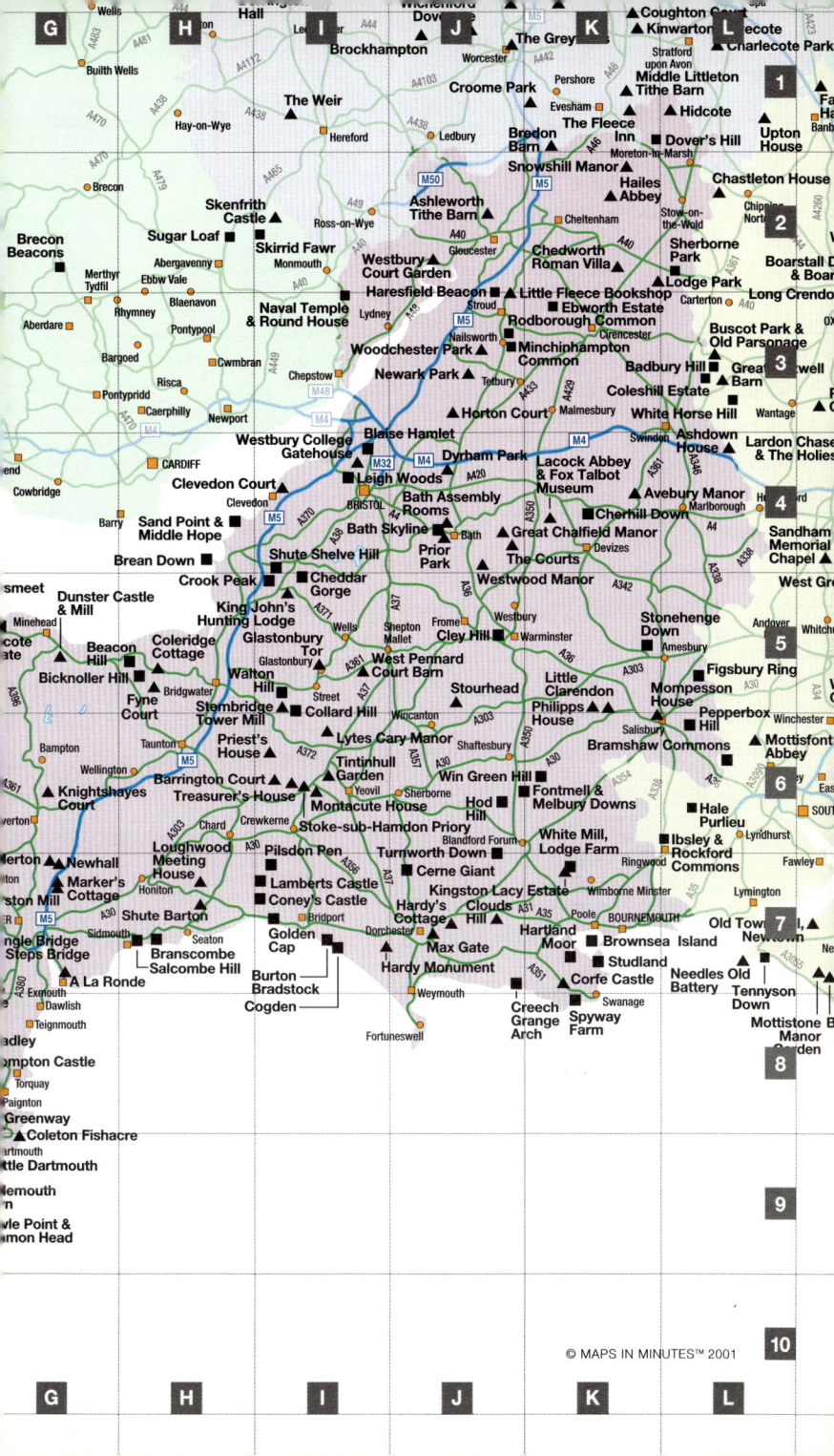

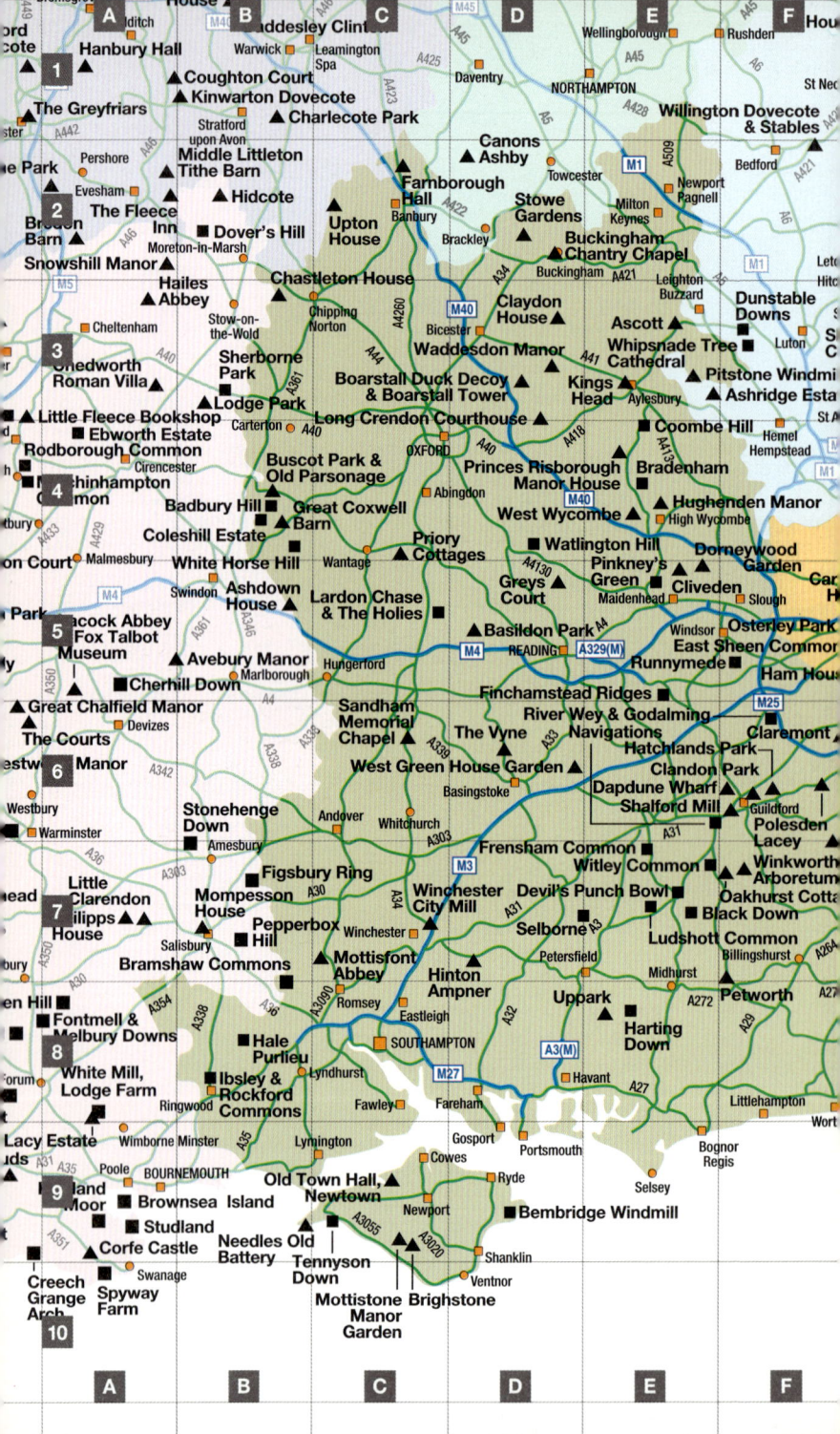

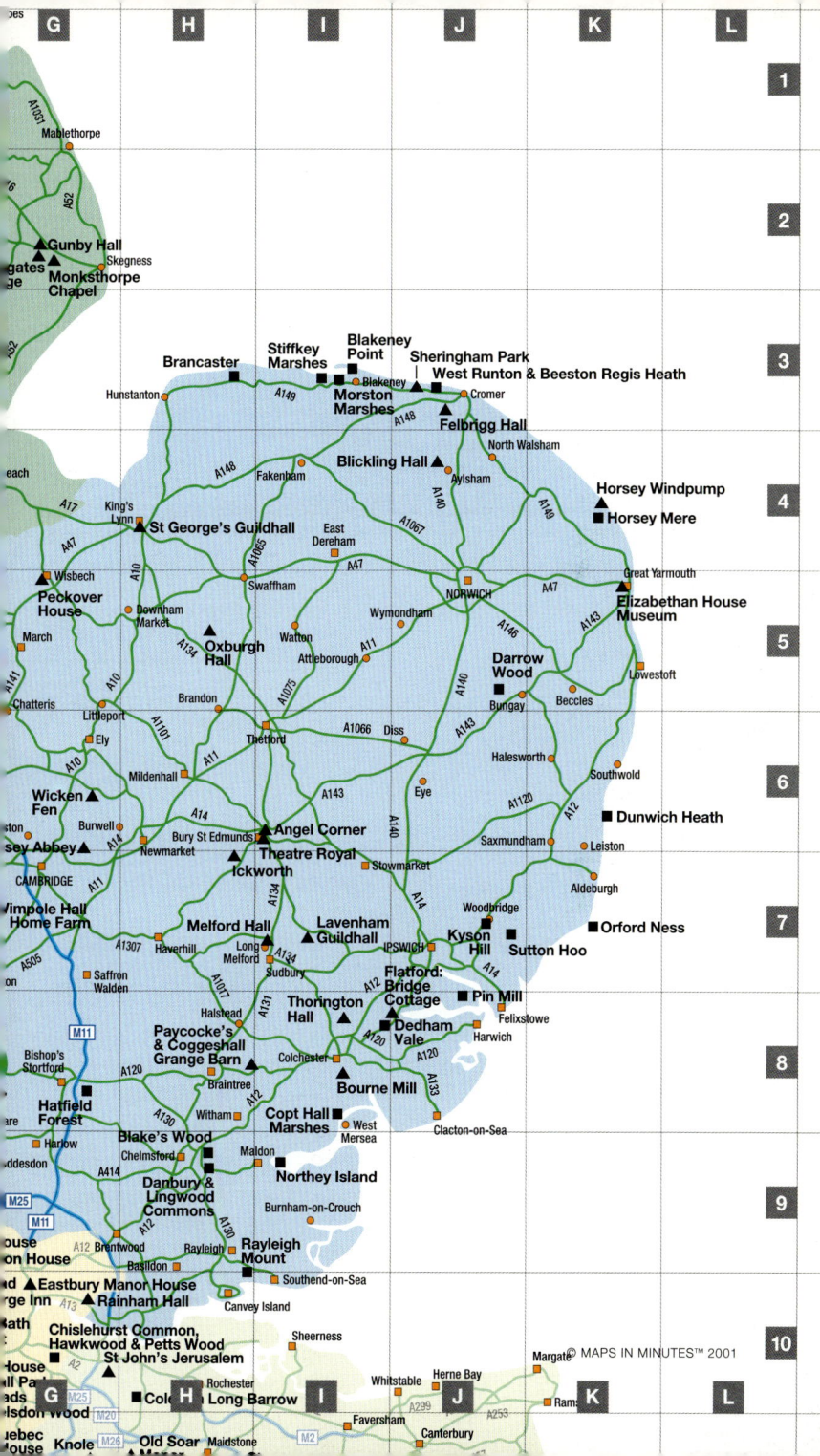

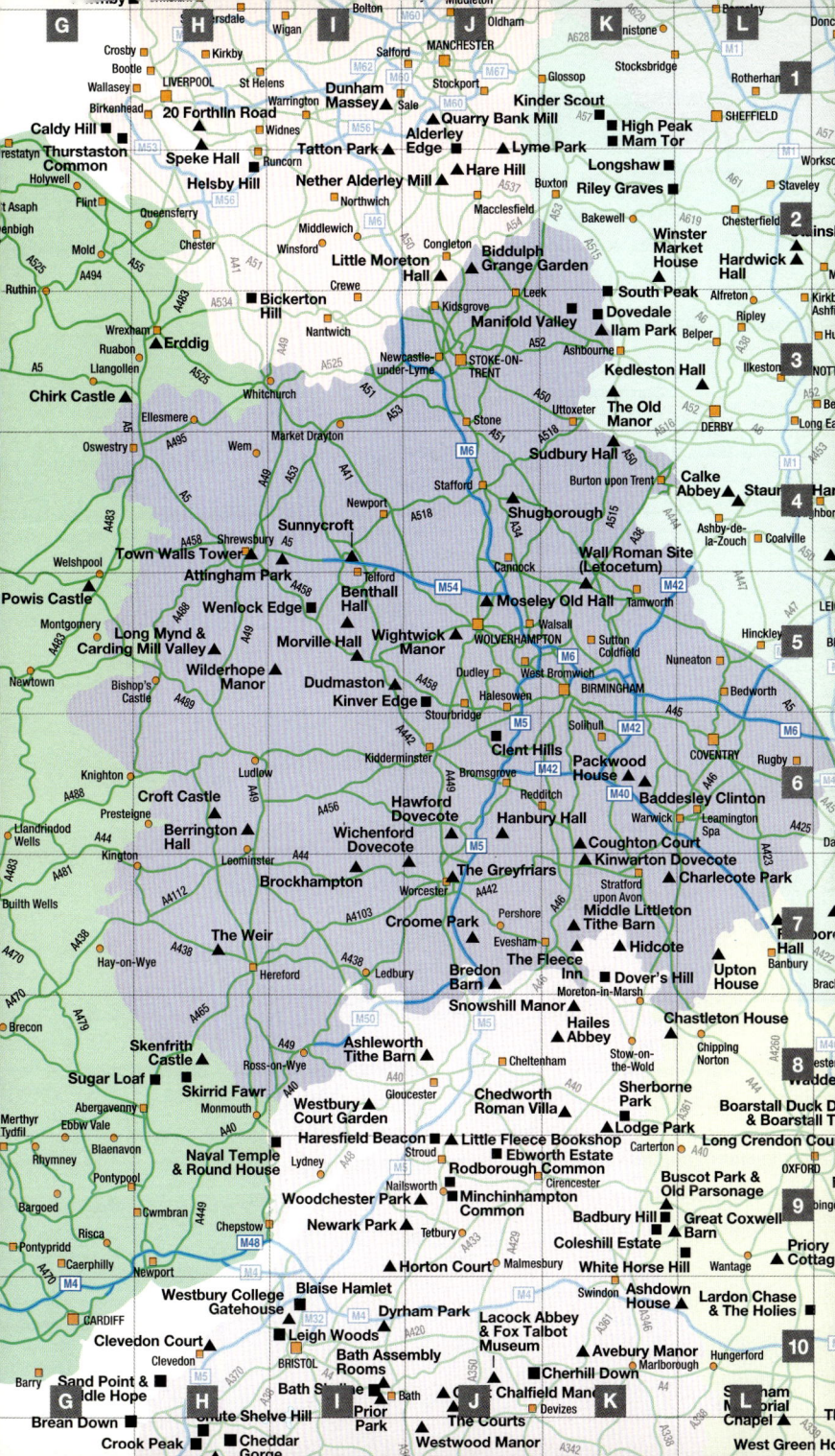

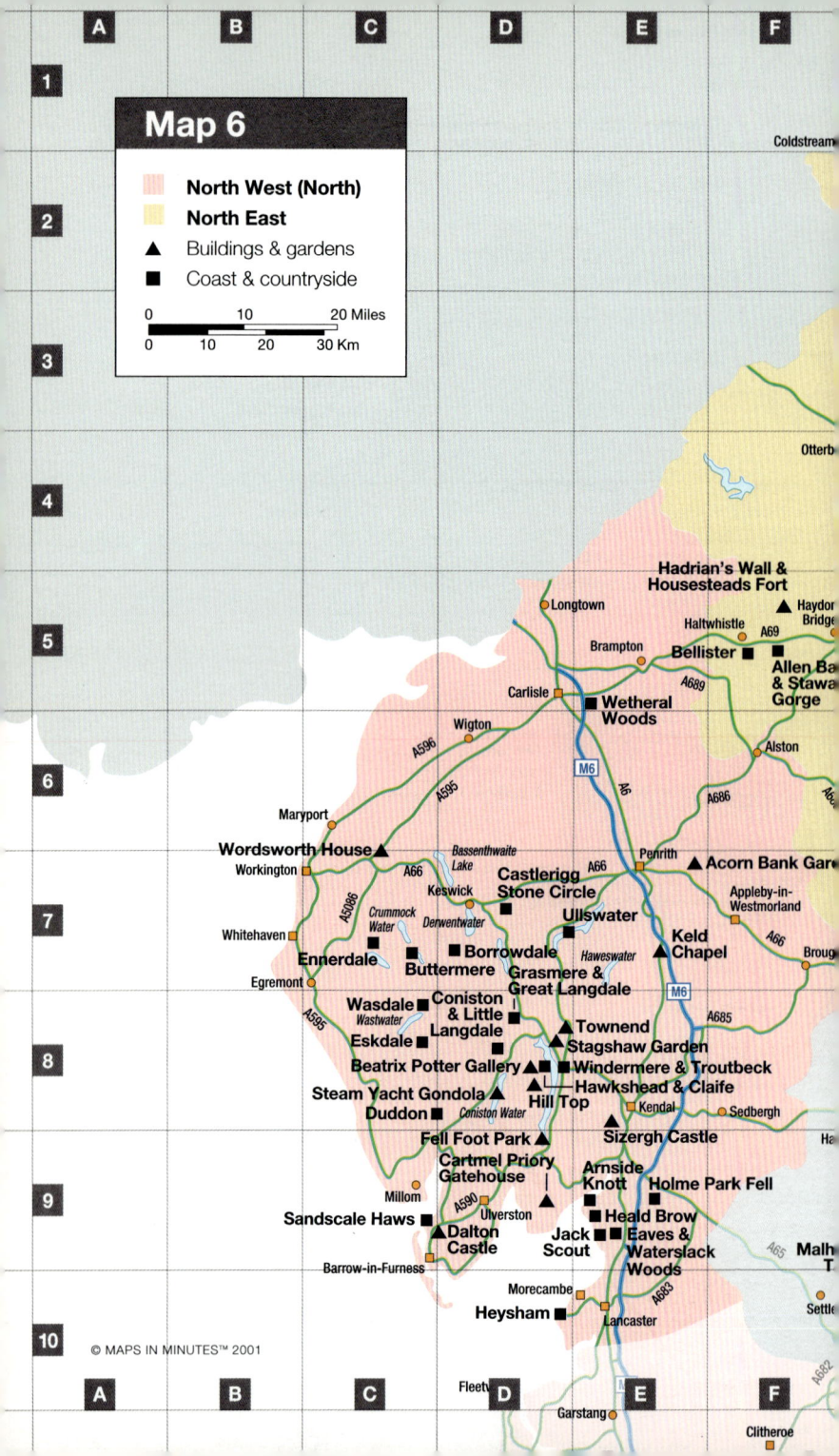

Brecon Beacons (NTPL/Joe Cornish)

Dyrham Park (NTPL/Rupert Truman)

# Introduction

## Life Below Stairs

The front cover for this edition of the Handbook shows the larder from the servants' quarters at Petworth House. Over the past few years, the National Trust has been restoring the areas below stairs in several of its houses and these have proved very popular: most of us have ancestors who were in domestic service.

Now visitors can enjoy exploring new parts of Penrhyn Castle in North Wales. While the state rooms of this extraordinary neo-Norman castle have been on show for many years, the service area was a mere shell, glimpsed by departing visitors. The Trust has now restored 14 service rooms to show how they would have looked in July 1894, when Lord Penrhyn entertained the Prince and Princess of Wales on a royal visit. You can see the lamp room, the sculleries and the pastry room, and admire the lavish feast that has been carefully recreated.

Penrhyn Castle (NTPL/Andreas von Einsiedel)

# INTRODUCTION · 21

Llanerchaeron in South Wales is a classic example of a small gentry estate with a house dating from 1795, designed by John Nash, gardens and a home farm complex that has survived with little alteration. The National Trust has restored the house and ancillary buildings, and these will be open to visitors from June 2002. Today Llanerchaeron is farmed organically.

Llanerchaeron (NTPL/Chris King)

## Just Desserts

Easter 2002 marks the opening to visitors of the Workhouse at Southwell in Nottinghamshire. The best surviving workhouse in England, it was built in 1824 and became a prototype for similar 'welfare' institutions throughout the country. Originally it consisted of a central hub housing the governor's lodgings, flanked by wings and work yards that segregated men, women and children. Segregation was very much the prevailing concept, with distinctions drawn between the sick and the aged, and the 'undeserving poor'.

'The workhouse should be a place of hardship, of coarse fare, of degradation and humility ... it should be as repulsive as is consistent with humanity.' (The Revd. H. H. Milman to Edwin Chadwick, 1832)

The Workhouse, Southwell (NTPL/Andrew Butler)

'Oliver Twist has asked for more' (*Oliver Twist*, Charles Dickens)

Was it intended to be a cruel system? Was it a fair one? Did the pauper children, like Oliver Twist, really go hungry? You can find out by listening to the sounds and stories of the 19th-century inhabitants as you explore the empty, evocative rooms. There are also a video and displays to enhance your visit.

Scutcheon on a hanging bowl found at Sutton Hoo (British Museum)

'Rime-crusted and ready to sail, a royal vessel with curved prow lay in harbour. They set their dear king amidships, close by the mast. A mass of treasure was brought there from distant parts. No ship, they say, was ever so well equipped with swords, corselets, weapons and armour.' (*Beowulf*)

## Travels through Time

Another National Trust property opening for the first time in 2002 is Sutton Hoo, the burial ground of the 7th-century kings of East Anglia which yielded up a spectacular Anglo-Saxon ship burial during excavations just before the outbreak of World War II. The remains from the ship were given to the British Museum, but visitors to the Treasury at Sutton Hoo will now be able to see the great ornamental shield, sword and gold and garnet belt fittings, on loan from the Museum.

Moving from the Dark Ages to the Middle Ages, visitors to Fountains Abbey and Studley Royal in North Yorkshire can now visit the 12th-century watermill that ground corn for the Cistercian monks of Fountains. Explore the three floors of this attractive, atmospheric building, see the waterwheel turning, and discover whether the turbine is producing electricity.

For something completely different, go to Petworth House, where there will be a major exhibition, *Turner at Petworth*, from July to September 2002 to commemorate the 150th anniversary of the death of Britain's greatest painter, J.M.W.Turner. (An illustrated catalogue of the exhibition will be published jointly by the Tate Gallery and the National Trust.) After buying one of Turner's paintings in 1802, the 3rd Earl Egremont not only invited the artist to Petworth but encouraged him to treat the house as if it were his own home, with a room over the chapel converted into a studio.

'The greatest Landscape Painter that ever lived.' (Thomas Phillips' description of his friend and fellow painter, J.M.W. Turner)

'The Artist and his Admirers' by J.M.W. Turner (© Tate, London 2001)

> **'He seems to paint with tinted steam, so evanescent and airy.'**
> **(John Constable)**

In 2002 four of Turner's most famous landscapes are returning to the Carved Room, for which they were commissioned. The exhibition will feature 70 gouaches, paintings and oils on loan from Tate Britain.

### Open to View

These are some of the new sites to visit. But remember that the National Trust offers hundreds of places to enjoy. The year 2001 was not a happy one: foot and mouth hit the Trust and our tenant farmers hard, and some properties were obliged to remain closed for part of the visitor season. So, go out and visit again, using this Handbook and other publications.

You can give our farmers a really helpful boost by consulting the *Farm Food and Crafts Guide* (phone 0870 458 4000; email **enquiries@thenationaltrust.org.uk** or see it on the web at **www.nationaltrust.org.uk**, and click on shopping). It contains over 100 entries for farm shops and other rural enterprises, including organic and seasonal produce, and many services such as cycle hire and internet designs. Go and stay at a farmhouse using the *Bed & Breakfast Guide* (as above), or take a National Trust Holiday Cottage (see page 361).

INTRODUCTION · **25**

# How to use this Handbook

The Handbook gives details of how you can visit National Trust properties, including opening arrangements for the period from March 2002 to the end of February 2003 inclusive, admission charges and available facilities. Property entries are arranged by area (see map on page 5) and are ordered alphabetically within each area. Maps for each appear on pages 6 to 18, and these show properties with a charge for entry together with a selection of coast and countryside places mentioned in the introduction to each area. They also show main population centres. A simple grid reference is given in each property entry, after the ➔ symbol. These refer first to the appropriate map number then to the appropriate grid square eg **3**:G6. Ordnance Survey grid references are also given; for coast and countryside properties with no individual entry, these appear within the box in the relevant area introduction.

To find properties within a particular county, please refer to the index by county at the back of this Handbook. County names are also given in individual property entries.

Property features are indicated by symbols alongside the property name. More detailed information about specific facilities is represented by symbols down the left-hand side of each entry. You will find the key to the symbols on the inside front cover.

Please note the following points about this year's Handbook:

- areas are shown in hectares (1ha = 2.47 acres) with the acres equivalent in brackets. Heights and short distances are shown in metres (1m = 3.28 feet); longer distances continue to be measured in miles (ml)

- although opening times and arrangements vary considerably from place to place and from year to year, most houses will be open during the period 23 March to 3 November inclusive, usually on three or more days per week between about noon and 5pm. **Please note that, unless otherwise stated in the property entry, last admission is 30 minutes before the stated closing time**

- we make every effort to ensure that property opening times and available facilities are as published, but very occasionally it is essential to change these at short notice. Always check the current Handbook for details and, if making a special journey, please telephone in advance for confirmation. You can also check our website on **www.nationaltrust.org.uk**

- **Jubilee Bank Holiday 3 and 4 June 2002**: Whilst we hope that as many of our properties as possible will be open on these days, at the time of going to press many have not been able to confirm this. In cases where it is not clearly stated, please telephone the property or consult the website.

- when telephoning a property, please remember that we can provide a better service if you call on a weekday morning, on a day when the property is open.

# Special Information about National Trust Membership

- Membership of the National Trust allows you free parking in Trust car parks and free entry to most Trust properties open to the public during normal opening times and under normal opening arrangements, **provided you can present a valid membership card.**

- **Please check that you have your card with you before you set out on your journey. We very much regret that you cannot be admitted free of charge without it, nor can admission charges be refunded subsequently, due to the administrative costs of doing so.**

- Membership cards are **not transferable**.

- If your card is lost or stolen, please contact the Membership Department (address on p.362), tel. 0870 458 4000.

- A replacement card can be sent to a temporary address if you are on holiday. Voluntary donations to cover the administrative costs of a replacement card are always welcome.

- Free entry is not guaranteed; additional charges may be made for the following:
  - when a special event is in progress at a property
  - when a property is opened specially for a National Gardens Scheme open day
  - where the management of a property is not under the National Trust's direct control, eg Tatton Park, Cheshire
  - where special attractions are not an integral part of the property, eg Steam Yacht *Gondola* in Cumbria, Wimpole Hall Home Farm in Cambridgeshire, Dunster Watermill in Somerset, the model farm and museum at Shugborough in Staffordshire and the Old Hall and farm at Tatton Park in Cheshire
  - where special access conditions apply, eg 20 Forthlin Road in Liverpool, where access is only by minibus from Speke Hall and Albert Dock, and **all** visitors (including Trust members) pay a fare for the minibus journey

- The National Trust encourages educational use of its properties. Education Group Membership is open to all non-profit-making educational groups whose members are in full-time education. Subscription rates are banded according to the nature of the organisation and the number on roll. Tel. 0870 458 4000 for further details.

- Life members of the National Trust who enrolled as such before 1968 have cards which admit one person only. Life members wishing to exchange these for 'admit two' cards, or those wishing to change from one category of life membership to another, should contact the Membership Department in Bromley for the scale of charges.

- Entry to properties owned by the Trust but maintained and administered by English Heritage or Cadw (Welsh Historic Monuments) is free to members of the Trust, English Heritage and Cadw.

- Members of the National Trust are also admitted free of charge to properties of The National Trust for Scotland, a separate charity with similar responsibilities. NTS properties include the famous Inverewe Garden, Bannockburn, Culloden and Robert Adam's masterpiece, Culzean Castle. Full details are contained in the *Guide to the National Trust for Scotland for 2002,* which can be obtained by sending a self-addressed adhesive label and £2.50 to The National Trust for Scotland (see address on p.363). Information is also available on the Internet at **www.nts.org.uk**

- Reciprocal visiting arrangements also exist with certain overseas Trusts, including Australia, New Zealand, Barbados, Bermuda, Canada, Jersey, Guernsey and the Manx Museum and National Trust on the Isle of Man. For a full list contact our Membership Department.

- National Trust members visiting properties owned by the National Trust for Scotland or overseas Trusts are only eligible for free entry on presentation of a valid membership card.

## How you can support the National Trust
# BECOME A MEMBER TODAY

You will be helping the Trust protect and care for much-loved countryside and coastline as well as the historic houses and gardens listed in this Handbook. Your subscription goes directly to support this work. Benefits include:

- free admission to most of the properties listed in this Handbook
- three mailings a year which include a free copy of this Handbook, three editions of the full colour *National Trust Magazine* (available also on tape) and two editions of your regional newsletter

There is a wide range of different membership categories for you to choose from (see form on following page).

### How to join

For immediate membership, you can join at almost all National Trust properties or shops during your visit, or join on-line at **www.nationaltrust.org.uk/join**

For postal applications, complete and return the form overleaf.

Or just telephone the National Trust Membership Department on 0870 458 4000. Enquiries and credit card applications are welcome. The lines are open Monday to Friday 9 am to 5.30 pm and from 9 am to 4 pm on Saturdays, Sundays and Bank Holidays (except Christmas Day and New Year's Day). Please allow 21 days for receipt of your membership card and new member's pack.

# Application for membership

TO: THE NATIONAL TRUST, FREEPOST MB1438, BROMLEY, KENT BR1 3BR

*Twelve-month membership*

- ☐ **Individual:** £32.50 and, for each additional member living at the same address, £21.50. One card for each member.
- ☐ **Family group:** £60 for two adults, living at the same address, and their children or grandchildren under 18. Please give names and dates of birth for all children. Two cards cover the family.
- ☐ **Family one adult:** £46 for one adult and his/her children under 18, living at the same address. Please give names and dates of birth for all children. One card covers the family.
- ☐ **Child:** £15 Must be under 13 at time of joining. Please give date of birth.
- ☐ **Young person:** £15 Must be 13 to 25 at time of joining. Please give date of birth.
- ☐ **Education group membership:** See Special Information for National Trust Members, and tel. 0870 458 4000 for further details.

*Life membership*

- ☐ **Individual:** £770 (£495 if aged 60 or over and retired). One card admits the named member and a guest.
- ☐ **Joint:** £935 for lifetime partners (£580 if either partner is aged 60 or over and retired). Two cards, each admitting the named member.
- ☐ **Family joint:** £1040 for two adults, living at the same address, and their children or grandchildren under 18. Please give names and dates of birth for all children. Two cards cover the family.

Rates valid until 28 February 2003.

| SOURCE D1215 | | | DATE | |
|---|---|---|---|---|
| FULL ADDRESS | | | | |
| | | | POSTCODE | |
| TITLE | INITIALS | SURNAME | DATE OF BIRTH | VALUE £ |
| | | | | |
| | | | | |
| | | | | |
| | | | | |

**AMOUNT ATTACHED:**
CHEQUE/POSTAL ORDER £
Delete as appropriate

Please allow 21 days for receipt of your membership card

Credit/debit card payments can be made by telephoning 0870 458 4000 (office hours)

Immediate membership can be obtained by joining at a National Trust property, shop or countryside information point

We promise that any information you give will be used for National Trust purposes only. If you do not wish to receive information about our holiday cottages, local members' groups and special products developed to support the National Trust, such as the National Trust Travel Collection, please tick this box. ☐

The National Trust is an independent registered charity (no. 205846)

## Making the most of your membership
## JOIN YOUR LOCAL MEMBERS' ASSOCIATION OR CENTRE

**National Trust Associations and Centres are local clubs run by members for members. There are now around 200 National Trust Associations and Centres in England, Wales and Northern Ireland, as well as Belgium and Germany.**

Associations and Centres exist to promote the work of the National Trust and make membership more enjoyable by allowing members to share their interest in the charity with like-minded people from their local area. Through an organised programme of talks, outings, holidays and social events members make friends, learn more about the National Trust and its properties, and support its work through fundraising.

To find out more, ask at any National Trust property for the free *Make the Most of your Membership* leaflet which gives contact details for every Association and Centre. Alternatively contact the Membership Department at PO Box 39, Bromley, Kent BR1 1XL, tel. 0870 458 4000 or search for your nearest group on our website **www.nationaltrust.org.uk/assocs**

## How you can support the National Trust in the USA
## JOIN THE ROYAL OAK FOUNDATION

More than 40,000 Americans belong to the Royal Oak Foundation, the Trust's US membership affiliate. A not-for-profit organisation, the Royal Oak helps the National Trust through the generous tax-deductible support of members and friends by making grants towards its work. Member benefits include the National Trust Handbook, three editions of *The National Trust Magazine*, the quarterly Royal Oak Newsletter, and free admission to properties of the National Trust and of the National Trust for Scotland.

Royal Oak also awards scholarships to US residents to study in Britain, and sponsors lectures, tours and events in both the US and the UK, designed to inform Americans of the Trust's work.

For further information please write, call, fax or email
**The Royal Oak Foundation, 26 Broadway, Suite 950, New York, NY 10004, USA tel. 001 212 480 2889, fax 001 212 785 7234**
email **general@royal-oak.org**
web **www.royal-oak.org**

# Making the most of your visits

This section of the handbook provides a range of information that will help you enjoy your visits to our properties. Please also take time to read the questions and answers on pp.36 and 37 as these also contain important information.

## Admission fees and opening arrangements

Members of the National Trust are admitted free to virtually all properties (see Special Information about National Trust Membership, p.26). Each property entry shows the normal adult admission fee. This includes VAT and is liable to change if the VAT rate is altered.

**Children:** under 5s are free. Children aged 5–16 pay half the adult price, unless stated. 17s and over pay the adult price. Children not accompanied by an adult are admitted at the Trust's discretion.

**Concessions:** as a registered charity completely independent of government, the National Trust cannot afford to offer concessions on admission fees.

**Education groups:** many properties offer educational facilities and programmes. Teachers are invited to make a free preliminary visit by prior arrangement with the property. Education Group Membership is recommended (see p.26 for more details).

**Group visits:** all groups are required to book in advance and confirm the booking in writing. Some properties have limited access for groups so early booking is recommended. A discount is usually available for groups of 15 or more at most properties. Full information on group visits to National Trust properties is available from the Travel Trade Office, tel. 020 7447 6700; fax. 020 7447 6701, and on our website at **www.nationaltrust.org.uk/traveltrade**

**National Garden Scheme days:** each year many of the National Trust's gardens are opened on extra days in support of the National Gardens Scheme. National Trust Members may have to pay for entry on NGS days. Money raised on these days is donated by NGS to support nurses' and gardeners' charities, including National Trust gardens (primarily for the provision of garden apprenticeships). The National Trust acknowledges with gratitude the generous and continuing support of the National Gardens Scheme Charitable Trust.

**Busy properties:** many properties are extremely popular at Bank Holidays and summer weekends. At some houses and gardens timed tickets may be issued to smooth the flow of people entering the property (but not to limit the duration of a visit), and all visitors (including NT members) are required to use these tickets. This system is designed to create better viewing conditions for visitors and to minimise wear-and-tear on the historic interiors or gardens. On rare occasions entry to the property may not be possible on that day. If you are planning a long journey, please telephone the property in advance of your trip. At a few properties special considerations apply and pre-booking is essential, eg Chastleton, Mr Straw's House.

**Anything new?** see *What's new in 2002* in each property entry for details of exciting changes ranging from special events to newly-opened features.

## Dogs

Dogs assisting visitors with disabilities are allowed inside Trust houses, gardens, restaurants and shops. We regret that these are the only circumstances in which dogs are allowed into houses.

The dog symbol is used in each property entry to indicate those places where dogs are welcome in the grounds only (not gardens). In these cases dogs must be kept on the lead at all times to minimise disturbance to deer, livestock, wildlife and other visitors. If a property does not feature the dog symbol, dogs are not allowed at all.

Dogs are welcome at most countryside properties, and considerable efforts are made to provide facilities. The Trust endeavours to provide a shady parking space in car parks, water for drinking bowls, hitching posts where dogs may be safely left and advice on suitable areas where dogs may be exercised. (Dogs should never be left alone in cars.) These facilities vary from property to property and according to how busy it may be on a particular day. The primary responsibility for the welfare of dogs remains, of course, with the dog's owner.

Dogs should be kept under close control at all times. Please observe local notices on the need to keep dogs on leads, particularly at sensitive times of year, for example during the breeding season for ground-nesting birds. Lambing time is still beset by sheep-worrying incidents despite sustained publicity over many years. This is also the period during which deer are calving.

On some beaches the Trust has found it increasingly necessary to introduce seasonal restrictions on dogs due to conflicts with other users, particularly families with children, and the problems of dog fouling. A list of Trust beaches where restrictions apply is available: see below for details.

Many local authorities implement legislation on dog fouling and this can include Trust property. Where the law applies, it is an offence not to clear up dog waste. Failure to do so could result in a fine of up to £1,000. Dog waste bins are installed at many heavily used sites. If bins are not provided, please dispose of the waste thoughtfully. Where access for dogs has been restricted, the Trust has attempted to find suitable alternative locations nearby.

For a free leaflet, *A Guide for Dog Owners*, sponsored by Petplan, please send a first class stamp to the Membership Department (see p.362).

## Events

The National Trust has a large, exciting and varied programme of events in 2002. During the late winter and spring there will be snowdrop days, Easter Egg trails and Spring Plant Fairs, with open-air theatre and concerts following in the summer months. Living history weekends will be held at a variety of properties throughout the season, with special Hallowe'en events and Christmas festivities including winter walks to round off the year.

Regional Events leaflets are available from April from the Membership Department. Full details of all events can be found on the internet at **www.nationaltrust.org.uk** in the **Things To Do** section.

## For families

The Trust is committed to providing a welcoming, worthwhile and enjoyable visit for families with children. Family tickets are offered in every region, although not necessarily at every property, and in general will admit two adults and up to three children. Many properties provide baby-feeding areas and baby-changing facilities (often combined in a purpose-designed parent and baby room). In restaurants there are high-chairs, together with children's menus, colouring sheets and, at some properties, play areas. There are children's guides, trails or quiz sheets, and Trust shops stock a wide range of interesting and inexpensive items for children.

Trusty the Hedgehog, the children's character, has been created especially for young members and visitors. As well as featuring on *Trust Tracks*, the newsletter for young members, Trusty appears at many events at Trust properties across the country and is proving immensely popular in helping to develop children's interest in the Trust's vital conservation work. Trusty has his own interactive home pages, specifically for young visitors. Children can view the special art gallery showing their own paintings, email reports about their favourite places and discover more about wildlife. You can email Trusty through his website at **www.trusty.org**. If you would like a free list of events for children and families, please telephone 0870 458 4000.

One note of caution on visiting historic houses: we ask parents to recognise the challenges which the Trust faces in preserving fragile interiors and delicate contents. Architecture, interior decoration and furnishings differ at every house, and therefore access arrangements for visitors vary too. We regret that at the majority of historic houses it is not possible to admit prams, pushchairs or baby back carriers, because of the considerable risk of accidents to babies and young children, damage to historic contents and inconvenience to other visitors on busy days. However, some houses are able to admit baby back carriers at all times; others may admit back carriers on quiet days mid-week, at the discretion of the staff on duty at the time – please telephone in advance to check.

For visitors with smaller babies, front slings are admitted and are usually available on loan, as are reins for toddlers at a few properties. Prams can be stored at the entrance at the staff's discretion. We regret that the restriction on back carriers, prams and pushchairs can cause particular difficulties for parents with older and/or heavier babies. If you are unsure about restrictions, do please telephone the property in advance of your visit to check. Once at a property, please ask staff for help and advice, and do bear in mind that there is often plenty for children to see and do outdoors, whether on an estate with a garden and park, or at nearby countryside or coastal sites.

## How to get there

At the end of each property entry is a brief description of location together with a grid reference and OS Landranger series map number. Car-parking is usually available reasonably close to the property.

Travelling on foot, by bike, boat, train or bus is environmentally friendly and enjoyable. Details of access by public transport are given throughout the Handbook (correct as of October 2001). Regular updates are issued during the year; contact the Trust's Membership Department (see p.362) and ask for *Green Transport News*. Please note that no indication of frequency of transport services is given, so check the times of services before setting out. 'Passing ☒' (NIR in N. Ireland) indicates the bus service passes the station entrance or approach road and 'Passing close ☒' indicates that a walk is necessary. Unless otherwise stated, bus services pass the property (although there may be a walk from the bus-stop!), and the railway station name is followed by the distance from the property.

**You can obtain further train details from the national rail enquiry line 0845 748 4950 (at local rates). Bus information is now available for the whole country by ringing a single number charged at national rates: 0870 608 2608.**

The government's Rural Bus Grant has been continued and is leading to even more new services passing properties.

Wheelchair users travelling by train should note that some stations are unstaffed. These are followed by a (U).

The National Trust is grateful to Barry Doe, a life member, for this travel information. If you experience difficulties following this information or have suggestions to make, he will be glad to reply to your comments. Please contact him at: 25 Newmorton Road, Moordown, Bournemouth, Dorset BH9 3NU (tel. 01202 528707; fax. 01202 519914).

**Cycling:** Cycling is a healthy and environmentally sensitive way of travelling and touring the countryside. The Trust actively promotes cycling as a means of reaching its properties, and we are working closely with organisations such as the Countryside Agency, the Cyclists Touring Club and Sustrans to help maximise opportunities for visitors to enjoy a 'journey of experience' whilst travelling to Trust destinations.

The National Cycle Network covers over 5,000 miles and, combined with existing bridleways, quiet roads and greenways, cycling visitors to Trust properties can now enjoy an alternative means of transport to access their favourite places.

The Cycle Touring Network has officially accredited Clumber Park in Nottinghamshire with Cycle Centre status. Clumber has an excellent cycle hire facility with two waymarked routes suitable for both novice and experienced riders and three cyclo-orienteering courses. Route 6 of the National Cycle Network runs through Clumber making it an ideal destination or a welcome stopping place on a longer journey.

Under each individual property entry, where relevant, the bicycle symbol gives details of facilities available for cyclists on site, such as cycle stands. At the *How to find the property* symbol ➡ you can find the nearest National Cycle Network (NCN) route. This is shown as in the following example: NCN 4, 2m (Severn & Thames). This denotes that the property is two miles from NCN route number 4, covered by the Severn & Thames map. For further information on NCN routes or for maps, please contact Sustrans on 0117 929 0888.

## Shopping and eating

The Trust's shops, restaurants, tea-rooms and holiday cottages are all managed by National Trust Enterprises. The profit they generate goes to support the work of the National Trust, and in 2000/2001 contributed over £11 million to funds.

New products will be introduced month by month, some of them suggested by our own supporters, and there will be a range of new gift ideas. Every purchase makes a vital contribution to the Trust's work, and we hope you will enjoy the new products on sale in our shops. You can see our full range of goods if you look at our website **www.nationaltrust.org.uk** and click on **shopping**.

**Shops:** Many Trust properties have shops offering a wide range of related merchandise, much of which is exclusive to the National Trust. These shops and their opening times are indicated in relevant property entries by the shop symbol. Many are also open for Christmas shopping and dates are given in the appropriate entries. In addition the Trust operates a number of shops in towns and cities throughout the country, which are open during normal trading hours.

**Town shops:** opening times vary so please telephone for details if you are making a special journey.

**Bath** Marshall Wade's House, Abbey Churchyard (tel. 01225 460249)

**Belfast** 57 Fountain Street (tel. 028 9032 0645)

**Birmingham International Airport** Main Terminal, Landside (tel. 0121 781 0153)

**Cambridge** 9 King's Parade (tel. 01223 311894)

**Canterbury** 24 Burgate (tel. 01227 457120)

**Christchurch** 18 Bridge St (tel. 01202 490478)

**Cirencester** Tourist Information Centre, Cornhall, Market Place (tel. 01285 654180)

**Dartmouth** 8 The Quay (tel. 01803 833694)

**Grasmere** Information Centre & Shop Church Stile, Grasmere (tel. 015394 35621)

**Greenhithe** Bluewater Shopping Centre, Unit U128B, The Guild Hall tel. 01322 423826)

**Haslemere** Haslemere Museum (tel. 01428 658063)

**Hexham** 25/26 Market Place (tel. 01434 607654)

**Kendal** K's Village, Lound Rd (tel. 01539 736190)

**London**
**Brentford** Syon Park (tel. 020 8569 7497)

**Victoria** Blewcoat School, 23 Caxton St (tel. 020 7222 2877)

**Melksham** 5 Church St (tel. 01225 791513)

**Monmouth** 5 Church St (tel. 01600 713270)

**St Alban's** Tourist Information Centre, Town Hall, Market Place (tel. 01727 864511)

**St David's** Captain's House, High St (tel. 01437 720385)

**Salisbury** 41 High St (tel. 01722 331884)

**Sidmouth** Old Fore St (tel. 01395 578107)

**Solihull** – Beatties (concession store) 700 Warwick Street (tel. 0121 705 8111)

**Stratford-upon-Avon** 45 Wood St (tel. 01789 262197)

**Street** Clark's Village, Farm Road (tel. 01458 440578)

**Truro** 9 River St (tel. 01872 241464)

**Wells** 16 Market Place (tel. 01749 677735)

**Windsor** 14 High St (tel. 01753 850433)

**Wolverhampton** – Beatties (concession store) 71-80 Victoria Street (tel. 01902 643345)

**York** – Shop & Tea-room 32 Goodramgate (tel. 01904 659050)

**Restaurants and tea-rooms:** The National Trust operates over 140 tea-rooms and restaurants. They are usually located in very special old buildings including castles, lighthouses, stables, and even hot-houses! We aim to offer a welcoming atmosphere, value for money and traditional home cooking, with many properties featuring menus with an historical theme. Tea-rooms and restaurants are often open at times of year when houses and gardens are closed and many offer special programmes of events, such as lecture lunches, as well as festive meals in the run-up to Christmas. For more information on functions and private parties at National Trust properties, contact the Membership Department on 0870 458 4000 or check our website.

## Visitors with disabilities

We warmly welcome visitors with disabilities to our properties; we also welcome assistance dogs (on harness) for visually impaired, hearing impaired and disabled people. Most properties have a good degree of access, and provide manual wheelchairs. Unless otherwise mentioned in the relevant property entry, all properties have adapted WCs. Self-drive and volunteer-driven powered vehicles are available at some larger gardens and parks. The Trust admits to its historic buildings users of powered wheelchairs and similar small vehicles, subject to the physical limitations of the building and any other temporary constraints which may apply on the day – please telephone the property in advance to check. The necessary companion of a disabled visitor is admitted free of charge on request, while the normal charge applies to the disabled visitor.

The Sympathetic Hearing Scheme operates at many properties, and Braille guides are available at most. General information and a free booklet on access (also available in large print and tape), are available from the National Trust Membership Department, FREEPOST MB 1438, Bromley, Kent BR1 3BR. Please enclose a first-class stamp.

*The National Trust Magazine* is available free on tape, as are several regional newsletters. Please contact the Trust's **Access For All** Adviser at our London Central Office – see p.362 for address – if you wish to receive these regularly.

## Voluntary Talks Service

The National Trust has a group of enthusiastic and knowledgeable volunteer speakers. They are available to give illustrated talks to groups of all sizes. Talks cover many different aspects of the Trust's work, from the Neptune Coastline Campaign to garden history, conservation, individual properties and regional roundups. Talks can also be tailored to meet your group's particular interests. To find out more, contact the Talks Service Co-ordinator at your local National Trust Regional Office (see p.362).

# Conservation and Access

## Your questions answered

These are some of the questions most commonly asked by visitors. If you need any further information regarding a visit you are planning, please telephone the relevant property or 0870 458 4000.

### May I take photographs?

We welcome amateur photography out-of-doors at our properties. We regret, however, that such photography is not permitted indoors when houses are open to visitors.

However, at most properties special arrangements can be made for interested amateurs (as well as voluntary National Trust speakers, research students and academics) to take interior photographs by appointment outside normal opening hours. **Applications must be made in writing to the property concerned, for a mutually convenient appointment. Please note that not all properties are able to offer this facility and those that do may make an admission charge (including NT members).**

All requests for commercial photography must be channelled through the Marketing & Communications Manager at the appropriate Regional Office.

### Why is it so dark inside some houses?

In order to prevent deterioration of light-sensitive contents, especially textiles and watercolours, light levels are regularly monitored and carefully controlled using blinds and sun-curtains. Visitors are recommended to allow time for their eyes to adapt to darker conditions inside houses, particularly in rooms where light levels are reduced to preserve vulnerable material.

Some historic houses offer special tours at weekends during the winter months, when house staff demonstrate traditional housekeeping practices and explain why National Trust conservation policies require low light levels inside houses and closure to visitors during the winter months. These events are advertised in the local press and the regional newsletter. You may obtain a programme of these and a variety of other events for people of all ages from the Membership Department (see p.362).

### May we picnic in the grounds?

Many properties welcome picnics; some have a designated picnic area, a few cannot accommodate them (this is usually indicated in the property entries). Fires and barbecues are generally not allowed. If you are planning a picnic at a Trust property for the first time, do please telephone the property in advance to check.

## Will there be somewhere to sit down?

Seats for visitors' use are provided at various points in all the Trust's historic houses and gardens. Those visitors who wish to sit down – whether elderly, infirm, pregnant or simply tired – should feel free to use the seats available, or ask a room steward if seating is not immediately obvious.

## Is there somewhere to leave large or bulky bags?

At some properties visitors will be asked to leave behind large items of hand luggage while they make their visit. This is to protect furniture and contents from accidental damage and to improve security. This restriction includes rucksacks, large handbags, carrier bags, bulky shoulder bags and camera/camcorder bags. These bags can be left safely at the entrance to any house where the restriction applies (principally historic houses with vulnerable contents, fragile decorative surfaces or narrow visitor routes). See the *For families* section on p.32 for additional information on back carriers and pushchairs.

## Are there any restrictions on type of footwear?

Any heel which covers an area smaller than a postage stamp can cause irreparable damage to all floors, carpets and rush matting. We regret, therefore, that sharp-heeled shoes are not permitted. When necessary, plastic slippers are provided for visitors with unsuitable or muddy footwear. Alternatively slippers are available for purchase.

We would also like to remind visitors that ridged soles trap grit and gravel, which scratch fine floors. Boot-scrapers and brushes are provided for visitors' use. Overshoes may be provided at properties with vulnerable floors.

Please remember to use appropriate footwear at all times in the countryside and in gardens.

## May I use my mobile telephone?

The use of mobile telephones can interfere with the correct operation of sensitive electronic environmental monitoring equipment, and visitors are therefore requested to switch off mobile telephones when entering houses and other buildings where such equipment is likely to be fitted. Visitors are also asked to exercise consideration when using mobile phones in gardens and other enclosed open spaces where ringing may cause disturbance to the quiet enjoyment of others.

## May I smoke?

Smoking is not permitted inside Trust houses, restaurants or shops. Smokers are also invited to exercise restraint in gardens, since the scent of flowers is such an important part of visitors' enjoyment of a garden.

# Introduction to the South West

In the far west of the area, the National Trust's holdings in Cornwall amount to 9,200ha (almost 23,000 acres), including 119 miles of one of Europe's most spectacular coastlines. This ownership includes magnificent country houses such as **Lanhydrock**, **Cotehele** and **Antony**, the renowned gardens of **Trelissick**, **Glendurgan** and **Trengwainton**, as well as fascinating reminders of Cornwall's industrial past, such as the **Cornish Mines and Engines** near Redruth. There are magnificent walks throughout the county, many with breathtaking views. Details of the Trust's extensive coast and countryside properties, and of the recreational opportunities they provide, are given in a series of leaflets (see Further Information).

In neighbouring Devon, the Trust protects 91 miles of coast, including **Foreland Point**, **Countisbury**, the wooded valleys of **Watersmeet** and the beautiful stretch between **Woody Bay** and Combe Martin on the Exmoor coast. The Trust also protects much of the coastal land between Ilfracombe and Croyde, including **Morte** and **Baggy Points**, between which there is a superb beach. At Bideford Bay, there are fine walks on the remote coastline between **Abbotsham, Portledge** and **Bucks Mills**, and also further west at **Brownsham** and **East Titchberry**, **Hartland** and **South Hole**.

South Devon has an equally interesting coastline. From **Bolt Tail** to **Overbecks** near Salcombe run six miles of rugged Trust-owned cliffland, crossed by the coastal footpath, which dips to give access to safe bathing at **Soar Mill Cove** and **Starehole Bay**. The recent purchase of **Southdown Farm** strengthens the protection of this coastline. The area between **Portlemouth Down** and **Prawle Point** offers low cliffs with walks, views and sandy coves. The cliffs become more impressive again towards **Gammon Head** to the east.

The River Dart is a famous beauty spot, and the Trust protects several woods along the estuary, as well as coast on either side of the mouth at **Little Dartmouth** and between **Kingswear** and Southdown Cliff, near Brixham. To the east the Trust owns three miles of coastline between **Salcombe Hill**, Sidmouth and **Branscombe**.

The Trust also owns extensive areas in and around the Dartmoor National Park, including fine walking country in the Teign Gorge, between **Whiddon Deer Park** and **Fingle Bridge**, below the impressive **Castle Drogo**. Downstream are the spectacular hanging oak-woods at **Steps Bridge**. To the south, on the fringe of the National Park, is **Parke Estate**, with delightful walks along the River Bovey. Near Buckfast are **Holne Woods** and **Hembury Woods**, in which there is an Iron Age hill-fort. Further west are **Hentor**, **Willings Walls** and **Trowlesworthy Warren**, on which there are also many archaeological sites, and the **Dewerstone**, a popular area for climbers. Nearer to Plymouth lie **Plym Bridge Woods**, interesting for their industrial archaeology.

The Dorset coast offers equally splendid walking opportunities. In total the Trust protects over 15 miles of Dorset coastline, including the highest cliff in Southern England, **Golden Cap**. From here there are breathtaking views along the coast to Portland Bill. To the east is **Cogden Beach**, where the dramatic Chesil Beach starts. At **Spyway Farm** in Purbeck there are information panels about the area and access to the sea at **Dancing Ledge**, while to the north lies **Studland**, noted for its rare birds, unspoilt heathland and glorious beach. Between **Corfe Castle** and Wareham is **Hartland Moor**, home to some of Britain's rarest reptiles. Adjacent to the moor is the site on which 160ha (400 acres) of ex-farmland is being restored to typical local heathland by the Trust.

Inland Dorset boasts some of England's classic landscapes, with rolling chalk

**There are special events at most Trust properties; please telephone 0870 458 4000 for details**

## SOUTH WEST · 39

downland and hidden valleys. This is an area rich in archaeological remains, such as those at **Hod Hill** and **Turnworth Down**, near Blandford, and **Pilsdon Pen**, **Lamberts Castle** and **Coney's Castle** near Bridport, as well as the famous ancient figure of the **Cerne Giant**, cut into the chalk near Cerne Abbas. The Fontmell Down Estate south of Shaftesbury includes **Melbury Beacon** and botanically rich chalk grassland at **Melbury Down**, from where there are magnificent views across the Blackmore Vale.

The prehistoric heritage of Wiltshire is celebrated worldwide. Apart from **Stonehenge Down** and **Avebury**, the Trust also owns Iron Age hill-forts at **Figsbury Ring** near Salisbury, **Cherhill Down** near Calne and **Cley Hill** near Warminster. These sites are also important for nature conservation and all give fine views over the surrounding countryside, as does **Pepperbox Hill** and its 17th-century folly overlooking Salisbury, and **Win Green Hill**, the highest point of Cranborne Chase.

To the north, the Cotswolds offer excellent walking, superb views and some of the most charming villages to be found anywhere in England. The natural limestone amphitheatre at **Dover's Hill** is the venue for the annual Cotswold 'Olympick Games' and at the other end of the escarpment **Haresfield Beacon**, the site of a prehistoric hill-fort, offers magnificent views across to Wales. The **Ebworth Estate** near Painswick (no parking facilities at present) has many delightful waymarked walks through protected beech-woods rich in wildlife, as well as a daytime conference centre (tel. 01452 814213 for details). Near Stroud are **Minchinhampton** and **Rodborough Commons**, an area of nationally-important limestone grassland forming a steep-sided open plateau with a wide variety of wild flowers and butterflies. Minchinhampton Common has many interesting archaeological features, and there are breathtaking views from the southern side of Rodborough Common. A series of waymarked walks allows the visitor to explore and enjoy the fascinating **Woodchester Park** valley with its extensive woodlands and chain of picturesque lakes.

---

**OS grid references for main properties with no individual entry (OS map series numbers given in brackets)**

|  |  |
|---|---|
| Abbotsham | [190] SS410277 |
| Bath Skyline | [172] ST777630 |
| Beacon & Bicknoller Hills | [181] ST124397 |
| Bolt Tail | [202] SX666398 |
| Brean Down | [182] ST297588 |
| Burton Bradstock | [194] SY492888 |
| Cley Hill | [183] ST838443 |
| Cogden Beach | [194] SY503883 |
| Collard Hill | [182] ST485345 |
| Coney's Castle | [193] SY372975 |
| Crook Peak | [182] ST387558 |
| Damage Cliffs | [180] SS470465 |
| Dewerstone | [201] SX539638 |
| Dover's Hill | [151] SP137397 |
| Ebworth Estate | [163] SO890097 |
| Figsbury Ring | [184] SU193338 |
| Fingle Bridge | [191] SX743898 |
| Fontmell & Melbury Downs | [183] ST885187 |
| Foreland Point | [180] SS754523 |
| Golden Cap: Langdon Hill | [193] SY413931 |
| Stonebarrow | [193] SY383934 |
| Hartland Moor | [195] SY963854 |
| Hembury Woods | [202] SX726685 |
| Hentor | [202] SX595653 |
| Holne Woods | [202] SX712708 |
| Holnicote: North Hill | [181] SS911476 |
| Webbers Post | [181] SS903439 |
| Kingswear | [202] SX885510 |
| Lamberts Castle | [193] SY366988 |
| Leigh Woods | [172] ST555730 |
| Minchinhampton | [162] SO850010 |
| Morte Point | [180] SS443457 |
| Parke Estate | [191] SX805785 |
| Pepperbox Hill | [184] SU212248 |
| Pilsdon Pen | [193] ST414012 |
| Plym Bridge Woods | [201] SX525587 |
| Portlemouth Down | [202] SX740375 |
| Rodborough | [162] SO850038 |
| Sand Point | [182] ST330660 |
| Sherborne Park | [163] SP162138 |
| Spyway Farm | [195] SY998778 |
| Steps Bridge | [202] SX802883 |
| Walton Hill | [182] ST474348 |
| Whiddon Deer Park | [191] SX725894 |
| Win Green Hill | [184] ST925206 |
| Woody Bay | [180] SS675487 |

---

For all your information needs check our website www.nationaltrust.org.uk

## SOUTH WEST

The **Sherborne Park Estate** at Northleach offers attractive waymarked walks and watermeadows. Also on the estate is **Lodge Park**, a unique example of a 17th-century deer course and grandstand. Gloucestershire is also home to two notable Trust gardens – celebrated **Hidcote**, at the northern end of the county and, in the west, the delightful 17th-century water garden at **Westbury Court**.

On the shores of the Bristol Channel near Weston-super-Mare there are fine coastal walks at **Sand Point** and **Middle Hope**. To the west is **Brean Down**, the site of a Roman temple, Iron Age hill-fort and other archaeological features. Nearby are **Crook Peak**, **Wavering Down** and **Shute Shelve Hill**, a limestone landscape with heath, scrub and woodland rich in wildlife. Inland, the Trust owns some dramatic parts of the Quantocks, including **Beacon** and **Bicknoller Hills**, east of Williton, and further east are **Glastonbury Tor** and **Walton** and **Collard Hills**, overlooking the remote expanse of the Somerset Levels. Further west, between Minehead and Porlock, the diverse landscape of the **Holnicote Estate** extends south from the Bristol Channel through farmland and ancient woodland to the high moorland of Exmoor.

### Highlights for Visitors with Disabilities ...

The upgraded path from **Salcombe Hill** car park gives magnificent views over Sidmouth; **Plym Bridge Woods, Figsbury Ring** and **Win Green Hill** have gates fitted with RADAR locks, whilst Plym Bridge Woods also has a fishing platform suitable for wheelchair access. In Dorset, there is easy access from the car park down a gentle slope to the shingle beach at **Burton Bradstock**. At **Hartland Moor** there is wheelchair access along Hartland Way to an adapted bird hide; there is a summer boardwalk onto the beach at **Studland**. **Stonebarrow Hill** at Golden Cap has an adapted WC and marvellous views, and nearby **Langdon Hill Wood** has a circular forest route suitable for powered vehicles (access either via kissing-gates or gates with RADAR locks). In Cornwall there are accessible viewpoints at many coastal properties such as **Bodigga Cliff** near Looe, **Carn Galver**, West Penwith and St Anthony Head. Two new easy access trails have been created on the Holnicote Estate at **North Hill** and **Webbers Post**, both offering fine views over moorland, woodland and coast. The viewpoint at **Dover's Hill** is wheelchair accessible. From **Haresfield Beacon** there is access onto Short Wood via a gate with RADAR padlock – superb views can be enjoyed from extensive grasslands.

### ... and for Families

The **Heddon Valley** in north Devon is especially recommended for children, with bridges and stepping stones along the river, meadows full of flowers and easy walks which start from the NT shop and information centre; **Plym Bridge Woods** is excellent for family walks and cycle rides and a good educational site for groups of all ages; **Leigh Woods**, on the Avon Gorge near Bristol, offers wonderful nature walks with varied trees, flowers and fungi. Conegar Capers on the **Kingston Lacy Estate** is a new woodland play area for children aged 5-13; **Dyrham Park** offers three parkland walks for families to discover stunning views, hidden history, magnificent trees and secret wildlife.

### Further Information

Please contact our Membership Department, PO Box 39, Bromley, Kent BR1 3XL. Tel. 0870 458 4000. Email: enquiries@thenationaltrust.org.uk

**Please remember – your membership card is always needed for free admission**

The *Coast of Cornwall* series of 22 informative map-guides, priced 60p–90p, covers the Trust's extensive coastal ownership and is available from NT shops in the county and by post from the Membership Department (please include a donation to cover postage): 1 Bude to Morwenstowe; 2 Crackington Haven; 3 Boscastle; 4 Tintagel; 5 Polzeath to Port Quin; 6 Trevose to Watergate Bay incl. Bedruthan Steps (not NT); 7 Crantock to Holywell Bay; 8 St Agnes & Chapel Porth; 9 Godrevy to Portreath; 10 West Penwith: St Ives to Pendeen; 11 West Penwith: Levant to Penberth; 12 Loe Pool and Mount's Bay; 13 The Lizard, West Coast: Gunwalloe Church Cove to Kynance; 14 The Lizard: Kynance, Lizard Point & Bass Point; 15 The Lizard, East Coast: Landewednack to St Keverne; 16 The Helford River; 17 Trelissick woodland walk; 18/19 The Roseland & St Anthony Head; 20 Nare Head & the Dodman; 21 Fowey; 22 East Cornwall: Lantic Bay to Sharrow Point.

A set of full-colour leaflets on coast and countryside properties in Devon is available including West Exmoor Coast, Watersmeet & Countisbury, Arlington, Killerton, Dartmouth, Salcombe, Castle Drogo and the Teign Valley, Bideford Bay to Welcombe Mouth, Wembury and Ayrmer Cove, and Ilfracombe to Croyde.

There is also a series of walks leaflets for the Wessex area. Titles include Bath Skyline, Cheddar Gorge & Crook Peak, Golden Cap (detailing walks from Stonebarrow and Langdon Hill), Kingston Lacy Estate, Isle of Purbeck (five walks), The Cerne Giant and Dorset Hill-forts, Holnicote Estate (eight walks) and Stourhead Estate. Also available are leaflets on Wildlife and Places to Visit in Dorset, Somerset and Wiltshire & South Glos; free copies from local NT properties and shops. Guidebooks to properties in these counties are available for the cover price plus 75p p&p.

# A LA RONDE

Devon

Summer Lane, Exmouth EX8 5BD · **Tel** 01395 265514

A unique 16-sided house built on the instructions of two spinster cousins, Jane and Mary Parminter, on their return from a grand tour of Europe. Completed *c.*1796, the house contains many 18th-century contents and collections brought back by the Parminters. The fascinating interior decoration includes a feather frieze and shell-encrusted gallery which, due to its fragility, can only be viewed on closed circuit television

- 21 March to 3 Nov: daily except Fri & Sat 11–5.30
- £3.50; child £1.70. No party reduction; unsuitable for coaches or large groups except by arrangement with the Custodian
- As house 10.30–5.45
- As house 10.30–5.30 (morning coffee, light lunches, afternoon teas)
- (1:G7) 2ml N of Exmouth on A376 [192: SY004834] **Bus**: Stagecoach in Devon 57 Exeter–Exmouth to within ¼ml **Station**: Lympstone Village (U) 1¼ml; Exmouth 2ml

**NT properties nearby** Branscombe, Killerton

## ANTONY

Cornwall

Torpoint, Plymouth PL11 2QA · **Tel** 01752 812191
**Email** antony@ntrust.org.uk

One of Cornwall's finest early 18th-century houses, faced in lustrous silvery-grey Pentewan stone, offset by colonnaded wings of red brick and set within grounds landscaped by Repton. These include the formal garden with the National Collection of day lilies and fine summer borders, and the superb woodland garden with its outstanding displays of rhododendrons, azaleas, camellias and magnolias. Also of note is the 18th-century dovecote and the 1789 Bath Pond House. Antony has been the home of the Carew family for almost 600 years

26 March to 31 May, 4 Sept to 31 Oct: Tues, Wed, Thur & BH Mons; June, July & Aug: daily except Mon, Fri & Sat (but open BH Mon). *Times*: 1.30–5.30; last admission 4.45. Bath Pond House can only be seen by written application to Custodian on days house is open. **Woodland garden** (Carew Pole Garden Trust, not NT): 1 March to 31 Oct: daily except Mon & Fri (but open BHols) 11–5.30

£4.40; family £10.75. Booked parties £3.60. NT garden only £2.20. Woodland garden £3 (NT members free when house open). Combined gardens-only ticket for Antony garden & woodland garden £3.70. Pre-booked parties £3

As house

House: stairclimber. Garden: largely accessible; recommended route. Ground floor of house, plus family history exhibition, shop & tea-room accessible

Braille guide

Tea-room 12.30–5.30

(1:E8) 5ml W of Plymouth via Torpoint car ferry, 2ml NW of Torpoint, N of A374, 16ml SE of Liskeard, 15ml E of Looe [201: SX418564] **Bus**: First Western National 80/1, from Plymouth (passing close ≥ Plymouth), alight Great Park Estate, ¼ml **Station**: Plymouth 6ml via vehicle ferry Ferry: Torpoint 2ml **Cycle**: NCN 27 2ml

**NT properties nearby** Cotehele, Saltram

## ARLINGTON COURT

Devon

Arlington, nr Barnstaple EX31 4LP · **Tel** 01271 850296 · **Fax** 01271 850711
**Email** arlingtoncourt@ntrust.org.uk

Nestling in the thickly-wooded valley of the River Yeo lies the 1,400-ha (3,500-acre) Arlington Court estate. At its centre stands Arlington Court, the intimate and intriguing Victorian home of Miss Rosalie Chichester. Crowded with treasures amassed from her travels, her collections include model ships, tapestry, pewter and shells. In the basement, from May to Sept visitors can view the comings and goings of Devon's largest colony of Lesser Horseshoe bats via the newly-installed 'batcam'. Arlington's stable block houses one of the best collections of 19th-century horse-drawn vehicles

**Please see the area introductions for details of coast & countryside properties**

## SOUTH WEST · 43

in the country and offers carriage rides around the grounds. The 12-ha (30-acre) gardens are largely informal, featuring a beautiful Victorian garden complete with conservatory and ornamental ponds leading to a partially-restored walled kitchen garden. Stunning walks take in historic parkland grazed by Jacob sheep and Shetland ponies, leafy woodlands, a tranquil lake with heronry and bird hide, deep forests and stream-fed valleys

- **House, carriage collection & Victorian garden**: 23 March to 3 Nov: daily except Tues (but open 4 June). *Times*: Gardens, shop, tea-rooms and bat lobby open 10.30, house and carriage collection open 11. Last admission 4.30, closes 5.30. Tues from 3 June to 3 Sept, gardens, shop, tea-rooms and bat lobby only 10.30–4.30. 4 Nov to 22 March 2003, grounds open during daylight hours

- £5.60; child £2.80; family £13.90. Parties of 15+ £4.80. Gardens & carriage collection only: £3.50; child £1.70. Tues (gardens & bat lobby only) £2.40; child £1.20

- 23 March to 3 Nov: 10.30–5 daily except Tues. Please tel. for autumn/winter opening times and events

- Close designated parking for disabled drivers. Ground-floor access to house and carriage collection. Gardens with gravel paths accessible. Wheelchairs and Batricar available

- Braille guides and 'touch tour' for house and carriage collection; audio guides available

- Garden tea-room and Old Kitchen tea-room (licensed) serve hot and cold meals and beverages all day, including breakfasts and picnics. Children's play area in Garden tea-room

- Baby-changing facilities, high chairs, children's menu, play area at reception and Garden tea-room, play carriages at stables

- Children's quizzes, batcam, sculpture trail. Warden-led schools' visits

- On short leads in gardens, grounds and carriage collection only

- (1:F5) 8 ml NE of Barnstaple on A39 [180: SS611405] **Bus**: First Red Bus 309, Barnstaple–Lynton (passing close ⇌ Barnstaple) (not Suns) **Station**: Barnstaple 8ml

**NT properties nearby** Dunster Castle, Knightshayes Court, North Devon coastline

**Unless indicated, last admission is always 30 mins before closing time**

## ASHLEWORTH TITHE BARN 🏛  Gloucestershire
Ashleworth · **Tel** 01985 843600 (Regional Office)
**Email** ashleworth@ntrust.org.uk

A 15th-century tithe barn, picturesquely located on the banks of the Severn and with an immense stone-tiled roof

**Note**: The barn may be closed during 2002 for major repairs; tel. to check

- 🅾 1 April to 31 Oct: daily (closed Good Fri) 9–6 or sunset if earlier. Other times by appointment
- 💷 £1
- ➜ (1:J2) 6ml N of Gloucester, 1¼ml E of Hartpury (A417), on W bank of Severn, SE of Ashleworth [162: SO818252] **Bus**: Swanbrook 51/2 Gloucester–Tewkesbury (passing close ≋ Gloucester), alight Ashleworth ¼ml **Station**: Gloucester 7ml

**NT properties nearby** Bredon Barn, May Hill, Westbury Court Garden

---

## AVEBURY 🏛 🌳  Wiltshire
nr Marlborough SN8 1RF · **Tel** 01672 539250 · **Fax** 01672 539388
**Email** avebury@ntrust.org.uk

One of the most important megalithic monuments in Europe and spread over a vast area, much of which is under Trust protection. The great stone circle, encompassing part of the village of Avebury, is enclosed by a ditch and external bank and approached by an avenue of stones. Many of the stones were re-erected in the 1930s by the archaeologist Alexander Keiller. West of Avebury, the Iron Age earthwork of Oldbury Castle crowns Cherhill Down, along with the conspicuous Lansdowne Monument. With the spectacular folds of Calstone Coombes, this area of open downland provides wonderful walking opportunities

**What's new in 2002**: The Barn gallery exhibition, *Avebury 6000 Years of Mystery* recounts the development of the Avebury landscape and the story of the people who discovered it, using interactive displays and CD-ROMs housed in the spectacular 17th-century thatched barn

- 🅾 **Stone circle**: daily. **Alexander Keiller Museum and Barn gallery** daily (closed 24, 25 Dec). *Times*: 1 April to 31 Oct 10–6 or dusk if earlier; 1 Nov to 31 March 2003: 10–4
- 💷 Alexander Keiller Museum including Barn gallery: £4; child £2; family (2 adults and 3 children) £10, or (1 adult and 3 children) £7. EH members free (tel. 01672 539250). A charge will be introduced for car parking in 2002.
- 🛍 1 April to 31 Oct: daily 10.30–5 (longer if fine); 1 Nov to 31 March 2003: daily except Mon & Tues 11.30–4; tel. 01672 539384
- ♿ Parking for disabled drivers in High St car park. Museum, Barn gallery & parts of circle: accessible

---

**There are special events at most Trust properties; please telephone 0870 458 4000 for details**

- Some items in Museum may be touched. Interactive exhibition in Barn gallery. Large-print guide for Museum and Barn gallery
- The Circle restaurant (licensed) serves vegetarian lunches and teas using organic and local products, tel. 01672 539514
- Children's guidebook
- Education room, bookings tel. 01672 539250
- *Walking around Avebury* guide features six local walks; from property or NT Wessex office (£2.50 plus 50p p&p)
- Rack near barn
- On leads in stone circle
- (1:K4) 6ml W of Marlborough, 1ml N of the Bath road (A4) on A4361 and B4003 [173: SU102699] **Bus**: First Badgerline/Thamesdown 48/A, 49/A Swindon–Trowbridge/Marlborough; Wilts & Dorset 5, 6 Salisbury–Swindon. All pass close ≋ Swindon. Also Hatts 43, X43 Calne–Avebury **Station**: Pewsey 10ml **Cycle**: NCN 4

**NT properties nearby** Lacock Abbey & Fox Talbot Museum

## AVEBURY MANOR AND GARDEN

Wiltshire

nr Marlborough SN8 1RF · **Tel** 01672 539250 · **Fax** 01672 539388
**Email** avebury@ntrust.org.uk

A much-altered house of monastic origin, the present buildings dating from the early 16th century, with notable Queen Anne alterations and Edwardian renovation by Colonel Jenner. The topiary and flower gardens contain medieval walls, ancient box and numerous 'rooms'

**Note**: The manor house is occupied and furnished by private tenants, who open a part of it to visitors. Owing to restricted space, timed tickets may be in operation at busy times. Following periods of prolonged wet weather it may be necessary to close the garden. No smoking in house or garden

- **House**: 31 March to 30 Oct: Tues, Wed, Sun & BH Mons 2–5.30; last admission 5 or dusk if earlier. **Garden**: 29 March to 6 Nov: daily except Mon and Thur (but open BH Mons) 11–5.30 or dusk if earlier
- £3.60; child £1.80; parties £3.30, children £1.60. Garden only £2.70; child £1.30; parties £2.40, children £1.10. A charge will be introduced for car parking in 2002
- See Avebury
- Garden: largely level and accessible
- Large-print guide
- (1:K4) As Avebury [SU099700]

**NT properties nearby** Lacock Abbey & Fox Talbot Museum

**For all your information needs check our website www.nationaltrust.org.uk**

## BARRINGTON COURT          Somerset

Barrington, nr Ilminster TA19 0NQ · **Tel/Fax** 01460 241938
**Email** barringtoncourt@ntrust.org.uk

An enchanting formal garden, influenced by Gertrude Jekyll and laid out in a series of walled rooms, including the White Garden, the Rose and Iris Garden and the Lily Garden. The working kitchen garden has espaliered apple, pear and plum trees trained along high stone walls. The Tudor manor house was restored in the 1920s by the Lyle family. It is let to Stuart Interiors as showrooms with antique furniture for sale, thereby offering NT visitors a different kind of visit

**What's new in 2002**: An innovative garden information area which incorporates plant sales. Access to the Long Gallery in the Court House is now fully accessible via a staircase built by Stuart Interiors

- March & Oct–3 Nov: Thur to Sun 11–4.30; 1 April to 30 June & Sept: daily except Fri 11–5.30. July & Aug: daily (Fri gardens only) 11–5.30. Coach parties by appointment only. **Events**: *She Stoops to Conquer*, 12 July (open air). All event details tel. 01985 843601
- £5.20; child £2.50; family £13. Parties £4.50
- As garden, tel. 01460 242112
- Garden: accessible but some paths uneven. Self-drive vehicle and manual wheelchairs. Restaurant & shop: accessible
- Braille guide and menu. Large-print guide to garden and house. Scented plants and flowers
- Licensed restaurant with fresh produce from kitchen garden and Beagle's self-service café, open as garden. Also available for functions and meetings (tel. 01460 241244)
- Baby-changing room. Children's menu and activities. Children's trail
- Racks in car park
- (1:I6) In Barrington village, 5ml NE of Ilminster, on B3168. M5 (Junction 25) A358 signposted Chard and Ilminster, then follow signs. If approaching from either

**Please remember – your membership card is always needed for free admission**

direction on A303 leave at Hayes End roundabout from where property is signposted [193:ST396182] **Bus**: First Southern National 630, 632/3 Martock–Ilminster with connections from Taunton on First Southern National 31 (passing close ≣ Taunton) **Station**: Crewkerne 7ml **Cycle**: NCN 30

**NT properties nearby** Lytes Cary Manor, Montacute House, Tintinhull Garden, Treasurer's House

---

## BATH ASSEMBLY ROOMS 　　　Bath & NE Somerset
Bennett Street, Bath BA1 2QH · **Tel** 01225 477789 · **Fax** 01225 428184

Designed by John Wood the Younger in 1769, at a time when Bath was becoming fashionable among polite society, the Assembly Rooms were both a meeting place and venue for public functions. Bombed in 1942, they were subsequently restored and are now let to Bath & North East Somerset Council, which has its Museum of Costume in the basement

- **O** Daily 10–5, when not in use for booked functions (closed 25/26 Dec). **Note**: Access is guaranteed in Aug, but at other times visitors should tel. in advance. The Assembly Rooms are available for weddings, tel. for details
- **£** Free to Rooms; admission charge to Museum of Costume (inc. NT members)
- When Rooms not in use for booked functions
- Daily
- Street parking not always available. Disabled visitors may be set down at door. Level access
- → (1:J4) N of Milsom Street, E of the Circus [156: ST749653] **Bus**: From ≣ Bath Spa and surrounding areas **Station**: Bath Spa ¾ml **Cycle**: NCN 4 ¼ml

**NT properties nearby** The Courts Garden, Dyrham Park, Great Chalfield Manor, Lacock Abbey, Prior Park, Westwood Manor

---

## BLAISE HAMLET 　　　Bristol
Henbury, nr Bristol · **Tel** 01985 843600 (Regional Office)

A hamlet of nine different picturesque cottages, designed by John Nash in 1809 for John Harford, to accommodate Blaise Estate pensioners

- **O** All year
- **£** Free. Access to green only; cottages not open. No WC
- Green accessible
- → (1:I4) 4ml N of central Bristol, W of Henbury village and just N of B4055 [172: ST559789] **Bus**: First City Line 1 from ≣ Bristol Temple Meads; also 43 from city centre **Station**: Sea Mills 3ml; Filton Abbey Wood 3½ml **Cycle**: NCN 4 ¾ml

**NT properties nearby** Clevedon Court, Dyrham Park, Horton Court, Leigh Woods

**For general enquiries, please telephone 0870 458 4000**

48 · SOUTH WEST

## BOSCASTLE                                                                Cornwall
**Tel** Shop 01840 250353 · **Email** boscastle@ntrust.org.uk

Much of the land in and around this picturesque north Cornish harbour and village is owned by the Trust, including the cliffs of Penally Point and Willapark which guard the sinuous harbour entrance, Forrabury Common, high above the village and divided into ancient 'stitchmeal' cultivation plots, and large areas of woodland and meadow in the lovely Valency Valley

- All year. The Old Forge shop and information centre April to end Oct: daily 10.30–5.30
- Pay-and-display car park (inc. NT members) behind harbour
- Occasional guided walks (see Council information centre in car park or seasonal newsletter *Coastlines*). *Coast of Cornwall* leaflet no. 3 includes map and details of circular walks in area, as well as information on local history, geology and wildlife
- As shop and information centre
- Flat surfaced access to harbour; WC in car park and at harbour
- Pubs and cafés (not NT) in village
- (1:D7) 5ml N of Camelford, 3ml NE of Tintagel on B3263 [190: SX097914] **Bus**: First Western National X10 from Exeter, passing ≡ Exeter St David's; 122/4/5, X4 Wadebridge–Bude (with some from ≡ Bodmin Parkway)

**NT properties nearby** Tintagel Old Post Office

## BRADLEY                                                                  Devon
Newton Abbot TQ12 6BN · **Tel** 01626 354513

A small medieval manor house, set in woodland and meadows

**Note**: The property was given to the National Trust by Mrs A H Woolner in 1938. Her family continues to live here and manage the house. There are no refreshments or WCs

- 3 April to 26 Sept: Wed and Thur 2–5
- £2.80. No party reduction; organised parties by appointment with Secretary. Lodge gates too narrow for coaches
- House: ground floor accessible. Garden: accessible
- Opportunities to touch less fragile contents
- (1:G8) Drive gate (with small lodge) is ½ml from town centre on Totnes road (A381); ¼ml walk to house from lodge [202: SX848709] **Bus**: Stagecoach in Devon X64, 75A, First Western National 175, Alansway 176, 189 from Newton Abbot (passing close ≡ Newton Abbot) **Station**: Newton Abbot 1½ml

**NT properties nearby** Compton Castle

---

**Please see the area introductions for details of coast & countryside properties**

SOUTH WEST · 49

## BRANSCOMBE – THE OLD BAKERY, MANOR MILL & FORGE

Devon

Branscombe, Seaton EX12 3DB · **Tel** 01297 680333 (Old Bakery)
01392 881691 (Manor Mill) · 01297 680481 (Forge)

The Old Bakery is a stone-built and partially rendered building beneath thatch, which until 1987 was the last traditional working bakery in Devon. The old baking equipment has been preserved in the baking room and the rest of the building now serves as a tea-room. Manor Mill, still in working order and recently restored, is a water-powered mill which probably supplied the flour for the bakery. The forge is open daily and the blacksmith sells the ironwork he produces

**O** **Old Bakery**: Easter to Oct: daily; winter: Sat & Sun 11–5. **Manor Mill**: 24 March to 3 Nov: Sun; also Wed in July & Aug. *Times*: 2–5. **Forge**: daily; tel. to check

**£** £1, Manor Mill only. Car park adjacent to village hall on opposite side of road, donations in well

At Old Bakery

On leads and only in garden and information room of Old Bakery

→ (1:H7) In the village of Branscombe off A3052 [192: SY198887] **Bus**: Axe Valley 899 Sidmouth–Lyme Regis (connections from ≋ Axminster or Honiton) **Station**: Honiton 8ml

**NT properties nearby** A La Ronde, Shute Barton

## BROWNSEA ISLAND

Dorset

Poole Harbour, BH13 7EE · **Tel** 01202 707744 · **Fax** 01202 701635
**Email** office@brownseaisland.fsnet.co.uk

A wonderfully atmospheric island of heath and woodland, privately owned until acquired by the Trust in 1962, and now a haven for a rich variety of wildlife, including red squirrels and many species of bird. Part of the island is leased as a nature reserve to the Dorset Wildlife Trust. There are many fine walks and spectacular views of Poole Harbour

**Unless indicated, last admission is always 30 mins before closing time**

**Note**: Boats run from Poole Quay and Sandbanks. Visitors may land from own boats at Pottery Pier at west end of island, accessible at all stages of the tide. Please note that the island's paths are uneven in places

**What's new in 2002**: Visitor centre exhibition on the island is now also open at weekends

**O** 23 March to 13 Oct: daily 10–5 (6 in July & Aug). **Events**: for details of open-air theatre and other events tel. 01985 843601

**£** Landing fee: £3.50; child £1.50; family £8.50 (2 adults and up to 3 children) £5 (1 adult and up to 3 children). Parties £3.20, child £1.20, by written arrangement with Property Manager

Guided tours of nature reserve; contact Dorset Wildlife Trust Warden (tel. 01202 709445)

23 March to 13 Oct: daily 10.30–4.45 (5.45 in July & Aug) (tel. 01202 700852)

Mainland parking near Poole Quay. All boats accept and help manual wheelchair users. Island: area around quay accessible; elsewhere paths hilly and rough. 4 self-drive vehicles (booking advisable) and 2 manual wheelchairs. Cafeteria & shop on quay: ask at reception desk for gates to be opened

Braille guide, large-print guide, audio guide

Coffee, snacks and teas in the café near landing quay: 23 March to 13 Oct: daily from 10.15; closes 30min before last boat departs (tel. 01202 700244). Tuck shop open daily

Nursing room, baby-changing facilities, 8 all-terrain baby buggies. Family trails. Children's guidebook

Teachers' resource book. Portman Study Centre. School groups welcome (tel. 01202 707744)

→ (1:K7) In Poole Harbour [195: SZ032878] **Bus**: Wilts & Dorset 150 Bournemouth–Swanage, alight Sandbanks; 152 Poole Quay–Sandbanks. Yellow Buses 30 Poole Quay–Boscombe (passes ≋ Poole), also 12 Christchurch Quay–Sandbanks, June–Sept only; also from surrounding areas to Poole bridge, few mins walk **Station**: Poole ½ml to quay; Branksome or Parkstone, both 3½ml to Sandbanks

**NT properties nearby** Clouds Hill, Corfe Castle, Kingston Lacy

---

## BUCKLAND ABBEY                                              Devon
Yelverton PL20 6EY · **Tel** 01822 853607 · **Fax** 01822 855448
**Email** bucklandabbey@ntrust.org.uk

---

Tucked away in its own secluded valley above the River Tavy, Buckland was originally a small but influential Cistercian monastery. The house, which incorporates the remains of the 13th-century abbey church, has rich associations with Sir Francis Drake and his sea-faring rival, Sir Richard Grenville, containing much interesting memorabilia from their time. There are exhibitions on Buckland's 700-year history as

---

**There are special events at most Trust properties; please telephone 0870 458 4000 for details**

well as a magnificent monastic barn, an unusual herb garden, delightful estate walks and several craft workshops. Recent developments include a hand-crafted plasterwork ceiling in the Drake Chamber, the Cot Lane rural crafts area and a new Elizabethan garden. The Abbey is managed jointly by the National Trust and Plymouth City Museum

23 March to 3 Nov: daily except Thur; 4 Nov to March 2003: Sat & Sun (some weekdays for booked parties); closed 23 Dec to 21 Feb 2003. It may be necessary to close the Abbey, or significant parts of it, during exhibition refurbishment, Nov 2002 to spring 2003. Please tel. after Oct for confirmation. *Times*: 23 March to 3 Nov: 10.30–5.30; 4 Nov to March 2003: 2–5. Last admission 45 min before closing. **Events**: 24–26 Aug, Medieval Life; 7, 8 Sept, Country Days; 5, 6 and 12, 13 Oct, Elizabethan Experience three weekends before Christmas, Abbey decorations; school holidays, daily family activities. Send s.a.e. for property events leaflet

£4.70; family £11.70. Grounds only £2.50. Booked parties of 15+ £3.90. Winter admission (4 Nov to March): reduced price for house; grounds free. Car park 150m, occasional charge of £1 (refundable on admission)

23 March to 3 Nov: as house; 4 Nov to March 2003: Sat & Sun 12.30–5, plus Fri in Nov & Dec until Christmas 12–4 (tel. 01822 853706). Independent craft workshops: variable opening (not Thur); tel. wood-turner (01364 631585), countryside artist (01752 783291)

Parking for disabled drivers near reception/shop. After admission at main reception, disabled passengers may be set down at the Abbey. Steep site, with access via gravel paths from car parks. Wheelchairs. Volunteer-driven buggy; ask in car park or at reception. Abbey: wheelchair stairclimber for access to middle floor (tel. to confirm). Restaurant: accessible via path with short steep slope. WC. Information leaflet on request

Braille and audio guides. Abbey 'touch' items. Scented herbs and plants. Advice leaflet on request

**For all your information needs check our website www.nationaltrust.org.uk**

**52 · SOUTH WEST**

- 🍽 Licensed self-service restaurant/tea-room open as shop. Restricted menu Nov to March 2003. Open Dec for booked Christmas lunches, candlelit dinners and events (tel. 01822 855024). Picnics in car park only
- 👶 Children's guide, parent and baby room, baby slings, children's menu; tel. for leaflet on children's activities and events
- 🎒 Sandford Award for Education. Resource books. Fully equipped schools' base, brass rubbing centre and kitchen handling collection; booking required. For further details contact our Education Officer
- 🚲 Lockable posts; discounted admission to house
- 🐕 On leads and only in car park; dog posts in shade
- ➔ (1:F8) 6ml S of Tavistock, 11ml N of Plymouth: turn off A386 ¼ml S of Yelverton [201: SX487667] **Bus**: Plymouth Citybus 55 from Yelverton (not Sun) (with connections from 🚆 Plymouth) **Station**: Bere Alston (U), 4½ml **Cycle**: NCN 27 2ml

**NT properties nearby** Antony, Cotehele, Lydford Gorge, Saltram

---

## CARNEWAS & BEDRUTHAN STEPS                    Cornwall
**Tel** 01637 860563 (Shop) · 01637 860701 (Café)

---

One of the most popular destinations on the Cornish coast, by virtue of the spectacular clifftop view of massive rock stacks marching into the distance across the sweep of Bedruthan beach (not NT). There are magnificent walks along the coast path between Carnewas and Park Head. The Trust has rebuilt the cliff staircase down to the beach, but it is **unsafe to bathe at any time** and visitors need to be aware of the risk of being cut off by the tide

- 🅾 All year. Shop and information centre in car park 29 March to end Oct: daily 10.30–5.30. Staircase closed 1 Nov to 28 Feb 2002
- 💷 Car park charge (NT members free)
- 🚶 Occasional guided walks (tel. for details). *Coast of Cornwall* leaflet no. 6 includes maps and details of circular walks in area, as well as information on local history, geology and wildlife
- 🛍 As shop and information centre
- ♿ Moderately flat access to viewpoint, but not designed for wheelchairs; WC
- 🍽 Tea-room and garden in Carnewas car park overlooking Bedruthan Steps, March to end Oct: daily 10–5; Nov & Dec: Sat & Sun 11–4
- ➔ (1:C8) Just off B3276 from Newquay to Padstow, 6ml SW of Padstow [200: SW849692] **Bus**: Western Greyhound 556 from 🚆 Newquay **Station**: Newquay 7ml

**NT properties nearby** Trerice

---

**Please remember – your membership card is always needed for free admission**

# CASTLE DROGO  Devon

Drewsteignton, nr Exeter EX6 6PB · **Tel** 01647 433306 · **Fax** 01647 433186
**Email** castledrogo@ntrust.org.uk

This granite castle, built between 1910 and 1930 for the self-made millionaire Julius Drewe, is one of the most remarkable works of Sir Edwin Lutyens. Perched on a moorland spur above the River Teign, it commands spectacular views of Dartmoor. The interior is designed for comfortable and elegant living, with an interesting kitchen and scullery and elaborately appointed bathrooms. There is a delightful formal garden with roses and herbaceous borders, as well as spring flowers and many fine walks in the estate

- **Castle**: 2–17 March: Sat & Sun (pre-season guided tours only); tel. for details. 23 March to 3 Nov: daily except Fri (but open Good Fri) 11–5.30. Guided tours each Fri 26 July to 30 Aug 11.00/1.00/3.00. **Garden**: all year: daily 10.30 to dusk

- £5.70; family £14.20. Garden & grounds only £2.90. Booked parties £4.80. Reduced rate for garden and grounds, Nov to Feb. Car park 400m. The croquet lawn is normally open; equipment can be hired at visitor reception

- Occasional guided walks on estate

- Shop & plant centre: 23 March to 3 Nov, daily 10.30–5.30; also 4 Nov to 22 Dec: daily except Mon & Tues 11–4.30 (tel. 01647 433563)

- Buggy service and wheelchairs. Close parking and access by arrangement, ask at visitor reception. Castle: reasonable access to hall, library, chapel and gun room; lift with seat (too small for most wheelchairs) to lower floor via 2 steps, dining and kitchen area. Garden: accessible. Tea-room, restaurant & shop: accessible. WC at visitor reception

- Braille guide; audio guide to castle. Scented plants

- Licensed restaurant 30 March to 29 Sept: as castle 12–5.30; Nov & Dec open for booked Christmas lunches and suppers (tel. 01647 432629). Tea-room 23 March to 3 Nov: daily 10.30–5.30; Nov & Dec: limited refreshments

- Children's guide, quizzes and events, children's menu, baby-changing facilities, babies in back carriers allowed. Playground near picnic site

- On leads and only in car park and on estate walks

- (1:F7) 5ml S of A30 Exeter–Okehampton road via Crockernwell or A382 Moretonhampstead–Whiddon Down road; coaches must use the latter and turn off at Sandy Park [191: SX721900] **Bus**: First Western National 173 Exeter–Newton Abbot (passing ≋ Exeter Central), Carmel 174 and First Western National 180 from ≋ Okehampton **Station**: Yeoford (U) 8ml

**NT properties nearby** Finch Foundry, Lydford Gorge

SNOWDROP

**For general enquiries, please telephone 0870 458 4000**

## CHEDWORTH ROMAN VILLA 🏛️     Gloucestershire

Yanworth, nr Cheltenham GL54 3LJ · **Tel** 01242 890256 · **Fax** 01242 890544
**Email** chedworth@ntrust.org.uk

The remains of one of the largest Romano-British villas in the country, set in a wooded Cotswold combe. Over one mile of walls survive and there are several fine mosaics, two bathhouses, hypocausts, a water-shrine and latrine. Excavated in 1864, the site still has a Victorian atmosphere and the site museum houses objects from the villa. A 15-minute audiovisual presentation gives visitors an insight into the history of this fascinating place

- 🅾️ 26 Feb to 31 March: 11–4; 2 April to 27 Oct: 10–5; 29 Oct to 17 Nov: 11–4. Daily except Mon (but open BH Mons). **Events**: Legio II Roman Legion July 27, 28; send s.a.e. for full programme
- 💷 £3.80; family £9.50 (additional charges for some special events, inc. NT members). School and other parties must book in advance. Party reduction negotiable. Free coach and car park. Audio tour £1
- 👤 For booked parties only; £12.50 for schools, £25 for others. Max. 30 people per guide
- 🛍️ As villa (not open for school parties outside normal hours)
- ♿ Reception building: ramped access; otherwise steps to most main features; some ramps
- 🎧 Free audio tour; sculpted stone details may be touched
- 👶 Free children's trails, activities for children throughout the school breaks, tel. the property. Baby-changing facilities. Children's guidebook and audio tours
- 🏫 School groups by arrangement. Activity room and resource book. Activity sheets. Living History days for schools, contact the property for details
- ➡️ (1:K2) 3ml NW of Fossebridge on Cirencester–Northleach road (A429), approach from A429 via Yanworth or from A436 via Withington (coaches must approach from Fossebridge) [163: SP053135] **Bus**: Cotswold Lion from Cirencester Wed & Sat June to Sept

**NT properties nearby** Lodge Park, Sherborne Park Estate, Snowshill Manor,

---

## THE CHURCH HOUSE 🏛️     Devon

Widecombe in the Moor, Newton Abbot TQ13 7TA · **Tel/Fax** 01364 621321

Originally a brewhouse dating back to 1537, this former village school is now leased as a village hall. The adjacent Sexton's Cottage is a NT shop and Dartmoor National Park information point

- 🅾️ Open to visitors when not in use as the village hall; tel. for access details
- 💷 Free (donation box)
- 🛍️ Shop & information point in Sexton's Cottage mid Feb to 24 Dec: daily from 10.30

---

**Please see the area introductions for details of coast & countryside properties**

♿ Ground floor accessible.

→ (1:F7) In centre of Dartmoor, N of Ashburton, W of Bovey Tracey [191: SX718768] **Bus**: First Western National 170/2 Newton Abbot–Totnes/Tavistock & 180 from Moretonhampstead (connections from Exeter) (June–Sept only) (tel. 01392 382800)

**NT properties nearby** Hembury Woods, Holne Woods, Parke

## CLEVEDON COURT

North Somerset

Tickenham Road, Clevedon BS21 6QU · **Tel** 01275 872257

An outstanding 14th-century manor house, with much of the original building still evident, incorporating a massive 12th-century tower and 13th-century great hall. Altered and added to by the Elizabethans, it has been home to the Elton family since 1709. The house contains many striking Eltonware pots and vases and a fascinating collection of Nailsea glass. There is also a beautiful 18th-century terraced garden

🔘 31 March to 29 Sept: Wed, Thur, Sun & BH Mons (also BH Tues 4 June) 2–5

£ £4.50; child £2. Parties and coaches by arrangement; no reduction. On-site parking, unsuitable for trailer caravans or motor caravans. No facilities for picnics

♿ House: ground floor accessible via 4 steps. Garden steep with many steps. No adapted WCs

👶 Children's guidebook. Nursery rhyme trail for younger children

🎓 Educational tours welcome, by arrangement

→ (1:I4) 1½ml E of Clevedon, on Bristol road (B3130), signposted from M5 exit 20 [172: ST423716] **Bus**: First Badgerline X7, 364, 662/3 from Bristol; X24/5, 824/5 from Weston-super-Mare (passing close ≠ Weston-super-Mare) **Station**: Yatton 3ml

**NT properties nearby** Dyrham Park, Horton Court

**Unless indicated, last admission is always 30 mins before closing time**

## CLOUDS HILL

Dorset

Wareham BH20 7NQ · **Tel** 01929 405616

A tiny isolated brick and tile cottage, bought in 1925 by T. E. Lawrence ('Lawrence of Arabia') as a retreat. The austere rooms inside are much as he left them and reflect his complex personality and close links with the Middle East

**What's new in 2002**: New guidebook

- 31 March to 27 Oct: daily except Mon, Tues & Wed (but open BH Mons and BH Tues 4 June) 12–5 or dusk if earlier; no electric light. Parties wishing to visit at other times must tel. in advance
- £2.80. No reduction for parties or children. Unsuitable for coaches or trailer caravans. No WC
- T. E. Lawrence books on sale
- Braille guide
- (1:J7) 9ml E of Dorchester, 1½ml E of Waddock crossroads (B3390), 4ml S of A35 Poole–Dorchester road, 1ml N of Bovington Camp [194: SY824909] **Bus**: First Southern 101–4, 107 National from ≋ Wool, alight Bovington, 1¼ml **Station**: Wool 3½ml; Moreton (U) 3½ml

**NT properties nearby** Brownsea Island, Corfe Castle, Hardy Monument, Hardy's Cottage, Kingston Lacy, Max Gate

## COLERIDGE COTTAGE

Somerset

35 Lime Street, Nether Stowey, Bridgwater TA5 1NQ · **Tel** 01278 732662

The home of Samuel Taylor Coleridge for three years from 1797, with mementoes of the poet on display. It was here that he wrote *The Rime of the Ancient Mariner*, part of *Christabel* and *Frost at Midnight*

- 24 March to 29 Sept: Tues, Wed, Thur & Sun 2–5
- £3; child £1.50. No reduction for parties which must book
- (1:H5) At W end of Nether Stowey, on S side of A39, 8ml W of Bridgwater [181: ST191399] **Bus**: First Southern National 15, 915 Bridgwater–Minehead (passing close ≋ Bridgwater) **Station**: Bridgwater 8ml

**NT properties nearby** Dunster Castle, Fyne Court, Holnicote Estate

## COLETON FISHACRE HOUSE & GARDEN

Devon

Coleton, Kingswear, Dartmouth TQ6 0EQ · **Tel** 01803 752466
**Fax** 01803 753017 · **Email** coletonfishacre@ntrust.org.uk

Spectacularly set in a stream-fed valley on a beautiful stretch of the NT South Devon coastline, the house was designed in 1925 for Rupert & Lady Dorothy D'Oyly Carte, who created the luxuriant garden around it. The house reflects the Arts & Crafts

There are special events at most Trust properties; please telephone 0870 458 4000 for details

tradition, but has refreshingly modern interiors; the garden has year-round interest with a gazebo, water features and fine collection of rare and exotic plants

- **Garden**: March: Sat & Sun only 11–5; 23 March to 3 Nov: daily except Mon & Tues (but open BH Mons & 3, 4 June) 10.30–5.30. **House**: from 23 March as garden 11–4.30. **Events**: tel. or send s.a.e. for details
- £4.90; child £2.40; family £12.20. Booked parties £4.20. Garden only £3.80; child £1.90. Booked parties £3.20 (coach parties must book in advance)
- Occasional guided walks by arrangement or as advertised under special events
- Small selection of gifts, postcards and unusual plants at reception
- House: ground-floor access only. Garden: limited access, upper paths reasonably flat with some grass paths, but steep slopes (strong companions for wheelchair users essential). Wheelchair can be booked. WC. Tea-garden: wheelchair accessible tables
- Braille guide to house and garden. Audio guide to house. Scented herbs and plants
- Tea-room as garden 10.30–5. Picnics in car park area only, where tables provided. Limited indoor seating in wet weather
- Baby-changing facilities; children's trail leaflets. Children's menu
- Rack; locks available
- On surrounding NT land only (must be on leads); tel. for details
- (1:G9) 3ml from Kingswear; take Lower Ferry road, turn off at toll house (take care on narrow lanes near property) [202: SX910508] **Bus**: Stagecoach in Devon 120 Torquay–Kingswear (passing ≷ Paignton); otherwise Stagecoach in Devon 22–4 Brixham–Kingswear (with connections from ≷ Paignton). On both, alight ¾ml SW of Hillhead, 1½ml walk to garden **Station**: Paignton 8ml; Kingswear (Paignton & Dartmouth Rly) 2¼ml by footpath, 2¾ml by road

**NT properties nearby** Bradley Manor, Compton Castle, Greenway, NT coastline on both sides of the Dart

---

# COMPTON CASTLE                                                                                  Devon
Marldon, Paignton TQ3 1TA · **Tel** 01803 875740 (answerphone) **Fax** 01803 875740

A magical fortified manor house, built between the 14th and 16th centuries and home to the Gilbert family for most of the last six hundred years. Sir Humphrey Gilbert (1539–1583) was coloniser of Newfoundland and half-brother to Sir Walter Ralegh. The dramatic towers and battlements shelter a stone courtyard, medieval great hall and minstrels' gallery. Also open are the courtyard, restored Great Hall, solar, chapel, rose garden and old kitchen

**Note**: Compton Castle is occupied and administered by Mr & Mrs G. E. Gilbert

- 1 April to 31 Oct: Mon, Wed & Thur (also 4 June) 10–12.15, 2–5
- £2.90. Booked parties £2.30; organisers should notify the Secretary. Additional parking at Castle Barton opposite entrance

---

**For all your information needs check our website www.nationaltrust.org.uk**

- Guidebooks, postcards and slides only
- Limited access
- Refreshments at Castle Barton (not NT) from 10 (tel. 01803 873314)
- Children's guidebook
- On leads in car park
- (1:G8) At Compton, 3ml W of Torquay, 1ml N of Marldon; from the Newton Abbot–Totnes road (A381) turn left at Ipplepen crossroads and W off Torbay ring road via Marldon [202: SX865648] **Bus**: Stagecoach Devon 7 Paignton–Marldon; First Western National 111 Dartmouth–Torquay (passing Totnes); 66 Brixham–Torquay. On all alight Marldon, 1½ml **Station**: Torquay 3ml

**NT properties nearby** Bradley Manor, Coleton Fishacre

## CORFE CASTLE    Dorset
Wareham BH20 5EZ · **Tel/Fax** 01929 481294 · **Email** corfecastle@ntrust.org.uk

One of Britain's most majestic ruins, the castle controlled the gateway through the Purbeck Hills and had been an important stronghold since the time of William the Conqueror. Defended during the Civil War by the redoubtable Lady Bankes, the castle fell to treachery from within, and was heavily slighted afterwards by the Parliamentarians. Many fine Norman and early English features remain

**What's new in 2002**: Seasonal, regular castle tours. New family guidebook. Improved on-site interpretation

- Daily all year (closed 25, 26 Dec and 1 day mid-March; tel. for details). *Times*: March: 10–5; April to Oct 10–6; Nov to Feb 2003 10–4. **Events**: living history events, archaeology weekend, traditional crafts, outdoor theatre, school holiday activities; tel. for details
- £4.30; child £2.15; family £10.80 (2 adults & 3 children); £6.50 (1 adult & 3 children). Parties £3.70, children £1.85. Car- & coach-parking available at Castle View off A351; also at Norden park-and-ride and West St (not NT). **Note**: All paying visitors arriving by public transport will be offered a reduction on the entry

**Please remember – your membership card is always needed for free admission**

price to the castle on production of a valid bus or train ticket. NT members arriving by bus or train will be offered a voucher which may be redeemed at the NT shop or tea-room in Corfe Castle (offer open until 31 Dec 2002)

- Castle View interactive family exhibition centre in NT car park. Guided tours often available during opening hours, April to Oct. Private groups by arrangement; tel. for details
- Daily (closed 25, 26 Dec). *Times*: March 10–5; April to Sept 10–6; Oct & March 2003 10–5; Nov to Feb 2003 10–4 (tel. 01929 480921)
- Ruins: Outer Bailey accessible. Shop, tea-room & exhibition centre with interactive displays: accessible. Adapted WC (RADAR lock; key from visitor centre and castle ticket office)
- Braille guide; many items and surfaces can be touched. Large-print guide
- Daily: March 10–5; April to Oct 10–5.30. Nov to Feb 2003 10–4 daily except Thur & Fri (closed 25, 26 Dec). Closed Jan/early Feb for redecoration, tel. 01929 481332 for dates
- Baby-changing facilities at visitor centre; baby carriers, highchairs and children's menu. Children's guidebook. Children must be accompanied by an adult within the castle
- Teachers' resource book, schools' study centre with hands-on materials; guided tours, contact Education Coordinator; tel. 01929 480609 for details
- Corfe Common walks leaflet from property or NT Wessex Office (50p plus 50p p&p)
- On leads only
- (1:K7) On A351 Wareham–Swanage road [195: SY959824] **Bus**: Wilts & Dorset 142/3/4 Poole–Swanage, Dorset Linkrider 29 Weymouth–Swanage. Both from Wareham **Station**: Mainline Wareham 4ml. Corfe Castle (Swanage Railway) a few minutes walk (park and ride from Norden Station). Discounted joint tickets available for visitors arriving from Swanage Railway (tel. 01929 425800)

## CORNISH MINES & ENGINES                                               Cornwall
Pool, nr Redruth · **Tel/Fax** 01209 315027

Cornwall's engine houses are dramatic reminders of the time when the county was a powerhouse of tin, copper and china clay mining. These two great beam engines were used for pumping water (from a depth of over 550m) and for winding men and ore. The engines were originally powered by high-pressure steam, introduced by the local engineer Richard Trevithick. Today one is rotated by electricity. The visit also includes the Industrial Discovery Centre at East Pool, which provides an overview of Cornwall's industrial heritage. Nearby is the Geological Museum of the Camborne School of Mines, where the Trust's Norris collection of minerals can be seen

**Note**: The property is managed by the Trevithick Trust on behalf of the National Trust. Trevithick Cottage is nearby at Penponds and is open April to Oct, Wed 2–5, free of charge (donations welcome)

## 60 · SOUTH WEST

- **Engine Houses and Industrial Discovery Centre**: 25 March to 3 Nov: daily except Sat (but open every day in Aug), 11–5. Nov to March 2003: by arrangement only; for details and group visits during this period tel./fax 01209 210900. For group visits at other times, contact the Trevithick Trust (tel./fax 01209 315027). **Geological Museum**: daily except Sat and Sun 9–5

- £5; family £13; concessions £4.60; students £3. Museum free

- Available

- As property

- Michell's Whim Engine: many flights of stairs. Industrial Discovery Centre and Taylor's Engine House: accessible by lift

- Braille guide for Michell's Whim Engine

- Mining diagrams and working models at both properties

- (1:B9) At Pool, 2ml W of Redruth on either side of A3047 [203: SW672415] **Bus**: From surrounding areas (some passing ≋ Redruth) **Station**: Redruth 2ml; Camborne 2ml **Cycle**: NCN 3 ½ml

**NT properties nearby** Glendurgan Garden, Trelissick Garden

---

# COTEHELE                                                               Cornwall

St Dominick, nr Saltash PL12 6TA · **Tel** 01579 351346 · **Infoline** 01579 352739
**Fax** 01579 351222 · **Email** cotehele@ntrust.org.uk

At the heart of this riverside estate, the house at Cotehele was mainly built 1485–1627 and was a home of the Edgcumbe family for centuries. Its granite and slatestone walls contain intimate chambers adorned with tapestries, original furniture and armour. Outside, the formal gardens overlook the richly planted valley garden below, with medieval dovecote, stewpond and Victorian summer-house, and 18th-century tower above. At the Quay there are interesting old buildings housing an art and craft gallery and an outstation of the National Maritime Museum. The restored Tamar sailing barge *Shamrock* is moored alongside. A network of footpaths throughout the estate provides a variety of riverside and woodland walks with a high nature conservation and industrial archaeology interest

**Note**: The number of visitors in the fragile house has to be limited to a maximum of 80 at a time and not more than 600 in one day. There is no electric light, so visitors should avoid dull days early and late in the season

- **House**: 23 March to 3 Nov: daily except Fri (but open Good Fri). *Times*: 23 March to 30 Sept 11–5; Oct–3 Nov 11–4.30; **Garden**: all year: daily 10.30 to dusk

---

**Please see the area introductions for details of coast & countryside properties**

£ £6.40; family £16. Garden & mill only £3.60; family £9. All parties only by written arrangement with the Property Manager, £5.40. Coach party organisers will be sent a copy of the route when they book. No parties Sun or BHols

🗓 23 March to 3 Nov: daily 11–5 or dusk if earlier. Nov & Dec: Christmas shop (tel. 01579 352713). Cotehele Quay Art & Craft Gallery: daily 12–5 or dusk if earlier; Nov & Dec: Christmas opening (tel. 01579 351494 or 351346)

♿ Close parking by arrangement. House: hall and kitchen accessible; ramps available at house. Garden: flat area around house, but valley very steep; loose gravel. Restaurant & shop: ramps available. Wheelchairs at reception. Quay tea-room: accessible. Woodland walks: some paths accessible

👁 Braille guides for house, garden and mill; some items in house and mill may be touched on request. Scented plants

☕ Licensed restaurant in the Barn, open as house (tel. 01579 352711). Light refreshments and ice creams at the Edgcumbe Arms on Cotehele Quay, daily during season (tel. 01579 350024); Nov & Dec: limited opening

🚼 Parent and baby room

🏫 Schools' resource pack. Environmental education facilities. National Maritime Museum outstation on Quay. Education rooms in garden and in Loft on Quay. All school enquiries, tel. 01579 351346

🐕 Under close control and only on woodland walks

➡ (1:E8) On W bank of the Tamar, 1ml W of Calstock by steep footpath (6ml by road), 8ml SW of Tavistock, 14ml from Plymouth via Saltash Bridge; 2ml E of St Dominick, 4ml from Gunnislake (turn at St Ann's Chapel); Calstock can be reached from Plymouth by water (contact Plymouth Boat Cruises Ltd, tel. 01752 822797) and from Calstock (tel. 01822 833331) [201: SX422685] **Bus**: First Western National 79, Callington–Tavistock (passing ≠ Gunnislake) **Station**: Calstock (U), 1½ml (signposted from station)

**NT properties nearby** Antony, Buckland Abbey, Lydford Gorge, Saltram

**Unless indicated, last admission is always 30 mins before closing time**

## COTEHELE MILL    Cornwall

see main Cotehele entry, · **Tel** (opening hours) 01579 350606 or 351346
**Email** cotehele@ntrust.org.uk

Tucked away in dense woodland, this water mill, restored to working order, is a fine reminder of the recent past when corn was ground here for the local community. Nearby, a range of agricultural outbuildings contains a collection of a blacksmiths', carpenters', wheelwrights' and saddlers' tools and are presented as workshops, giving an insight into the working life of local craftsmen.

**What's new in 2002**: A small exhibition explains other aspects of the working estate and provides details of walks to inspire visitors to explore the riverside and surrounding countryside. Occasional corn-grinding days, please tel. for details

- 23 March to 30 June, 1 Sept to 3 Nov: daily except Fri (but open Good Fri); July & Aug: daily. *Times*: 23 March to 30 June & Sept 1–5.30; July & Aug 1–6; 1 Oct to 3 Nov 1–4.30.
- £3.60; family £9. Also admits to Cotehele garden, 1 ml away. Parties by written arrangement only
- See main Cotehele entry
- Limited close parking by prior arrangement. Water wheel and ground-floor workshops accessible
- Noisy machinery. Workshop tools may be handled
- See main Cotehele entry
- Guided schools' visits by prior arrangement. General school enquiries, tel. 01579 351346
- Under close control on woodland walk to mill. Dogs not allowed in the mill buildings
- (1:) see main Cotehele entry

**Note**: there is no parking at the mill except by prior arrangement for visitors with disabilities. All visitors must park at Cotehele Quay and walk 0.3 ml through the woods. Do not forget your membership card!

## THE COURTS GARDEN    Wiltshire

Holt, nr Trowbridge BA14 6RR · **Tel/Fax** 01225 782340
**Email** courtsgarden@ntrust.org.uk

One of Wiltshire's best-kept secrets, the English garden style at its best, full of charm and variety. There are many interesting plants and an imaginative use of colour, with surrounding topiary, water features and garden ornaments. Complemented by an arboretum with natural planting of spring bulbs

**What's new in 2002**: Tea-room and garden exhibition in the house to open during the season, tel. for details of opening times

**There are special events at most Trust properties; please telephone 0870 458 4000 for details**

SOUTH WEST · 63

- [O] 24 March to 13 Oct: daily (closed Sat), 12–5.30. Out of season by appointment only. **Events**: series of garden-based walks and talks (tel. 01985 843601 for details)
- [£] £4; child £2. Parties by arrangement with the Head Gardener. No WC
- NT shop in Lacock (tel. 01249 730302)
- Parking in village, not NT (50 metres). Garden: largely accessible. One wheelchair. WC in village hall, not NT
- Scented plants; Braille guide and large-print guide
- Cycle rack
- → (1:J4) 3ml SW of Melksham, 2½ml E of Bradford-on-Avon, on S side of B3107 [173: ST861618] **Bus**: First Badgerline 237/8 Trowbridge–Corsham/Calne (passing close ≷ Trowbridge) **Station**: Bradford-on-Avon 2½ml; Trowbridge 3ml **Cycle**: NCN 4 1¼ml

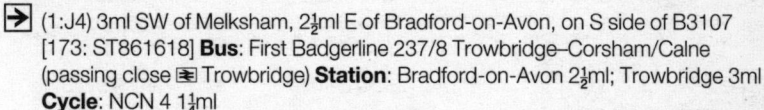

**NT properties nearby** Lacock Abbey & Fox Talbot Museum, Great Chalfield Manor, Westwood Manor

YELLOW FLAG

---

## DUNSTER CASTLE  Somerset

Dunster, nr Minehead TA24 6SL · **Tel** 01643 821314 · **Infoline** 01643 823004 **Fax** 01643 823000 · **Email** dunstercastle@ntrust.org.uk

Dramatically sited atop a wooded hill, there has been a castle here since at least Norman times. The 13th-century gatehouse survives, but the present building was remodelled in 1868–72 by Antony Salvin for the Luttrell family, who lived here for 600 years. The fine oak staircase and plasterwork of the 17th-century house he adapted can still be seen. There is a sheltered terrace to the south on which tender plants and shrubs grow, and beautiful parkland in which to walk

**What's new in 2002**: Tenants' Hall exhibition – Feudal Stronghold and Family Home – reveals the significance of Dunster Castle to Britain's turbulent history

- [O] **Castle**: 23 March to 3 Nov: daily except Thur & Fri (but open Good Fri). *Times*: 23 March to 25 Sept: 11–5; 28 Sept to 3 Nov: 11–4. **Garden & park**: daily (closed 25, 26 Dec). *Times*: Jan to March, 28 Sept to 31 Dec: 11–4; 23 March to 27 Sept: 10–5. **Events**: very varied programme; for full details tel. 01985 843601
- [£] Castle, garden & park £6.20; child (under 16) £3.10; family £15.50. Booked parties £5.20. Garden & park only £3; child (under 16) £1.50; family £7.50. Castle is a 10min steep climb from car park, but multiseater vehicle available to give lifts if necessary. Car park in grounds
- Contact Visitor Services tel. 01643 821314 for details of out of hours guided tours of house and/or attics and basements

**For all your information needs check our website www.nationaltrust.org.uk**

## 64 · SOUTH WEST

- Daily: 23 March to 27 Sept 10–5; 28 Sept to 1 Jan 11–4. Closed 25, 26 Dec and 2 to 31 Jan 2003. Feb & March 2003 daily 11–4 (tel. 01643 821626)
- Castle and garden are on a steep hill. Volunteer-driven multiseater and self-drive vehicle for transport from car park. Castle: accessible to manual wheelchairs via stairclimber. Property plan shows wheelchair-friendly routes. Shop: accessible, but cobbled floor
- Braille and large-print guides; audio tapes. Wide variety of contents can be touched. Scented plants and flowers in conservatory and garden
- Picnic area in park. Large choice of refreshments in Dunster village and tea-garden at watermill (not NT)
- Baby-changing facilities. Buggy park; back carriers, slings and reins from front porch. Children's guidebook; activity trails and colouring sheets. Activity days; tel. for details
- Study centre. Teachers' resource book (£3.50). For assistance and bookings, contact Education Coordinator
- Racks in main car park
- On leads and only in park
- (1:G5) In Dunster, 3ml SE of Minehead. NT car park approached direct from A39 [181: ST995435] **Bus**: First Southern National 39 from Minehead; otherwise 28, 300, 928 Taunton–Minehead (passing ≣ Taunton), or 15, 915 Bridgwater–Minehead, alight Dunster Steep, ½ml **Station**: Dunster (W Somerset Steam Rly) 1ml

**NT properties nearby** Arlington Court, Coleridge Cottage, Dunster Mill, Holnicote Estate

---

## DUNSTER WORKING WATERMILL     Somerset
Mill Lane, Dunster, nr Minehead TA24 6SW · **Tel** 01643 821759

---

Built on the site of a mill mentioned in the Domesday Survey of 1086, the present mill dates from the 18th century and was restored to working order in 1979.

**Note**: The mill is a private business and all visitors, including NT members, are asked to pay the admission charge

- 23 March to 3 Nov: daily. *Times*: 10.30–5
- £2.20; family tickets; party rates by arrangement. The mill is run and maintained by private funding; NT members pay normal admission charge. Parking ¼ml
- For groups by arrangement
- Selling mill flour, muesli & mill souvenirs
- Ground floor accessible free
- Riverside tea-room (not NT): 1 April to 31 Oct daily except Fri (open Good Fri and Fris in July & Aug): 10.30–5

**Please remember – your membership card is always needed for free admission**

SOUTH WEST · 65

- School parties welcome, but must book
- (1:G5) On River Avill, beneath Castle Tor; approach via Mill Lane or Castle Gardens on foot; from car park in Dunster village or in old park [181: ST995435] **Bus**: As Dunster Castle

**NT properties nearby** Arlington Court, Coleridge Cottage, Dunster Castle, Holnicote Estate

## DYRHAM PARK

South Gloucestershire

nr Chippenham SN14 8ER · **Tel/Fax** 01179 372501
**Email** dyrhampark@ntrust.org.uk

Crowned with a balustrade and with fine views over its ancient deer park, Dyrham was built between 1691 and 1702 for William Blathwayt, William III's Secretary at War and Secretary of State. The rooms have changed little since they were furnished by Blathwayt and their contents are recorded in his housekeeper's inventory. There are many fine textiles and paintings, as well as items of blue-and-white delftware, reflecting the contemporary taste for Dutch fashions. Restored Victorian domestic rooms open (and for extended period, see below), including kitchen, bells passage, bakehouse, larders, tenants' hall and Delft-tiled dairy. Car park has been relocated to the East Lodge, and a free bus now takes visitors to and from the house, thereby restored to its original, car-free, setting. Audio tours of the house, colour souvenir guidebook and CD-ROM available to purchase

**House**: 23 March to 3 Nov: 12–5.30 (last admissions to house 4.45): daily except Wed & Thur. **Garden**: 23 March to 3 Nov: 11–5.30 (or dusk if earlier) daily except Wed & Thur. **Park**: daily (closed 25 Dec) 11–5.30 or dusk if earlier. **Winter opening for domestic rooms**: 9 Nov to 15 Dec: Sat & Sun 12–4. **Note**: Property closed 5–8 July for concerts. **Events**: 6/7 July Music Festival; also opera in West Garden; for details tel. 01985 843601. Picnics welcome in park, but parties of 20+ please tel. in advance. No barbecues

£7.90; child £3.90; family £19.50. Grounds only £3; child £1.50; family £7. Park only (on days when house and garden closed) £2; child £1. Winter: park and domestic rooms £4; child £2. Party rate weekdays only; contact Property Manager. Coaches by arrangement

23 March to 3 Nov: as house; 9 Nov to 15 Dec: Sat & Sun 12–4 (tel. 0117 937 4300)

Free accessible bus from car park to house. House: ground floor accessible; stairclimber on West Terrace; access to domestic areas; only four upstairs rooms inaccessible and photograph album of these rooms available. Wheelchairs. Orangery, terrace, restaurant & shop: accessible

For general enquiries, please telephone 0870 458 4000

## 66 · SOUTH WEST

- 👁 Braille and tape guides to house. Hearing loop in reception buildings and some rooms in house. Braille menu. Large-print guide
- 👂 Sympathetic Hearing Scheme
- 🍽 Licensed restaurant: as house 11–5.30, last orders 5; also 9 Nov to 15 Dec, Sat & Sun 12–4. Also available for private functions tel. (01179 374293). Possible kiosk service in top car park, tel. for times (01179 374293)
- 👶 Baby-changing facilities. Children's guidebook illustrated by member of the Blathwayt family
- 📚 Teachers' resource material. Study centre. For all details, including domestic areas open outside normal hours, contact the Education Co-ordinator, tel. 0117 937 2501
- 🐕 Only in dog-walking area
- ➡ (1:J4) 8ml N of Bath,12ml E of Bristol; approached from Bath–Stroud road (A46), 2ml S of Tormarton interchange with M4, exit 18 [172: ST743757] **Bus**: Special link ⇌ Bath Spa into Dyrham **Station**: Bath Spa 8ml

**NT properties nearby** Horton Court, Lacock Abbey & Fox Talbot Museum

---

# FINCH FOUNDRY                                                            Devon
Sticklepath, Okehampton EX20 2NW · **Tel** 01837 840046

---

A fascinating 19th-century water-powered forge, which produced agricultural and mining hand tools. Still in working order with regular demonstrations throughout the day, the foundry has three waterwheels driving the huge tilt hammer and grindstone

- 🅾 23 March to 3 Nov: daily except Tues (but open 4 June) 11–5.30
- 💷 £3; child £1.50. **Note**: access to car park is narrow and unsuitable for coaches and wide vehicles
- 🏪 As foundry
- ♿ Disabled drivers may park in front of building. Foundry: can be viewed through shop windows. Workshop & museum: access difficult. Shop: accessible
- 👁 Braille guide; objects can be touched; volunteers will explain history of foundry
- 🍽 As foundry, serving light lunches and cream teas
- 🚲 Secure parking at back of foundry
- 🐕 Dogs welcome in Foundry and surroundings
- ➡ (1:F7) 4ml E of Okehampton off the A30 [191:SX641940] **Bus**: First Western National X9/10 Exeter–Bude, passing ⇌ Exeter St David's **Station**: Okehampton (Sun, Jun–Sept only) 4½ml

**NT properties nearby** Castle Drogo, Lydford Gorge

---

**Please see the area introductions for details of coast & countryside properties**

## FYNE COURT
Somerset

Broomfield, Bridgwater TA5 2EQ · **Tel** 01823 451587

Formerly the pleasure grounds of the now demolished home of the pioneer electrician, Andrew Crosse (1784–1855), this nature reserve is now the headquarters of the Somerset Wildlife Trust and a visitor centre for the Quantocks

- All year 9–6 or sunset if earlier
- Free. Car park charge. Coach-parking by arrangement only
- Easter to Christmas: daily 2–5 (not NT)
- Trail for disabled visitors. Tea-room patio: accessible in fine weather
- May to Sept: teas on Sun and BHols (not NT). Picnic sites
- (1:H5) 6ml N of Taunton; 6ml SW of Bridgwater [182: ST222321] **Station**: Taunton 6ml

**NT properties nearby** Dunster Castle, Holnicote Estate

## GLASTONBURY TOR
Somerset

nr Glastonbury · **Tel** 01985 843600 (Regional Office)

The dramatic and evocative Tor dominates the Somerset Levels and offers spectacular views over Somerset, Dorset and Wiltshire. At the summit of this very steep hill an excavation has revealed the plans of two superimposed churches of St Michael, of which only the 15th-century tower remains

**Note**: During summer 2002 the tower will be under extensive repairs and repointing

- All year
- Free. Information leaflet (50p) available from mobile recruitment Land Rover April to Oct or from NT Wessex Regional Office (please add 50p for p&p). Please use council run park-and-ride from centre of Glastonbury from April to Sept. No parking at Tor except for orange badge holders
- In Wells
- Large-print guide available from regional office
- On leads only
- (1:I5) Signposted from Glastonbury, from where seasonal park-and-ride (not NT) operates [182/183: ST512386] **Bus**: First Badgerline 29, 929 from ⇌ Taunton, 173 from ⇌ Bath Spa (Sun only), 376/7, 929, 976/7 from ⇌ Bristol Temple Meads, 377, 977 from Yeovil. All pass within ½ml of the Tor **Cycle**: NCN 3

**NT properties nearby** Lytes Cary Manor, Stourhead

---

**Unless indicated, last admission is always 30 mins before closing time**

## GLENDURGAN GARDEN    Cornwall

Mawnan Smith, nr Falmouth TR11 5JZ ·
**Tel** 01326 250906 (opening hours only) or 01872 862090 · **Fax** 01872 865808
**Email** glendurgan@ntrust.org.uk

A valley garden of great beauty, created in the 1820s and running down to the tiny village of Durgan and its beach. There are many fine trees and rare and exotic plants, with outstanding spring displays of magnolias and camellias. Late in the season a glorious display of wild flowers carpets the valley slopes. The laurel maze, dating from 1833, puzzles young and old. The house is privately occupied

**What's new in 2002**: Reconstruction of original schoolroom in cob and thatch

- 16 Feb to 2 Nov: daily except Sun & Mon (but open BH Mons & closed Good Fri) 10.30–5.30; last admission 4.30
- £3.90; family £9.75. Booked parties £3.20
- Shop & plant sales as garden
- The garden is not really suited to wheelchairs. All paths are steep; a viewing point is accessible but a strong companion is needed
- Braille guide
- Snacks and light refreshments
- Giant's Stride (a pole with ropes to swing from) and the maze
- (1:C9) 4ml SW of Falmouth, ½ml SW of Mawnan Smith, on road to Helford Passage [204: SW772277] **Bus**: Truronian T4 from Falmouth (passing close Penmere) **Station**: Penmere (U) 4ml

**NT properties nearby** Trelissick Garden

## THE GODOLPHIN ESTATE    Cornwall

**Tel** 01326 561407 (Lizard Countryside Office) · **Fax** 01326 562882
**Email** godolphin@ntrust.org.uk

The Trust acquired this ancient estate of 236ha (585 acres) in 2000; improvements to public access have been and continue to be made. The historic landscape includes Godolphin Hill, from which there are wonderful views over west Cornwall, and more than 400 recorded archaeological features ranging from Bronze Age enclosures to dramatic 19th-century mine buildings

- Open all year

---

**There are special events at most Trust properties; please telephone 0870 458 4000 for details**

## SOUTH WEST · 69

- 🚶 Occasional guided walks, tel. for details
- ♿ Newly created riverside path, plus track through woods to Count House, suitable for wheelchairs
- 🍴 Refreshments at Godolphin House when open, and nearby at Godolphin Cross and Townshend
- 🎓 Education base in the Godolphin Count House. For bookings and information tel. Lizard Countryside Office
- 🐕 Welcome on leads and under control
- ➡ (1:B9) From Helston take A394 to Sithney Common, turn right onto B3302 and follow signs. From Hayle take B3302 through Leedstown. From the west, take B3280 through Goldsithney **Bus**: First Western National 39 Camborne–Helston (passing close ≋ Camborne) **Station**: St Erth 5ml

**Note: GODOLPHIN HOUSE (tel./fax. 01736 763194) is PRIVATELY OWNED but shares the Trust's car parks and, when open, offers facilities to complement the estate. OPEN: from Easter Monday to end Sept; for days and times please tel. Group tours by arrangement only. Refreshments and plant sales available during house opening times**

**NT properties nearby** St Michael's Mount

---

## GREAT CHALFIELD MANOR 🏠✝✿                                                          Wiltshire
nr Melksham SN12 8NJ · **Tel** 01225 782239 · **Fax** 01225 783379

A charming manor house, enhanced by a moat and gatehouse and with beautiful oriel windows and a great hall. Completed in 1480, the manor and gardens were restored earlier last century, *c.*1905–11, by Major R. Fuller, whose family live here and manage the property. The garden, designed by Alfred Parsons, to complement the manor, has been replanted

- 🕐 2 April to 31 Oct: Tues, Wed, Thur by guided tours only at 12.15, 2.15, 3, 3.45 & 4.30. The tours take 45min and numbers are limited to 25. Visitors arriving during a tour can visit the adjoining parish church and garden first. **Note**: Group visits are welcome on Fri & Sat (not BHols) by written arrangement with Mrs Robert Floyd. Organisers of coach parties should allow 2hrs because of limits on numbers in house
- 💷 £4. No reduction for children or parties
- ♿ Garden: limited access
- ➡ (1:J4) 3ml SW of Melksham off B3107 via Broughton Gifford Common (sign for Atworth, drive on left) [166: ST860630] **Bus**: First Badgerline 237/238 Trowbridge–Corsham/Calne (passing close ≋ Trowbridge), alight Holt, 1ml by footpath **Station**: Bradford-on-Avon, 3ml **Cycle**: NCN 4

**NT properties nearby** The Courts Garden, Lacock Abbey & Fox Talbot Museum, Westwood Manor

---

**For all your information needs check our website www.nationaltrust.org.uk**

## GREENWAY 🏠✤                                             Devon

Greenway Road, Galmpton, nr Churston Ferrers TQ5 0ES · **Tel** 01803 842382
**Email** greenway@ntrust.org.uk

Greenway is a glorious woodland garden on the banks of the River Dart that time seems to have passed by. Renowned for rare half-hardy plants underplanted by native wild flowers, a true 'secret' garden of peace and tranquillity. A unique and important estate on the Dart estuary

**Note**: To protect the amenities of local people living on the roads leading to Greenway, the Trust is required to restrict the number of visitors' vehicles admitted to the property. **All visitors (both members and non-members) intending to arrive by car/mini-coach (max 25-seaters) must tel. 01803 842382 to book a parking space before arriving at this property**. Visitors arriving without having booked a parking space will not be admitted. There are no parking spaces on the narrow country lanes leading to the property

- ⭕ 6 March to 5 Oct: Wed, Thur, Fri & Sat 10.30–5. Please note, this property will be **closed** on Mon 3 and Tues 4 June
- £ £3.50; child £1.75. Booked parties and visitors arriving on foot £2.75; child £1.40
- 🛍 Shop and plant sales as garden
- ♿ Many paths are steep, some parts of the garden wheelchair accessible with a strong pusher. Blue paths and red paths to distinguish ease of route
- ☕ Café serving light meals, organic and vegetarian food
- ➡ (1:G8) Green transport routes to Greenway: Dartmouth to Dittisham 'Red and Yellow' ferry (tel. 01803 833206), park in Dartmouth Park & Ride, the ferry leaves from North Embankment double steps. Car to Goodrington Park & Ride, steam train to Churston station, walk down Greenway Road (30 mins). **Bus**: Alansway 106 ≋ Paignton–Galmpton, thence 1½ml **Station**: Paignton 4½ml; Churston (Paignton & Dartmouth Rly) 2 ml

CHIFFCHAFF

**NT properties nearby** Bradley Manor, Coleton Fishacre, Compton Castle, NT coastline on both sides of Dart

---

## HAILES ABBEY ✝🛡                                   Gloucestershire

nr Winchcombe, Cheltenham GL54 5PB · **Tel** 01242 602398
**Email** customers@english-heritage.org.uk · **Web** www.english-heritage.org.uk

Founded in 1246 and once a celebrated pilgrimage site, this Cistercian abbey now lies in ruins. Remains of the dramatic cloister arches survive and there is a small museum

---

**Please remember – your membership card is always needed for free admission**

## SOUTH WEST · 71

**Note**: Hailes Abbey is financed, managed and maintained by English Heritage. For further information contact EH Regional Office, tel. 0117 975 0700

**What's new in 2002**: 750th anniversary year of the Abbey

- **Site & Museum**: April to end Oct: daily, 10–6 (10–5 in Oct). Nov to end March 2003: closed. **Events**: tel. for details
- £2.80; concessions £2.10; children (5–15) £1.40 (inc. tape guide). NT members charged admission on special event days
- EH shop in museum
- Site and museum: largely accessible
- Braille guide; tape guides, including basic tape for people with learning disabilities; touch prints
- Loop system for hearing-impaired visitors
- Ice creams and soft drinks
- Baby-changing facilities
- Teachers' handbook. Free admission for booked school parties; tel. for information
- On leads and only in grounds
- (1:K2) 2ml NE of Winchcombe, 1ml E of Broadway road (B4632, originally A46) [150: SP050300] **Bus**: Castleways from Cheltenham (passing close ≋ Cheltenham) alight Didbrook, 1½ml, or more frequent to Greet, 1¾ml by footpath **Station**: Cheltenham 10ml

**NT properties nearby** Hidcote Manor Garden, Snowshill Manor

---

## HARDY MONUMENT                                         Dorset

Black Down, Portesham · **Tel** 01202 882493 (Dorset Estates Office)
**Fax** 01202 841855 (Dorset Estates Office)

---

A monument erected in 1844 in memory of Vice-Admiral Sir Thomas Masterman Hardy, Flag-Captain of HMS *Victory* at the Battle of Trafalgar. It has been recently restored by the Trust. Tremendous views across Dorset countryside

- 31 March to 29 Sept: Sat & Sun 11–5. May close in bad weather. Staffed by volunteers. Numbers at the top of the monument are limited. Children must be accompanied by an adult
- £1; no reduction for children. No WC
- (1:I7) From the B3157 Weymouth–Bridport road, turn off at Portesham; the road climbs steeply to a car park signposted 'Hardy Monument' [194: SY613876] **Bus**: First Southern National X53 ≋ Weymouth–Exeter, alight Portesham, then 1¾ml by footpath **Station**: Dorchester South or Dorchester West (U), both 6ml

**NT properties nearby** Clouds Hill, Hardy's Cottage, Max Gate

**For general enquiries, please telephone 0870 458 4000**

## HARDY'S COTTAGE 🏠✼ — Dorset
Higher Bockhampton, nr Dorchester DT2 8QJ · **Tel** 01305 262366

The small cob and thatch cottage where novelist and poet Thomas Hardy was born in 1840 and from where he would walk to school every day in Dorchester, six miles away. It was built by his great-grandfather and is little altered since. The interior has been furnished by the Trust (see also Max Gate)

- 🅞 1 April to 4 Nov: daily except Fri & Sat (but open Good Fri) 11–5 (or dusk if earlier). Cottage is 10min walk through woods from car park. No coach-parking
- £ £2.80. No reduction for children or parties. School parties and coaches by arrangement only. No WC
- 🛍 At 65 High West St, Dorchester (tel. 01305 267535); Hardy's works on sale
- ♿ Car-parking arrangements with Custodian. Garden: accessible
- 👁 Large-print guide
- ➔ (1:J7) 3ml NE of Dorchester, ½ml S of A35 [194: SY728925] **Bus**: Wilts & Dorset X84, 184–6 Weymouth–Salisbury, 187–9 Poole–Dorchester (all pass ⮕ Dorchester South & close Dorchester West), alight Bockhampton Lane, ½ml **Station**: Dorchester South 4ml; Dorchester West (U) 4ml

**NT properties nearby** Clouds Hill, Hardy Monument, Max Gate

## HEDDON VALLEY SHOP 🏊🚗🚶 — Devon
Heddon Valley, Parracombe, Barnstaple EX31 4PX · **Tel** 01598 763402

An information centre and gift shop set in a spectacular NT-owned wooded valley on Exmoor's coast. The area offers many beautiful coastal and woodland walks

- 🅞 23 March to 3 Nov: daily. *Times*: March, April, May & Oct 11–5; June to Sept 10.30–6
- £ Free. Donations welcome. Car park
- 🚶 See local listings for programme of guided walks on the surrounding coastal estate. Walks leaflet from shop
- 🛍 Gift shop
- ☕ Confectionery, ice creams and cold drinks
- 🎒 By arrangement with the Warden (tel. 01598 763306)
- ➔ (1:F5) Halfway between Combe Martin and Lynton, off the A39 at Hunters Inn [180:SS655481] **Bus**: First Red Bus 309, 310 Barnstaple–Lynton (passing close ⮕ Barnstaple), alight just N of Parracombe, thence 2ml

**NT properties nearby** Arlington Court, Dunster Castle, Watersmeet

---

**Please see the area introductions for details of coast & countryside properties**

SOUTH WEST · 73

# HIDCOTE MANOR GARDEN

Gloucestershire

Hidcote Bartrim, nr Chipping Campden GL55 6LR · **Tel** 01386 438333
**Infoline** 01684 855370 · **Fax** 01386 438817
**Email** hidcote@ntrust.org.uk

One of England's great gardens, an 'Arts & Crafts' masterpiece created by the horticulturist Major Lawrence Johnston. A series of outdoor rooms, each with a different character and separated by walls and hedges of many different species, the garden is famous for its rare shrubs and trees, outstanding herbaceous borders and unusual plant species from all over the world. The varied styles of the outdoor rooms peak at different times of year, making for an interesting visit at any time

**Note**: Hidcote is liable to overcrowding on BH Mons and fine Suns. As the number of parties is limited per day, party leaders should check with property before booking transport

- 23 March to end May, Aug to 3 Nov: daily except Thur & Fri (but open Good Fri); June & July: daily except Fri. *Times*: March to end Sept 10.30–6.30; Oct to 3 Nov 10.30–5.30; last admission 1hr before closing or dusk if earlier.
  **Events**: send s.a.e. for details

- £5.80; family £14.50. Coaches & parties by appointment only (tel. 01386 438333); no party reduction. No picnicking and no games in garden. Free car park

- 23 March to 3 Nov: as garden 11–5.30; 8 Nov to 15 Dec: Fri, Sat & Sun 12–4. Plant sales centre as garden to end Sept 10.30–5.30

- Gravelled car park; disabled visitors may be set down at entrance. Garden: partly accessible; steps and informal stone-paved paths. Restaurant: contact Restaurant Manager to arrange level access. Tea bar: accessible. Two power-assisted wheelchairs

- Braille and tape guides. Scented plants

- Licensed Garden Restaurant (waitress service) 23 March to 3 Nov: as garden 12–2.30 & 3–5.30; 8 Nov to 15 Dec: Fri, Sat & Sun 12–4. The restaurant is unable to accept reservations, except for parties of 10–30 people, between 23 March and 3 Nov. Booking essential at all other times. Tea bar for light refreshments 23 March to end Sept: as garden 10.30–5.30 (opening subject to weather). Further details from Property Catering Manager, tel. 01386 438703

- (1:L1) 4ml NE of Chipping Campden, 1ml E of B4632 (originally A46), off B4081. Coaches are not permitted through Chipping Camden High Street [151: SP176429] **Station**: Honeybourne (U) 4½ml **Cycle**: NCN 5 1¼ml

**NT properties nearby** Chastleton House, Charlecote Park, Dover's Hill, The Fleece Inn, Snowshill Manor, Upton House

**Unless indicated, last admission is always 30 mins before closing time**

## HOLNICOTE ESTATE 🏠✝🚶            Somerset
Selworthy, Minehead TA24 8TJ · **Tel** 01643 862452 · **Fax** 01643 863011
**Email** holnicote@ntrust.org.uk

The Holnicote Estate covers 5042ha (12,500 acres) of Exmoor National Park and includes the high tors of Dunkery and Selworthy Beacons, with breathtaking views in all directions. Its traditional cottages and farms are grouped in and around the villages and hamlets, which include Selworthy, Allerford, Bossington, Horner and Luccombe. The Estate also covers 4ml of coastline between Porlock Bay and Minehead, where the South West Peninsula Coastal Path begins. There are over 100ml of footpaths to enjoy through the fields, woods, moors and villages. The area is noted for its diversity of wildlife and many rare species can be found in the Horner and Dunkery National Nature Reserve

**What's new in 2002**: A new leaflet, *Selworthy Green*, is available, price 60p, from local NT shops, or by post, tel. 01985 843601. Also *Holnicote Walks* pack, for villages, coastline, archaeology and wildlife. 8 walks, each 60p (£3.99 for the set)

- ⓞ All year
- 🛍 Shop & information centre on *Selworthy Green*; mid March to end April: daily 11–4; May to Sept: daily 10–5; Oct: daily 11–4; Nov: Sat & Sun 10–4
- ♿ Easy access trails at North Hill (SS911477) and Webbers Post (SS903439). Adapted bird hide (SS907463). Other parts also accessible; tel. for details
- 🍴 Tea-rooms (not NT and seasonal only) at Allerford, Bossington, Horner, Luccombe and Selworthy
- 📚 Teachers' resource book. Study centre. Contact the Estate Office 01643 862452
- → (1:G5) Off A39 Minehead–Porlock, 3ml W of Minehead [181: SS920469]
  **Bus**: First Southern National 38, 300, Minehead–Porlock, alight Holnicote, thence ½ml **Station**: Minehead (West Somerset Rly) 5ml

**NT properties nearby** Arlington Court, Dunster Castle, Watersmeet House

## HORTON COURT 🏠🏠          South Gloucestershire
Horton, nr Chipping Sodbury, Bristol BS17 6QR · **Tel** 01249 730141
**Fax** 01454 320510

A Norman hall and an exceptionally fine detached ambulatory are all that remain of what is probably the oldest rectory in England. There are interesting early Renaissance features, including stucco caricatures of classical figures. House not open to the public. Horton Camp, an Iron Age hill-fort with open access, is situated 500m south of Horton Court

- ⓞ 3 April to 2 Nov: Wed & Sat 2–6 or dusk if earlier. Other times by written appointment with tenant
- £ £2; child £1. Unsuitable for coaches. No WC
- ♿ Close parking on application to tenant. Ambulatory accessible

**There are special events at most Trust properties; please telephone 0870 458 4000 for details**

→ (1:J3) 3ml NE of Chipping Sodbury, ¾ml N of Horton, 1ml W of the Bath–Stroud road (A46) [172: ST766851] **Station**: Yate 5ml

**NT properties nearby** Dyrham Park, Lacock Abbey & Fox Talbot Museum

## KILLERTON
Devon

Broadclyst, Exeter EX5 3LE · **Tel** 01392 881345 · **Fax** 01392 883112
**Email** killerton@ntrust.org.uk

The house, home of the Aclands, was rebuilt in 1778 to the design of John Johnson. Furnished as a comfortable family home, it houses the Paulise de Bush costume collection, displayed in period rooms, and a Victorian laundry. There is an introductory exhibition in the stable courtyard and an interesting 19th-century chapel. The delightful hillside garden features rhododendrons, magnolias, herbaceous borders and rare trees, as well as an ice house and early 19th-century rustic style summer-house known as The Bear's Hut. The surrounding parkland and woods offer a number of beautiful circular walks giving access to the 2500-ha (6100-acre) estate, and there is also a discovery centre offering varied activities. See also entries below for *Clyston Mill*, *Marker's Cottage* and *Newhall Equestrian Centre*

**Note**: Killerton House has a major reservicing project planned from September 2002. The house should reopen for Easter 2003. Please tel. to check reopening date

**What's new in 2002**: Exhibition on lace

**House**: 9 March to 2 Sept: daily except Tues (but open 4 June) 11–5.30; also closed Mons in March; daily in Aug. **Park & garden**: daily 10.30–dusk. **Events**: tel. for full programme; 13, 14 July, Exeter Festival open-air concerts. Send s.a.e. for programme. **Note**: On 13, 14 July the house closes at 4.30 and only ticket holders for the Exeter Festival concerts will be admitted to the garden after 4.30

£5.40; family £13.50. Garden and park only £3.90. Garden and park reduced rate Nov to Feb. Booked parties and cyclists £4.50

Introductory talks on house and garden by arrangement

Shop & plant centre 9 March to 3 Nov: daily; 4 to 30 Nov: daily except Mon & Tues; Dec: daily; Jan & Feb 2003: Sat & Sun; March 2003: daily. *Times*: 9 March to 30 Sept 11–5.30 (Tues 11–5); Oct to 22 Dec 11–5; Jan to mid-March 2003 11–4. In winter the shop may not open in bad weather, tel. 01392 881912

Volunteer-driven buggy to take disabled drivers from car park to house and garden when house open. House: 3 steps at entrance (ramp on request); stairclimber to costume displays, please book as not available every day. Wheelchairs. Garden: gravel paths and grass in lower part; upper part steep. Shop: wheelchair lift to upper level

Braille guides for house and costume collection; musicians may play grand piano and organ. Scented plants. Audio guide

Licensed restaurant as house 12–5 (may close weekdays in March) closed 3 Sept to Easter 2003. Tea-room 1 March to end Oct: daily; 1 Nov to 22 Dec daily except Mon & Tues; Jan 2003 weekends only; Feb & March: daily except Mon &

Tues; *Times*: 9 March to 30 Sept: 10.30–5.30; Oct: 10.30–4.30; Nov & Dec: 11–4.30; Jan to 8 March 2003: 11–4. In winter the tea-room may not open in bad weather, tel. 01392 881345

👶 Table and chair in women's WCs near stable courtyard and at house; children's guide; quiz sheet for house; children's menu and highchairs; babies in back carriers and single pushchairs allowed in all areas. Discovery centre open most weekends when house open. Play area for children and picnic area by car park. Family activities in school holidays

📖 Education programme, including Victorian days, environmental activities and orienteering for booked parties. Tel. for details

🐕 On leads and only in park; shaded parking in overflow car park

➔ (1:G7) Off Exeter–Cullompton road (B3181, formerly A38); from M5 northbound, exit 30 via Pinhoe and Broadclyst; from M5 southbound, exit 28 [192:SS9700] **Bus**: Stagecoach in Devon 54/A Cullompton–Exeter (passing close ≋ Exeter Central) to the house on summer Sun, otherwise alight Killerton Turn ¾ml **Station**: Pinhoe (U), not Sun, 4½ml; Whimple (U), not Sun, 6ml; Exeter Central & St David's, both 7ml

**NT properties nearby** Clyston Mill, Knightshayes Court, Marker's Cottage, Newhall Equestrian Centre

## KILLERTON: CLYSTON MILL ☒                                                    Devon
Broadclyst, Exeter EX5 3EW · **Tel** 01392 462425

A water-powered grain mill in working order, believed to date from the early 19th century

**Note**: There are no refreshments or WCs, but picnic area in the orchard. The nearest WCs are in the village car park

🅾 31 March to 29 Oct: Sun, Mon, Tues 2–5

£ £1.50, £2.50 for joint ticket with Marker's Cottage. Mill unsuitable for coach parties. Parking in village car park

♿ Access difficult

🐕 No dogs in mill

➔ (1:G7) Off Exeter–Cullompton road (B3181) in village of Broadclyst. Park in village car park, walk towards church and follow signs through churchyard [192: SX981973] **Bus**: Stagecoach in Devon 54 Exeter-Collompton (passes close ≋ Exeter Central) **Station**: Pinhoe (U), not Sun, 2½ml; Polsloe Bridge (U) 4ml; Whimple (U) 4½ml; Exeter Central 5½ml; Exeter St David's 6ml

**NT properties nearby** Killerton, Marker's Cottage, Newhall Equestrian Centre

**Please remember – your membership card is always needed for free admission**

## KILLERTON: MARKER'S COTTAGE  Devon
Broadclyst, Exeter EX5 3HR · **Tel** 01392 461546

A fascinating medieval cob house, containing a cross-passage screen decorated with a painting of St Andrew and his attributes

- **O** 31 March to 29 Oct: Sun, Mon, Tues 2–5
- **£** £1.50, £2.50 for joint ticket with Clyston Mill. House unsuitable for coach parties. Parking in village car park
- Access difficult; 4 steps into house
- → (1:G7) Off Exeter–Cullompton road (B3181) in village of Broadclyst. Turn right opposite church (coming from Exeter direction) and then second right [192:SX985973] **Bus**: Stagecoach in Devon 54 Exeter–Cullompton (passes close Exeter Central) **Station**: Pinhoe (U), not Sun, 2½ml; Polsloe Bridge (U) 4ml; Whimple (U) 4½ml; Exeter Central 5½ml; Exeter St David's 6ml

**NT properties nearby** Killerton, Newhall Equestrian Centre

## KILLERTON: NEWHALL EQUESTRIAN CENTRE  Devon
Broadclyst, Exeter EX5 3LW · **Tel** 01392 462453

The finest range of vernacular farm-buildings on the Killerton Estate. Listed Grade II*, the buildings are arranged around two courtyards and retain many original features. They are now used as a livery yard and equestrian centre, with exhibitions of equestrian art, a small carriage museum and pets' corner

**Note**: The property is leased and managed on the Trust's behalf by Mr & Mrs D. Llewellin who have extensively renovated the buildings

- **O** 9 March to 3 Nov: daily 10.30–5.30
- **£** £2.50; child £1.25 (inc. NT members). Party rates on aplication, coaches welcome
- Guided tours can be arranged; also self-guided with leaflet
- As centre
- Livery yard, carriage collection & tea-room all accessible
- Braille guide; items to touch; also some farm animals and horses
- Tea-room as centre
- On short leads at all times
- → (1:G7) As for Killerton

**NT properties nearby** Clyston Mill, Killerton, Marker's Cottage

## KING JOHN'S HUNTING LODGE 🏠     Somerset
The Square, Axbridge BS26 2AP · **Tel** 01934 732012

An early Tudor merchant's house, extensively restored in 1971

**Note**: The property is run as a local history museum by Axbridge and District Museum Trust, in cooperation with Sedgemoor District Council, Somerset County Museums Service and Axbridge Archaeological and Local History Society

- 🅾 29 March to 30 Sept: daily 1–4
- 💷 Free. School parties by arrangement. Council car park, 2min walk
- ♿ Ground floor accessible
- ➜ (1:l5) In the Square, on corner of High Street [182: ST431545] **Bus**: First Badgerline 126, 826 Weston-super-Mare–Wells (passing close ≋ Weston-super-Mare) **Station**: Worle (U) 8ml

**NT properties nearby** Clevedon Court, Prior Park

## KINGSTON LACY 🏠✿♣🏊🚶♥     Dorset
Wimborne Minster BH21 4EA
**Tel** 01202 883402 (Mon to Fri 9–5) & 01202 842913 (Sat & Sun 11–5)
**Infoline** 01202 880413 · **Fax** 01202 882402 · **Email** kingstonlacy@ntrust.org.uk

Home of the Bankes family for over 300 years, having replaced the ruined family seat at Corfe Castle, this 17th-century house was radically altered in the 19th century by Sir Charles Barry. The house contains the outstanding collection of paintings and other works of art accumulated by William Bankes. It is famous for its dramatic Spanish Room, with walls hung in magnificent gilded leather. The house and garden are set in a wooded park with attractive waymarked walks and a fine herd of Red Devon cattle. The surrounding estate is crossed by many paths (leaflet available from shop) and dominated by the Iron Age hill-fort of **Badbury Rings**. The botanically rich rings are managed by grazing and dogs are not permitted. Point-to-point races are held 23 Feb, 23 March & 13 April and on these days a charge is made for car-parking

**Note**: House may be partially scaffolded in 2002

**What's new in 2002**: Open Good Friday. Events and exhibition to celebrate the centenary of the birth of Ralph Bankes, donor of Kingston Lacy. New garden guide

- 🅾 **House**: 23 March to 3 Nov: daily except Mon & Tues (open BHols inc. BH Tues 4 June) 12–5.30 (last admission 4.30). **Garden & park**: 2 Feb to 17 March: Sat & Sun only, 11–4; 23 March to 3 Nov, daily 11–6; 8 Nov to 22 Dec: Fri, Sat & Sun 11–4; special snowdrop days in early 2003: for details tel. infoline
- 💷 £6.50; child £3; family £17. Park & garden only £3; child £1.50. Booked parties (15+) £5
- 🚶 Parties of 15+; for details tel. 01202 883402

**Please see the area introductions for details of coast & countryside properties**

SOUTH WEST · 79

- 2 Feb to 17 March: Sat & Sun 11–4; 23 March to 3 Nov: daily 11–5.30; 8 Nov to 22 Dec: Fri, Sat & Sun 11–4 (tel. 01202 841424)
- House: access very difficult; two days (June & Sept) reserved to enable wheelchair users to visit main state rooms; tel. 01202 883402 for details. Volunteer-driven buggy from car park to WCs, restaurant, house and garden. Restaurant & shop: accessible. Wheelchairs available. Garden and some woodland walks accessible, some thick gravel. Estate: specially made trailer with room for 8 wheelchairs may be booked for guided tours of estate; otherwise some wheelchair access; several routes have stiles for ambulant visitors with impaired mobility
- Braille guide; bronzes, wood carvings and some marblework may be touched. Large-print guide
- Licensed restaurant as shop. For party bookings, special occasions and Christmas lunches tel. 01202 889242. Picnics in park only
- Baby-changing facilities in all WCs. In the house baby slings and reins available. No back carriers or pushchairs. Highchairs in restaurant. Children's guidebook. Playgrounds on woodland walk
- Teachers' resource material, study centre and active education programme, contact the Education Coordinator, tel. 01202 883402
- Estate walks leaflet from property or NT Wessex office (tel. 01985 843601)
- On leads and only in park and woods
- (1:K7) On B3082 Blandford–Wimborne road, 1½ml W of Wimborne [195: SY980019] **Bus**: Wilts & Dorset 132/3, 182/3 from Bournemouth, Poole (passing ≋ Bournemouth & close ≋ Poole), alight Wimborne Square 2½ml **Station**: Poole 8½ml

**NT properties nearby** Brownsea Island, Corfe Castle, White Mill

## KNIGHTSHAYES COURT

Devon

Bolham, Tiverton EX16 7RQ · **Tel** 01884 254665 · **Fax** 01884 243050
**Email** knightshayes@ntrust.org.uk

Designed by William Burges and begun in 1869, Knightshayes is a rare survival of his work. The rich interiors combine medieval romanticism with lavish Victorian decoration, and the smoking and billiard rooms, elegant boudoir and drawing room all give an atmospheric insight into grand country house life. The celebrated garden features a water lily pool and topiary, fine specimen trees, rare shrubs and delightful seasonal colours. Attractive woodland walks lead through the grounds

- **House**: 23 March to 3 Nov: daily except Fri (but open Good Fri). *Times*: 23 March to 30 Sept; 11–5.30; 1 Oct to 3 Nov: 11–4. **Garden**: 16 March to 3 Nov: daily. *Times*: 11–5.30. Visitor reception tel. 01884 257381
- £5.50; family £13.70, park & garden only £3.90. Booked parties £4.80. Children half price. Parking 400m

**Unless indicated, last admission is always 30 mins before closing time**

## 80 · SOUTH WEST

🛈 Guided tours of house and garden for parties by arrangement during season and also on Sun during Nov & Dec; tel. for details

🛒 Shop & plant centre Sat & Sun 16, 17 March; 23 March to 3 Nov: daily; 6 Nov to 20 Dec: daily except Mon & Tues. *Times*: 16, 17 March 11–4; 23 March to 3 Nov 11–5; 6 Nov to 20 Dec 11–4 (shop tel. 01884 259010, plant centre tel. 01884 243464)

♿ Disabled drivers may park near house after passing through stables reception. House: ground floor accessible; small lift to first floor suitable if visitor can stand and wheelchair fold. Garden: some gravel paths, but recommended signed routes. Shops, restaurant and picnic areas in car park: accessible

👁 Braille guide; audio guide indicating tactile objects, including Epstein bronzes and pianos, which musicians may play. Scented plants

☕ Licensed self-service restaurant as shops; also open for booked Christmas lunches and candlelit dinners, tel. 01884 259416. In Oct opening hours may vary, although light refreshments are always available during opening hours; tel. to check. Picnic area in car park and parkland

🚸 Children's quizzes for house and garden; changing facilities in women's WC; baby back- or front-carriers welcome in all areas. Children's menu; highchair

🚲 Racks by plant centre

🐕 Welcome on leads in stables, woodland and park

➡ (1:G6) 2ml N of Tiverton; turn right off Tiverton–Bampton road (A396) at Bolham [181: SS960151] **Bus**: First Southern National 398 Tiverton–Minehead, alight Bolham, thence ¾ml. Otherwise Stagecoach in Devon 373 from ▬ Tiverton Parkway; 55/A/B Exeter–Tiverton (passing close ▬ Exeter Central), alighting Tiverton 1¾ml **Station**: Tiverton Parkway 8ml **Cycle**: NCN 3

**NT properties nearby** Killerton, Marker's Cottage, Newhall Equestrian Centre

**There are special events at most Trust properties; please telephone 0870 458 4000 for details**

# LACOCK ABBEY, FOX TALBOT MUSEUM & VILLAGE

Wiltshire

Lacock, nr Chippenham SN15 2LG · **Tel** Abbey tel/fax 01249 730227
Museum tel 01249 730459 · **Fax** 01249 730501

Founded in 1232 and converted into a country house *c.*1540, the fine medieval cloisters, sacristy, chapter house and monastic rooms of the Abbey have survived largely intact. The handsome 16th-century stable courtyard has half-timbered gables, a clockhouse, brewery and bakehouse. The Victorian woodland garden boasts a fine display of spring flowers, magnificent trees, an 18th-century summer-house, Victorian rose garden and ha-ha. The Museum of Photography commemorates the achievements of a former resident of the Abbey, William Fox Talbot (1800–77), inventor of the modern photographic negative and whose descendants gave the Abbey and village to the Trust in 1944. The village, which dates from the 13th century and has many limewashed half-timbered and stone houses, was used as a location in the TV and film productions of *Pride and Prejudice, Moll Flanders* and *Emma*. The Abbey also featured in the film of Harry Potter

**What's new in 2002**: New planting in the Botanic Garden

**Museum, cloisters & garden**: 16 March to 3 Nov: daily 11–5.30 (closed Good Fri). **Abbey**: 30 March to 3 Nov: daily 1–5.30 (closed Tues & Good Fri, but open Tues 4 June). Museum open winter weekends, but closed 21 Dec to 29 Dec; tel. for details. **Events**: send s.a.e. for leaflet. Garden open outside normal opening times for spring flowers under National Gardens Scheme, charges apply (inc. NT members)

Abbey, museum, cloisters & garden: £6.20; child £3.40; family £16.80; parties £5.70; children £2.90. Garden, cloisters & museum only: £4; child £2.40; family £11.30. Abbey & garden only: £5; child £2.80; family £12.70

Guided tours by arrangement

In village: 30 March to 24 Dec, 27 to 31 Dec; 2 Jan to end March 2003: daily. *Times*: 30 March to 3 Nov 10–5.30; 4 Nov to end March 11–4 (tel. 01249 730302). Museum shop selling photographic books, films and postcards

Limited parking in Abbey courtyard by arrangement. Abbey: difficult, 4 sets of steps. Garden, cloisters & museum: accessible (non-wheelchair stairlift in museum); wheelchairs and self-drive vehicle at museum

Braille, tape and large-print guides to Abbey. Pre-booked guided tours at Abbey

Picnic area in The Pound, opposite museum. Tea-rooms (not NT) in village

Children's guide to Abbey

Teachers' resource book, Abbey open to schools before public opening hours. For details of Abbey tours tel. 01249 730227. For other information about the Abbey, Village and Museum contact the Education Coordinator tel. 01249 730141

Racks in Red Lion car park in High St

**For all your information needs check our website www.nationaltrust.org.uk**

✈ (1:K4) 3ml S of Chippenham, just E of A350; signposted to car park [173: ST919684] **Bus**: First Badgerline 234 Chippenham–Frome (passing close ≋ Chippenham), 237 Trowbridge–Corsham. Both pass close ≋ Trowbridge **Station**: Chippenham 3½ml **Cycle**: NCN 4

**NT properties nearby** The Courts Garden, Great Chalfield Manor, Westwood Manor

---

## LANHYDROCK  Cornwall
Bodmin PL30 5AD · **Tel** 01208 73320 · **Fax** 01208 74084
**Email** lanhydrock@ntrust.org.uk

One of the most fascinating late 19th-century houses in England, full of period atmosphere and the trappings of a high Victorian country house. Although the gatehouse and north wing (with magnificent 32m-long gallery with plaster ceiling) survive from the 17th century, the rest of the house was rebuilt following a disastrous fire in 1881 with the latest in contemporary living, including central heating. The garden features a stunning collection of magnolias, rhododendrons and camellias, and offers fine colours right through into autumn. All this is set in a glorious estate of 364ha (900 acres) of woods and parkland running down to the Fowey River. There is an extensive network of footpaths and a guide to estate walks

**Note**: 50 rooms are open to visitors, who should allow at least 1½ hours to tour the house. The car park is 600m from the house. Secure locker system for large bags

○ **House**: 23 March to 3 Nov: daily except Mon (but open BH Mons).
*Times*: 23 March to 30 Sept 11–5.30; Oct & Nov 11–5. **Garden**: daily 10–6.
**Events**: tel. for details

THE GATEHOUSE

---

**Please remember – your membership card is always needed for free admission**

## SOUTH WEST · 83

**£** £7; family £17.50. Garden & grounds only £3.80. Booked parties £6

**◧** 16 Feb to 23 Dec: daily. *Times*: Feb, March, Nov & Dec 11–4; 23 March to 30 Sept 11–5.30; Oct 11–5. Plant sales (in car park): 1 March to 3 Nov: daily. *Times*: 1 March to 30 Sept 11–5.30; Oct & Nov: 11–5 (tel. 01208 74099)

**♿** Close parking, ask at reception building. Disabled visitors may be set down at gatehouse. House: access via ramp to restaurant; most ground-floor rooms accessible; small lift to first floor. Shop: some steps. Powered self-drive buggy; please book. Indoor and outdoor wheelchairs. Garden: some level access, wheelchair route and map. Information leaflet on access for disabled visitors

**👁** Braille guides for house and garden; large-print guide for house and tactile route guide sheet (with handcloth). Musicians may play piano, access via a few steps. Aromatic plants; water sounds

**☕** 16 Feb to 3 Nov: licensed restaurant, light refreshments and ice creams daily. Nov, Dec & Jan: limited opening (tel. 01208 74331)

**👶** Children's guide and quizzes. Parent and baby room; baby slings and harnesses; pushchair storage area in house; pushchair loan. Adventure play area near main car park. Organised activities in school holidays

**🏫** Schools' base; handling collection; education stewards

**🐕** On leads and only in park and woods

**➡** (1:D8) 2½ml SE of Bodmin, overlooking valley of River Fowey; follow signposts from either A30, A38 Bodmin–Liskeard or B3268 Bodmin–Lostwithiel roads [200: SX085636] **Bus**: First Western National 55, from ≋ Bodmin Parkway **Station**: Bodmin Parkway 1¾ml by original carriage-drive to house, signposted in station car park; 3ml by road **Cycle**: NCN 3

**NT properties nearby** Trerice

## LAWRENCE HOUSE  Cornwall
9 Castle Street, Launceston PL15 8BA · **Tel** 01566 773277

A Georgian house given to the Trust to help preserve the character of the street, and now leased to Launceston Town Council as a museum and civic centre

**◯** April to early Oct: daily except Sat & Sun 10.30–4.30. Other times by appointment

**£** Free, but contributions towards museum expenses welcome

**◧** Small shop open as museum

**👁** Braille guide

**➡** (1:E7) [201: SX330848] **Bus**: First Western National 76, X76 from Plymouth (passing ≋ Plymouth); First Western National X10 from ≋ Exeter St David's

**NT properties nearby** Cotehele

**For general enquiries, please telephone 0870 458 4000**

84 · SOUTH WEST

## THE LEVANT STEAM ENGINE  Cornwall

Trewellard, Pendeen, nr St Just · **Tel** 01736 786156 (opening hours only) 01736 796993 (Penwith Countryside Office) · **Fax** 01736 786059

In its tiny engine house perched on the cliff edge, the famous Levant beam engine is steaming again after sixty idle years. The sight, sounds and smells of this 160-year-old engine conjure up the feel of Cornwall's industrial past. ½ml along the cliff is Geevor mine (not NT) and a mining museum

**What's new in 2002**: A short underground tour included, from the miners' dry to the man engine shaft via a spiral staircase

- Open and steaming: March, April: Fri and BH Sun & Mon. May: Tue, Fri and BH Sun & Mon. June: Sun, Wed, Thur, Fri. July to Sept: daily except Sat. Oct: Tues & Fri only. Open but not steaming: Nov to March: Fri only. *Times*: 11–5 summer; 11–4 winter

- £4; family £10; concessions £3.50; students £2. Stewarded by volunteer members of the Trevithick Society. Members are invited to contribute to the cost of the project

- Available

- Limited access; assistance if required

- Machinery sounds, smells and atmosphere; old boiler and controls may be touched. Braille guide to Penwith Coast

- At Geevor mine or Pendeen village

- Groups (max. 40) only by appointment

- (1:A9) 1ml W of Pendeen, on B3306 St Just–Zennor road [203: SW368346] **Bus**: First Western National 10A from Penzance **Station**: Penzance 7ml

**NT properties nearby** St Michael's Mount, Trengwainton Garden

## LITTLE CLARENDON  Wiltshire

Dinton, Salisbury SP3 5DZ · **Tel** 01985 843600 (Regional Office)

A Tudor house, altered in the 17th century and with a 20th-century Catholic chapel. The three principal rooms on the ground floor are open to visitors and furnished with vernacular oak furniture

- 1 April to 28 Oct: Mon 1–5 & Sat 10–1

- £2. No reduction for parties. No pushchairs or prams. No coaches. Parking at Dinton Post Office. No WC

- House: access via 3 steps

- (1:K5) ¼ml E of Dinton church, close to post office; take B3089 from Salisbury to Dinton [184: SU015316] **Bus**: As for Philipps House

**NT properties nearby** Mompesson House, Philipps House and Dinton Park, Stonehenge Down, Stourhead

**Please see the area introductions for details of coast & countryside properties**

## LITTLE FLEECE BOOKSHOP 🏠  Gloucestershire
Bisley Street, Painswick GL6 6QQ · **Tel** 01452 812103

A 17th-century building, originally part of a former inn and restored in an exemplary 'Arts & Crafts' style in 1935. Now open as a bookshop, with the ground-floor room only on view

- 2 April to 31 Oct: daily except Sun & Mon (closed Good Fri); Nov & Dec: Sat only. *Times*: 10–1, 2–5

- (1:J3) 3ml N of Stroud A46, 6ml SE of Gloucester B4073. Off main High Street, Painswick [162: S0868098] **Bus**: Stagecoach in the Cotswold/Swanbrook 46 Nailsworth–Cheltenham Spa (passes close ≋ Stroud) **Station**: Stroud 4ml

**NT properties nearby** Ebworth Estate, Haresfield Beacon, Minchinhampton & Rodborough Commons, Woodchester Park

## THE LIZARD AND KYNANCE COVE  Cornwall
**Tel** 01326 561407 (Lizard Countryside Office) · **Fax** 01326 562882
**Email** lizard@ntrust.org.uk

The Lizard is the most southerly point of mainland Britain and the turning point of one of the busiest shipping lanes in the world. The coastline on either side offers dramatic cliff walks, masses of rare wild flowers and unique geology, as well as having played a key role in the history of modern communications. Marconi's historic wireless experiments on the Lizard in 1901 are celebrated at the restored **Lizard Wireless Station**, Bass Point, and the new **Marconi Centre** at Poldhu (tel. for opening details). Two miles north of Lizard Point lies Kynance Cove – white sand, turquoise water and multi-coloured serpentine islands with stacks and arches hidden amongst the towering cliffs – long considered one of the most beautiful places in Cornwall

- All year

- Car parks at Kynance and the Lizard (charge, NT members free). Free parking in Lizard town, whence a footpath leads to Lizard Point

- Occasional guided walks; tel. for details. *Coast of Cornwall* leaflet no. 14 includes maps and details of circular walks in area, as well as information on local history, geology and wildlife

- Access to viewpoints above Kynance and Lizard Point; WC at both car parks

- Seasonal refreshments at Kynance car park and in the newly acquired café on beach

- Bicycle racks in both car parks

- Welcome, but seasonal bans on some beaches including Kynance

- (1:C10/B10) From Helston take A3083 to Lizard Town [203: SW690133 (Kynance)] **Bus**: Truronian T3 Helston–Kynance Cove, June–Oct only (with connections from ≋ Redruth; otherwise T1 Perranporth–Lizard (passing ≋ Truro), thence Kynance Cove 1½ml; to Lizard Point 1ml

**Unless indicated, last admission is always 30 mins before closing time**

## LODGE PARK & SHERBORNE ESTATE

Gloucestershire

Aldsworth, nr Cheltenham GL54 3PP
**Tel** 01451 844130 · 01451 844257 (Estate Office) · **Infoline** 01684 855369
**Fax** 01451 844131 · **Email** lodgepark@ntrust.org.uk

Situated on the picturesque Sherborne Estate in the Cotswolds, Lodge Park was created in 1634 by John 'Crump' Dutton. Inspired by his passion for gambling and banqueting it is a unique survival of a grandstand, deer course and park. It was the home of Charles Dutton, 7th Lord Sherborne, until 1982 when he bequeathed his family's estate to the National Trust. The grandstand has been reconstructed to its original form and is the first project of its kind undertaken by the Trust that relies totally on archaeological evidence. The park behind was designed by Charles Bridgeman in 1725. The Sherborne Estate is 1650ha (4000 acres) of rolling Cotswold countryside with sweeping views down to the River Windrush. Much of the village of Sherborne is owned by the Trust, including the post office and shop, school and social club. There are walks for all ages around the estate, which include the restored and working water meadows

**What's new in 2002**: Lodge Park is now licensed for weddings and available for events. Tel. property for details

- **House**: 1 March to 4 Nov: Fri, Sat, Sun & Mon. *Times*: 11–4. Slide talks at regular intervals during the day. **Estate**: open daily throughout the year

- House: £4; family £10. Estate: free to pedestrians. Car park £1

- Out of hours guided tours and walks can be arranged for Lodge Park, the Bridgeman Landscape and the Sherborne Estate; tel. for details

- Wheelchair available for ground floor use only. Virtual tour of Lodge Park on website

- Braille guide; video introduction with hearing loop; personal guided 'touch' tour by prior appointment

- Post office & shop in Sherborne village: ice creams, sweets and soft drinks, also licensed, closed all day Wed & Sun, and Sat pm. Social club open Sun 12–2 for soft drinks, also licensed

- (1:K2/L2) 3ml E of Northleach; approach from A40 [163: SP146123]
  **Bus**: Swanbrook 53 Oxford–Gloucester (passing ≋ Gloucester and close ≋ Oxford)

**NT properties nearby**
Chastleton House,
Chedworth Roman Villa,
Hidcote Manor Gardens,
Snowshill Manor

---

There are special events at most Trust properties; please telephone 0870 458 4000 for details

## LOUGHWOOD MEETING HOUSE ✠ — Devon
Dalwood, Axminster EX13 7DU · **Tel** 01392 881691 · **Fax** 01392 881954

Built *c.*1653 by the Baptist congregation of Kilmington, who attended services here at the risk of imprisonment or transportation. A simple but interesting building, with an interior fitted in the early 18th century

- **O** All year
- **£** Free (box for donations)
- **→** (1:H7) 4ml W of Axminster; turn right on Axminster–Honiton road (A35), 1ml S of Dalwood, 1ml NW of Kilmington [192/193: SY253993] **Bus**: Stagecoach in Devon 380 Axminster–Exeter (passing close ☒ Axminster) **Station**: Axminster 2½ml

**NT properties nearby** Shute Barton

## LUNDY — Devon
Bristol Channel, EX39 2LY · **Tel** 01237 431831 · **Fax** 01237 431832
**Email** info@lundyisland.co.uk · **Web** www.lundyisland.co.uk

A unique and unspoilt island, undisturbed by cars and home to a fascinating array of wildlife amidst dramatic scenery. There is a small village with an inn and Victorian church, and nearby the 13th-century Marisco Castle keeps guard

**Note**: The island is financed, administered and maintained by the Landmark Trust

- **O** Always. Sea passages all year round from Bideford by the island vessel MS *Oldenburg* (300 tons, 267 passengers, refreshments on board) and also from Ilfracombe in summer. For sailing details tel. 01271 863636
- **£** Entrance fee inc. in fare for passengers on MS Oldenburg, but £3.50 per person for those arriving by other means. Discount for NT members who book in advance and arrive on MS Oldenburg (day trips only)
- Shop selling the famous Lundy stamps, souvenirs and postcards, plus general supplies and groceries
- Visitors with disabilities should tel. in advance so that disembarking arrangements may be made
- Available at the Marisco Tavern. Accommodation: 23 holiday cottages; camping site for up to 40 people. For bookings, apply to: The Landmark Trust, Shottesbrooke, Maidenhead, Berkshire SL6 3SW (tel. 01628 825925)
- Baby-changing facilities in women's WC. Children always find Lundy fascinating
- **→** (1:D5) 11ml N of Hartland Point, 25ml from Ilfracombe, 30ml S of Tenby [180: SS1345] **Bus**: Bus services available from ☒ Barnstaple to Bideford or Ilfracombe **Station**: Barnstaple: 8½ml to Bideford **Cycle**: NCN 31 (at Bideford)

**NT properties nearby** North Devon coastline including Baggy Point and Morte Point

## LYDFORD GORGE

Devon

The Stables, Lydford Gorge, Lydford, nr Okehampton EX20 4BH
**Tel** 01822 820441/820320 · **Fax** 01822 822000
**Email** lydfordgorge@ntrust.org.uk

This famous gorge is 1½ml long and can be viewed from a circular walk, which starts high above the river and passes through attractive oak-woods before dropping down to the spectacular 30m-high White Lady waterfall. The path then proceeds along an enchanting riverside walk through the steeply sided ravine, scooped out by the River Lyd as it plunges into a series of whirlpools, including the thrilling Devil's Cauldron

**Note**: The walk is arduous in places; visitors should wear stout footwear. Unsuitable for visitors with heart complaints or walking difficulties and very young children

- Daily. *Times*: 23 March to 30 Sept: 10–5.30; Oct to 3 Nov: 10–4; 4 Nov to 31 March 2003: 10.30–3. **Note**: 4 Nov to 31 March access is from waterfall entrance to waterfall only. There are delays at the Devil's Cauldron during busy periods. Free car parks at both entrances

- £3.70. Booked parties £3.10

- Shop & information at main entrance 23 March to 3 Nov as gorge. Small shop at waterfall entrance 23 March to 3 Nov as gorge

- Picnic area, shop and tea-room accessible. New accessible level path with seats, viewpoints and bird hide (access from waterfall entrance)

- Tapping rail on new path (see above). Large-print guides for route. Audio tapes available from entrance

- At main entrance 23 March to 30 Sept: 10.30–5; Oct to 3 Nov: 10.30–4

- Children's guide; children's menu; baby-changing facilities; unsuitable for pushchairs due to terrain and width of some paths; back carriers and baby slings available; parent and baby room at waterfall entrance

- Teachers' geology pack (primary school level and A-Level), guide and new resource book

- Stands. Property is close to three cycle routes: Devon Coast to Coast, West Devon Way and Plym Valley. Discounted entry for cyclists

- On leads only

- (1:F7) At W end of Lydford village; halfway between Okehampton and Tavistock, 1ml W off A386 opposite Dartmoor Inn; main entrance at W end of Lydford; second entrance near Mucky Duck Inn [191 & 201: SX509846] **Bus**: First Western National 86, Plymouth–Barnstaple (most passing ≋ Plymouth); 187 ≋ Gunnislake– ≋ Okehampton, Sun, June to Sept only; bus stop at main entrance and waterfall entrance to gorge. Reduced entry on production of valid bus ticket and for those arriving by cycle. **Cycle**: NCN 27, 31

**NT properties nearby** Buckland Abbey, Castle Drogo, Cotehele, Finch Foundry

---

**Please remember – your membership card is always needed for free admission**

## LYTES CARY MANOR 🏠✝❋  Somerset
nr Charlton Mackrell, Somerton TA11 7HU
**Tel** 01985 843600 (Regional Office), 01458 224471 (Property)
**Email** lytescarymanor@ntrust.org.uk

A charming manor house with a 14th-century chapel and 15th-century Great Hall, much added to in the 16th century and rescued from dereliction in the 20th century by Sir Walter Jenner. The interiors were refurnished in period style and are complemented by the attractive hedged garden with mixed borders

**What's new in 2002**: There is a new section to the waymarked river walk open at the same times as house and garden (leaflet available from house). New property guidebook

- 🅾 23 March to 30 Oct: Mon, Wed & Sat 2–6 or dusk if earlier; also Fri in June, July & Aug: 2–6. (Open BH Tues 4 June 2–6)
- 💷 £4.60; child £2. No party reduction. Small coaches only, by arrangement (max. of 7.5m, 30 people)
- ♿ Garden accessible
- 👁 Braille guide. Scented plants
- 🚸 Children's trail
- 🐕 On leads and only in car park and on river walk
- ➡ (1:l6) Signposted from Podimore roundabout at junction of A303, A37 take A372 [183: ST529269] **Bus**: First Badgerline 376/7 Bristol–Yeovil (passing ≋ Bristol Temple Meads); First Southern National 54 Taunton–Yeovil (passing close ≋ Taunton). Both pass within ¾ml ≋ Yeovil Pen Mill. On both, alight Kingsdon, 1ml **Station**: Yeovil Pen Mill 8½ml; Castle Cary 9ml; Yeovil Junction 10ml

**NT properties nearby** Barrington Court, Montacute House, Priest's House, Stembridge Tower Mill, Tintinhull Garden, Treasurer's House

## MAX GATE 🏠❋  Dorset
Alington Avenue, Dorchester DT1 2AA · **Tel** 01305 262538 · **Fax** 01305 250978
**Web** www.thomas-hardy.connectfree.co.uk

Novelist and poet Thomas Hardy designed and lived in this house from 1885 till his death in 1928. Here he wrote *Tess of the d'Urbervilles*, *Jude the Obscure* and *The Mayor of Casterbridge*, as well as much of his poetry. The house contains several pieces of his furniture

- 🅾 1 April to 30 Sept: Mon, Wed & Sun 2–5. **Note**: Only dining and drawing rooms open. Private visits, tours and seminars by schools, colleges and literary societies by appointment with the tenants, Mr & Mrs Andrew Leah
- 💷 £2.30; child £1.20
- 🛍 At 65 High West St, Dorchester (tel. 01305 267535)

- House: some level access to ground floor
- Braille guide. Large-print guide
- (1:J7) 1ml E of Dorchester on the A352 Wareham road. From Dorchester follow A352 until you reach the roundabout named Max Gate (at the junction of the A35 Dorchester bypass). Turn left and left again into the cul-de-sac outside the house [194:SY704899] **Bus**: Southern National D from town centre **Station**: Dorchester South 1ml; Dorchester West (U) 1ml

**NT properties nearby** Clouds Hill, Hardy's Cottage, Hardy Monument

## MOMPESSON HOUSE

Wiltshire

The Close, Salisbury SP1 2EL · **Tel** 01722 335659 · **Fax** 01722 321559
**Email** mompessonhouse@ntrust.org.uk

An elegant and spacious 18th-century house in the Cathedral Close, featured in the award-winning film *Sense and Sensibility*, and with magnificent plasterwork and a fine oak staircase. As well as pieces of good quality period furniture, the house also contains the Turnbull collection of 18th-century drinking glasses. Outside, the delightful walled garden has a pergola and traditional herbaceous borders

**What's new in 2002**: New short guide to house

- 23 March to 29 Sept: daily except Thur & Fri (but open Good Fri) 12–5.30
- £3.90; child £1.95. Garden only 80p. Visitor sitting room. Parties £3.40. Parking in city centre nearby. Coach-parking in central car park
- Out of hours tours of house and/or garden by arrangement

**Please see the area introductions for details of coast & countryside properties**

SOUTH WEST · **91**

- At 41 High Street, Salisbury (tel. 01722 331884)
- Ground floor, garden, WC & tea-room: accessible
- Braille and large-print guides. Scented plants
- Garden Room as house 12–5
- Children's guide
- (1:K6) On N side of Choristers' Green in the Cathedral Close, near High Street Gate [184: SU142295] **Bus**: From surrounding areas **Station**: Salisbury ½ml

**NT properties nearby** Little Clarendon, Mottisfont Abbey, Philipps House and Dinton Park, Stourhead

---

## MONTACUTE HOUSE                                                           Somerset
Montacute TA15 6XP · **Tel/Fax** 01935 823289 **Email** montacute@ntrust.org.uk

A glittering Elizabethan house, adorned with elegant chimneys, carved parapets and other Renaissance features, including contemporary plasterwork, chimney pieces and heraldic glass. The magnificent state rooms, including a long gallery which is the largest of its type in England, are full of fine 17th- and 18th-century furniture and Elizabethan and Jacobean portraits from the National Portrait Gallery. There are also good quality textiles, including an exhibition of 17th-century samplers. The formal garden includes mixed borders and old roses and is surrounded by a landscape park. Montacute featured in the award-winning film of *Sense and Sensibility*

**Note**: Some rooms in the house do not have electric light, so visitors wishing to make a close study of tapestries, textiles or paintings should avoid visiting on dull days

- **House**: 23 March to 3 Nov: daily (except Tues, but open BH Tues 4 June) 11–5. **Garden & park**: 23 March to 3 Nov: daily except Tues (but open 4 June); 6 Nov to March 2003: daily except Mon & Tues. *Times*: 23 March to 3 Nov: 11–5; 6 Nov to March 2003: 11.30–4.

- £6.20; child £3; family £15. Booked parties (15+) £5.50, children £2.80. Limited parking for coaches which must be booked in advance. Garden and park only: 23 March to 3 Nov: £3.40; child £1.50; 6 Nov to March 2003: £2; child £1. Party organisers please book in writing to House Manager with s.a.e.

- Guided tours for groups by arrangement with House Manager

- 23 March to 3 Nov: as house 11–5; 6 Nov to 22 Dec (Christmas shop) & March 2003: daily except Mon & Tues 11–4 (tel. 01935 824575)

- Designated parking for disabled drivers near garden entrance. House: many steps and stairs. Garden: accessible; 2 wheelchairs. Restaurant & shop: accessible.

- Braille and large-print guides for house. Braille menu. Many items in house may be touched. Scented plants and shrubs

- Sympathetic Hearing Scheme

---

**Unless indicated, last admission is always 30 mins before closing time**

92 · SOUTH WEST

- 🍴 Licensed restaurant 23 March to 3 Nov: 11–5.30 (tel. 01935 826294). Christmas menu and booked parties catered for 6 Nov to 22 Dec: Fri, Sat & Sun 11–4; March 2003: Fri, Sat & Sun 11–4 (light refreshments only). Party organisers must book lunches and teas in writing with the House Manager. Picnic area by car park
- 👶 Parent and baby room. Children's guidebook and quiz sheets. Children's portions; highchairs
- 📕 Teachers' resource book
- 🚲 Racks in car park
- 🐕 On leads and only in park; some shaded parking
- ➡️ (1:I6) In Montacute village, 4ml W of Yeovil, on S side of A3088, 3ml E of A303; signposted [183 & 193: ST499172] **Bus**: Safeway 681 Yeovil–South Petherton/Crewkerne (passing within ¾ml ☒ Yeovil Pen Mill) **Station**: Yeovil Pen Mill 5½ml; Yeovil Junction 7ml; Crewkerne 7ml

**NT properties nearby** Barrington Court, Lytes Cary Manor, Priest's House, Stourhead, Tintinhull Garden, Treasurer's House

---

## NEWARK PARK 🏠 🐕     Gloucestershire

Ozleworth, Wotton-under-Edge GL12 7PZ · **Tel** 01453 842644
**Email** michael@newark98.freeserve.co.uk

A Tudor hunting lodge, converted into a castellated country house by James Wyatt. An atmospheric house set in spectacular countryside

**Note**: The property is let and the tenant is responsible for the showing arrangements

- 🕐 April & May: Wed & Thur 11–5; June to Sept: Wed, Thur, Sat & Sun 11–5. Open BH Mons (but not Easter BH) 11–5
- 💷 £3. No party reduction. Car park
- ➡️ (1:J3) 1½ml E of Wotton-under-Edge, 1¾ml S of junction of A4135 & B4058 (house is not signposted from main road) follow signs for Ozleworth [172: ST786934] **Bus**: First Badgerline 306, 309, 310 Bristol–Dursley, alight Wotton-under-Edge, 1¾ml. Frequent services link ☒ Bristol Temple Meads with the bus station **Station**: Stroud 10ml

**NT properties nearby** Dyrham Park, Horton Court, Woodchester Park

---

There are special events at most Trust properties; please telephone 0870 458 4000 for details

## THE OLD MILL

Wembury Beach, Wembury PL9 0HP · **Tel** 01752 862314

Devon

A café housed in a former mill house, standing on a small beach near the Yealm estuary (not NT)

- **O** 29 March to 3 Nov: daily 10.30–5 (except in bad weather) or dusk if earlier
- **£** Free, but parking charge for non-members
- Regular guided rock pool rambles and other marine-related events are led by the Devon Wildlife Trust wardens from Wembury Marine Centre (open Easter to end Sept), for details tel. 01752 862538
- Access difficult, several stone steps
- Café serving hot and cold snacks and ice cream, some beach goods and souvenirs
- On beach, 1 Oct to 31 March only
- (1:F9) At Wembury, nr Plymouth [201: SX517484] **Bus**: First Western National 48 from Plymouth, thence ½ml **Station**: Plymouth 10ml

**NT properties nearby** Overbecks, Saltram

## OVERBECKS MUSEUM AND GARDEN

Sharpitor, Salcombe TQ8 8LW
**Tel** 01548 842893 · **Fax** 01548 845020 · **Email** overbecks@ntrust.org.uk

Devon

This elegant Edwardian house contains the eclectic collections of the scientist who lived here from 1928–37, Otto Overbeck. Among the items on show are late 19th-century photographs of the area, local shipbuilding tools, model boats, toys, shells, animals, a nautical collection and some of Mr Overbeck's drawings. The beautiful and luxuriant garden, with spectacular views over the Salcombe estuary, enjoys a warm microclimate and so is home to many rare plants, trees and shrubs

- **O** **Museum**: 24 March to end July, Sept: daily except Sat; Aug: daily; Oct: daily except Fri & Sat. *Times*: 11–5.30; Oct 11–5. **Garden**: all year: daily. **Events**: tel. for details
- **£** £4.20; family ticket £10.50; garden only £3, children half price. Small car park near house; charge refundable on admission. Roads leading to Overbecks are steep and single track and therefore unsuitable for coaches or large vehicles
- By arrangement, outside normal opening hours
- As museum
- Ground floor, shop & tea-room: accessible by ramp into museum; wheelchair. Garden: steep; some gravel paths; strong companion needed. Tel. for details of parking and other facilities
- Braille guides to museum for adults and children; also Braille ghost hunt certificate!

**For all your information needs check our website www.nationaltrust.org.uk**

## 94 · SOUTH WEST

- As museum 11.30–4.15. Picnics in some parts of garden
- Secret room with dolls, toys and other collections; quiz guide; ghost hunt for children; baby-changing facilities, single pushcairs admitted to house and garden
- Youth hostel on site (tel. 01548 842856)
- Only on coastal walks from car park
- (1:F9) 1½ml SW of Salcombe, signposted from Malborough and Salcombe (narrow approach road) [202: SX728374] **Bus**: Stagecoach in Devon X64, Tally Ho! 164, 606 from ≋ Totnes; also First Western National 92 from Plymouth. On all alight Salcombe, 1½ml

**NT properties nearby** Coastline both sides of estuary, Coleton Fishacre, Saltram

---

# PHILIPPS HOUSE AND DINTON PARK    Wiltshire
Dinton, Salisbury SP3 5HH · **Tel** 01985 843600 (Regional Office)

A neo-Grecian house by Jeffry Wyatville for William Wyndham, completed in 1820 and recently restored. The principal rooms on the ground floor are open to visitors and possess fine Regency furniture. The surrounding landscape park has recently been restored and offers many attractive walks

- **House**: 1 April to 28 Oct: Mon 1–5 & Sat 10–1. **Park**: all year. **Note**: Visitors to house only should park at house. Visitors to park should at all times use St Mary's Road car park at which walks start. **Events**: tel. 01985 843601 for details
- £3. Park free. No WC
- House: showrooms accessible via ramp. Park: access limited, but good views of the lake from main access point from St Mary's Road car park
- Large-print guide
- A series of walks around the park start from the car park; leaflet from property (when open), and from the village shop/post office, NT shop in Salisbury and NT Wessex office (50p plus 50p p&p)
- In park only
- (1:K5) 9ml W of Salisbury, on N side of B3089; in Dinton take St Mary's Road at crossroads. Park car park opposite cricket ground and house entrance 200m further on left [184: SU004319] **Bus**: Wilts & Dorset 25, 26, 27 from Salisbury (passing ≋ Salisbury & Tisbury) **Station**: Tisbury 5ml

**NT properties nearby** Little Clarendon, Mompesson House, Stonehenge Down, Stourhead

SYCAMORE LEAVES

---

**Please remember – your membership card is always needed for free admission**

# PRIEST'S HOUSE 🏠 Somerset

Muchelney, Langport TA10 0DQ · **Tel** 01458 252621

A late medieval hall house, built by Muchelney Abbey in 1308 for the parish priest and little altered since the hall was divided in the early 17th century. Interesting features include the Gothic doorway, beautiful double height tracery windows and a massive 15th-century stone fireplace. The house is occupied and furnished by tenants

- ⓞ 24 March to 30 Sept: Sun & Mon 2.30–5.30; last admission 5.15
- £ £2. No reductions for parties or children. No WC. Unsuitable for coaches and trailer caravans
- 🚲 Muchelney is on the South Somerset cycle trail
- ➔ (1:l6) 1ml S of Langport [193: ST429250] **Bus**: First Southern National 54 Yeovil–Taunton (passing close ≋ Taunton & within ¾ml Yeovil Pen Mill), alight Huish Episcopi, ¾ml

**NT properties nearby** Barrington Court, Lytes Cary Manor, Montacute House, Stembridge Tower Mill, Tintinhull Garden, Treasurer's House

# PRIOR PARK LANDSCAPE GARDEN ❁ Bath & NE Somerset

Ralph Allen Drive, Bath BA2 5AH · **Tel** 01225 833422 · **Infoline** 09001 335242
**Email** priorpark@ntrust.org.uk

A beautiful and intimate 18th-century landscape garden, created by local entrepreneur Ralph Allen with advice from the poet Alexander Pope and 'Capability' Brown, and set in a sweeping valley with magnificent views of the City of Bath. The many interesting features include a Palladian bridge and three lakes. The restoration of the garden is continuing. Prior Park College, a co-educational school, operates from the mansion (not NT)

**What's new in 2002**: Interpretation panels detailing the history and ongoing restoration of Prior Park

- ⓞ Feb to Nov: daily except Tues (but open BH Tues 4 June); Dec & Jan 2003: Fri, Sat & Sun (closed 25, 26 Dec & 1 Jan 2003). *Times*: 11–5.30 (or dusk if earlier)
- £ £4; child £2. To thank visitors for using public transport, all those who produce a valid bus or train ticket receive £1 off admission; NT members receive £1 voucher, which can be used for purchases such as guidebooks. There is a bus and coach drop-off point outside the gates to the garden. Coach parties must book in advance, tel. 01225 833422; every passenger receives a discount
- 🛍 In Abbey Churchyard, Bath (tel. 01225 460249)
- ♿ 3 parking bays for disabled drivers, booking essential, tel. 01225 833422. Garden: top, with wonderful views, easily accessible; elsewhere very steep
- 📖 Braille and large-print guides

**For general enquiries, please telephone 0870 458 4000**

🏛 For details of arrangements for schools, contact the Education Coordinator, tel. 01225 833422

🚲 Racks

➡ (1:J4) All visitors must use public transport as there is no parking at Prior Park or nearby. To obtain a leaflet explaining how to reach the garden, tel. 01225 833422 [172:ST760633] **Bus**: First Badgerline 2, 4 🚆 Bath–Combe Down. As Bath is very congested, use park-and-ride to centre **Station**: Bath Spa 1ml **Cycle**: NCN 4 1½ml

**NT properties nearby** The Courts Garden, Dyrham Park, Great Chalfield Manor, Lacock Abbey & Fox Talbot Museum, Westwood Manor

---

# ST ANTHONY HEAD                                           Cornwall

**Tel** 01872 862945 (Fal Countryside Office) · **Fax** 01872 865619
**Email** stanthonyhead@ntrust.org.uk

---

At the southernmost tip of the Roseland peninsula, St Anthony Head overlooks the spectacular entrance to one of the world's largest natural harbours – Carrick Roads and the Fal estuary. The starting point for a number of excellent coastal and sheltered creekside walks, the Head also bears newly revealed remains of a century of defensive fortifications

🅾 All year

💷 Car park charge (NT members free)

🚶 *Coast of Cornwall* leaflet no. 18/19 includes maps and details of circular walks in area, as well as information about local history, geology and wildlife

♿ Accessible paths to gun emplacements and viewpoint, and through defensive rock-cut ditch to WW2 Battery Observation Post and bird hide; WC. Two adapted holiday cottages in converted officers' quarters (tel. 01225 791133 for brochure)

🍴 Nearest refreshments (not NT) in Gerrans and St Mawes

➡ (1:C9) S of St Mawes off A3078 [204: SW846314] **Bus**: First Western National 51 Truro–St Mawes, alight St Mawes for ferry to Place, thence 1½ml or alight Portscatho, thence 3ml (tel. 01209 719988) **Station**: Penmere, via ferry to St Mawes then to Place, 6ml Foot ferry: Falmouth to St Mawes (all year, but no Sun service in winter); St Mawes to Place (1ml from St Anthony Head along coast path), daily in summer only

**NT properties nearby**
Trelissick Garden

GREATER BLACK-BACKED GULL

---

**Please see the area introductions for details of coast & countryside properties**

## ST MICHAEL'S MOUNT     Cornwall

Marazion, nr Penzance TR17 0EF · **Tel** 01736 710507 · **Fax** 01736 711544
**Email** godolphin@manor-office.co.uk · **Web** www.stmichaelsmount.co.uk

Originally the site of a Benedictine priory and approached by a causeway at low tide (and ferry boats at high tide – weather permitting), the dramatic castle on top of this famous rocky island dates from the 12th century. It was converted into a private house in the 17th century and contains fascinating early rooms, an armoury, a rococo Gothic drawing room and, at the highest point, a 14th-century church. There are magnificent views towards Land's End and The Lizard

**Note**: There are no facilities for dogs on the island. Sensible shoes are advisable, as many walking surfaces are uneven. Passages in the castle are narrow, so some delays may occur at the height of the season. On Sundays from June to Sept a short non-denominational service is held in the church at 11am

- 25 March to 1 Nov: daily except Sat & Sun. *Times*: 10.30–5.30, last admission 4.45. These times are from the visitors' entrance to the island and ample time should be allowed for travel from the mainland. **The castle and gardens are also open most weekends during the season; these are special charity open days and NT members must pay for admission**. Private garden (not NT): open daily April & May. Nov to end March: essential to tel. in advance for the opening arrangements for any day

- £4.60; family £13. Booked parties £4.20. No NT car park; public car park in Marazion. Private garden (not NT): £2.50

- Introductory video in cinema

- 25 March to 1 Nov daily (tel. 01736 711067)

- Unsuitable for wheelchairs, prams and pushchairs: steep site, cobbled causeway and paths

- Braille guides

- The Sail Loft restaurant (licensed), plus light refreshments and ice creams, 25 March to 1 Nov daily (but closed Sat in Oct); limited out of season opening (tel. 01736 710748). Island café (not NT) 25 March to 1 Nov daily

- Schools' resource pack (tel. 01736 710507)

**Unless indicated, last admission is always 30 mins before closing time**

## SOUTH WEST

→ (1:B9) ½ml S of A394 at Marazion, whence there is access on foot over the causeway at low tide or, during summer months only, by ferry at high tide. Tide and ferry information only: tel. 01736 710265/710507 [203: SW515298]
**Bus**: First Western National 2, 2A Penzance–Falmouth; 17A Penzance–St Ives, 32 Penzance–Camborne. All pass ⊞ Penzance **Station**: Penzance 3ml
**Cycle**: NCN 3 ¾ml

**NT properties nearby** Godolphin Estate, Trengwainton Garden

---

## SALTRAM
Devon

Plympton, Plymouth PL7 1UH · **Tel** 01752 333500 · **Fax** 01752 336474
**Email** saltram@ntrust.org.uk

---

A remarkable survival of a George II mansion, complete with its original contents and set in an attractive landscape park. Robert Adam worked here on two occasions to create the magnificent state rooms. There is exquisite plasterwork throughout and three rooms are decorated with the original Chinese wallpaper. The house contains fine period furniture, china and pictures, including many portraits by Reynolds and Angelica Kauffmann. Three new rooms including the Parker children's doll's house and hands-on 18th-century-inspired activities for children. The superb 18th-century gardens contain an orangery, the Chapel Art Gallery and several follies, as well as beautiful shrubberies and imposing specimen trees

**O** House: 24 March to 3 Nov: daily except Fri (but open Good Fri). *Times*: 24 March to 30 Sept: 12–4.30; 1 Oct to 3 Nov: 11.30–3.30 (due to poor light). Garden, Chapel Art Gallery, shop & tea-room: 24 March to 3 Nov: daily except Fri (but open Good Fri) 11–5; 4 Nov to 19 Dec: daily except Fri 11–4. Jan 2003: garden & shop: daily except Fri 11–4, tea-room & gallery weekends only. Feb and March: garden daily except Fri 11–4; tea-room, shop & gallery weekends only:11–4.
**Events**: Craft Fairs 17, 18 Aug & 30 Nov to 1 Dec. Entry £2 incl. NT members. Summer Jazz Picnic: 20 July. Tel. 01752 333500 for events leaflet

**£** £6; garden only £3. Discount for booked parties, rates on application. Parking 500m. February only, garden entry reduced to £1.50

Special theme lectures. Booking essential, tel. 01752 333500

Shop as above, tel. 01752 330034. Chapel Art Gallery as above, selling local arts and crafts. Exhibition and Craft Fair details contact Gallery Manager, tel. 01752 347852

Visitors with disabilities may be set down at front door by arrangement. House: accessible; lift for those who can transfer from wheelchair to seat in lift to view first floor. Garden: accessible. Chapel Art Gallery: ground floor accessible. Tea-room accessible. WCs in stables. Wheelchairs available from house and reception

Braille and audio guides. Scented plants

Refreshments daily in tea-room or restaurant. Please check which facility is open at reception. Bookings tel. 01752 333500

---

**There are special events at most Trust properties; please telephone 0870 458 4000 for details**

- Pushchairs, children's guide, baby-changing facilities on request at entrance hall. Highchairs, children's menu, baby foods
- Education room and workshops; advance booking essential; educational activities for school groups, bookings on request, tel. for details
- On leads and only in park. Shaded 'dog park' near stable block entrance and dog bins installed
- (1:F8) 3½ml E of Plymouth city centre, between Plymouth–Exeter road (A38) and Plymouth–Kingsbridge road (A379); take Plympton turn at Marsh Mills roundabout [201: SX520557] **Bus**: Plymouth Citybus 19/A/B, 20–2, 51 from Plymouth, alight Plymouth Road–Plympton Bypass Jct, ¾ml footpath. Reduced entry fee for visitors arriving by public transport on production of valid ticket **Station**: Plymouth 3½ml **Cycle**: NCN 27

**NT properties nearby** Buckland Abbey, coastline near Wembury

## SHUTE BARTON

Devon

Shute, nr Axminster EX13 7PT · **Tel** 01297 34692

One of the most important surviving non-fortified manor houses of the Middle Ages. Begun in 1380 and completed in the late 16th century, then partly demolished in the late 18th century, the house has battlemented turrets, late Gothic windows and a Tudor gatehouse

- 3 April to 30 Oct: Wed & Sat 2–5.30. Guided tours only. The house is tenanted; there is access to most parts of the interior
- £1.80. No party reduction; unsuitable for coaches or large groups. No WC
- (1:H7) 3ml SW of Axminster, 2ml N of Colyton on Honiton–Colyton road (B3161) [177/193: SY253974] **Bus**: First Southern National 20 Taunton–Seaton (passes ☒ Honiton) **Station**: Axminster 3ml

**NT properties nearby** Branscombe, Loughwood Meeting House

## SNOWSHILL MANOR

Gloucestershire

Snowshill, nr Broadway WR12 7JU · **Tel/Fax** 01386 852410
**Infoline** 01684 855376
**Email** snowshillmanor@ntrust.org.uk

A Cotswold manor house containing Charles Paget Wade's extraordinary collection of craftmanship and design, including musical instruments, clocks, toys, bicycles, weavers' and spinners' tools and Japanese armour. There is a delightful organic garden, and Mr Wade's cottage can also be visited. The Snowshill costume collection can be viewed by appointment only at Berrington Hall, please tel. 01568 613720 on Thur or Fri

**Note**: Entry to the Manor may be restricted from 4 Sept to 3 Nov due to essential building work. Please ring to confirm opening arrangements for Sept, Oct and Nov

For all your information needs check our website www.nationaltrust.org.uk

100 · SOUTH WEST

- **House**: 29 March to 3 Nov: Wed to Sun 12–5, but open BH Mons & Tues 4 June; also Mons July & Aug: Garden, shop and restaurant: 11–5.30. **Note**: entry to the house is by timed ticket
- £6; family £15. Garden, restaurant & shop only £3.50. Coach and school parties by written appointment only. Photography only by written arrangement with Property Manager
- 29 March to 3 Nov: as garden; 9 Nov to 15 Dec: Sat & Sun 12–4
- House & grounds: access very limited (buggy available). Visitor facilities accessible. Adapted WC
- Braille guide of house and garden; audio tape; touch list
- As shop; tel. 01386 858685
- No pushchairs or baby back-carriers in house. Parent and baby room
- Racks
- (1:K2) 2½ml SW of Broadway; turn from A44 Broadway bypass into Broadway village and by village green turn uphill to Snowshill [150: SP096339] **Bus**: Castleways ≋ Evesham–Broadway, thence 2½ml **Station**: Moreton-in-Marsh 7ml

**NT properties nearby** Chastleton House, Hidcote Manor Garden, Lodge Park

---

## STEMBRIDGE TOWER MILL 🕱              Somerset
High Ham TA10 9DJ · **Tel** 01458 250818

The last thatched windmill in England, dating from 1822 and in use until 1910

- 24 March to 30 Sept: Sun, Mon & Wed 2–5; special arrangements may be made for coach and school parties
- £2; child £1. Parties by arrangement with the tenant; no reduction. Parking for coaches ¼ml. No WC

---

**Please remember – your membership card is always needed for free admission**

SOUTH WEST · 101

→ (1:I5) 2ml N of Langport, ½ml E of High Ham; take the Somerton road from Langport and follow High Ham signs. Take road opposite cemetery in High Ham. Mill is along on right [182: ST432305] **Bus**: First Southern National 54 Yeovil–Taunton (passing close ⇌ Taunton & within ¾ml Yeovil Pen Mill), alight Langport, 2½ml **Station**: Bridgwater 10ml

**NT properties nearby** Barrington Court, Lytes Cary Manor, Montacute House, Priest's House, Tintinhull Garden, Treasurer's House

---

## STOKE-SUB-HAMDON PRIORY                     Somerset
North Street, Stoke-sub-Hamdon TA4 6QP · **Tel** 01985 843600 (Regional Office)

A complex of buildings begun in the 14th century for the priests of the chantry chapel of St Nicholas (now destroyed)

○ 23 March to 3 Nov: daily 10–6 or dusk if earlier. **Note**: Only Great Hall open

£ Free. No WC

→ (1:I6) Between A303 and A3088. 2ml W of Montacute between Yeovil and Ilminster [193:ST473175] **Bus**: Safeway 681 Yeovil–South Petherton/Crewkerne (passing within ¾ml ⇌ Yeovil Pen Mill) **Station**: Crewkerne or Yeovil Pen Mill, both 7ml

**NT properties nearby** Barrington Court, Lytes Cary Manor, Montacute House, Priest's House, Stembridge Tower Mill, Tintinhull Garden, Treasurer's House

---

## STONEHENGE DOWN                             Wiltshire
Amesbury, nr Salisbury SP4 7DE ·
**Tel** 01985 843600 (National Trust) Open Countryside · 01980 623108 (English Heritage) Monument and Visitor Centre

The Trust owns 758ha (1873 acres) of downland surrounding the famous monument, including some fine Bronze Age barrow groups and the Cursus, variously interpreted as an ancient racecourse or processional way. There are recommended walks and an archaeological leaflet (£1) from the leaflet dispenser in the car park or from the NT Wessex office (add 50p p&p)

**Note**: The monument itself is owned and administered by English Heritage

○ Tel. English Heritage for details. NT members free. NT land north of visitor centre open at all times, but parts may be closed at the Summer Solstice (21 June) for up to 2 days

🛍 EH shop adjacent to the monument

♿ Area around monument accessible and access to grassland north of visitor centre via adjacent byway

🎧 Tape guide for monument; also refers to the landscape

🐕 Not on archaeological walks

**For general enquiries, please telephone 0870 458 4000**

## SOUTH WEST

➜ (1:K5) Monument 2ml W of Amesbury, at junction of A303 & A344/A360 [184: SU1242] **Bus**: Wilts & Dorset 3 ☒ Salisbury–Stonehenge **Station**: Salisbury 9½ml

**NT properties nearby** Little Clarendon, Mompesson House, Philipps House and Dinton Park, Stourhead

---

## STOURHEAD                                                                 Wiltshire
The Estate Office, Stourton, Warminster BA12 6QD · **Tel** 01747 841152
**Fax** 01747 842005 · **Email** stourhead@ntrust.org.uk

An outstanding example of the English landscape style, this splendid garden was designed by Henry Hoare II and laid out between 1741 and 1780. Classical temples, including the Pantheon and Temple of Apollo, are set around the central lake at the end of a series of vistas, which change as the visitor moves around the paths and through the magnificent mature woodland with its extensive collection of exotic trees. The house, begun in 1721 by Colen Campbell, contains furniture by the younger Chippendale and fine paintings. King Alfred's Tower, an intriguing red-brick folly built in 1772 by Henry Flitcroft, is almost 50m high and gives breathtaking views over the estate. Much of the estate woodland and downland is managed for nature conservation and there are two interesting Iron Age hill-forts, Whitesheet Hill and Park Hill Camp. There are also waymarked walks and an exhibition about the estate in the reception building. Leaflet of estate walks available from shop and NT Wessex office 50p (plus 50p p&p)

**What's new in 2002**: New restaurant, shop and plant centre. Specialist guided tours of house each Thur 28 March to 31 Oct. Please book in advance. Education Room open summer 2002. New colour souvenir guide to garden. New farm walk in walks leaflet

**Garden**: daily 9–7 or sunset if earlier. **House**: 23 March to 3 Nov: daily 12–5.30 or dusk, except Thur & Fri (but open Good Fri). **King Alfred's Tower**: 23 March to 3 Nov: daily except Mon (but open BH Mons). *Times*: Tues to Fri 2–5.30; Sat, Sun & BH Mon 11.30–5.30 or dusk. **Events**: tel. for events leaflet from estate office; book via Regional Box Office 01985 843601

Garden & house £8.70; child £4.10; family £20.50; booked (15+) parties by appointment £8.20. Garden or house March to 3 Nov: £4.90; child £2.70; family £12.30; booked parties £4.40. Garden only 4 Nov to end Feb: £3.80; child £1.85; family £9.20; booked parties £3.60. King Alfred's Tower £1.65, child 85p, family £4.10

Tours of house and garden by arrangement; tel. for details and information on group packages

Shop and plant centre daily all year: 23 March to 3 Nov 10–6; 4 Nov to 24 March 2003 11–4 (tel. 01747 842040; fax 01747 842041)

Close parking at house and garden. House: access via 13 steps; thereafter all showrooms on one level. House congested at weekends and in May and June. Garden: 1½ml path around lake accessible, but steep in places; at least two strong companions essential. Wheelchairs for house and garden; also (in peak

---

**Please see the area introductions for details of coast & countryside properties**

season) volunteer-driven vehicle from car park to garden and house entrances and 2-seater self-drive vehicle for garden. Shop, plant centre and restaurant: accessible. King Alfred's Tower: level walk across grass and along 2½ml terrace walk to house. WCs at main car park and Spread Eagle courtyard

- 'Touch tour' guide for house (must be booked; tel. 01747 842020; fax 01747 842022). Large-print guide for house. Braille garden guide. Scented azaleas in early summer

- Sympathetic Hearing Scheme

- Self-service restaurant daily all year: 23 March to 3 Nov 9.30–5.30; 4 Nov to 28 March 2003 10.30–4 (tel. 01747 842047; fax 01747 842049). Picnics near car parks and in garden. Spread Eagle Inn close to garden entrance also open all year. Weekend and mid-week breaks available 1 Nov to end March (tel. 01747 840587; fax 01747 840954)

- Parent and baby room by reception building in main car park. Children's guidebook, house, garden and King Alfred's Tower quizzes

- For details of education arrangements, contact the Education Coordinator, tel. 01747 842012

- On short fixed leads in garden 4 Nov to end Feb and under close control on wider estate throughout year. Dogs must be on leads near farm stock. Dogs are not allowed in King Alfred's Tower, but may be tied up outside

- (1:J5) At Stourton, off B3092, 3ml NW of Mere (A303), 8ml S of Frome (A361). Parking 400m from house and garden, adjacent to catering facilities. **King Alfred's Tower**: 3½ml by road from Stourhead House; parking 350m [183: ST7834]] **Bus**: Wilts & Dorset 25/6, Brue Travel 125 Salisbury–Stourhead (Tues, Wed, Fri only); Wakes 80 Frome to ≋ Gillingham (Wed, sat only); otherwise First Southern National 58/A ≋ Shaftesbury–Yeovil, some to Stourhead, but on others alight Zeals, 1¼ml **Station**: Gillingham 6½ml; Bruton (U) 7ml

**NT properties nearby** Barrington Court, Lytes Cary Manor, Mompesson House, Montacute House, Tintinhull Garden

**Unless indicated, last admission is always 30 mins before closing time**

## STUDLAND BEACH & NATURE RESERVE — Dorset
Countryside Office, Studland, Swanage BH19 3AX · **Tel** 01929 450259
**Email** studlandbeach@ntrust.org.uk

Fine sandy beaches stretch continuously for 3ml from South Haven Point to the chalk cliffs of Handfast Point and Old Harry Rocks, and include Shell Bay and a designated naturist area. The heathland behind the beach is a National Nature Reserve and a haven for many rare birds and other forms of wildlife. There are several public paths and two nature trails here. Bird hides at Little Sea

**Note**: WCs at Knoll and Middle Beach, and Shell Bay (summer only)

- All year. **Car parks**: Shell Bay: all year: daily 9am–11pm; The Knoll & Middle Beach: Easter to Sept daily 9–8 (reduced parking area in winter); South Beach: all year: daily 9am–11pm
- Car parks (Shell Bay, The Knoll, Middle Beach and South Beach): Easter to April: £3 (£1.50 after 2, £1 after 4); May & June £4 (£3 after 2, £1.50 after 4); 1 July to 31 Aug £5.50 (£4 after 2, £2 after 4); 1 to 15 Sept £4.50 (£3 after 2, £2 after 4); 16 to 30 Sept: £2.50 (£1.50 after 2, £1 after 4); Rest of year, donations only. NT members free. Coaches £15 (£5 after 4), motorcycles £2 (£1 after 2). Boat launching: single hull £4.50 per day, twin hull £10 per day, weekly and season tickets available. No powered boats permitted
- Guided tours of nature reserve by wardens; tel. 01929 450259 for details
- Knoll visitor centre shop daily. *Times*: 1 March to 30 June, 8 Sept to Feb 2003: 11–4;·1 July to 7 Sept: 10–5. **Note**: Hours may be longer in fine weather and shorter when weather bad (tel. 01929 450500)
- Knoll car park: accessible. Part of Knoll Beach and visitor facilities accessible via boardwalks in summer. Some wheelchair access. Specially designed wheelchair suitable for beach use available from the Knoll visitor centre
- NT beach café at Knoll Beach open as Knoll visitor centre shop (tel. 01929 450305). Concessionary café at Middle Beach and fish restaurant at Shell Bay
- Baby-changing facilities in WC at Knoll
- Studland Study Base open for educational visits. For full details of teachers' and students' resources and guided walks, contact the Education Coordinator tel. 01929 480609. Information in Knoll visitor centre and coastguard hut at Middle Beach
- Purbeck walks pack describes local walks; from local NT shops and NT Wessex office £2.75 (plus 50p p&p)
- Racks in all car parks; lockable posts in the Knoll, Middle Beach and South Beach car parks
- Only on main beaches from first Mon in Sept to last Fri in June (must be on leads from 1 May). Last Sat in June to first Sun in Sept inclusive: prohibited from Knoll and Middle Beaches; permitted on Shell Bay Beach and South Beach. No fouling of the beaches: 'Poop Scoops' on sale at the visitor centre. Permitted all year on nature reserve footpaths

**There are special events at most Trust properties; please telephone 0870 458 4000 for details**

→ (1:K7) [195: SZ036835] **Bus**: Wilts & Dorset 150 Bournemouth–Swanage (passing ≣ Branksome) to Shell Bay & Studland. Also 152 Poole–Sandbanks (passing close ≣ Parkstone); Yellow Buses 12 Christchurch–Sandbanks, summer only then vehicle ferry from Sandbanks to Shell Bay
**Station**: Branksome or Parkstone, both 3½ml to Shell Bay or 6ml to Studland via vehicle ferry

**NT properties nearby** Brownsea Island, Clouds Hill, Corfe Castle, Hardy's Cottage, Kingston Lacy, Max Gate

---

## TINTAGEL OLD POST OFFICE                Cornwall
Tintagel PL34 0DB · **Tel/Fax** 01840 770024 (opening hours only)
**Email** tintageloldpo@ntrust.org.uk

---

One of the Trust's most delightful small buildings and enhanced by a small garden, this 14th-century manor house is well furnished with local oak pieces. One room was used in the 19th century for nearly fifty years as the letter-receiving office for the district and is now restored to that period and function

O 23 March to 3 Nov: daily. *Times*: 23 March to 30 Sept 11–5.30; Oct & Nov 11–4

£ £2.30; family £5.70. Booked parties £1.80

As property

Access very limited

Braille guide

→ (1:D7) In centre of village [200: SX056884] **Bus**: First Western National X10 from ≣ Exeter St David's; also First Western National 122/4/5, X4 Wadebridge–Bude (with some from ≣ Bodmin Parkway)

**NT properties nearby** Boscastle

---

## TINTINHULL GARDEN                Somerset
Farm St, Tintinhull, Yeovil BA22 9PZ · **Tel** 01935 822545
**Email** tintinhull@ntrust.org.uk

---

A delightful formal garden, created last century around a 17th-century manor house. Small pools, varied borders and secluded lawns are all neatly enclosed within walls and clipped hedges, and there is also an attractive kitchen garden

O 23 March to 29 Sept: daily except Mon & Tues 12–6 (but open BH Mons and BH Tues 4 June)

£ £3.80; child £1.80. No party reduction. Coach parties by arrangement in advance with the Gardener

In advance with the Gardener

Parking in courtyard by arrangement. Garden: difficult; cobbles, uneven paths and steps, but accessible with helper

**For all your information needs check our website www.nationaltrust.org.uk**

Roses, honeysuckle and other scented plants. Large-print guide

Tea-room as property 12–5.30

Cycles can be left in courtyard

(1:I6) 5ml NW of Yeovil, ½ml S of A303, on E outskirts of Tintinhull [183: ST503198] **Bus**: First Southern National 52 Yeovil–Martock (passing within ¾ml ⚏ Yeovil Pen Mill) **Station**: Yeovil Pen Mill 5½ml; Yeovil Junction 7ml

**NT properties nearby** Barrington Court, Lytes Cary Manor, Montacute House

## TREASURER'S HOUSE                                Somerset
Martock TA12 6JL · **Tel** 01935 825801

A small medieval house, recently refurbished by the Trust. The Great Hall was completed in 1293 and the solar block, with an interesting wall painting, is even earlier. There is also a kitchen added in the 15th century

24 March to 30 Sept: Sun, Mon & Tues 2–5. **Note**: Only medieval hall, wall painting and kitchen are shown. Parking is limited and unsuitable for coaches and trailer caravans

£2; child £1. Parties (no reduction) only by arrangement with tenant; tel. for details. No WC

Large-print guide

(1:I6) Opposite church in middle of village; 1ml NW of A303 between Ilminster and Ilchester [193: ST462191] **Bus**: First Southern National 52 Yeovil–Martock (passing within ¾ml ⚏ Yeovil Pen Mill) **Station**: Crewkerne 7½ml; Yeovil Pen Mill 8ml

**NT properties nearby** Barrington Court, Lytes Cary Manor, Montacute House, Priest's House, Stembridge Tower Mill, Tintinhull Garden

## TRELISSICK GARDEN                                Cornwall
Feock, nr Truro TR3 6QL · **Tel** 01872 862090 · **Fax** 01872 865808
**Email** trelissick@ntrust.org.uk

Beautifully positioned at the head of Fal estuary, the estate commands panoramic views over the area and has extensive park and woodland walks beside the river. At its heart is the tranquil garden, set on many levels and containing a superb collection of tender and exotic plants which bring colour throughout the year. The display of spring blossom is particularly delightful. The house is not open, but there is an art and craft gallery, shop, two restaurants and fine Georgian stable block

**Note**: Copeland China collection open 6 to 10 May and 9 to 13 Sept by appointment. Tel. 01872 862248

**Garden**: 16 Feb to 3 Nov: daily. *Times*: 10.30–5.30 (Sun 12.30–5.30) or dusk if earlier. **Woodland walks**: all year, daily. **Events**: programme of theatrical and

**Please remember – your membership card is always needed for free admission**

## SOUTH WEST · 107

musical events, winter and spring programmes, tel. for details.
**1–4 May: Cornwall Gardens Society Show here. All access to site via Park and Ride service**

- £ £4.50; family £11.25. Booked parties £3.70. Car park £1.60, refundable on admission

- Shop & plant sales 16 Feb to 3 Nov: daily as garden; 4 Nov to 23 Dec: 11–4 and 27 to 31 Dec: 11–3 (tel. 01872 865515). Art & craft gallery as shop (tel. 01872 864084)

- Close parking. Garden: upper parts reasonably flat, loose gravel paths. Shop & restaurant: accessible. Gallery: ground floor accessible. Wheelchairs and guide for disabled visitors from reception. Self-drive single-seater (tel. to book)

- Braille guide. Small garden with aromatic plants near entrance

- Trelissick Barn licensed restaurant 16 Feb to 3 Nov: daily as garden (Sun open 12); 4 Nov to 23 Dec: 11–4 & 27 to 31 Dec: 11–3 (tel. 01872 863486). Courtyard Room (light refreshments), limited opening

- Parent and baby changing room just beyond the gallery

- Schools' resource pack

- On leads in park and on woodland walks only

- (1:C9) 4ml S of Truro, on both sides of B3289 above King Harry Ferry [204: SW837396] **Bus**: Truronian T7 from Truro (passing close ≷ Truro); First Western National 89B from ≷ Truro, Sun only **Station**: Truro 5ml; Perranwell (U), not Sun, except July & Aug, 4ml **Cycle**: NCN 3

**NT properties nearby** Glendurgan Garden, Trerice

---

## TRENGWAINTON GARDEN                                    Cornwall

nr Penzance TR20 8RZ · **Tel** 01736 362297 (opening hours only)
**Fax** 01736 362297 · **Email** trengwainton@ntrust.org.uk

---

A unique garden, perhaps more favoured for the cultivation of exotic trees and shrubs than any other on mainland Britain. The walled garden in particular contains many species which cannot be grown in the open anywhere else in the country. Intimate and closely linked to the stream running through its valley, the garden leads up to a terrace and summer-houses with splendid views of Mount's Bay and The Lizard

- O 17 Feb to 3 Nov: daily except Fri & Sat (but open Good Fri). *Times*: 1 April to 30 Sept 10–5.30; Feb, March, Oct & Nov 10–5

- £ £3.90; family £9.75. Booked parties £3.20

- Shop & plant sales

**For general enquiries, please telephone 0870 458 4000**

## 108 · SOUTH WEST

- ♿ Map available to show advised route taking in Jubilee, Lower Stream and Walled Gardens. Two wheelchairs. Strong companion advised because of gradients in this valley garden. Shop, plant sales and new tea-house fully accessible
- 👁 Fragrant plants, stream, pools, water sounds
- ☕ Light refreshments in tea-house in the walled garden
- 🐕 On leads only and not in the tea-house garden
- ➡ (1:B9) 2ml NW of Penzance, ½ml W of Heamoor off Penzance–Morvah road (B3312), ½ml off St Just road (A3071) [203: SW445315] **Bus**: First Western National 10/A Penzance–St Just **Station**: Penzance 2ml **Cycle**: NCN 3 2½ml

**NT properties nearby** Levant Steam Engine, St Michael's Mount

---

# TRERICE 🏠 ✼ 🛡 🔔                                             Cornwall
Kestle Mill, nr Newquay TR8 4PG · **Tel** 01637 875404 · **Fax** 01637 879300
**Email** trerice@ntrust.org.uk

---

This delightful small Elizabethan manor house enjoys a secluded setting and contains fine fireplaces, plaster ceilings, oak and walnut furniture, interesting clocks and Stuart portraits. The highlight of the interior is the magnificent great chamber with its splendid barrel ceiling. The attractive garden has some unusual plants and an orchard with old varieties of fruit trees, and in the barn there is an exhibition on the history of the lawnmower

- 🕐 24 March to 15 July, 11 Sept to 3 Nov: daily except Tues & Sat (but open 4 June); 16 July to 10 Sept: daily except Sat. *Times*: 24 March to 30 Sept 11–5.30; Oct & Nov 11–5. **Events**: send SAE for programme
- 💷 £4.40; family £11. Booked parties £3.60
- 🛍 Shop & plant sales as house
- ♿ Close parking by arrangement. House: ground and upper (via grass slope) floors accessible. Tea-room & shop: accessible. Garden: limited access; some loose gravel and cobbles

**Please see the area introductions for details of coast & countryside properties**

- Braille guide and tape tour; access leaflet; many items may be touched
- The Barn open as house, last serving 5 (4.30 in Oct & Nov). Organisers of parties should arrange for meals beforehand (tel. 01637 875404)
- Parent and baby room. Free age-related quizzes for children
- Schools may visit the house from 10.30 by appointment with the Property Manager. School hut. Schools are welcome to picnic in the orchard
- On leads and only in car park. Shade provided in car park
- (1:C8) 3ml SE of Newquay via A392 and A3058 (turn right at Kestle Mill) [200: SW841585] **Bus**: First Western National 50 from Newquay–Trerice (May to Sept only) otherwise X89, X90 Newquay–Truro, alight Kestle Mill, ¾ml **Station**: Quintrell Downs (U), not Sun, except July & Aug, 1½ml **Cycle**: NCN 32

**NT properties nearby** Lanhydrock

## WATERSMEET HOUSE                                                    Devon
Watersmeet Road, Lynmouth EX35 6NT · **Tel** 01598 753348

A fishing lodge, built *c.*1832 in a picturesque valley at the confluence of the East Lyn and Hoar Oak Water, and now a NT shop, with refreshments and information. The site has been a tea-garden since 1901 and is the focal point for several beautiful walks

- 23 March to 3 Nov: daily 10.30–5.30 (4.30 Oct & Nov)
- Free. Pay-and-display car park, or free car parks at Combepark, Hillsford Bridge and Countisbury
- See local listings for programme of guided walks on Watersmeet Estate. Walks leaflet from shop
- As property
- Access limited; arrangements strictly by appointment with Catering Manager (tel. 01598 753348)
- In tea-garden beside river, as property. Party catering by arrangement
- Baby-changing facilities in both men's and women's WCs. Children's quiz
- By arrangement with the Warden (tel. 01598 763306)
- Cycles can be left in town council car park
- On leads and only in car parks and on the walks
- (1:F5) 1½ml E of Lynmouth, in valley on E side of Lynmouth–Barnstaple road (A39) [180: SS744487] **Bus**: First Red Bus 309, 310 Barnstaple–Lynmouth (passing close ☒ Barnstaple), 300 Minehead–Ilfracombe. On both, alight Lynmouth, thence walk through NT Gorge

**NT properties nearby** Arlington, Dunster Castle, Heddon Valley, Holnicote

**Unless indicated, last admission is always 30 mins before closing time**

## WEST PENNARD COURT BARN — Somerset

West Pennard, nr Glastonbury · **Tel** 01985 843600 (Regional Office)

A 15th-century barn of five bays with a roof of interesting construction. Repaired and given to the Trust by the Society for the Protection of Ancient Buildings in 1938

- Visitors collect key from Mr P H Green, Court Barn Farm, West Bradley, Somerset, by arrangement, tel. 01458 850212
- Free
- (1:15) 3ml E of Glastonbury, 7ml S of Wells, 1½ml S of West Pennard (A361) [182/183: ST547370] **Bus**: First Badgerline 669 Shepton Mallet–Street or 969 Bath–Glastonbury, both to within 1ml **Station**: Castle Cary 8ml **Cycle**: NCN 3 2½ml

**NT properties nearby** Glastonbury Tor, Lytes Cary Manor, Stourhead

## WESTBURY COLLEGE GATEHOUSE — Bristol

College Road, Westbury-on-Trym · **Tel** 01985 843600 (Regional Office)

The 15th-century gatehouse of the College of Priests (founded in the 13th century), of which John Wyclif was prebend. There is an interesting church (not NT) nearby

- Access by key only, to be collected by written appointment with the vicar, The Vicarage, 44 Eastfield Road, Westbury-on-Trym, Bristol BS9 4AG, tel. 0117 962 1536/0117 950 8644
- £1.10; child 50p
- (1:14) 3ml N of the centre of Bristol [172: ST572775] **Bus**: Frequent from surrounding areas **Station**: Clifton Down (U) not Sun, 2ml **Cycle**: NCN 4 1ml

**NT properties nearby** Blaise Hamlet, Clevedon Court, Dyrham Park, Horton Court, Leigh Woods, Prior Park

## WESTBURY COURT GARDEN — Gloucestershire

Westbury-on-Severn GL14 1PD · **Tel** 01452 760461 · **Infoline** 01684 855377
**Email** westburycourt@ntrust.org.uk

A rare and beautiful survival: the only restored Dutch water garden in the country, laid out 1696–1705. The National Trust's first garden restoration, it was restored in 1971 and is planted with species dating from before 1700

- 1 March to 30 June: daily except Mon & Tues (but open BH Mons & 4 June). 1 July to 31 Aug: daily. 1 Sept to 27 Oct: Wed to Sun. *Times*: 10–5. Other months by appointment
- £3. Free car park. Parties of 15+ by written appointment
- Small selection of NT goods on sale: bookmarks, postcards etc

**There are special events at most Trust properties; please telephone 0870 458 4000 for details**

Garden: accessible; wheelchair
Braille guide. Scented plants
No tea-room, but picnic area
(1:J2) 9ml SW of Gloucester on A48 [162: SO718138] **Bus**: Stagecoach in South Wales/Duke's 73 Gloucester–Newport (passing close Newport); Stagecoach in Wye & Dean 31 Gloucester–Coleford **Station**: Gloucester 9ml

**NT properties nearby** Ashleworth Tithe Barn, May Hill

## WESTWOOD MANOR
Wiltshire
Bradford-on-Avon BA15 2AF · **Tel** 01225 863374 · **Fax** 01225 867316

A 15th-century stone manor house, altered in the early 17th century, with late Gothic and Jacobean windows and fine plasterwork. There is a modern topiary garden

**Note**: Westwood Manor is administered for the National Trust by the tenant

31 March to 29 Sept: Sun, Tues & Wed 2–5. At other times parties by written application with s.a.e. to the tenant

£4. No reduction for parties or children. No WC

Large-print guide

(1:J4) 1½ml SW of Bradford-on-Avon, in Westwood village, beside the church; village signposted off Bradford-on-Avon to Rode road (B3109) [173: ST812590] **Bus**: Bodmon 94/96 from Trowbridge (passing close Trowbridge); otherwise from surrounding areas to Bradford-on-Avon, thence 1½ml **Station**: Avoncliff (U), 1ml; Bradford-on-Avon 1½ml **Cycle**: NCN 4 ¾ml

**NT properties nearby** The Courts Garden, Great Chalfield, Lacock

## WHITE MILL
Dorset
Sturminster Marshall, nr Wimborne BH21 4BX · **Tel** 01258 858051
**Fax** 01258 857184

Rebuilt in 1776 on a site marked as a mill in the Domesday Book, this cornmill was extensively repaired in 1994 and still retains its original elm and applewood machinery (now too fragile to be operative). The setting, next to the River Stour, is delightful and there is a riverside picnic area nearby

23 March to 27 Oct: Sat, Sun & BH Mons, inc. BH Tues 4 June, 12–5. Booked parties at other times, tel. 01258 857184

£2.50; child £1.50. Parties by arrangement. No WC

The mill is shown by guided tour and numbers within the building are restricted for safety reasons

Some parking by mill. Mill: ramped access to most of ground floor; viewing platform and internal mirrors enable visitors to see most of the upper floors

**For all your information needs check our website www.nationaltrust.org.uk**

- Large-print and audio guides; handling collection
- Not in mill, but shaded areas in grounds and car park
- (1:K7) On the River Stour north of Sturminster Marshall. From B3082 Blandford to Wimborne road take right-hand turn signposted Sturminster Marshall. Follow road for 1ml to junction. Mill car park is on left, mill on right [195:ST958006] **Bus**: Wilts & Dorset X8 Poole–Blandford (passes close ≠ Poole); 182/3 Bournemouth–Shaftesbury (passes ≠ Bournemouth), alight Sturminster Marshall, ½ml **Station**: Hamworthy 7ml; Poole 8½ml

**NT properties nearby** Brownsea Island, Corfe Castle, Kingston Lacy

---

## WOODCHESTER PARK  Gloucestershire

Old Ebworth Centre, Ebworth Estate, The Camp, Stroud GL6 7ES
**Tel** 01452 814213 · **Fax** 01452 810055 · **Email** woodchesterpark@ntrust.org.uk

A beautiful secluded valley near Stroud, in the Cotswolds. The valley contains the remains of an 18th- and 19th-century landscape park, a chain of five lakes, fringed by woodland pasture and an unfinished Victorian mansion (not NT), which is open to the public on specified days from Easter to Oct. There are also waymarked trails (steep and strenuous in places) through delightful scenery

**Note**: Woodchester mansion is not NT; for details, contact the Woodchester Mansion Trust, tel. 01453 750455 or website: www.the-mansion.co.uk

- **Park**: daily all year. *Times*: May to Sept 9–8; Oct to April: 9–5
- Car park £1 (NT members free). Last admission to car park 1hr before closing
- Under strict control, on leads where requested
- (1:J3) 4ml SW of Stroud off B4066 Stroud–Dursley road; NT car park accessible from Nympsfield road, 300m from the junction with B4066 [162: SO797012] **Station**: Stroud 5ml

**NT properties nearby** Coaley Peak, Ebworth Estate, Haresfield Beacon, Minchinhampton & Rodborough Commons, Newark Park

---

**Please remember – your membership card is always needed for free admission**

# Introduction to the South and South East

Although this is one of England's most densely populated and urbanised areas, it includes some remarkably extensive and beautiful open spaces, as well as miles of dramatic coastline. The fact that so much has survived is due largely to the work of the National Trust, which over many decades has acquired and protected land threatened by development and insensitive use.

The Trust owns many properties within easy reach of London, including most of the delightful village of **Chiddingstone** in Kent, complete with cobbled streets and the famous Chiding Stone, from which it takes its name. Nearby are **Chartwell**, Sir Winston Churchill's former home, the beautiful moated **Ightham Mote** and the enchanting **Emmetts Garden**. The Trust's founder, Octavia Hill, knew this area well, and a woodland is named after her at **Toys Hill**, from where there are magnificent views.

One of the South East's most mysterious areas is Romney Marsh, still peaceful and relatively inaccessible. Here the Trust owns $3\frac{1}{2}$ miles of the **Royal Military Canal**, between Appledore and Warehorne. The canal was built in 1804–7 as a defence against Napoleonic invasion and there are pleasant walks along its banks. On the edge of the Marsh is **Smallhythe Place**, former home of the great Victorian actress, Ellen Terry.

The **White Cliffs of Dover** need no introduction. Information about this fascinating area can be found in the **Saga Gateway to the White Cliffs Visitor Centre**, which provides access to miles of outstanding coastline and walking country, as well as the chance to visit the lighthouse at **South Foreland**. Recent years have seen much development in this part of Kent due to the Channel Tunnel, but man's presence has been felt here for many thousands of years – at **Coldrum Long Barrow**, near Trottiscliffe, the Trust owns a Neolithic burial chamber, in which skeletal remains have been found.

Much of the Sussex coast is now under tarmac and concrete, but Trust-owned land on the **Seven Sisters**, including **Birling Gap** and **Crowlink**, offers delightful

SOUTH FORELAND LIGHTHOUSE

**For general enquiries, please telephone 0870 458 4000**

walks over open downland with spectacular coastal views. East Head offers a mile of unspoilt sandy beach and dunes at the entrance to Chichester Harbour. Access through the West Wittering Estate. Further inland, **Chyngton Farm** and **Frog Firle Farm** at Alfriston are classic South Downs country, rich in natural history and with splendid views over the Cuckmere valley. Nestling in the gentle countryside just north of the Downs is the charming manor house, **Bateman's**, Rudyard Kipling's former home. West along the South Downs Way are important areas of downland, such as **Devil's Dyke** and **Harting Down**. Both are rich in downland flora and fauna, and reward those who leave the beaten track.

The Trust cares for 17 miles of beautiful coastline on the Isle of Wight and 9 per cent of countryside, including the major downland areas – Ventnor, St Catherine's, Bembridge and Culver, Afton, Brook, Compton and Mottistone – as well as the **Needles Headland** with the **Old Battery**, overlooking the famous stacks of rock. From here there are excellent walks to enjoy as far as **Tennyson Down**, where the great poet once strolled. The ancient port of **Newtown**, with its Old Town Hall and important nature reserve, is also an interesting place to visit.

The West Weald includes several large expanses of rare lowland heath. **Black Down**, probably the most wooded of these, is the highest point in West Sussex, and over the border in Surrey there are large expanses of heathland at **Frensham** and **Hindhead**, including the dramatic **Devil's Punch Bowl**. The issues involved in the management of heathland and its associated wildlife are interpreted at the **Witley Centre**. In Hampshire, there is further rolling heath at **Ludshott** and hammer ponds at **Waggoners Wells**, while **Selborne Hill and Common** were made famous by the 18th-century naturalist Gilbert White. The Trust also cares for some 1,200ha (3,000 acres) in the magnificent New Forest, including **Hale Purlieu** and **Bramshaw Commons**, and the recently acquired **Ibsley** and **Rockford Commons**, which offer excellent walking.

The Surrey Hills, rising to **Reigate Hill**, **Box Hill** and **Leith Hill** at their highest point, provide a picturesque backdrop to some of the Trust's classic country estates, including **Polesden Lacey** and the exquisite **Hatchlands Park**. This is idyllic countryside, offering a variety of walks with breathtaking views. Running for nearly 20 miles between Godalming and Weybridge are the **River Wey Navigations**, dating back to the 17th century and once part of London's lost route to the sea. Information on this important waterway is available at **Dapdune Wharf** in Guildford.

The Chilterns offer some of the finest scenery in southern England and from their highest point, **Coombe Hill**, there are spectacular views over three counties. To the south-west lies another notable beauty spot, **Watlington Hill**, 210 metres high and celebrated for its chalk-loving flora and fine yew forest. There are some beautiful villages in this area, including **West Wycombe** and **Bradenham**, which both serve as ideal centres for good walking through typical Chiltern beech-woods. Exploration on foot is also the best way to enjoy the steep heather-clad slopes of the **Finchampstead Ridges** near Wokingham, overlooking the River Blackwater and a haven for wildlife and naturalists alike.

Further west, in Oxfordshire, the **Buscot** and **Coleshill Estates** offer wide expanses of unspoilt countryside, including **Badbury Hill**, offering splendid views over the upper Thames valley. Buscot and Coleshill are both attractive villages built of Cotswold stone, and there is a popular picnic area at **Buscot Weir**. Not far from here is **White Horse Hill**, with its famous horse cut into the chalk escarpment. The hill is crowned by the Bronze

**Please see the area introductions for details of coast & countryside properties**

Age hill-fort of **Uffington Castle** and nearby **Dragon Hill**, where St George allegedly slew the beast. The Ridgeway Path gives good access to these sites.

**Highlights for Visitors with Disabilities ...**
Particularly recommended are The Old Brick & Tile Works at **Pinkney's Green**, a nature reserve near Maidenhead with specially adapted paths and viewing platforms, as well as a tapping rail (access by RADAR key). **St Helen's Duver** on the Isle of Wight has a level shingle walk suitable for accompanied wheelchair users, and also an accessible holiday cottage.

**... and for Families**
Plenty of space to run around and play at **Box Hill**, with open heathland of **Headley Common** close by, **Leith Hill**, **Polesden Lacey**, **Coombe Hill**, the **White Cliffs of Dover** and the **Seven Sisters**. **Devil's Dyke** and the **Witley Centre** offer a wide range of activities for children and school groups. Also, the **Saga Gateway to the White Cliffs Visitor Centre** and spectacular **Bodiam Castle** have much to offer families on a day out. The interactive exhibits and boat trip at **Dapdune Wharf** are always popular with the under 10s

| OS grid references for main properties with no individual entry (OS map series numbers given in brackets) | |
|---|---|
| Badbury Hill | [163] SU250940 |
| Birling Gap | [199] TV554960 |
| Black Down | [186] SU922308 |
| Bramshaw Commons | [184] SU297178 |
| Chiddingstone | [188] TQ501451 |
| Coldrum Long Barrow | [188] TQ654607 |
| Coombe Hill | [165] SP849066 |
| Crowlink | [199] TV544975 |
| Devil's Dyke | [186] TQ260110 |
| F'hampstead Ridges | [175] SU808634 |
| Frensham Common | [186] SU859419 |
| Frog Firle Farm | [199] TQ517012 |
| Hale Purlieu | [184] SU200180 |
| Hindhead area | [186] SU891358 |
| Ibsley & Rockford Commons | [184] SU175095 |
| Ludshott Common | [186] SU835358 |
| Pinkney's Green | [175] SU860825 |
| Royal Military Canal | [189] TQ958292 |
| Selborne | [186] SU742335 |
| Tennyson Down | [196] SZ325853 |
| Toys Hill | [188] TQ465517 |
| White Horse Hill, Uffington Castle & Dragon Hill | [163] SU301866 |

**For further information**
Please contact the Membership Department, PO Box 39, Bromley, Kent BR1 3XS. Tel. 0870 458 4000. Email: enquiries@thenationaltrust.org.uk

There is a series of leaflets on walks in Kent and East Sussex, A *Stroll the South Downs* walks leaflet pack with details of walks in Surrey, West Sussex, Hampshire and the Isle of Wight, and also a series of leaflets covering walks in Berks, Bucks and Oxon. For details of these please contact the Membership Department.

There is also a North Downs Countryside Pack, available from Box Hill Shop (tel. 01306 888793) and West Weald countryside leaflets, available from the Witley Centre (tel. 01428 683207).

A leaflet on *Walks & Places to Visit on the Isle of Wight* is available, free of charge, from the NT IoW Office (tel. 01983 741020). A book of *Walks Around the Wey and Godalming Navigations* is available from Dapdune Wharf or Thames Lock (tel. 01483 561389).

## ALFRISTON CLERGY HOUSE 🏠 ❀     East Sussex

The Tye, Alfriston, Polegate BN26 5TL · **Tel** 01323 870001 · **Fax** 01323 871318
**Email** alfriston@ntrust.org.uk

Step back into the Middle Ages with a visit to this 14th-century thatched Wealden 'hall house'. Trace the history of this building which, in 1896, was the first to be acquired by the National Trust. Discover why the chalk floor is soaked in sour milk and visit the excellent shop with its local crafts. Explore the delightful cottage garden and savour the idyllic setting beside Alfriston's parish church, with stunning views across the meandering River Cuckmere

**What's new in 2002**: Opening in Nov & Dec

- ⭕ 2 to 17 March: Sat & Sun 11–4; 23 March to 3 Nov: daily except Tues & Fri (but open Good Fri) 10–5. 6 Nov to 22 Dec: daily except Mon & Tues 11–4

- £ £2.80; child £1.40; family £7. Booked parties £2.40. WCs and parking in car park at other end of village (not NT)

- 🛍 As house. 6 Nov to 22 Dec: Christmas shop daily except Mon & Tues 11–4; tel. for details

- ♿ House unsuitable for wheelchairs, but limited access to garden by arrangement

- 📖 Braille guide

- ➜ (2:H8) 4ml NE of Seaford, just E of B2108, in Alfriston village, adjoining The Tye and St Andrews Church [189: TQ521029] **Bus**: RDH 125 from Lewes, Renown 126 from Eastbourne & Seaford (pass close ≋ Lewes and Seaford), Cuckmere Valley Rambler bus, summer weekends only from ≋ Berwick **Station**: Berwick (U) 2½ml **Cycle**: NCN 2

**NT properties nearby** Bateman's, Monk's House, Sheffield Park Garden

---

## ASCOTT 🏠 ❀     Buckinghamshire

Wing, nr Leighton Buzzard LU7 0PS · **Tel** 01296 688242 · **Fax** 01296 681904
**Email** info@ascottestate.co.uk

Originally a half-timbered Jacobean farmhouse, Ascott was bought in 1876 by the de Rothschild family and considerably transformed and enlarged. It now houses a quite exceptional collection of fine paintings, Oriental porcelain and English and French furniture. The extensive gardens are a mixture of the formal and natural, containing specimen trees and shrubs, as well as an herbaceous walk, lily pond, Dutch garden and remarkable topiary sundial

- ⭕ **House & garden**: 2 to 30 April, 6 Aug to 13 Sept: daily except Mon. *Times*: 2–6; last admission 5. **Garden only**: 1 May to 1 Aug: every Wed and last Sun in each month; 18 & 25 Sept. *Times*: 2–6; last admission 5

---

**There are special events at most Trust properties; telephone 0870 458 4000 for details**

**SOUTH AND SOUTH EAST · 117**

£ £5.60; child £2.80. Garden only £4; child £2. No reduction for parties, which must book. Parking 220m

♿ Close parking by prior arrangement. House: ground floor accessible. 3 wheelchairs. Garden: some steep slopes; several level paths with superb views

Braille guide

🐕 On leads and only in car park

➔ (2:E3) ½ml E of Wing, 2ml SW of Leighton Buzzard, on S side of A418 [165: SP891230] **Bus**: Arriva The Shires X15 Aylesbury–Milton Keynes (passing close ≋ Aylesbury & Leighton Buzzard) **Station**: Leighton Buzzard 2ml

**NT properties nearby** Ashridge Estate, Claydon House

---

## ASHDOWN HOUSE                                      Oxfordshire
Lambourn, Newbury RG16 7RE · **Tel** 01488 72584
**Email** ashdownhouse@ntrust.org.uk

---

An extraordinary Dutch-style 17th-century house, perched on the Berkshire Downs and famous for its association with Elizabeth of Bohemia ('The Winter Queen'), Charles I's sister, to whom the house was 'consecrated'. The interior has an impressive great staircase rising from hall to attic, and important paintings contemporary with the house. There are spectacular views from the roof over the formal parterre, lawns and surrounding countryside, as well as beautiful walks in neighbouring **Ashdown Woods**. Nearby **Weathercock Hill** and **Alfred's Castle**, an Iron Age defended settlement where in 871 King Alfred is rumoured to have defeated the Danes, offer fine walking (there is a car park 250m from the house, but please note the estate is closed on Fri)

**Note**: No WCs

🔴 **Hall, staircase & roof**: April to end Oct: Wed & Sat by guided tour only at 2.15, 3.15 & 4.15 from front door. **Garden**: April to end Oct: Wed & Sat 2–5. **Woodland**: All year: daily except Fri, dawn to dusk

£ £2.10. Woodland free. No reduction for parties, which must book in writing. Car park 250m

♿ Grounds: accessible. House: difficult for people with impaired mobility

No tea-room, but picnic area by car park

🚲 Lockable post in woodland car park

🐕 On leads and only in woodland

➔ (2:B5) 2½ml S of Ashbury, 3½ml N of Lambourn, on W side of B4000 [174: SU282820] **Bus**: Thamesdown 47 Swindon–Lambourn, with connections from Newbury (passing close ≋ Swindon & Newbury)

**NT properties nearby** Avebury, Buscot Park, Great Coxwell Barn, White Horse Hill

---

**For all your information needs check our website www.nationaltrust.org.uk**

## BASILDON PARK 🏛️❋🌳🎭            Berkshire

Lower Basildon, Reading RG8 9NR · **Tel** 0118 984 3040 · **Infoline** 01494 755558
**Fax** 0118 984 1267 · **Email** basildonpark@ntrust.org.uk

This beautiful Palladian mansion was built in 1776–83 by John Carr for Francis Sykes, who had made his fortune in India. The interior is notable for its original delicate plasterwork and elegant staircase, as well as for the unusual Octagon Room. The house fell on hard times in the early part of last century, but was rescued by Lord and Lady Iliffe, who restored it and filled it with fine pictures and furniture. The early 19th-century pleasure grounds are currently being restored, and there are waymarked trails through the parkland. At the top of Streatley Hill 2ml away is a car park giving access to **The Holies**, **Loughdown** and **Lardon Chase**, an outstanding area of downland and woodland with many beautiful walks and breathtaking views

- **House**: 23 March to 3 Nov: daily except Mon & Tues (open BH Mons and Tues 4 June) 1–5.30. **Park, garden & woodland walks**: as house 12–5.30. **Note**: Property closes at 5 on 16/17 Aug for 60s and 70s concerts. **Events**: for details send s.a.e. marked 'Events' to Box Office, P.O.Box 180, High Wycombe, Bucks HP14 4XT

- £4.40; child £2.20; family £11. Park & garden only £2; child £1; family £5. Parties of 15+ £3, only on application to Property Manager. Parking in grounds, 400m from house

- Special tours by arrangement with Property Manager; tel. for details

- 23 March to 3 Nov: as house 12–5.30; also 6 Nov to 22 Dec: Wed to Sun 12–4 (tel. 01491 671738)

- Close parking; contact ticket office near car park for information. Staff-driven buggy service available from car park to house. House: ground floor only, comprising Garden Room & Restaurant. Garden: firm gravel paths. Restaurant: ramped access. Shop: accessible

- Braille guide

- Restaurant 23 March to 3 Nov, 12–5.30. Groups by arrangement (tel. 0118 984 3040). Picnics in grounds except on main lawns near house

- Highchair

- On leads and only in park, woodland and grounds; not on main lawns near house

- (2:D5) Between Pangbourne and Streatley, 7ml NW of Reading, on W side of

---

**Please remember – your membership card is always needed for free admission**

## SOUTH AND SOUTH EAST · 119

A329; leave M4 at exit 12 and follow brown NT signs to Pangbourne. From A34 take Oxford ring road and leave at Henley/Reading junction, then turn right at roundabout for Wallingford bypass, cross over river and take first left onto A329 [175:SU611782] **Bus**: Thames Travel 105 Wallingford–Reading (passes ≋ Pangbourne) **Station**: Pangbourne 2½ml; Goring & Streatley 3ml

**NT properties nearby** Greys Court, The Holies & Lardon Chase, Loughdown, The Vyne

---

# BATEMAN'S    East Sussex
Burwash, Etchingham TN19 7DS · **Tel** 01435 882302 (House)
**Fax** 01435 882811 · **Email** batemans@ntrust.org.uk

---

The home of Rudyard Kipling from 1902–36, the interior of this beautiful Jacobean house reflects the author's strong associations with the East. There are many oriental rugs and artefacts, and most of the rooms – including his book-lined study – are much as Kipling left them. The delightful grounds run down to the small River Dudwell, where there is a watermill, and contain roses, wild flowers and herbs. Kipling's Rolls-Royce is also on display

**What's new in 2002**: Weekend opening of the wild garden in March

- 2 to 17 March: Sat & Sun (wild garden only), 11–4; 23 March to 29 Sept: daily except Thur & Fri (but open Good Fri). *Times*: 11–5 (grounds close 5.30); last admission 4.30. The mill grinds corn most Sats at 2

- 2–17 March: £2.60; child £1.30; family £6.50; booked parties £2.20. 23 March to 29 Sept: £5.20; child £2.60; family £13. Booked parties £4.40, no reduction Sun, BH Mons & Good Fri

- 23 March to 29 Sept: as house 11–5. 30 Sept to 3 Nov: daily except Thur & Fri 11–5. 6 Nov to 22 Dec daily except Mon & Tues 11–4. Christmas shop: Nov to 23 Dec: daily except Mon & Tues 11–4; tel. for details

- House: ground floor accessible. Garden: accessible, with routes to avoid steps; map available. Tea-room: accessible

- Braille introduction to house. Scented plants and flowers; watermill sounds (Sat only)

- Licensed tea-room 23 March to 29 Sept: as house 11–5. 30 Sept to 3 Nov: as shop. 6 Nov to 22 Dec: as shop. Picnic area in copse adjacent to car park only

- Baby-changing facilities. Children's guide

- Teachers' resource booklet

- On leads and only in car park; dog crèche

- (2:H8) ½ml S of Burwash (A265); approached by road leading S from W end of village or N from Woods Corner (B2096) [199: TQ671238] **Bus**: Autopoint/RDH 318 Hawkhurst–Heathfield (passing ≋ Etchingham) **Station**: Etchingham 3ml

**NT properties nearby** Bodiam Castle, Scotney Castle Garden, Sissinghurst Castle Garden

**For general enquiries, please telephone 0870 458 4000**

## BEMBRIDGE WINDMILL ☒     Isle of Wight

NT Office, Longstone Farmhouse, Strawberry Lane, Mottistone, Newport PO30 4EA · **Tel** 01983 873945 (opening hours only)

Built *c*.1700 and still with its original wooden machinery, the windmill is the only one surviving on the Island

- 🅞 28 March to end June, Sept to 25 Oct: daily except Sat (but open Easter Sat); July & Aug: daily. *Times*: 10–5
- 💷 £1.70. No party reduction. All school groups are conducted by a NT guide; special charge applies. Parking 100m. No WC
- 🚶 Conducted school groups and special visits March to end Oct (but not July or Aug), by written appointment
- 🛍 Small shop, as mill
- ♿ Mill: difficult; steep stairs; grab ropes only. Area around mill: accessible
- Braille guide
- ☕ Coffees and ice creams
- 📖 Educational quiz sheets; guided tours (see above)
- → (2:D9) ½ml S of Bembridge on B3395 [196: SZ639874] **Bus**: Southern Vectis 1 from Cowes (passing ≋ Ryde Esplanade); 2 from Shanklin **Station**: Brading (U) 2ml by footpath. Ferry: Ryde (Wightlink Ltd) 6ml (tel. 0870 582 7744); E Cowes (Red Funnel) 13ml (tel.023 8033 4010)

**NT properties nearby** Brighstone Shop and Museum, Mottistone Manor Garden, Needles Old Battery, Newtown Old Town Hall

---

## BOARSTALL DUCK DECOY 🦆🚶     Buckinghamshire

Boarstall, nr Aylesbury HP18 9UX · **Tel** 01844 237488
**Email** boarstall@ntrust.org.uk

A rare survival of a 17th-century decoy in working order, set on a tree-fringed lake, with nature trail and exhibition hall

- 🅞 23 March to 25 Aug: Wed 5–8; Sat, Sun & BH Mons 10–5. Talk/demonstration Sat, Sun & BH Mons if Warden available; tel. for details
- 💷 £2.10; family £5. Parties of 6+, which must book, £1
- ♿ Ramped access to nature trail, exhibition, bird hide and decoy in dry weather; wheelchair

---

**Please see the area introductions for details of coast & countryside properties**

SOUTH AND SOUTH EAST · **121**

- School parties by arrangement
- On leads and only in car park
- (2:D3) Midway between Bicester and Thame, 2ml W of Brill [164 or 165: SP624151] **Station**: Bicester Town (U), not Sun, 6½ml; Bicester North, 7½ml

**NT properties nearby** Boarstall Tower, Claydon House

---

## BOARSTALL TOWER                              Buckinghamshire
Boarstall, nr Aylesbury HP18 9UX · **Tel** 01844 239339
**Email** rob.dixon@boarstall.com

The 'superb' 14th-century gatehouse (listed Grade I), and gardens with large moat, of Boarstall House (demolished 1778). John de Haudlo built 'Buckinghamshire's only complete medieval fortified building' in 1312, both as defences for his house and as an expression of his status. Although updated in 1615 for use as a banqueting pavilion or hunting lodge, and to reflect the latest taste, including 'handsome' oriel windows and the upgrading of its 'fine' top floor chamber, it retained its medieval belfry, crossloops, crenellations and other features, so keeping its fortified look, still fashionable in Jacobean times. Today, the exterior and many rooms remain virtually unchanged from that time.

- 27 March to 30 Oct: Wed & BH Mons and Tues 4 June 2–6. Also Sat by prior arrangement with tenant
- £2.10; child £1.05. No reduction for parties
- Close parking. House: ground floor accessible (1 step). Garden: accessible
- In car park only
- (2:D3) Midway between Bicester and Thame, 2ml W of Brill [164, 165: SP624141] **Station**: as for Boarstall Duck Decoy above

**NT properties nearby** Boarstall Duck Decoy, Claydon House, Long Crendon Courthouse, Waddesdon Manor

---

## BODIAM CASTLE                                     East Sussex
Bodiam, nr Robertsbridge TN32 5UA · **Tel** 01580 830436 · **Fax** 01580 830398
**Email** bodiamcastle@ntrust.org.uk

One of the most famous and evocative castles in Britain, Bodiam was built in 1385, both as a defence and a comfortable home. The exterior is virtually complete and the ramparts rise dramatically above the moat below. Enough of the interior survives to give an impression of castle life, and there are spiral staircases and battlements to explore.

**Note**: Bodiam Castle is often used by education groups during mornings in term time

- 1 Jan; 5 Jan to 9 Feb: Sat & Sun 10–4. 10 Feb to 1 Nov: daily 10–6. 2 Nov to mid-Feb 2003 Sat & Sun: 10–4. Last admission 1 hr before closing

---

**Unless indicated, last admission is always 30 mins before closing time**

**122** · SOUTH AND SOUTH EAST

£ £3.90; child £1.95; family £9.75. Booked parties £3.30. Car park ¼ml, £2 (NT members free); coaches £5

1 Jan; 5 Jan to 9 Feb: Sat & Sun 11–4. 10 Feb to 1 Nov: daily 10–5 or dusk if earlier; 2 Nov to mid-Feb 2003: Sat & Sun 11–4

Castle is ¼ml from car park over uneven ground; for alternative access tel. Administrator in advance. Castle: ground floor accessible. Shop & restaurant: accessible. WC in car park

Braille guides for adults and children; large-print guide; raised map; video with soundtrack in castle

Tea-room: as shop

Parent and baby room. Children's guide and quiz. Highchairs; children's menu

Teachers' resource books. Education rooms with hands-on resources; booked tours; tel. for details

On leads and only in grounds

(2:17) 3ml S of Hawkhurst, 2ml E of A21 Hurst Green [199: TQ782256] **Bus**: Stagecoach in E Sussex 254, 349 Tunbridge Wells–⇌ Hastings (passing ⇌ Wadhurst); Autopoint 19 from ⇌ Battle **Station**: Robertsbridge 5ml, Bodiam (Kent & E Sussex steam Rly) ¼ml

**NT properties nearby** Bateman's, Scotney Castle Garden, Sissinghurst Castle Garden, Smallhythe Place

---

# BOX HILL         Surrey
The Old Fort, Box Hill Road, Box Hill, Tadworth KT20 7LB · **Tel** 01306 885502 **Fax** 01306 875030 **Email** boxhill@ntrust.org.uk

---

An outstanding area of woodland and chalk downland, long famous as a destination for day-trippers from London, but surprisingly extensive and with much to offer the rambler and naturalist. There are many beautiful walks and spectacular views towards the South Downs. On the summit there is an information centre, shop with plant sales, servery and a fort dating from the 1890s (which is partly open to the public)

All year. **Events**: 12 Dec special Christmas shopping day, all welcome, especially visitors with disabilities, free glass of sherry and mince pie

£ Countryside free. Coaches must not use the zig-zag road from Burford Bridge on W side of the hill as a weight restriction applies, but must approach from E side of the hill B2032 or B2033; car/coach parks at top of hill; pay-and-display £1.50 (free to NT members displaying membership cards). Annual car park pass available from information centre or North Downs Office (tel. 01306 742809)

---

**There are special events at most Trust properties; telephone 0870 458 4000 for details**

SOUTH AND SOUTH EAST · **123**

- Guided walks throughout the year. Groups by arrangement with the Warden (tel. 01306 885502)
- Shop & information centre: daily (closed 25, 26 Dec) 11–5 or dusk if earlier, later in summer weather permitting (tel. 01306 888793). Plant sales at back of shop March to Sept; Christmas trees on sale from 1 Dec
- Parking behind servery. Summit area: accessible. Wheelchair path to viewpoint and beyond. Shop & servery: accessible.
- Braille guides for short walk and nature walk
- Servery for snacks and hot and cold drinks daily (closed 25, 26 Dec) 11–5 or dusk if earlier, later in summer weather permitting (tel. 01306 888793)
- Education room. Educational groups for day visits and residential groups by arrangement with North Downs Education Officer (tel. 01306 742809)
- 3 cycle ports at shop
- Under close control (where sheep grazing)
- (2:F6) 1ml N of Dorking, 2½ml S of Leatherhead on A24 [187: TQ171519] **Bus**: Contact property for details – new service proposed for 2002 **Station**: Boxhill & Westhumble ½ml

**NT properties nearby** Headley Heath, Polesden Lacey

---

## BRADENHAM VILLAGE                                          Buckinghamshire
nr High Wycombe · **Tel** 01494 528051 (Regional Office)

The church and 17th-century manor house (not open) provide an impressive backdrop to the sloping village green. The manor was once the home of Isaac D'Israeli, father of Benjamin Disraeli, who lived nearby at Hughenden Manor (see p.138). A network of paths provides easy access for walkers to explore the delightful surrounding countryside, which includes hills, farmlands and classic Chilterns beech-woods

- All year. Parking on the village green
- Free
- (2:E4) 4ml NW of High Wycombe, off the A4010 [165: SU825970] **Bus**: Arriva 332 High Wycombe–Princes Risborough **Station**: Saunderton 1ml

**NT properties nearby** Hughenden Manor, West Wycombe Park

---

## BRIGHSTONE SHOP AND MUSEUM                                  Isle of Wight
NT Shop, North Street, Brighstone PO30 4AX · **Tel** 01983 740689

An attractive terrace of thatched vernacular cottages, containing a NT shop and Village Museum (run by Brighstone Museum Trust)

- 2 Jan to 31 March: Mon–Sat 10–1; 1 April to 26 May: Mon–Sat 10–4; 27 May to 28 Oct: Mon–Sat 10–5, Sun 12–5; 29 Oct to 31 Dec: Mon–Sat 10–4

**For all your information needs check our website www.nationaltrust.org.uk**

**124** · SOUTH AND SOUTH EAST

£ Free entry, donations welcome

→ (2:C9) [196:SZ428828] **Bus**: Southern Vectis 7B Newport–Alum Bay Ferry: Yarmouth (Wightlink Ltd) 8ml (tel. 0870 5827744); E Cowes (Red Funnel) 12ml (tel. 023 8033 4010)

**NT properties nearby** Bembridge Windmill, Mottistone Manor Garden, Needles Old Battery, Newtown Old Town Hall

---

## BUCKINGHAM CHANTRY CHAPEL ✝    Buckinghamshire
Market Hill, Buckingham · **Tel** 01494 528051 (Regional Office)

A 15th-century chapel, the oldest building in Buckingham and incorporating a fine Norman doorway. Later used as a school, it was restored by Gilbert Scott in 1875

O Daily: by written appointment with the Buckingham Heritage Trust, c/o Old Gaol Museum, Market Hill, Buckingham MK18 1JX (tel. 01280 823020)

£ Free. No WC

♿ Chapel: accessible

→ (2:D2) On Market Hill [152 or 165: SP693340] **Bus**: Stagecoach Express X5 Cambridge–Oxford (passes ≋ Milton Keynes Central and Bicester North); Jeffs 32 from Milton Keynes (passing close ≋ Milton Keynes Central); Arriva The Shires 66 from Aylesbury (passing close ≋ Aylesbury) **Station**: Wolverton 10ml

**NT properties nearby** Claydon House, Stowe Gardens

---

## BUSCOT OLD PARSONAGE 🏠 ✲    Oxfordshire
Buscot, Faringdon SN7 8DQ · **Tel** 01793 762209 (Coleshill Estate Office)
**Email** buscot@ntrust.org.uk

An early 18th-century house of Cotswold stone, set on the banks of the Thames and with a small garden

O April to end Oct: Wed 2–6 by appointment in writing with tenant

£ £1.20. Not suitable for parties. No WC

→ (2:B4) 2ml from Lechlade, 4ml from Faringdon on A417 [163: SU231973] **Bus**: Stagecoach in Oxford 64 Swindon–Carterton, Stagecoach in Swindon 77 Swindon–Cirencester (both passing close ≋ Swindon). On both, alight Lechlade, 1½ml

**NT properties nearby** Buscot Park, Great Coxwell Barn

WREN

---

**Please remember – your membership card is always needed for free admission**

## BUSCOT PARK 🏛️✽♠ Oxfordshire

Estate Office, Faringdon SN7 8BU · **Tel** 01367 240786 · **Infoline** 0845 345 3387
**Fax** 01367 241794 · **Email** estbuscot@aol.com
**Web** www.buscot-park.com

The late 18th-century neo-classical house, set in parkland, contains the fine paintings and furniture of the Faringdon Collection Trust. The grounds include various avenue walks, and an Italianate water garden, designed in the early 20th century by Harold Peto

**Note**: This property is administered on behalf of the National Trust by Lord Faringdon, and the contents of the house are owned by The Faringdon Collection Trust

**O** **House and grounds**: 29 March to 29 Sept: every Wed, Thur and Fri, plus weekends 2–6 (inc. Easter Sat & Sun): 30/31 March, 13/14 & 27/28 April. 11/12 & 25/26 May; 8/9 & 22/23 June, 13/14 & 27/28 July, 10/11 & 24/25 Aug, 14/15 & 28/29 Sept. *Times*: 2–6. **Grounds only**: 29 March to 29 Sept: Mon (inc. BH Mons) and Tues 2–6

**£** House & Grounds £5; child £2.50. Grounds only £4; child £2. No reduction for parties which must book in writing or by fax or email to the Estate Office stating numbers and time of arrival

🛍️ No shop

♿ House: sheer flight of 14 steps to front door. Grounds: testing gradients and thick gravel paths. Visitors with walking difficulties may be set down at House, by arrangement made at Ticket Office on arrival

☕ As house 2.30–5.30. Also BH Mons when Grounds only open

➡️ (2:B4) Between Lechlade and Faringdon, on A417 [163: SU239973]
**Bus**: Thamesdown 67 Swindon–Faringdon (Fri only); otherwise as for Buscot Old Parsonage (see above) but 2¾ml walk from Lechlade

**NT properties nearby** Buscot Old Parsonage, Great Coxwell Barn

## CHARTWELL 🏛️✽🚶 Kent

Westerham TN16 1PS · **Tel** 01732 868381 · **Infoline** 01732 866368
**Fax** 01732 868193 · **Email** chartwell@ntrust.org.uk

The home of Sir Winston Churchill from 1924 until the end of his life. A delightful family home, with stunning views over the Weald, which became the place from which Sir Winston drew inspiration. The rooms and gardens remain much as he left them, with pictures, maps and personal mementoes strongly evoking the career and wide-ranging interests of this great statesman. The beautiful terraced gardens contain the lakes Sir Winston created, the water garden where he fed his fish, Lady Churchill's rose garden and the Golden Rose Walk, a Golden Wedding anniversary gift from their children. Many of Sir Winston's paintings can be seen in the garden studio

**What's new in 2002**: Circular estate walk offering magnificent views of Chartwell and the Weald and access to woodland with bluebells and foxgloves in spring

🅾 **House, garden & studio**: 23 March to 30 June, 1 Sept to 3 Nov: daily except Mon & Tues (but open BH Mons); July & Aug: daily except Mon (but open BH Mon). *Times*: 11–5; last admission 4.15. Picnics permitted in area off car park. Tel. infoline for details. Car park: year-round opening (except 25 Dec) for countryside access; gates locked at 5.30 or dusk if earlier. **Events**: open-air concerts, painting days, lecture lunches, garden tours and family garden party

💷 Individuals and groups: £5.80; child £2.90; family £14.50. Garden & studio only £2.90. Coaches and groups please book (concessions to couriers and drivers). Tel. for information and booking pack

🚶 Private guided tours and special talks by arrangement. Details and charges on request.

🛍 23 March to 3 Nov: days as house, 11–5.30; 6 Nov to 22 Dec: daily except Mon & Tues 11–4

♿ Close parking for house; contact Visitor Centre on arrival at main car park. House: ground floor accessible, 2 steps to small lift to first floor which is limited to one wheelchair at a time. Garden: partial access. Shop: accessible. Restaurant & ground floor: accessible with close parking. For information on access and wheelchairs tel. 01732 868381

👁 Braille guide. Rose garden; scented plants; tel. 01732 868381 to arrange touch tour or for info sheet (also available at Visitor Centre)

🍴 Licensed self-service restaurant, days as house, 10.30–5. Also 6 Nov to 22 Dec: days as shop. Function rooms for social and business entertainment. Wedding parties catered for. Tel. 01732 863087

👶 Baby-changing facility. Children's guidebook and quiz. Children's meals. No pushchairs in house; baby carriers on loan from Visitor Centre

🚲 Racks alongside visitor centre

🐕 On leads and only in grounds

➡ (2:G6) 2ml S of Westerham, fork left off B2026 after 1½ml [188: TQ455515]
**Bus**: Metrobus 246 ☒ Bromley North–Edenbridge (passing ☒ Bromley S)
**Station**: Edenbridge (U) 4ml; Edenbridge Town 4½ml; Sevenoaks 6½ml

**NT properties nearby** Emmetts Garden, Ightham Mote, Knole, Quebec House

---

**Please see the area introductions for details of coast & countryside properties**

# CHASTLETON HOUSE

Oxfordshire

Chastleton, Moreton-in-Marsh GL56 0SU · **Tel/Fax** 01608 674355 ·
**Bookings** 01494 755585 · same day 01608 674355 · **Infoline** 01494 755560
**Email** chastleton@ntrust.org.uk

Chastleton House is one of England's finest and most complete Jacobean houses. It is filled not only with a mixture of rare and everyday objects, furniture and textiles collected since its completion in 1612, but also with the atmosphere of 400 years of continuous occupation by one family. The gardens have a typical Elizabethan and Jacobean layout with a ring of fascinating topiary at their heart and it was here in 1865 that the rules of modern croquet were codified. Since acquiring the property, the Trust has concentrated on conserving it rather than restoring it to a pristine state

**Note**: As Chastleton House is relatively fragile and the access roads are quiet and narrow, the maximum number of visitors is restricted to 175 per day. Admission is by timed ticket. **We regret that on Sats and during peak holiday periods, visitors who have not booked in advance may face disappointment. For advance bookings see below.** On quiet days a same-day tel. call to 01608 674355 is often sufficient. For up-to-date information on ticket availability tel. the 24-hour infoline. The largest vehicles that can be accommodated are 25-seater, 7.5m long minicoaches. There are WCs but no shop or tea-room

- 23 March to 2 Nov: daily except Sun, Mon & Tues. *Times*: April to Sept: 1–5, last admission 4; Oct to Nov: 1–4, last admission 3. **Note**: to book tickets tel. 01494 755585 Mon to Fri 9.30–4 or write to the National Trust Box Office, PO Box 180, High Wycombe, Bucks HP14 4XT (please do not include payment)

- £5.40; child £2.70; family £13.50. Groups (min. 11, max. 25) by appointment only. No access for coaches (see above). Car park on hill 270m from house; return walk includes a short but steep hill. Sensible shoes recommended

- Out-of-hours guided 'Private View' Wed morning at 10am, £7 (inc. NT members); must be booked in advance, tel. 01494 755585

- Tel. for information about access and parking

- Braille guide

- Lockable posts in car park; bicycles can be hired from Country Lanes at Moreton-in-Marsh station, Easter to 30 Sept (tel. 01608 650065)

- (2:B3) 6ml from Stow-on-the-Wold. Approach only from A436 between the A44 (west of Chipping Norton) and Stow [163: SP248291] **Station**: Moreton-in-Marsh 4½ml; Kingham 5ml

**NT properties nearby** Hidcote Manor Garden, Snowshill Manor, Stowe, Upton House

**Unless indicated, last admission is always 30 mins before closing time**

## CLANDON PARK 🏛 🔭 ❀ 🍴 🔔                                     Surrey

West Clandon, Guildford GU4 7RQ · **Tel** 01483 222482 · **Infoline** 01483 225971
**Fax** 01483 223479 · **Email** clandonpark@ntrust.org.uk

A grand Palladian mansion, built c.1730 by the Venetian architect Giacomo Leoni, and notable for its magnificent two-storeyed Marble Hall. The house is filled with the superb collection of 18th-century furniture, porcelain, textiles and carpets acquired in the 1920s by the connoisseur Mrs David Gubbay, and also contains the Ivo Forde Meissen collection of Italian comedy figures and a series of Mortlake tapestries. The attractive gardens contain a parterre, grotto, sunken Dutch garden and a Maori house with a fascinating history

**Note**: The Queen's Royal Surrey Regiment Museum (tel. 01483 223419) is based at Clandon Park and open to visitors the same days as the house 12–5 (free entry)

**What's new in 2002**: Object in Focus – one artefact specially displayed and described

🅾 **House**: 24 March to 3 Nov: daily except Mon, Fri & Sat (but open Good Fri, Easter Sat & BH Mons) 11–5. **Museum**: as house 12–5. **Garden**: all year: as house 11–5. **Events**: for details of concerts in the Marble Hall tel. property to be put on mailing list. The Saloon and Marble Hall are available for civil weddings and wedding receptions (tel. 01483 224912 for details), as well as private and corporate functions (all enquiries welcome, tel. 01483 225804)

£ House & gardens: £6; family £15. Combined ticket with Hatchlands Park £9; families £22.50. Groups £5 Tues, Wed & Thur only. Parking 300m

🍴 Coach parties welcome Tues, Wed & Thur and after 2pm on Sun; tel. 01483 222482 to book. Morning guided tours by arrangement (extra charge) and free, but pre-arranged, introductory talks

🛍 March: Sun 12–4; 24 March to 3 Nov: as house 12–5; 5 Nov to 23 Dec: daily 12–4; tel. 01483 211412

♿ Close parking for 3 disabled drivers. Disabled visitors may be set down at house. House: ground floor accessible via 8 steps at front entrance; lower-ground floor accessible from north courtyard; 40 steps to first-floor porcelain collections. Garden: ramped access. Restaurant & shop: accessible. Seatwalker and 3 wheelchairs available

📖 Braille guide

---

**There are special events at most Trust properties; telephone 0870 458 4000 for details**

## SOUTH AND SOUTH EAST · 129

- Licensed restaurant open March: Sun; 24 March to 3 Nov: as house; Nov: daily except Mon, Fri & Sat; 1 to 23 Dec: daily except Fri & Sat. *Times*: 10.30–5.30. Advance bookings for lunch advisable, especially on Sun; tel. 01483 222502. Picnicking in grounds and gardens; tables in car park area
- Changing table available. Pushchairs allowed in house Tues, Wed & Thur. Children's menus; highchairs. Children's quizzes for house and garden
- Racks next to reception in car park
- On leads and only in car park area
- (2:F6) At West Clandon on A247, 3ml E of Guildford; if using A3 follow signposts to Ripley to join A247 via B2215 [186: TQ042512] **Bus**: Arriva Surrey & W Sussex/Northdown 418, 478/9 Guildford–Kingston (pass close ≥ Guildford). New hopper bus service planned for 2002, contact property for details **Station**: Clandon 1ml, turn left on main road

**NT properties nearby** Claremont Landscape Garden, Hatchlands Park, Polesden Lacey, River Wey and Dapdune Wharf

## CLAREMONT LANDSCAPE GARDEN                                                 Surrey

Portsmouth Road, Esher KT10 9JG · **Tel** 01372 467806 · **Fax** 01372 464394
**Email** claremont@ntrust.org.uk

Claremont's creation and development involved some of the great names in garden history, including Sir John Vanbrugh, Charles Bridgeman, William Kent and 'Capability' Brown. The first gardens were begun *c*.1715 and later the delights of Claremont were famed throughout Europe. Since 1975 the Trust has been restoring this layout following years of neglect. The many features include a lake, island with pavilion, grotto, turf amphitheatre, viewpoints and vistas

**Note**: The house (Claremont Fancourt School) is not NT and is not open to the public

**What's new in 2002**: New colour guidebook

- **Garden**: April to end Oct: daily; Nov to end March: daily except Mon. *Times*: April to end Oct: Mon to Fri 10–6, Sat, Sun & BH Mons 10–7. Late night opening 25 May, 1, 8 and 15 June until 9pm; Nov to end March 10–5 or sunset if earlier. **Note**: closed 25 Dec; and closes at 2 on major event days in July. Belvedere Tower open first weekend each month April to Oct. **Events**: tel. 01372 467806 for information

For all your information needs check our website www.nationaltrust.org.uk

**130** · SOUTH AND SOUTH EAST

- £ £3.80. 50p discount if arriving on public transport (please present valid ticket) or bicycle; family £9.50. Groups of 15+ £3.20. Coach parties must book; no coaches on Sun or BHols. Parking at entrance
- Guided tours for booked groups (min. 15) £1 extra per person. Unbooked tours 1st and 3rd Sat, 2nd Wed and last Sun of each month. 2pm meet at entrance kiosk; tel for further details
- April to end Oct: daily except Mon (but open BH Mons); Nov to 15 Dec: daily except Mon & Tues. 12 Jan to end March 2003: Sat & Sun. *Times*: 11–5 or sunset if earlier
- Parking by entrance. Grassland level; level firm gravel path around lake. 2 wheelchairs; please book. Tea-room & shop: accessible
- Braille guide
- Tea-room as shop. In bad weather tea-room and shop may be closed, tel. to check 01372 469421
- Baby-changing facilities in WC. Highchairs
- Lockable stands
- On leads and only Nov to end March
- (2:F6) On S edge of Esher, on E side of A307 (no access from Esher bypass) [187: TQ128634] **Bus**: Tellings-Golden Miller/Northdown 515 Kingston–Guildford (passing close ≠ Esher) **Station**: Esher 2ml; Hersham 2ml; Claygate 2ml

**NT properties nearby** Clandon Park, Ham House, Hatchlands Park, The Homewood, Polesden Lacey

---

## CLAYDON HOUSE     Buckinghamshire

Middle Claydon, nr Buckingham MK18 2EY · **Tel** 01296 730349
**Infoline** 01494 755561 · **Fax** 01296 738511
**Email** claydon@ntrust.org.uk

---

One of England's most extraordinary houses displaying some of the most remarkable 18th-century rococo and chinoiserie decoration. Features of the house include the unique Chinese Room and parquetry Grand Stairs. In continuous occupation by the Verney family for over 350 years, the house has mementoes of their relation Florence Nightingale, who was a regular visitor.

**Note**: All Saints' Church (not NT) in the grounds is also open to the public. Evensong at 4pm: 19 May, 16 June, 21 July, 18 Aug

**What's new in 2002**: Verney Archive Exhibition on transport

- 23 March to 3 Nov: daily except Thur & Fri. House 1–5; grounds 12–6; Secondhand bookshop: 1–5 (house closes at 4 on events days). Leaflets available in French, German and Spanish. **Events**: for details tel. 01494 755572 or send s.a.e. to Box Office, P.O.Box 180, High Wycombe, Bucks HP14 4XT

---

**Please remember – your membership card is always needed for free admission**

SOUTH AND SOUTH EAST · 131

- £ £4.40; child £2.20; family £11. Parties of 15+ Sat, Mon to Wed, £3.60. Garden only £1
- Out of hours tours, tel. for details
- Close parking. House: access via 3 steps, ramp; ground floor accessible. Wheelchairs. Garden: ramped access. Tea-room: accessible. **Note**: Disabled visitors unable to climb stairs will be charged half-price admission
- Braille guide. Guided tours by arrangement
- Courtyard House Restaurant (not NT) 11.30–2.30. Blackboard menu. Tea-room 1–5.30. Snacks and afternoon teas. Essential to pre-book for groups of 12 or more. Tel. 01296 730004. Special diets catered for
- Baby-changing facilities
- School parties by arrangement
- Lockable posts in car park
- On leads and only in park
- (2:D3) In Middle Claydon 13ml NW of Aylesbury, 3½ml SW of Winslow; signposted from A413 & A41 (M40 jct 9 12ml); entrance by N drive only [165: SP720253] **Bus**: Red Rose 16 from Aylesbury (passing close ≋ Aylesbury) **Cycle**: NCN 51

**NT properties nearby** Stowe, Waddesdon Manor

---

# CLIVEDEN                                                   Buckinghamshire

Taplow, Maidenhead SL6 0JA · **Tel** 01628 605069 · **Infoline** 01494 755562
**Fax** 01628 669461 · **Email** cliveden@ntrust.org.uk

---

This spectacular estate overlooking the River Thames has a series of gardens, each with its own character, featuring topiary, statuary, water gardens, a formal parterre, informal vistas, woodland and riverside walks. The present house, the third on the site, was built by Charles Barry for the Duke of Sutherland in 1851. Once the home of Nancy, Lady Astor, it is now let as an hotel and is open only on certain days

For general enquiries, please telephone **0870 458 4000**

- **Estate & garden**: 13 March to 31 Dec: daily. *Times*: 13 March to 31 Oct 11–6; 1 Nov to 31 Dec 11–4. **House (part)**: April to Oct: Thur & Sun 3–5.30; entry by timed ticket from information kiosk. **Octagon Temple (Chapel)**: as house. **Note**: in bad ground conditions some areas of formal garden may be roped off. **Woodlands car park**: all year: daily 11–5.30 (closes at 4 from Nov to March); no WC at woodlands. **Events**: full programme, inc. concerts, open-air theatre, children's theatre held throughout the season; send s.a.e. to Estate Secretary or contact Regional Box Office on 01494 755572

- Grounds £6; child £3; family £15. House £1 extra; child 50p. Group rate £5.50 (must book; apply to Estate Secretary). Woodlands car park £3; child £1.50; family £7.50. **Note**: Mooring charge on Cliveden Reach (£2 up to 4hrs, £6 per 24hrs, season ticket £30; inc. NT members) does not include entry fee to Cliveden. Tickets from River Warden. Mooring at suitable locations for more than ½ml downstream from Cliveden boathouse

- Shop adjacent to main car park 13 March to 15 Dec: daily except Mon & Tues (but open Good Fri and BH Mons). *Times*: March to end Oct 12–5.30; Nov to 15 Dec 12–4 (tel. 01628 665946). Open every day July & Aug

- Car park 200m from house, but alternative arrangements for disabled drivers. Disabled visitors may be driven to and collected from restaurant. House (part): accessible, but some steps. Terrace: ramped access. Garden & grounds: largely accessible; route-maps; 4 wheelchairs and 4 self-drive powered vehicles available. Restaurant & shop: accessible

- Braille guide. Scented and tactile plants; fountains and water garden

- Licensed conservatory restaurant, 13 March to 27 Oct: daily except Mon & Tues (open Good Fri & BH Mons) 11–5; 2 Nov to 15 Dec: Sat & Sun 11.30–2.30. Parties 20+ must book (tel. 01628 661406). Refreshment kiosk in main car park daily. Two picnic areas; no picnics or barbecues in formal gardens

- Baby-changing facilities in WCs near main car park and near conservatory restaurant. Highchairs

- Lockable posts in car park

**Please see the area introductions for details of coast & countryside properties**

## SOUTH AND SOUTH EAST · 133

- Under close control and only in specified woodlands (not in formal garden)
- (2:E5) 2ml N of Taplow; leave M4 at exit 7 onto A4, or M40 at exit 4 onto A404 to Marlow and follow brown signs. Entrance by main gates opposite Feathers Inn [175: SU915851] **Station**: Bourne End 2ml; Taplow (not Sun) 2½ml; Burnham 3ml

**NT properties nearby** Greys Court, Hughenden Manor, West Wycombe Park

---

## DEVIL'S PUNCH BOWL CAFÉ                                    Surrey
London Road, Hindhead Common, Surrey GU26 6AB
**Tel** 01428 608771 · **Fax** 01428 608767

Local people, visitors from further afield and those journeying along the A3 can all enjoy the stunning scenery of the Devil's Punch Bowl and Hindhead Commons from the viewpoint 50m from the café. A selection of hot and cold food is available all day in this recently refurbished café and gateway to the Surrey Hills

- Open daily 8–5 or dusk if earlier. Closed 25, 26 Dec and 1 Jan
- Car park charges will apply after the first hour. Coaches by appointment. No lorries
- (2:E7) [187: TQ250520/265522] **Bus**: Stagecoach in Hants & Surrey 18, 19, 71 ❊ Haslemere–❊ Aldershot **Station**: Haslemere 3ml

---

## DORNEYWOOD GARDEN                                 Buckinghamshire
Dorneywood, Burnham SL1 8PY · **Tel** 01494 528051 (Regional Office)
**Email** dorneywood@ntrust.org.uk

The house was given to the Trust as an official residence for either a Secretary of State or Minister of the Crown. Only the garden is open, with herbaceous borders, a rose garden, cottage and kitchen gardens maintained in the style of the 1930s

- Garden open by written appointment only on 26 June, 17 July & 3 Aug: 2–5. Write for tickets giving at least one week's notice to the Secretary, Dorneywood Trust, at above address
- £3. No party reduction
- Garden: limited access
- Teas available
- (2:E5) Located on Dorneywood Road, SW of Burnham Beeches, 1½ml N of Burnham village, 2ml E of Cliveden [175: SU938848] **Bus**: Arriva The Shires/First Bee Line 74 High Wycombe–Heathrow Airport (passing close ❊ Slough & Beaconsfield), alight Farnham Common, 1½ml walk through Burnham Beeches **Station**: Burnham 2½ml

**NT properties nearby** Cliveden, Hughenden Manor, West Wycombe Park

---

*Unless indicated, last admission is always 30 mins before closing time*

## EMMETTS GARDEN               Kent

Ide Hill, Sevenoaks TN14 6AY · **Tel** 01732 750367 · 01732 868381 (Enquiries) **Fax** 01732 750490 · **Email** emmetts@ntrust.org.uk

Influenced by William Robinson, this charming and informal garden – with the highest treetop in Kent – was laid out in the late 19th century, with many exotic and rare trees and shrubs from across the world. While there are glorious shows of spring flowers and shrubs, a rose garden and rock garden, Emmetts is equally attractive for its spectacular views at all times and for its autumn colours

**What's new in 2002**: Wheelchair path giving improved access to some paths and slopes

- 23 March to 30 June: daily except Mon & Tues (but open on BH Mons) 11–5; 6 July to 3 Nov: Sat, Sun & Wed, plus BH Mon 11–5; last admission 4.15. **Events**: garden tours and open-air jazz concerts in summer
- Individual and group: £3.50; child £1.75; family £8.75
- Coaches and groups please book (introductory talk, concessions to couriers and drivers), tel. 01732 868381. An ideal tour combination with Chartwell (3 ml). Pre-booking preferred. Please tel. for information and booking pack
- Shop in tea-room, days as garden 11–5
- Volunteer-driven buggy can take visitors and one folded wheelchair from car park to ticket hut. Garden: largely accessible via wheelchair path, but steps and slopes in some areas. 3 wheelchairs. Shop & tea-room: accessible. Caution: sheer drop at end of shrub garden
- Braille guide. Scented azaleas and bluebells in spring, roses in summer; fountain; small waterfall
- Tea-room as garden 11–5.
- Baby-changing facilities. Family picnic area with tables in woodland near car park. Tree trail
- Tree trail
- Racks in car park
- On leads only
- (2:G6) 1½ml S of A25 on Sundridge to Ide Hill road, 1½ml N of Ide Hill off B2042, leave M25 at exit 5, then 4ml [188: TQ477524] **Bus**: Camden 404 from ≠ Sevenoaks, alight Ide Hill, 1½ml **Station**: Sevenoaks 4½ml; Penshurst (U) 5½ml

**NT properties nearby** Chartwell, Ightham Mote, Knole, Quebec House

## GREAT COXWELL BARN 🏠     Oxfordshire

Great Coxwell, Faringdon · **Tel** 01793 762209 (Coleshill Estate Office)
**Email** greatcoxwellbarn@ntrust.org.uk

A 13th-century monastic barn, stone-built with a stone-tiled roof and interesting timber structure

- **O** Daily at reasonable hours
- **£** 50p. No WC
- 🐕 On leads only
- ➜ (2:B4) 2ml SW of Faringdon between A420 and B4019 [163: SU269940]
  **Bus**: Stagecoach in Swindon 65/6 Swindon–Oxford (passing close ≋ Swindon & passing ≋ Oxford), alight Great Coxwell Turn, ¾ml **Station**: Swindon 10ml

**NT properties nearby** Ashdown House, Coleshill Estate, White Horse Hill

## GREYS COURT 🏛 🏠 ✤ 🛡     Oxfordshire

Rotherfield Greys, Henley-on-Thames RG9 4PG · **Tel** 01491 628529
**Infoline** 01494 755564 · **Email** greyscourt@ntrust.org.uk

A picturesque and intriguing house, originally 14th-century but much added to later, with a beautiful courtyard and one surviving tower dating from 1347. The house has an interesting history and was involved in Jacobean court intrigue. Inside, the intimate rooms contain some outstanding 18th-century plasterwork. The outbuildings include a Tudor wheelhouse, beautiful walled gardens full of old-fashioned roses and wisteria, and an ornamental vegetable garden

- **O** **House (part of ground floor only)**: 22 March to 27 Sept: Wed, Thur, Fri, BH Mons and Tues 4 June (closed Good Fri) 2–6. **Garden**: 22 March to 27 Sept: daily except Sun & Mon (closed Good Fri but open BH Mons and Tues 4 June) 2–6. **Events**: for details tel. 01494 755572
- **£** £4.80; child £2.40; family £12. Garden only £3.20; family £8. Parking 220m. Reduction for coach parties, which must book in advance (send s.a.e. for booking form). £1 entry or free cup of tea for those arriving by public transport or bicycle
- ♿ House: please contact the Custodian. Garden: partly accessible; some steep and uneven paths
- ☕ Teas in Cromwellian stables 4 April to end Sept: Wed to Sat (closed Good Fri but open BH Mons and Tues 4 June) 2.15–5.15
- 🚲 Lockable posts near ticket office
- 🐕 On leads and only in car park and on footpaths around the estate
- ➜ (2:D5) W of Henley-on-Thames. From Nettlebed mini-roundabout on A4130 take the B481 and the property is signed to the left after about 3 miles. There is also a direct (unsigned) route from Henley-on-Thames town centre if you follow

the signs to Peppard and Greys for about 3 miles [175: SU725834]
**Bus**: Chiltern Bus from Henley-on-Thames. Alight Rotherfield Greys Church and follow signed footpath to Greys Court (approx ½ml) **Station**: Henley-on-Thames 3ml

**NT properties nearby** Basildon Park, Cliveden

## HATCHLANDS PARK
Surrey

East Clandon, Guildford GU4 7RT · **Tel** 01483 222482 · **Infoline** 01483 225971 **Fax** 01483 223176 · **Email** hatchlands@ntrust.org.uk

Built in the 1750s for Admiral Boscawen, hero of the Battle of Louisburg, and set in a beautiful 170-ha (430-acre) Repton park offering a variety of park and woodland walks, Hatchlands contains splendid interiors by Robert Adam, decorated in appropriately nautical style. It houses the Cobbe Collection, the world's largest group of keyboard instruments associated with famous composers such as Purcell, J C Bach, Chopin, Mahler and Elgar, as well as with Marie Antoinette. There is also a small garden by Gertrude Jekyll, flowering from late May to early July. Beautiful bluebell wood in May

**What's new in 2002**: New flora and fauna interpretation in the Old Barn on the Long Walk

- **House**: 1 April to 31 Oct: daily except Mon, Fri & Sat (but open BH Mon and Fri in Aug). *Times*: 2–5.30. **Garden**: as house. **Park walks**: April to Oct: daily 11–6. **Events**: tel. 01483 225804 to be put on mailing list; Cobbe Collection Trust concerts lunchtimes Weds April to June, and end Sept to Nov, for details/bookings tel. 01483 211474 or see website www.cobbecollection.co.uk

- House and grounds £6; family £15. Park walks and garden only £2.50. Combined ticket with Clandon Park £9; families £22.50. Groups £5 (Tues to Thur only). Coach parties welcome weekdays and after 2pm on Sun; tel. 01483 222482 to book. Parking 300m

- No guided tours, but new audio tour of house and keyboard instruments for hire (Standard and Basic Language versions) £2 (inc. NT members)

- As house 1–5 (tel. 01483 224523)

- Parking by entrance kiosk; then staff-driven buggy from car park to house, ask at kiosk. House: all showrooms and terrace accessible. Garden: partly accessible. Wheelchairs and seatwalker. Restaurant: accessible. Fanny Boscawen walk short and relatively flat

- Braille and audio guides

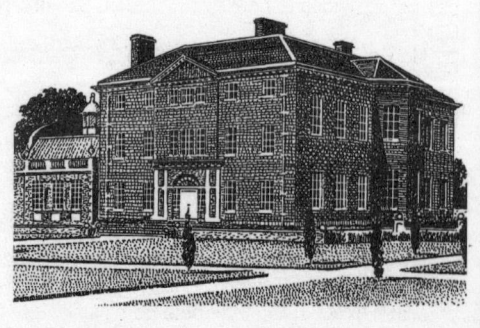

**Please remember – your membership card is always needed for free admission**

# SOUTH AND SOUTH EAST · 137

- Personal induction loops with audio guide
- Licensed self-service restaurant open as house 11–5 (tel. 01483 211120). Lunch served 12–2.30 (busy for lunch on Wed concert days). Picnicking in grounds
- Facilities in ladies' WC for nursing mothers; changing table. Children's menu; highchairs. Children's quizzes for both house and garden
- Racks at kiosk in car park
- On leads and only in car park area
- (2:F6) E of East Clandon, N of A246 Guildford–Leatherhead road [187: TQ063516] **Bus**: Arriva Surrey & W Sussex 418, 478/9 Guildford–Kingston (pass close ≋ Guildford) **Station**: Clandon 2½ml, Horsley 3ml

**NT properties nearby** Clandon Park, Polesden Lacey, River Wey & Dapdune Wharf

---

## HINTON AMPNER GARDEN 🏠✿ Hampshire
Bramdean, nr Alresford SO24 0LA · **Tel** 01962 771305 · **Fax** 01962 793101
**Email** hintonampner@ntrust.org.uk

---

One of the great gardens of the 20th century. A masterpiece of design by Ralph Dutton, 8th and last Lord Sherborne, uniting a formal layout with varied and informal plantings in pastel shades. A garden of all-year-round interest with scented plants and magnificent vistas over the park and rolling Hampshire countryside. The house, which is tenanted, contains Ralph Dutton's fine collection of English furniture, Italian paintings and hard-stones

- **Garden**: 17 & 24 March, then 30 March to end Sept: daily except Thur & Fri 11–5. **House**: 2 April to end Sept: Tues & Wed, plus Sat & Sun in Aug 1.30–5
- House & garden £5. Garden only £4. Special entrance for coaches, which must book in advance. No group bookings in Aug. Tel. for party rate
- Close parking, ask at kiosk. House: accessible. Garden: accessible via grass ramps and gentle slopes; map of wheelchair route. 4 wheelchairs. Tea-room: accessible
- Braille guides to house and garden. Scented plants
- Tea-room as garden 11–5 (light lunches 12–2). Picnics in grass car park only
- Cycles can be secured to gate in view of entry kiosk
- (2:D7) On A272, 1ml W of Bramdean village, 8ml E of Winchester, leave M3 at exit 9 and follow signs to Petersfield [185: SU597275] **Bus**: Stagecoach in Hampshire 67 Winchester–Petersfield (passing close ≋ Winchester & passing ≋ Petersfield). Winchester 9ml **Station**: Winchester 9m

**NT properties nearby** Mottisfont, The Vyne, Winchester City Mill, Uppark

**For general enquiries, please telephone 0870 458 4000**

## HUGHENDEN MANOR     Buckinghamshire

High Wycombe HP14 4LA · **Tel** 01494 755573 · **Infoline** 01494 755565
**Fax** 01494 463310 · **Email** hughenden@ntrust.org.uk

The home of Victorian prime minister and statesman Benjamin Disraeli from 1848 until his death in 1881. Most of his furniture, books and pictures remain in this, his private retreat from the rigours of parliamentary life in London. There are beautiful walks through the surrounding park and woodland, and the garden is a recreation of the colourful design of his wife, Mary Anne

**Note**: Certain rooms have little electric light. Visitors wishing to make a close study of the interior of the house should avoid dull days early and late in the season

**What's new in 2002**: Refurbishment of upper floors now complete

- **House**: 2 to 31 March: Sat & Sun; 3 April to 3 Nov: daily except Mon & Tues (but open BH Mons and Tues 4 June). *Times*: 1–5. **Note**: At BHols, Suns and other busy days entry is by timed ticket, on a first come, first served basis. **Garden**: as house 12–5. **Park & woodland**: all year. **Events**: for details tel. 01494 755572. **Fri 10 May – closed to all visitors until 2.30**

- £4.40; child £2.20; family £11. Garden only £1.50; child 75p. Park and woodland free. Parties must pre-book, tel. for details. Small parties only. No parties at weekends or BHols. Parking space for only one coach; car park 200m from house (overflow car park 400m).

- Guided tours for booked parties; tel. for details and rates

- 2 to 31 March: as house; April to 3 Nov: as house 12–5; 7 Nov to 15 Dec: daily except Mon & Tues 11–4 (tel. 01494 755575)

- Parking 110m from house. House: ground floor accessible, photo album of first-floor rooms. Garden: best seen from terrace; steep paths. Shop & restaurant: accessible. Park & woodland: very hilly. Wheelchairs available. Exhibition and WC in stableyard

- Braille and tape guides; large-print guides available on loan

**Please see the area introductions for details of coast & countryside properties**

SOUTH AND SOUTH EAST · 139

- Restaurant March: weekends only; April to 3 Nov: as house; Nov to 15 Dec: Sat & Sun. *Times*: March to Oct:12–5. Nov to 15 Dec 11–4 (available for private bookings, Christmas lunches and winter events, tel. 01494 755573)
- Baby-changing facilities. Baby front slings and toddler reins; loan of all-terrain buggy for outdoors. Children's guidebook. Children's menu; highchairs
- Study base for booked groups. Guided tours linked to Victorian history and environmental education can be arranged. Victorian handling collection. Rates and details from Education Warden, tel. 01494 755596
- Locking cycle posts in car park near stable yard
- Under close control and only in park and woodland; shaded parking; dog rings in stable yard
- (2:E4) 1½ml N of High Wycombe; on W side of the Great Missenden road (A4128) [165: SU866955] **Bus**: Arriva The Shires 323/4 High Wycombe–Aylesbury (passing close ≋ High Wycombe). **Note**: Long and steep walk to house entrance **Station**: High Wycombe 2ml

**NT properties nearby** Claydon House, Cliveden, King's Head, Waddesdon Manor, West Wycombe Park

## IGHTHAM MOTE                                                                 Kent

Ivy Hatch, Sevenoaks TN15 0NT · **Tel** 01732 810378 · **Infoline** 01732 811145
**Fax** 01732 811029 · **Email** ighthammote@ntrust.org.uk

A superb moated manor house, nestling in a sunken valley and dating from 1330. The main features of the house span many centuries and include the Great Hall, old Chapel, crypt, Tudor chapel with painted ceiling, drawing room with Jacobean fireplace, frieze and 18th-century wallpaper and billiards room. There is an extensive garden and interesting walks in the surrounding woodland. A comprehensive ongoing programme of repair was begun in 1988 and is the subject of a 'Conservation in Action' exhibition in the Ticket Office

**What's new in 2002**: Reopening of Great Hall following conservation work. Housekeeper's Room on show. Occasional limited access to the Tower. Work due to start on the South West Quarter to facilitate the eventual opening of the Robinson apartments. Interpretation panels illustrate the work in progress

- **House**: 24 March to 3 Nov: daily except Tues & Sat 10–5.30. **Car park**: daily dawn to dusk. New estate walks leaflet
- £5.40; child £2.70; family £13.50. Booked parties of 15+ weekdays £4.70 (no reduction Sun & BHols). Foreign language guides on sale
- Free introductory talks. Regular garden tours. Booked special guided tours for groups of 15+ on open weekday mornings only; for details tel. 01732 810378
- As house (tel. 01732 811203)
- Close parking and dropping-off point: contact Property Manager in advance or ask at ticket office on arrival. 3 wheelchairs. House: most of ground floor

**Unless indicated, last admission is always 30 mins before closing time**

accessible, some changes of level; courtyard cobbled. Garden: some gravel paths. Conservation exhibition & tea pavilion: accessible. Shop: ground floor accessible. Woodland estate walk: accessible. Estate buggies for loan

- Braille guide; many items to be enjoyed by touch
- Tea pavilion as house (tel. 01732 811314). Oct hours vary depending on weather. Picnic area in car park. No picnics in gardens
- Baby-feeding/changing facilities. Children's quiz. Children's guide. Baby slings
- New teachers' resource book. Special tours for schools, contact Property Manager for details. Woodland shelter in grounds for use by groups. Environmental handling collection
- On leads and only on estate walks
- (2:H6) 6ml E of Sevenoaks, off A25, and 2½ml S of Ightham, off A227 [188: TQ584535] **Bus**: Camden 222 ⇆ Tunbridge Wells–⇆ Borough Green (passing ⇆ Tonbridge), alight Fairlawne, thence ½ml (footpath); 404 Sevenoaks– Shipbourne (passing ⇆ Sevenoaks), alight Ivy Hatch, ¾ml; otherwise Arriva Kent Thameside 306/8 ⇆ Sevenoaks–Gravesend (passing ⇆ Borough Green), alight Ightham Common, 1½ml **Station**: Borough Green & Wrotham 3½ml; Hildenborough 4ml

**NT properties nearby** Chartwell, Knole, Old Soar Manor

---

# KING'S HEAD

Buckinghamshire

King's Head Passage, Market Square, Aylesbury HP20 2RW · **Tel** 01296 381501 **Fax** 01296 381502 · **Email** kingshead@ntrust.org.uk

A coaching inn, dating from 1450 and of particular interest for its large mullioned window, containing fragments of 15th-century glass carrying the arms of Henry VI and his wife, Margaret of Anjou. Limited opening to pre-booked groups

- Access during normal public house hours. Groups (max 4 visitors per tour) must be booked in advance on tel. 01296 381501
- £2 (NT members £1)
- Limited access; tel. for details
- (2:E3) At NW corner of Market Square [165:SP818138] **Bus**: from surrounding areas **Station**: Aylesbury 400m

**NT properties nearby** Claydon House, Waddesdon Manor

---

There are special events at most Trust properties; telephone 0870 458 4000 for details

# KNOLE 🏛️✳️♠️🎭         Kent

Sevenoaks TN15 0RP · **Tel** 01732 462100 · **Infoline** 01732 450608
**Fax** 01732 465528 · **Email** knole@ntrust.org.uk

One of the great treasure houses of England, set in a magnificent deer park. The original 15th-century house was enlarged and embellished in 1603 by the 1st Earl of Dorset, one of Queen Elizabeth's 'favourites', and has remained unaltered ever since – a rare survival. The thirteen state rooms open to the public contain magnificent collections: 17th-century royal Stuart furniture, including three state beds, silver furniture and the prototype of the famous Knole Settee, outstanding tapestries and textiles, and important portraits by Van Dyck, Gainsborough, Lely, Kneller and Reynolds

**Note**: Please do not feed the deer; they can be dangerous

- ⭕ **House**: 23 March to 3 Nov Wed to Sun 11–4; Good Fri & BH Mons 11–4. Booked groups welcome by arrangement. **Park**: daily for pedestrians only, by courtesy of Lord Sackville. Parking available for cars visiting house during normal opening hours (£2.50). Outside these times, park in nearby town centre. **Garden**: May to Sept: first Wed in each month only, by courtesy of Lord Sackville 11–4; last admission 3

- £ House: £5; child £2.50; family £12.50. Booked groups (15+) £4.25. Parking £2.50. Park free to pedestrians. Garden (note limited opening): £2; child £1

- 🎭 Guided tours for booked groups (15+ by arrangement)

- 🛍️ 23 March to 3 Nov. *Times*: Wed to Sun 10.30–5; Good Fri and BH Mons 10.30–5; Christmas shop Nov & Dec: daily except Mon & Tues 11–4. (tel. 01732 743748)

- ♿ Close parking. Great Hall, Stone Court, Green Court, shop & restaurant: accessible. Wheelchair. Garden: accessible when open. Park: accessible. WCs in Green Court and near tea-room

- 👁️ Braille guide; some items can be touched. Herb and wilderness gardens (limited opening)

**For all your information needs check our website www.nationaltrust.org.uk**

## 142 · SOUTH AND SOUTH EAST

- Audio loop system
- Tea-room 23 March to 3 Nov; as shop
- Baby-changing facilities. Children's guide and worksheets. Highchairs; children's menu
- Education room, handling and costume collections. Strong links to Tudor and Stuart aspects of curriculum, teachers' guide. Excellent collection of historical portraits. Special needs groups welcome. Contact Education Officer for details (tel. 01732 462100)
- On leads and only in park
- (2:H6) Park entrance in Sevenoaks town centre off A225 Tonbridge Road, leave M25 at Junction 5 [188: TQ532543] **Bus**: Arriva 402 ≣ Bromley North–Tunbridge Wells (passing ≣ Bromley South, Sevenoaks ≣). Arriva 402 Tunbridge Wells–Bromley North. Bus station ¾ml **Station**: Sevenoaks 1½ml

**NT properties nearby** Chartwell, Ightham Mote

## LAMB HOUSE                                East Sussex
West Street, Rye TN31 7ES · **Tel** 01372 453401 (Regional Office)

A delightful brick-fronted house dating from the early 18th century and typical of the attractive town of Rye. This was the home of writer Henry James from 1898 to 1916, and later of author E. F. Benson. Some of James's personal possessions can be seen and there is a charming walled garden

**Note**: The house is administered and largely maintained on the Trust's behalf by a tenant

- 3 April to 2 Nov: Wed & Sat 2–6
- £2.60; child £1.30; family £6.50. Groups by arrangement £2.20. No WC. Car park and WCs in town
- (2:J8) In West Street, facing W end of church [198: TQ920202] **Bus**: From surrounding areas to Rye **Station**: Rye ½ml **Cycle**: NCN 2

**NT properties nearby** Bodiam Castle, Smallhythe Place

## LEITH HILL                                Surrey
Coldharbour · **Tel** 01306 711777 · **Fax** 01306 712153

The highest point in south-east England, crowned by an 18th-century Gothic tower, from which there are magnificent views. The surrounding woodland contains ancient stands of hazel and oak and there is a colourful display of rhododendrons in May and June

- **Tower**: 29 March (Good Fri) to end Sept: Wed 10–5; Sat, Sun & BHols 10–5. Oct to end March 2003: Sat, Sun & BHols (except 25 Dec) 10–3.30.
  **Rhododendron wood & estate**: all year: daily

**Please remember – your membership card is always needed for free admission**

## SOUTH AND SOUTH EAST · 143

**£** Tower: £1.50; child 75p. No reduction for groups. (01306 712434) Rhododendron wood: £1.50 per car. Parking in designated areas along road at foot of the hill, ½ml walk from tower, some steep gradients. No direct vehicular access to summit. No coaches. Display in information room and telescope on top of tower. Circular trail guide available from dispenser £1. No WCs

🚶 Guided walks throughout the year. Groups by arrangement with the Warden (tel. 01306 711777)

♿ Car park. Access path to upper part of rhododendron wood

☕ Light refreshments when tower open. Picnic areas beside tower and in rhododendron wood

🏛 Educational groups for day visits and residential groups by arrangement with North Downs Education Officer; tel. 01306 742809

🐕 On leads in rhododendron wood (not in picnic area or tower)

➔ (2:F7) On summit of Leith Hill, 1ml SW of Coldharbour A29/B2126 [187: TQ139432] **Station**: Holmwood (U), not Sun, 2½ml; Dorking 5½ml

**NT properties nearby** Box Hill, Clandon Park, Hatchlands Park, Polesden Lacey, Ranmore Common

---

## LONG CRENDON COURTHOUSE    Buckinghamshire
Long Crendon, Aylesbury HP18 9AN · **Tel** 01494 528051 (Regional Office)

A 15th-century two-storeyed building, partly half-timbered and probably first used as a wool store. The manorial courts were held here from the reign of Henry V until Victorian times

🕐 Upper floor only, 23 March to end Sept: Wed 2–6; Sat, Sun & BH Mons 11–6

**£** £1. No party reduction. No WC

➔ (2:D4) 2ml N of Thame, via B4011, close to the church [165: SP698091] **Bus**: Arriva The Shires 260/1, Aylesbury–Thame (passing ≈ Haddenham & Thame Parkway) **Station**: Haddenham & Thame Parkway 2ml by footpath, 4ml by road

**For general enquiries, please telephone 0870 458 4000**

## MONK'S HOUSE

East Sussex

Rodmell, Lewes BN7 3HF · **Tel** 01372 453401 (Regional Office)

A small weather-boarded house, the home of Leonard and Virginia Woolf until Leonard's death in 1969. The rooms reflect the life and times of the literary circle in which they moved

**Note**: The house and garden are administered and largely maintained on the Trust's behalf by a tenant

- 3 April to 2 Nov: Wed & Sat 2–5.30

- £2.60; child £1.30; family £6.50. Groups of 10 or more by prior arrangement during normal opening hours. Larger groups may also be accommodated on Thur by arrangement with the tenants (please book at least 4 weeks in advance). Car park 50m; village street too narrow for coaches; drivers must set passengers down at main road junction, then park elsewhere

- (2:G8) From A27 SW of Lewes, follow signs for Kingston and then Rodmell village, where turn left at Abergavenny Arms pub, thence ½ml [198: TQ421064] **Bus**: Metrobus 123 Lewes–Newhaven (passing ≷ Lewes) **Station**: Southease (U) 1¼ml

**NT properties nearby** Alfriston Clergy House, Sheffield Park Garden

## MOTTISFONT ABBEY GARDEN, HOUSE & ESTATE

Hampshire

Mottisfont, nr Romsey SO51 0LP · **Tel** 01794 340757 · **Infoline** 01794 341220
**Fax** 01794 341492 · **Email** mottisfontabbey@ntrust.org.uk

Set amidst glorious countryside along the River Test, this 12th-century Augustinian priory was converted into a private house after the Dissolution, and still retains the spring or 'font' from which its name is derived. The abbey contains a drawing room decorated by Rex Whistler and Derek Hill's 20th-century picture collection, but the key attraction is the grounds with magnificent trees, walled gardens and National Collection of Old-fashioned Roses. The estate includes Mottisfont village and surrounding farmland and woods

**What's new in 2002**: The phased programme of renovation to the Rose Garden is nearing completion. Opening Thur in June, July and August

- **Garden & grounds**: 23 March to 3 Nov: daily except Thur & Fri (but open Good Fri and Thur June, July & Aug) 11–6 or dusk if earlier. Special opening for rose garden 8 to 23 June: daily 11–8.30; last admission 1 hr before closing. **House (Whistler Room & cellarium)**: as garden 11–6 (last admission 5). **Derek Hill Picture Collection**: Sun, Mon & Tues 11–6 (last admission 5); also open at other times, tel. for confirmation. **Events**: for details tel. 01794 340757. Rooms in the house are available for social and business entertainment, civil weddings and receptions; contact Catering and Functions Manager

- £6, family £15. No party reduction. **Note**: As the roses are renowned for their

**Please see the area introductions for details of coast & countryside properties**

scent, please do not smoke in the walled garden during the rose season. To appreciate the roses evening viewing is recommended

- Shop and plant sales as garden 11–5.30; 8 to 23 June 11–8; Oct 11–5 (tel. 01794 341901)
- Rose garden: accessible. Elsewhere: extensive lawns, gravel drive can be difficult for narrow-wheeled wheelchairs. Wheelchairs and volunteer-driven buggy
- Braille guide. Many scents in rose garden
- Licensed restaurant as garden 12–5. During June groups are strongly recommended to book a private room for lunch or tea to avoid long queuing; contact Catering and Functions Manager. Outdoor refreshment kiosk open at peak times. Tea-room: 11–6 (last orders 5.30)
- Baby-changing facilities; children's menus. Children's quiz
- Only in car park (no shade) and on lead; under close control on woodland walks in Spearywell Woods and Great Copse. Walks leaflet from entrance kiosk (20p). 7ml estate path now open (leaflet £1), access from main car park (open 9–6)
- (2:C7) 4½ml NW of Romsey, 1ml W of A3057 [185: SU327270] **Station**: Dunbridge (U) ¾ml

**NT properties nearby** Hinton Ampner Garden, Winchester City Mill

---

# MOTTISTONE MANOR GARDEN          Isle of Wight

The Gardener, Manor Cottage, Hoxall Lane, Mottistone PO30 4ED
**Tel** 01983 741302

---

A garden noted for its colourful herbaceous borders, grassy terraces planted with fruit trees and its sea views. The 16th- and 17th-century manor house, which is tenanted, lies at the heart of the Mottistone Estate, which offers delightful walks between the Downs and the coast

**What's new in 2002**: Additional shrub border

- **Garden**: 24 March to 30 Oct: Sun, Tues, Wed & BH Mons. *Times*: Tues & Wed 11–5.30, Sun & BH Mons 2–5.30. Groups (during opening hours) by written appointment. **House**: Aug BH Mon 2–5.30; guided tours for NT members on that day, 10–12. **Events**: summer open-air concerts. Plant fair
- Garden £2.60. No party reduction. Parking 50m
- Limited access due to steep slopes; tel. for details
- Teas in garden

---

**Unless indicated, last admission is always 30 mins before closing time**

## 146 · SOUTH AND SOUTH EAST

🐕 On leads only

➜ (2:C9) At Mottistone, 2ml W of Brighstone on B3399 [196: SZ406838]
**Bus**: Southern Vectis 7B Newport–Alum Bay Ferry: Yarmouth (Wightlink Ltd) 6ml (tel. 0870 582 7744) E Cowes (Red Funnel) 12ml (tel. 023 8033 4010)

**NT properties nearby** Bembridge Windmill, Brighstone Shop & Museum, Needles Old Battery, Old Town Hall Newtown

---

## THE NEEDLES OLD BATTERY 🏠 🏛     Isle of Wight
West Highdown, Totland PO39 0JH · **Tel** 01983 754772 (Opening hours only)

---

The threat of a French invasion prompted the construction in 1862 of this spectacularly sited fort, which still retains its original gun barrels. The laboratory, searchlight position and position-finding cells have all been restored and a 65m tunnel leads to stunning views of the Hampshire and Dorset coastline

**What's new in 2002**: New exhibition on history of the Battery

🅾 28 March to 28 June, 2 Sept to 31 Oct: daily except Fri & Sat (but open Easter weekend); July & Aug: daily. *Times*: 10.30–5. **Note**: Property closes in bad weather; tel. on day of visit to check

💷 £3; family £7.50. No reduction for groups; school groups can be conducted by a NT guide by arrangement; a special charge applies. No vehicular access to Battery (visitors with disabilities by arrangement). Many paths are steep and not suitable for people with walking difficulties. Access to the searchlight is by narrow spiral staircase, with further steps to tea-room and headland beyond the Battery. Parking 1ml away at Alum Bay (not NT; minimum charge £3), or park in Freshwater Bay (IOW Council) or Highdown car park (NT) and walk over Downs (or see bus services below)

🧒 School groups, special visits 1 April to 1 Nov (but not Aug) by appointment

♿ Parking 1ml from Battery, but accompanied wheelchair users may park nearer by arrangement; access limited

☕ Tea-room, with spectacular views, as Battery 11–5 (last order 4.30)

👶 Children's guide and quiz sheets; the children's exhibition tells the story of 'The Needles at War' and cartoon information boards throughout explain how the Battery functioned

🐕 On leads only

➜ (2:B9) At Needles Headland, W of Freshwater Bay and Alum Bay (B3322) [196: SZ300848] **Bus**: Southern Vectis 42 Yarmouth–Needles, April to Oct only; otherwise any service to Alum Bay, thence 1ml **Station**: Ferry: Yarmouth (Wightlink Ltd) 5ml (tel. 0870 582 7744); E Cowes (Red Funnel) 16ml

**NT properties nearby** Bembridge Windmill, Brighstone Shop & Museum, Mottistone Manor Garden, Old Town Hall Newton

---

**There are special events at most Trust properties; telephone 0870 458 4000 for details**

## NYMANS GARDEN   West Sussex

Handcross, nr Haywards Heath RH17 6EB · **Tel** 01444 400321/405250
**Fax** 01444 400253 · **Email** nymans@ntrust.org.uk

One of the great gardens of the Sussex Weald, and still retaining much of its distinctive family style in the historic collection of plants, shrubs and trees. This is reflected also in the surrounding estate, with its woodland walks and wild garden, and in the many rare and exotic species collected from overseas. The Messel family's creativity is much in evidence in Lady Rosse's library, drawing room and forecourt garden

- **Garden**: 1 March to 3 Nov: daily except Mon & Tues (but open BH Mons & 4 June); Nov to March 2003: Sat & Sun (but closed 28, 29 Dec). *Times*: March to 4 Nov 11–6 or sunset if earlier; Nov to March 2003 11–4, but may be restricted if ground very wet; tel. for information. **House**: 27 March to 3 Nov: Lady Rosse's library, drawing room and small dining room: 11–5. **Events**: tel. 01444 400321 for details

- £6; family £15. Booked groups of 15+ £5, Wed to Fri only. Joint ticket with same-day entry to Standen £9, available Wed to Fri. Car park at entrance; coaches must book in advance (no coaches Suns mid-March to end June); reduced admission for groups arriving by coach in Sept & Oct. Winter weekends £3; child £1.50; family £7.50; booked groups £2.50

- Shop & plant centre 1 March to end Nov: daily except Mon & Tues (but open BH Mons) 11–6; 1 to 24 Dec: Christmas shop 11–4 (tel. 01444 400157). Also open winter weekends as garden

- House: difficult; some access at quiet times. Garden: accessible; wheelchair route indicated; map. Tea-room & shop: accessible. Powered vehicles, to book tel. 01444 400321. Wheelchairs

- Braille guide to garden, woodland and family rooms. Old roses and other scented plants. Audio garden guide

- Licensed self-service restaurant as shop 11–5. Refreshment kiosk (weather permitting). Limited menu in tea-room Nov to end Feb 11–4. Christmas lunches: from 3 to 20 Dec (except Mons); restaurant also open 21, 22 Dec (closed 23–25

**For all your information needs check our website www.nationaltrust.org.uk**

Dec). Picnics welcome outside formal gardens, eg in Pinetum. The restaurant and entrance hall are available for private and commercial functions; tel. for details (01444 400161/400321)

Changing table in WCs at car park and tea-room. Highchair. Children's garden quizzes

Cycle stand near entrance

On leads and only in car park

(2:G7) On B2114 at Handcross, 4½ml S of Crawley, just off London–Brighton M23/A23 [187: TQ265294] **Bus**: Arriva Surrey & W Sussex 73 Brighton–Crawley Down, Metrobus E Surrey 271 Haywards Heath–Crawley. All pass ≋ Crawley and stop at Nymans **Station**: Balcombe 4½ml; Crawley 5½ml

**NT properties nearby** Sheffield Park, Standen, Wakehurst Place

## OAKHURST COTTAGE                                                    Surrey

Hambledon, nr Godalming GU8 4HF · **Tel** 01428 684090
**Email** oakhurstcottage@ntrust.org.uk

A small 16th-century timber-framed cottage, restored and furnished as a simple labourer's dwelling. There is a delightful garden containing typical Victorian plants

23 March to 3 Nov: daily except Mon, Tues & Fri (but open BH Mons) 2–5, all visits by appointment only

£3, inc. guided tour. No party reduction. Schools and groups by special arrangement any day or evening. Parking 200m. No WC

(2:F7) [186:SU967389] **Bus**: Arriva Surrey & W Sussex 503 from Godalming (Wed only) (passes close ≋ Godalming); otherwise Stagecoach in Hants & Surrey 71 Guildford–Hindhead (passes close ≋ Godalming), alight Lane End 1ml **Station**: Witley 1½ml

**NT properties nearby** Petworth House & Park, Winkworth Arboretum, Witley Centre

## OLD SOAR MANOR                                                      Kent

Plaxtol, Borough Green TN15 0QX · **Tel** 01732 810378 · **Infoline** 01732 811145

The solar block of a late 13th-century knight's dwelling

6 April to 29 Sept: daily except Fri 10–6

Free. Exhibition on Manor and surrounding areas. No WCs

(2:H6) 2ml S of Borough Green (A25); approached via A227 and Plaxtol; narrow lane, unsuitable for coaches [188: TQ619541] **Bus**: Camden 222 ≋ Tunbridge Wells–≋ Borough Green (passing ≋ Tonbridge); 404 Sevenoaks–Shipbourne (passing ≋ Sevenoaks); on both alight E end of Plaxtol, thence ¾ml by footpath **Station**: Borough Green & Wrotham 2½ml

**NT properties nearby** Chartwell, Ightham Mote, Knole

**Please remember – your membership card is always needed for free admission**

SOUTH AND SOUTH EAST · 149

## OLD TOWN HALL, NEWTOWN 🏠                   Isle of Wight

The Custodian, Ken Cottage, Upper Lane, Brighstone PO30 4AT
**Tel** 01983 531785 (opening hours only)

The small, now tranquil, village of Newtown once sent two members to Parliament and the Town Hall was the setting for often turbulent elections. An exhibition inside depicts the exploits of 'Ferguson's Gang', an anonymous group of Trust benefactors in the 1920s and 1930s

- 27 March to end June, Sept to 30 Oct: Mon, Wed & Sun (but open Good Fri & Easter Sat); July & Aug: daily except Fri & Sat. *Times*: 2–5
- £1.50. No party reduction
- Guided tours by written appointment
- Braille guide
- School groups welcome by appointment
- (2:C9) Between Newport and Yarmouth, 1ml N of A3054 [196: SZ424905]
  **Bus**: Southern Vectis 35, 47 from Newport; otherwise 7 🚆 Ryde Esplanade–Freshwater (passing Yarmouth Ferry Terminal), alight Barton's Corner, 1ml Ferry: Yarmouth (Wightlink Ltd) 5ml (tel. 0870 582 7744); E Cowes (Red Funnel) 11ml (tel. 023 8033 4010)

**NT properties nearby** Bembridge Windmill, Brighstone Shop & Museum, Mottistone Manor Garden, Needles Old Battery

## PETWORTH HOUSE AND PARK 🏠🌳😊          West Sussex

Petworth GU28 0AE · **Tel** 01798 342207 · **Infoline** 01798 343929
**Fax** 01798 342963 · **Email** petworth@ntrust.org.uk

A magnificent late 17th-century mansion set in a beautiful park, landscaped by 'Capability' Brown and immortalised in Turner's paintings. The house contains the Trust's finest and largest collection of pictures, with numerous works by Turner, Van Dyck, Reynolds and Blake, as well as ancient and neo-classical sculpture, fine furniture and carvings by Grinling Gibbons. The Servants' Quarters contain interesting kitchens (inc. a splendid copper *batterie de cuisine* of over 1000 pieces) and other service rooms. On weekdays, additional rooms are open to visitors by kind permission of Lord and Lady Egremont (see below)

**What's new in 2002**: Major Turner exhibition, 6 July to 29 Sept. The Carved Room and Red Room are restored to their 19th-century appearance. 11am opening for escorted tours

- House & Servants' Quarters: 23 March to 3 Nov: daily except Thur & Fri (but open Good Fri). Extra rooms shown weekdays (but not BH Mons) as follows: Mon, White & Gold Room and White Library; Tues & Wed, three bedrooms on first floor. *Times*: 11–5.30. Morning opening of the house for escorted tours.
  **Pleasure Ground and car park** (for walks, picnics and access to restaurant,

For general enquiries, please telephone 0870 458 4000

## 150 · SOUTH AND SOUTH EAST

shop and Petworth town): open as House and Servants' Quarters. *Times*: 11–6. Special opening for spring bulbs 9, 10 and 16, 17 March. *Times*: 12–4. **Park**: daily 8 to sunset (closes for concerts). **Events**: Turner at Petworth exhibition, open-air concerts (charge for NT members). Lecture lunches, behind-the-scenes tours and Christmas events during Nov and Dec. For details of all events send s.a.e. to Petworth House. Winter opening: Servants' Quarters, Pleasure Ground: 20 Nov to 14 Dec: Wed to Sat. *Times*: 11–3. Shop open early Jan for sale

£ House, Pleasure Ground & Servants' Quarters: £7; child £4; family £18. Booked groups of 15+ £6.50. Pleasure Ground only £1.50; child free. Park: free. Coach parties alight at Church Lodge entrance, coaches then park in NT car park. Coach parties must book in advance as parking limited; contact Administration Office

Guided tours for groups and school parties by arrangement; contact Administration Office

As house 11–5. Also open 10, 16, 17 March. Christmas shopping 6 Nov to 22 Dec, Wed to Sat 10.30–3.30. Also Jan for sale

Car park 800m from house; vehicle takes elderly and disabled visitors to house, tel. for timetable. Disabled and elderly visitors may also be set down at the Church Lodge entrance; contact Administration Office. House: ground floor accessible; wheelchairs. Illustrated folder of first-floor bedrooms. Shop & tea-room: accessible. Pleasure Ground: accessible. Park: mostly rough grass

Braille and large-print guides to House and Servants' Quarters. Touch tours (must be booked). List of the items that can be touched during normal opening hours is available

Licensed restaurant as house 11–5. Also open for Mothering Sunday lunches 10 March, and 16, 17 March 10.30–3.30. Winter opening 6 Nov to 22 Dec Wed to Sat 10.30–3.30. Private functions catered for; also booked Christmas lunches (tel. 01798 344975)

Baby-feeding and changing facilities. No prams in house but pushchairs admitted. Highchairs. Free quizzes

Details of educational programme from Education Officer (tel. 01798 344976)

Racks in car park

Under close control and only in park (not in Pleasure Ground)

(2:F7/F8) In centre of Petworth (A272/A283); house car park well signposted, car parks for house and park on A283; pedestrian access from Petworth town and from A272. No vehicles in park [197: SU976218] **Bus**: Stagecoach Coastline 1 Worthing–Midhurst (passing ≋ Pulborough); 65, 95 Horsham–Petworth (passing ≋ Horsham) **Station**: Pulborough 5¼ml

**NT properties nearby** Slindon, Uppark

---

**Please see the area introductions for details of coast & countryside properties**

## PITSTONE WINDMILL 🗙                            Buckinghamshire
Ivinghoe · **Tel** 01494 528051 (Regional Office)

One of the oldest post-mills in Britain, dating from 1627 and restored entirely by volunteers

- **O** June to end Aug: Sun & BHols: 2.30–6

- **£** £1; child 30p. Group organisers, contact David Goseltine, Holland Cottage, Whipsnade, Dunstable, Beds LU6 2LG (tel. 01582 872303). Parking 200m (by B488). No WC

- 🚶 Access difficult: long track from car park; long flight of wooden steps to mill machinery

- → (2:E3) ½ml S of Ivinghoe, 3ml NE of Tring, just W of B488 [165: SP946158]
  **Bus**: Arriva The Shires 61 Aylesbury–Luton (passing close ⇌ Aylesbury & Luton)
  **Station**: Tring 2½ml; Cheddington 2½ml

**NT properties nearby** Ashridge Estate, Dunstable Downs

---

## POLESDEN LACEY 🏠 ❀ 🌳 🚶 ▼                 Surrey
Great Bookham, nr Dorking RH5 6BD · **Tel** 01372 452048 · **Infoline** 01372 458203
**Fax** 01372 452023 · **Email** polesdenlacey@ntrust.org.uk

In an exceptional setting on the North Downs, this originally Regency house was extensively remodelled in 1906–9 by the Hon. Mrs Ronald Greville, a well-known Edwardian hostess. Her collection of fine paintings, furniture, porcelain and silver are displayed in the reception rooms and galleries, as they were at the time of her celebrated house parties. There are extensive grounds, a walled rose garden, lawns and landscape walks. King George VI and Queen Elizabeth The Queen Mother spent part of their honeymoon here in 1923

- **O** **House**: 23 March to 3 Nov: daily except Mon & Tues (but open BH Mons and Tues 4 June) 11–5. **Garden**: daily 11–6 or dusk if earlier. **Events**: Summer festival: for booking form send s.a.e. to the above address or tel. 01372 452048. Surrey Hills Country Fair – additional charge for all visitors, inc. NT members. Tel. 01372 452048 for information about marquee wedding receptions or to join guided walks and events mailing list. Estate has YHA hostel, tel. 01306 877964

- **£** Garden, grounds & walks: £4; family £10; house £7; family £17.50. Combined booked tickets (garden & house) £6 for groups of 15+. Parking 200m. Croquet lawns; equipment for hire from house (book in advance)

- 🛍 Shop: 20 Jan to 28 Feb: Sat & Sun only. Shop & plant sales: March & April, Sept to end Nov: daily except Mon & Tues; May to Aug & 1 to 23 Dec: daily.
  **Note**: Open all BH Mons. *Times*: Jan to end March, Nov & Dec: 11–4; April to Oct (& BH Mons) 11–5

- 🚶 Disabled visitors may be driven to and collected from house front door. Car park

**Unless indicated, last admission is always 30 mins before closing time**

close to house, WC, shop and tea-room, all of which are accessible. Garden: some gravel and paved surfaces. Wheelchairs and self-drive single-seat powered vehicle by arrangement with house. Walk with firm surface through farm and woodland (strong pusher recommended)

- Braille guide to house. By arrangement, house staff will describe contents and indicate those to touch. Rose and lavender gardens

- Tea-room 20 Jan, Feb, March and Nov: daily except Mon & Tues; April to end Oct and 1 to 23 Dec: daily. *Times*: Jan, Feb, March, Nov & Dec 11–3, April to Oct & BH Mons 11–5. **Note**: limited menu Jan to March, Nov & Dec and light refreshments only on Mons & Tues. Pre-booked Christmas lunches 10–14 and 17–21 Dec, tel. 01372 456190

- Changing tables in men's and women's WCs. No prams, pushchairs or baby back-carriers in house. Highchairs

- Not in rose garden, on paths or on lawns, under close control in remainder of grounds and on walks

- (2:F6) 5ml NW of Dorking, 2ml S of Great Bookham, off A246 Leatherhead–Guildford road [187: TQ136522] **Bus**: New service planned for 2002. Contact property for details **Station**: Box Hill & Westhumble 2ml, by quiet lane and then along estate drive (past Bagden Lodge)

**NT properties nearby** Box Hill, Clandon Park, Claremont Landscape Garden, Dapdune Wharf, Hatchlands Park

---

# PRINCES RISBOROUGH MANOR HOUSE

Princes Risborough HP17 9AW                                  Buckinghamshire
**Tel** 01494 528051 (Regional Office)

---

A 17th-century red-brick house with Jacobean staircase

- House (hall, drawing room and staircase) & front garden, only by written appointment with the owner, April to Oct: Wed 2.30–4.30

- £1.20. No party reduction. Public car park 50m

- Admitted by arrangement with the owner

- (2:E4) Opposite church, off market square [165: SP806035] **Bus**: Arriva The Shires 323/4 High Wycombe-Aylesbury (passing close ≅ Aylesbury) **Station**: Princes Risborough 1ml

**NT properties nearby** Hughenden Manor, West Wycombe Park and Village

---

**There are special events at most Trust properties; telephone 0870 458 4000 for details**

## PRIORY COTTAGES 🏠                                       Oxfordshire

1 Mill Street, Steventon, Abingdon OX13 6SP
**Tel** 01793 762209 (Coleshill Estate Office)

Former monastic buildings, now converted into two houses. South Cottage contains the Great Hall of the original priory

- 🅾 April to end Sept: Wed 2–6 by written appointment with tenant. **Note**: Only the Great Hall in South Cottage is shown

- 💷 £1. No party reduction. No WC. Unsuitable for coach parties

- ➡ (2:C4) 4ml S of Abingdon, on B4017 off A34 at Abingdon West or Milton interchange on corner of The Causeway and Mill Street, entrance in Mill Street [164: SU466914] **Bus**: Stagecoach in Oxford 32A, Oxford Bus 35A Oxford–🚆 Didcot Parkway (passing close 🚆 Oxford) **Station**: Didcot Parkway 5ml **Cycle**: NCN 5 3ml

**NT properties nearby** Ashdown House, Greys Court, Watlington Hill, White Horse Hill

---

## QUEBEC HOUSE 🏠                                                            Kent

Westerham TN16 1TD · **Tel** 01372 453401 (Regional Office)

General Wolfe spent his early years in this gabled, red-brick 17th-century house. The low-ceilinged, panelled rooms contain memorabilia relating to his family and career and the Tudor stable block houses an exhibition about the Battle of Quebec (1759)

**Note**: The property is administered and maintained on the Trust's behalf by a tenant

- 🅾 2 April to 29 Oct: Tues & Sun 2–6. Parties by written arrangement with the tenant

- 💷 £2.60; child £1.30; family £6.50. Booked parties £2.20 (inc. exhibition). Public car park 150m E of house

- ♿ Public parking about 60m to east, ramped access to pavement leading past front gates to level side entrance. House: ground floor accessible (portable ramps on request). Garden: accessible

- 👆 Opportunities to touch on request

- 🚫 No picnicking

- ➡ (2:G6) At E end of village, on N side of A25, facing junction with B2026 Edenbridge road [187: TQ449541] **Bus**: Metrobus 246 🚆 Bromley North–Edenbridge (passing 🚆 Bromley S) **Station**: Sevenoaks 4ml; Oxted 4ml

**NT properties nearby** Chartwell, Emmetts Garden, Ightham Mote, Knole

---

For all your information needs check our website www.nationaltrust.org.uk

## RIVER WEY & GODALMING NAVIGATIONS AND DAPDUNE WHARF

Surrey

Navigations Office and Dapdune Wharf, Wharf Road, Guildford GU1 4RR
**Tel** 01483 561389 · **Fax** 01483 531667 · **Email** riverwey@ntrust.org.uk

The Wey was one of the first British rivers to be made navigable, and opened to barge traffic in 1653. This 15½ml waterway linked Guildford to Weybridge on the Thames, and thence to London. The Godalming Navigation, opened in 1764, enabled barges to work a further 4ml upriver. Dapdune Wharf in Guildford is the home of *Reliance*, a restored Wey barge with an interactive exhibition telling the story of the waterway, the people who lived and worked on it and the barges built there

**What's new in 2002**: A hands-on discovery room in the old Gunpowder Store, where visitors can try their hand at lifting a load, tie a nautical knot and find out more about cargoes carried on the Wey

- **Dapdune Wharf**: 23 March to 3 Nov: Thur to Mon and Tues 4 June 11–5. River trips 11–5 (conditions permitting).

- Dapdune Wharf: £2.50; child £1.50; family £6.50; reduced rate for booked groups. Separate charge for river trips on electric launch (sponsored by Panasonic Batteries) subject to weather conditions. Charge applies to children over 1yr and NT members; max. 12 passengers. Navigations: the entire 19½ml towpath is open to walkers and moorings for visiting boats: no charge. Navigation licences (inc. all lock tolls) payable on all craft are issued for the year; visitor passes issued for up to 21 days. NT members have 10% reduction on production of current membership card for visitor passes only. There are insurance and safety requirements and restrictions on engine size to protect the property; check with Navigations Office in advance. Horse-drawn boat trips on narrow boat Iona (tel. 01483 414938); rowboats, punts, canoes and narrow boats at Farncombe Boat House (tel. 01483 421306); restaurant boats, excursion boats, rowboats and canoes at Guildford Boat House (tel. 01483 504494)

- Booked guided tours of Dapdune Wharf for groups, also guided walks; tel. for details

- Small shop run by volunteers at Dapdune Wharf

- Main exhibition at Dapdune Wharf: Wey barge accessible with care. Some parts of towpath and some fishing sites accessible, details from Navigations Office

- Braille and large-print guides

- Small servery (drinks, ice creams) run by volunteers at Dapdune Wharf, normally open as wharf. Riverside picnic areas. Also Farncombe Boathouse Tea-room (not NT); tel. 01483 418769 for details

- Baby-changing facilities at Dapdune Wharf, children's trails, colouring corner

- Education centre can be booked for slide talks or school sessions with NT staff, using handling collection and children's costumes. Worksheets, teachers' pack and GNVQ information sheets. School parties by appointment only

**Please remember – your membership card is always needed for free admission**

SOUTH AND SOUTH EAST · **155**

🚲 Cyclists welcome, but the towpath is very narrow and cyclists are asked to give way to other users and to dismount in lock areas

🐕 On leads within lock areas; elsewhere under control

➡ (2:E6/F6) Dapdune Wharf is on Wharf Road to rear of Surrey County Cricket Ground, off Woodbridge Rd (A322), Guildford. Car park, also easy access from town centre on foot via towpath; tel. Navigation Office for details. Access to rest of Navigations from A3 & M25. Visiting craft can enter from the Thames at Shepperton or slipways at Guildford or Pyrford. Visitor moorings available at Dapdune Wharf and along towpath side of Navigations [186:SU993502]
**Station**: 🚆 Addlestone, Byfleet & New Haw, Guildford, Farncombe & Godalming all close to the Navigations

**NT properties nearby** Clandon Park, Hatchlands Park, Shalford Mill

## RUNNYMEDE 🚤 🚶 ♿                                                       Surrey
Egham · **Tel** 01784 432891 · **Fax** 01784 479007 · **Email** runnymede@ntrust.org.uk

Runnymede is an attractive area of riverside meadows, grassland and broadleaved woodland, rich in diversity of flora and fauna, and part-designated a Site of Special Scientific Interest. It was on this site, in 1215, that King John sealed Magna Carta, an event commemorated by the American Bar Association Memorial and John F. Kennedy Memorial. Also here are the Fairhaven Lodges, designed by Lutyens. On the opposite bank of the Thames from Runnymede lies the important archaeological site of Ankerwycke, an area of parkland acquired by the National Trust in 1998 and containing the remains of the 11th-century St Mary's Priory and the Ankerwycke Yew, a magnificent tree believed to be over 2000 years old

**Note**: The information given below relates to the Runnymede side of the river

🅾 All year. Riverside grass car park: April to 30 Sept: daily when ground conditions allow, 9–7. Tea-room car park (hard-standing) daily all year: 8.30–5, later in summer

£ Fees payable for parking (free to NT members displaying membership cards). Fishing: day permits only; all year except 15 March to 15 June; tickets available from riverbank. 24-hr mooring, fees payable, inc. NT members

🚶 Hand-held self-guided audio 'wand' tour for hire. Leaflet available. Extensive programme of guided walks throughout the year; tel. for details

🛍 Small shop in tea-room

♿ Riverbank: good access for vehicles in summer. Memorials: access difficult. Meadows & tea-room: limited access by arrangement. Riverboats provide for people with disabilities. Contact Warden for further information

✋ Braille guide

☕ Not NT. April to end Sept: daily 8.30–5.30; Oct to end March 2003: daily (closed 25 Dec) 9.30–4.30. Coach parties welcome by arrangement (tel. 01784 477110)

🚲 Cycling permitted on Thames Path

**For general enquiries, please telephone 0870 458 4000**

## 156 · SOUTH AND SOUTH EAST

➡ (2:F5) Runnymede: on the Thames, 2ml W of Runnymede Bridge, on S side of A308 (M25, exit 13), 6ml E of Windsor. Ankerwycke: 3ml E of Windsor, 2ml W of Staines off B376 Staines to Wraysbury road, 1½ml from M25 (exit 13) [176: TQ007720] **Bus**: Ashford Coaches 305 Staines–Colnbrook, alight Magna Carta Lane. Nightingale Coaches 560 Slough–Wraysbury Village, alight Village Green **Station**: Egham ½ml from Runnymede; Wraysbury 1ml from Ankerwycke **Cycle**: NCN 4 (Runnymede only)

**NT properties nearby** Claremont Landscape Garden, Cliveden, River Wey Navigations

---

## ST JOHN'S JERUSALEM 🏠 ✝ ❋      Kent
Sutton-at-Hone, Dartford DA4 9HQ · **Tel** 01372 453401 (Regional Office)

A large garden, moated by the River Darent. The chapel was once the east end of a Knights Hospitaller Commandery church built in the 13th century, of which the remainder was converted into a private residence. Access to the chapel only. The tranquil garden contains some magnificent trees

**Note**: The property is occupied as a private residence and is administered and managed by a tenant on the Trust's behalf

🅾 3 April to 30 Oct: Wed 2–6. **Note**: only the former chapel and garden are open

💷 £1; child 50p; family £2.25

♿ Garden: accessible

➡ (2:H5) 3ml S of Dartford at Sutton-at-Hone, on E side of A225. Turn into entrance gate near 'Ernest Doe'; parking 500m at end of drive [177: TQSS8703] **Bus**: Arriva Kent Thameside 413–5 from ☒ Dartford **Station**: Farningham Road ¾ml **Cycle**: NCN 1 2¾ml

---

## SANDHAM MEMORIAL CHAPEL ✝      Hampshire
Burghclere, nr Newbury RG20 9JT · **Tel/Fax** 01635 278394
**Email** sandham@ntrust.org.uk

This red-brick chapel was built in the 1920s for the artist Stanley Spencer to fill with murals inspired by his experiences in WW1. Influenced by Giotto's Arena Chapel in Padua, Spencer took five years to complete what is arguably his finest achievement. The chapel is set amidst lawns and orchards with views across Watership Down

**Note**: As there is no lighting in the chapel, it is best to view the paintings on a bright day

🅾 March & Nov: Sat & Sun; 23 March to 3 Nov: daily except Mon & Tues (but open BH Mons and Tues 4 June); Dec to Feb 2003: by appointment only. *Times*: March & Nov 11–4; April to end Oct 11–5

💷 £2.80. No party reduction. Parking in lay-by opposite chapel

---

**Please see the area introductions for details of coast & countryside properties**

SOUTH AND SOUTH EAST · 157

- ♿ Wheelchair users can enter through main gates; access via grass ramp. Chapel: accessible via steps; portable ramp
- 👁 Braille and large-print guides
- 🍴 Picnicking on front lawn. Refreshments 100m away at Carpenter's Arms (not NT), 11–3; tel. 01635 278251 (parties must book)
- 🐕 On leads only
- ➜ (2:C6) 4ml S of Newbury, ½ml E of A34 [174: SU463608] **Bus**: Burghfield minicoaches 123/4 from Newbury (passing close ☒ Newbury) **Station**: Newbury 4ml

**NT properties nearby** Basildon Park, The Vyne

---

## SCOTNEY CASTLE GARDEN AND ESTATE

Lamberhurst, Tunbridge Wells TN3 8JN                            Kent
**Tel** 01892 891081 · **Fax** 01892 890110 · **Email** scotneycastle@ntrust.org.uk

One of England's most romantic gardens, designed in the picturesque style around the ruins of a 14th-century moated castle. There are rhododendrons and azaleas in profusion, with wisteria and roses rambling over the old ruins. Wonderful vistas and viewpoints abound and there are beautiful woodland and estate walks

**What's new in 2002**: Extended weekend opening hours – now open 11–6

- 🅾 **Garden**: 23 March to 3 Nov: daily except Mon & Tues (but open BH Mons and closed Good Fri) 11–6, last admission 1hr before closing. **Old Castle**: May to 15 Sept: days and times as garden. **Estate**: walks and car park open all year
- £ £4.40; child £2.20; family £11. Booked parties £3.80 (no party reduction on Sat, Sun or BH Mons). Car park and estate walks: no charge
- 🛍 As garden (tel. 01892 890912)
- ♿ Garden: very steep in places; wheelchair users need strong companion; manual wheelchairs available
- 👁 Tape, Braille and large-print guides free. Herb garden; roses
- 🍴 Picnicking adjacent to car park and in the parkland
- 👶 Baby-changing facilities. Children's quiz
- 🚶 Estate walkers' guide on sale at garden entrance and shop
- 🚲 Racks in car park
- 🐕 Guide dogs are permitted in the garden. Dogs on leads welcome on estate walks
- ➜ (2:H7) 1ml S of Lamberhurst on A21 [188: TQ688353] **Bus**: Tunbridge Wells Heritage Hopper from ☒ Tunbridge Wells weekends and certain other days May–Sept; otherwise Coastal Coaches 256 Tunbridge Wells–Wadhurst (passing ☒ Tunbridge Wells), alight Lamberhurst Green, 1ml **Station**: Wadhurst 5½ml

**NT properties nearby** Bateman's, Bodiam Castle, Sissinghurst Castle Garden

*Unless indicated, last admission is always 30 mins before closing time*

## SHALFORD MILL  Surrey

Shalford, nr Guildford GU4 8BS · **Tel** 01483 561389

A large 18th-century watermill on the River Tillingbourne, given in 1932 by a group of anonymous NT benefactors calling themselves 'Ferguson's Gang'

**Note**: Owing to fire regulations, visitors cannot go higher than the first floor

- **O** Daily 10–5
- **£** Free but donations in the box (emptied daily) most welcome. No parking at property. Children must be accompanied by an adult
- **→** (2:F6) 1½ml S of Guildford on A281 opposite Sea Horse Inn [186:TQ001476] **Bus**: Arriva Surrey & W Sussex 21/4/5, 32, 53, 63 from Guildford (pass close ≋ Guildford) **Station**: Shalford (U) ½ml; Guildford 1½ml

**NT properties nearby** Clandon Park, Dapdune Wharf and the River Wey Navigations, Hatchlands Park

---

## SHEFFIELD PARK GARDEN  East Sussex

Sheffield Park TN22 3QX · **Tel** 01825 790231 · **Fax** 01825 791264
**Email** sheffieldpark@ntrust.org.uk

A magnificent landscape garden, laid out in the 18th century by 'Capability' Brown and further developed in the early years of the 20th century by its owner, Arthur G. Soames. The centrepiece is the original four lakes. There are dramatic shows of daffodils and bluebells in spring, and the rhododendrons, azaleas and stream garden are spectacular in early summer. Autumn brings stunning colours from the many rare trees and shrubs. Enjoy winter walks in this garden for all seasons

- **O** Jan & Feb: Sat & Sun; March to 22 Dec: daily except Mon (but open BH Mon). *Times*: Jan, Feb, Nov & Dec 10.30–4; March to Oct 10.30–6 (closes dusk if earlier); last admission 1hr before closing. **Events**: Easter egg hunt; bat walk; bird walk; garden tours; teddy bears' picnic; children's trail. Please tel. for details
- **£** £4.80; child £2.40; family £12. Pre-booked parties only £4
- Booked tours for groups of 10+: tel. for rates
- As garden; tel. 01825 790655
- Disabled parking near entrance. Garden: accessible, except woodland path beyond lower lakes; most paths firm and level; 3 self-drive vehicles and 4 wheelchairs. Recommended route map
- Water sounds; scented trees and shrubs (especially mid May to early June)
- Restaurant (not NT) and picnic area by car park; no picnics in garden

BLUEBELLS

SOUTH AND SOUTH EAST · 159

- 👶 Baby-changing facilities; all-terrain pushchair and back carriers. Children's tree trail guide
- 🐕 On leads and only in car park
- ➡️ (2:G7) Midway between East Grinstead and Lewes, 5ml NW of Uckfield, on E side of A275 (between A272 & A22), ½ml from Sheffield Park station (Bluebell Rly) [198: TQ415240] **Bus**: Bluebell Rly link from ⛉ East Grinstead to Kingscote, thence train to Sheffield Park; RDH 121 from Lewes (passing close ⛉ Lewes) (Sat only); 246 from Uckfield (Mon–Fri only); otherwise RDH 31 ⛉ Haywards Heath–⛉ Uckfield), alight Chailey Crossroads, 1¾ml **Station**: Sheffield Park (Bluebell Rly) ¾ml; Uckfield 6m; Haywards Heath 7ml

**NT properties nearby** Nymans Garden, Standen, Wakehurst Place

---

## SISSINGHURST CASTLE GARDEN 🏠 🏡 ✿ ⛱ Kent

Sissinghurst, nr Cranbrook TN17 2AB · **Tel** 01580 710700
**Infoline** 01580 710701 · **Fax** 01580 710702 · **Email** sissinghurst@ntrust.org.uk

One of the world's most celebrated gardens, the creation of Vita Sackville-West and her husband Sir Harold Nicolson. Developed around the surviving parts of an Elizabethan mansion with a central red-brick prospect tower, a series of small, enclosed compartments, intimate in scale and romantic in atmosphere, provide outstanding design and colour through the season. The study, where Vita worked, and library are also open to visitors

**Note**: The library and Vita Sackville-West's study close each day at 5.30. Tower and library opening may be restricted early and late season. Please phone to check details. No tripods or easels in the garden. Visitors are asked not to smoke in the garden and to switch off mobile telephones before entering

**What's new in 2002**: Changed opening times

- 🅾️ 23 March to 3 Nov: daily except Wed & Thur. *Times*: Mon, Tues & Fri 11–6.30; Sat, Sun & BHols 10–6.30. Last admission 1hr before closing, ½hr before dusk if earlier. **Events**: Painting in the garden, artists with easels Wed & Thur £15. Please phone for further details tel. 01580 710700
- 💷 £6.50. Coaches and parties by appointment only. Contact Bookings Secretary, tel. 01580 710700 or fax 01580 710702
- 🛍️ 23 March to 3 Nov: daily except Wed & Thur 11–5.30; autumn and Christmas shopping 6 Nov to 24 Dec 10.30–4.30, daily except Mon & Tues, for details tel. 01580 710703
- ♿ Disabled drivers may park near ticket office. Disabled visitors may be set down at ticket office. Garden: paths narrow and uneven, so admission restricted to 2 wheelchair users at a time. Unsuitable for large powered vehicles; if transfer to a manual wheelchair is impossible tel. in advance. Wheelchairs. Plan of wheelchair route. Restaurant on two levels & shop: accessible. Christmas shopping 1–24 Dec daily except Mon & Tues park by shop

**For all your information needs check our website www.nationaltrust.org.uk**

## 160 · SOUTH AND SOUTH EAST

- Braille garden plan and guide. Scented plants and flowers; herb garden. Trained companions for visually impaired visitors may be available; tel. in advance
- Granary Restaurant (licensed – no spirits) 23 March to 3 Nov daily except Wed & Thur 11–5.30. Christmas shopping 6 Nov to 22 Dec daily except Mon & Tues 11–4. Christmas menu 1–24 Dec. Lecture lunches from 6 Nov. Picnics in car park or in front of garden entrance. Tel. 01580 710704
- Not ideal for children. No pushchairs admitted, as paths are narrow and uneven but baby carriers available. No children's games in garden. Baby changing facilities
- Racks and lock-up facilities. Bridlepaths approved for use by cycles. Cycle hire at Tonbridge and Canterbury stations (discount for train passengers)
- No dogs in garden or picnic areas, but on leads in surrounding areas
- (2:I7) 2ml NE of Cranbrook, 1ml E of Sissinghurst village (A262) [188: TQ8138] **Bus**: Arriva Kent & E Sussex 4/5 Maidstone–Hastings (passing ≋ Staplehurst), alight Sissinghurst, 1¼ml. Direct bus link operating mid-May to Aug BH, Tues & Sun (tel. 01580 710700 for info) **Station**: Staplehurst 5½ml

**NT properties nearby** Bateman's, Bodiam Castle, Scotney Castle Garden, Smallhythe Place, Stoneacre

## SMALLHYTHE PLACE 🏠✿🛡 Kent

Smallhythe, Tenterden TN30 7NG · **Tel/Fax** 01580 762334
**Email** smallhytheplace@ntrust.org.uk

An early 16th-century half-timbered house, home of the Victorian actress Ellen Terry from 1899 to 1928, and containing many personal and theatrical mementoes. The charming cottage grounds include her rose garden and the Barn Theatre, which is open most days by courtesy of the Barn Theatre Society

- 23 March to 3 Nov: daily except Thur & Fri (but open Good Fri) 11–5; last admission 4.30 or dusk. **Note**: The Barn Theatre may be closed some days at short notice
- £3.20; child £1.60; family £8. Pre-booking for coach parties essential. No coach parties in Aug
- Braille and large-print guides; touch list; pictorial album

**Please remember – your membership card is always needed for free admission**

- Restaurant and picnic area (not NT) at Tenterden Vineyard Park, 500m from property
- Children's quiz; children must be accompanied by an adult
- (2:I7) 2ml S of Tenterden, on E side of the Rye road (B2082) [189: TQ893300] **Bus**: Arriva Kent & Sussex 12 ≋ Rye–Tenterden **Station**: Rye 8ml; Appledore 8ml; Headcorn 10ml

**NT properties nearby** Bodiam Castle, Scotney Castle Garden, Sissinghurst Castle Garden

## SOUTH FORELAND LIGHTHOUSE — Kent

St Margaret's at Cliffe · **Tel** 01304 852463 · **Fax** 01304 205295
**Email** southforeland@ntrust.org.uk

A distinctive landmark used by Marconi for his first ship-to-shore radio experiments

- 1 March to 31 Oct: daily 11–5.30; July & Aug daily 11–5.30
- £2; child £1; family £5; booked groups £1.50. No access to lighthouse by car; visitors must walk from main car park situated at Langdon Cliffs (2ml) or from St Margaret's village or bay
- Range of souvenirs
- Limited parking (tel. in advance) but no access up tower (spiral staircase)
- Sympathetic Hearing Scheme
- Exhibition
- Teachers' pack; fact sheets on various subjects; Key stages 1 & 2
- (2:L6) **Bus**: Stagecoach in E. Kent 90, 91, 111, 211 Dover– St Margaret's, then ½ml **Station**: Dover Priory 2½ml

**NT properties nearby** The White Cliffs of Dover

## SPRIVERS GARDEN — Kent

Horsmonden TN12 8DR · **Tel** 01372 453401 (Regional Office)

A small formal garden with walled and hedged compartments, herbaceous borders and a rose garden

**Note**: This property is administered and maintained on the Trust's behalf by a tenant

- 25 May, 1 & 22 June: 2–5
- £2; child £1; family £5. Parking limited; space for one coach only. No WC
- (2:H7) 3ml N of Lamberhurst on B2162 [188: TQ6940] **Bus**: Arriva Kent & Sussex/Nu-Venture 297 ≋ Tunbridge Wells–Tenterden **Station**: Paddock Wood 4ml

**NT properties nearby** Scotney Castle Garden, Sissinghurst Castle Garden

**For general enquiries, please telephone 0870 458 4000**

## STANDEN    West Sussex

East Grinstead RH19 4NE · **Tel** 01342 323029 · **Fax** 01342 316424
**Email** standen@ntrust.org.uk

A family house built in the 1890s, designed by Philip Webb, friend of William Morris, and a showpiece of the Arts & Crafts Movement. It is decorated throughout with Morris carpets, fabrics and wallpapers, complemented by contemporary paintings, tapestries and furniture. The house retains many of its original electrical fittings. The beautiful hillside garden gives fine views over the Sussex countryside and there are delightful woodland walks

**What's new in 2002**: New presentation of kitchen. New information and exhibition space. Lifelong learning and school education programme

- **House**: 23 March to 3 Nov: daily except Mon & Tues (but open BH Mons and 4 June). *Times*: 11–5. **Garden**: 23 March to 3 Nov: daily except Mon & Tues (but open BH Mons & 4 June); 8 Nov to 15 Dec: Fri, Sat & Sun. *Times*: 23 March to 3 Nov 11–6; 8 Nov to 15 Dec 11–3. **Note**: Property may close for short periods on Sun and BHols to avoid overcrowding. **Events**: 'Behind the Scenes' Tues 17 Sept, 'Putting the House to Bed', lecture lunches, carol concerts; send s.a.e. or tel. for details

- £5.50; family £13.75. Garden only £3. Joint ticket with same-day entry to Nymans Garden £9, available Wed to Fri. Groups £4.50 Wed to Fri only, if booked in advance; other times by arrangement with Property Manager. Parking 180m

- By special arrangement

- 23 March to 3 Nov: as house 11–5; 8 Nov to 15 Dec: Fri, Sat & Sun 11–3. Shop specialises in Arts & Crafts Movement merchandise

- Close parking for disabled drivers. House: ground floor accessible, but some steps; wheelchairs. Garden: partly accessible but on hillside, so steps and steep slopes; gravel paths. Restaurant & shop: accessible

- Braille guide to house and garden; descriptive and touch tours, advance notice helpful. Scented plants and flowers. Guided tours by arrangement. Large-print guide available

- Licensed restaurant (offering 'historical' menu) 23 March to 3 Nov: as house 11–5; 8 Nov to 15 Dec: as shop (light refreshments only). Picnics in lower car park and picnic area

- 2 reins, 2 baby carriers suitable for children aged up to 16 months; no baby back-carriers or pushchairs in house

**Please see the area introductions for details of coast & countryside properties**

SOUTH AND SOUTH EAST · **163**

- Adult and school education groups welcome; tel. for details
- Cycles can be left near ticket kiosk
- On leads and only in lower car park; under close control on woodland walks (via lower car park)
- (2:G7) 2ml S of East Grinstead, signposted from B2110 (Turners Hill road) [187: TQ389356] **Bus**: Metrobus 84 East Grinstead–Crawley (passing Three Bridges), alight at approach road just north of Saint Hill, ½ml, or at Saint Hill, thence ½ml by footpath **Station**: E Grinstead 2ml; Kingscote (Bluebell Rly) 2ml **Cycle**: NCN 21 1¼ml

**NT properties nearby** Nymans Garden, Sheffield Park, Wakehurst Place

## STONEACRE           Kent
Otham, Maidstone ME15 8RS · **Tel/Fax** 01622 862157

A half-timbered yeoman's house with a great hall and crownpost, dating from the late 15th century and surrounded by a delightful recently restored cottage garden

**Note**: This property is occupied as a private residence and is administered and maintained on the Trust's behalf by a tenant

**What's new in 2002**: Open Bank Holiday Mondays

- 23 March to 16 Oct: Wed & Sat 2–6; but open BH Mons 2–6, last admission 5
- £2.60; child £1.30; family £6.50. Booked groups £2.20. Car park 100m; drive narrow, unsuitable for coaches. No WC
- Rose gardens; other scented plants
- (2:I6) At N end of Otham village, 3ml SE of Maidstone, 1m S of A20 [188: TQ800535] **Bus**: Arriva Kent & E Sussex 13 Maidstone–Hollingbourne (passing close Maidstone E & W), alight Otham, ½ml **Station**: Bearsted 2ml

**NT properties nearby** Scotney Castle Garden, Sissinghurst Castle Garden

## STOWE LANDSCAPE GARDEN           Buckinghamshire
Buckingham MK18 5EH
**Tel** 01280 822850 · **Infoline** 01494 755568 · **Fax** 01280 822437
**Email** stowegarden@ntrust.org.uk

One of the finest Georgian landscape gardens, made up of valleys and vistas, narrow lakes and rivers with more than 30 temples and monuments designed by many of the leading architects of the 18th century. At the centre is Stowe House (not NT), occupied by Stowe School, and all around is Stowe Park. The creation of the Temple family, Stowe has been described as 'a work to wonder at' in its size, splendour and variety. Many of the garden buildings have now been conserved, and thousands of new trees and shrubs have been planted in recent years. Work continues on this as well as on the house itself

**Unless indicated, last admission is always 30 mins before closing time**

**Note**: Stowe House and the deer park are undergoing restoration with the support of the Heritage Lottery Fund

**What's new in 2002**: Four newly restored monuments: the Fane of Pastoral Poetry and Lord Cobham's Monument in the garden, and the Conduit House and Wolfe's Obelisk in the park. Restoration of the North Front and Colonnades of the house

**Gardens**: 2 March to 22 Dec: daily except Mon & Tues (open BH Mons and Tues 4 June) (closed Sat 25 May). *Times*: March to Oct 10–5.30; last admission 4. Nov and Dec 10–4, last admission 3 (opening times may vary; tel. to check 01280 818282/818280). **Note**: Visitors should allow plenty of time as gardens are extensive. Gardens may close in bad weather; tel. to check. **House**: (not NT) 21 March to 14 April: 10 July to 6 Sept: daily except Mon & Tues, 12–5pm, last admission 4; 30 Oct to 3 Nov and 18 to 22 Dec: daily except Mon & Tues, 11–3, last admission 2 (tel. 01280 818282 or 818280). **It may be necessary to close the house at times when it is being used for private functions, please tel. to check. Events**: for details send s.a.e. to Box Office, Stowe Gardens 01280 823334. Licensed for civil weddings, tel. 01280 818809 for details

£ Gardens £4.80; child £2.40; family £12. House (inc. NT members) £3. Group visits must be pre-booked, tel. garden 01280 822850, house 01280 818282

Guided tours by arrangement. Group visits to house by arrangement throughout the year, tel. 01280 818282

Gift shop, open as gardens

Gardens: unsuitable for manual wheelchairs and private battery-powered vehicles; self-drive powered 2-seaters, booking essential. Tea-room: accessible

Braille and tape guides; raised maps

Licensed tea-room as gardens 10.30–5, Nov and Dec Sat & Sun 12–3. Parties of 20+ must pre-book, tel. 01280 815819

Highchairs

School visits welcomed

Lockable cycle posts in car park

On leads only

→ (2:D2) 3ml NW of Buckingham via Stowe Avenue, off A422 Buckingham–Banbury road [152: SP665366] **Bus**: Stagecoach Express X5 Cambridge–Oxford (passing ≋ Milton Keynes Central & Bicester North); Jeffs 32 from Milton Keynes (passing close ≋ Milton Keynes Central); Arriva The Shires 66 from Aylesbury (passing close ≋ Aylesbury). On all, alight Buckingham, thence 3ml

**NT properties nearby** Claydon House, Waddesdon Manor

OXFORD BRIDGE AND LODGE

---

**There are special events at most Trust properties; telephone 0870 458 4000 for details**

# UPPARK

West Sussex

South Harting, Petersfield GU31 5QR · **Tel** 01730 825415
**Infoline** 01730 825857 · **Fax** 01730 825873 · **Email** uppark@ntrust.org.uk

A fine late 17th-century house set high on the South Downs with magnificent sweeping views to the sea. An extensive, award-winning exhibition tells the dramatic story of the 1989 fire and restoration of the house and its collections. The elegant Georgian interior houses a famous Grand Tour collection that includes paintings, furniture and ceramics. An 18th-century dolls' house with original contents is one of the star items in the collection. The complete servants' quarters in the basement are shown as they were in Victorian days when H.G. Wells' mother was housekeeper. The beautiful and peaceful garden is now fully restored in the early 19th-century 'picturesque' style, in a downland and woodland setting

- 24 March to 31 Oct: daily except Fri & Sat.
  *Times*: **Grounds, exhibition, garden, shop & restaurant**: 11–5. **House**: 1–5. Last admission to house 4.15 (opens 11 on BH Mons and 12 on Suns in Aug). On BH Suns & BH Mons and Suns in Aug, entry to house is by timed ticket (inc. NT members). **Events**: tel. for details

- £5.50; family £13.75. Groups weekdays only and must book

- Booked group guided tours: by arrangement, tel. for details

- As grounds, from 11. Christmas opening: tel. for details.

- Disabled visitor drop-off points. House: accessible, lift to basement. Stairlift to upper floor of exhibition. Garden: accessible. Shop: accessible. Wheelchairs. Disabled visitors advised to tel. in advance

- Braille guide to house; items to handle available from stewards

- Licensed restaurant as grounds from 11. Picnic areas near car park and in woodland

- Front carriers available on loan, no back carriers. No pushchairs on Suns & BH Mons; changing facilities; highchairs. Children's guide, hands-on items in exhibition

- On leads and only in car park and on woodland walk (**no shade in car park**)

- (2:E8) 5ml SE of Petersfield on B2146, 1½ml S of South Harting [197: SU775177] **Bus**: Stagecoach Sussex Bus 54 ➤ Petersfield–➤ Chichester, not Sun **Station**: Petersfield 5½ml

**NT properties nearby** Harting Down, Hinton Ampner, Petworth

## THE VYNE                                                              Hampshire

Sherborne St John, Basingstoke RG24 9HL · **Tel** 01256 883858
**Infoline** 01256 881337 · **Fax** 01256 881720 · **Email** thevyne@ntrust.org.uk

Built in the early 16th century for Lord Sandys, Henry VIII's Lord Chamberlain, the house acquired a classical portico in the mid-17th century (the first of its kind in England) and contains a fascinating Tudor chapel with Renaissance glass, a Palladian staircase and a wealth of old panelling and fine furniture. The attractive grounds feature herbaceous borders and a wild garden, with lawns, lakes and woodland walks

**What's new in 2002**: New visitor route, car park and lavatories. Volunteer-driven buggy service. Woodland access from car park and new woodland leaflet. Restored Summerhouse open to visitors for first time. Refurbished restaurant opens late spring

- **House**: 23 March to 3 Nov: daily except Thur & Fri 11–5 (but open Good Fri). **Grounds**: weekends in Feb & March 11–5; 23 March to 3 Nov: daily except Thur & Fri 11–5 (but open Good Fri). **Events**: for details tel. 01256 883858. **Weddings and functions**: Stone Gallery licensed for civil weddings. Receptions, private and corporate functions in Brewhouse Restaurant or Walled Garden. All enquiries welcome: tel. 01256 883858

- £6.50; family £16.25. Grounds only £3. Parties (Mon, Tues & Wed only) £5. Joint party ticket with West Green House Garden £9 (Mon & Tues only)

- As grounds Feb & March 11–3; 23 March to 3 Nov 11–5. Also Christmas shopping 14 Nov to 22 Dec, Thur, Fri, Sat & Sun 1–4.

- Volunteer-driven buggy service. House: ground floor accessible via ramps. Garden, lawns & lake: accessible. Shop, tea-garden & restaurant: accessible. Wheelchairs at ticket office and house. New purpose-built WC for disabled visitors

- Braille guide. Touch tours available. Scented plants

- During the refurbishment of the Brewhouse Restaurant, there will be only limited catering facilities until May. Open as grounds Feb & March 11–3; 23 March to 1 May 11–5. Special feature Easter weekend: hog roast. Licensed Brewhouse Restaurant (increased capacity and improved facilities), open as grounds. 4 May to 3 Nov 11–5. Also 14 Nov to 22 Dec Thur, Fri, Sat & Sun. Christmas lunches 12/13/14/19/20/21 Dec (bookings only). Coach parties by arrangement only, tel. for details. Picnics in car park field only

- Baby-changing facilities at car park and restaurant WCs

**Please remember – your membership card is always needed for free admission**

SOUTH AND SOUTH EAST · **167**

🐕 On leads and only in car park and Morgaston Wood

➔ (2:D6) 4ml N of Basingstoke between Bramley and Sherborne St John. From Basingstoke Ring Road, follow Basingstoke District Hospital signs until property signs are picked up. Follow A340 Aldermaston Road towards Tadley. Right turn into Morgaston Road. Right turn into Vyne Road [175 & 186: SU637566]
**Bus**: Stagecoach in Hampshire 45 from Basingstoke (passing ≢ Basingstoke)
**Station**: Bramley 2½ml; Basingstoke 4ml

**NT properties nearby** Basildon Park, Sandham Memorial Chapel, West Green House

---

# WADDESDON MANOR 🏠 ♣ ♠ ☻ 🔔   Buckinghamshire
Waddesdon, nr Aylesbury HP18 0JH · **Tel** 01296 653203
**Bookings** 01296 653226 · **Infoline** 01296 653211 · **Fax** 01296 653212
**Email** waddesdonmanor@ntrust.org.uk · **Web** www.waddesdon.org.uk

---

A Renaissance-style château, its towers rising above the trees, crowns a hill. This ensemble was created by Baron Ferdinand de Rothschild in the 1870s for his house parties. The unique collection of 18th-century French objects includes buttons, gold boxes, cabinets, carpets and porcelain. There are 18th-century English faces in the magnificent Gainsborough portraits, as well as paintings by Bakst. The mature gardens, famous for specimen trees, a colourful parterre and striking seasonal displays, also offer naturalised bulbs and wildflowers in grassland. The rococo revival Aviary houses breeding pairs of exotic birds. The wine cellars contain thousands of bottles of vintage Rothschild wines. Since 1996 Waddesdon has won many awards for its immaculate restoration and for the quality of its shops and visitor services

**Note**: All visitors inc. NT members require timed tickets to enter the House, available from the Ticket Office. In order to enjoy Waddesdon to the full, visitors should allow at least one-and-a-half hours to tour the House and another hour for the garden. Last recommended admission to the House 2.30

**What's new in 2002**: Illustrated biography of Manor; Baron's Walk; 3-D carpet bedding for the Queen's Jubilee; exotic planting; edible bedding; the Rothschild wine story

⭕ **Grounds (inc. gardens, aviary, restaurant & shops)**: 27 Feb to 22 Dec: daily except Mon & Tues (open BH Mons and Tues 4 June) 10–5 (sculpture in garden uncovered week before Easter, weather permitting). **House (inc. wine cellars)**: 27 March to 3 Nov: daily except Mon & Tues (open BH Mons and Tues 4 June) 11–4. **Note**: Entry is by timed ticket, available from 10am on a first-come, first-served basis from the ticket office. Tickets can be booked 24hrs+ in advance Mon to Sun 10–4, tel. 01296 653226 (booking charge £3 per transaction).
**Bachelors' Wing**: 27 March to 3 Nov: Wed, Thur & Fri 11–4; space is limited and entry cannot be guaranteed. Children welcomed under parental supervision, babies must be carried in front slings. **Events**: study days, floodlit opening, wine tastings, children's and other activities throughout the year; for details tel. 01296 653226. Conference and wedding enquiries 01296 653243

**For general enquiries, please telephone 0870 458 4000**

**168** · SOUTH AND SOUTH EAST

[£] Grounds: (inc. gardens, aviary, restaurant & shops): £3; child £1.50; family £7.50; 6 Nov to 22 Dec: free. House: £7; child £6. Bachelors' Wing: £1. Audio tour £1. To visit the House a grounds ticket must be purchased

[i] Drop-in presentations on the Rothschilds, Waddesdon & Wine in the Powerhouse. Free accompanied walks around the garden including 'Meet the Keeper' and 'Wildlife Walks'. Guidebooks (French & German), workshops, courses and special events for families, individuals and groups; for details tel. 01296 653226

[🛍] Gift and wine shops 27 Feb to 22 Dec: daily except Mon & Tues (but open BH Mons and Tues 4 June) 10–5. Mail order tel. 01296 653247. Online shop www.waddesdon.org.uk

[♿] Disabled visitors may be set down at house. House: accessible, lift to first floor. (Bachelors' Wing Wine Cellars not accessible to wheelchairs). Garden: accessible, some gravel; free route map. Restaurant & shops: accessible, but Stables approached via steep incline. Wheelchairs for House and garden, but for safety reasons only 2 allowed on each floor at a time

[👁] Braille and audio guides (in English and French) to House. Scented plants and trees

[☕] **Manor Restaurant**: waitress service 27 Feb to 22 Dec, Wed to Sun (open BH Mons and Tues 4 June) 10–5. **Stables Restaurant**: assisted service 27 March to 3 Nov, Wed to Sun (but open BH Mons and Tues 4 June) 10–5. The Stables Restaurant can be booked by groups. **Summer-house**: al fresco snacks open in good weather

[👶] Baby-changing facilities. Children's garden. Children's trails and events

[🐕] Only guide dogs and only in the grounds; some shaded parking

[→] (2:D3) Access via Waddesdon village, 6ml NW of Aylesbury on A41; M40 (westbound) exit 6 or 7 via Thame & Long Crendon or M40 (eastbound) exit 9 via Bicester [165: SP740169] **Bus**: Arriva The Shires 16/17 from Aylesbury (passing close ≋ Aylesbury) **Station**: Aylesbury 6ml; Haddenham & Thame Parkway 9ml

**NT properties nearby** Claydon House, King's Head Aylesbury, Stowe Gardens

**Please see the area introductions for details of coast & countryside properties**

## WAKEHURST PLACE 🏛️❀🛡️  West Sussex

Ardingly, nr Haywards Heath RH17 6TN · **Tel** 01444 894066 · **Fax** 01444 894069
**Email** wakehurst@kew.org · **Web** www.kew.org

Often described as Kew's country garden, Wakehurst Place contains a series of ornamental features with many plants from across the world providing year-round colour and interest. Extensive woodlands, including an informal arboretum and secluded valley, offer delightful walks. Information about the garden and its many interesting features is available within the Elizabethan mansion. The Loder Valley nature reserve may also be visited by permit (24 hours' notice required)

**Note**: Wakehurst Place is administered and maintained by the Royal Botanic Gardens, Kew; tel. 01444 894066 for up-to-date information

**What's new in 2002**: The Wellcome Trust Millennium Building, adjacent to Wakehurst Place, aims to house seeds from ten per cent of the world's flora by 2009, to save species from extinction in the wild. Enjoy the Millennium Seed Bank interactive public exhibition in the Orange Room and follow the journey of a seed from identification and collection, through to drying and cold storage in the massive underground vaults. Entry free for NT members, and included in gardens entry fee

- 🅾 Daily (closed 25 Dec & 1 Jan). *Times*: Feb & Oct 10–5; March 10–6; April to end Sept 10–7; Nov to end Jan 2003 10–4. **Note**: Mansion closes 1 hr before gardens. **Events**: tel. for information about all events. NT members may be charged for some events

- £ £6.50, concessions £4.50, under-17s free. Discounts for booked groups of 10+. Parking 400m from mansion. Exhibition in mansion

- 🚶 Guided tours available Tues, Thur, Sat, Sun & BHols: tel. 01444 894004 for times & availability. Booked tours on request; write to Administrator

- 🛍 Garden and gift shops (Kew Enterprises)

- ♿ Disabled visitors may be set down at the mansion by arrangement. Upper garden: largely accessible; steep paths elsewhere. Wheelchairs available. Restaurant: ramped access. Shop: one shallow step

- 👃 Year-round scents

- ☕ Licensed self-service restaurant (not NT) open all year, closes 1 hr before garden. Picnics welcome in gardens

- 🚼 Baby-changing rooms in all WCs

- 🎓 Contact Education Officer (tel. 01444 894094)

- 🚲 Rack in car park

- 🐕 Only guide dogs permitted

- ➡ (2:G7) 1½ml NW of Ardingly, on B2028 [187: TQ339314] **Bus**: Metrobus 81, 82, 88 🚂 Haywards Heath–🚂 Crawley or 🚂 East Grinstead **Station**: Balcombe 5ml; Haywards Heath 6ml; E Grinstead 6½ml; Horsted Keynes (Bluebell Rly) 3¾ml

**NT properties nearby** Nymans Garden, Sheffield Park, Standen

**Unless indicated, last admission is always 30 mins before closing time**

## WEST GREEN HOUSE GARDEN  Hampshire
West Green, Hartley Wintney RG27 8JB · **Tel/Fax** 01252 844611

A delightful series of walled gardens surrounding a charming 18th-century house. The largest features herbaceous beds with wonderful colour combinations and a superb ornamental kitchen garden. In the areas of the Nymphaeum and the Lake Field new restoration work is ongoing and, at the discretion of the lessee, restrictions are frequently necessary for the development and protection of the garden

**Note: The property has been leased by the Trust by way of a long-term private tenancy agreement and the house is not open to visitors. The lessee has kindly agreed to the opening of the gardens and is responsible for all arrangements and facilities (see below for access arrangements for NT members). There are limited visitor facilities**.

- 27 April to 1 Sept: Wed to Sun 11–4.30. Also weekends in Sept 11–4.30. **Note**: Entry is free to NT members on Wed only and NT groups **who can book Mon & Tues only (normally not open days)**. **Events**: send s.a.e. for details
- £4. No reduction for groups, which must book in advance, except for group joint tickets with The Vyne at £9 (combined full-rate is £11) available Mon & Tues only
- Garden: steps and gravel paths
- Simple refreshments only; picnics in the old orchard. Group lunches by arrangement
- (2:D6) 1ml W of Hartley Wintney, 10ml NE of Basingstoke, 1ml N of A30 [175: SU745564] **Bus**: Stagecoach in Hampshire 200 Basingstoke–Camberley (passing ☒ Winchfield), alight Phoenix Green 1ml **Station**: Winchfield 2ml

**NT properties nearby** Basildon Park, Sandham Memorial Chapel, The Vyne

---

## WEST WYCOMBE PARK  Buckinghamshire
West Wycombe HP14 3AJ · **Tel** 01494 513569

A perfectly preserved rococo landscape garden, created in the mid-18th century by Sir Francis Dashwood, founder of the Dilettanti Society and the Hellfire Club. The house is among the most theatrical and Italianate in England, its façades formed as classical temples. The interior has Palmyrene ceilings and decoration, with pictures, furniture and sculpture dating from the time of Sir Francis

**Note**: The West Wycombe Caves and adjacent café are privately owned and NT members must pay admission fees

- **Grounds only**: 1 April to 31 May: Sun to Thur & BHols 2–6. **House & grounds**: 1 June to 31 Aug: daily except Fri & Sat, 2–6. Weekday: entry by guided tour every 20 mins (approx). Last admission 5.15
- House & grounds £4.80; child £2.40; family £12. Grounds only £2.60. Groups by arrangement; no reductions. Parking 250m from house

---

**There are special events at most Trust properties; telephone 0870 458 4000 for details**

SOUTH AND SOUTH EAST · 171

- Tours of house on weekdays. Tours of grounds by written arrangement
- Designated parking 150m from house. House: some access to ground floor. Grounds: limited access; some steep slopes. Wheelchair (please book)
- Braille guide
- Refreshments at West Wycombe Garden Centre (not NT). No picnics in park
- On leads in car park only
- (2:E4) At W end of West Wycombe, S of the Oxford road (A40) [175: SU828947] **Bus**: Wycombe Bus 275 High Wycombe–Oxford; 331/2, 340/1 High Wycombe–Thame (all pass close ⮕ High Wycombe) **Station**: High Wycombe 2½ml

**NT properties nearby** Hughenden Manor, West Wycombe Village

## WEST WYCOMBE VILLAGE AND HILL  Buckinghamshire
West Wycombe · **Tel** 01494 528051 (Regional Office)

This Chilterns village comprises buildings spanning several hundred years, with particularly fine examples from the 16th to 18th centuries. The hill, with its fine views, is surmounted by an Iron Age hill-fort and is part of the original landscape design of West Wycombe Park. It is now the site of a church and the Dashwood Mausoleum

**Note**: The church, mausoleum and caves do not belong to the National Trust

- All year. Parking at top of hill and in village. Village architectural trail leaflet from village store (50/51 High St) and newsagent (36/37 High St)
- George and Dragon and Swan public houses.
- (2:E4) 2ml W of High Wycombe, on both sides of A40. Public transport: as for West Wycombe Park [175:SU828946]

**NT properties nearby** Bradenham Village, Hughenden Manor, West Wycombe Park

## THE WHITE CLIFFS OF DOVER  Kent
Langdon Cliffs, nr Dover CT16 1HJ · **Tel** 01304 202756 · **Fax** 01304 205295
**Email** whitecliffs@ntrust.org.uk

The White Cliffs of Dover are internationally famous. The 'Gateway to the White Cliffs' visitor centre has spectacular views and introduces the visitor to five miles of coast and countryside through imaginative displays and interpretation. Much of the chalk downland along the clifftops is an SSSI, AONB and Heritage Coast with interesting flora and fauna, and the visitor centre is an excellent place to watch the world's busiest shipping lanes

**Note**: The Gateway visitor centre is sponsored by Saga Group Ltd

- **Car park**: daily 9–6 (closes later in summer); **Gateway visitor centre**: 1 March to 31 Oct: daily 10–5; 1 Nov to 28 Feb 2003 (closed 25 Dec) 11–4. **South Foreland Lighthouse**: see page 161

**For all your information needs check our website www.nationaltrust.org.uk**

## 172 · SOUTH AND SOUTH EAST

- £ Car park £1.50; 75p concession (NT members free). Coaches £5. Lighthouse: see page 161
- Range of souvenirs
- Parking adjacent to visitor centre which is fully accessible; WC. Accessible path to viewpoint. Lighthouse: see page 161
- Sympathetic Hearing Scheme
- Coffee shop in visitor centre. Serves a range of drinks, ice creams, snacks and light lunches to eat in or take away. Coach parties welcome. Functions and corporate events by arrangement
- Parent and baby room. High-chairs and children's menu
- Key Stages 1 & 2 packs
- Cycle racks
- Under close control at all times (stock grazing)
- (2:K7) From A2/A258 roundabout take road to Dover Castle, turn left at brown sign to Upper Road before Castle Hill [138: TR336422] **Bus**: Stagecoach in E Kent 91 (Suns); otherwise 100, 200 Dover–Margate to within ½ml. Also local open-top bus tour **Station**: Dover Priory 2½ml **Cycle**: NCN 1 50m

**NT properties nearby** Bockhill Farm, Kingsdown Leas, South Foreland Lighthouse, St Margaret's Leas

---

## WINCHESTER CITY MILL                                      Hampshire

Bridge Street, Winchester SO23 8EJ · **Tel/Fax** 01962 870057
**Email** winchestercitymill@ntrust.org.uk · **Web** www.winchestercitymill.co.uk

Spanning the River Itchen, this water-powered corn mill has had a chequered past. Rebuilt in 1744, it remained a working watermill until the turn of the century and has recently been restored to full working order. Milling demonstrations throughout the season, and something to delight everyone, including impressive mill-races and pretty island garden

**What's new in 2002**: New exhibition display and working models

- O 1 March to 30 June: Wed to Sun and BH Mons; 1 July to 31 Aug: daily; 1 Sept to 4 Nov: Wed to Sun. *Times*: 11–5
- £ £2, family £5. No party reduction. Parking in public car park, 200m
- Groups by arrangement
- 1 March to 30 June: Wed to Sun and BH Mons; 1 July to 31 Aug: daily; 1 Sept to 4 Nov: Wed to Sun; 5 Nov to 24 Dec: daily. *Times*: March to end Oct 11–5; Nov & Dec 9–5
- Access difficult; many steps
- Braille guide; some items may be touched; sound of rushing water. Informal talks can be arranged

**Please remember – your membership card is always needed for free admission**

SOUTH AND SOUTH EAST · 173

- Exploratory family quiz and fun hands-on displays. Video and guide sheets for adults and children
- School groups welcome by appointment
- Stands
- (2:C7) At foot of High Street, beside City Bridge [185: SU487294] **Bus**: From surrounding areas **Station**: Winchester 1ml

**NT properties nearby** Hinton Ampner, Mottisfont Abbey

## WINKWORTH ARBORETUM                                    Surrey
Hascombe Road, Godalming GU8 4AD · **Tel** 01483 208477 · **Fax** 01483 208252
**Email** winkwortharboretum@ntrust.org.uk

A hillside woodland, created in the 20th century and now containing over 1,000 different shrubs and trees, many of them rare. The most impressive displays are in spring with magnolias, bluebells and azaleas, and in autumn for stunning colours. There are two lakes and wildlife in abundance. For details of seasonal events and 'plant of the month' tel. or consult website

**Note**: The car park is only for visitors to the arboretum

**What's new in 2002**: 2002 marks the 50th anniversary of the Trust's ownership of Winkworth Arboretum. Special events are being organised. A new guidebook is also available from the shop

- Daily during daylight, but may be closed if weather bad (especially in high winds)
- £3.50; child £1.75; family £8.75. Discounts for groups of 10 or more. Coach parties must book in writing with Head of Arboretum to ensure parking space
- Guided tours (10+) £2 extra per person. All groups must book in writing to Head of Arboretum
- 23 March to 17 Nov: daily except Mon & Tues (but daily during bluebell and autumn colour times) 11–4 or dusk if earlier; 17 Nov to 15 Dec and 13 Jan to 23 March 2003: Sat & Sun 11–5 or dusk. (**Note**: Open all BH Mons, but may be closed in bad weather especially high winds)
- Viewpoint: accessible from upper car park via level paths. Lake & boathouse: access (ramp) from lower entrance gate (tel. in advance for key). Adapted WC (RADAR key)
- Scented trees and shrubs; water sounds, birdsong
- Tea-room for light refreshments as shop (tel./fax 01483 208265 when tea-room open). Picnickers welcome
- Baby-changing facilities. Children's quiz
- Racks
- On leads only

**For general enquiries, please telephone 0870 458 4000**

→ (2:F7) Near Hascombe, 2ml SE of Godalming on E side of B2130. Discount for cycle and public transport users. [169/170/186: SU990412] **Bus**: Arriva Surrey & W Sussex 42/4 Guildford–Cranleigh (passing close ≷ Godalming) **Station**: Godalming 2ml

**NT properties nearby** Clandon Park, Devil's Punchbowl Café, Oakhurst Cottage, River Wey and Dapdune Wharf, Witley Centre, open countryside at Witley and Hindhead

---

## THE WITLEY CENTRE               Surrey

Witley Centre, Witley, Godalming GU8 5QA
**Tel** 01428 683207 · **Fax** 01428 685040 · **Email** witleycentre@ntrust.org.uk

A purpose-built visitor education centre surrounded by a fascinating mix of woodland and heath. The Centre, with its countryside exhibition, also hosts school groups and children's holiday activities

**Centre**: 23 March to 3 Nov: daily except Mon. *Times*: Tues to Fri 11–4, Sat, Sun & BHols 11–5. Common and car park: all year. **Events**: Fun days and children's holiday events; tel. for details

Free. Parking 100m from centre

Small shop in centre with limited range of souvenirs

Centre: ground floor accessible. Nature trail accessible with strong companion. Batricar available

Braille guides to Witley and Milford Commons. Touch table

Ice creams and soft drinks. Picnic tables

Educational parties by arrangement with West Weald Education Officer (tel. 01428 683207)

Racks outside centre

Under close control

→ (2:E7) 7ml SW of Guildford between London–Portsmouth A3 and A286 roads, 1ml SW of Milford [186: SU9341] **Bus**: Stagecoach in Hants & Surrey/Coastline 70 Guildford–Midhurst, 71 Guildford–Haslemere (both passing close ≷ Godalming & passing ≷ Haslemere) **Station**: Milford 2ml

**NT properties nearby** Black Down, Devil's Punch Bowl Café, Frensham, Ludshott and Selborne, Oakhurst Cottage, Winkworth Arboretum, large areas of open countryside at Hindhead

# Introduction to London

The National Trust owns a surprisingly wide range of buildings in the London area, from elegant town houses like **Carlyle's House** in Chelsea to the 17th-century splendour at **Ham House** and to Southwark's **George Inn**, still a working pub. Equally, these span the many centuries of the area's role as a major settlement and economic centre, from the remains of the '**Roman' Bath** in Strand Lane to Ernö Goldfinger's seminal 1930s house in Hampstead, **2 Willow Road**.

Many of the Trust's London properties date from the time when the countryside was still within sight of the heart of the city. Large estates such as **Osterley Park** are green lungs in the midst of suburbia, and **Sutton House** in Hackney, once part of a small village, is now ideally located for its role as a centre for the Trust's work in inner city schools.

Despite being one of the world's major conurbations, London still contains green and relatively tranquil areas. The Trust has played a major role in securing fragments of the city's once extensive common land, including **East Sheen Common** (not far from **Ham House**) and **Chislehurst Common**. Nearby at **Petts Wood** and **Hawkwood** there are attractive areas of heath, farm and woodland with fine walks. Interesting features of an ancient agricultural landscape can be seen at **Morden Hall Park** and there are woods and open grassland at **Selsdon Wood** near Croydon. At **Watermeads**, managed as a nature reserve, on the River Wandle at Mitcham (key for latter may be obtained from the Property Manager, for a small annual fee), there is a fascinating wetland and river environment.

**OS grid references for properties with no individual entry (OS map series numbers given in brackets)**

| | | |
|---|---|---|
| Chislehurst Common | [177] | TQ440700 |
| East Sheen Common | [176] | TQ197746 |
| Hawkwood | [177] | TQ441690 |
| Petts Wood | [177] | TQ450681 |
| Selsdon Wood | [177] | TQ357615 |
| Watermeads | [176] | TQ274677 |

### Highlights for Visitors with Disabilities ...
Particularly recommended are the accessible paths through the rose garden and along the river at **Morden Hall Park**.

### ... and for Families
Lots of space to run around and play at **Osterley Park**.

HAM HOUSE

### Further Information
Please contact the Membership Department, PO Box 39, Bromley, Kent BR1 3XS. Tel. 0870 458 4000. Email: enquiries@thenationaltrust.org.uk

**Unless indicated, last admission is always 30 mins before closing time**

## BLEWCOAT SCHOOL GIFT SHOP   London (Westminster)
23 Caxton Street, Westminster SW1H 0PY · **Tel/Fax** 020 7222 2877

Built in 1709 by a local brewer to provide an education for poor children and in use as a school until 1926. It is now the NT London Gift Shop and Information Centre

- Daily except Sat & Sun (closed BHols) 10–5.30. Thur only 10–7. Christmas opening: Sats 16, 23, 30 Nov, 7, 14, 21 Dec
- Free
- Access difficult, several steps
- (2:G5) Near the junction with Buckingham Gate. Frequent local services (tel. 020 7222 2877)
[176:TQ295794] **Bus**: Frequent local services (020 7222 1274) **Station**: Victoria ¼ml **Underground**: St James's Park, 100m **Cycle**: NCN 4 ¾ml

**NT properties nearby** Carlyle's House, Fenton House, 2 Willow Road

## CARLYLE'S HOUSE   London (Kensington & Chelsea)
24 Cheyne Row, Chelsea SW3 5HL
**Tel** 020 7352 7087 · **Infoline** 01494 755559 · **Fax** 020 7352 5108
**Email** carlyleshouse@ntrust.org.uk

In a quiet and beautiful residential area of London, this Queen Anne house was the home of Thomas Carlyle, the 'Sage of Chelsea', for some 47 years until his death in 1881. The skilful Scottish home-making of his wife Jane is much in evidence: the Victorian period decor, the furniture, pictures, portraits and books are all still in place. As an historian, social writer, ethical thinker and powerful public speaker, Thomas is honoured in the house, while Jane's strong belief in his genius and her own brilliant wit and gift for writing are recognised in the many existing letters. Their academic and domestic lives can be experienced today in the evocative atmosphere of the house

- 23 March to 3 Nov: daily except Mon & Tues (open BH Mons and Tues 4 June): Wed, Thur & Fri: 2–5; Sat, Sun and BH Mon: 11–5. **Events**: Send s.a.e. for details
- £3.60; child £1.80
- Groups welcome; introductory talk can be booked in advance
- Not suitable for wheelchairs: 4 steps up from pavement to front door, 2 steps down from hall to garden door, 3 steps down from door into garden, 1 step up from paved area to garden level. Narrow halls, steep stairs (73 stairs from bottom to top)

**There are special events at most Trust properties; please telephone 0870 458 4000 for details**

LONDON · 177

→ (2:F5) Off Chelsea Embankment between Albert and Battersea Bridges. NT sign on corner of Cheyne Row. Or via Kings Rd and Oakley St. NT sign on corner of Upper Cheyne Row. [176: TQ272777] **Bus**: 11, 19, 22, 49, 239 **Station**: Victoria 1½ml Underground: Sloane Square and South Kensington **Cycle**: NCN 4

**NT properties nearby** Blewcoat School NT Shop, Fenton House, 2 Willow Road

## EASTBURY MANOR HOUSE

Barking IG11 9SN   London (Barking & Dagenham)
**Tel** 020 8507 0119 · **Fax** 020 8507 0118

An important example of a medium-sized brick-built Elizabethan manor house. The house is architecturally distinguished and well preserved. Recent restoration has revealed notable wall paintings. Described by Daniel Defoe in *A Tour Through the Whole Island of Great Britain* as 'where tradition says the Gunpowder Treason Plot was first contrived'. The house is managed by the London Borough of Barking and Dagenham

**Note**: From Jan to Dec 2002 the East Wing of the building will be closed to the public for major development works

○ 2 March to 7 Dec: first Sat in every month except Aug 10–4. **Events**: Guided tours, tea-room exhibitions, displays and activities; tel. for details. Corporate and private hire. Licensed for civil weddings; tel. for rates

£ £1.90; child 65p; family £4.50. Concessions £1. Group visits by arrangement; tel. for details. Evening tours also available

♿ House: ground floor accessible: Garden: accessible

Braille guide

As house

Teachers' resource book. School visits by arrangement

On leads and only in garden

→ (2:G5) In Eastbury Square, 10min walk S from Upney station [177: TQ457838] **Bus**: TLT 287, 368 ⇌ Barking–Rainham/Chadwell Heath (tel. 020 7222 1234) **Station**: Barking, then one stop on Underground District line to Upney ¼ml

**NT properties nearby** Rainham Hall

## FENTON HOUSE

London (Camden)

Windmill Hill, Hampstead NW3 6RT · **Tel/Fax** 020 7435 3471
**Infoline** 01494 755563 · **Email** fentonhouse@ntrust.org.uk

A late 17th-century house with an outstanding collection of porcelain and early keyboard instruments, most of which are in working order. The delightful walled garden includes fine displays of roses, an orchard and a vegetable garden

**For all your information needs check our website www.nationaltrust.org.uk**

**Note**: For audition to use the early keyboard instruments, apply in writing one month in advance to the Keeper of Instruments, c/o Fenton House

**What's new in 2002**: Website

- 🅞 2 to 17 March: Sat & Sun 2–5; 23 March to 3 Nov: daily except Mon & Tues (open BH Mons and Tues 4 June). *Times*: 2–5; weekends & BHols 11–5. Parties at other times by appointment. Short guides available in French, German, Italian and Japanese. **Events**: for details of summer concerts and other events send s.a.e.

- £ £4.40; child £2.20; family £11. Booked parties of 15+ £3.70. No parking facilities. Joint ticket with 2 Willow Road £6.30

- 🯅 Demonstration tours (max. 20) of instruments by the Keeper, 29 March, 25 April, 30 May, 6 June (young persons' tour), 4 July, 1 Aug, 3 & 24 Oct at 2pm. Porcelain tours 18 April, 16 May, 12 Sept, 10 Oct at 11am. £10 (inc. NT members), 1½–2hrs; apply to Custodian

- ♿ Ground floor: accessible. Garden: can be seen from upper walk. For access use entrance on Hampstead Grove. Photograph album of upper floors and garden

- 👁 Braille guide, large-print short guide

- 🯅 Children's quiz

- 🎵 Tape of music played on Benton Fletcher Collection of Instruments available for hire (£1) during visit

- ➔ (2:G4) Visitors' entrance on W side of Hampstead Grove [176:TQ262860]
  **Bus**: Frequent local services (tel. 020 7222 1234). Underground: Hampstead 300m **Station**: Hampstead Heath 1ml

**NT properties nearby** Carlyle's House, Sutton House, 2 Willow Road

---

## GEORGE INN 🍺                                          London (Southwark)

The George Inn Yard, 77 Borough High St, Southwark SE1 1NH
**Tel** 020 7407 2056

---

The last remaining galleried inn in London, famous as a coaching inn during the 17th century and mentioned by Dickens in *Little Dorrit*. Leased to a private company and still in use as a public house

- 🅞 During licensing hours

- 🍽 Bar food daily; à la carte restaurant Mon to Fri & Sat evening; tel. for reservations

- 🯅 Children admitted subject to normal licensing regulations

- 🐕 On leads and only in courtyard

- ➔ (2:G5) On E side of Borough High Street, near London Bridge Stn
  [176:TQ326801] **Bus**: Frequent local services (tel. 020 7222 1234)
  **Station**: London Bridge 🚊 & Underground, few mins walk **Cycle**: NCN 4 300m

---

**Please remember – your membership card is always needed for free admission**

# HAM HOUSE  London (Richmond-upon-Thames)

Ham, Richmond TW10 7RS · **Tel** 020 8940 1950 · **Fax** 020 8332 6903
**Email** hamhouse@ntrust.org.uk

Ham House is unique in Europe as the most complete survival of 17th-century fashion and power. It was built in 1610 and then enlarged in the 1670s when it was at the heart of Restoration court life and intrigue. The garden is significant as one of the few formal gardens to survive the English Landscape Movement in the 18th century. The garden restoration, begun in 1973, has influenced recent restorations of some of the great gardens in Europe

**What's new in 2002**: An exhibition about the history and development of the garden accompanied by a video of the history of the house in the 18th-century Dairy buildings; opening of the interior of the earliest identified Still House in England; development of a 17th-century kitchen garden with the produce served in the Orangery restaurant

- **House**: 23 March to 3 Nov: daily except Thur & Fri 1–5 (open Good Fri). **Garden**: all year: daily except Thur & Fri 11–6 or dusk if earlier. Closed 25, 26 Dec & 1 Jan. **Events**: Open-air concerts during the summer. Jubilee events including a garden party; house and ghost tours; school holiday family events; tel. for details 020 8940 1950. Great Hall licensed for weddings, Orangery and surrounding gardens for receptions, also corporate functions: contact Functions Manager, tel. 020 8332 6644

- Formal gardens with Ice House, Still House, Dairy and exhibition: £2, child £1, family £5; House (with over 20 historic rooms on view) formal gardens and outbuildings: (as above), £6, child £3, family £15. Discount for pre-booked groups of 15+. Free parking 400m (not NT)

- Guided tours of house and gardens available by arrangement

- 23 March to 3 Nov daily except Thur & Fri 11–5.30; March, Nov and Dec weekends 11–4. Special Christmas shop, contact shop manager tel. 0208 948 2035

- Parking near house. Gardens: level access to all areas but some deep gravel. Powered single-seater; tel. to book. Tea-room: ramped access. Shop: accessible. House: steps to front, stairclimber available; small lift to all floors on request. Two wheelchairs available

- Braille guide to house. Scented plants

- Sympathetic Hearing Scheme

- Orangery tea-room (licensed) with historic menus, home-grown produce and tea terrace 23 March to 3 Nov, daily except Thur & Fri 11–5. March, Nov and Dec, weekends 11–4. Christmas lunches in Dec. Special rates for weekday group bookings with separate room for coach parties, tel. 020 8940 0735

- Children welcome: baby-changing facility, reins and slings available for house. Quiz. Highchairs, children's menu (inc. home-made vegetarian option). Special events, tel. for details.

- School visits all year round, teachers' guide available. Special areas offered in Stuart life, Victorian domestic life and arts events and activities, contact Administrative Assistant, tel. 020 8940 1950
- Rack on north terrace
- (2:F5) On S bank of Thames, W of A307, between Richmond and Kingston; Ham gate exit of Richmond Park, readily accessible from M3, M4 and M25 [176: TQ172732] **Bus**: TfL 65 Ealing Broadway–Kingston, alight Ham Polo Ground, Petersham Rd, 15 mins walk down historic avenues; 371 Richmond station–Kingston, alight Royal Oak pub, 10 mins walk Ham (tel. 020 7222 1234) **Station**: Richmond & District line Underground 1½ml via Thames towpath, 2ml by road; Kingston 2ml. **Cycle**: NCN 4 passes entrance. Also seasonal foot/bike ferry Twickenham (Marble Hill House).

**NT properties nearby** Claremont Landscape Garden, Morden Hall Park, Osterley Park

---

## LINDSEY HOUSE   London (Kensington & Chelsea)
100 Cheyne Walk SW10 0DQ · **Tel** 01494 528051 (Regional Office)

Built on the former site of Sir Thomas More's garden and now part of Cheyne Walk. The house claims one of the finest 17th-century exteriors in London

- The ground-floor entrance hall, main staircase to first floor, and the front and rear gardens open by written appointment only: 15 May, 12 June, 11 Sept & 9 Oct 2–4. Write (enclosing s.a.e.) to The Secretary, 100 Cheyne Walk, London SW10 0DQ
- Free. No parking (nearest car park Battersea Park, south of Thames)
- (2:G5) On Cheyne Walk, W of Battersea Bridge near junction with Milman Street on Chelsea Embankment [176: TQ268775] **Bus**: Frequent local service (tel. 020 7222 1234) **Station**: Victoria 1¾ml **Underground**: South Kensington 1¼ml **Cycle**: NCN 4

**NT properties nearby** Carlyle's House, Fenton House, 2 Willow Road

---

## MORDEN HALL PARK   London (Merton)
Morden Hall Road, Morden SM4 5JD · **Tel** 020 8648 1845 · **Fax** 020 8687 0094
**Email** mordenhall@ntrust.org.uk

A green oasis in the heart of London suburbia, this former deer park has an extensive network of waterways, ancient hay meadows, an impressive avenue of trees and an interesting collection of old estate buildings. The workshops now house local craftworkers, whose work is on show, and there is an independently managed city farm on Bunce's Meadow

- **Park**: all year during daylight. **Note**: Car park by the café/shop and garden centre closes at 6. **Events**: 4–6 May, Craft Fair; details from Four Seasons Events (tel. 01276 679419). There is a charge for all visitors to the fair, inc. NT members

---

**Please see the area introductions for details of coast & countryside properties**

- £ Free
- 🚶 Free guided walks and talks monthly and guided tours by arrangement; contact Property Office
- 🏛 Daily (closed 25, 26 Dec & 1, 15 & 16 Jan 2003) 10–5 (tel. 020 8687 0881). Garden centre run by Capital Gardens plc as National Trust tenants (tel. 020 8646 3002). Craft workshops closed on Tues
- ♿ Wheelchair path through rose garden and beside river. Café, shop & garden centre: accessible. 2 wheelchairs on request
- 🔊 Flowing water sounds by mill
- ☕ Licensed café daily (closed 25, 26 Dec & 1 Jan 2003) 10–5 (tel. 020 8687 0881)
- 👶 Baby-changing facilities. Highchairs
- 🏫 Snuff Mill Environmental Centre for educational groups, nature club and holiday activities; contact Education Officer (tel. 020 8542 4232)
- 🚴 8 cycle spaces in car park
- 🐕 On leads around buildings, paths and picnic area; under close control elsewhere
- ➡ (2:G5) Off A24, and A297 S of Wimbledon, N of Sutton [176: TQ259687] **Bus**: Frequent from surrounding areas (tel. 020 7222 1234) Tramlink: Phipps Bridge ½ml. Underground: Morden 500m

**NT properties nearby** Claremont Landscape Garden, Ham House

## OSTERLEY PARK London (Hounslow)

Jersey Road, Isleworth TW7 4RB · **Tel** 020 8232 5050 · **Infoline** 01494 755566
**Fax** 020 8232 5080 · **Email** osterley@ntrust.org.uk

In 1761 the founders of Child's Bank commissioned Robert Adam to transform a crumbling Tudor mansion into an elegant neo-classical villa. This was their house in the country, created for entertainment and to impress friends and business associates. Today the spectacular interiors contain one of Britain's most complete examples of Adam's work. The magnificent 16th-century stables survive largely intact and are still in use. The house is set in extensive park and farm land, complete with Pleasure Grounds and garden buildings

**What's new in 2002**: The Jersey Galleries feature contemporary art in a programme of exhibitions from April to Oct, admission free. Artist in residence – please tel. 020 8232 5050 for information

🕐 **House**: 2 to 24 March: Sat & Sun; 27 March to 3 Nov: daily except Mon & Tues (closed Good Fri but open BH Mons and Tues 4 June). *Times*: 1–4.30. **Jersey Galleries**: as house. **Grand Stables**: Sun afternoons in summer. **Park & Pleasure Grounds**: daily 9–7.30 or sunset if earlier. **Note**: Park closes early before major events. Car park closed Good Fri & 25, 26 Dec. **Events**: for details of annual summer concerts and other events tel. 01494 755572

**Unless indicated, last admission is always 30 mins before closing time**

**£** House £4.40; child £2.20; family £11. Park & Pleasure Grounds free. Parties £3.80, must pre-book. Discounts for house visitors arriving by public transport with valid LT travelcard: non-members £1 off adult ticket, adult NT members receive £1 voucher towards guidebook or cream tea. Coach-parking free, otherwise car park £2.50

**👤** Booked out-of-hours 'Private View' with morning coffee Wed to Fri mornings £8 per person (inc. NT members). Minimum charge £120. Groups with own guide must book

**🏛** 2 to 24 March: Sat & Sun; 27 March to 3 Nov: daily except Mon & Tues (closed Good Fri but open BH Mons and 4 June) 1–5.30. 6 Nov to 22 Dec: daily except Mon & Tues 12–4; (tel. 020 8232 5062)

**♿** Car park 250m from house; electric shuttle takes less mobile visitors to house, shop and tea-room when house open. House: access via stairclimber (notify car park staff on arrival). Not suitable for electric wheelchairs. Tea-room, walled tea-garden & shop: accessible. Park: level and accessible. Indoor and outdoor wheelchairs available. Self-drive powered vehicles available Wed, Thur, Sun & BH Mons and 4 June 2–5 in summer; no booking necessary. Tel. 020 8232 5050 for further details

**👁** Braille guide; staff will describe contents

**🎧** Sympathetic Hearing Scheme

**☕** 2 to 24 March: Sat & Sun; 27 March to 3 Nov: daily except Mon & Tues (closed Good Fri but open BH Mons and 4 June) 11–30–5; 6 Nov to 22 Dec: daily except Mon & Tues 12–4. Groups of 20+ must book, tel. 020 8232 5057

**👶** Baby-changing facilities in WC. No pushchairs or baby back-carriers in house. Highchairs. Children's quiz and guidebook

**🎓** Full education programme. Study base in stable block for groups of up to 60. Details from Education Coordinator (tel. 020 8232 5069 or fax 020 8232 5078)

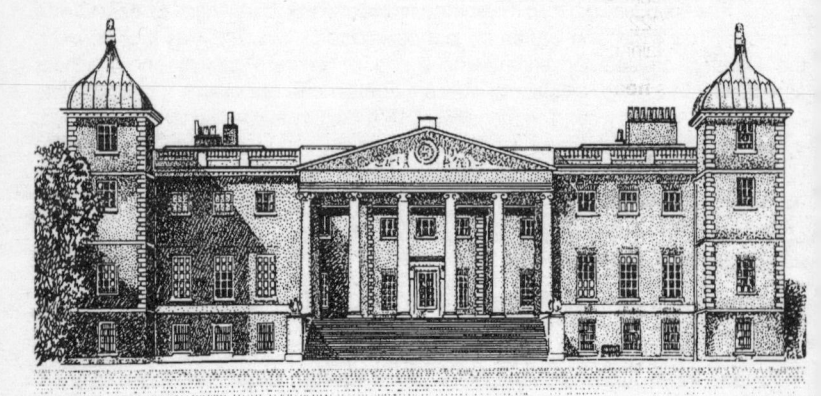

**There are special events at most Trust properties; please telephone 0870 458 4000 for details**

LONDON · **183**

🚲 Hitching posts in stableyard; links to London cycle network
🐕 Only in park and on leads unless indicated
➡ (2:F5) Follow brown tourist signs on A4 between Gillette Corner and Osterley underground station (access via Thornbury Rd & Jersey Rd); M4, Jn 3 then follow A312/A4 towards central London [176: TQ146780] **Bus**: TfL H91 Hounslow–Hammersmith, LT H28 Hounslow–Osterley (not Sun) to within ½ml (tel. 020 7222 1234). Underground: Osterley (Piccadilly line), turn left on leaving station, ½ml **Station**: Syon Lane 1½ml

**NT properties nearby** Carlyle's House, Fenton House, Ham House, 2 Willow Road

---

## RAINHAM HALL 🏠                                London (Havering)
The Broadway, Rainham RM13 9YN · **Tel** 01494 528051 (Regional Office)

An elegant Georgian house, built in 1729 to a symmetrical plan and with fine wrought iron gates, carved porch and interior panelling and plasterwork

🅾 April to end Oct: Wed & BH Mons 2–6; Sat by written appointment with tenant

💷 £2.10. No party reduction. Parking limited. No WC

♿ Please contact tenant if bringing a guide dog

➡ (2:H5) Just S of the church, 5ml E of Barking [177: TQ521821] **Bus**: Frequent local services (tel. 020 7222 1234) **Station**: Rainham, 200m

**NT properties nearby** Eastbury Manor, Sutton House

---

## 'ROMAN' BATH 🏛                                London (Westminster)
5 Strand Lane WC2 · **Tel** 020 7641 5264 · Mobile 0850 745162
**Fax** 020 7641 5215

The remains of a bath, restored in the 17th century and believed by some to be Roman

**Note**: The Bath is administered and maintained by Westminster City Council. Please note that extensive building work is being carried out to the adjacent building and the approach to the Baths is via a covered pavement.

🅾 Bath visible through window from pathway all year. Otherwise May to end Sept: every Wed 1–5 by appointment only (24hrs' notice) during office hours

---

**For all your information needs check our website www.nationaltrust.org.uk**

184 · LONDON

£ 50p. Children under 16 and OAPs 25p. No WC

→ (2:G5) Just W of Aldwych station (Piccadilly Line now closed), approach via Surrey Street [176: TQ309809] **Bus**: Frequent local services (tel. 020 7222 1234) **Station**: Blackfriars or Charing Cross, both ½ml **Underground**: Temple, not Sun, few metres; Embankment ½ml **Cycle**: NCN 4 ½ml

**NT properties nearby** Carlyle's House, The George Inn

---

## SUTTON HOUSE 🏠 🎭  London (Hackney)

2 & 4 Homerton High Street, Hackney E9 6JQ · **Tel** 020 8986 2264
**Email** suttonhouse@ntrust.org.uk

---

A unique survival in London's East End, Sutton House was built in 1535 by Sir Ralph Sadleir, a rising star at the court of Henry VIII. It became home to successive merchants, Huguenot silk-weavers, Victorian schoolmistresses and Edwardian clergy, and although altered over the years, remains an essentially Tudor house. Oak-panelled rooms and carved fireplaces survive intact and an exhibition tells the history of the house and its former occupants

○ **Historic rooms**: 6 Feb to 22 Dec and from 17 Jan 2003: Fri, Sat, Sun, BH Mons and Tues 4 June, 2–5. Lively programme of events for all ages, tel. for details of full programme. Art gallery open as historic rooms

£ £2.10; child 50p; family £4.70. Group visits by arrangement; tel. for rates

👤 Guided tours; tel. for rates

🛍 As historic rooms

♿ House: ground floor, shop and refreshment area accessible; adapted WC

👁 Braille guide; tactile items; tel. before a visit

☕ As historic rooms

👶 Family trails. Baby-changing facilities in WC

🎒 School and educational group visits by arrangement

🚲 Room for cycles on railings outside property

→ (2:G4) At the corner of Isabella Road and Homerton High Street [176: TQ352851] **Bus**: Frequent local services (tel. 020 7222 1234) **Station**: Hackney Central ¼ml; Hackney Downs ½ml **Cycle**: NCN 1 1¼ml

**NT properties nearby** Eastbury Manor, Fenton House, Rainham Hall, 2 Willow Road

---

**Please remember – your membership card is always needed for free admission**

## 2 WILLOW ROAD

London (Camden)

2 Willow Road, Hampstead NW3 1TH · **Tel/Fax** 020 7435 6166
**Infoline** 01494 755570 · **Email** 2willowroad@ntrust.org.uk

The former home of Ernö Goldfinger, designed and built by him in 1939. The central house of a terrace of three, it is one of Britain's most important examples of Modernist architecture and is filled with furniture also designed by Goldfinger. The art collection includes a number of significant British and European 20th-century works, Bridget Rileym Max Ernst and Henry Moore being represented amongst others

**Note**: 1998 London Tourism Awards Small Attraction of the Year. Extended opening until 14 Dec

- Public afternoons: 2 to 23 March, Sat only, 12–5. Last admission 4. Introductory film shown at interval throughout the afternoon. 28 March to 2 Nov: Thur, Fri & Sat 12–5, last admission 4. Visits by guided tour only. Entry by non-bookable timed ticket. Tours every 45 mins from 12.15 until 4. Tour lasts approx 1 hour inc. 15-min introductory film. 9 Nov to 14 Dec: as March. Private parties are welcome throughout the year outside public afternoon opening times. Groups must be of 4+ and must book in advance. Tel./fax/email for details

- £4.40; child £2.20; family £11. No parking at house. Limited on-street parking. East Heath Road municipal car park (100m), open intermittently. Joint ticket with Fenton House £6.30

- Walks April–Oct, every 1st Thur of month. Guided walk around Modern Movement Architecture in Hampstead, followed by optional tour of house. Meet Hampstead Underground 10.30. Walk and tour of house: £7 (NT members £5); walk only: £5 (NT members £3). Booking advisable

- Sole access to main part of house via spiral staircase. Filmed tour of house available on ground floor. Cinema equipped with induction loop. Limited parking nearby

- Braille floor plans

- (2:G4) [176:TQ270858] **Bus**: Frequent local services (tel. 020 7222 1234) **Station**: Hampstead Heath ¼ml **Underground**: Hampstead or Belsize Park ½ml

**NT properties nearby** Fenton House

# Introduction to the East of England

The East of England is characterised by wide expanses of open countryside and sweeping views under huge skies. Here also is a remote and beautiful coastline, studded with unspoilt fishing villages, ancient historical sites and internationally renowned nature reserves.

The North Norfolk coast is one of the most scenic areas of Britain, and is particularly important for its birdlife. At **Morston Marshes** and **Stiffkey Marshes** a range of seabirds can be seen, as well as seals at **Blakeney Point**. **Brancaster** is noted for its coastal flora and the site of the Roman fort of **Branodonum**. There are several National Trust-owned properties in the Sheringham area, including the highest point in Norfolk at **West Runton**, beautiful landscape and woodland at **Sheringham Park** and woods and heathland at **Beeston Regis Heath**. Spectacular views can be had from **Incleborough Hill**. Inland are the celebrated country houses and parks of **Blickling** and **Felbrigg**.

On the edge of Norfolk's famous Broads is **Horsey Mere**, where the Trust owns over 800ha (1900 acres) of marshland, marrams and farmland, as well as **Horsey Windpump**. In the past much of East Anglia was subject to regular flooding and drainage mills such as this were essential to maintain water levels. Another example can be seen at **Wicken Fen** in Cambridgeshire, a haven for rare wildlife and virtually the last remnant of the extensive fenland that once covered much of eastern England, with 18 footpath routes. The imposing Houghton Mill near Huntingdon with its riverside meadow makes an ideal spot from which to explore the wider countryside along the Riiver Great Ouse

The remote character of the east coast led to the construction of the fascinating military research buildings at **Orford Ness** in Suffolk. The Ness is also an important site for breeding and overwintering birds. There are many interesting natural habitats in this area, including **Dunwich Heath**, a surviving fragment of the sandy heaths locally known as the Sandlings, and **Minsmere Beach**, adjacent to the famous bird reserve. Further south, there are pleasant walks and fine views at **Kyson Hill** near Woodbridge, and at **Pin Mill** on the River Orwell, where a wealth of sailing boats is usually present.

The picturesque qualities of the Essex/Suffolk border became famous through the work of John Constable, and at Bridge Cottage at **Flatford** there is an exhibition of his work and a range of other facilities. Fine walks lead into the beautiful **Dedham Vale**.

There are good birdwatching opportunities on the Essex coast, especially on the reserve of **Northey Island** in the Blackwater estuary (access by advance permit only from the Warden, Northey Cottage, Northey Island, Maldon, tel. 01621 853142). **Copt Hall Marshes**, near Little Wigborough, is another noted site, particularly for overwintering birds, and can be viewed from a waymarked circular route.

The ancient landscapes of East Anglia include **Danbury** and **Lingwood Commons**, a survival of the medieval manors of St Clere and Herons and a former area of common grazing, and **Blake's Wood**, an area of hornbeam and chestnut coppice, renowned in spring for its display of bluebells. **Hatfield Forest** near Bishop's Stortford is an outstanding ancient woodland and rare surviving example of a medieval royal hunting forest offering excellent walking. All these areas are designated SSSIs and are rich in wildlife.

**Please see the area introductions for details of coast & countryside properties**

The Trust is also fortunate in owning two motte-and-bailey castles: **Darrow Wood**, near Harleston in Norfolk, and **Rayleigh Mount** in Essex, recorded in the Domesday Book and offering excellent recreational space in the heart of Rayleigh town.

East Anglia's involvement in the wool trade brought it much wealth in the past, and provided the means for building the many grand churches and buildings that dot the landscape. **St George's Guildhall** at King's Lynn and the **Guildhall of Corpus Christi** at Lavenham are two splendid examples. The other chief source of wealth was land, forming the basis of the magnificent country estates that once extended across much of eastern England. Although many of these estates were reduced dramatically in size during the 20th century, the country houses that were once their focal point can still be enjoyed. These range from the intimate red brick of moated **Oxburgh Hall**, tucked away in a remote corner of rural Norfolk, to the extravagant grandeur of **Wimpole Hall**, complete with its **Home Farm** and marvellous ark with walks to the Folly and through woodland belts.

**OS grid references for main properties with no individual entry (OS map series numbers given in brackets)**

| | | |
|---|---|---|
| Beeston Regis Heath | [133] | TG173418 |
| Blake's Wood | [167] | TL773067 |
| Copt Hall Marshes | [168] | TL981146 |
| Danbury & Lingwood Commons | [167] | TL773068 |
| Darrow Wood | [156] | TM265894 |
| Horsey Mere | [134] | TG456223 |
| Incleborough Hill | [133] | TG189423 |
| Kyson Hill | [169] | TM269477 |
| Morston Marshes | [132] | TG010445 |
| Northey Island | [168] | TL872058 |
| Pin Mill | [169] | TM214380 |
| Stiffkey Marshes | [133] | TG956439 |
| West Runton | [133] | TG184414 |

One of the National Trust's most unusual properties in this part of England is **Whipsnade Tree Cathedral**, where different species of tree have been planted in the form of a nave and transepts. There are many excellent walks to be had on the nearby downs.

Arguably one of the most underrated counties in terms of scenery, Hertfordshire offers superb opportunities for outdoors recreation in beautiful and varied landscapes. The **Ashridge Estate** has many miles of footpaths giving superb views over the Chilterns and providing access to the area's magnificent woods and chalk downland, both of which are home to many species of interesting birds and plants. At the other end of the county is the charming and evocative **Shaw's Corner**, once home to the great playwright George Bernard Shaw.

## Highlights for Visitors with Disabilities ...
Many properties have powered vehicles (see individual entries); **Wicken Fen** and **Sheringham Park** both have accessible pathways; **Orford Ness** is holding a special access day, tel. Warden on 01394 450900 for details; **Ickworth** has a special scented walk.

## ... and for Families
All NT restaurants in East Anglia have special play areas for children; there are children's playgrounds at **Blickling, Ickworth** and **Wimpole**; **Wimpole Home Farm** is a must for families with young children.

*Unless indicated, last admission is always 30 mins before closing time*

## 188 · EAST OF ENGLAND

**Further Information**
Please contact the Membership Department, PO Box 39, Bromley BR1 3XL. Tel. 0870 458 4000. Email: enquiries@thenationaltrust.org.uk

Walks leaflets are available at the following properties: Blickling, Dunwich Heath, Felbrigg, Hatfield Forest, Ickworth Park, Orford Ness, Sheringham Park, West Runton, Wicken Fen and Wimpole Hall. For leaflets on walks and events please contact the Membership Deartment.

## ANGEL CORNER                                                    Suffolk

8 Angel Hill, Bury St Edmunds IP33 1UZ
**Tel** 01284 763233 (St Edmundsbury BC) · **Fax** 01284 757137

A fine Queen Anne house, containing the parlour of the Mayor of St Edmundsbury

- By appointment only. Details from The Mayor's Secretary, St Edmundsbury Borough Council, 8 Angel Hill, Bury St Edmunds IP33 1UZ; tel. 01284 757135
- £1, inc. coffee and biscuits
- Difficult steps up to front door. Wheelchair ramp at rear by prior appointment
- Refreshments inc. in admission charge
- (3:I6) In Bury St Edmunds [155: TL855643] **Bus**: From surrounding areas **Station**: Bury St Edmunds ½ml

**NT properties nearby** Ickworth Estate, Theatre Royal

---

## ANGLESEY ABBEY AND GARDEN                                Cambridgeshire

Lode, Cambridge CB5 9EJ · **Tel/Fax** 01223 811200
**Email** angleseyabbey@ntrust.org.uk

The house, dating from 1600 and built on the site of a 12th-century priory, houses a unique collection representing the tastes of one man, Huttleston Broughton, 1st Lord Fairhaven. The many paintings include notable works by Claude Lorraine, fine examples of furniture, silver and tapestries and one of the Trust's largest collections of clocks. It is surrounded by 39ha (98 acres) of landscape garden and arboretum with over 100 pieces of sculpture. There is all-year-round floral interest in the garden with the Winter Walk and extensive snowdrop collection in January and February; hyacinth displays in the spring, herbaceous borders and dahlia gardens in the summer and magnificent autumn foliage. A working watermill regularly mills grain for sale

- **House**: 27 March to 27 Oct: daily except Mon & Tues (but open BH Mons and 4 June) 1–5. 12 noon opening for pre-booked groups. **Garden**: 27 March to 30 June: daily except Mon & Tues (but open 4 June); 1 July to 1 Sept: daily & late opening Thur to 8; 4 Sept to 27 Oct: daily except Mon & Tues 10.30–5.30. **Winter**: 30 Oct to 22 Dec, 1 Jan to 23 March 2003: daily except Mon & Tues 10.30–4.30 or dusk if earlier. **Lode Mill**: As for garden except 1–4.30; **Winter**: Sat & Sun only 11–4. **Note**: March to Oct: last admission to house and mill 4.30, 3.30 winter. Timed entry to house on Suns & BH Mons. **Closed Good Fri**. **Winter**: part of gardens only. **Events**: send s.a.e. for details

**There are special events at most Trust properties; please telephone 0870 458 4000 for details**

EAST OF ENGLAND · 189

£ £6.25, family discounts. Groups £5.25. Garden and mill only £3.85 (groups £3.35). Group visits information pack (no groups Suns & BH Mons). £3.25 winter season

🛍 As garden

♿ House: 2 ground-floor rooms accessible; photographic record of upper rooms, which are accessible via stairclimber (booking essential). Garden, Winter Walk, shop, plant centre & restaurant: accessible. Single-seat self-drive vehicles and wheelchairs. Lode Mill: ground floor accessible

👁 Braille guide to house; items to touch on request in most rooms. Winter and spring gardens heavily scented; other scented plants and shrubs

🍽 As garden. Self-service licensed restaurant. Picnic area adjacent to restaurant

👶 Children's guide. Baby slings. Children's menu, baby food, highchairs, drawing sheets; small outside play area

📖 All ages, lifelong programme

🚲 Racks at visitor centre and special entry price

🐕 On leads and only in car park and on public footpaths

➡ (3:G6/G7) 6ml NE of Cambridge on B1102 [154: TL533622] **Bus**: Stagecoach in Cambridge 111, 122 from Cambridge (frequent services link 🚉 Cambridge and bus station) **Station**: Cambridge 6ml

**NT properties nearby** Wicken Fen, Wimpole Estate

---

## ASHRIDGE ESTATE          Hertfordshire

Ringshall, Berkhamsted HP4 1LT · **Tel** 01442 851227 · **Infoline** 01494 755557
**Fax** 01442 850000 · **Email** ashridge@ntrust.org.uk

This magnificent and varied estate runs across the borders of Herts and Bucks, along the main ridge of the Chiltern Hills. There are woodlands, commons and chalk downland supporting a rich variety of wildlife and offering splendid walks through outstanding scenery. The focal point of the area is the Monument, erected in 1832 to the Duke of Bridgewater. There are also splendid views from Ivinghoe Beacon, accessible from Steps Hill

**What's new in 2002**: Full programme of wildlife-themed events for all seasons. Workshops, talks, walks and trails etc

O **Estate**: all year. **Visitor Centre**: 29 March to 3 Nov: daily except Fri (but open Good Fri). **Times**: Mon to Thur & Good Fri: 2–5; Sat, Sun, BH Mons and Tues 4 June: 12–5; **Monument**: Sat, Sun, BH Mons and Tues 4 June: 12–5; Mon to Thur by arrangement, weather permitting. **Events**: for details tel. 01442 851227

£ Countryside free. Monument £1; child 50p. Tel. for further information, shop and party bookings. Riding permits from riding warden, tel. 01442 842716

🛍 As visitor centre; 2 Nov to 8 Dec: Sat & Sun 12–4 or dusk if earlier, weather permitting

**For all your information needs check our website www.nationaltrust.org.uk**

**190 · EAST OF ENGLAND**

- ♿ Parking near visitor centre. Monument area, monument drive & visitor centre: accessible. Self-drive powered vehicles and manual wheelchair from visitor centre April to end Oct (not Fri); booking advisable. Extensive routes with fine views; some routes may be difficult in bad weather
- 👁 Volunteer Basecamp for use by groups of visually impaired people with sighted companions; details from Estate Office, tel. 01442 841800
- ☕ Refreshments at visitor centre, weather permitting
- 🏛 Full educational programme and study base. Details from the Education Warden (tel. 01442 851227)
- 🚲 Racks at visitor centre; cyclists' guide
- 🐕 Under close control
- → (3:E8/E9) Between Northchurch & Ringshall just off B4506 [165: SP970131] **Bus**: Monument; Seamarks 27; Arriva The Shires 30/1 from ☒ Tring, alight Aldbury, ½ml. Beacon; Arriva The Shires 61 Aylesbury–Luton (passing close ☒ Aylesbury & Luton); Seamarks 327 from Tring to Monument and Beacon, Sun, June–Sept only **Station**: Monument: Tring 1¾ml; Beacon: Cheddington 3½ml

**NT properties nearby** Dunstable Downs, Pitstone Windmill, Shaw's Corner, Whipsnade Tree Cathedral

---

## BLAKENEY POINT                                              Norfolk

The Warden, 35 The Cornfield, Langham, Holt NR25 7DQ
**Tel** 01263 740480 (April to Sept) · 01263 740241 (Oct to March)
**Fax** 01263 740241 · **Email** blakeneypoint@ntrust.org.uk

One of Britain's foremost bird sanctuaries, the Point is a 3½ml long sand and shingle spit, noted in particular for its colonies of breeding terns and for the rare migrants that pass through in spring and autumn. Both common and grey seals can be seen, as well as an interesting range of seaside plants. An information centre at Morston Quay provides further details on the area's attractions

- 🅾 All year
- £ No landing fee. Access on foot from Cley Beach (3¼ml) or by ferry from Morston and Blakeney (tidal). Restricted access to certain areas of the Point during the main bird breeding season (May to July). Car park at Blakeney Quay and Morston Quay £2, NT members free
- 🏛 For booked school parties and special interest groups (small charge)
- ♿ Contact Warden in advance
- 👁 Sea and bird sounds; atmosphere
- ☕ April to Sept light refreshments in the Old Lifeboat House subject to tide times
- 🐕 On leads only. No dogs west of Old Lifeboat House on Blakeney Point, April to Sept

---

**Please remember – your membership card is always needed for free admission**

EAST OF ENGLAND · 191

→ (3:I3) Morston Quay, Blakeney and Cley are all off A149 Cromer–Hunstanton road [133: TG0046] **Bus**: Norfolk Green 36 ⇌ Sheringham–Hunstanton **Station**: Sheringham (U) 8ml

**NT properties nearby** Felbrigg, Sheringham Park

## BLICKLING HALL, GARDEN & PARK

Blickling, Norwich NR11 6NF  Norfolk
**Tel** 01263 738030 · **Fax** 01263 731660 · **Email** blickling@ntrust.org.uk

Built in the early 17th century and one of England's great Jacobean houses, Blickling is famed for its spectacular long gallery, superb plasterwork ceilings and fine collections of furniture, pictures, books and tapestries. The gardens are full of colour throughout the year and the extensive parkland features a lake and a series of beautiful woodland and lakeside walks

**What's new in 2002**: Revised exhibition in Document Room, 50,000 additional spring bulbs in wilderness areas of garden

**O House**: 23 March to 3 Nov: daily except Mon & Tues (but open BH Mons and Tues 4 June). *Times*: March to Sept: 1–5; Oct & Nov: 1–4. Taster tours of House at 12 on most House open days (check on day for availabilty, £2.50 extra, incl. NT members) and Attic Tours on Tues in Aug. **Garden**: Open 10.15–5.30 (last admission 5.15), same days as house; also Tues in Aug; 7 Nov to 22 Dec: daily

For general enquiries, please telephone 0870 458 4000

## 192 · EAST OF ENGLAND

except Mon, Tues & Wed 11–4; 4 Jan to end March 2003: Sat & Sun 11–4. **Park & woods**: daily dawn to dusk. **Events**: extensive programme; tel. Box Office on 0870 010 4900 or send s.a.e. for full programme, also series of art exhibitions and book sales in Lothian Barn throughout season

£ £6.70. Garden only £3.80. Family and group discounts. Groups must book with s.a.e. to Property Office. Free access to South Front, shop, restaurant, plant centre, bookshop and Estate Barn. Coarse fishing in lake; permits from Warden, tel. 01263 734181. A car parking charge (members free) is planned for 2002

Private and school party guided tours of house (outside normal opening hours), garden and estate.

Shop, plant centre and bookshop open as garden. Plant centre closed Nov to end March 2003. Estate Barn (Countryside & RAF exhibition) open as house

Close parking. Ramp at East Gate. House: ramped entrance; ground floor on one level; lift to upper floor. Garden: routes avoiding steps; self-drive vehicles, push wheelchairs & walking frames with seats. Shop, restaurant & Estate Barn: ramped access. Plant centre and bookshop: accessible.

Braille guide, also some items in house can be touched by visually impaired visitors

Licensed restaurant open as garden. Wedding receptions (licensed for civil ceremonies). Private lunch, supper and dinner parties in house by arrangement (tel. 01263 738045). Picnic area in orchard

Children's guide. Baby slings, baby-changing facilities. Children's menu, large-handled cutlery, baby food, highchairs, scribble sheets. Play area in orchard (dog-free area), garden quizzes

Education groups welcome. Workshops available. Education Officer for details on 01263 738050

On leads at all times and only in park. A shaded area for dogs is planned for 2002 next to main car park

→ (3:J4) 1½ml NW of Aylsham on B1354. Signposted off A140 Norwich (15ml S) to Cromer (10ml N) road [133: TG178286] **Bus**: First Eastern Counties/Sanders 43, 50/A/B, X50 Norwich–Holt (passing close ≥ Norwich) to Blickling June–Sept otherwise alight Aylsham 1½ml **Station**: Aylsham (Bure Valley Railway from ≥ Hoveton & Wroxham) 1¾ml, North Walsham (U) 8ml. Grand Days Out scheme offering combined rail and bus link to Blickling on selected days. Tel. 01603 764776 for details

**NT properties nearby** Felbrigg Hall, Sheringham Park

---

## BOURNE MILL    Essex
Bourne Road, Colchester CO2 8RT · **Tel** 01206 572422

---

The mill was originally built as a fishing lodge in 1591 and features stepped 'Dutch' gables. There is a millpond, and some of the machinery, including the waterwheel, is intact and working

**Please see the area introductions for details of coast & countryside properties**

EAST OF ENGLAND · 193

**O** All BH Suns and BH Mons, plus June, July & Aug: Sun & Tues 2–5. Closed 25, 26 December. No WC

**£** £2. Children must be accompanied by an adult. No reduction for parties

**→** (3:I8) 1ml S of centre of Colchester, in Bourne Road, off the Mersea Road (B1025) [168: TM006238] **Bus**: Arriva Colchester 8/A/B, First Eastern National 67/A from Colchester (passing ⇌ Colchester). Colchester tour bus from Colchester Castle **Station**: Colchester Town ¾ml; Colchester 2ml **Cycle**: NCN 1 1¼ml

**NT properties nearby** Coggeshall Grange Barn, Copt Hall Marshes, Flatford, Paycocke's

---

## BRANCASTER                                                      Norfolk

Brancaster Millennium Activity Centre, Dial House, Brancaster Staithe, King's Lynn PE31 8BW · **Tel** 01485 210719
**Email** brancaster@ntrust.org.uk

---

An extensive area of salt marsh, intertidal mud and sand flats, and including the site of the Roman fort of Branodunum

**Note**: A boat can be hired at Brancaster Staithe (weather permitting) to take visitors to the National Nature Reserve on Scolt Head Island. It is managed by English Nature (EN Warden: tel. 01328 711866). The island is an important breeding site for four species of tern, oystercatcher and ringed plover. Nature trail. It is dangerous to walk over the salt marshes and sand flats at low tide. Ferry tel. 01485 210638/210456.

The Brancaster Millennium Activity Centre offers residential courses for schools, from Key Stage 2 to A level, with cutting-edge environmental technology. Also field studies and outdoor pursuits, inc. birdwatching, coastal processes, woodlands, salt marshes, orienteering, sailing, kayaking and cycling. Family Fun Weeks and a wide range of adult courses. Tel. Centre for information.

**O** All year

**£** Golf club car park at Brancaster Beach, parking charge (inc. NT members)

**🐕** Under control at all times on the beach; not on Scolt Head Island mid April to mid Aug. Dog-free area on Brancaster Beach, W of golf clubhouse May to Sept

**→** (3:H3) Brancaster Staithe is halfway between Wells and Hunstanton on A149 coast road [132: TF800450] **Bus**: Norfolk Green 36 ⇌ Sheringham–Hunstanton

**NT properties nearby** Blakeney Point

---

*Unless indicated, last admission is always 30mins before closing time*

194 · EAST OF ENGLAND

## COGGESHALL GRANGE BARN                                Essex
Grange Hill, Coggeshall, Colchester CO6 1RE · **Tel** 01376 562226

One of the oldest surviving timber-framed barns in Europe, dating from the 12th century and originally part of a Cistercian monastery. It was restored in the 1980s by The Coggeshall Grange Barn Trust, Braintree DC and Essex CC, and contains a small collection of farm carts and wagons. The Essex Way long-distance footpath passes the barn

- 31 March to 13 Oct: Tues, Thur, Sun and BH Mons 2–5
- £1.70; joint ticket with Paycocke's £3.40. No party reduction. Car parking at Grange Barn during opening times only
- Barn accessible, parking nearby
- Structure, including main aisle posts, may be touched
- Refreshments (not NT) in town
- (3:H8) Signposted off A120 Coggeshall bypass; ½ml from centre of Coggeshall, on Grange Hill (signposted) [168: TQ848223] **Bus**: First Eastern National 70 Braintree–Colchester (passing close ≠ Marks Tey) **Station**: Kelvedon 2½ml

**NT properties nearby** Bourne Mill, Paycocke's

## DUNSTABLE DOWNS COUNTRYSIDE CENTRE & WHIPSNADE ESTATE                                Bedfordshire
Whipsnade Road, Kensworth, Dunstable LU6 2TA · **Tel** 01582 608489
**Fax** 01582 671826
**Email** dunstabledowns@ntrust.org.uk

Commanding outstanding views over the Vale of Aylesbury and surrounding countryside, 206 ha (510 acres) of grassland and farmland SW of Dunstable, this local beauty spot offers an opportunity for many forms of recreation, including walking and kite-flying. The Countryside Centre is located at the top of the hill

- **Downs**: all year. **Countryside Centre**: 23 March to 2 Nov: daily except Mon. *Times*: Tues to Sat 10–5, Sun & BHols and Tues 4 June 10–6. School holidays open daily weather permitting
- As Countryside Centre
- Parking near to Dunstable Downs Countryside Centre (B4541) limited access; steep slopes, some paths may be difficult in bad weather
- Kiosk for refreshments only. Open every day except 25 Dec, 10–dusk

ROSEBAY WILLOWHERB

**There are special events at most Trust properties; please telephone 0870 458 4000 for details**

EAST OF ENGLAND · 195

- Limited programme, details from Education Warden, tel 01582 608489
- Under close control
- (3:E8/F8) At W end of Dunstable, 4ml NE of Ashridge between B4540 and B4541, car parking off both roads, and at Whipsnade Tree Cathedral & Whipsnade Crossroads **Bus**: As for Whipsnade Tree Cathedral, p.211

**NT properties nearby** Ashridge Estate, Whipsnade Tree Cathedral

## DUNWICH HEATH: COASTAL CENTRE & BEACH

Suffolk

Dunwich, Saxmundham IP17 3DJ · **Tel** 01728 648505/648501
**Fax** 01728 648384

A remnant of the once extensive Sandlings heaths and one of Suffolk's most important nature conservation areas. There are many excellent walks, including access to the neighbouring bird reserve of Minsmere, and an observation room in the converted Coastguard Cottages

- Daily. Dawn to dusk. **Events**: many family events; send s.a.e. for details
- Parking charge: season tickets 6 mths £11.50 & 1 yr £17; cars (pay-and-display) £1.80; coaches £20 (unless booked to use enterprise or education facilities). Members should display membership card on dashboard or obtain pass from Coastguard Cottages
- Guided walks with Warden throughout the year and on request for groups; send s.a.e for details
- In Coastguard Cottages. Jan & Feb: Sat & Sun only; March to mid-July and mid-Sept to end Oct: Wed to Sun; Easter, mid-July to mid-Sept and all half-terms: daily. Nov & Dec: Thur to Sun from 10am. Closed Christmas. Also open 4 June
- Car park viewing point and some footpaths accessible. Stairlift to viewing room. Shop & tea-room: accessible. Chauffeur-driven/self-drive single and two-seater vehicles (booking essential). Further information from the Warden
- Braille guide; guided walks for visually impaired people
- Licensed tea-room in Coastguard Cottages: open as shop
- Baby-changing facilities. Children's menu, baby food, highchairs, scribble sheets; outdoor play area
- Education Officer and Field Study Centre. Groups must book in advance (tel. 01728 648501)
- Under close control at all times. Dog-free area on beach
- (3:K6) 1ml S of Dunwich, signposted from A12 [156: TM475683]
  **Station**: Darsham (U) 6ml

**NT properties nearby** Flatford, Orford Ness, Sutton Hoo

**For all your information needs check our website www.nationaltrust.org.uk**

## ELIZABETHAN HOUSE MUSEUM

Norfolk

4 South Quay, Great Yarmouth NR30 2QH
**Tel** 01493 855746 (745526 out of season only) · **Fax** 01493 745459

A 16th-century building with rooms displayed to reflect the lives of the families who have lived here through history. Of particular interest are a Tudor bedroom and dining-room, Victorian kitchen, scullery and parlour, and the Conspiracy Room, where the trial and execution of King Charles I was allegedly plotted. There is also a special children's room with replica toys and there are hands-on activities throughout the house

**Note**: The house is leased to Norfolk Museums Service

- 25 March to 31 Oct: Mon to Fri 10–5; Sat & Sun 1.15–5. Tel. for details of additional opening times
- Tel. for current admission prices (2001 prices £2; child £1; family (2 adults & 4 children) £4.70. Concessions £1.50)
- As museum
- Education Officer
- (3:K5) In Great Yarmouth [134: TG523073] **Bus**: Local services from surrounding areas **Station**: Great Yarmouth ½ml

**NT properties nearby** Stroll further along the Quay to discover more of Great Yarmouth's heritage and visit two newly displayed 17th-century houses typical of Great Yarmouth Rows (managed by English Heritage, discount for NT members)


## FELBRIGG HALL, GARDEN AND PARK

Norfolk

Felbrigg, Norwich NR11 8PR · **Tel** 01263 837444 · **Fax** 01263 837032
**Email** felbrigg@ntrust.org.uk

One of the finest 17th-century houses in East Anglia, the Hall contains its original 18th-century furniture and Grand Tour paintings, as well as an outstanding library. The walled garden has been restored and features a working dovecote, a small orchard and the National Collection of Colchicum. The park is renowned for its fine and aged trees. The former deer park is being restored to woodland pasture. There are way-marked walks to the church and lake, and through the woods

- **House**: 23 March to 3 Nov: daily except Thur & Fri. *Times*: 1–5; BH Sun & BH Mons 11–5. Guided tour 12 noon each open day (except BH, numbers limited, additional charge, inc. members). **Note**: House will close at 4pm (last entries 3.30) on and after 27 Oct. **Garden**: 23 March to 3 Nov: daily except Thur & Fri. *Times*: 11–5.30. Walled Garden only, also open Thur & Fri 18 July to 30 Aug, 12–4. **Estate walks**: daily, dawn to dusk. **Events**: throughout year. Send s.a.e. to Property Manager for details

**Please remember – your membership card is always needed for free admission**

**£** Estate free to pedestrians and cyclists, parking charge (members free). House and garden: £5.90; child £2.90; family £14.70. Garden only £2.30. Parties (except BHols) £4.90; please book with s.a.e. to Property Manager at least one week ahead of proposed visit

**i** Introductory tour of house at 12 noon on open days except BHols (charge inc. NT members). Special guided group tours of Hall outside normal opening times; guided group tours of gardens; guided group walks of estate. Tel. to discuss options and requirements

**🏠** 23 March to 3 Nov: daily except Thur & Fri 11–5.30; 7 Nov to 22 Dec: daily except Mon, Tues & Wed; 4 Jan to March 2003: Sat & Sun 11–4 (tel. 01263 837040). **Second-hand bookshop**: 23 March to 3 Nov: daily except Thur & Fri 11–4.45. 7 Nov to 22 Dec: daily except Mon, Tues & Wed; 4 Jan to March 2003: Sat & Sun 11–4

**♿** Designated parking area in main car park; visitors with disabilities may be set down at visitor reception by arrangement. Wheelchairs for house and garden from visitor reception (100m). Self-drive battery cars. Hall: ground floor accessible; photograph album of first floor. Garden: accessible. Shop, second-hand bookshop (ramp), Turret tea-room and Park Restaurant: accessible. All-weather accessible path in woods

**👁** Braille guide to house

**🍴** Park restaurant (waited service) & Turret tea-room (counter service) both licensed. 23 March to 3 Nov: daily except Thur & Fri, 11–5.15; 7 Nov to 22 Dec: daily except Mon, Tues & Wed; 4 Jan to March 2003: Sat & Sun 11–3.30. Occasionally only one may be open. Booking advisable for Park restaurant. Special themed suppers monthly, send s.a.e to Property Manager for details. Private functions catered for, tel. 01263 838237

**👶** Parent and baby-changing room. Baby slings for visiting Hall. High-chairs, children's menu and drawing sheets in Park restaurant. High-chairs and toys in family room of Turret tea-room

**📚** Educational activities for schools by arrangement. Family Living History in school holidays. Send s.a.e. to Property Manager for details

**🚲** Racks in stable courtyard

**🐕** On leads or under very close control in parkland when sheep and cattle grazing. Under close control in woodland

**→** (3:J3) Nr Felbrigg village, 2ml SW of Cromer; entrance off B1436, signposted from A148 and A140 [133: TG193394] **Bus**: First Eastern Counties 780 from ≋ Sheringham, Suns April–Sept only, otherwise 50 Norwich–Holt, alight near Felbrigg village, then 1½ml on to Hall **Station**: Cromer (U) or Roughton Road (U). Visitors with valid bus or train tickets £1 off entrance price to house and garden. Both 2¼ml

**NT properties nearby** Blickling Hall, Sheringham Park

## FLATFORD: BRIDGE COTTAGE                                  Suffolk

Flatford, East Bergholt, Colchester CO7 6OL · **Tel** 01206 298260
**Fax** 01206 299193
**Email** flatford@ntrust.org.uk

A 16th-century thatched cottage, just upstream from Flatford Mill and housing an exhibition on John Constable, several of whose paintings famously depict this property. There is a tea-garden, shop, information centre and boat hire, and access is possible on foot to Trust land in the beautiful Dedham Vale

**Note**: Flatford Mill, Valley Farm and Willy Lott's House are leased to the Field Studies Council which runs arts-based courses for all age groups. For information on courses tel. 01206 298283. There is no general public access to these buildings, but the Field Studies Council will arrange tours for groups

- March and April: daily except Mon & Tues, 11–5.30; May to end Sept: daily 10–5.30; Oct: daily 11–5.30; Nov & Dec: daily except Mon & Tues, 11–3.30; Jan & Feb 2003: Sat & Sun only, 11–3.30. Closed Christmas and New Year. **Events**: special evening events in tea-room; tel. or send s.a.e. for details

- Bridge Cottage free. Parking 200m; private car park, charge (inc. NT members). Guided walks (when guides available) £1.90, accompanied children free; at other times audio tapes can be hired (£1.90 per tape, £5 deposit)

- Guided walks of the area: Easter, BHols and every afternoon May to end Sept when guides available (tel. to check). Booked guided walks for school and coach parties

- As cottage

- Close parking 25m from cottage; main car park, 200m. Tea-garden & shop: accessible. Wheelchair, self-drive buggy and walking aid at Bridge Cottage

- Braille guide and menus; large-print guides; audio commentaries for raised images of Constable's The Haywain and The Leaping Horse

- Licensed tea-room as cottage

- Flatford trail. Baby carriers. Children's menu, baby food, highchairs, scribble sheets, play table

- School visits welcome. Guided walks of sites depicted in Constable's paintings available for booked educational parties; tel. for details

- Lockable posts

- (3:I8) On N bank of Stour, 1ml S of East Bergholt (B1070). Accessible on foot from East Bergholt, Dedham and Manningtree [168: TM077332] **Bus**: First Eastern Counties/Carters 93/4 Ipswich–Colchester (passing Ipswich and close Colchester Town), alight E Bergholt, ¾ml **Station**: Manningtree 1¾ml by footpath, 3½ml by road

**NT properties nearby** Dedham Vale, Thorington Hall

## HATFIELD FOREST

Essex

Takeley, nr Bishop's Stortford CM22 6NE · **Tel** 01279 870678 · **Fax** 01279 871938
**Email** hatfieldforest@ntrust.org.uk

An outstanding ancient woodland and rare surviving example of a medieval royal hunting forest. The pollarded hornbeams and oaks support a wide variety of wildlife and there are many excellent walks and nature trails, as well as fishing in the lake

- Daily. Dawn to dusk. Vehicle access restricted to entrance car park Nov to Easter. **Events**: Wood Fair in Sept and family events throughout the year; send s.a.e for details

- Car park £3; minibuses £5; coaches £20; school coaches £10. Pay and display machines £1 Nov to Easter and outside normal opening times Easter to Oct. Parties must book in advance. Riding for members of Hatfield Forest Riding Association only; tel. for details

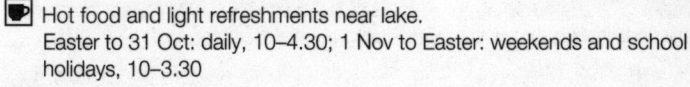

- Reserved car-parking; accessible paths and grassland; bookable self-drive vehicle

OAKLEAVES AND ACORNS

- Hot food and light refreshments near lake. Easter to 31 Oct: daily, 10–4.30; 1 Nov to Easter: weekends and school holidays, 10–3.30

- Baby-changing facilities

- Full education programme; details from Education Officer

- Several miles of track suitable for cycling; cycles excluded only from area of lake and gravel pit

- On leads where cattle and sheep are grazing and around lake. There is a dog-free area near the lake

- (3:G8) Signposted off A120 at Takeley, E of Bishop's Stortford [167: TL547208/546199] **Bus**: First Eastern National 33 ⇌ Stansted Airport–⇌ Chelmsford; London Transit 316 ⇌ Bishop's Stortford–Great Dunmow; Village Link 7 ⇌ Bishop's Stortford–⇌ Elsenham. All services alight Takeley Street (Green Man), thence ¾ml **Station**: Bishops Stortford 4ml

## HORSEY WINDPUMP

Norfolk

Horsey, Great Yarmouth NR29 4EF **Tel** 01493 393904 (open days only) 0870 609 5388 (Regional Office) · **Email** horsey@ntrust.org.uk

A drainage windmill, severely damaged by lightning in 1943 and since restored

- 1 April to 30 Sept: daily 11–5

**Unless indicated, last admission is always 30 mins before closing time**

## 200 · EAST OF ENGLAND

[£] Adult £1.50, child 80p. No party reduction. Car-parking 30p per hour for non-members. **Note**: Mooring fees payable by all boat users (inc. NT members) to the Horsey Estate

[🛍] Small shop open as windpump

[♿] Mill: steep wooden stairs. Wheelchair access to ground floor. Shop: accessible. 450m path to viewpoint over Horsey Mere

[🍽] Light refreshments

[🚲] Lockable posts

[🐕] Guide dogs only

[➡] (3:K4) 2½ml NE of Potter Heigham, 11ml N of Yarmouth near B1159 [134: TG457223] **Bus**: First Blue Bus 603/4 Lowestoft–Martham (passing close ⇌ Yarmouth), alight W Somerton School, 1¾ml **Station**: Acle (U) 10ml

**NT properties nearby** Elizabethan House Museum

---

## HOUGHTON MILL [✖][↕]    Cambridgeshire
Houghton, nr Huntingdon PE28 2AZ · **Tel** 01480 301494 · **Fax** 01480 469641

A large timber-built watermill on an island in the Great Ouse, with intact machinery which is still operational. An art gallery exhibits work by local artists

**What's new in 2002**: Major repair and decoration project recently completed. New interactive display; regular milling. Sun & BH Mons: flour for sale

[O] **Mill**: 30 March to 19 May, 28 Sept to 27 Oct: Sun & BH Mons; 25 May to 25 Sept: daily except Thur & Fri. *Times*: 2–5.30; last admission 5.15. Parties and school groups at other times by arrangement with Custodian. **Art gallery**: July & Aug: as mill

[£] £3; family discounts

[🧑] By arrangement

[♿] Ground floor accessible; steep wooden stairs

[👁] Braille guide. Many items (wheat grains, wholemeal) can be touched. Water sounds and machinery noises

[🍽] Light refreshments as mill

[🧒] Hands-on display and working models. Trails for mill and riverbank

[🏫] Guided tours for booked school parties

[➡] (3:F6) In village of Houghton, signposted off A1123 to Huntingdon, to St Ives [153: TL282720] **Bus**: Huntingdon & District 554, Whippet 1A, 4 from Huntingdon (passing close ⇌ Huntingdon) **Station**: Huntingdon 3½ml

**NT properties nearby** Anglesey Abbey, Wicken Fen, Wimpole Hall

---

**There are special events at most Trust properties; please telephone 0870 458 4000 for details**

# ICKWORTH HOUSE, PARK & GARDEN

Ickworth, The Rotunda, Horringer, Bury St Edmunds IP29 5QE  Suffolk
**Tel** 01284 735270 · **Fax** 01284 735175 · **Email** ickworth@ntrust.org.uk

The eccentric Earl of Bristol created this equally eccentric house, with its central rotunda and curved corridors, in 1795 to display his collections. These include spectacular paintings by Titian, Gainsborough and Velasquez and a magnificent Georgian silver collection. The house is surrounded by an Italianate garden and set in a 'Capability' Brown park with woodland walks, deer enclosure, vineyard, Georgian summer-house, church, canal and lake

- **House**: 23 March to 3 Nov: daily except Mon & Thur (but open BH Mons) 1–5 (closes 4.30 in Oct). **Garden**: 23 March to 3 Nov: daily 10–5; 4 Nov to 21 Dec: daily except Sat & Sun 10–4; 2 Jan to 22 March 2003: daily 10–4. **Park**: daily 7–7. **Note**: Garden & park closed 25 Dec. **Events**: many throughout the season, also Christmas programme; tel. for details 01284 735961

- £5.95; child £2.60; family discounts. Park & garden only (inc. access to shop & restaurant) £2.70; child 80p. Booked parties £4.95; child £2.10. No party rate Sun & BH Mons

- Taster tours each day except Mon & Thur during open season at 12 noon: £2 per person (inc. NT members). House admission extra. Pre-booked guided tours and special openings of house for groups with particular interests. Also booked tours for groups of Italianate garden, woods, parkland and vineyard. Details from property

- 23 March to 3 Nov: daily except Mon & Thur (but open BH Mons); 5 Nov to 21 Dec: Sat & Sun. *Times*: March to Oct 12–5; Nov & Dec 11–4

**For all your information needs check our website www.nationaltrust.org.uk**

- ♿ Disabled drivers may park outside the house. Disabled visitors may be set down at house. House: ramped access; restricted access in house for large powered vehicles/chairs; lift to first floor; stairlift to basement (shop and restaurant) suitable for wheelchair users able to transfer; wheelchair on each floor. Adapted WC on ground floor. Garden: largely accessible, some changes of level; gravel drive and paths. 1½ml level woodland walk. Two self-drive vehicles for park and garden
- 👁 House: Braille guide and self-guided touch trail; handling collections. Garden: scented woodland walk with tapping rail (under restoration), level surface tactile route; audio tour. Activity trails and exploration packs for house, park and garden (obtain from house)
- 🦻 Hearing loop at reception.
- ☕ Self-service licensed restaurant in Servants' Hall in basement open as shop. Programme of themed restaurant events/meals. Tel. for details 01284 735086
- 👶 All-terrain pushchair. Parent and baby room. Children's guide to house, Tracker packs and replica costumes for children. Baby slings. Children's portions, baby foods, highchairs, activity table, scribble books and activities. Challenging play area near car park. Family trim trail in woods and family cycle route (see below)
- 🏫 School groups welcome; booked tours and activities on request. Many holiday activities. Contact Education Officer on 01284 735961
- 🚲 Family cycle route (2½ml), various surfaces with some steep gradients; helmets advised. Parental supervision advised
- 🐕 On leads and only in park
- ➡ (3:H7) In Horringer, 3ml SW of Bury St Edmunds on W side of A143 [155: TL8161] **Bus**: First Eastern Counties 141-5 Bury St Edmunds–Haverhill passes close ⇌ Bury St Edmunds **Station**: Bury St Edmunds 3ml

**NT properties nearby** Lavenham, Melford Hall

# LAVENHAM: THE GUILDHALL OF CORPUS CHRISTI

Market Place, Lavenham, Sudbury CO10 9QZ  
Suffolk  
**Tel** 01787 247646 · **Email** lavenhamguildhall@ntrust.org.uk

This early 16th-century timber-framed building overlooks and dominates the town's market place. Inside are exhibitions on local history, farming and industry, as well as the story of the medieval woollen cloth trade. There is also an attractive walled garden with dye plants, and 19th-century lock-up and mortuary

- 🕐 2-24 March: Sat & Sun 11-4; 25 March to 31 May: Wed to Sun 11-5 (open BH Mon, closed Good Fri); June to end Sept: daily 11-5; Oct: Wed to Sun 11-5; Nov: Sat & Sun 12-4. Parts of the building may be closed occasionally for community use
- £ £3. Accompanied children free. Parties £2.50. School parties by arrangement, 60p per child
- 🛍 March to Oct: as Guildhall; 1 Nov to 22 Dec: daily except Mon, Tues & Wed 11-4

**Please remember – your membership card is always needed for free admission**

- ♿ Shop & tea-room: accessible
- ✋ Studwork and carved wood can be touched
- ☕ Tea-room as Guildhall (closed Mon, but open BH Mon)
- 🚸 Children's guidebook. Children's menu, highchairs, scribble sheets
- ➔ (3:I7) A1141 and B1071 [155: TL917494]
  **Bus**: Chambers 753 Bury St Edmunds–Colchester (passing close ≋ Bury St Edmunds & passes ≋ Sudbury); Chambers 90C Haverhill–Ipswich (passes ≋ Sudbury and Ipswich)
  **Station**: Sudbury (U) 7ml

**NT properties nearby** Ickworth, Melford Hall

## MELFORD HALL 🏛 ❁ Suffolk

Long Melford, Sudbury CO10 9AA · **Tel** 01787 880286
**Email** melford@ntrust.org.uk

One of East Anglia's most celebrated Elizabethan houses, little changed externally since 1578 and with an original panelled banqueting hall. There is also a Regency library, as well as Victorian bedrooms and good collections of furniture and porcelain. Small collection of Beatrix Potter memorabilia. The garden contains some spectacular specimen trees and a charming banqueting house, and there is an attractive walk through the park

**What's new in 2002**: Beatrix Potter Tour. May to Sept, 1st Wed of month 2.30. £1 per adult (some steps/slopes in house & garden)

- 🅾 23 March to 30 April and 1 Oct to 3 Nov: Sat, Sun & BH Mons; May to end Sept: daily except Mon & Tues (but open BH Mons and 4 June). *Times*: 2–5.30
- 💷 £4.50. Booked parties daily except Sun, Mon & Tues £3.40; write with s.a.e. to Senior Visitor Reception Assistant
- ♿ Disabled visitors may be set down at the hall; parking spaces for disabled drivers. Hall: wheelchairs; ramp; stairlift to first floor. Garden: some steps/slopes. Small powered mobility aids may be admitted to ground floor at quiet times – please phone first
- ✋ Braille and large-print guides
- ☕ In village (not NT)
- 🚸 Children's guide; carry-slings
- 🏛 Introductory talks and tours of house exterior (please tel. for details)
- 🐕 On leads, in car park and park walk only

**For general enquiries, please telephone 0870 458 4000**

**204 · EAST OF ENGLAND**

→ (3:I7) In Long Melford off A134, 14ml S of Bury St Edmunds, 3ml N of Sudbury [155: TL867462] **Bus**: Beestons/Chambers/Felix various services (but frequent) from Sudbury; Chambers 753 Bury St Edmunds–Colchester (passes close ≋ Bury St Edmunds); Chambers 90C Haverhill–Ipswich (passes ≋ Ipswich). All pass ≋ Sudbury **Station**: Sudbury (U) 4ml

**NT properties nearby** Ickworth, Flatford, Lavenham Guildhall

---

# ORFORD NESS                                        Suffolk

Quay Office, Orford Quay, Orford, Woodbridge IP12 2NU
**Tel/Fax** 01394 450900 · **Infoline** 01394 450057
**Email** orfordness@ntrust.org.uk

---

The largest vegetated shingle spit in Europe, containing a variety of habitats including shingle, salt marsh, mudflat, brackish lagoons and grazing marsh. An important location for breeding and passage birds as well as for the shingle flora, which includes a large number of nationally rare species. The Ness was a secret military site from 1913 until the mid 1980s. Visitors follow a 5ml route, which can be walked in total or in part (the full walk involves walking on shingle). Other walks are open seasonally

**Note**: Access around the site is on foot only, but tractor-drawn trailer tours operate 1st Sat of the month July to Sept, booking essential. No dogs

◯ 30 March to 29 June & 5 to 26 Oct: Sat only and 4 June. 2 July to 28 Sept: daily except Sun & Mon. The only access is by ferry from Orford Quay, with boats crossing regularly between 10 & 2 and the last ferry leaving the Ness at 5. Open throughout the year to booked parties of 12+. **Events**: contact Warden for details of full programme

£ Admission inc. ferry crossing: adult non-NT member £5.60; adult NT member £3.60; children half-price (under 3s free). Pay-and-display car-parking in Orford town

🎟 July to Sept; contact warden for details

♿ Wheelchair. Special access day for visitors with disabilities 22 July 2002, booking essential

👶 Children's 'Spy Trail' and quizbook

▦ Displays on natural history and history of the site. For education visits or resource information, contact Education Officer, tel. 01728 648501. Basecamp accommodation

🚫 No dogs

→ (3:K7) Access from Orford Quay, Orford town 10ml E of A12 (B1094/1095), 12ml NE of Woodbridge B1152/1084 [156:TM425495] **Cycle**: NCN 1

**NT properties nearby** Dunwich Heath, Kyson Hill, Sutton Hoo

---

Please see the area introductions for details of coast & countryside properties

# OXBURGH HALL, GARDEN AND ESTATE

Oxborough, King's Lynn PE33 9PS  
**Tel** 01366 328258 · **Fax** 01366 328066 · **Email** oxburghhall@ntrust.org.uk

Norfolk

This quintessential moated manor house, with its magnificent Tudor gatehouse, was built in 1482 by the Bedingfeld family, who still live here. The rooms show the development from medieval austerity to Victorian comfort, and include an outstanding display of embroidery done by Mary, Queen of Scots and Bess of Hardwick. The attractive gardens include a French parterre and there are delightful woodland walks, as well as an interesting Catholic chapel. Picnic tables in car park and woodlands

- **House**: 23 March to 3 Nov: daily except Thur & Fri. *Times*: 1–5, BH Mons 11–5. **Garden**: 2–17 March, Sat & Sun; 23 March to 3 Nov, daily except Thur & Fri but daily in Aug. *Times*: 2 to 17 March 11–4, 23 March to 3 Nov 11–5.30. **Events**: send s.a.e. for full details

- £5.50; child £2.80, family ticket £14.50. Garden & estate only £2.80. Booked parties £4.50 (except BHs); book with s.a.e. to Property Manager

- As garden 11–5, and every weekend 9 Nov to 22 Dec 11–4

- Parking adjoining ticket office, 200m from hall. Hall: shallow ramp to 4 ground-floor rooms; difficult stairs to upper floors. Garden: largely accessible; gravel paths; route map available; care necessary near moat. Restaurant & shop: accessible. Wheelchairs at ticket office. Chapel: 100m from Hall, access via ramp

- Braille guide; some items may be touched

- Licensed restaurant in Old Kitchen as garden 11–5. 9 Nov to 22 Dec Sat & Sun 11–4. Private functions catered for. Light refreshments in car park, opening times vary according to season

- Children's guide. Baby-changing facilities; baby slings. Children's menu, baby foods, highchairs, scribble sheets, toys

- School groups welcome. Selection of tours and activities available from the Oxburgh Explorer pack. Please contact Education Officer at property

- (3:H5) At Oxborough, 7ml SW of Swaffham on S side of Stoke Ferry road [143: TF742012] **Station**: Downham Market 10ml

**NT properties nearby**  
Peckover House,  
St George's Guildhall

---

**Unless indicated, last admission is always 30 mins before closing time**

## PAYCOCKE'S  Essex

West Street, Coggeshall, Colchester CO6 1NS · **Tel/Fax** 01376 561305

A merchant's house, dating from *c.*1500 and containing unusually rich panelling and wood carving. Coggeshall was famous for its lace, examples of which are displayed inside the house, and there is also a very attractive cottage garden

- 31 March to 13 Oct: Tues, Thur, Sun & BH Mons 2–5.30
- £2.30; joint ticket with Coggeshall Grange Barn £3.40. Parties of 10+ must book in advance with the tenant. No party reduction. Children must be accompanied by an adult. Parking at Grange Barn (10min walk) until 5
- Ground floor: accessible, but one awkward step at front door; house very small. Garden: accessible
- Braille guide
- Refreshments (not NT) in village
- (3:H8) Signposted off A120, on S side of West Street, about 300m from centre of Coggeshall, on road to Braintree next to the Fleece Inn, 5½ml E of Braintree [168: TL848225] **Bus**: First Eastern National 70 Colchester–Braintree (passing ᚕ Marks Tey) **Station**: Kelvedon 2½ml

**NT properties nearby** Bourne Mill, Coggeshall Grange Barn, Flatford Bridge Cottage

---

## PECKOVER HOUSE & GARDEN  Cambridgeshire

North Brink, Wisbech PE13 1JR · **Tel/Fax** 01945 583463
**Email** peckover@ntrust.org.uk

This outstanding Victorian garden includes an orangery, summerhouses, roses, herbaceous borders, fernery, croquet lawn and Reed Barn. The town house, built *c.*1722, is renowned for its very fine plaster and wood rococo decoration

**What's new in 2002**: Shop; displays on Peckover family. 17th-century thatched Reed Barn recently refurbished and available for weddings and functions. The house and garden will be open on occasional weekends during Feb & March 2003, tel. for details

- **Garden**: 23 March to 3 Nov: daily except Fri 12.30–5. **House**: 23 March to 3 Nov: Wed, Sat, Sun, Good Fri, BH Mons & 4 June, also Thur in May, June, July and Aug, 1.30–4.30. Please note on House open days the garden opens one hour before the House. Parties welcome when house open and at other times by appointment. **Events**: tel. or send s.a.e. for details
- Adults £4 (£2.50 on garden open days); child £1.50. Parties £3. Note that Peckover House does not have its own car park. Parking is located 300m from the property in a large free public car park
- Out of hours tours of house and/or garden; tel. for details
- As house

---

**There are special events at most Trust properties; please telephone 0870 458 4000 for details**

♿ Parking (with blue badge) on road in front of Peckover House. Batricar (please tel. to check availability). Garden and Reed Barn accessible.

👃 Scented flowers and plants

☕ In Reed Barn (or Servants' Hall some Sats); hours as House; historical menus change monthly. Reed Barn available for private functions and weddings

➡ (3:G5) On N bank of River Nene, in Wisbech (B1441) [143: TF458097] **Bus**: First Eastern Counties X94 ≥ Peterborough–Lowestoft; X94 and Norfolk Green 46 from King's Lynn (passing close ≥ King's Lynn) **Station**: March 9½ml **Cycle**: NCN 1 ¼ml

**NT properties nearby** Oxburgh Hall, St George's Guildhall at King's Lynn

Please note: Octavia Hill Birthplace Museum (not NT) within walking distance. Open Wed, Sat, Sun and BH from 2–5.30 (last admission 5) from third Wed in March to end of October (open throughout the year by appointment, 01945 476358; admission £1.50 (NT members)/£2 (non-NT members)

## RAMSEY ABBEY GATEHOUSE 🏠  Cambridgeshire
Abbey School, Ramsey, Huntingdon PE17 1DH
**Tel** 0870 609 5388 (Regional Office)

The remnants of a former Benedictine monastery, built on an island in the Fens. The late 15th-century gatehouse is richly carved and contains an ornate oriel window

🅾 1 April to end Oct: daily 10–5. Other times by written application to Curator

£ Free (but box for donations). No WC

➡ (3:F6) At SE edge of Ramsey, at point where Chatteris road leaves B1096, 10ml SE of Peterborough [142: TL291851] **Bus**: Stagecoach in Peterborough 330/1 Huntingdon–Peterborough (passing close ≥ Huntingdon & Peterborough) **Station**: Huntingdon 10ml

**NT properties nearby** Houghton Mill, Peckover House, Ramsey (not NT), Ramsey Rural Museum, Wood Lane,

## RAYLEIGH MOUNT  Essex
Rayleigh · **Tel** 0870 609 5388 (Regional Office)

The former site of the Domesday castle erected by Sweyn of Essex

🅾 Daily. Summer 7am–7.30pm; winter 7am–5pm

£ Free

➡ (3:H10) 6ml NW of Southend, path from Rayleigh station (A129) [178: TQ805909] **Bus**: From surrounding areas **Station**: Rayleigh 200m

**NT properties nearby** Danbury & Lingwood Commons

## ST GEORGE'S GUILDHALL 🏛️ 🎭                     Norfolk

27–29 King Street, King's Lynn PE30 1HA · **Tel** 01553 765565
**Bookings** 01553 764864 · **Fax** 01553 762141 · **Web** www.west-norfolk.gov.uk

The largest surviving English medieval guildhall and now converted into an arts centre, but with many interesting surviving features

- 🅾 Daily except Sat and Sun (closed Good Fri, BHols, 24 Dec to 1st Mon in Jan). *Times*: 10–2 (opening times may vary in July & Aug). The Guildhall is not usually open on days when there are performances in the theatre. Phone box office in advance for details. **Events**: July, King's Lynn Festival. Performances, workshops and art exhibitions throughout year; tel. box office for further information and brochure

- 💷 Free

- 🛍️ Crafts, Christmas shop from mid Nov

- ♿ Access to galleries: tel. 01553 779095 in advance

- ☕ Crofters Coffee Bar at Guildhall. Also Riverside Restaurant open for lunch and dinner Mon to Sat

- ➡️ (3:H4) On W side of King Street close to the Tuesday Market Place [132: TF616202] **Bus**: From surrounding areas **Station**: King's Lynn ¾ml **Cycle**: NCN 1 ¼ml

---

## SHAW'S CORNER 🏛️ ✤ 🎭                   Hertfordshire

Ayot St Lawrence, nr Welwyn AL6 9BX · **Tel/Fax** 01438 820307
**Infoline** 01494 755567 · **Email** shawscorner@ntrust.org.uk

An Edwardian Arts & Crafts-influenced house, the home of Bernard Shaw from 1906 till his death in 1950. The rooms remain much as he left them, with many literary and personal effects evoking the individuality and genius of this great dramatist. The kitchen and outbuildings are evocative of early 20th-century domestic life. Shaw's writing hut is hidden at the bottom of the garden, which has richly-planted borders and views over the Hertfordshire countryside

**What's new in 2002**: Walks leaflet linking local landmarks

- 🅾 27 March to 3 Nov: daily except Mon & Tues (open BH Mons) 1–5. House closes 3.30 on events days; tel. 01494 755572 for details. **Note**: On exceptionally busy days admission is by timed ticket. **Events**: for details tel. 01494 755572

- 💷 £3.60; child £1.80; family £9. Parties by prior appointment only (no party reduction)

- 🚶 Introductory talks for booked groups Wed to Sun, mornings only; tel. for details

- ♿ House: ramped access. Garden: accessible, via grass slope. Wheelchair. **Note**: House small and quickly congested; visits during quiet periods recommended; tel. for details

---

**Please remember – your membership card is always needed for free admission**

EAST OF ENGLAND · 209

- ⌾ Braille and large-print guides to house; monocular; items to touch. Scented plants
- ⚲ No baby back-carriers in house, but front sling baby carrier for loan
- ▮ School and adult groups welcome by arrangement, Wed to Sun mornings only
- ⚙ Lockable cycle posts in car park
- ⚑ On leads and only in car park
- → (3:F8) A1(M) junction 4 or M1 junction 10; follow B653 signed to Wheathamstead, then The Ayots and Shaw's Corner [166: TL194167] **Bus**: Shaw Shuttle 900, Wed & Suns from ⇌ Welwyn Garden City; Sovereign 304 ⇌ St Albans City–Hitchin, alight Gustard Wood, 1¼ml **Station**: Welwyn Garden City 4ml; Harpenden 5ml

**NT properties nearby** Ashridge Estate

---

# SHERINGHAM PARK                                    Norfolk

Warden: Gardener's Cottage, Sheringham Park, Upper Sheringham NR26 8TB
**Tel/Fax** 01263 823778
**Email** sheringhampark@ntrust.org.uk

---

One of Humphry Repton's most outstanding achievements, the landscape park contains fine mature woodlands, and the large woodland garden is particularly famous for its spectacular show of rhododendrons and azaleas (flowering mid May to June). There are stunning views of the coast and countryside from the viewing towers and many delightful waymarked walks, including a route to the North Norfolk Railway Station (a private full-gauge steam railway)

- ◯ **Park**: daily. Dawn to dusk. **House**: Sheringham Hall is privately occupied. April to Sept: limited access by written appointment with the tenant
- £ £2.70 per car. Coaches (must book for May/June visits) £8.10. Pay-and-display car park. Members should display membership card in windscreen

**For general enquiries, please telephone 0870 458 4000**

## 210 · EAST OF ENGLAND

[&] Raised walkway from car park to viewpoints. Self-drive vehicle and wheelchair when car park staff present, Easter to end Sept (weekends only in Sept) except in poor weather

[☕] Light refreshments Easter to end Sept

[🚲] Lockable rails; pannier lockers; cycle route restricted during rhododendron season

[🐕] On leads when among grazing stock

[➔] (3:J3) 2ml SW of Sheringham, access for cars off A148 Cromer–Holt road; 5ml W of Cromer; 6ml E of Holt [133: TG135420] **Bus**: First Eastern Counties/Sanders 50/A/B, X50 Norwich–Holt (passes close ⇌ Norwich and passes ⇌ Sheringham) **Station**: Sheringham (U) 2ml

**NT properties nearby** Blickling Hall, Felbrigg Hall

---

# SUTTON HOO                                              Suffolk
Woodbridge · **Tel** 01394 389700

Opening spring 2002. The Anglo-Saxon royal burial site where the priceless Sutton Hoo treasure was discovered in a huge ship grave. New facilities and exhibition hall opening March 2002. The exhibition tells the story of the site – which has been described as 'page one of English history' – and displays some original objects as well as replicas of the treasure. The burial site forms part of the 99-ha (245-acre) estate given to the National Trust by the Annie Tranmer Trust in 1998. Excellent walks

[O] Shop, restaurant and Exhibition Hall: 14 March to 31 May and Oct, Wed to Sun 10–5; 1 June to end Sept daily 10–5; Nov to end Feb 2003, Sat & Sun 10–4. The estate will be closed on certain Sats between Nov and Feb. Please tel. in advance

[£] £3.50; child £2; group rate £3; school group £1.50. Car park charge (when visitor facilities and exhibition closed) £2.50

[👤] Guided tours available at set times at weekends, additional charge

[🛍] As Exhibition Hall

[&] Visitor vacilities and Exhibition Hall: accessible. Hard, level path to burial ground (500m). Waymarked paths round estate

[✋] Items to touch in Exhibition Hall

[☕] As Exhibition Hall

[👶] Play area, handling collection and dressing-up box in exhibition, children's menu, baby food, high-chairs, drawing sheets

[🚲] Racks in car park, secure lockers at reception

[🐕] On leads at all times

[➔] (3:J7) 2 ml east of Woodbridge on B1083 **Station**: Melton 1½ml

**NT properties nearby** Dunwich Heath, Orford Ness

---

**Please see the area introductions for details of coast & countryside properties**

## THEATRE ROYAL 🎭 Suffolk

Westgate Street, Bury St Edmunds IP33 1QR · **Tel** 01284 769505
**Fax** 01284 706035 · **Email** admin@theatreroyal.org
**Web** www.theatreroyal.org

A rare example of a late Georgian playhouse, built in 1819 and still in use, presenting a year-round programme of professional drama, comedy, dance, mime, pantomime and amateur works. It boasts a national reputation and attracts the best touring companies in the country

- 🅾 May to end Sept. Tues & Thur: 11–1 & 2–4; Sat: 11–1. No access when theatrical activity is in progress. Please check in advance that theatre is open, tel. 01284 769505. **Events**: send large s.a.e. for details
- £ Free. Limited parking in Westgate Street. No parking in front of the theatre
- 🚶 Short guided tours at 11.30 & 2.30 Tues & Thur, and 11.30 Sat. £2 for NT members, bookable in advance through Theatre Royal Box Office, 01284 769505. For tours and talks at other times tel. 01284 755127
- ♿ Ramped access to boxes. Induction loop system. Signed performances. For full details tel. 01284 769505
- ☕ Licensed bar in theatre for performances.
- 🏫 For details of education initiatives tel. 01284 755127
- ➡ (3:I6) On Westgate Street on S side of A134 from Sudbury (one-way system) [155: TL855637] **Bus**: From surrounding areas **Station**: Bury St Edmunds ¾ml

## THORINGTON HALL 🏠 Suffolk

Stoke by Nayland, Colchester CO6 4SS · **Tel** 0870 609 5388 (Regional Office)

An oak-framed, plastered and gabled house, built *c.*1600 and later extended

- 🅾 Only by written appointment with the tenant
- ➡ (3:I8) 2ml SE of Stoke by Nayland [155: TM013355] **Bus**: Carters 755 from Colchester (passing ≋ Colchester) **Station**: Colchester 7ml **Cycle**: NCN 1 1½ml

**NT properties nearby** Flatford Bridge Cottage, Lavenham Guildhall, Melford Hall

## WHIPSNADE TREE CATHEDRAL Bedfordshire

nr Dunstable · **Tel** 01582 872406

Created following WW1 in 'Faith, hope and reconciliation', the Tree Cathedral covers a tranquil 10.5ha (26 acres) and contains many tree species uniquely planted in the plan of a medieval cathedral. Grass avenues form chancel, nave, transepts, chapels and cloisters, and there is also a dew pond. Nearby are Whipsnade Downs, where the Trust owns a farm and an area of botanically rich chalk grassland, to which there is unrestricted access on foot

**Unless indicated, last admission is always 30 mins before closing time**

## 212 · EAST OF ENGLAND

- **O** All year. **Events**: an annual interdenominational service is held on 16 June; tel. for details or see website
- **£** Free car park (signposted off B4540)
- **♿** Some routes may be difficult in bad weather. Motorised wheelchairs by appointment
- **🐕** Under close control
- **→** (3:F8) 2ml S of Dunstable, off B4540 [165/166: TL008180] **Bus**: Arriva The Shires 43 Luton–Hemel Hempstead (passing close ≠ Luton & Hemel Hempstead)

**NT properties nearby** Ascott, Ashridge Estate, Dunstable Downs, Whipsnade Downs

---

## WICKEN FEN NATIONAL NATURE RESERVE

Lode Lane, Wicken, Ely CB7 5XP  
**Tel/Fax** 01353 720274 · **Email** wickenfen@ntrust.org.uk  
**Web** www.wicken.org.uk

Cambridgeshire

---

Britain's oldest nature reserve and a unique fragment of the wilderness that once covered East Anglia. A haven for birds, plants, insects and mammals alike, the Fen can be explored by the traditional wide droves and lush green paths, and there is a boardwalk nature trail giving access to several hides. The William Thorpe Visitor Centre provides a range of facilities and information about this fascinating place

- **O** **Reserve**: daily except 25 Dec, dawn to dusk. Some paths are closed in very wet weather. **Visitor centre**: daily except Mon 10–5 (may occasionally be closed in winter). Open BHols. **Fen Cottage**: April to Oct: Sun & BH Mons 2–5 (and some other days in summer). **Events**: tel. for details of guided walks, children's activities and family events
- **£** £3.80; child £1.20. Cottage only £1.50. Booked parties £2.90, special rates for school/educational groups; contact the Education Officer or write with s.a.e.
- **👤** Guided tours by special arrangement
- **🛍** Books and gifts in visitor centre. Binoculars for hire
- **♿** Close parking by arrangement. Visitor centre: accessible. Raised boardwalk & adapted bird hides accessible. Fen Cottage: limited access by arrangement
- **🍴** Hot and cold drinks, light snacks and ice creams in visitor centre

REDSHANK

---

There are special events at most Trust properties; please telephone 0870 458 4000 for details

EAST OF ENGLAND · 213

- 👶 Children's activities in visitor centre. Family events throughout year. Boardwalk suitable for pushchairs
- 🏫 Full-time Education Officer. Science, geography and history activities for school or educational groups at all levels
- 🐕 On leads only; not in Fen Cottage
- ➡️ (3:G6) S of A1123, 3ml W of Soham (A142), 9ml S of Ely, 17ml NE of Cambridge via A10 [154: TL563705] **Bus**: Stagecoach in Cambridge 122 Cambridge–Ely (Sun only); Greys 117 from Ely (Thur, Sat only); otherwise Stagecoach in Cambridge X12, 122 from Cambridge, Ely & Newmarket, alight Soham Downfields 3ml, or X7–9 Cambridge–Ely, alight Stretham 3½ml. All pass ≋ Ely **Station**: Ely 9ml

**NT properties nearby** Anglesey Abbey, Ickworth, Wimpole Hall

## WILLINGTON DOVECOTE & STABLES   Bedfordshire
Willington, nr Bedford · **Tel** 0870 609 5388 (Regional Office)

A distinctive 16th-century stable and stone dovecote, lined internally with nesting boxes for 1,500 pigeons

- 🅾️ April to end Sept: by appointment with Mrs J. Endersby, 21 Chapel Lane, Willington MK44 3QG (tel. 01234 838278)
- 💷 £1. No party reduction. Car park 30m. No WC
- ♿ Accessible, ground floor only but floors uneven
- ➡️ (3:F7) 4ml E of Bedford, just N of the Sandy road (A603) [153: TL107499] **Bus**: Stagecoach United Counties 171/2, 174/8/9 Bedford–Biggleswade (passing ≋ Bedford St John's & Biggleswade and close ≋ Sandy), alight Willington crossroads, ½ml **Station**: Bedford St John's (U), not Sun, 4ml; Sandy 4½ml; Bedford 5ml

**NT properties nearby** Ashridge Estate, Dunstable Downs, Stowe Gardens, Wimpole Hall & Home Farm

## WIMPOLE HALL   Cambridgeshire
Arrington, Royston SG8 0BW · **Tel** 01223 207257 · **Fax** 01223 207838
**Email** wimpolehall@ntrust.org.uk · **Web** www.wimpole.org

This magnificent 18th-century house, the largest in Cambridgeshire and set in grand style in an extensive wooded park, has an extraordinary pedigree. The interior features work by Gibbs, Flitcroft and Soane, and the park – complete with grand folly, Chinese bridge and lakes – was landscaped by Bridgeman, Brown and Repton. There is a series of spectacular avenues and extensive walks through the delightful grounds. The garden has thousands of daffodils in April and colourful parterres in July and Aug. Walled garden restored to a working vegetable garden, best seen from June to Aug

**What's new in 2002**: Handling collection and Gallery

**For all your information needs check our website www.nationaltrust.org.uk**

## 214 · EAST OF ENGLAND

**O** 23 March to 31 July & 3 Sept to 3 Nov: daily except Mon & Fri (but open Good Fri and BH Mons); Aug: daily except Mon (but open BH Mon); 10, 17 & 24 Nov: Sun only. *Times*: 1–5 (BH Mons 11–5; closes 4 after 27 Oct). **Garden**: as Farm (below). **Park**: daily sunrise to sunset. **Events**: tel. for details of full programme throughout year

**£** £6.20; child £2.80. Joint ticket with Home Farm £9; child £4.50; family £22. Garden only £2.50. Adult party rate (12 +) £5.20; child party rate £2.30. Car park 200m, parking charge (members free). No group rates on Sun & BH Mon

By special arrangement outside normal opening hours

23 March to 3 Nov: daily except Mon & Fri (open BH Mons) 10.30–5.30; Nov to March 2003: daily except Mon & Fri 11–4 (closed 25, 26 Dec)

Parking near stable block. Disabled visitors may be set down near Hall. Hall: tel. for details. Garden: accessible; gravel paths. Restaurant: accessible

Braille guide; some items may be touched by arrangement

Licensed restaurant. 23 March to 3 Nov: as Hall; 5 Nov to 22 Dec: daily except Mon and Fri. *Times*: March to 27 Oct 11–5.30; 29 Oct to March 2003 11–4. Stable block: light refreshments available most weekends through year and midweek at busy times 11–5 (closes 4 in winter). Closed 25, 26 Dec. Picnic area

Parent and baby room in stable block; baby slings. Children's menu, baby food, highchairs, scribble sheets

Full education programme; details from Education Officer (tel. 01223 207801)

On leads and only in park

→ (3:G7) 8ml SW of Cambridge (A603), 6ml N of Royston (A1198) [154: TL336510] **Bus**: Whippet 175/7 Cambridge–Biggleswade (passing close ≠ Biggleswade & Cambridge) **Station**: Shepreth 5ml

**NT properties nearby** Anglesey Abbey, Ickworth, Wicken Fen

**Please remember – your membership card is always needed for free admission**

EAST OF ENGLAND · **215**

# WIMPOLE HOME FARM　Cambridgeshire

As Wimpole Hall · **Tel** 01223 207257 · **Fax** 01223 207838
**Email** wimpolefarm@ntrust.org.uk · **Web** www.wimpole.org

A model farm, built by Soane in 1794 and now home to a fascinating range of rare animal breeds, including sheep, goats, cattle, pigs and horses. The Great Barn has a collection of farm implements dating back 200 years and interpretive displays

**What's new in 2002**: Interpretation displays. Adventure playground

- 23 March to 30 June, 3 Sept to 3 Nov: daily except Mon & Fri (but open Good Fri and BH Mons); July & Aug: daily except Mon (but open BH Mon); Nov to March 2003: Sat & Sun (open Feb half-term week). *Times*: 23 March to 3 Nov 10.30–5; 5 Nov to March 2003 11–4. **Events**: Spring lambing in April. Tel. for details of full programme throughout year

- NT members £2.60; child £1.60; non-members £4.90; child (over 3) £2.80. Joint ticket with hall £9; child £4.50; family £22. Adult party rate (12+) £3.90; child party rate £2.20, book with s.a.e. to Property Manager, Wimpole Hall. School parties welcome (Education Group members £1.60 per child). No group rates on Sun & BH Mon. Parking 400m from farm, parking charge (members free)

- By special arrangement

- As farm 11–5

- Ask for directions and parking at stable block. Level access throughout farm; ramps to most buildings. Stableyard refreshments & shop: accessible. Wheelchairs. Bookable self-drive vehicle at stable block

- Braille guide. Animal sounds and smells; some animals may be patted and stroked

- Light refreshments as farm 11–5. Children's birthday parties catered for

- Baby-changing room. Special children's corner; woodland adventure playground; children's publications. Special events for children April, May and Aug

- Full education programme; details from Education Officer (tel. 01223 207801)

- (3:G7) As Wimpole Hall [154:TL336510] **Bus**: As Wimpole Hall

**NT properties nearby** Anglesey Abbey, Ickworth, Wicken Fen

NORFOLK HORN

**For general enquiries, please telephone 0870 458 4000**

# Introduction to the East Midlands

The East Midlands is an area of immensely diverse scenery, ranging from the flat agricultural landscapes of southern Lincolnshire through the wooded estates of the Dukeries in Nottinghamshire to the upland drama of the Derbyshire Pennines, which lie within one of England's most famous and heavily visited national parks. The National Trust cares for over 12 per cent of the Peak District National Park, the different properties being grouped into three estates: **High Peak, Longshaw** and **South Peak**. High Peak includes the **Hope Woodlands**, less wood than wild and dramatic Pennine moorland, adjoining the impressive 600-metre high **Kinder Scout** and with superb views. Nearby are the stunning valley of **Edale**, where the Trust owns several farms, and the landmark of **Mam Tor**, next to the spectacular limestone gorge of **Winnats Pass**. The **Derwent** and **Howden Moors** are important historic landscapes lying above Ladybower and Howden Reservoirs. Deeply incised by many spectacular cloughs or valleys in which run fast-flowing streams, the moors are important for upland breeding birds and stands of relict woodland. On the eastern edge of the Peak District, the **Longshaw Estate** is an outstanding area of moorland, woodland and farmland with the Duke of Rutland's former shooting lodge, now a visitor centre, as its focal point.

The South Peak Estate straddles the Derbyshire/Staffordshire border and includes **Dovedale**, famous for its ashwoods and geological features, as well as the former **Leek & Manifold Valley Light Railway**, now a surfaced track leading through dramatic limestone scenery. Nearby **Ilam Park** has a range of visitor facilities and local information and there is an information shelter at **Milldale**. Not far from the Peak District are four of the Trust's most celebrated country houses, all in Derbyshire – **Calke Abbey**, **Hardwick Hall**, **Kedleston Hall** and **Sudbury Hall**.

Further east are the extensive parkland, heaths and woods of **Clumber Park**, a significant area for wildlife and a remnant of the vast estates that once covered much of Nottinghamshire. Also in Nottinghamshire is Mr Straw's House, a semi-detached Edwardian house unaltered since the 1930s, and **The Workhouse** at Southwell; built in 1824, it is one of the few surviving examples.

Lincolnshire is perhaps one of England's most enigmatic counties, rich in ancient history and atmosphere, and offering the opportunity to explore some of the country's less well-known historic houses. Near Skegness lies charming **Gunby Hall**, complete with walled garden and set in an open landscape under often dramatic skies. **Monksthorpe Chapel** on this estate, is one of the two best surviving English examples of a Baptist Chapel from the late 17th century. Further inland the moated **Tattershall Castle**, one of the area's most important and dramatic medieval buildings, affords the chance to look out over the expanse of the Lincolnshire Fens towards the famous Boston 'Stump'. Near Grantham are **Belton House**, a splendid late 17th-century house set in magnificent parkland, and **Woolsthorpe Manor**, the birthplace and family home of Sir Isaac Newton.

**OS grid references for main properties with no individual entry (OS map series numbers given in brackets)**

| | |
|---|---|
| Derwent Moors | [110] SK173893 |
| Dovedale | [119] SK148510 |
| Hope Woodlands | [110] SK109914* |
| Kinder Scout | [110] SK083889 |
| Leek & Manifold | [119] SK095561 |
| Mam Tor | [110] SK128836 |
| Milldale | [119] SK139548 |

*car park for access (not NT)

**There are special events at most Trust properties; please telephone 0870 458 4000 for details**

The attractive rolling countryside of Northamptonshire provides the setting for the unusual **Lyveden New Bield**, an unfinished 16th-century lodge, and for stunning **Canons Ashby**, one of England's most interesting Elizabethan manor houses.

### Highlights for Visitors with Disabilities ...
Particularly recommended are **Clumber Park**, with excellent pathways and visitor facilities, and the **Manifold** track, which is very suitable for wheelchair access.

### ... and for Families
The **Museum of Childhood at Sudbury Hall** is of special interest; bicycles can be hired at **Clumber Park**; **Wildlife Discovery Centre** and extensive outdoor adventure playground at **Belton House**; and children always find much to see and do at **Tattershall Castle**.

### Further Information
Contact the Membership Department, PO Box 39, Bromley BR1 3XL. Tel. 0870 458 4000. Email: enquiries@thenationaltrust.org.uk

---

## BELTON HOUSE    Lincolnshire
Grantham NG32 2LS · **Tel** 01476 566116 · **Fax** 01476 579071
**Email** belton@ntrust.org.uk

---

The crowning achievement of Restoration country house architecture, Belton was built in 1685–88 and later altered by James Wyatt. The stunning interiors contain exceptionally fine plasterwork and wood-carving, as well as important collections of paintings, furniture, tapestries and silverware. There are also formal gardens, an orangery, a magnificent landscape park and a large adventure playground

**What's new in 2002**: Coach House touchscreen visit

- **House**: 23 March to 3 Nov: daily except Mon & Tues (but open BH Mons, Good Fri and Tues 4 June) 12.30–5. **Garden & park** (inc. adventure playground): as house 11–5.30 (closes 4.30 20 July) but 10.30–5.30 in Aug. **Garden**: 9 Nov to 22 Dec, Sat & Sun, 12–4. **Park**: all year on foot only from Lion Lodge gates. **Note**: No access from this entrance to house, garden or adventure playground. Park may be closed occasionally for special events. **Bellmount Woods**: daily, access from separate car park. **Events**: send s.a.e. for details. Licensed for civil weddings

- £5.60; child £2.80; family £14. Discount for parties

- Guided tours in house 11.30–12.30 on open days during Aug. Guided tours for parties, outside normal hours only, by arrangement

- 23 March to 3 Nov: as house 12–5.30, but 11–5.30 in Aug; 9 Nov to 22 Dec: Sat & Sun 12–4

- Close parking by arrangement. House: difficult; contact Property Manager for details. Wheelchair for house. Garden, park, restaurant, shop & refreshment kiosk: accessible; rough paths to playground difficult in wet weather

- Braille and audio guides

---

**For all your information needs check our website www.nationaltrust.org.uk**

## EAST MIDLANDS

- Sympathetic Hearing Scheme
- Licensed restaurant as shop 12–5, but 11–5 in Aug. Open for functions and booked parties throughout year; write (with s.a.e) for details
- Activity room in house; Wildlife Discovery Centre; extensive outdoor adventure playground with under-6s 'corral'; miniature train rides in summer. Children's guide. Parent and baby facilities; front baby slings on loan. Children's portions
- Educational visits from school parties welcomed to both house and grounds. Education Officer, schoolrooms, teachers' resource book and workshops
- Parking for 5 cycles
- On leads and only in parkland
- (3:E3) 3ml NE of Grantham on A607 Grantham–Lincoln road, easily reached, and signposted from A1 [130: SK929395] **Bus**: Road Car 601 Grantham–Lincoln; 609 Grantham–Sleaford (both pass close ≥ Grantham) **Station**: Grantham 3ml

**NT properties nearby** Tattershall Castle, Woolsthorpe Manor

---

## CALKE ABBEY                                                                 Derbyshire

Ticknall, Derby DE73 1LE · **Tel** 01332 863822 · **Fax** 01332 865272
**Email** calkeabbey@ntrust.org.uk

---

This baroque mansion, built 1701–3 and set in a stunning landscape park, has become famous as a graphic illustration of the English country house in decline. Little restored, the house contains the spectacular natural history collection of the Harpur Crewe family, as well as a magnificent 18th-century state bed and interiors that are essentially unchanged since the 1880s. The open parkland is managed for its nature conservation value and the attractive grounds feature a beautiful walled garden and an interesting collection of garden buildings, including a newly restored orangery

**Please remember – your membership card is always needed for free admission**

# EAST MIDLANDS · 219

**Note**: All visitors (inc. NT members) require a house and garden (or garden only) ticket from the ticket office. Delays in entry to house are possible at BHols. The house, church and garden are closed on Sat 17 Aug for annual concert. One-way system operates in the park; access only via Ticknall entrance

**◯ House, garden & church**: 23 March to 3 Nov: daily except Thur & Fri. *Times*: House: 1–5.30 (ticket office opens 11). Garden & church: 11–5.30; 11–7 Tues & Wed in July & Aug. **Park**: Most days until 9pm or dusk if earlier. **Events**: Full programme of events, send s.a.e. for details

**£** £5.40; child £2.70; family £13.50. Garden only: £3. Discount for parties. Vehicles £2.60, refundable on entry to the house when open (NT members free)

Morning guided tours for parties (but not Sun or BH weekends). Tours last approx. 1hr 20min (extra charge inc. NT members); evening meals available with house tours. Party organisers tel. for details and bookings

23 March to 3 Nov: as house 10.30–5.30; 9 Nov to 22 Dec: Sat & Sun 11–4, also 2 to 18 Dec: Mon, Tues & Wed 11–4. Jan to March 2003: Sat & Sun 11–4 (tel. 01332 865699)

House: ground floor accessible; house congested at peak times; photo album of inaccessible rooms. Garden & park: partly accessible. Stables, shop & restaurant: accessible. Church: some steps. 5-seater volunteer-driven buggy to take visitors to house (ask at ticket office)

Braille guide; some items may be touched

Sympathetic Hearing Scheme

Licensed restaurant 23 March to 3 Nov: as house 10.30–5; 9 Nov to 22 Dec: as shop 11–4. Jan to March 2003: as shop. Booked meals for groups. Kiosk for snacks and ice creams on busy afternoons plus Thur & Fri in July & Aug. Corporate events by arrangement (tel. 01332 864803)

Parent and baby facilities. Highchairs; children's menu

Tours and workshops available for education groups. Education Officer and teachers' resource book

On leads and only in park; no shaded parking

→ (3:C4) 10ml S of Derby, on A514 at Ticknall between Swadlincote and Melbourne. Access from M42/A42 Jn 13 and A50 Derby South [128: SK356239] **Bus**: Arriva Derby 68/9, Derby–Swadlincote (passing close ≠ Derby), alight Ticknall, thence 1¼ml walk through park to house **Station**: Derby 9½ml; Burton-on-Trent 10ml

**NT properties nearby** Kedleston Hall, Staunton Harold Church, Sudbury Hall

**For general enquiries, please telephone 0870 458 4000**

## CANONS ASBY HOUSE — Northamptonshire

Canons Ashby, Daventry NN11 3SD · **Tel** 01327 860044 · **Fax** 01327 860168
**Email** canonsashby@ntrust.org.uk

The home of the Dryden family since its construction, this Elizabethan manor house has survived more or less unaltered since *c*.1710. The intimate and atmospheric interior contains wall paintings and Jacobean plasterwork of the highest quality. There are also a formal garden, an orchard featuring varieties of fruit trees from the 16th century and a surprisingly grand church – all that remains of the Augustinian priory from which the house takes its name

- **House, gardens, park & church**: 23 March to 3 Nov: daily except Thur & Fri. *Times*: House 1–5.30; 12–4.30 in Oct & Nov. Gardens, park & church 11–5.30; 11–4.30 Oct & Nov, access through garden; 9 Nov to 22 Dec: Sat & Sun 11–3. **Events**: Send s.a.e for details

- £5.20; child £2.60; family £13; garden only £1. Donation box for church. Parking 200m. Discount for parties; coaches and parties must book, write (with s.a.e.) to the Property Manager

- Guided house tours for pre-booked parties (inc. schools) March to 3 Nov: daily except Sun; Nov & Dec: Mon to Fri

- As house 12–5 but 12–4.30 in Oct & Nov; 9 Nov to 22 Dec Sat & Sun 11–3

- Close parking in stable yard by arrangement. House: access via 7 steps. Wheelchairs. Garden: access via 3 steps. Tea-room: accessible (portable ramp if required)

- Braille and tape guides

- Tea-room open as house 12–5 but 12–4.30 in Oct & Nov; 9 Nov to 22 Dec, Sat & Sun 11–3. Party bookings by arrangement. Picnics in car park

- Education groups welcome; teachers' resource book

- Lockable posts

- On leads and only in Home Paddock

- (3:D7) Easy access from either M40, exit 11 or M1, exit 16. From M1, take A45 (Daventry) and at Weedon crossroads turn left onto A5; 3ml S turn right onto unclassified road through Litchborough. From M40 at Banbury, take A422 (Buckingham) and after 2ml turn left onto B4525; after 3ml turn left onto unclassified road signposted to property [152: SP577506] **Bus**: Occasional Sun services from Northampton **Station**: Banbury 10ml

**NT properties nearby** Farnborough Hall, Stowe Gardens, Upton House

**Please see the area introductions for details of coast & countryside properties**

# CLUMBER PARK  Nottinghamshire

The Estate Office, Clumber Park, Worksop S80 3AZ · **Tel** 01909 484977/476592 **Fax** 01909 500721

A wide expanse of parkland, peaceful woods, open heath and rolling farmland with a superb serpentine lake at its heart. Part of Nottinghamshire's famed 'Dukeries', Clumber was formerly home to the Dukes of Newcastle. The house was demolished in 1938, but many fascinating features of the estate remain, including an outstanding Gothic Revival Chapel, Hardwick village and the Walled Kitchen Garden.

**What's new in 2002**: New Park security and traffic management arrangements

- **Park**: daily throughout the year except 13 July & 10 Aug (concert days) and 25 Dec. April to Sept: last vehicle admission 7pm, park closes 9pm. Oct to March: last vehicle admission 5pm, park closes 7pm. **Walled kitchen garden**: April to Sept: Wed & Thur 10.30–5.30, Sat, Sun & BH Mon 10.30–6. **Chapel**: April to Sept: daily 10.30–5.30 (closes 6 on Sat & Sun); Oct to 12 Jan 2003: daily 10.30–4. 166-berth caravan site run by Caravan Club; open to non-members (tel. 01909 484758). Camp site run by Camping & Caravanning Club of Great Britain: April to Sept, limited spaces, booking advisable (tel. 01909 482303)

- Pedestrians, cyclists and coaches free. Cars and motorbikes £3.50 (NT members free); minibuses and cars with caravans £4.50. Walled kitchen garden 70p. Orienteering by arrangement (orienteering packs £1.95). Horse riding by permit only, £6 day permit or £50 annual season ticket. Coarse fishing: 16 June to 14 March; 7am to dusk; £4 day ticket or £50 annual season ticket

- Daily (closed 25, 26 Dec). *Times*: April to Sept: 10.30–5.30 (closes 6 on Sat, Sun & BH Mons); Oct to March 2003: 10.30–4. Plant sales April to Sept as shop

- Park: 13ml tarmac roads, off-road paths uneven in places. Ramped access to shop and tea-room, walled kitchen garden & Chapel. Wheelchairs (inc. child's) and 2 powered self-drive vehicles and adapted cycle (trandem) free from cycle hire (must be booked, ID essential)

- Tea-room as shop, opens 10 Sat & Sun (closed 25, 26 Dec), lunches 12–2

- Highchairs; children's portions. Cycles with child carriers or buggies; open parkland ideal for family activities

- Group bookings and education groups welcome; education workshops; tours and lectures; Education Officer; Education Centre; teachers' resource book and field studies equipment. Tel. 01909 476592

**Unless indicated, last admission is always 30 mins before closing time**

## 222 · EAST MIDLANDS

🚲 Cycle hire available April to Sept: daily; Oct to March: Sat & Sun and school holidays. *Times*: Opens 10, variable closing. £4 for 2hrs, ID essential. Tandems, child seats, trailer bikes and trike available. 2 waymarked cycle routes (5ml and 13ml)

🐕 Welcome in park. Must be on leads in chapel grounds and sheep enclosures

➡ (3:D2) 4½ml SE of Worksop, 6½ml SW of Retford, 1ml from A1/A57, 11ml from M1 exit 30 [120: SK645774 or 120: SK626746] **Bus**: Stagecoach in Bassetlaw 251/2 from Heanor & Hucknall and 252 from Nottingham, both Sun only; otherwise 33 Worksop–Nottingham (passing close ≋ Worksop), alight Carburton, ¾ml **Station**: Worksop 4½ml; Retford 6½ml **Cycle**: NCN 6

**NT properties nearby** Hardwick Hall, Mr Straw's House, The Workhouse

---

## GRANTHAM HOUSE 🏠✼🌳      Lincolnshire
Castlegate, Grantham NG31 6SS · **Tel** 01909 486411 (Regional Office)

Dating from 1380, the house has been extensively altered since then and presents an attractive mixture of styles. There are delightful walled gardens running down to the river

🅾 **Ground floor only**: 27 March to end Sept: Wed 2–5 by written appointment only with the tenant, Major-General Sir Brian Wyldbore-Smith

💷 £1.50. Limited space; max. seven in parties. No WC

➡ (3:E4) Immediately E of Grantham Church [130: SK916362] **Bus**: Road Car 601 Grantham–Lincoln, to within ¼ml **Station**: Grantham 1ml

**NT properties nearby** Belton House, Woolsthorpe Manor

---

## GUNBY HALL 🏠🐕☺      Lincolnshire
Gunby, nr Spilsby PE23 5SS · **Tel** 01909 486411 (Regional Office)

A fine red-brick house, dating from 1700 (with later extensions) and located in one of England's most remote corners. Many of the rooms are panelled and there is a beautiful oak staircase, as well as many fine paintings and items of furniture and china. The exquisite walled garden is planted with traditional English vegetables, fruit and flowers

🅾 **House**: 27 March to end Sept: Wed 2–6. **Note**: Only ground floor and basement are shown. **Garden**: 27 March to end Sept: Wed & Thur 2–6. House & garden also open Tues, Thur and Fri by written appointment only with Mr J. D. Wrisdale at above address. **Events**: occasional concerts

💷 £3.70. Garden only £2.60. No party reduction. Access roads unsuitable for coaches which must park in lay-by at gates ½ml from house

♿ Courtyard cobbled. Garden: accessible. Wheelchair

🌹 Rose and herb garden

---

There are special events at most Trust properties; please telephone 0870 458 4000 for details

🐕 On leads and only in garden

➡️ (3:G2) 2½ml NW of Burgh le Marsh, 7ml W of Skegness on S side of A158 (access off roundabout) [122: TF467668] **Bus**: Road Car 6 Skegness–Lincoln (passing close ⊠ Skegness) **Station**: Skegness 7ml

**NT properties nearby** Monksthorpe Chapel, Tattershall Castle

---

## GUNBY HALL ESTATE: MONKSTHORPE CHAPEL ✠

Monksthorpe, nr Spilsby   Lincolnshire
**Tel** 01909 486411 (Regional Office)

---

One of the two best surviving English examples of a Baptist Chapel from the late 17th century. This remote Chapel, originally a brick barn, with outdoor baptistry was used by local Baptists as a secluded place of worship. The Chapel was substantially altered to its present appearance in the early 19th century

🕐 April to end of Sept: Wed & Thur 2–5 (access by collection of the key from Gunby Hall – £10 returnable deposit required). Chapel open and stewarded from 1–5 on Sats: 13 Apr, 11 May, 15 June, 13 July, 10 Aug, 14 Sept

£ Entrance is free, but a £1 donation per visitor is requested towards the upkeep of the Chapel

♿ Chapel accessible (parking available close to the chapel)

➡️ (3:G2) From A158 in Candlesby, turn off main road opposite Royal Oak pub, following signs to Monksthorpe. Follow road for about 1½ ml and turn left. After 50m turn left at dead end sign. Parking is on the left at the entrance to the avenue [122:TF462651] **Station**: Skegness 9ml

---

## GUNBY HALL ESTATE: WHITEGATES COTTAGE 🏠

Mill Lane, Bratoft, nr Spilsby   Lincolnshire
**Tel** 01909 486411 (Regional Office)

---

A small thatched cottage, built c.1770 to provide accommodation for estate workers. Notable for its mud and stud walling, it has been restored using traditional methods and materials

🕐 27 March to end Sept: Wed 2–6 by written appointment only with the tenant, Mr J. Zaremba

£ £1.50. Parties should not exceed six at any one time, as rooms small. WCs at Gunby Hall (above)

➡️ (3:G2) 2ml W of Burgh le Marsh, 8ml W of Skegness. Approached by Gunby Lane off A158 just W of the roundabout N of Gunby Hall. **Public transport**: as for Gunby Hall, above [122:TF462651]

**NT properties nearby** Gunby Hall, Monksthorpe Chapel, Tattershall Castle

## HARDWICK HALL                                                                 Derbyshire

Doe Lea, Chesterfield S44 5QJ · **Tel** 01246 850430 · **Fax** 01246 854200
**Email** hardwickhall@ntrust.org.uk

One of Britain's foremost Elizabethan houses and a magnificent statement of the wealth and authority of its builder, Bess of Hardwick. Like a huge glass lantern, the house dominates the surrounding area and contains outstanding collections of 16th-century furniture, tapestries and needlework. Walled courtyards enclose fine gardens, orchards and a herb garden, and the surrounding country park contains rare breeds of cattle and sheep

**Note**: Extensive building work throughout 2002 may lessen visitors' enjoyment. Due to limited lighting, visitors wishing to make a close study of tapestries and textiles should avoid dull days early and late in the season. To avoid congestion, access to the house may be limited at peak periods. Visitors are advised to allow 45 minutes to tour the house. The remains of Hardwick Old Hall in the grounds are in the guardianship of English Heritage (01246 850431)

**What's new in 2002**: Return of Gideon tapestries and Lapiere Canopy

- **Hall**: 27 March to 27 Oct: daily except Mon, Tues & Fri (but open BH Mons, Good Fri & Tues 4 June) 12.30–5; 12.30–4 in Oct. **Garden**: 27 March to 27 Oct: daily except Tues, 11–5.30. **Parkland**: daily. **Old Hall (EH)**: 23 March to 31 Oct: daily except Tues & Fri 11–6. **Stainsby Mill**: see p.229. **Events**: send s.a.e. for details

- £6.40; child £3.20; family £16. Garden only £3.40; child £1.70; family £8.50. Reduction for parties of 15+ by written arrangement with Property Manager; please send s.a.e. Vehicles £2 (NT/EH members free). Country park car park 80p for non-members (season ticket £10). Joint ticket for Hall (NT) & Old Hall (EH): £8.50; child £4.25; family £21.25 (NT members free). Children under 15 must be accompanied by an adult

- Tours of stonemasons' yard Wed/Thur pm (except 29, 30 May), £1 (inc. NT members). Hall guided tours and school visits Mons in July & Aug (not BH Mon) 12.15–4

- 27 March to 27 Oct: daily except Mon, Tues & Fri (but open BH Mons, Good Fri, Tues 4 June and Mons in July & Aug) 12–5 (12–4.30 in Oct (shop/restaurant tel. 01246 854088)

- House: ramped entrance; ground floor accessible; illustrated booklet of upper floors. Great Kitchen & shop: ramped access. Garden: accessible. Park: access around Miller's Pond and Great Pond. Bookable wheelchairs for ground floor and garden

- Braille guide, tactile maps of garden and park walks; large-print introductory guides. Herb & flower garden. Herbs and some objects in house can be touched, ask at reception for details

- Licensed restaurant in Great Kitchen as shop. Lunches 12–2, teas 2–5, 2–4.30 in Oct. Last orders 30min before closing. Party bookings by written application with s.a.e. Picnics in car park and parkland only

**Please remember – your membership card is always needed for free admission**

EAST MIDLANDS · 225

[👶] Parent and baby facilities accessible from car park; baby carriers. Highchair, children's portions

[🎒] School parties to house Wed and Thur, also Mons in July; also to park, Stainsby Mill and Old Hall; pre-booking essential. Teachers' resource books available for New Hall, Garden and Stainsby Mill

[🐕] On leads and only in park

[→] (3:C2) **Note**: A one-way traffic system operates in the Park; access only via Stainsby Mill entrance (leave M1, exit 29, follow brown signs), exit only via Hardwick Inn. Park gates shut 6 in summer, 5.30 in winter. 6½ml W of Mansfield, 9½ml SE of Chesterfield; approach from M1 (exit 29) via A6175 [120: SK463638] **Bus**: Cosy Coaches C1 from ⇌ Chesterfield to Hall (Sun, June–Aug only); otherwise Stagecoach Express 737, 747 Sheffield/Chesterfield–Nottingham, 48 Chesterfield–Bolsover (local buses link with Chesterfield ⇌ station), alight Glapwell 'Young Vanish', 1½ml **Station**: Chesterfield 8ml

**NT properties nearby** Calke Abbey, Kedleston Hall, Stainsby Mill

---

# HIGH PEAK ESTATE            Derbyshire

High Peak Estate Office, Edale End, Hope Valley S33 2RF · **Tel** 01433 670368
**Fax** 01433 670397
**Email** highpeakestate@ntrust.org.uk

---

The High Peak is outstanding walking country, stretching from the heather-clad moors of Park Hall to the gritstone of Derwent Edge, and from the peat bogs of Bleaklow to the limestone crags of Winnats Pass. The wild and dramatic Pennine moorlands are of international importance for their populations of breeding birds, including golden plover, merlin and red grouse. Sites of particular interest include Mam Tor, with its spectacular views, landslip and prehistoric settlement; Odin Mine, one of the oldest lead mines in Derbyshire; Kinder Scout, the highest point for fifty miles around and where the Mass Trespass of 1932 took place; and the unspoilt valley of Snake Pass. The Trust also owns several farms in the beautiful Edale valley

[O] Open and unrestricted access to walkers all year to moorland, subject to occasional management closures (which are advertised locally). Access to farmland is via public rights of way and permitted paths. Five information shelters are open all year: Lee Barn (110:SK096855) on Pennine Way near Jacob's Ladder; Dalehead (110: SK101843) in Edale; South Head Farm (SK060854) at Kinder; Edale End (SK161864) between Edale and Hope; Grindle Barns above Ladybower Reservoir (SK189895). **Events**: send s.a.e or email for details of events and wide range of leaflets

[£] Many free car parks (not NT) in area. Also pay-and-display (not NT) at Edale, Mam Nick, Castleton, Bowden Bridge and Hayfield

[♿] Excellent views from various sites, including Mam Nick, Blue John and Snake Pass; leaflet available from Estate Office

[🎒] Many opportunities for educational groups; new teachers' resource book; contact Education Officer

**For general enquiries, please telephone 0870 458 4000**

➡ (3:B1) The estate covers the area N & S of the A57 on the Sheffield side of Snake Top, E of Hayfield and W of Castleton [110:SK100855] **Bus**: First Mainline 403 New Mills–Castleton operates to within 1ml of South Head Farm, weekends only, April–Oct only. Frequent services to Castleton from surrounding areas; also to Edale from Castleton, weekends only **Station**: Edale is 1½ml from Dale Head, 2ml from Lee Barn and 3ml from Edale End; Chinley is 3ml from South Head Farm; Hope is 3ml from Edale End

**NT properties nearby** Longshaw Estate, Lyme Park

## KEDLESTON HALL
Derbyshire

Derby DE22 5JH · **Tel** 01332 842191 · **Fax** 01332 841972
**Email** kedlestonhall@ntrust.org.uk

A classical Palladian mansion built 1759–65 for the Curzon family who have lived in the area since the 12th century. The house boasts the most complete and least-altered sequence of Robert Adam interiors in England, with the magnificent state rooms retaining their great collections of paintings and original furniture. The Eastern Museum houses a fascinating range of objects collected by Lord Curzon when Viceroy of India (1899–1905)

- **House**: 23 March to 3 Nov: daily except Thur & Fri (but open Good Fri) 12–4.30. **Garden**: as house 10–6. **Park**: 23 March to 22 Dec: daily; 5 Jan to 17 March 2003, Sat & Sun. *Times*: 23 March to 3 Nov 10–6; Nov to March 2003 10–4. **Events**: tel. for details of events programme. Licensed for civil weddings

- £5.30; child £2.60; family £13.20. Park & garden only: £2.40; child £1.10 (refundable against tickets for house). Thur & Fri £2 per vehicle for park (other facilities closed). £1 reduction for booked parties of 15+

- Introductory talks from 18th-century housekeeper. Guided walks around park and/or gardens can be booked, tel. 01332 842393/842338

- 23 March to 3 Nov: as house 11.30–5.30; Nov to 22 Dec: Sat & Sun 12–4. Tel. 01332 843405

- House: access via stairclimber (last entry 3.30). Garden: accessible. Restaurant & shop: accessible. Wheelchairs and self-drive vehicle for garden and limited use in park (subject to availability)

- Braille guide. Many items can be touched

- Sympathetic Hearing Scheme

- Licensed restaurant as house 11–5. Nov to 22 Dec: Sat & Sun light meals and teas 12–4. Party bookings by written application with s.a.e. Tel. 01332 843404

**Please see the area introductions for details of coast & countryside properties**

# EAST MIDLANDS · 227

- WC with baby-changing facility. Children's guide and quiz; children's portions
- Education groups welcome, contact property
- On leads and only in park
- (3:C3) 5ml NW of Derby, entrance off Kedleston Road and signposted from roundabout where A38 crosses A52 close to Markeaton Park [SK312403] **Bus**: Arriva Derby 109 ☒ Derby–Ashbourne calls at Hall on Sun, otherwise alight the Smithy, thence 1ml **Station**: Duffield (U) 3½ml; Derby 5½ml

**NT properties nearby** Calke Abbey, Sudbury Hall and Museum of Childhood

## LONGSHAW ESTATE                                             Derbyshire

Sheffield S11 7TZ
**Tel** 01433 631708 (Visitor Centre) · 01433 631757 (Wardens' Office)
**Fax** 01433 631757 (Wardens' Office)
**Email** longshaw@ntrust.org.uk

A wide expanse of open moorland, woodland and farms within the Peak District National Park, with dramatic views and excellent walking

- **Estate**: all year. Lodge is not open. **Visitor centre** (tea-room, shop and information centre): 2 Jan to 31 March, Nov & Dec: Sat & Sun; April, May & Oct: daily except Mon & Tues (but open BH Mons); June, July, Aug & Sept: daily. *Times*: 10.30–5 or sunset if earlier. Parties at other times by arrangement. **Events**: 5–7 Sept, Longshaw Sheepdog Trials
- £1. Car park 200m from visitor centre [SK266800]; access difficult for coaches; no coaches at weekends or BHols. Car parks for estate at Haywood [110/119: SK256778] and Wooden Pole [110/119: SK267790]. Riding permits available. Longshaw walks and leaflets from visitor centre
- Groups may book guided walks around the estate, contact Wardens' office
- As visitor centre. Christmas tree sales in main car park in Dec
- Access limited to carriage drive; map available. 1 car-parking space at visitor centre, book with Visitor Centre Manager
- At visitor centre
- Baby-changing facilities. Highchairs
- Education groups welcome
- On leads only; not in visitor centre
- (3:C2) 7¼ml from Sheffield, next to A625 Sheffield–Hathersage road; Woodcroft car park is off B6055, 200m S of junction with A625 [110/119: SK266802] **Bus**: First Mainline 240 Sheffield–Bakewell (passing ☒ Grindleford); 272 Sheffield–Castleton (passing ☒ Hathersage). All pass close ☒ Sheffield **Station**: Grindleford (U) 2ml

**NT properties nearby** Hardwick Hall, High Peak Estate, Stainsby Mill

**Unless indicated, last admission is always 30 mins before closing time**

## LYVEDEN NEW BIELD 🏠✝✤🎭     Northamptonshire

nr Oundle, Peterborough PE8 5AT · **Tel** 01832 205358
**Email** lyvedennewbield@ntrust.org.uk

An incomplete Elizabethan garden house and moated garden. Begun in 1595 by Sir Thomas Tresham to symbolise his Catholic faith, Lyveden remains virtually unaltered since work stopped when Tresham died in 1605

- 🅞 House, Elizabethan water garden and visitor information room: 23 March to 3 Nov open daily except Mon & Tues (but open BH Mons and Tues 4 June), 10.30–5; 4 Nov to end March 2003 Sat & Sun 10.30–4. Parties by arrangement with custodian. **Events**: send s.a.e. for details

- £ £2. Limited roadside parking; access on foot ½ml along farm track; parking for coaches by arrangement

- 🚶 Tours for groups

- 🛍 Small selection of gifts

- ♿ Drivers with disabilities may park at the house

- 🎒 Education groups welcome

- 🐕 On leads only

- ➔ (3:F6) 4ml SW of Oundle via A427, 3ml E of Brigstock, off Harley Way [141: SP983853] **Bus**: Stagecoach in Northants X4 Northampton–Peterborough (passing close ☒ Peterborough); alight Lower Benefield, 2ml by bridlepath; Stagecoach United Counties/Blands 8 Kettering Corby, alight Brigstock, 2½ml. Both pass close ☒ Kettering **Station**: Kettering 10ml

**NT properties nearby** Canons Ashby, Houghton Mill

---

## THE OLD MANOR 🏠🏠✝✤     Derbyshire

Norbury, Ashbourne DE6 2ED · **Tel** 01909 486411 (Regional Office)

A stone-built hall, dating from the 13th to 15th centuries and of specialist architectural interest only. The adjacent church (not NT) is also worth visiting

**Note**: It is uncertain as to whether the property will be open in 2002. Please contact Regional Office for current information

- 🅞 27 March to end Sept: Tue, Wed & Sat, by written appointment only with the tenant. Coaches need to drop passengers at top of drive

- £ £1.50

- ➔ (3:B3) [128:SK125424] **Bus**: Arriva North Midlands 409 Uttoxeter–Ashbourne (passing close ☒ Uttoxeter), alight Ellastone, ¾ml **Station**: Uttoxeter (U) 7½ml

**NT properties nearby** Kedleston Hall, Sudbury Hall and Museum of Childhood

---

**There are special events at most Trust properties; please telephone 0870 458 4000 for details**

## PRIEST'S HOUSE 🏠            Northamptonshire

Easton on the Hill, nr Stamford · **Tel** 01909 486411 (Regional Office)

A pre-Reformation priest's lodge, of specialist architectural interest only and containing a small museum of village bygones

- **O** Unmanned. Names of keyholders on property noticeboard. Appointments for groups may be made through local representative Mr Paul Way, 39 Church St, Easton on the Hill, Stamford PE9 3LL
- **£** Donation of 50p requested. Unsuitable for coaches
- House: ground-floor room accessible
- → (3:F5) Approx. 2ml SW of Stamford off A43 [141: TF011045] **Bus**: Blond/Searle/Stagecoach in Peterborough 44, 180 from Stamford (passing close ≋ Stamford), alight Easton, ½ml (tel. 01522 553135) **Station**: Stamford 2ml

**NT properties nearby** Lyveden New Bield, Woolsthorpe Manor

## STAINSBY MILL: HARDWICK ESTATE        Derbyshire

Doe Lea, Chesterfield S44 5QJ · **Tel** 01246 850430 (Hardwick Hall)
**Fax** 01246 854200 · **Email** stainsbymill@ntrust.org.uk

A remarkably complete water-powered flour mill, with newly reconstructed 1849–50 machinery and still in good working order

- **O** 23 March to 31 May, 1 Oct to 3 Nov: daily except Mon, Tues & Fri (but open BH Mons and Good Fri. 1 June to 30 Sept: daily except Mon & Tues (but open BH Mon, Tues 4 June and Mons July & Aug). *Times*: 11–4.30. **Events**: 11/12 May, National Mills Day
- **£** £2.10; child £1; family £5.20. Children under 15 must be accompanied by an adult. Parties (no reduction) only by arrangement with Property Manager, Hardwick Hall. **Note**: No WC at mill, but available at Hardwick Hall car park
- On request at the mill. For private out-of-hours tours contact Property Manager
- At Hardwick Hall
- Mill: limited access to ground floor
- Braille guide. Panelling and millstones on display may be touched
- At Hardwick Hall
- School parties Wed & Thur, plus Fri June to Sept; teachers' technology resource book; contact Property Manager at Hardwick Hall
- On leads and only in park
- → (3:C2) From M1 exit 29 take A6175 signposted to Clay Cross then first left and left again to Stainsby Mill [120:SK455653] **Bus**: As for Hardwick Hall, but, except for the C1, alight Heath, thence 1ml (1½ml on X2) **Station**: Chesterfield 9ml

**NT properties nearby** Calke Abbey, Hardwick Hall, Kedleston Hall

For all your information needs check our website www.nationaltrust.org.uk

## STAUNTON HAROLD CHURCH ✝ 🌳     Leicestershire

Staunton Harold, Ashby-de-la-Zouch · **Tel** 01332 863822 · **Fax** 01332 865272
**Email** stauntonharold@ntrust.org.uk

One of the very few churches built during the Commonwealth, set in attractive parkland. The interior retains its original 17th-century cushions and has fine panelling and painted ceilings

**Note**: A one-way system in operation on the estate; coaches follow alternative brown sign route

- ⭕ 23 March to 29 Sept: daily except Mon & Tues; Oct: Sat & Sun. *Times*: 1–5 or sunset if earlier
- 💷 Donations of £1 requested, collection box. WCs (not NT) 300m
- ♿ Church & park: largely accessible
- ☕ Light refreshments at Hall (Sue Ryder Foundation)
- ➡ (3:C4) 5ml NE of Ashby-de-la-Zouch, W of B587. Access from M42/A42, jct13 [128: SK379208] **Bus**: Arriva Derby 68/9 Derby–Swadlincote (passing close ≋ Derby), alight Melbourne, 3½ml or Ticknall via Calke Park, 3ml **Cycle**: NCN 6 2½ml

**NT properties nearby** Calke Abbey, Kedleston Hall, Sudbury Hall

---

## MR STRAW'S HOUSE 🏠 🛡     Nottinghamshire

7 Blyth Grove, Worksop S81 0JG · **Tel** 01909 482380
**Email** mrstrawshouse@ntrust.org.uk

This modest semi-detached Edwardian house provides a fascinating insight into everyday life in the early part of the 20th century. The interior has remained unaltered since the 1930s and features contemporary wallpaper, Victorian furniture and household objects. There are also new displays of family costume and memorabilia and a typical suburban garden

**Note**: Blyth Grove is a private road; there is no access without advance booking. There is a car park with picnic area opposite the house for visitors with timed tickets. On arrival please go to reception at 5 Blyth Grove

- ⭕ 23 March to 2 Nov: daily except Sun & Mon (but closed BH Mons, Good Fri and Tues 4 June) 11–4.30. Admission for all visitors (inc. NT members) is by timed ticket, **which must be booked in advance**. All bookings by tel. or letter (with s.a.e.) to Custodian. On quiet days a same-day tel. call is often sufficient. **Events**: send s.a.e. for details

---

**Please remember – your membership card is always needed for free admission**

EAST MIDLANDS · 231

- £ £4.20; child £2.10; family £10.50. **Note**: Booked morning and evening guided tours for groups (max. 24) by arrangement (extra charge, inc. NT members, £1 for morning and £2.50 evening)
- Access: difficult, house small and soon congested; tel. in advance. No wheelchair access
- Braille guide; audio cassette; some items may be touched
- Education groups welcome. Workshops available; contact Custodian
- (3:D2) In Worksop, follow signs to Bassetlaw General Hospital. House signposted from Blyth Road (B6045) [120: SK590802] **Bus**: From surrounding areas **Station**: Worksop ½ml **Cycle**: NCN 6 ¾ml

**NT properties nearby** Clumber Park, Hardwick Hall, Stainsby Mill

## SUDBURY HALL                                                        Derbyshire

Sudbury, Ashbourne DE6 5HT · **Tel** 01283 585305 · **Fax** 01283 585139
**Email** sudburyhall@ntrust.org.uk

One of the most individual of late 17th-century houses, with rich interior decoration including wood carving by Gibbons, superb plasterwork, and decorative painted murals and ceilings by Laguerre. The Great Staircase is one of the finest of its kind in an English house

**Note**: Owing to low light levels, visitors wishing to study the Hall's plasterwork or paintings in detail should avoid dull days and late afternoons towards end of season

- **Hall**: 16 March to 3 Nov: daily except Mon & Tues (but open BH Mons, Good Fri & Tues 4 June). *Times*: 1–5 (dusk if earlier). **Grounds**: as Hall 10–5. **Events**: send s.a.e. for details. Licensed for civil weddings

For general enquiries, please telephone 0870 458 4000

- £3.90; child £2; family £9.80. Joint ticket for Hall & Museum £6.30; child £3.10; family £15.60. Parties by arrangement with the Bookings Secretary
- Guided and specialist tours of Hall; 'Behind the Scenes' tours; for details contact Property Manager
- 16 March to 3 Nov: as Hall 12.30–5
- Hall: access difficult, contact Property Manager in advance; wheelchair for inside use. Garden: difficult. Lake, tea-room & shop: accessible. Multi-seater volunteer-driven buggy to take visitors from car park to property
- Braille guide
- Coach House tea-room as house 12–5 (last orders 4.30). Coaches by appointment only, write (with s.a.e.) to Property Secretary for booking form
- Baby-changing facilities in stable block. Children's portions. No back carriers in Hall; front slings, reins and indoor buggy available
- Activities linked to National Curriculum for school parties by arrangement with Education Officer (tel. 01283 585022)
- On leads and only in car park
- (3:B4) 6ml E of Uttoxeter at jct of A50 Derby–Stoke and A515 Ashbourne [128: SK160323] **Bus**: Arriva North Midlands Stevensons 1 Burton-on-Trent–Uttoxeter (passing ≠ Tutbury & Hatton and close ≠ Burton-on-Trent **Station**: Tutbury & Hatton (U) 5ml

**NT properties nearby** Calke Abbey, Kedleston Hall

---

## SUDBURY HALL – THE NATIONAL TRUST MUSEUM OF CHILDHOOD
Derbyshire

As Sudbury Hall, Ashbourne DE6 5HT · **Tel** 01283 585305
**Email** museumofchildhood@ntrust.org.uk

---

Housed in the 19th-century service wing of Sudbury Hall, the Museum contains fascinating and innovative displays about children from the 18th century onwards. There are chimney climbs for adventurous 'sweep-sized' youngsters, and Betty Cadbury's fine collection of toys and dolls is on show

- 16 March to 3 Nov: daily except Mon & Tues (but open BH Mons, Good Fri & Tues 4 June) 1–5 or dusk if earlier. **Events**: special Christmas opening with family activities and tea with Santa Claus: 7, 8 Dec and 14, 15 Dec: 12–4 (last admission 3.30)
- £3.90; child £2; family £9.80. Joint ticket for Hall & Museum £6.30; child £3.10; family £15.60. Parties by arrangement with the Bookings Secretary
- Guided tours; contact Property Manager
- Days as Sudbury Hall. *Times*: 12.30–5; also special Christmas opening 7, 8 & 14, 15 Dec 12–4

---

**Please see the area introductions for details of coast & countryside properties**

- ♿ Museum: largely accessible; wheelchair
- Handling collections
- ☕ Coach House tea-room days as Museum. *Times*: 16 March to 3 Nov 12–5 (last orders 4.30). Special Christmas opening 7, 8 & 14, 15 Dec 12–4. Coaches by written appointment (with s.a.e.) only
- 👶 Baby-changing facilities; baby back-carriers allowed; pushchairs difficult
- Educational materials. Special schools' facilities as for Sudbury Hall. Also special events and activities for children; send s.a.e. to Education Officer for details
- 🐕 On leads and only in car park
- ➔ (3:B4) As Sudbury Hall [128: SK160323]

**NT properties nearby** Calke Abbey, Kedleston Hall

## TATTERSHALL CASTLE — Lincolnshire

Tattershall, Lincoln LN4 4LR · **Tel/Fax** 01526 342543
**Email** tattershallcastle@ntrust.org.uk

A vast fortified and moated red-brick tower, built in medieval times for Ralph Cromwell, Lord Treasurer of England. The building was rescued from becoming derelict by Lord Curzon 1911–14 and contains four great chambers with enormous Gothic fireplaces, tapestries and brick vaulting. There are spectacular views from the battlements and a guardhouse with museum room

- 🕐 23 March to 3 Nov: daily except Thur & Fri 11–5.30 (11–4 in Oct), also open Thur in Aug; 9 Nov to 15 Dec: Sat & Sun 12–4. Ground floor of castle may occasionally be closed for functions or events, tel. to check. Licensed for civil weddings
- £ £3.20; child £1.60; family £8. Discount for parties, contact Custodian. Free audio guide. Coach parties must book
- 🛍 As castle
- ♿ Close parking for disabled drivers, contact Custodian for details. Castle: ramps to ground floor. Photograph album of inaccessible parts of castle. Shop: accessible. Grounds: accessible, gravel paths
- Braille guide
- ☕ Some drinks and ice creams available in shop. Picnicking welcome in grounds
- 👶 WC with baby-changing facility; child back-carriers allowed; family guidebook; I-Spy sheet
- Castle is particularly suitable for school groups; teachers' resource book; workshops

**Unless indicated, last admission is always 30 mins before closing time**

## 234 · EAST MIDLANDS

- 🚲 Cycles can be attached to paling fence and helmets left in office
- 🐕 On leads and only in car park; no shaded parking; dog hooks in shade by entrance to grounds
- ➡️ (3:F3) On S side of A153, 15ml NE of Sleaford; 10ml SW of Horncastle [122: TF209575] **Bus**: Road Car/Brylaine 5 Lincoln–Boston (passing close ≋ Lincoln and Boston) **Station**: Ruskington (U) 10ml

**NT properties nearby** Belton House, Gunby Hall, Monksthorpe Chapel

---

## ULVERSCROFT NATURE RESERVE 🐦   Leicestershire
nr Loughborough · **Tel** 01909 486411 (Regional Office)

---

Part of the ancient forest of Charnwood, especially beautiful in spring during the bluebell season

- 🅾️ Access by permit only from The Secretary, Leicestershire & Rutland Wildlife Trust, Longfellow Road, Knighton Fields, Leicester LE2 6BT (tel. 0116 270 2999)
- ➡️ (3:D5) [129:SK493118] **Bus**: Arriva Fox County 117–9, 217/8 Leicester–Swadlincote (passing close ≋ Leicester) **Station**: Barrow upon Soar 7ml, Loughborough 7½ml

**NT properties nearby** Calke Abbey, Staunton Harold Church

---

## WINSTER MARKET HOUSE 🏠   Derbyshire
nr Matlock · **Tel** 01335 350245

---

A market house of the late 17th or early 18th century, now restored and housing a NT information room

- 🅾️ 23 March to 3 Nov: daily (times vary)
- 💷 Free. Public WC in side street near house
- ➡️ (3:B3) 4ml W of Matlock on S side of B5057 in main street of Winster [119: SK241606] **Bus**: Hulley's 172 Matlock–Bakewell (passing close ≋ Matlock) **Station**: Matlock (U) 4ml **Cycle**: NCN 1 1¼ml (via A153)

**NT properties nearby** Hardwick Hall, Ilam Park

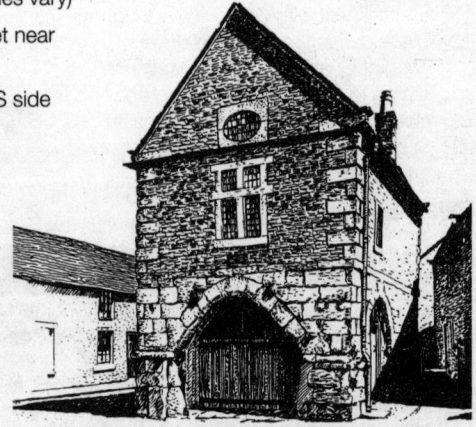

---

**There are special events at most Trust properties; please telephone 0870 458 4000 for details**

EAST MIDLANDS · **235**

# WOOLSTHORPE MANOR 🏠  Lincolnshire
23 Newton Way, Woolsthorpe-by-Colsterworth, nr Grantham NG33 5NR
**Tel/Fax** 01476 860338 · **Email** woolsthorpemanor@ntrust.org.uk

A small 17th-century manor house, the birthplace and family home of Sir Isaac Newton, who formulated some of his major works here during the Plague years (1665–67). An early edition of his *Principia* is on display. The orchard includes a descendant of the famous apple tree. Science Discovery Centre and exhibition

- **House & Science Discovery Centre**: 1 to 22 March Sat & Sun 1–5; 23 March to 29 Sept: daily except Mon & Tues (but open BH Mons, Good Fri & Tues 4 June) 1–5, but 1–6 during July & Aug; 5 Oct to 3 Nov: Sat & Sun 1–5 but Wed to Sun 1–5 half-term week. **Note**: In the interests of preservation, the numbers of visitors admitted may be limited, particularly at busy weekends and BHols. **Events**: 'The Science of Christmas' 14, 15 & 21, 22 Dec. Please tel. property for details

- £3.50; child £1.70; family £8.70. No reduction for parties, which must book in advance with Custodian as parking for coaches is limited to one at a time

- Tours of house and Science Discovery Centre to booked parties by arrangement with Custodian throughout year

- Sloping site. Close parking. House: ground floor accessible; photograph album of upper rooms

- Braille guides for adults and children

- Well equipped for education groups: teachers' resource book; education room; interactive science exhibition; workshops

- On leads and only in car park

- (3:E4) 7ml S of Grantham, ½ml NW of Colsterworth, 1ml W of A1 (not to be confused with Woolsthorpe near Belvoir). Leave A1 at Colsterworth roundabout via B676, at second crossroads turn right following NT signs [130: SK924244] **Bus**: Road Car 606–8 Grantham–South Witham (passing close ≥ Grantham) **Station**: Grantham 7ml

**NT properties nearby** Belton House, Tattershall Castle

For all your information needs check our website www.nationaltrust.org.uk

## THE WORKHOUSE, SOUTHWELL  Nottinghamshire

Upton Road, Southwell NG25 0PT · **Tel** 01636 817250 · **Fax** 01636 817251
**Email** theworkhouse@ntrust.org.uk

The Workhouse at Southwell is a formidable 19th-century brick institution with a story to tell about the care of the poor in Britain. The revolutionary but harsh 'welfare' system introduced here in 1824 was adopted nation-wide in the New Poor Law. The building is the least altered workhouse in existence today, a survivor from the hundreds that once covered the country. Discover the people who lived and worked here, what life was like and how things have changed today

**What's new in 2002**: As this is a new property, The Workhouse will be a popular attraction and a booking service is available at no extra charge. Visitors are strongly advised to book for peak times, including weekends, Bank Holidays and the spring. Groups welcome but please book in advance

- 13 March to 3 Nov: daily except Mon & Tues (but open BH Mons) 12–5 but 11–5 during Aug. Also open every day week commencing 27 May and Tues to Sun week commencing 21 Oct.
- £4; child £2; family £10. Introductory video, displays and audio guide included
- Ground floor access only; wheelchairs on upper floors for pre-booking – please ring for details of special access
- Standard audio guide tour
- Audio loops from reception; video and audio guide
- Tea-room and restaurant facilities in nearby Southwell and the surrounding area
- Parent and baby facilities accessible from car park; activity handling room
- Excellent property for education groups in many subject areas. Education Officer and facilities, school tours and activities (booking essential)
- Cycle racks
- (3:D3) 13ml from Nottingham on A612 and 8ml from Newark on A617 and A612 **Bus**: Pathfinder 100/1 ≠ Newark North Gate–Nottingham; Stagecoach in Mansfield 29/A Newark–Mansfield (passing ≠ Fiskerton). All pass ≠ Newark Castle **Station**: Fiskerton (U) 2ml, Newark North Gate 7$\frac{1}{2}$ml

**Please remember – your membership card is always needed for free admission**

# Introduction to the West Midlands

The West Midlands is an intriguing mix of urban areas and delightful unspoilt countryside of much variety and charm. There are surprisingly extensive tracts of open moorland and hills, as well as picturesque villages, grand country houses and some notable gardens.

The area's key upland properties lie to the west – the **Clent Hills** in Worcestershire, splendid country for walkers with an easy-access trail from **Nimmings Wood Car Park and Cafe** to the viewing platform near the summit of the hill with breathtaking views in all directions, and Shropshire's **Long Mynd**. The Mynd is an area of upland heath and a Site of Special Scientific Interest. Excellent access is possible via the **Carding Mill Valley**. The Trust owns seven miles of nearby **Wenlock Edge**, a geologically interesting wooded escarpment near the village of Much Wenlock. Elegant **Attingham Park**, the great rolling estate at Dudmaston and the Elizabethan **Wilderhope Manor** lie not far away. Just beyond the western fringe of the Peak District National Park is **Biddulph Grange**, one of England's most extraordinary gardens. The South Peak Estate straddles the Derbyshire/Staffordshire border and includes **Dovedale**, famous for its ashwoods and geological features, as well as the former **Leek & Manifold Valley Light Railway**, now a surfaced track leading through dramatic limestone scenery. Nearby **Ilam Park** has a range of visitor facilities and local information and there is an information shelter at **Milldale**.

The borderland of England and Wales runs south from here into the green rolling countryside of Herefordshire, where excellent walking is possible. The **Croft Castle Estate** offers either a circular walk or other open routes that provide access to the woodland and the Iron Age hill-fort of **Croft Ambrey**. The site is famous for its veteran trees but also has a rich diversity of wildlife including fallow deer, white-clawed crayfish, redstart and curlew.

Many Trust properties lie within easy distance of the central conurbation of Birmingham, including the beautiful medieval manor of **Baddesley Clinton** and nearby **Packwood House**. A little further away is **Charlecote Park**, rich in associations with William Shakespeare. To the west of Birmingham is the dramatic escarpment of Kinver Edge, with its fascinating Rock Houses. On the edge of Wolverhampton are **Wightwick Manor** – an Arts & Crafts masterpiece with wonderful gardens – and **Moseley Old Hall**, with its romantic Charles II associations.

## Highlights for Visitors with Disabilities ...

The **Brockhampton Estate** has a nature trail with touchable sculptures. The trail may not suit all visitors so please contact the property for information.

## ... and for Families

Regular family events at **Attingham Park** and **Moseley Old Hall**; **Shugborough**, with its working historic farm; new children's quiz at **Biddulph Grange Garden**.

**OS grid references for main properties with no individual entry (OS map series numbers given in brackets)**

| | |
|---|---|
| Clent Hills | [139] SO932803 |
| Croft Ambrey | [137] SO449656 |
| Long Mynd | [137] SO430940 |
| Wenlock Edge | [138] SO595988 |

## Further Information

Contact the Membership Department, PO Box 39, Bromley BR1 3XL. Tel. 0870 458 4000. Email: enquiries@thenationaltrust.org.uk

## ATTINGHAM PARK

Shropshire

Shrewsbury SY4 4TP · **Tel** 01743 708162 · **Infoline** 01743 708123
**Fax** 01743 708175 · **Email** attingham@ntrust.org.uk

One of the great houses of the Midlands. The elegant mansion was built in 1785 for the 1st Lord Berwick to the design of George Steuart and has a picture gallery by John Nash. The magnificent Regency interiors contain collections of ambassadorial silver, Italian furniture and Grand Tour paintings. The park was landscaped by Repton and has attractive walks along the River Tern and through the deer park

- **House**: 23 March to 3 Nov: daily except Wed & Thur 1–4.30. Costumed guided tours from 1. (Open BH Mons 11–5). **Deer park & grounds**: daily (closed 25 Dec). *Times*: March to end Oct 9–8; Nov to Feb 2003 9–5. **Events**: send s.a.e. for programme

- £4.60; family £11.50. Park & grounds only £2.20. Booked parties (15+) £4

- Tours for booked parties at 11; £5.50 per head (inc. NT members)

- 23 March to 3 Nov: 12–5 (BH Mons 11–5)

- Disabled visitors may be set down by tea-room or in outer courtyard on request. House: access by rear lift with staff help, book in advance. Tea-room: access difficult; outside tables accessible. Mile Walk: accessible; self-drive vehicle

- Braille and large-print guides

- Licensed tea-room 23 March to 3 Nov: daily except Wed & Thur 12–5 (BH Mons 11–5). Also Nov to March: Sat & Sun 12.30–4. Closed 22–26 Dec. Lunches and suppers at other times for booked parties. Separate tea-room available. Picnic sites along Mile Walk

- Baby-changing facilities. Highchairs

- Environmental education resource pack; park exhibition in Bothy. Booked visits welcome; organised activities in environmental science, geography, history, art and technology; education room (max. 30)

- On leads in immediate vicinity of house, but not allowed in deer park

- (4:I4) 4ml SE of Shrewsbury, on N side of B4380 in Atcham village [126: SJ550099] **Bus**: Arriva North Midlands/Elcock/Pete's Travel 81, 96 Shrewsbury–Telford (all passing close ≠ Shrewsbury & Telford Central **Station**: Shrewsbury 5ml

**NT properties nearby** Benthall Hall, Dudmaston, Morville Hall, Powis Castle, Sunnycroft

**Please see the area introductions for details of coast & countryside properties**

# BADDESLEY CLINTON 🏠✝❋🌳👤🛡 Warwickshire

Rising Lane, Baddesley Clinton Village, Knowle, Solihull B93 0DQ
**Tel** 01564 783294 · **Fax** 01564 782706
**Email** baddesleyclinton@ntrust.org.uk

A romantic and atmospheric moated manor house, dating from the 15th century and little changed since 1634. The interiors reflect the house's heyday in the Elizabethan era, when it was a haven for persecuted Catholics – there are no fewer than three priest-holes. There is a delightful garden with stewponds, a lake walk and nature walk

- **House**: 6 March to 3 Nov: daily except Mon & Tues (closed Good Fri, open BH Mons & Tues 4 June). *Times*: March, April, Oct & Nov 1.30–5, May to end Sept 1.30–5.30. **Grounds**: 6 March to 15 Dec: daily except Mon & Tues (open BH Mons, Tues 4 June and Good Fri). *Times*: March, April, Oct & 1 to 3 Nov: 12–5; May to end Sept: 12–5.30; 6 Nov to 15 Dec: 12–4.30. **Events**: tel. or send s.a.e. for details

- £5.80; family £14.50. Grounds, restaurant & shop only £2.90. Combined ticket for Baddesley Clinton and Packwood House £8.50; family £21.25; garden only £4.25. Free parking. Parties of 15+ and coaches are welcome by written arrangement. **Note**: Admission to house is by timed ticket, but visitors may then stay as long as they wish

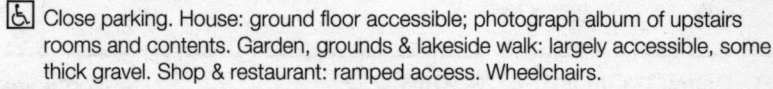

- Wed, Thur evenings by appointment. Supper can be included

BULLFINCH

- As grounds. Tel. 01564 785569

- Close parking. House: ground floor accessible; photograph album of upstairs rooms and contents. Garden, grounds & lakeside walk: largely accessible, some thick gravel. Shop & restaurant: ramped access. Wheelchairs.

- Braille guide; tactile route around the house

- Licensed restaurant as grounds. Party lunches and dinners arranged. Picnic tables near entrance. Tel. 01564 783010

- Baby-changing facilities and baby slings. No baby back-carriers, prams or pushchairs in house. Children's guide. Children's menu, highchairs

- School parties by appointment: Wed, Thur & Fri mornings. Teachers' resource book

- Lockable posts near ticket office

- On leads and only in car park (reasonable walks nearby)

- (4:K6) ¾ml W of A4141 Warwick–Birmingham road, at Chadwick End, 7½ml NW of Warwick, 6ml S of M42 junction 5; 15ml SE of central Birmingham [139: SP199715] **Station**: Lapworth (U), 2ml; Birmingham International 9ml

**NT properties nearby** Charlecote Park, Hanbury Hall, Packwood House

---

**Unless indicated, last admission is always 30 mins before closing time**

## BENTHALL HALL 🏠✝❋🛡  Shropshire

Broseley TF12 5RX · **Tel** 01952 882159
**Email** benthall@ntrust.org.uk

Situated on a plateau above the gorge of the Severn, this 16th-century stone house has mullioned and transomed windows and a stunning interior with carved oak staircase, decorated plaster ceilings and oak panelling. There is an intimate and carefully restored plantsman's garden, old kitchen garden and interesting Restoration church

**Note**: Benthall Hall is the home of Mr & Mrs Richard Benthall

- **House and garden**: 31 March to 29 Sept: Wed, Sun & BH Mons 1.30–5.30. **Events**: church services alternate Suns; visitors welcome
- £3.60; child £1.80. Garden only £2.30
- Booked parties by prior arrangement Wed & Sun only. Reduced rates. Coaches by appointment
- Hall: ground floor accessible. Garden: partly accessible
- Braille and large-print guides
- Regret no teas at Benthall Hall, but group catering available at nearby Dudmaston by prior arrangement. No picnics
- (4:I5) 1ml NW of Broseley (B4375), 4ml NE of Much Wenlock, 1ml SW of Ironbridge [127: SJ658025] **Bus**: Arriva North Midlands 9, 39, 99 Wellington–Bridgnorth, alight Broseley, 1ml (pass close ⇌ Telford Central) **Station**: Telford Central 7½ml

**NT properties nearby** Attingham Park, Dudmaston, Kinver Edge, Morville Hall, Sunnycroft, Wightwick Manor

## BERRINGTON HALL 🏠❋🛡  Herefordshire

nr Leominster HR6 0DW · **Tel** 01568 615721 · **Fax** 01568 613263
**Email** berrington@ntrust.org.uk

Beautifully set above a wide valley with sweeping views to the Brecon Beacons, this elegant Henry Holland house was built in the late 18th century and is set in parkland designed by 'Capability' Brown. The rather austere external appearance belies a surprisingly delicate interior, with beautifully decorated ceilings and a spectacular staircase hall. There are good collections of furniture and paintings, as well as a nursery, Victorian laundry, Georgian dairy and an attractive garden. The walled garden contains an historic collection of local apple trees

**Note**: Costume collection not displayed, but can be viewed by pre-booking. Please write to the property or contact the Costume Curator on 01568 613720

- **House**: 23 March to 3 Nov: daily except Thur & Fri (but open Good Fri) 1–5, closes 4.30 in Oct & Nov. **Garden**: as house 12–5, closes 4.30 in Oct & Nov. **Park walk**: 1 July to 3 Nov: as house. **Events**: send s.a.e. for details

**There are special events at most Trust properties; please telephone 0870 458 4000 for details**

WEST MIDLANDS · 241

[£] £4.40; family £11. Grounds only £3. Parties of 15+ only by written arrangement. Free car and coach park

[👤] By arrangement with Property Manager

[🛍] 23 March to 3 Nov: as house 12–5 (4.30 in Oct & Nov); Nov to 22 Dec: Sat & Sun 12–4.30

[♿] Parking for disabled drivers, enquire at ticket office. House: 2 wheelchairs. Garden: accessible; firm gravel paths. Self-drive single-seater batricar. Restaurant: access by 5 steps; in fine weather a table can be put in the courtyard on request

[👁] Braille and audio guides; staircase balustrades are interesting to touch

[☕] Servants' Hall restaurant and Edwardian tea-room (counter service) both licensed. 23 March to end Sept: daily except Thur & Fri 12–5, Oct 12–4.30. Also open weekends in Nov & Dec, hours as shop. Tel. 01568 610134. Picnic tables near car park and play area

[👶] Baby-changing facilities. Children's outdoor and indoor quizzes; play area in walled garden. Outdoor orienteering course

[🏫] School visits by arrangement

[➡] (4:H6) 3ml N of Leominster, 7ml S of Ludlow on W side of A49 [137: SO510637] **Bus**: First Midland Red/Caradoc 192, 292 Birmingham–Hereford (passing close ≷ Ludlow & Leominster), alight Luston, 2ml **Station**: Leominster (U) 4ml

**NT properties nearby** Brockhampton Estate, Croft Castle, The Weir

For all your information needs check our website www.nationaltrust.org.uk

## BIDDULPH GRANGE GARDEN ❇️ 🌿     Staffordshire

Biddulph Grange, Biddulph, Stoke-on-Trent ST8 7SD · **Tel** 01782 517999
**Fax** 01782 510624 · **Email** biddulphgrange@ntrust.org.uk

One of Britain's most exciting and unusual gardens. A series of connected 'compartments', designed in the mid 19th century by James Bateman to display specimens from his extensive and wide-ranging plant collection. Visitors are taken on a miniature tour of the world, featuring the Egyptian Court and imitation of the Great Wall of China, as well as a pinetum, fernery and rock gardens

- ⭕ 23 March to 3 Nov: daily except Mon and Tues (but open BH Mons & 4 June, closed Good Fri); 11 Nov to 22 Dec: Sat & Sun. *Times*: 23 March to 11 Nov: Wed to Fri 12–5.30, Sat, Sun & BH Mons 11–5.30; last admission 5 or dusk if earlier; 11 Nov to 22 Dec: 12–4 or dusk. **Events**: send s.a.e. for details
- 💷 23 March to 3 Nov: £4.50; child £2.40; family £11.50. 11 Nov to 22 Dec: free. Free car park 50m. Party rate £3.80 (15+ must book). Voucher available when purchasing full-price adult ticket at Biddulph Grange Garden to visit Little Moreton Hall at a reduced admission price. See ticket seller on arrival
- 🚶 Booked guided tours in groups of 10+, at 10 on Wed, Thur & Fri; £6.50 per person (inc. NT members)
- 📷 As property
- ♿ Garden: difficult, uneven levels; unsuitable for wheelchairs. Terrace with views over garden: accessible. Tea-room: accessible. Contact Garden Office for full access details
- 👁 Braille and large-print guides
- ☕ Tea-room as property, light lunches 12–2. Picnics in car park only
- 👶 2 highchairs
- 🏫 School visits by arrangement
- 🐕 On leads and only in car park
- ➡️ (4:J2) ½ml N of Biddulph, 3½ml SE of Congleton, 7ml N of Stoke-on-Trent. Access from A527 (Tunstall–Congleton road). Entrance on Grange Road [118: SJ895591] **Bus**: Bakers B23 from Leek, First PMT 98/9 from Congleton (passing ≋ Congleton) **Station**: Congleton 2½ml

**NT properties nearby** Little Moreton Hall

---

## BREDON BARN 🏠     Worcestershire

Bredon, nr Tewkesbury · **Tel** 01985 843600 (Regional Office)
**Email** bredonbarn@ntrust.org.uk

A 14th-century barn, beautifully constructed of local Cotswold stone and noted for its dramatic aisled interior and unusual stone chimney cowling

---

**Please remember – your membership card is always needed for free admission**

- ◯ April to 30 Nov: daily except Mon, Tues & Fri 10–6 or sunset if earlier. At other times by appointment only
- £ £1
- → (4:J7) 3ml NE of Tewkesbury, just N of B4080 [150: SO919369]
  **Bus**: Boomerang 540/5 Evesham–Cheltenham (passing ☰ Evesham)
  **Station**: Pershore (U) 8½ml

**NT properties nearby** Ashleworth Tithe Barn, Croome Park, Hailes Abbey, Snowshill Manor

---

## BROCKHAMPTON ESTATE  Herefordshire
Bringsty WR6 5TB · **Tel** 01885 482077 (Estate Office) or 01885 488099
**Email** brockhampton@ntrust.org.uk

---

This 688ha (1700-acre) estate was bequeathed to the National Trust in 1947 and still maintains traditional farms and extensive areas of woodland, including ancient oak and beech. Visitors can enjoy a variety of walks through both park and woodland, which combine to form a rich habitat for wildlife such as the dormouse, buzzard and raven. A stone-flagged trail leads to the Lawn Pool and provides some access for those with disabilities. At the heart of the estate lies Lower Brockhampton House, a late 14th-century moated manor house with a beautiful timber-framed gatehouse and interesting ruined chapel

**What's new in 2002**: Additional bedroom open at Lower Brockhampton House

- ◯ **Estate**: woods and parkland walks open daily throughout the year during daylight hours. **House**: 29 March to 3 Nov: daily except Mon & Tues (but open BH Mons & 4 June). *Times*: April to Nov 12–5 (closes 4 in Oct & Nov). **Note**: The medieval hall, parlour, minstrels' gallery, information room, gatehouse and chapel ruins are shown. **Events**: tel. for details
- £ Estate free to pedestrians, car park non-members £2 (refundable on entry to house). House £3; family £7.50
- 🛍 A selection of NT goods, local artists' pictures, greetings cards, bookmarks and postcards at Old Apple Store tea-room
- ♿ Estate: 'challenging' stone-flagged trail with sculptures to Lawn Pool; walks leaflet available from tea-room. House: ground floor and chapel ruins accessible. Please phone for information
- 👆 Braille guide; timber-framing and oak furniture may be touched
- ☕ Old Apple Store tea-room in estate car park, open as house
- 🐕 In woods and parkland only, on leads
- → (4:I7) 2ml E of Bromyard on Worcester road (A44); reached by a narrow road through 1½ml of woods and farmland [149: SO682546] **Bus**: First Midland Red Duke's 419/420 Worcester–Hereford (passing ☰ Worcester Foregate Street & close ☰ Hereford)

**NT properties nearby** Berrington Hall, Croft Castle, The Greyfriars, The Weir

## CARDING MILL VALLEY & LONG MYND — Shropshire

Chalet Pavilion, Carding Mill Valley, Church Stretton SY6 6JG
**Tel** 01694 722631 · **Fax** 01694 723068

An extensive area of historic upland heath, part of the Long Mynd and with stunning views across the Shropshire and Cheshire plains and Black Mountains. This is excellent walking country with much of interest to the naturalist; the Chalet Pavilion in Carding Mill Valley offers information about the area, as well as a tea-room and shop

- **Heathland**: daily. **Chalet Pavilion (tea-room, shop & information centre)**: 23 March to 27 Oct: daily 11–5; 2 Nov to end March 2003: Sat & Sun 11–4 (or dusk if earlier), closed 21–26 Dec but open daily 27–29 Dec. **Note**: Closed 12 June for staff training
- Car parking: car £2 (Nov to end March £1); motorcycle 50p; minibus £2.50; coach £5. Education coaches £5 if booked, £10 if unbooked
- Guided walks in summer
- In Chalet Pavilion (closed 12 June for staff training)
- Close parking. Tea-room, shop & information centre: accessible
- In Chalet Pavilion (closed 12 June for staff training)
- Baby-changing facilities. Highchairs
- Environmental education programme. School parties must book, tel: 01694 724536
- Must be under control and only on moorland
- (4:H5) 15ml S of Shrewsbury, W of Church Stretton valley and A49; approached from Church Stretton and, on W side, from Ratlinghope or Asterton [137: SO443945] **Bus**: Arriva North Midlands 60, Whittle 435 Shrewsbury–Ludlow, alight Church Stretton, ½ml **Station**: Church Stretton (U) 1m

**NT properties nearby** Wenlock Edge, Wilderhope Manor

## CHARLECOTE PARK — Warwickshire

Warwick CV35 9ER · **Tel** 01789 470277 · **Fax** 01789 470544
**Email** charlecotepark@ntrust.org.uk

The home of the Lucy family for over 700 years, the mellow brickwork and great chimneys of Charlecote seem to sum up the very essence of Tudor England. There are strong associations with both Queen Elizabeth and Shakespeare, who knew the house well – he is alleged to have been caught poaching the estate deer. The rich early Victorian interior contains many important objects from Beckford's Fonthill Abbey and, outside, the balustraded formal garden gives onto a fine deer park landscaped by 'Capability' Brown

**What's new in 2002**: Education Officer, school room & teachers' resource book for house. Education visits/school parties welcome. Tel. property for details

---

**Please see the area introductions for details of coast & countryside properties**

## WEST MIDLANDS · 245

**O** **House**: 23 March to 3 Nov: daily except Wed & Thur 12–5. **Park & Gardens**: 23 March to 3 Nov: daily except Wed & Thur 11–6. 9 Nov to 15 Dec: Sat & Sun 11–4; 1 Feb to 16 March 2003: Sat & Sun 11–4. **Events**: send s.a.e. for details

**£** House & grounds; £5.80; grounds only: £3; family £14.50. Parties (min. 15) by arrangement £4.80. Car and coach park 300m. Video film of life at Charlecote Park in the Victorian period. Croquet set available £2.50 per hour

Evening guided tours for booked parties May to Sept: Tues 7.30–9.30 (£6.80 inc. NT members; minimum charge £150)

Shop & Victorian kitchens as house 11–5.30. Also 9 Nov to 15 Dec & 1 Feb to 16 March: Sat & Sun 11–4

Parking for disabled visitors, ask at kiosk. House: accessible; no access for wheelchair users to museum on upper floor of gatehouse or main house. Wheelchairs. Buggy. Restaurant & shop: accessible. Video can be viewed in the gatehouse information room.

Braille guide

Sympathetic Hearing Scheme

Licensed Orangery restaurant 11–5. Picnics in deer park only

Changing and feeding room. Children's play area

School parties by arrangement

On leads and only in car park (reasonable walks nearby)

→ (4:K7) 1ml W of Wellesbourne, 5ml E of Stratford-upon-Avon, 6ml S of Warwick on N side of B4086 [151: SP263564] **Bus**: Stagecoach in Warwickshire 18, X18 Coventry–Stratford-upon-Avon (passing ⇌ Leamington Spa) **Station**: Stratford-upon-Avon, 5½ml; Warwick 6ml; Leamington Spa 8ml

**NT properties nearby** Baddesley Clinton, Coughton Court, Hidcote Manor Gardens, Packwood House, Upton House

---

## COUGHTON COURT           Warwickshire

nr Alcester B49 5JA · **Tel** 01789 400777 · **Infoline** 01789 762435
**Fax** 01789 765544 · **Web** www.coughtoncourt.co.uk

---

One of the great Tudor houses, Coughton has been the home of the Throckmorton family since 1409. It has important associations with the Gunpowder Plot, about which there is an exhibition, and also saw much activity during the Civil War. The impressive central gatehouse and half-timbered courtyard are particularly noteworthy and inside there are fine collections of furniture, porcelain and paintings. Two churches, a lake, riverside walk, walled flower garden and bog garden provide additional interest

**Note**: Coughton Court is lived in, opened and managed by the Throckmorton family. National Trust vouchers or discounts do not apply at this property, nor is it possible to become a NT member at Coughton Court

**Unless indicated, last admission is always 30 mins before closing time**

## 246 · WEST MIDLANDS

- **House & gardens**: 23 March to 30 June & Sept: daily except Mon & Tues (but open BH Mons and Tues 4 June and closed Good Fri and Sat 22 June); July and Aug: daily except Mon (but open BH Mon). 5–26 Oct: Sat & Sun. *Times*: house 11.30–5 (11 BH Mons), gardens 11–5.30, walled garden 11.30–4.30. Last admissions 4.30. **Note**: On busy days entry to the house is by timed ticket. **Events**: Send s.a.e. for details
- £9.45; family £29.25. Garden only £6.95. Walled garden (created by the family) £2.50 for NT members (inc. in admission price for non-members). Parties of 15+ by arrangement (not BHols)
- Evening guided tours for booked parties Wed to Fri. Garden tours by appointment. No party rate or membership concessions for out of hours visits
- Shop & plant sales as gardens (managed by family)
- House: 3 ground-floor rooms accessible. Wheelchairs. Garden, grounds & riverside path: accessible. Restaurant & shop: accessible
- Braille guide
- Restaurant (managed by family) as house 11–5.30
- School visits by arrangement
- On leads and only in car park
- (4:K6) 2ml N of Alcester on A435 [150: SP080604] **Bus**: First Midland Red 146, Swanbrook/Woodstones 165 Birmingham–Evesham (passing Redditch & close Evesham; Stagecoach in Warwickshire 26 from Stratford-upon-Avon (passing close Stratford-upon-Avon) **Station**: Redditch 6ml **Cycle**: NCN 5

**NT properties nearby** Baddesley Clinton, Charlecote Park, Hanbury Hall, Packwood House

---

# CROFT CASTLE         Herefordshire

nr Leominster HR6 9PW · **Tel** 01568 780246 · **Fax** 01568 780462
**Email** croftcastle@ntrust.org.uk

---

Croft Castle will be undergoing major structural works during 2002 and will therefore be closed to the public. The Castle gardens will however remain open, as will the parkland and Croft Ambrey. The park contains a superb avenue of 350-year-old Spanish chestnuts. The walled garden is independently maintained by the Croft Trust and contains various historic fruit trees and plants (plants for sale throughout the season) open same days as gardens

**Note**: Access to an Interpretation Centre will be available, open same days as gardens, showing video film of work in progress and the Castle interior, together with family, estate history and an archaeology exhibition. There will also be occasional opportunities during the closure to view the work in progress inside the Castle, and various events are planned covering archaeology, park and garden tours, Shakespeare performances and other entertainment. Please tel. 01568 780246 for details

---

There are special events at most Trust properties; please telephone 0870 458 4000 for details

## WEST MIDLANDS · 247

- ⭕ **Castle**: closed. **Gardens & Grounds**: 23 March to 3 Nov: 11–5, daily except Mon & Tues (open Good Fri, BH Mons & 4 June). **Park & Croft Ambrey**: daily
- 💷 Garden: £3; car park £2 per car (refundable on entry to garden); £10 per coach. Parties of 15+ by written arrangement
- ♿ Close parking. Garden: gravelled terrace accessible. Grounds: largely accessible. Wheelchairs
- ☕ Tea-room 11–5, same days as garden
- 👫 Children's gardens quiz
- 🐕 On leads and only in parkland
- ➡️ (4:H6) 5ml NW of Leominster, 9ml SW of Ludlow; approach from B4362, turning N at Cock Gate between Bircher and Mortimer's Cross; signposted from Ludlow–Leominster road (A49) and from A4110 at Mortimer's Cross [137: SO455655] **Bus**: First Midland Red/Caradoc 192, 292 Birmingham–Hereford (passing close ≋ Ludlow & Leominster), alight Gorbett Bank, 2¼ml **Station**: Leominster (U) 7ml

**NT properties nearby** Berrington Hall, Brockhampton Estate, The Weir

---

# CROOME PARK ✝ ✤ 🌳 ⚓ 👤                                Worcestershire
NT Estate Office, The Builders' Yard, High Green, Severn Stoke WR8 9JS
**Tel** 01905 371006 · **Fax** 01905 371090 · **Email** croomepark@ntrust.org.uk

---

Croome was 'Capability' Brown's first complete landscape, making his reputation and establishing a new style of parkland design which became universally adopted over the next fifty years. The elegant park buildings and other structures are mostly by Robert Adam and James Wyatt. The Trust acquired 270ha of the park in 1996 with substantial grant aid from the Heritage Lottery Fund

**Note**: The Trust has embarked on a 10-year restoration plan, including dredging the water features, clearance and replanting of the gardens and parkland. Royal & SunAlliance is making a major financial contribution towards the cost of this restoration

---

**For all your information needs check our website www.nationaltrust.org.uk**

**248 · WEST MIDLANDS**

**What's new in 2002**: Further work in the gardens, including the restoration of park buildings and new shrubbery planting in 18th-century style

- 24 March to 3 Nov: Fri to Mon (and 4 June). *Times*: 11–5. [**Croome Church**: open as garden, in association with the Churches Conservation Trust, which owns the church]
- Garden £3.40; family £8.50. Car parking £2 (refundable on entrance to garden)
- Out of hours pre-booked guided tours for groups of 10 or more: £5 (inc. NT members). Please write to the Property Manager
- Limited access; tel. in advance
- Picnic area in wilderness walk
- On leads only
- (4:J7) 8ml S of Worcester and E of A38 and M5, 6ml W of Pershore, and A44 [150: SO887453] **Bus**: First Midland Red 372–4 Worcester–Gloucester, alight Severn Stoke, thence 2ml **Station**: Pershore 6ml

**NT properties nearby** Brockhampton Estate, The Greyfriars, Hanbury Hall

---

# DUDMASTON                                                Shropshire

Quatt, nr Bridgnorth WV15 6QN · **Tel** 01746 780866 · **Fax** 01746 780744
**Email** dudmaston@ntrust.org.uk

A late 17th-century house with intimate family rooms containing fine furniture and Dutch flower paintings, as well as interesting contemporary paintings and sculpture. The delightful gardens are a mass of colour in spring and include a walk in the Dingle, a wooded valley. There are also estate walks starting from Hampton Loade. Dudmaston is the home of Colonel and Mrs Hamilton-Russell

- **House**: 31 March to 29 Sept: Tues, Wed & Sun, plus BH Mons 2–5.30. **Garden**: Mon, Tues, Wed & Sun 12–6. **Events**: send s.a.e. for details
- £3.95; child £2; family £9. Garden only £2.90. Booked groups (15+) £3.30. Parking 100m
- **House**: for booked parties, Mon only 2–5.30. **Garden**: free tours Mon afternoons
- As garden 1–5.30
- House: ramped entrance; main and inner halls, Library, Oak Room, Modern Art Gallery, Darby Gallery and Old Kitchen accessible. Garden & grounds: signed route (some steep slopes). Tea-room: accessible. Shop: accessible via ramp. Wheelchairs and self-drive vehicle
- Braille and large-print guides for house and woodland; tape guide with cassette player for house. Scented plants
- Sympathetic Hearing Scheme
- Tea-room as garden 11.30–5.30. Light lunches. Booked parties by arrangement. **Note**: the tea-room is open to the general public and not restricted to those visiting the house or garden

---

**Please remember – your membership card is always needed for free admission**

WEST MIDLANDS · 249

- 👶 Baby-changing facilities; baby slings. Highchairs
- 🐕 On leads and only in the Dingle and on the estate walks
- ➡️ (4:I5) 4ml SE of Bridgnorth on A442 [138: SO746887] **Bus**: Shropshire Bus 297 Bridgnorth–Kidderminster (passing close ☒ Kidderminster) **Station**: Hampton Loade (Severn Valley Rly) 1½ml; Kidderminster 10ml

**NT properties nearby** Attingham Park, Benthall Hall, Berrington Hall, Kinver Edge, Morville Hall, Sunnycroft, Wightwick Manor

---

## FARNBOROUGH HALL 🏛️ ✳️ 🌳   Warwickshire
Banbury OX17 1DU · **Tel** 01295 690002 · **Email** farnboroughhall@ntrust.org.uk

A beautiful honey-coloured stone house, built in the mid-18th century and the home of the Holbech family for over 300 years. The interior plasterwork is quite outstanding and the charming grounds contain 18th-century temples, a terrace walk and an obelisk

**Note**: Farnborough Hall is occupied and administered by Mr & Mrs Holbech

- ⭕ **House & grounds**: April to end Sept: Wed & Sat 2–6, also 5, 6 May 2–6. **Terrace walk**: April to end Sept: Thur & Fri 2–6 (closed Good Fri) by prior arrangement, please telephone
- 💷 £3.50. Garden and terrace walk only £1.75. Terrace walk only (Thur & Fri) by prior telephone appointment £1. Parties by written arrangement only, no reduction. Coach and car park. Strong shoes advisable for terrace
- ♿ House: ground floor accessible. Garden: accessible; terrace walk: very steep
- 🐕 On leads and only in grounds
- ➡️ (2:C2) 6ml N of Banbury, ½ml W of A423 [151: SP430490] **Station**: Banbury 6ml

**NT properties nearby** Canons Ashby House, Charlecote Park, Upton House

**For general enquiries, please telephone 0870 458 4000**

## THE FLEECE INN 🏠 — Worcestershire

Bretforton, nr Evesham WR11 5JE · **Tel** 01386 831173
**Email** fleeceinn@ntrust.org.uk

---

A black and white half-timbered medieval farmhouse, largely unaltered since first becoming a licensed house in 1848

**Note**: The Inn is managed by a commercial tenant

- During normal licensing hours. Car-parking in village square. Coaches by written appointment only
- Food available lunchtime and evening
- (4:K7) 4ml E of Evesham, on B4035 [150: SP093437]
  **Bus**: Barry's/Cresswell/Spring & Son 554 from Evesham **Station**: Evesham 3ml

**NT properties nearby** Dovers Hill, Hidcote Manor Garden, Middle Littleton Tithe Barn, Snowshill Manor

---

## THE GREYFRIARS 🏠 ❖ ♥ — Worcestershire

Friar Street, Worcester WR1 2LZ · **Tel** 01905 23571
**Email** greyfriars@ntrust.org.uk

---

A fine timber-framed merchant's house, built in 1480 next to the Franciscan friary. Rescued from demolition and carefully restored, the panelled interior contains interesting textiles and furnishings. An archway leads through to the delightful walled garden

- 1 April to 31 Oct: Wed, Thur & BH Mons & 4 June, 2–5. During three Choirs Festival: 17 Aug & 19–24 Aug; 11–1 and 2–5
- £3; family £7.50; guided tours £5. Parties of 15+ by written appointment. No party reduction. Unsuitable for large parties of children. Public car park in Friar Street. No WC
- (4:J7) In centre of Worcester [150: SO852546] **Bus**: From surrounding areas **Station**: Worcester Foregate Street ½ml

**NT properties nearby** Brockhampton Estate, Croome Park, Hanbury Hall

---

## HANBURY HALL 🏠🏠❖♠♥🔔 — Worcestershire

Droitwich WR9 7EA · **Tel** 01527 821214 · **Fax** 01527 821251
**Email** hanburyhall@ntrust.org.uk

---

Built in 1701, this elegant William & Mary-style house is famed for its beautiful painted ceilings and staircase, and has other unusual features including an Orangery, Ice House, Moorish gazebos and working Mushroom House. The recreated early 18th-century garden is surrounded by 160ha (395 acres) of parkland, has a Parterre, Wilderness, Fruit Garden and Grove. The tercentenary exhibition in the Long Gallery opened in 2001, interprets the social, family, gardens and architectural history

**Please see the area introductions for details of coast & countryside properties**

**What's new in 2002**: Recreated 18th-century bowling green

- ⭕ 24 March to 30 Oct: Sun to Wed 1.30–5.30 (but open Good Fri); last admission 5 or dusk if earlier. Garden: 12–5. **Events**: send s.a.e. for details

- 💷 £4.60; family £11.50; garden only £2.90. Property available for wedding ceremonies, receptions and private parties; tel. for details. Free car and coach-parking

- 🚶 Private guided tours for booked parties, April to Oct, £6 (inc. NT members), min. charge £120

- 🛍 12–5

- ♿ Disabled visitors may be set down at house. House: ground floor accessible. Garden: accessible. Tea-room: accessible. Self-drive vehicle. Wheelchair

- 👁 Braille guide; some items may be touched

- ☕ Tea-room serving light lunches and refreshments, as garden 12–5

- 🐕 Not in garden but on leads in park on footpaths

- ➡ (4:J6) 4½ml E of Droitwich, 1ml N of B4090, 6ml S of Bromsgrove, 1½ml W of B4091 [150: SO943637] **Bus**: First Midland Red 142/4 Worcester–Birmingham (passing close ≋ Droitwich Spa), alight Wychbold, 2½ml **Station**: Droitwich Spa 4ml

**NT properties nearby** Coughton Court, The Clent Hills, The Greyfriars

---

# HAWFORD DOVECOTE 🏠                              Worcestershire

Hawford · **Tel** 01743 708100 (Regional Office)
**Email** hawforddovecote@ntrust.org.uk

A 16th-century half-timbered dovecote, the remnant of a former monastic grange

- ⭕ April to 31 Oct: daily (closed Good Fri) 9–6 or sunset if earlier. Other times by appointment with Regional Office. **Note**: access is on foot via the drive of the adjoining house

- 💷 £1

- ➡ (4:J6) 3ml N of Worcester, ½ml E of A449 [150: SO846607] **Bus**: First Midland Red 303 Worcester–Kidderminster (passing ≋ Worcester Foregate Street & Kidderminster), alight Hawford Lodge, ¼ml **Station**: Worcester Foregate Street 3ml; Worcester Shrub Hill 3½ml

**NT properties nearby** The Greyfriars, Hanbury Hall, Wichenford Dovecote

---

**Unless indicated, last admission is always 30 mins before closing time**

## ILAM PARK  Staffordshire

Ilam, Ashbourne DE6 2AZ · **Tel** 01335 350245 · **Email** ilampark@ntrust.org.uk

A beautiful area of open park and woodland, running on both banks of the River Manifold and with spectacular views towards Dovedale

- **Grounds and park**: daily. Hall is let to YHA and not open. **Note**: Small caravan site run by NT (basic facilities) open to Caravan Club/NT members Easter to Oct (tel. 01335 350310)
- Free. Pay-and-display car park (NT members free)
- Guided walks around the estate may be booked by groups, contact Education Warden (tel. 01335 350503)
- Shop & information centre with an exhibition on Ilam and the South Peak Estate 5 Jan to 23 March, 27 Oct to 22 Dec, 2 Jan to end March 2003: Sat & Sun 11–4; 24 March to 26 Oct: daily 11–5
- Grounds: limited access near hall. Wheelchair. Information centre & shop: accessible via cobbled courtyard; ramps available
- Braille leaflet and tea-room menu
- Manifold Tea-room 5 Jan to 23 March, 27 Oct to 22 Dec, 2 Jan to end March 2003: Sat & Sun 11–4; 24 March to 12 May: Sat & Sun 11–5; 13 May to end Oct: daily except Wed & Thur 11–5
- Children's portions
- Education Centre and wide range of educational activities and materials for all ages. Teachers' resource book for Dovedale. Details from Education Officer, South Peak Estate Office, Home Farm, tel. 01335 350549/01335 350503
- On leads only
- (4:K3) 4½ml NW of Ashbourne [119: SK132507] **Bus**: Warrington 443 from Ashbourne, Thur & Sat only, with connections from Derby; also various services from ⇌ Buxton and Derby, summer Sun only; otherwise First PMT X1 Derby–Manchester (passing close ⇌ Derby & Macclesfield), alight Ilam Cross Roads, 2ml

**NT properties nearby** Kedleston Hall, Sudbury Hall and Museum of Childhood

## KINVER EDGE  Staffordshire

The Warden's Lodge, The Compa, Kinver, nr Stourbridge DY7 6HU · **Tel** 01384 872418
**Email** kinveredge@ntrust.org.uk

A sandstone ridge, covered in woodland and heath and from which there are dramatic views across surrounding counties. The famous Holy Austin rock houses, which were inhabited until the 1950s, have now been restored and parts are open to visitors at selected times

- **Kinver Edge**: all year. **Holy Austin rock house grounds**: daily. *Times*: April to

There are special events at most Trust properties; please telephone 0870 458 4000 for details

Sept 9–7, Oct to March 2003 9–4. **Upper terrace**: Wed, Sat & Sun. *Times*: April to Sept 2–5, Oct to March 2–4. **Lower rock houses**: Sat only, 2–4 and at other times for guided tours by arrangement with custodian (tel. 01384 872553)

£ Kinver Edge: free; Lower rock houses: 40p; child 20p

**Lower rock houses**: by arrangement with custodian; charges apply

Roadside parking. Wheelchair route to lower caves at Holy Austin rock; limited access to escarpment from east

On leads within grounds of rock houses

(4:J5) 5ml W of Stourbridge, 6ml N of Kidderminster. 2½ml off A458 [138: SO836836] **Bus**: Hansons 228, Travel West Midlands 242 Stourbridge–Kinver **Station**: Stourbridge Town 5ml

**NT properties nearby** Clent Hills, Dudmaston

## KINWARTON DOVECOTE                                              Warwickshire
Kinwarton, nr Alcester · **Tel** 01743 708100 (Regional Office) · **Email** kinwartondovecote@ntrust.org.uk

A circular 14th-century dovecote, still housing doves and retaining its potence, an unusual pivoted ladder from which access is possible to the nesting boxes

April to 31 Oct: daily (closed Good Fri) 9–6 or sunset if earlier. Other times by appointment with Regional Office

£ £1

(4:K7) 1½ml NE of Alcester, just S of B4089 [150: SP106585] **Bus**: Stagecoach in Warwickshire 25 from Stratford-upon-Avon; otherwise as for Coughton Court, but alight Alcester, 1½ml **Station**: Wilmcote (U), 5ml; Wootton Wawen (U), not Sun, 5ml **Cycle**: NCN 5

**NT properties nearby** Charlecote Park, Coughton Court

## MIDDLE LITTLETON TITHE BARN                                    Worcestershire
Middle Littleton, Evesham · **Tel** 01743 708100 (Regional Office) · **Email** middlelittleton@ntrust.org.uk

One of the largest and finest tithe barns in the country, dating from the 13th century

1 April to 4 Nov: daily 2–5. Directions for access on barn door

£ £1

(4:K7) 3ml NE of Evesham, E of B4085 [150: SP080471] **Bus**: First Midland Red 146, Swanbrook/Woodstones 165 Evesham–Birmingham (passing close Evesham), alight Middle Littleton School Lane, ½ml **Station**: Honeybourne (U) 3½ml; Evesham 4½ml

**NT properties nearby** Charlecote Park, Hidcote Manor Garden, Snowshill Manor

For all your information needs check our website www.nationaltrust.org.uk

## MORVILLE HALL  Shropshire

nr Bridgnorth WV16 5NB · **Tel** 01743 708100 (Regional Office)
**Email** morvillehall@ntrust.org.uk

An Elizabethan house of mellow stone, converted in the 18th century and set in attractive gardens

- By written appointment only with the tenants, Dr & Mrs C Douglas
- Access is by guided tour only
- House: ground floor accessible. Garden: largely accessible
- (4:I5) [138: SO668940] **Bus**: Arriva North Midlands/Pete's 436/7 Shrewsbury–Bridgnorth (passing close ≋ Shrewsbury & Severn Valley Rly Bridgnorth) **Station**: Bridgnorth (Severn Valley Rly) 3½ml

**NT properties nearby** Benthall Hall, Dudmaston, Wightwick Manor, Wilderhope Manor

## MOSELEY OLD HALL  Staffordshire

Moseley Old Hall Lane, Fordhouses, Wolverhampton WV10 7HY ·
**Tel/Fax** 01902 782808
**Email** moseleyoldhall@ntrust.org.uk

An Elizabethan house, altered in the 19th century and famous for its association with Charles II, who hid here after the Battle of Worcester (1651). The story of his escape is recounted in an exhibition in the barn, and there is an interesting garden full of 17th-century plants

- 23 March to 3 Nov: Sat, Sun, Wed, BH Mons and following Tues; 10 Nov to 15 Dec: Sun (guided tours only). *Times*: March to end Oct 1–5, garden & tea-room from 12 (BH Mons & 4 June 11–5); Nov & Dec 1–4. Sun 3 March, special opening of garden and ground floor of house, tea-room and shop 1–4 (suggested donation £1). Booked parties at other times, inc. evening tours. **Events**: send s.a.e. for full programme
- £4.20; family £10.50. Groups of 15+ £3.60
- Optional free guided tours; last guided tour 3.45
- 23 March to 3 Nov: as house; 10 Nov to 15 Dec: Christmas shop Sun 1–4
- House: ground floor accessible. Garden: accessible. Tea-room: 2 tables for wheelchair users on ground floor. Wheelchair
- Braille and large-print guides; some items, including fabric samples, may be touched
- Tea-room in 18th-century barn, 23 March to 3 Nov: as house 12–5; 10 Nov to 15 Dec: Sun 12–4. Other times for parties by arrangement
- Highchair

**Please remember – your membership card is always needed for free admission**

- Education programme includes living history
- (4:J5) 4ml N of Wolverhampton; S of M54 between A449 and A460; traffic from N on M6 leave motorway at exit 11, then A460; traffic from S on M6 & M54 take exit 1; coaches must approach via A460 to avoid low bridge [127: SJ932044] **Bus**: Arriva North Midlands 870–2 Wolverhampton–Cannock, alight Bognop Road, ¾ml; Travel West Midlands 613 from Wolverhampton, thence ¾ml (all pass close ≋ Wolverhampton) **Station**: Wolverhampton 4ml

**NT properties nearby** Attingham Park, Benthall Hall, Sunnycroft, Wightwick Manor

## PACKWOOD HOUSE — Warwickshire

Lapworth, Solihull B94 6AT · **Tel** 01564 783294 · **Fax** 01564 782706
**Email** packwood@ntrust.org.uk

The house, originally 16th-century, is a fascinating 20th-century evocation of domestic Tudor architecture. Created by Graham Baron Ash, its interiors were restored during the period between the world wars and contain a fine collection of 16th-century textiles and furniture. The gardens have renowned herbaceous borders and a famous collection of yews

- **House**: 6 March to 3 Nov: daily except Mon & Tues (but open BH Mons, 4 June and Good Fri) 12–4.30. **Note**: On busy days entry may be by timed ticket. **Garden**: 6 March to 3 Nov: daily except Mon & Tues (but open BH Mons, 4 June and Good Fri). *Times*: March, April, Oct & Nov 11–4.30; May to Sept 11–5.30. **Park and woodland walks**: all year, daily. **Events**: tel. or send s.a.e. for details
- £5.20; family £13. Garden only £2.60. Combined ticket for Baddesley Clinton and Packwood House; £8.50, family £21.25; garden only £4.25. Parties of 15+ and coaches welcome by written arrangement (free parking)
- As garden
- House: ground floor accessible, except great hall which can be seen from doorway. Garden: largely accessible. Wheelchairs. Contact property in advance about access arrangements. WC: large cubicle with handrails, otherwise unadapted; also ground-floor cloakroom in house
- Braille guide; tactile route around house. Yew trees and hedges may be touched
- Kiosk serving light refreshments (times vary, tel. for details); picnic area near car park
- School parties by appointment Wed, Thur & Fri mornings
- (4:K6) 2ml E of Hockley Heath (on A3400), 11ml SE of central Birmingham [139: SP174722] **Bus**: Stagecoach in Warwickshire X20 Birmingham–Stratford-upon-Avon, alight Hockley Heath, 1¾ml **Station**: Lapworth (U) 1½ml; Birmingham International 8ml

**NT properties nearby** Baddesley Clinton, Charlecote Park, Hanbury Hall

**For general enquiries, please telephone 0870 458 4000**

## SHUGBOROUGH ESTATE — Staffordshire

Milford, nr Stafford ST17 0XB · **Tel** 01889 881388 · **Fax** 01889 881323
**Web** www.staffordshire.gov.uk

The magnificent seat of the Earls of Lichfield, now being restored as a 19th-century working estate. The late 17th-century house was enlarged *c*.1750 and again at the turn of the 19th century, and contains interesting collections of china, silver, paintings and furniture. The stable block houses the original servants' quarters. There is a working laundry and brewhouse

**Note**: Shugborough is financed and administered by Staffordshire County Council. NT members have free entry to the house, but must pay for vehicle admission as well as entry to the county museum and farm and any special event charges. Admission charges and opening arrangements may vary when special events are held

- **House, county museum, farm & gardens** 30 March to 29 Sept: daily except Mon (open BH Mons); Oct first 3 Suns: *Times*: 11–5 (last admission 4.15). Opening times vary; tel. to check. See below for guided tours. **Events**: inc. open-air concerts and themed activities, Christmas evenings and craft festivals; civil wedding ceremonies and corporate bookings can be arranged; tel. for details

- Tel. for details. NT members free to house but must pay entry to parkland (£2 per vehicle) and to the county museum and farm, and to special events. Discounted saver tickets available. Evening visits for booked parties; tel. for prices. Guided tours available for school parties at £2 per head per site (2 sites for £3, 3 sites for £5); working demonstrations throughout the year from £3–£5; schools must book in advance

- Wide range of tours for booked groups daily from 10.30, inc. garden tours, connoisseur talks and tours for special-interest groups. Evening tours also available. Tel. for details of all tours

- NT shop at main site: 30 March to 29 Sept: daily 11–5; 30 Sept to 23 Dec: daily except Sat 11–4 (tel. 01889 882122)

- House: ground floor accessible via stairclimber by arrangement. County museum & farm: accessible. Tours and demonstrations can be arranged. Self-drive vehicles and wheelchairs for park and garden. Accessible picnic tables

- Braille, tape and large-print guides. Rose garden

- Lady Walk tea-rooms as house; dinners available for booked parties (min. 25). Tea-room at farm for light refreshments as house. Picnic sites at main and farm car parks

- Farm gives children chance to see and touch domestic and rare breeds of animal and poultry. Games gallery in corn mill. Play area. Major puppet collection in museum. Baby-changing facilities. Highchairs

- Extensive schools and adult demonstration programme

- Racks available at all sites

- On leads and only in parkland

**Please see the area introductions for details of coast & countryside properties**

➡️ (4:J4) Signposted from M6 exit 13; 6ml E of Stafford on A513; entrance at Milford. Pedestrian access from E, from the canal/Little Haywood side of the Estate [127: SJ992225] **Bus**: Arriva North Midlands 825 ➡ Stafford–Tamworth (passing close ➡ Lichfield City) **Station**: Rugeley 5ml; Stafford 6ml

---

## SUNNYCROFT 🏠 📷 ✣      Shropshire
200 Holyhead Road, Wellington, Telford TF1 2DR · **Tel** 01952 242884

A late Victorian gentleman's suburban villa, typical of the many thousands of such houses that were built for prosperous business and professional people on the fringes of Victorian towns and cities. Sunnycroft is one of the very few – perhaps the only one – to have survived largely unaltered and complete with its contents, of which a remarkable range remain. The grounds amount to a 'mini-estate', with pigsties, stables, kitchen garden, orchards, conservatory, flower garden and superb Wellingtonia avenue

**Note**: There is no car-parking at the property except for disabled visitors, who may also be dropped at the house. Visitors must use the public car park at Wrekin Road

🅾 1 April to 30 Oct: Sun, Mon & Tues 4 June 2–6. Entrance to house by timed ticket only. Guided tours for groups on Tues. Last entry to house 5

💷 £4.20; child £2.10

♿ Grounds: accessible. House: tel. in advance for details. Limited designated parking

➡️ (4:I4) Exit M54 jct 7, follow B5061 towards Wellington [127: SJ652109]
**Bus**: Arriva North Midlands 15 from ➡ Wellington Telford West
**Station**: Wellington Telford West ½ml

**NT properties nearby** Attingham Park, Benthall Hall, Dudmaston, Morville Hall, Moseley Old Hall

**Unless indicated, last admission is always 30 mins before closing time**

## TOWN WALLS TOWER 🏠                                                           Shropshire

Shrewsbury SY1 1TN · **Tel** 01743 708162 (Attingham Park)
**Fax** 01743 708175 (Attingham Park)

Shrewsbury's last remaining watchtower, built in the 14th century and overlooking the River Severn

- By written appointment only with the tenant, Mr A. A. Hector, Tower House, 26a Town Walls, Shrewsbury SY1 1TN

- (4:H4) A few mins walk from town centre, on S of Town Walls [126:SJ490122]
  **Bus**: From surrounding areas **Station**: Shrewsbury ½ml

**NT properties nearby** Attingham Park

## UPTON HOUSE 🏠✿♥                                               Warwickshire

Banbury OX15 6HT · **Tel** 01295 670266
**Email** uptonhouse@ntrust.org.uk

The house, built in 1695 of mellow local stone, was purchased and remodelled 1927–29 by Walter Samuel, 2nd Viscount Bearsted, Chairman of Shell 1921–46 and son of the founder of that company. Upton contains his outstanding collection of English and continental Old Master paintings including works by Hogarth, Stubbs, Guardi, Canaletto, Brueghel and El Greco; tapestries; French porcelain; Chelsea figures and 18th-century furniture. There is also an exhibition of paintings and publicity posters commissioned by Shell during Viscount Bearsted's chairmanship. The garden is very fine, with terraces, herbaceous borders, kitchen garden, ornamental pools and an interesting 1930s water garden together with the National Collection of Asters

**What's new in 2002**: New licensed restaurant. Tactile route for visitors

---

There are special events at most Trust properties; please telephone 0870 458 4000 for details

- **House:** 23 March to 3 Nov: Sat to Wed (inc BHols and Good Fri) 1–5. **Garden:** 23 March to 3 Nov: Sat, Sun & BHols 11–5; other Mons, Tues & Weds 12.30–5. 9 Nov to 15 Dec: Sat & Sun 12–4. **Events:** fine arts study tours, jazz concert and other events; send s.a.e. or tel. for details
- £6; family £15. Garden only £3. Parties of 15+ by written arrangement. Free parking
- Evening guided tours by written arrangement. Refreshments can be included
- As house. Plants and garden produce on sale (when available) by admission kiosk. Also 9 Nov to 15 Dec, Sat & Sun 12–4, limited seasonal range available
- Close parking. House: ground floor accessible via ramped side door; access to lower floor by prior arrangement. Wheelchair for use in house. Restaurant and shop: accessible. Garden: upper part accessible; motorised buggy with driver for lower garden
- Braille guide, tactile route around house
- Licensed restaurant (opening during 2002 season): 23 March to 3 Nov: Sat, Sun, BHols 11–5; other Mons, Tues & Weds: 12–5, last teas 4.30. 9 Nov to 15 Dec: Sat & Sun 12–4. Party lunches and dinners by arrangement, tel. property for details
- Parent and baby room. Baby-changing facilities. High-chairs. Children's quiz. No baby back-carriers, prams or pushchairs in house.
- Park by railings in main car park
- (2:C2) On A422, 7ml NW of Banbury, 12ml SE of Stratford-upon-Avon [151: SP371461] **Bus:** Johnson's 270 from Banbury **Station:** Banbury 7ml

**NT properties nearby** Canons Ashby House, Charlecote Park, Chastleton House, Farnborough Hall, Hidcote Manor Garden

---

## WALL ROMAN SITE (LETOCETUM) BATHS & MUSEUM

Staffordshire

Watling Street, Wall, nr Lichfield WS14 0AW · **Tel** 01543 480768

The excavated bathhouse of a Roman staging post on Watling Street, and the most complete example of its kind. An interesting museum displays local finds

**Note:** Letocetum is in the guardianship of English Heritage

- 1 April to 30 Sept: daily 11–5. **Events:** send s.a.e. for details
- £2.40; child £1.20; concessions £1.80 (all prices provisional). Parties of 11+ 15% discount. School booking, tel. 0121 625 6820
- As property
- Museum: accessible; ground uneven elsewhere
- Audio tape (NT members £1)

**For all your information needs check our website www.nationaltrust.org.uk**

- Free entry for education groups who book 14 days in advance
- On leads only
- (4:K5) On N side of A5 at Wall, near Lichfield [139: SK099067]
  **Station**: Shenstone 1½ml **Cycle**: NCN 5 2¼ml

**NT properties nearby** Moseley Old Hall, Shugborough

## THE WEIR Herefordshire

Swainshill, nr Hereford HR4 8BS · **Tel** 01981 590509 · **Infoline** 01743 708100
**Email** theweir@ntrust.org.uk

A delightful, tranquil riverside garden, particularly spectacular in early spring. Beautiful views over the River Wye and to the Black Mountains

- 19 Jan to 10 Feb: Sat & Sun 11–4; 13 Feb to 3 Nov: Wed to Sun, BH Mons & 4 June: 11–6
- £3; family £7.50; free car park (unsuitable for coaches). No WC
- Guided tours by arrangement. Tel. property for details
- On leads and only in car park (no shade or water)
- (4:H7) 5ml W of Hereford on A438 [149: SO435421] **Bus**: Yeoman's Canyon 446 from Hereford; otherwise Midland Red West 101 Hereford–Credenhill (both passing close ≋ Hereford), thence 1½ml **Station**: Hereford 5ml

**NT properties nearby** Berrington Hall, Croft Castle

## WICHENFORD DOVECOTE Worcestershire

Wichenford · **Tel** 01743 708100 (Regional Office)
**Email** wichenforddovecote@ntrust.org.uk

A 17th-century half-timbered black and white dovecote

- April to 31 Oct: daily (closed Good Fri) 9–6 or sunset if earlier. Other times by appointment with Regional Office
- £1
- (4:J7) 5½ml NW of Worcester, N of B4204 [150: SO788598] **Bus**: First Midland Red 310/2/3 from Worcester (passing close ≋ Worcester Foregate Street), alight Wichenford, ½ml
  **Station**: Worcester Foregate Street 7ml; Worcester Shrub Hill 7½ml

**NT properties nearby**
The Greyfriars, Hanbury Hall, Hawford Dovecote

HAZEL NUTS

**Please remember – your membership card is always needed for free admission**

## WIGHTWICK MANOR

West Midlands

Wightwick Bank, Wolverhampton WV6 8EE · **Infoline** 01902 761108
**Fax** 01902 764663 · **Email** wightwickmanor@ntrust.org.uk

One of only a few surviving examples of a house built and furnished under the influence of the Arts & Crafts Movement. The many original William Morris wallpapers and fabrics, Pre-Raphaelite paintings, Kempe glass and de Morgan ware help conjure up the spirit of the time. An attractive garden reflects the style and character of the house

- **House**: 1 March to 31 Dec & March 2003: Thur & Sat (also Good Fri, BH Sun & Mon & Tues 4 June for ground floor only) 1.30–4.30. Also family openings Weds in Aug 1.30–5. **Note**: viewing is by timed ticket, issued from Visitor Reception from 11, and by guided tour only. Many of the contents are fragile and some rooms cannot always be shown, so tours vary. **Garden**: Wed, Thur, Sat & BHols 11–6. Other days by appointment. **Events**: special events and garden tours; tel. 01902 761400 for details

- £5.60; children, students £2.80. Garden only £2.50, children free. Family ticket £13. Parking: car park (120m) at bottom of Wightwick Bank (please do not park in Elmsdale opposite the property). For coach parking please tel. 01902 761400

- Booked parties Wed, Thur & Sat and evenings (except BHols)

- William Morris Arts & Crafts shop Wed, Thur, Sat & BHols 1–5.30. Pottery (not NT) open as shop. **Note**: William Morris shop, tea-room and pottery are open to the general public, independent of visiting the house and garden

- Parking: ring for advice. House: steps to ground floor (5 rooms). Garden: accessible, but site slopes steeply

- Braille guides to house and Pre-Raphaelite collection

- Tea-room, Wed, Thur, Sat & BHols 11–5 (limited seating)

## 262 · WEST MIDLANDS

- Special family openings Weds in Aug, inc. family tours and hands-on activities
- Booked school visits on Wed & Thur, tel. for details
- On leads and only in garden
- (4:J5) 3ml W of Wolverhampton, up Wightwick Bank (off A454 beside the Mermaid Inn) [139: SO869985] **Bus**: Arriva North Midlands 890 Wolverhampton–Bridgnorth; 516 Wolverhampton–Pattingham (both pass close Wolverhampton) **Station**: Wolverhampton 3ml

**NT properties nearby** Dudmaston, Benthall Hall, Moseley Old Hall

---

## WILDERHOPE MANOR                                         Shropshire
Longville, Much Wenlock TF13 6EG · **Tel** 01694 771363

A gabled and unspoilt manor house, dating from 1586 and with fine views. Although unfurnished, the interior is of interest for its remarkable wooden spiral staircase and fine plaster ceilings. There are two circular walks through farmland and woods

- April to end Sept: Wed & Sat; Oct to end March 2003: Sat. *Times*: 2–4.30
- £1. No party reduction
- YHA shop
- House: accessible via steep path (strong companion needed); ground floor accessible. Shop (not NT): accessible
- On leads and only around Manor
- (4:I5) 7ml SW of Much Wenlock, 7ml E of Church Stretton, ½ml S of B4371 [138: SO545929] **Station**: Church Stretton (U) 8ml

**NT properties nearby** Carding Mill Valley

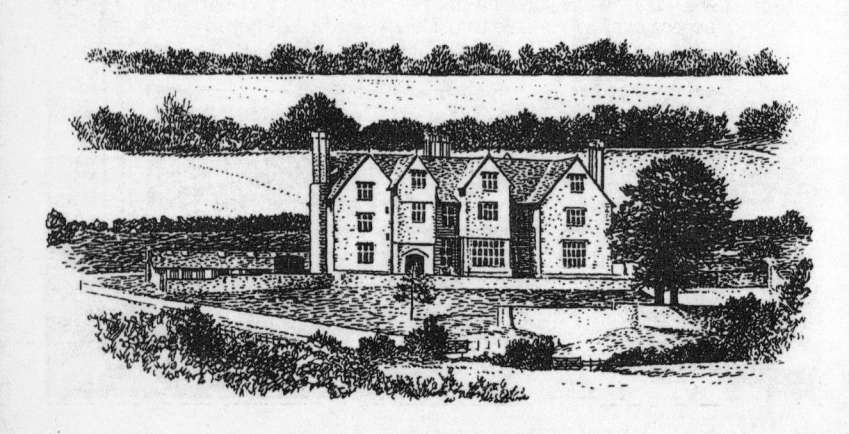

---

**Please see the area introductions for details of coast & countryside properties**

# Introduction to the North West

The North West of England contains some of Britain's most impressive scenery. In the north, the dramatic grandeur of the Lake District offers unparalleled opportunities for outdoor recreation. To the south, the urban centres of Manchester and Liverpool have good access to unspoilt countryside and splendid country houses, as well as to interesting reminders of the area's industrial heritage.

The National Trust is responsible for the conservation and management of approximately one quarter of the Lake District National Park, including England's highest mountain, **Scafell Pike**, her deepest lake, **Wastwater**, and over 90 farms. Almost all of the central fell area and major valley heads are owned or leased by the Trust, together with 24 lakes and tarns. This heart of the Lake District constitutes almost one quarter of the Trust's entire holding across England, Wales and Northern Ireland. The acquisition of this great estate – piece by piece over 100 years, since the purchase of **Brandelhow Park** on the shore of Derwentwater in 1902 – is one of the Trust's greatest achievements; its continued care and protection against the pressures of changing agricultural policies and mass tourism will be one of the Trust's greatest challenges. A growing set of leaflets gives more information about the Trust's countryside ownership in the area; tel. 015394 35599 for details.

In addition to the Lake District properties detailed in this Handbook, the Trust also cares for many other sites in Cumbria. These include the tiny medieval **Keld Chapel** near Shap (access at all reasonable times; key in village, see notice on chapel door), and further south, the fascinating **Cartmel Priory Gatehouse**. There are delightful

| OS grid references for properties with no individual entry (OS map series numbers given in brackets) | |
| --- | --- |
| Alderley Edge | [118] SS860775 |
| Arnside Knott | [97] SD456775 |
| Bickerton Hill | [117] SJ504529 |
| Brandelhow Park | [97] NY250205 |
| Caldy Hill | [108] SJ224855 |
| Castlerigg Circle | [89] NY292236 |
| Cross Keys Temperance Inn | [98] SD698969 |
| Eaves & Waterslack Woods | [97] SD465758 |
| Heald Brow | [97] SD467742 |
| Helsby Hill | [117] SJ492754 |
| Heysham | [97] SD419618 |
| Jack Scout | [90] SD459737 |
| Keld Chapel | [90] NY554145 |
| Sandscale Haws | [96] SD200756 |
| Tarn Hows | [96] SD328998 |
| Thurstaston Common | [108] SJ244853 |
| Wetheral Woods | [86] NY470553 |

### Landscape Tours in the Lake District

Relax and ride with the National Trust's Lake District Landscape Tours. From Easter to October a range of full and half-day tours run to the northern, southern and western lakes, including visits to Trust properties. The height of the minibuses offers unrestricted views over the drystone walls and allows everyone to appreciate fully the spectacular views. There are pick-up points at Keswick, Grasmere and Ambleside, and bookings can be made direct on 017687 73780 (Lakeside NT Information Centre) in season, or at the Tourist Information Centres in Windermere, Bowness, Keswick, Hawkshead and Coniston. Reduced ticket prices are available for Trust members.

**Unless indicated, last admission is always 30 mins before closing time**

walks through **Wetheral Woods**, along the River Eden near Carlisle, and on the south-west coast near Barrow is **Sandscale Haws**, a superb dune system.

Both **Arnside Knott** in Cumbria and, in Lancashire, the Silverdale properties of **Eaves** and **Waterslack Woods** offer the opportunity to enjoy a wide variety of wild flowers and butterflies, with fine views over limestone countryside. Near Kendal is **Holme Park Fell**, rercently acquired by the Trust and an important example of limestone pavement. A number of footpaths provide access to this interesting landscape. Further south the Trust has begun to protect the coastline at **Heysham**, with its small, ruined Saxon chapel and unique rock-cut graves. In east Lancashire the **Stubbins Estate** and **Holcombe Moor** serve as an important green lung to the North Manchester conurbation and are noted for their moorland bird species. Equally important for wildlife are the sand dunes and pinewoods at **Formby**, and the ancient woodland of **Stocktons Wood**, part of the historic landscape surrounding the magnificent **Speke Hall** on Merseyside.

Across the Mersey, the Wirral peninsula has a 12 mile-long country park, several parts of which are owned by the Trust. **Caldy Hill** gives spectacular views across the mouth of the River Dee, home to a wide variety of wildfowl and waders, some of which congregate here in huge numbers. At **Thurstaston Common** there is a rare surviving fragment of acid heathland, rich in insect life. To the south east lies **Helsby Hill**, from the summit of which there are breathtaking views over the Mersey and the mountains of North Wales. Several of the Trust's beauty spots in the south of the area are very near the great industrial conurbations of Liverpool and Manchester. The wooded sandstone escarpment of **Alderley Edge** gives fine views over the Cheshire Plain. A path from here links up with neighbouring **Hare Hill Garden**. Nearby **Styal Country Park** offers both pleasant riverside walks and much historic interest at **Quarry Bank Mill** and the factory colony village of Styal. There is another interesting watermill at **Nether Alderley**. Some of the area's most impressive country houses are also to be found on the fringes of Manchester, including **Lyme Park**, **Tatton Park** and **Dunham Massey**.

The south of the area runs towards the Welsh border and comprises beautiful mixed woodland, heathland and fields, with excellent walking opportunities. **Bickerton Hill** lies at the southern tip of the Peckforton Hills, a wooded ridge crossed by a 30 mile-long footpath, the Sandstone Trail, which passes a variety of dwellings from black-and-white cottages to prehistoric hill-forts.

### Highlights for Visitors with Disabilities ...
Wheelchair access to **Tarn Hows**; **Friar's Crag** at Derwentwater; **White Moss Common**, Grasmere; and at **Claife**, near Hawkshead, among many others. There is adapted holiday accommodation at Restharrow on the shores of **Windermere** and at **Acorn Bank Garden** east of Penrith (tel. 01225 791133 for details).

### ... and for Families
Particularly recommended are **Fell Foot Park**, **Lyme Park**, **Dunham Massey**, **Speke Hall**, **Formby**, **Quarry Bank Mill** and Steam Yacht *Gondola* on Coniston Water.

### Further Information
Please contact the Membership Department, PO Box 39, Bromley BR1 3XL. Tel. 0870 458 4000. Email: enquiries@thenationaltrust.org.uk

**There are special events at most Trust properties; please telephone 0870 458 4000 for details**

A leaflet detailing boating and fishing opportunities on Trust-managed waters in the Lake District is available from local NT information centres or the North West Regional Office; another leaflet lists car parks where NT members can park free (please send s.a.e.). A campsite leaflet is also available.

A free booklet *Wildlife, Wild Places*, describing the fascinating variety of wildlife habitats in the Trust's care in the North West, is also available from the Regional Office; please enclose two second-class stamps with your request.

## ACORN BANK GARDEN AND WATERMILL    Cumbria

Temple Sowerby, nr Penrith CA10 1SP · **Tel** 017683 61893 · **Fax** 017683 61467
**Email** acornbank@ntrust.org.uk

Ancient oaks and the high enclosing walls of this delightful garden keep out the worst of the Cumbrian climate, resulting in a spectacular display of shrubs, roses and herbaceous borders. Sheltered orchards contain a variety of traditional fruit trees and the famous herb garden is the largest collection of medicinal and culinary plants in the North. A circular woodland walk runs along Crowdundle Beck to Acorn Bank watermill, which although under restoration is open to visitors. The house is not open to the public

- 23 March to 3 Nov: daily except Tues, 10–5. **Events**: Tel. for details
- £2.50; child £1.20; family £6.20. Booked parties £1.80
- Shop and plant sales as garden
- Herb garden, herbaceous borders & greenhouse: accessible. Watermill: accessible path from car park, access to exterior and exhibition room. 2 wheelchairs
- Braille guide. Herbs, sounds of water from beck
- Tea-room: 31 March to 4 Nov 11–4.30. Tea-room available for evening functions and out of season, tel. 017683 61467
- Baby-changing facilities
- Rack in garden courtyard
- On leads on woodland walk
- (6:E7) Just N of Temple Sowerby, 6ml E of Penrith on A66 [91: NY612281] **Bus**: Stagecoach in Cumbria 563 Penrith–Brough, to within 1ml (passes close ≊ Penrith & ≊ Appleby) **Station**: Langwathby (U) 5ml; Penrith 6ml

**NT properties nearby** Ullswater and Aira Force

TARRAGON

## BEATRIX POTTER GALLERY

Cumbria

Main Street, Hawkshead LA22 0NS · **Tel** 015394 36355 · **Fax** 015394 36187
**Email** beatrixpottergallery@ntrust.org.uk

An annually changing exhibition of original sketches and watercolours painted by Beatrix Potter for her children's stories. This 17th-century building, which became known as Tabitha Twitchit's shop, was once the office of her husband, William Heelis. The interior remains substantially unaltered since his day, giving an interesting insight into a Victorian law office

- 24 March to 31 Oct: daily except Fri and Sat (but open Good Fri) 10.30–4.30. **Note**: Admission is by timed ticket (inc. NT members)

- £3; child £1.50; family £7.50. No party reduction. Car- and coach-parking in village car park, 200m. Joint Hill Top and Beatrix Potter Gallery tickets £7, child £2, family £16

- In the Square, Hawkshead; 1 March to 31 Oct: daily 10.30–4.30; Nov to 24 Dec: Sat, Sun & Mon 10.30–4.30; Jan & Feb 2003: Sat, Sun, Mon 10.30–4.30 (tel. 015394 36471 to check)

- Braille guide

- Children's quiz guidebook on Beatrix Potter. Free children's quiz sheets and trails. The Gallery is too small for baby back-carriers or pushchairs

- (6:D8) In The Square [96: SD352982] **Bus**: Stagecoach in Cumbria 505/6 Ambleside–Coniston (connections from ➥ Windermere) **Station**: Windermere 6½ml via ferry

**NT properties nearby** Hill Top, Tarn Hows

## BORROWDALE

Cumbria

Unit 2A, 13 High Hill, Keswick CA23 5LU · **Tel/Fax** 017687 74649
**Email** borrowdale@ntrust.org.uk

The location of the Trust's first acquisition in the Lake District: Brandelhow Woods, on the shore of Derwentwater. Total NT protection in the area today covers 11,806ha (29,173 acres), including eleven farms, half of Derwentwater (including the main islands), the hamlet of Watendlath, and well-known sites such as the Bowder Stone, Friar's Crag, Ashness Bridge and Castlerigg Stone Circle, a free-standing megalithic monument of 38 stones near Keswick

- All year. Information Centre at Keswick lakeside: 23 March to end Oct: 10–5; also some winter weekends, for details tel. 017687 73780

- Six NT pay-and-display car parks in valley (NT members free)

- Guided walks available; tel. for details

- Shop in Information Centre at Keswick lakeside (tel. 017687 73780)

**Please remember – your membership card is always needed for free admission**

NORTH WEST · 267

- ♿ Access to Friar's Crag, the Bowder Stone, Crow Park, Cat Bells Terrace, Calf Close Bay, Castlerigg Stone Circle and the shore of Derwentwater at Brandelhow; strong helpers recommended at all sites
- ☕ Café at Caffle House, Watendlath; teas at the Flock-In, Rosthwaite, at Ashness Farm, nr Ashness Bridge, at Knotts View, Stonethwaite and at Seathwaite – properties owned, but not managed, by the Trust
- ☎ Tel. Regional Office for details of minibus tours and resource information
- 🚲 Stands at Great Wood, Surprise View, Watendlath, Bowder Stone, Rosthwaite and Seatoller car parks
- → (6:D7) S of Keswick [90: NY266228 – Keswick Lakeside Information Centre]
  **Bus**: To Information Centre: Stagecoach in Cumbria X4/5 ▶ Penrith–Workington, 555/6 Lancaster–Keswick (pass close ▶ Lancaster, Kendal & Workington). Derwentwater launch service to various NT properties around lake, tel. 017687 72263

**NT properties nearby** Derwent Island House

---

## BUTTERMERE AND ENNERDALE   🏛 ⚓ 🚶   Cumbria

Beckfoot, Ennerdale CA23 2AU · **Tel/Fax** 019468 61235
**Email** buttermere@ntrust.org.uk

3588ha (8866 acres) of fell and commonland, including the lakes of Buttermere, Crummock and Loweswater, seven farms and woodland, as well as lakeshore access to Ennerdale Water. The high fells to the south include the famous Pillar Rock, and there are extensive prehistoric settlements on the fells south of Ennerdale

- 🅾 All year
- 💷 Three NT pay-and-display car parks (NT members free), inc. one on Honister Pass
- 🚶 Events programme organised throughout year. Fishing and boats available on Buttermere, Crummock Water and Loweswater, tel. for details
- ♿ 2ml route along SW side of Buttermere lake; strong pusher recommended; some short, steep gradients and uneven surfaces. Adapted gate by car park at Lanthwaite Woods leads to short route on firm gravel to Crummock Water
- ☎ Education programme for schools and other groups. Tel. for details
- → (6:C7) 8ml S of Cockermouth [89: NY1815 – Buttermere]
  **Bus**: Services from ▶ Penrith, Whitehaven, ▶ St Bees & Keswick

**NT properties nearby** Wordsworth House

For general enquiries, please telephone 0870 458 4000

## CARTMEL PRIORY GATEHOUSE    Cumbria

Cavendish Street, Cartmel, Grange-over-Sands LA11 6QA · **Tel** 015395 36874
**Fax** 015395 36636
**Email** cartmelpriory@ntrust.org.uk

All that is left, apart from the church, of a 12th-century Augustinian priory, which was later strengthened following devastating raids by Robert the Bruce. After the Dissolution in the mid-16th century, it served as a grammar school from 1624 to 1790. It is managed by the Cartmel Village Society as a village centre that depicts the history of the building, Cartmel village and the Cartmel peninsula

- **O** Easter to end Oct: daily except Mon & Tues 10–4; winter: Sat & Sun 10–4. Tel. for full opening details
- **£** Small entrance fee. Free to NT members. Parking nearby in village
- **→** (6:D9) [96: SD378788] **Bus**: Stagecoach in Cumbria 530/2 Kendal–Cartmel (passing ≋ Grange-over-Sands and ≋ Cork) **Station**: Cark (U) 2ml

**NT properties nearby** Fell Foot Park

## CONISTON AND LITTLE LANGDALE    Cumbria

Boon Crag, Coniston LA21 8AQ · **Tel/Fax** 015394 41197
**Email** coniston@ntrust.org.uk

A mixture of fell and woodland covering some 2608ha (6444 acres) and including eleven farms and the well-known Tarn Hows beauty spot. There is also access to the lakeshore of Coniston Water. Little Langdale shows several signs of early settlement, including the Thingmount (a Norse meeting place) by Fell Foot Farm

- **O** All year
- **£** Pay-and-display car park (NT members free) at Tarn Hows
- Guided walks available; tel. for details
- Accessible path from car park to halfway round Blea Tarn, with views to Great Langdale. Clockwise circuit of Tarn Hows possible. Two strong pushers needed for each route
- Trail around Tarn Hows using audio equipment (small deposit) from NT Land Rover in car park
- Tel. Regional Office for details of minibus tours and resource information
- Cycle tracks along Coniston lakeshore (west) and in woodland south of Tarn Hows. Racks at Tarn Hows car park
- **→** (6:D8) Little Langdale valley starts 4ml N of Coniston village [89/90: NY2904 – Blea Tarn Farm] **Bus**: NT minibus service 'Tarn Hows Tourer' linking Hawkshead, Tarn Hows and Coniston with Gondola, with connections from Ambleside and ≋ Windermere, Sun only during main season; leaflet from Regional Office

**NT properties nearby** Beatrix Potter Gallery, Gondola

**Please see the area introductions for details of coast & countryside properties**

## DALTON CASTLE

Cumbria

Market Place, Dalton-in-Furness LA15 8AX · **Tel/Fax** 01524 701178
**Email** daltoncastle@ntrust.org.uk

A 14th-century tower in the main street of the town, with a local exhibition by the Friends of Dalton Castle and a display about the painter George Romney, a native of Dalton

- Easter to end Sept: Sat 2–5
- Free but donations welcome
- (6:C9/D9) In main street of Dalton [96: SD226739] **Bus**: From surrounding areas **Station**: Dalton ¼ml

**NT properties nearby** Sandscale Haws (see Arnside & Silverdale)

## DERWENT ISLAND HOUSE

Cumbria

In Derwentwater · **Tel** 0870 609 5391 · **Email** derwent@ntrust.org.uk

An intriguing Italianate house of the 1840s, set on an idyllic wooded island in Derwentwater, with a restrained classical interior and restored garden

- The house is privately let, but parts are open to the public by booked timed ticket on: Sun 26 May, Sun 23 June, Wed 24 July, Sun 25 Aug, Sun 8 Sept. For booking form send s.a.e. to: The National Trust (Derwent Island Bookings), The Hollens, Grasmere, Ambleside, Cumbria LA22 9QZ
- £3.90; child £2. Launch to island (inc. NT members) £1.90; child £1
- At Keswick lakeside
- Access onto to the island is difficult for those with disabilities; no wheelchair access
- At Keswick lakeside
- No dogs
- (6:D7) [90: NY261224] **Bus**: Stagecoach in Cumbria X4/5 Penrith-Workington; 555/6 Lancaster–Keswick (pass close Lancaster, Kendal & Workington) **Cycle**: NCN 71 1ml (C2C)

**NT properties nearby** Borrowdale

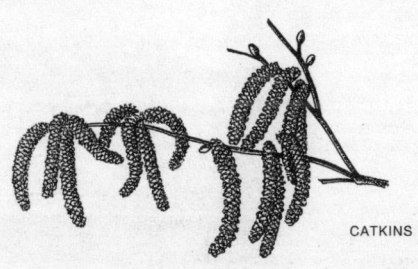

CATKINS

**Unless indicated, last admission is always 30 mins before closing time**

## DUNHAM MASSEY  Greater Manchester

Altrincham WA14 4SJ · **Tel** 0161 941 1025 · **Infoline** 0161 928 4351
**Fax** 0161 929 7508 · **Email** dunhammassey@ntrust.org.uk

An early Georgian house, Dunham Massey was extensively reworked in the early years of the 20th century. The result is one of Britain's most sumptuous Edwardian interiors, housing exceptional collections of 18th-century walnut furniture, paintings and Huguenot silver, as well as extensive servants' quarters. One of the North West's great plantsman's gardens with richly planted borders and majestic trees, as well as an orangery, Victorian bark house and well house. The ancient deer park contains a series of beautiful avenues and ponds

**House**: 23 March to 3 Nov: daily except Thur & Fri. *Times*: 23 March to 26 Oct 12–5; BH Sun & BH Mon & 4 June 11–5; 27 Oct to 3 Nov 12–4. **Park**: daily 9–5 (closes 7.30 23 March to 26 Oct); guided walks every Mon, Wed & Fri. **Garden**: 23 March to 3 Nov: daily 11–5.30 (27 Oct to 3 Nov: closes 4.30). **Mill**: Due to extensive restoration work, please tel. for details. **Events**: send s.a.e. for details

Park only £3 per car, £1 per motorbike, £5 per coach/minibus, refundable on purchase of adult house and garden ticket. Coaches bringing booked parties park free. NT members free. House & garden £5.50; child £2.75; family £13.75; booked groups £4.40. House or garden only £3.50; child £1.75. Reduced admission for bus ticket holders

Optional guided tours of house most afternoons at no extra charge. Pre-booked evening tours of house and garden at a charge

Daily (closed 25, 26 Dec). *Times*: 23 March to 26 Oct 10.30–5; 27 Oct to end March 2003 10.30–4; tel. 0161 928 6820

Close parking by arrangement. Shuttle service operates most days between car park and visitor facilities 23 March to 3 Nov. House: steps to ground floor and throughout house; stairclimber by prior arrangement. Garden & park: accessible, smooth, level paths. Shop & restaurant: accessible across cobbled yard, restaurant by lift. Wheelchairs and self-drive vehicles by arrangement

Braille guide, large-print guide; musicians may play Bechstein piano

Sympathetic Hearing Scheme

Licensed self-service Stables Restaurant: daily (closed 25 Dec). *Times*: 23 March to 26 Oct 10.30–5; 27 Oct to end March 2003 10.30–4. Booked functions welcome except Sun (tel. 0161 941 2815). Picnics welcome in North Park near main car park, but not in deer park or garden

**There are special events at most Trust properties; please telephone 0870 458 4000 for details**

NORTH WEST · 271

🚼 Baby-changing room; baby slings and reins. Children's menu, highchairs; free park trail; quiz sheets in house and garden

🏫 Victorian living history in house and park; environmental studies in deer park. Based on National Curriculum Key Stages 1, 2 & 3; by arrangement with Education Officer (tel. 0161 941 4986)

🐕 Good walks around estate, but must be on leads in deer park at all times

➔ (5:D8) 3ml SW of Altrincham off A56; exit 19 off M6; exit 7 off M56 [109: SJ735874] **Bus**: Arriva NW 38 ≥ Altrincham Interchange–Warrington **Station**: Altrincham (BR & Metro) 3ml; Hale 3ml **Cycle**: NCN 62 1ml

**NT properties nearby** Hare Hill, Lyme Park, Nether Alderley Mill, Quarry Bank Mill & Styal Estate

## DUNHAM MASSEY: WHITE COTTAGE 🏠 👤

Little Bollington, Altrincham WA14 4TJ                  Greater Manchester

An important timber-framed cottage, built c.1500 as a cruck-trussed open hall and altered in the 17th century. Recently restored by the Trust using traditional materials and techniques and now a private residence, open to visitors by kind permission of the tenants

⭕ April to end Oct: last Sun of month 2–5. All visits must be booked through the Stamford Estates Office, tel. 0161 928 0075 Mon to Fri 9–5

£ Box for donations in White Cottage

➔ (5:D8) As Dunham Massey

**NT properties nearby** Dunham Massey, Quarry Bank Mill & Styal Estate, Tatton Park

## FELL FOOT PARK 🌺 🍴                                  Cumbria

Newby Bridge, Ulverston LA12 8NN · **Tel** 015395 31273 · **Fax** 015395 30049
**Email** fellfootpark@ntrust.org.uk

This Victorian park, restored to its former glory, offers substantial access to the lakeshore of Windermere, where there are leisure facilities in season. Fine picnic areas and boat hire make this property particularly rewarding for families. Spring and early summer bring impressive displays of daffodils, followed by rhododendrons, and there are magnificent views of the Lakeland fells

**Note**: No launching or landing of speedboats or jet-skis

⭕ Daily 9–7 or dusk if earlier. Facilities, eg rowing boat hire (buoyancy aids available), 31 March to 4 Nov: daily 11–4.30. **Events**: summer activity programme; tel. for details

£ Car park £2 (up to 2hrs), £5 (all day). Coaches £15 by arrangement. **Note**: Car park has pay-and-display meters so NT membership card or season ticket must be displayed in car. Season tickets from most NT outlets in Cumbria

**For all your information needs check our website www.nationaltrust.org.uk**

## 272 · NORTH WEST

🏠 31 March to 4 Nov: daily 11–5

♿ Park: accessible but sloping site with unfenced water. Communications system, sponsored by BAe, in both car parks. Tea-room & shop: accessible. Three 2-seater self-drive buggies. Adapted WC with RADAR lock

👆 Braille guide

☕ 31 March to 4 Nov: as shop. Tea-room available for evening functions all year and during the day out of season; tel. the Catering Manager

👶 Highchairs, Trusty the Hedgehog lunch boxes, scribble sheets

🐕 On leads only

➔ (6:D9) At the extreme S end of Lake Windermere on E shore, entrance from A592 [96/97: SD381869] **Bus**: Stagecoach in Cumbria 618 Ambleside–Barrow-in-Furness (connections from 🚆 Windermere **Station**: Grange-over-Sands 6ml; Windermere 8ml

**NT properties nearby** Sizergh Castle & Garden

---

## FORMBY

Merseyside

Victoria Road, Freshfield, Formby L37 1LJ · **Tel** 01704 878591
**Fax** 01704 874949 · **Email** formby@ntrust.org.uk

A wonderful stretch of unspoilt coastline, made up of rolling sand dunes and attractive pine woods set between the sea and Formby town. There are interesting plants and birds to be found, and this is one of the last places in England where visitors may catch a glimpse of the rare red squirrel

🅾 Daily during daylight. **Events**: send s.a.e. for details

£ £2.90 per car (NT members free). Coaches £15. Coaches and group visits must book; tel. 01704 874949

♿ Hard-surfaced paths to red squirrel viewing area and Cornerstone Walk. Boardwalk from car park in sand dunes to viewing platform. Picnic sites. WC (RADAR key)

👶 Children's red squirrel booklet £1. Baby-changing facilities in WC

🎒 Every school group must book in advance. Maximum numbers enforced. Environmental education programme; for information tel./fax 01704 874949

🚲 Cycle parking

🐕 On leads around the squirrel walk

➔ (5:B7) 15ml N of Liverpool, 2ml W of Formby, 2ml off A565 [108: SD275080] **Bus**: ABC 160/1/4/5, 🚆 Formby–BR Freshfield, to within ½ml **Station**: Freshfield 1ml **Cycle**: NCN 62 3ml

**NT properties nearby** 20 Forthlin Road, Rufford Old Hall, Speke Hall

---

**Please remember – your membership card is always needed for free admission**

NORTH WEST · 273

## 20 FORTHLIN ROAD, ALLERTON  Liverpool

L24 1YP · **Bookings** 0151 427 7231 · **Infoline** 0870 900 0256
**Email** 20forthlinroad@ntrust.org.uk · **Web** www.spekehall.org.uk

This 1950s terraced house is the former home of the McCartney family, where the Beatles met, rehearsed and wrote many of their earliest songs. Displays include contemporary photographs by Michael McCartney and early Beatles memorabilia. The audio tour features contributions from both Michael and Sir Paul McCartney

**Note**: Any photography inside 20 Forthlin Road or duplication of audio tour material is strictly prohibited. You will be asked to deposit all handbags, cameras and recording equipment at the entrance to the house to be returned on your departure. Unauthorised reproduction is contrary to law

- 23 March to 26 Oct: Wed, Thur, Fri & Sat; 3 Nov to 8 Dec: Sat only. There is no need to book in advance, but visitors may do so if they prefer. Tours depart by minibus from Speke Hall and from Albert Dock. Ring infoline to check times and pick-up points. **There is no direct access by car**

- £6; child £2.80 (includes admission to garden and grounds of Speke Hall). NT members £3 to cover minibus

- At nearby Speke Hall

- Wheelchair-accessible minibus from Speke. Access to garden and parts of ground floor only

- At nearby Speke Hall

- (5:B8) See entry for Speke Hall **Station**: West Allerton, not Sun ½ml, Mossley 1½ml

**NT properties nearby** Formby, Rufford Old Hall, Speke Hall

## GAWTHORPE HALL  Lancashire

Padiham, nr Burnley BB12 8UA · **Tel** 01282 771004 · **Fax** 01282 770178
**Email** gawthorpehall@ntrust.org.uk

An Elizabethan gem in the heart of Lancashire, Gawthorpe resembles the great Hardwick Hall and is very probably by the same architect, Robert Smythson. In the middle of the 19th century Sir Charles Barry was commissioned to restore the house, thereby creating the opulent interiors we see today. There are many notable paintings on loan from the National Portrait Gallery, and an unparalleled collection of needlework, assembled by the last family member to live here, Rachel Kay-Shuttleworth. The wooded grounds and riverside location offer good summer walks

**Note**: Gawthorpe Hall is financed and administered by Lancashire County Council

- **Hall**: 1 April to 31 Oct: daily except Mon & Fri (but open Good Fri & BH Mons) 1–5. **Garden**: all year 10–6. **Events**: events and exhibitions all season, tel. for details and events guide

- £3; child £1.30; concessions £1.50; family £8 (prices may change). Garden free. Parties by arrangement. Free parking 150m

**For general enquiries, please telephone 0870 458 4000**

## 274 · NORTH WEST

- ♿ Access to grounds only; tel. for details
- 🌹 Rose garden
- ☕ Tea-room as Hall, 12.30–5. Available for evening functions all year, tel. 01282 779346
- 👶 Unsuitable for baby back-carriers or pushchairs. Highchair in tea-room
- 🏫 Role-play for Key Stage 2. Through role-play and interactive sessions with our Victorian Butler and Housekeeper children can gain valuable insight into how a grand Victorian house was organised and run. Available during term times from 10; for details tel. 01282 771004. Private study of the Rachel Kay-Shuttleworth collections can be arranged; tel. 01282 773963
- 🐕 In grounds only and under close control
- ➔ (5:D6) On E outskirts of Padiham; ¾ml drive to house on N of A671; M65 jct 8 towards Clitheroe, then signposted from second traffic light junction [103: SD806340] **Bus**: Frequent services from Burnley. All pass close ≠ Burnley Barracks & Burnley Manchester Road **Station**: Rose Grove (U) 2ml

**NT properties nearby** East Riddlesden Hall, Holcombe Moor, Rufford Old Hall, Stubbins Estate

---

# GONDOLA                                                Cumbria

NT Gondola Bookings Office, The Hollens, Grasmere LA22 9QZ
**Tel** 015394 41288 · **Bookings** 015394 63856 (15+ groups and charters)
**Fax** 015394 35353 · **Email** gondola@ntrust.org.uk

---

The steam yacht *Gondola* was first launched in 1859 and now, completely renovated by the Trust, provides a steam-powered passenger service in its opulently upholstered saloons. The perfect way to view Coniston's spectacular scenery

- 🅾 Steam yacht *Gondola* sails from Coniston Pier daily 1 March to 31 Oct, weather permitting. The National Trust reserves the right to cancel sailings in the event of high winds. Piers at Coniston and Brantwood (not NT). Parties from Coniston Pier only. Free parking and WC at Coniston Pier. *Gondola* is also available for private hire

**Please see the area introductions for details of coast & countryside properties**

💷 Ticket prices and timetable on application and published locally. Family ticket available. No reduction for NT members as Gondola is an enterprise and not held solely for preservation. Parties & private charters by prior arrangement; tel. 9–5

🛍 Guidebook and *Gondola* souvenirs available on board

➔ (6:D8) Coniston (½ml to Coniston Pier) [96:SD316978] **Bus**: Stagecoach in Cumbria 505/6 from Ambleside (connections from 🚊 Windermere). Tarn Hows tourer links with Gondola on Sun see p.253 **Station**: Foxfield (U), not Sun, 10ml; Windermere 10ml via vehicle ferry

**NT properties nearby** Beatrix Potter Gallery

## GRASMERE AND GREAT LANGDALE  Cumbria
High Close, Loughrigg, Ambleside LA22 0LQ · **Tel** 015394 37663
**Fax** 015394 37131 · **Email** grasmere@ntrust.org.uk

4925ha (12,170 acres) and ten farms, including the protection of the famous Langdale Pikes. The area includes the popular White Moss Common, the glaciated valley of Mickleden, a Victorian garden at High Close (currently being restored) and dramatic Dungeon Ghyll, as well as the bed of Grasmere lake and part of Rydal Water

**Note**: There is a NT campsite at Great Langdale, open all year [NY286059]; charge (inc. NT members); for details tel. 015394 37668

🅾 All year. Grasmere Information Centre (near church): March to end Oct: 10–5; Nov to mid Dec: 10–4 (tel. 015394 35621)

💷 Five NT pay-and-display car parks in the two valleys (NT members free), but none in Grasmere village

🛍 Shop in Grasmere Information Centre

♿ Designated parking. Accessible path at White Moss Common and Elterwater

🎦 Contact Regional Office for details of minibus tours and resource information

➔ (6:D8) Great Langdale valley starts 4ml W of Ambleside [89/90: NY2906]
**Bus**: To Grasmere Information Centre: Stagecoach in Cumbria 555/6, 599 from 🚊 Windermere **Station**: Windermere 8ml

**NT properties nearby** Stagshaw Garden, Townend

## HARE HILL  Cheshire
Over Alderley, Macclesfield SK10 4QB · **Tel** 0870 609 5391 (Regional Office)

A woodland garden with azaleas, rhododendrons and a delightful walled garden at its heart, containing a pergola and wire sculptures. The surrounding parkland has attractive walks, including a link path to Alderley Edge (2ml)

🅾 1 April to 30 Oct: daily except Mon, Tues & Fri (but open BH Mons & Tues 4 June); 10–30 May: daily (for rhododendrons and azaleas). *Times*: 10–5.30

**Unless indicated, last admission is always 30 mins before closing time**

## 276 · NORTH WEST

[£] £2.50. Entrance per car £1.50 refundable on entry to garden (NT members free). Parties either by written appointment c/o Garden Lodge, Oak Road, Over Alderley, Macclesfield SK10 4QB, or tel. Gardener-in-charge on 01625 828981. Not suitable for school parties

[&] Ample car-parking, but on slope; gravel paths, strong companion advisable. Wheelchair

[👁] Braille guide. Scented plants in walled garden; scents and sounds of wooded parkland

[🐾] Not in garden, elsewhere only on leads

[→] (5:E8) Between Alderley Edge and Prestbury, turn off north at B5087 at Greyhound Road [118: SJ875765] **Bus**: Bakers 287 Wilmslow–Macclesfield (passing ⇌ Prestbury), to within ¾ml **Station**: Alderley Edge 2½ml; Prestbury 2½ml

**NT properties nearby** Alderley Edge

---

# HAWKSHEAD AND CLAIFE   Cumbria
Unit 9, Scutcheon Bldgs, Far Sawrey LA22 9HH · **Tel/Fax** 015394 47997
**Email** hawkshead@ntrust.org.uk

---

Hawkshead is a classic Lakeland village, surrounded by beautiful scenery, much of which is owned by the Trust. Claife Woodlands and the low-lying small farms between the village and Lake Windermere are typical of the area. Just north of Hawkshead itself there is the Courthouse, which dates from the 15th century and is all that remains of the village manorial buildings (once held by Furness Abbey). Claife Station, on the west bank of Windermere, is a former Victorian viewing station with glimpses of the lake. Wray Castle is currently let as a college, with limited access to the grounds and occasional access to the castle, tel. property office for details

**Note**: There is a NT campsite at Low Wray, open Easter to end Oct [NY372012]; charge (inc. NT members); tel. 015394 32810

[O] All year. Hawkshead Courthouse: 31 March to 4 Nov: daily 10–5, access by key from NT shop, The Square, Hawkshead; free admission, but no parking facilities

[£] Pay-and-display car park (NT members free) at Ash Landing, close to Lake Windermere (Ferry Nab)

[🚶] Tel. for details of guided walks

[🛍] In The Square, Hawkshead (see Beatrix Potter Gallery, p.266, for opening times)

[&] Walk at Claife, from Red Nab NT car park to High Wray Bay along W shore of Windermere; follow signs in High Wray village, 2m NE of Hawkshead. Adapted holiday cottage at Restharrow on Windermere lakeside

[■] Contact Regional Office for details of minibus tours and resource information

[🚲] Lakeshore track from Harrowslack (SD388960) to St Margaret's Church (NY374006) along Windermere lakeshore (west)

---

**There are special events at most Trust properties; please telephone 0870 458 4000 for details**

➜ (6:D8) Hawkshead is 6ml SW of Ambleside [96/97: SD352982]
**Bus**: Stagecoach in Cumbria 505/6 Ambleside–Coniston (connections from ☒ Windermere). Boat & Goat bus service **Station**: Windermere 6ml via vehicle ferry

**NT properties nearby** Beatrix Potter Gallery, Hill Top

## HILL TOP
Cumbria
Near Sawrey, Ambleside LA22 0LF · **Tel** 015394 36269 · **Fax** 015394 36118
**Email** hilltop@ntrust.org.uk

Beatrix Potter wrote many of her famous children's stories in this little 17th-century house and it has been kept exactly as she left it, complete with her furniture and china. There is a traditional cottage garden attached. A selection of her original illustrations may be seen at the Beatrix Potter Gallery (p.266).

**Note**: Hill Top is a very small house and a timed entry and booking system is operated. The number of visitors is monitored to avoid overcrowding and to protect the fragile interior. This is a unique and popular property, and visitors sometimes have to wait to enter. We regret that occasionally some visitors may not gain entry at all. School holidays are particularly busy and, as a general rule, visitors are advised to come at the beginning or end of the season if at all possible

**What's new in 2002**: 2002 is the 100th anniversary of the commercial publication of Peter Rabbit. To celebrate, additional activities and talks are being arranged, as well as extended opening – tel. for details

⊙ 23 March to 3 Nov: daily except Thur & Fri (but open Good Fri). *Times*: March to May 11–4.30; June to Aug 10.30–5; Sept & Oct 11–4.30; last admission is always 30mins before closing. Booking by telephone (015394 36269) prior to visit is strongly advisable to guarantee entry. Advance payment required for non-members. Sustainable transport pilot scheme to be introduced in 2002

£ £4.50; child £1; family ticket £10. No party reduction. Parking 200m; no parking for coaches. Joint Hill Top and Beatrix Potter Gallery tickets £7; child £2; family ticket £16

**For all your information needs check our website www.nationaltrust.org.uk**

## 278 · NORTH WEST

- 📅 23 March to 3 Nov: daily. *Times*: March to May: 10.30–4.30; June to Aug 10–5; Sept to 3 Nov: 10.30–4.30
- ♿ House: ground floor accessible by arrangement. House very small and often crowded
- 👁 Braille guide, some items may be touched
- 🍴 Bar lunches and evening meals at the Tower Bank Arms (NT owned and let to tenant) next door, during licensing hours (tel. 015394 36334)
- 👶 Unsuitable for back carriers or pushchairs. Children's guidebook on Beatrix Potter
- ➡ (6:D8) 2ml S of Hawkshead, in hamlet of Near Sawrey, behind the Tower Bank Arms [96/97: SD370955] **Bus**: Stagecoach in Cumbria 505/6 Ambleside–Coniston service (connections from ≋ Windermere); also frequent service from ≋ Windermere to Bowness Pier, thence ferry and 2ml walk **Station**: Windermere 4½ml via vehicle ferry

**NT properties nearby** Beatrix Potter Gallery

---

## LITTLE MORETON HALL 🏠✝✹🎭                              Cheshire
Congleton CW12 4SD · **Tel** 01260 272018
**Email** littlemoretonhall@ntrust.org.uk

---

Britain's most famous and arguably finest timber-framed moated manor house. The drunkenly reeling south front, topped by a spectacular long gallery, opens onto a cobbled courtyard and the main body of the Hall. Magnificent wall paintings and a notable knot garden are of special interest.

**What's new in 2002**: Musical evenings, suppers and special tours

- 🅾 23 March to 3 Nov: daily except Mon & Tues (but open BH Mons, Tues 4 June and Good Fri); 9 Nov to 22 Dec: Sat & Sun (access in Dec restricted to ground floor, garden, shop and restaurant only). *Times*: 11.30–5 or dusk if earlier; 9 Nov to 22 Dec 11.30–4. Special openings at other times for booked parties. **Events**: 23 March to 22 Dec: Chapel service every Sun 3.45. Open-air theatre by ACT in July, plus family events, connoisseur tours and regular events during normal opening hours
- £ £4.50; child £2.25; family £11. Booked parties £3.75. Reduced price ticket for Biddulph Grange Garden. 30 Nov to 22 Dec: free. Extra charge for special openings. Parking 150m £2, refundable on entry to Hall (NT members free); car park open from 11am
- 🚶 Optional free guided tours most afternoons 23 March to 24 Nov
- 📅 As house
- ♿ Disabled visitors may be set down at house. House: ground floor and Chapel accessible (ramp available). Garden: accessible. Restaurant, shop & exhibition room: accessible. Self-drive vehicle and wheelchairs by arrangement. Photograph album of upper-floor rooms

---

**Please remember – your membership card is always needed for free admission**

## NORTH WEST · 279

- Braille and large-print guides; some items may be touched
- Small licensed restaurant (waited service) as house (no reservations); available for private functions and evenings. Picnic area by car park
- Baby-changing unit. Children's guidebook. Highchairs; children's portions
- School parties April to mid-Dec: Wed, Thur & Fri by arrangement. Schoolroom; teachers' resource pack
- Racks in car park
- On leads and only in car park
- (5:E9) 4ml SW of Congleton, on E side of A34 [118: SJ832589] **Bus**: First PMT 77 Congleton–Hanley (passing close ⇌ Kidsgrove & Congleton), alight Brownlow Heath, 1½ml **Station**: Kidsgrove 3ml; Congleton 4½ml

**NT properties nearby** Biddulph Grange Garden

---

## LYME PARK                                                                 Cheshire
Disley, Stockport SK12 2NX · **Tel** 01663 762023/766492 · **Fax** 01663 765035
**Email** lymepark@ntrust.org.uk

Originally a Tudor house, Lyme was transformed by the Venetian architect Leoni into an Italianate palace. Some of the Elizabethan interiors survive and contrast dramatically with later rooms. The state rooms are adorned with Mortlake tapestries, Grinling Gibbons wood-carvings and an important collection of English clocks. The 6.8ha (17-acre) Victorian garden boasts impressive bedding schemes, a sunken parterre, an Edwardian rose garden, Jekyll-style herbaceous borders, reflection lake, a ravine garden and Wyatt conservatory. The garden is surrounded by a medieval deer park of almost 566ha (1400 acres) of moorland, woodland and parkland, containing an early 18th-century hunting tower. Lyme appeared as 'Pemberley' in the BBC's recent adaptation of the Jane Austen novel *Pride and Prejudice*

**Note**: Lyme Park is owned and managed by the NT and partly financed by Stockport Metropolitan Borough Council

**What's new in 2002**: Restored Tapestry Dressing Room

- **House**: 29 March to 30 Oct: daily (except Wed & Thur) 1–5 (BH Mon & Tues 4 June 11–5). Timed tickets on BH Mons & Tues 4 June. **Park**: daily. *Times*: April to 31 Oct 8am–8.30pm; Nov to 31 March 2003 8–6. **Garden**: 29 March to 30 Oct: daily; Nov to 18 Dec: Sat & Sun. *Times*: April to Oct: Fri to Tues 11–5; Wed & Thur 1–5; Nov to 18 Dec 12–3. **The Cage** (early 18th-century hunting tower): April to Oct on 2nd and 4th weekends of each month. **Paddock Cottage** (17th-century hunting lodge): April to Oct on 3rd weekend of month 12–4. **Events**: send s.a.e. to Estate Office for details
- Park only £3.50 car, £2 motorbike, £6 coach/minibus, refundable on purchase of adult house & garden ticket. Coaches bringing booked parties – Park admission free. NT members free. House and garden £5.50, House only £4, garden only £2.50. Family ticket £12

**For general enquiries, please telephone 0870 458 4000**

## 280 · NORTH WEST

[K] Taster tours of house at noon on open days. Guided tours available on some days, limited places. Enquire at ticket office on arrival. House tours by arrangement outside normal opening hours (min. charge £120)

[🛍] 30 March to 30 Oct: daily 11–5; Nov to March 2003: Sat & Sun and 27–30 Dec, 2–6 Jan 2003 12–4. Shops located in old workshop yard and house courtyard

[♿] Disabled visitors may be set down at house. Limited close parking also available, ask on arrival. House: first floor accessible. Wheelchairs. Courtesy minibus: tel. for details. Refreshments/shops in courtyard and park accessible. Garden: accessible through Rose Garden. Park: steep terrain

[☕] Licensed table service. Ale Cellar Restaurant located in the House 30 March to 30 Oct daily 11–5 (except Wed & Thur). Booked functions welcome in the Servants' Hall. The Old Workshop tea-room located by the Mill Pond 30 March to 30 Oct daily 11–5; Nov to March Sat & Sun 12–4. Ice cream available on some days in the car park

[👶] Baby-changing facilities. Children's guide to house and quiz to park. Playground for 11-years and under. Highchairs, bottle-warming facilities. Children's menu

[🎓] Extensive education programme in house and park. Orienteering on request. Tel. Education Officer for details

[🚲] Lockable racks in main car park and workshop courtyard

[🐕] Under close control and only in park. Limited shaded parking, dog hooks and water bowls in workshop courtyard. Please clear up after your dog

[→] (5:E8) Entrance on A6, 6½ml SE of Stockport, 9ml NW of Buxton (house and car park 1ml from entrance) [109:SJ965825] **Bus**: Holly 362 from ≋ New Mills Central (passing ≋ Disley) Suns, June–Sept only, otherwise Stagecoach in Manchester 361 Stockport–Glossop, Trent 199 Buxton–Manchester Airport both to park entrance **Station**: Disley, ½ml from park entrance. NT courtesy bus from park entrance and car park to house for pedestrians on days house is open, tel. property for details

**NT properties nearby** Hare Hill

**Please see the area introductions for details of coast & countryside properties**

## NETHER ALDERLEY MILL                        Cheshire

Congleton Road, Nether Alderley, Macclesfield SK10 4TW · **Tel** 01625 584412
**Email** netheralderleymill@ntrust.org.uk

A fascinating and unusual watermill, dating from the 15th century. It has overshot tandem wheels and is powered by water from a lake, beside which the mill is built. After lying derelict for thirty years, the Victorian machinery was restored in the 1960s and is now in full working order, with regular flour-grinding demonstrations

- April, May & Oct: Wed, Sun & BH Mons & Tues 4 June; June to Sept: daily except Mon (but open BH Mon). *Times*: April, May & Oct 1–4.30; June to Sept 1–5
- £2; child £1. Parties (max. 20) by arrangement. No WC
- As required
- Sounds of working machinery
- Visits by arrangement. Parking space for one coach at a time; must book in advance. Teachers' resource book. Bookings: Cheshire Countryside Office, Foresters Lodge, Nether Alderley, Macclesfield, Cheshire SK10 4UB. Tel. 01625 584412
- (5:E8) 1½ml S of Alderley Edge, on E side of A34 [118: SJ844763] **Bus**: Arriva North Midlands 130 Manchester–Macclesfield (passing ≋ Alderley Edge) **Station**: Alderley Edge 2ml

**NT properties nearby** Alderley Edge, Hare Hill, Quarry Bank Mill

## QUARRY BANK MILL AND STYAL ESTATE
                                                Cheshire

Wilmslow SK9 4LA · **Tel** 01625 527468 · **Fax** 01625 539267
**Email** quarrybankmill@ntrust.org.uk · **Web** www.quarrybankmill.org.uk

Quarry Bank Mill and Styal Estate comprises four distinct elements, all once belonging to the Greg family who founded the Mill and gave the land to the National Trust:

The Georgian working water-powered cotton mill still spins and weaves cotton to be sold in the shop. The Mill includes demonstrations of the development of the textile industry from hand spinning to noisy weaving factory. See a spinning jenny and a mule in action; hear and feel the thump of the weaving shed, alongside the most powerful waterwheel in Europe, and one of the earliest steam-powered beam engines. Allow at least one-and-a-half hours to visit the mill.

The Apprentice House and its historic organic garden where you can see and hear how pauper children were boarded whilst they were indentured to the Mill. Guided tours take about 45 mins.

The colony village of Styal, which housed many of the workers in idyllic rural surroundings, provides a view of allotments, school and chapels.

**Unless indicated, last admission is always 30 mins before closing time**

## 282 · NORTH WEST

The Estate of riverside, farmland and woodland walks in the valley of the River Bollin, planted by the Gregs, provides a delightful contrast to the throb of machinery and other industrial heritage sights

**What's new in 2002**: New ramps and improved access to part of the estate should be available for disabled visitors, along with a children's playground themed on the Mill

- **Mill**: all year; 23 March to end Sept: daily 10.30–5.30, last admission 4pm. Oct to March: daily except Mon, 10.30–5, last admission 3.30. **Apprentice House and Garden**: open everry weekday (term time) except Mon, from 2. School holidays and weekends from 11. **Note**: entry to Apprentice House is by timed ticket only, available from Mill on arrival. **Park**: open daily during daylight hours

- Mill/Apprentice House £6.50; child/concessions £3.70; family £16.50. Mill only £5; child/concessions £3.40. Advance booking essential for groups of 10+ (send s.a.e. for booking form at least 3 weeks in advance; guides may be booked at same time). Reductions for groups of 20+. Parking £2.50 partially refundable on entry to Mill (NT members free)

- Available for booked groups from 9.30 except weekends and BH Mons; plus some evenings in May, June & Sept. Guided tours of woodlands and village from main car park on 2nd Sun of each month at 2.30

- As Mill, selling goods made from cloth woven in the Mill and wide range of gifts and souvenirs. Mail order catalogue for Styal Calico available. Tel. 01625 537529

- Disabled visitors may be set down in Mill yard. Mill: Mill owner and Mill worker exhibitions, power galleries, waterwheel and audiovisual theatre accessible. Apprentice House: 3 rooms on ground floor accessible, photographs of upper floors. Wheelchair on request. Tel. for access leaflet. 2 ml circular woodland route at southern end of the estate from the Twinnies Bridge car park (not NT) and opening through to Mill Yard this year

- Braille and large-print guides; talking map; cotton samples and other items to handle. Varied smells and noises from machinery

- Sympathetic Hearing Scheme

- Mill Kitchen licensed restaurant. Mill Pantry for snacks, drinks and ice creams. Conference and banqueting facilities. Tel: 01625 526238

- Parent and baby room; back carriers admitted; baby sling and back carriers available

- Education programme for booked parties linked to National Curriculum; living history, hands-on science and technology activities and textile workshops. Information from Education Dept, tel. 01625 532034

- (5:D8) 1½ml N of Wilmslow off B5166, 2½ml from M56, exit 5, 10ml S of Manchester [109: SJ835835] **Bus**: Styal Shuttle 200/1 ≋ Manchester Airport–Wilmslow **Station**: Styal, ½ml (not Sun); Manchester Airport 2ml; Wilmslow 2½ml

**NT properties nearby** Dunham Massey, Lyme Park, Nether Alderley Mill, Tatton Park

---

**There are special events at most Trust properties; please telephone 0870 458 4000 for details**

# RUFFORD OLD HALL

Lancashire

Rufford, nr Ormskirk L40 1SG · **Tel/Fax** 01704 821254
**Email** ruffordoldhall@ntrust.org.uk

One of Lancashire's finest 16th-century buildings, famed for its spectacular Great Hall with an intricately carved movable wooden screen and dramatic hammerbeam roof. It is rumoured that Shakespeare performed in this hall for the owner, Sir Thomas Hesketh, to whose family Rufford belonged for over 400 years. The house contains fine collections of 16th- and 17th-century oak furniture, arms, armour and tapestries

- **House**: 23 March to 30 Oct: daily except Thur & Fri. *Times*: 1–5. **Garden**: as house 11–5.30. **Events**: send s.a.e. for details. Great Hall available for wedding ceremonies and grounds for wedding photos; tel. for details

- £4; child £2; family £10. Garden only £2. Booked parties £2.75 (no parties Sun & BH Mons)

- 31 March to 4 Nov: as garden. Tel. for details of winter opening of shop and restaurant. Christmas gifts and lunches available Nov & Dec

- Parking on firm gravel; level paths to house and garden. House: ground floor accessible, otherwise many steps and narrow passages; photograph album of inaccessible rooms. 2 wheelchairs. Restaurant, shop & garden: accessible

- Braille guide and large-print house guide; great screen and carved oak doors may be touched. Audio tour

- Sympathetic Hearing Scheme

- Old Kitchen Restaurant (licensed) 31 March to 4 Nov: as hall 12–5; tel for winter opening details and Christmas dinners. Picnic site by car park. Restaurant available for private functions; contact Catering Manager

- Unsuitable for baby back-carriers or pushchairs, but baby slings for loan. Baby-changing facility in women's WC, bottle-warming service. Highchairs; children's menu; children's quiz sheet; scribble sheets; early learning toys

- Accompanied visits and teachers' pack

- Rack

- On leads and only in grounds; fresh water and bowl available; tether rings in yard

- (5:C6) 7ml N of Ormskirk, in village of Rufford on E side of A59 [108: SD463160] **Bus**: Arriva North West 303 Preston–Ormskirk; Stagecoach in Lancashire 758 Liverpool–Blackpool; Blue Bus 347 Southport–Chorley **Station**: Rufford (U), not Sun, ½ml; Burscough Bridge 2½ml

**NT properties nearby** Formby, Gawthorpe Hall, Speke Hall

For all your information needs check our website www.nationaltrust.org.uk

## SIZERGH CASTLE & GARDEN  Cumbria

Sizergh, nr Kendal LA8 8AE · **Tel** 015395 60070 · **Fax** 015395 61621
**Email** ntrust@sizerghcastle.fsnet.co.uk

The home of the Strickland family for over 760 years, the medieval castle was extended in Elizabethan times and has an exceptional series of oak panelled interiors with intricately carved chimneypieces and early oak furniture, culminating in the magnificent Inlaid Chamber. The castle is surrounded by handsome gardens which include a particularly imposing and beautiful rock garden. The estate has flower-rich limestone pasture and ancient woodland supporting numerous species of butterfly

**What's new in 2002**: A two-year programme of structural repairs to Sizergh Castle is due to begin in 2002 and parts of the exterior of the building may be obscured

- **Castle**: 24 March to 31 Oct: daily except Fri & Sat 1.30–5.30. **Garden**: 24 March to 31 Oct: daily except Fri & Sat 12.30–5.30. **Events**: tel. for details
- £5; child £2.50; family £12.50. Garden only £2.50. Parties of 15+ £4 by arrangement (not BHols). Car park 100m
- 24 March to 31 Oct: as garden, 12.30–5.30. Also open Nov & Dec, tel. for details
- Castle: Lower Hall accessible; photograph album of inaccessible rooms. Garden: gravel paths; self-drive vehicles and manual wheelchairs. Tea-room: 3 steps at entrance. Accessible picnic tables
- Braille guide; some wooden items may be touched
- Tea-room in castle, hours as castle. Picnic tables and refreshment kiosk in car park, open at peak times
- Children's guide. Unsuitable for baby back-carriers and pushchairs
- Country walks on estate. Leaflet from shop
- (6:E8) 3½ml S of Kendal, signposted off A590 [97: SD498878] **Bus**: Stagecoach in Cumbria 555 Keswick–Lancaster (passing close ≠ Lancaster and Kendal) **Station**: Oxenholme 3ml; Kendal (U) 3½ml

**NT properties nearby** Fell Foot Park

**Please remember – your membership card is always needed for free admission**

NORTH WEST · 285

## SPEKE HALL, GARDEN & ESTATE  Liverpool

The Walk, Liverpool L24 1XD · **Tel** 0151 427 7231 · **Infoline** 08457 585702
**Fax** 0151 427 9860
**Email** spekehall@ntrust.org.uk · **Web** www.spekehall.org.uk

One of the most famous half-timbered houses in the country, dating from 1490. The unique and atmospheric interior spans many periods: the Great Hall and priest holes evoke Tudor times, while the Oak Parlour and smaller rooms, some with William Morris wallpapers, show the Victorian desire for privacy and comfort. There is also fine Jacobean plasterwork and intricately carved furniture. A fully equipped Victorian kitchen and servants' hall enable visitors to see 'behind the scenes'. The restored garden has spring bulbs, a rose garden, summer border and stream garden, and there are woodland walks and magnificent views of the Mersey basin from the Bund, a high bank. Home Farm, a 5-min walk from Speke Hall, is a model Victorian farm building, restored and part-adapted to provide a new restaurant, shop, visitor reception and WCs, and offers estate walks, children's play area and orchard. There is a buggy service for the elderly and visitors with disabilities

**Note**: Speke Hall is administered and financed by the National Trust with the help of a grant through the National Museums & Galleries on Merseyside

- **House**: 23 March to 27 Oct: daily except Sun, Mon & Tues (but open BH Mons & Tues 4 June); 30 Oct to 8 Dec: Sat only. *Times*: 28 March to mid-Oct: 1–5.30; mid-Oct to Dec 1–4.30. **Garden & Estate**: daily throughout year. Closed 24, 26 Dec, 31 Dec, 1 Jan. *Times*: March to mid-Oct: 11–5.30; mid-Oct to end March 2003: 11–4. **Home Farm**: 23 March to 27 Oct: daily except Mon (open BH Mons); Nov & Dec: Sat & Sun. *Times*: 11–5.30.

- Estate: £3 per car (NT members free). Garden: £2.50; child £1.50; family £6. House & garden: £5; child £3; family £14; car park fee refunded to visitors to garden and house

- Group tours of gardens and estate by prior arrangement. Write or telephone Interpretation & Education Officer

- As Home Farm 11–5.30

- Car park adjacent to Home Farm. Free transport to and from Speke Hall. House: ground floor accessible. 4 wheelchairs at house. Gardens & woodland: accessible path. One self-drive vehicle for grounds available by prior arrangement

- Braille and large-print guides; guided tours by arrangement

- Sympathetic Hearing Scheme

- As Home Farm. Parties advised to pre-book. Picnic area and family area. Private function facilities if pre-booked

- Baby-changing facilities including feeding room at Home Farm. Baby changing also at Speke Hall. Children's menu, highchairs and children's table. Children's play area adjacent to Home Farm. Children's guidebook and quiz for house

- Education service available for pre-booked schools and groups. Details from Interpretation & Education Officer

**For general enquiries, please telephone 0870 458 4000**

- 🚶 Bund and other estate walks. Leaflet guide. Free entry to estate for pedestrians, cyclists and those arriving by public transport
- 🚲 Cycle parking at Home Farm
- 🐕 On leads around woodland and estate walks
- ➡️ (5:B8/C8) On N bank of the Mersey, 1ml off A561 on W side of Liverpool airport. Follow airport signs from M62 exit 6, A5300; M56 exit 12. Follow brown signs [108: SJ419825] **Bus**: Arriva North West 80, 180 ≥ Liverpool Lime Street–Liverpool Airport (passing ≥ Garston) or 82 ≥ Liverpool Lime Street–Speke, both to within ½ml **Station**: Garston 2ml; Hunt's Cross 2ml **Cycle**: NCN 62 1¾ml

**NT properties nearby** Formby, 20 Forthlin Road, Rufford Old Hall

## STAGSHAW GARDEN 💠   Cumbria

Ambleside LA22 0HE · **Tel/Fax** 015394 46027
**Email** stagshaw@ntrust.org.uk

A woodland garden, created by the late Cubby Acland, Regional Agent for the Trust. It contains a fine collection of shrubs, including many notable rhododendrons, azaleas and camellias. Adjacent to the garden are **Skelghyll Woods**, which offer delightful walks and access to the fells beyond

- 🕐 1 April to end June: daily 10–6.30; July to end Oct: by appointment, send s.a.e. to Property Office, St Catherine's, Patterdale Road, Windermere LA23 1NH
- 💷 £1.50. No party reduction. Parking very limited; access dangerous due to poor visibility; visitors may park at Waterhead car park and walk to Stagshaw. No access for coaches: park in Waterhead car park, Ambleside. No WC
- 🚶 Difficult for pushchairs
- ➡️ (6:D8) ½ml S of Ambleside on A591 [90: NY380029] **Bus**: Stagecoach in Cumbria 555/6, 599 from ≥ Windermere **Station**: Windermere 4ml

**NT properties nearby** Ambleside Roman Fort, Townend

---

**Please see the area introductions for details of coast & countryside properties**

## TATTON PARK  Cheshire

Knutsford WA16 6QN · **Tel** 01625 534400 · **Bookings** 01625 534428
**Infoline** 01625 534435 · **Fax** 01625 534403
**Email** tatton@cheshire.gov.uk · **Web** www.tattonpark.org.uk

One of the most complete historic estates open to visitors. The early 19th-century Wyatt house sits amid a landscaped deer park and is opulently decorated, providing a fine setting for the Egerton family's collections of pictures, books, china, glass, silver and specially commissioned Gillow furniture. The theme of Victorian grandeur extends into the garden, with fernery, orangery, rose garden, pinetum and Italian and Japanese gardens. There are also the Tudor Old Hall, a working farm, a children's play area and many walks, including 'Wartime Tatton'. The trail around the lake offers the chance to see many varieties of waterfowl. The garden, gift shop and speciality food shop offer a variety of home produce and giftware. **Events**: tel. for programme

**Note**: Tatton Park is financed, administered and maintained by Cheshire County Council. Without this commitment the Trust would not have been able to acquire this property. Members only have free admission to the mansion and gardens, except during special events, and half-price entry to the Tudor Old Hall & Farm. Members must pay car entry charges, and full admission to any special events, such as the RHS Flower Show on 17–21 July 2002

**What's new in 2002**: Guided tours of the Japanese gardens are sometimes available during the high season, please tel. 01625 534425 for further information. Completion of work on the restoration of the walled kitchen garden and new visitor facilities in stable yard. Guided tours of Mansion Tues to Sun, 12 and 12.15, then free-flow until last entry 4

- Mansion: 23 March to 29 Sept: daily except Mon but open BH Mons. Special opening Oct half-term & Christmas events in Dec. *Times*: 1–5, last entry 4. Guided tours Tues to Sun 12 and 12.15 by timed ticket (available from garden shop from 10.30) on first-come first-served basis. Limited number of tickets per tour. **Gardens**: all year: daily except Mon but open BH Mons; 23 March to 29 Sept 10.30–6, last entry 5. Oct to March 2003: 11–4, last entry 3. **Tudor Old Hall**: 23 March to 29 Sept daily except Mon but open BH Mons. Guided tours only Tues to Fri 3 & 4 and hourly Sat & Sun 12–4. **Park**: 23 March to 29 Sept: daily 10–7, last entry 6. Oct to March 2003: daily except Mon, 11–5, last entry 4. **Farm**: 23 March to 29 Sept: daily except Mon, but open BH Mons 12–5, last entry 4; Oct to March 2003: Suns only, 11.30–4, last entry 3.

- Tel. for details. NT members free to mansion (except guided tours) & gardens, but must pay for entry to park, Tudor Old Hall and farm. Saver tickets; discounts for groups of 12+

- Tel. infoline for details of guided tours outside normal hours: 01625 534435

- Tatton Gifts (not NT), Housekeeper's Store (selling estate and local food produce) and Garden Shop: daily except Mon, but open BH Mons, from 11.30

- Designated area in main car park, at Tudor Old Hall and Farm. Mansion: ramp to ground floor; contact cashier for access. Access leaflet. Garden, park, farm

**Unless indicated, last admission is always 30 mins before closing time**

restaurant & shop: accessible. Self-drive vehicles at garden and farm. Limited number of wheelchairs at main attractions. Walking and fishing facilities

- Braille guide. Some items in mansion may be touched; also farm animals
- Sign language interpreters and lip-speakers by arrangement
- 23 March to 29 Sept: Mon–Fri 10–5, Sat & Sun 10–6; Oct to March 2003: Tues to Sun 11–4
- Adventure playground
- Living history and education programme for schools, for details tel. 01625 534428.
- Not in gardens; on leads at Farm and under close control in Park
- (5:D8) 3½ml N of Knutsford, 4ml S of Altrincham, 5ml from M6, exit 19; 3ml from M56, exit 7, well signposted on A556; entrance on Ashley Road, 1½ml NE of jn A5034 with A50 [109/118: SJ745815] **Bus**: From surrounding areas to Knutsford, thence 2ml. Tel. 01244 602666 **Station**: Knutsford 2ml

**NT properties nearby** Dunham Massey, Little Moreton Hall, Quarry Bank Mill & Estate

---

# TOWNEND     Cumbria

Troutbeck, Windermere LA23 1LB · **Tel** 015394 32628
**Email** townend@ntrust.org.uk

A very fine example of Lake District vernacular architecture and an exceptional survival. Largely 17th-century, the solid stone and slate house belonged to a wealthy yeoman farming family and contains carved woodwork, books, papers, furniture and fascinating domestic implements from the past, largely accumulated by the Browne family who lived here from 1626 to 1943

- 2 April to 31 Oct: daily except Sat & Mon (but open BH Mons) 1–5 or dusk if earlier. **Events**: regular living history and other events; tel. for details

There are special events at most Trust properties; please telephone 0870 458 4000 for details

## NORTH WEST · 289

**£** £3; child £1.50; family £7.50. No reduction for parties which must book. Townend and the village are unsuitable for coaches; 12–15-seater minibuses are acceptable; permission to take coaches to Townend must be obtained from the Transportation and Highways Dept, Cumbria CC, Carlisle. Car park (no coaches)

Braille guide; many items may be touched

Unsuitable for baby back-carriers or pushchairs. Children's quiz sheet

→ (6:D8) 3ml SE of Ambleside at S end of Troutbeck village [90: NY407023] **Bus**: Stagecoach in Cumbria 555/6, 599 from ⇌ Windermere, alight Troutbeck Bridge, thence 1½ml **Station**: Windermere 2½ml

**NT properties nearby** Ambleside Roman Fort, Stagshaw Garden

---

# ULLSWATER – INCLUDING AIRA FORCE   Cumbria

Tower Buildings, Watermillock, Glenridding CA11 0JS · **Tel/Fax** 017684 82067
**Email** ullswater@ntrust.org.uk

Dramatic walks around Aira Force waterfalls provide one of the highlights of the Trust's ownership in this valley, which totals 5173ha (12,782 acres) of fell and woodland, as well as six farms (including Glencoyne, the largest). There is access to parts of Ullswater and Brotherswater lakes

**O** All year

**£** Two NT pay-and-display car parks at Aira Force and Glencoyne Bay (NT members free)

Tel. for details of guided walks

Parking in public car park. At Aira Force, access to Victorian Glade and tea-room, but no access to waterfalls. Access to Aira Green on shore of Ullswater

Trail around Victorian arboretum at Aira Force using audio equipment from NT Land Rover or car park attendant (small deposit)

Tea-rooms (not NT) at Aira Force; and at Side Farm, Patterdale (walkers only, no parking)

Tel. Regional Office for details of minibus tours and resource information

Rack at Aira Force car park

→ (6:D7) 7ml S of Penrith [90: NY4020 – Aira Force] **Bus**: Stagecoach in Cumbria 108 ⇌ Penrith–Patterdale **Station**: Penrith 10ml **Cycle**: NCN 71 2ml

**NT properties nearby** Acorn Bank Garden, Townend

LINNET

**For all your information needs check our website www.nationaltrust.org.uk**

## WASDALE, ESKDALE AND DUDDON      Cumbria

The Lodge, Wasdale Hall, Wasdale CA20 1ET · **Tel** 019467 26064
**Email** wasdale@ntrust.org.uk

Here the Trust owns England's highest mountain, Scafell Pike, and deepest lake, Wastwater. Almost the whole of the head of Wasdale is NT-owned, including Great Gable and the famous historic wall patterns at the valley head. Lower down, there is the wooded and tranquil Nether Wasdale Estate. Over 7000ha (17,000 acres) and eleven farms are covered. In neighbouring Eskdale, Trust protection covers extensive areas of fell, six farms and Hardknott Roman Fort. In the beautiful and tranquil Duddon valley the Trust cares for almost 3000ha (7400 acres) and nine farms.

**Note**: There is a NT campsite at Wasdale Head, open Easter to end Oct (and Nov to Easter 2003 with limited facilities) [NY183076]; charge (inc. NT members); tel. 019467 26220

- All year
- NT pay-and-display car park (NT members free) at Wasdale Head
- Tel. for details of guided walks
- Tel. Regional Office for details of minibus tours and resource information
- (6:C8) Wasdale: 9ml E of A595 Cumbrian coast road from Barrow to Whitehaven, turning at Santon Bridge Eskdale: 10ml E of A595, turning at Santon Bridge and Eskdale Green Duddon: 7ml N of A595, turning at Broughton-in-Furness [89: NY178003 – Boot] **Station**: Drigg 8ml; Dalegarth (Ravenglass & Eskdale Rly) $\frac{1}{4}$ml from Eskdale; Foxfield 8ml from Duddon

**NT properties nearby** Dalton Castle, Sandscale Haws

---

## WINDERMERE AND TROUTBECK      Cumbria

St Catherine's, Patterdale Road, Windermere LA23 1NH · **Tel/Fax** 015394 46027
**Email** windermere@ntrust.org.uk

This property includes the beautiful and secluded head of the Troutbeck valley, as well as several sites next to Lake Windermere and six farms. One of these, Troutbeck Park, was once farmed by Beatrix Potter and was her largest farm. Ambleside Roman Fort, tiny Bridge House in Ambleside, and Cockshott Point on the lake at Bowness-on-Windermere, are all popular places to visit. Footpaths lead from Ambleside over Wansfell to the Troutbeck Valley and offer high level views and contrasting valley landscapes. See also **Townend**, **Fell Foot Park** and **Stagshaw Garden**

- All year. Bridge House Information Centre & shop: April to end Oct: 10–5 (tel. for details). **Events**: annual *Out-and-About* events leaflet; tel for copy.
- At Bridge House, Ambleside (tel. 015394 32617)
- Level path runs from the Glebe in Bowness to Cockshott Point, lakeside access for wheelchair users

---

**Please remember – your membership card is always needed for free admission**

- Tel. Regional Office for details of minibus tours and resource information
- (6:D8) Troutbeck is signposted E of the A591 Windermere to Ambleside road [90: NY407023 – Townend] **Bus**: Stagecoach in Cumbria 555/6, 599 from ⇌ Windermere, alight Troutbeck Bridge, thence 1½ml **Station**: Windermere 2½ml

**NT properties nearby** Stagshaw Gardens, Townend

## WORDSWORTH HOUSE — Cumbria

Main Street, Cockermouth CA13 9RX · **Tel/Fax** 01900 824805
**Email** wordsworthhouse@ntrust.org.uk

The Georgian town house where William Wordsworth was born in 1770. Several rooms contain some of the poet's personal effects. His childhood garden with terraced walk, attractively restored, has views over the River Derwent, referred to in *The Prelude*

- 1 April to 1 Nov: daily except Sat & Sun (but open BHol Sats and all Sats in June, July & Aug). *Times*: 10.30–4.30. **Events**: throughout the season, tel. for details
- £3.50; child £1.50; family £8. Booked parties (15+) £2.50. Parking in the town. Reciprocal discount ticket, available from Wordsworth House, allows visitors to enjoy Dove Cottage and Rydal Mount (nr Grasmere, not NT) at reduced prices; ask for details
- 1 April to 1 Nov: daily except Sun, 10–5. Nov, Dec 2002 & March 2003: daily except Sun, 10–4
- House & restaurant: access by steps. Garden, shop & stables: easy access
- Braille guide. Herbs and aromatic plants
- Licensed tea-room as house. Available for private hire (tel. for details)
- House is too small for baby back-carriers and pushchairs, which should be left at main entrance; baby sling (up to 6 mths). Mother and baby facilities. Children's menu, quiz sheet, toys and books, highchair,
- Education programme available for schools and other groups. Tel. for details
- (6:C7) Parking in town centre car parks. Map of car parks available at main entrance and shop [89: NY118307] **Bus**: Stagecoach in Cumbria X4/5 ⇌ Penrith–Workington, 35/6 Workington–Cockermouth. All pass close ⇌ Workington **Station**: Maryport 6½ml **Cycle**: NCN 71 (C2C)

**NT properties nearby** Countryside properties of Buttermere & Ennerdale

# Introduction to Yorkshire

Yorkshire is world-renowned for the beauty and scale of its scenery. Many of the county's most outstanding stretches of coast and countryside are in the care of the National Trust, and are managed carefully to ensure their future protection. The upland properties of **Malham Tarn Estate** and **Upper Wharfedale** protect some of the finest landscapes in the Yorkshire Dales, with limestone pavements, waterfalls, and flower-rich hay meadows criss-crossed with stone walls and studded with traditional field barns. This is magnificent walking country

| OS grid references for main properties with no individual entry (OS map series numbers given in brackets) | |
|---|---|
| Cayton Bay | [101] TA063850 |
| Farndale | [94] SE654994 |
| Hayburn Wyke | [101] TA010970 |
| Hudswell Woods | [92] NZ153005 |
| Newbiggin Cliffs | [93] TA827105 |
| Peak Alum Works | [94] NZ973024 |
| Scarthwood Moor | [94] SE465995 |

through dramatic and varied scenery. At the gateway to Swaledale, on the edge of Richmond, lie **Hudswell Woods**, an area of semi-natural ancient woodland adjacent to the River Swale, reputedly England's fastest flowing river.

There is further wild and open country due east at **Scarthwood Moor**, from where there are fine views over the Pennines. Further east is the delightful valley of **Farndale**, famed in spring for its dramatic display of wild daffodils. The Trust also owns **Bridestones**, **Crosscliff** and **Blakey Topping**, within the North York Moors National Park, as well as the bent pinnacle of **Roseberry Topping**, used as a beacon station at the time of the Armada and again when Napoleon threatened invasion. To the north west, on the edge of urban Middlesbrough, is fascinating **Ormesby Hall**.

The spine of the Pennine chain runs through the south west of the area, and at **Hardcastle Crags**, near Hebden Bridge, there are waymarked trails and a rich variety of birdlife. Not far away is **East Riddlesden Hall**, a classic and charming West Riding manor house.

To the south lies the **Marsden Moor Estate**, with many interesting archaeological remains and much wildlife interest, including significant numbers of breeding moorland birds. This whole area rewards exploration on foot. There are also good walking opportunities at the strange and fantastic geological formations of **Brimham Rocks** near Pateley Bridge, set in open moorland overlooking Nidderdale. Nearby is the magnificent **Fountains Abbey** and **Studley Royal**, Yorkshire's only World Heritage Site with one of Europe's most important designed landscapes.

In the heart of the historic city of York, **Treasurer's House** provides a splendid backdrop to the Minster, and within easy travelling distance are **Beningbrough Hall and Gardens** and **Nunnington Hall**.

The Trust cares for 12 miles of Yorkshire's wild and rugged coastline, including **Newbiggin Cliffs**, where razorbills and guillemots nest, and **Cayton Bay** and **Hayburn Wyke** near Scarborough. These areas of wooded valley and cliffs are notable for their abundance of wild flowers. Further north, Trust land at **Runswick** and **Port Mulgrave** is best viewed from the Cleveland Way long distance footpath. At the **Old Coastguard Station** in Robin Hood's Bay and the Trust's Coastal Centre in Ravenscar there are fascinating insights into the local wildlife and geology, while the **Peak Alum Works** explain the alum industry and history of this early industrial site.

**Please see the area introductions for details of coast & countryside properties**

### Highlights for Visitors with Disabilities ...
Special arrangements can be made at **Malham Tarn** and **Brimham Rocks** for visitors with disabilities (tel. for details).

### ... and for Families
**The Old Coastguard Station** and Coastal Centre at **Ravenscar** have rockpool aquariums; **Townhead Barn** at Malham has hands-on displays for children.

### Further Information
Please contact the Membership Department, PO Box 39, Bromley BR1 3XL. Tel. 0870 458 4000. Email: enquiries@thenationaltrust.org.uk

---

# BENINGBROUGH HALL AND GARDENS
North Yorkshire

Beningbrough, York YO30 1DD · **Tel** 01904 470666 · **Fax** 01904 470002
**Email** beningbrough@ntrust.org.uk

York's 'country house and garden', this imposing Georgian mansion was built in 1716 and contains one of the most impressive baroque interiors in England. Exceptional wood carving, an unusual central corridor running the full length of the house and over 100 pictures on loan from the National Portrait Gallery can be found inside. There is also a fully equipped Victorian laundry, delightful walled garden and some interesting sculptures in wood

**Note**: Most rooms have no electric light. Visitors wishing to make a close study of the interior and portraits should avoid dull days early and late in the season

- **House**: 23 March to 30 June and 1 Sept to 3 Nov: daily except Thur & Fri (but open Good Fri); July & Aug: daily except Thur. *Times*: **House**: 12–5. **Grounds**: 11–5.30. **Events**: Spring Plant Fair 12 May; family events throughout year. Licensed for wedding ceremonies and receptions; tel. Visitor Services Manager for details

- £5.20; child £2.60; family (2 adults & 3 children, or 1 adult & 4 children) £13. Garden & exhibition only: £3.60; child £1.80; family £9. Discount for cyclists. Contact property for details of party rates and group visits information

- Garden walks most weekends

- As grounds, tel. 01904 470082

- Parking spaces by stable block. House: ramped access to ground floor; inform reception on arrival. Garden: accessible, level paths (embedded gravel); walled garden has wide level paths for wheelchair access. Restaurant, shop: accessible. Wheelchairs

- Braille guide for house. Guided tours by arrangement

- Licensed restaurant open 11–5. Hot food 12–2. Refreshments kiosk open on busy days. Functions and parties by arrangement, tel. 01904 470513

**Unless indicated, last admission is always 30 mins before closing time**

## 294 · YORKSHIRE

- Baby-changing and feeding room. No pushchairs in house, baby slings available. Children's quizzes in house and garden. Family activity packs in house. Children's menu; high-chairs. Wilderness playground
- School groups by arrangement. Victorian 'below stairs'; artwork with portraits
- Racks and lockers available
- (5:G4) 8ml NW of York, 2ml W of Shipton, 2ml SE of Linton-on-Ouse (A19) [105: SE516586] **Bus**: Stephensons/Hutchinson 31 York–Easingwold (passing close ≋ York) **Station**: York 8ml **Cycle**: NCN 65

**NT properties nearby** Nunnington Hall, Rievaulx Terrace & Temples, Treasurer's House

---

## BRAITHWAITE HALL
North Yorkshire
East Witton, Leyburn DL8 4SY · **Tel** 01969 640287

A remote 17th-century stone farmhouse with fine original features including fireplaces, panelling and oak staircase

- By arrangement with the tenant, Mrs David Duffus
- £1, inc. leaflet. No reduction for children. No access for coaches. No WC
- (5:F3) 1½ml SW of Middleham, 2ml W of East Witton (A6108) [99: SE117857] **Bus**: Dales & District 159 Ripon–Richmond

**NT properties nearby** Fountains Abbey and Studley Royal

---

## BRIDESTONES, CROSSCLIFF AND BLAKEY TOPPING
North Yorkshire
Smout House, Bransdale, Fadmoor, York YO62 7JL · **Tel/Fax** 01751 431693
**Email** bridestones@ntrust.org.uk

The Bridestones and Crosscliff Estate covers an area of 488ha (1205 acres) and is a mixture of farmland, open moorland and woodland. Bridestones Moor, named after its peculiar rock formations created from sandstone laid down under the sea during the Jurassic period, is a SSSI and nature reserve with typical moorland vegetation, including three species of heather, an ancient woodland estimated to date from the end of the last Ice Age, and herb-rich meadows. The Bridestones Nature Trail is approximately 1½ml long and leads visitors through a range of habitats. Blakey Topping at the northern end of Crosscliff Moor is the result of massive erosion by glacial meltwater and today gives a superb 360-degree view from its summit

- All year. **Events**: guided walks and other events; tel. for details
- Access by car is via the Forestry Commission's Forest Drive, for which a toll is charged (inc. NT members). The drive runs from Dalby, near Thornton le Dale, towards Scarborough. Further parking at either Staindale Lake or Crosscliff Viewpoint

---

**There are special events at most Trust properties; please telephone 0870 458 4000 for details**

➔ (5:I3) [94: SE8791] **Bus**: To Bridestones: Moorsbus from Thornton le Dale (connections from York and Scarborough) (Sun, June–Sept and daily in Aug); otherwise Yorkshire Coastline 840 Leeds–Whitby (passing ≋ York) to within 2¼ml. To Blakey Topping: Yorkshire Coastliner as above, but to within 1½ml

**NT properties nearby** Nunnington Hall, Ormesby Hall, Rievaulx Terrace & Temples, Yorkshire Coast

---

# BRIMHAM ROCKS                                           North Yorkshire

Summerbridge, Harrogate HG3 4DW · **Tel** 01423 780688 · **Fax** 01423 781020
**Email** brimhamrocks@ntrust.org.uk

---

At a height of nearly 300m, Brimham Rocks enjoy spectacular views over the surrounding countryside. Set within the Nidderdale AONB, this fascinating moorland is filled with strange and fantastic rock formations and is rich in wildlife

**Note**: The property can be extremely busy in July and August

- **O** All year: 8am till dusk. Facilities may close in bad weather

- **£** Pay-and-display car park £2.50 up to 4 hrs, £3.50 over 4 hrs; motorcycle free; minibus £6 all day; coach £12 all day (NT members free); members' season ticket available from property to display in car

- Shop with exhibition room, 16 March, April, May and Oct: Sat & Sun, BHs and local school hols 11–5; 25 May, June to Sept: daily 11–5; Nov & Dec: Sun, 26 Dec & 1 Jan: weather permitting; Feb 2003: local school hols

- Some hard surfaced paths giving access among the rock formations; wheelchair; WC. Shop: access difficult

- Braille guide and large-print guide

- Light refreshments, as shop

- Racks

- Under strict control at all times and on lead during April, May & June (ground-nesting birds)

- ➔ (5:F4) 10ml NW of Harrogate off B6165, 10ml SE of Ripon, 4ml E. of Pateley Bridge off B6265 [99: SE2165]
  **Bus**: Keighley & District 802 Bradford–Leyburn (Sun, June–Oct only); otherwise Harrogate & District 24 ≋ Harrogate–Pateley Bridge, alight Summerbridge, 2ml

**NT properties nearby** Fountains Abbey & Studley Royal

CURLEW

---

**For all your information needs check our website www.nationaltrust.org.uk**

# EAST RIDDLESDEN HALL    West Yorkshire

Bradford Road, Keighley BD20 5EL · **Tel** 01535 607075 · **Fax** 01535 691462
**Email** eastriddlesden@ntrust.org.uk

A characterful 17th-century manor house and buildings with distinctive architectural details, set in mature grounds with beech trees, ducks and a pond. The house has as wonderful ambience and is furnished with textiles, Yorkshire oak furniture and pewter. There is also a handling collection for you to discover. The Starkie Wing façade provides a dramatic backdrop to the garden designed by Graham Stuart Thomas, planted with lavender, flowers and a fragrant herb border. Wild flowers, bulbs, perennials and apple trees provide a changing carpet of colour throughout the year in the orchard garden. A magnificent 17th-century oak-framed barn also stands in the grounds. New children's play area

- 23 March to 3 Nov: daily except Mon, Thur & Fri (but open Good Fri, BH Mons and Mon in July & Aug). *Times*: 12–5 (Sat 1–5). **Events**: 12 May Plant Fair; 2, 3 Nov Craft Festival and themed events. Licensed for civil ceremonies and wedding receptions. Please tel. for additional days in the school holidays

- £3.60; child £1.80; family £9. Parking 100m. Contact property for discounted party rates and group visit information. Coaches must book

- Shop and information area in Bothy as house, opens 12 on Sat. Christmas opening, tel. for details

- Some designated parking. Disabled visitors may be set down near house. House: ground floor accessible. Photograph albums of contents of the house. Garden: some uneven surfaces; loose gravel paths. Shop: 2 steps at entrance, 1 inside. Tea-room on first floor of Bothy; tel. for arrangements. Great Barn (uneven floor) and Airedale Barn accessible for events. Wheelchair

- Braille and large-print guides, tactile book; panelling, carving and handling collection; guided tours by arrangement

**Please remember – your membership card is always needed for free admission**

- 🦻 Sympathetic Hearing Scheme
- ☕ Tea-room as house, but opens 12 on Sat. Christmas opening, tel. for details. Picnic area in field
- 👶 Changing facilities and feeding room. Children's guide. Children's menu; highchairs. Quiz sheets and activity days. Grass maze. No pushchairs in the house, slings available. Children's play area
- 🎒 School groups by arrangement; Living History days; teachers' resource book
- 🚲 Racks
- 🐕 On leads and only in grounds
- ➡ (5:F5) 1ml NE of Keighley on S side of the Bradford Road in Riddlesden, close to Leeds & Liverpool Canal [104: SE079421] **Bus**: Frequent services from railway, Bradford Interchange, Bingley, Keighley & Leeds **Station**: Keighley 1½ml

**NT properties nearby** Gawthorpe Hall, Fountains Abbey & Studley Royal, Hardcastle Crags, Malham Tarn Estate

---

## FOUNTAINS ABBEY & STUDLEY ROYAL WATER GARDEN

North Yorkshire

Fountains, Ripon HG4 3DY · **Tel** 01765 608888 (enquiries and infoline)
**Fax** 01765 601002 · **Web** www.fountainsabbey.org.uk

---

One of the most remarkable places in Europe and a World Heritage Site, comprising the spectacular ruin of a 12th-century Cistercian abbey and monastic watermill, an Elizabethan mansion and one of the best surviving examples of a Georgian water garden. Elegant ornamental lakes, canals, temples and cascades provide a succession of dramatic eye-catching vistas. St Mary's Church provides a majestic focus to the medieval deer park, home to 500 deer and a wealth of flora and fauna

**Note**: The National Trust (NT) works in partnership with English Heritage (EH) to care for this site. EH maintains the Abbey (which is owned by the NT) and owns St Mary's Church (managed by the NT)

- 🅾 **Abbey, Fountains Hall & water garden**: daily (except Fri in Nov, Dec & Jan 2003; closed 24, 25 Dec). *Times*: April to Sept 10–6 (closes 4 on 12, 13 July); Oct to March 2003: 10–4 or dusk if earlier. **Deer park**: daily during daylight. **Mill**: tel. for details. **Floodlighting**: 23 Aug to 12 Oct: Abbey is floodlit on Fri & Sat evenings until 10pm. **St Mary's Church**: daily 1 April to 30 Sept 1–5.
**Events**: extensive programme throughout year: open-air Shakespeare, opera, fireworks and Christmas concerts; details from Box Office, tel. 01765 609999. All outside major events wheelchair-accessible. Join free events mailing list. Extensive programme of wildlife and historical tours, music events and family activities, tel. 01765 608888. For details of wedding receptions and ceremonies, corporate hospitality/entertaining and conference facilities tel. 01765 601003

- £ Fountains Abbey & Studley Royal water garden and mill: £4.80; child £2.50; family (2 adults, 3 children) £12. Booked groups of 15–30 £4.20, children £2.30;

## 298 · YORKSHIRE

groups of 31+ £3.80, children £2.10. Visitor centre, deer park, St Mary's Church: free. Parking: visitor centre free; deer park £2 (pay-and-display; NT members free – members' season ticket to display in car available from property).
**Note**: Charges may be reduced if access to estate is restricted because of events

Free guided tours of the Abbey and water garden April to Oct plus extended tours of the complete estate, available throughout the year. Floodlit tours of the Abbey: 23 Aug to 12 Oct every Fri 7.45pm & 8.15pm. Specialist guides for booked groups (£1 per person) (tel. 01765 601005)

Visitor Centre shop daily (closed 24, 25 Dec & each Fri in Jan 2001). *Times*: April to Aug 10–6, Sept to March 10–5 or dusk if earlier (tel. 01765 601004). Lakeside shop: daily. Tel. 01765 601004 for detailed opening times

Extensive facilities for visitors with disabilities. Two four-wheeled self-drive vehicles and wheelchairs available by booking (tel. 01765 601005). Good access to visitor centre and its facilities, but paths from the centre are steep and unsuitable for any vehicle, including wheelchairs. Minibus from visitor centre to Studley Royal and Fountains Hall. Owners of three-wheeled vehicles are strongly advised that the estate is unsuitable for them owing to steep terrain. A free map shows accessible routes across whole estate. Abbey: level access from West Gate/Fountains Hall follow signs from visitor centre to West Gate/Fountains Hall. Good access to outdoor estate events

Braille and large-print guides; tactile model of Abbey at visitor centre

Sympathetic Hearing Scheme; hearing loop in Fountains Abbey Mill audiovisual room

In visitor centre. Licensed restaurant open as visitor centre shop except Sept closes 5pm. Childrens' menu and activity area in restaurant. Group bookings and functions welcome, tel. 01765 601003. Lakeside tea-room: April to end Sept: daily 10–5.30, school holidays and Sun Oct to March 2003 10.30–4.30 or dusk if earlier, tel. 01765 601003

Parent and baby rooms, menus and activity area at visitor centre and near Fountains Hall. Highchairs. Children's guide. Programme of children's activities, trails and indoor activity base throughout year, tel. 01765 608888

Wide range of educational activities and materials for all ages. Free preliminary teacher's visit. Booking essential, tel. 01765 601005

Racks

On short leads only. Enclosed dog walk/toilet at Visitor Centre

(5:F4) 4ml W of Ripon off B6265 to Pateley Bridge, signposted from the A1, 10ml N of Harrogate (A61) [99: SE271683] **Bus**: Reliance 812 from York, with connections from Harrogate on Harrogate & District 36, Suns, June–Oct only; Keighley & District 802 from Bradford and Leeds, Suns, June–Oct only; otherwise Abbots 145 from Ripon (with connections from Harrogate) Thur & Sat only (tel. 01609 780780)

**NT properties nearby** Beningbrough Hall & Gardens, Brimham Rocks, East Riddlesden Hall

**Please see the area introductions for details of coast & countryside properties**

YORKSHIRE · 299

## HARDCASTLE CRAGS
West Yorkshire

Estate Office, Hollin Hall, Crimsworth Dean, Hardcastle Crags, Hebden Bridge HX7 7AP · **Tel/Fax** 01422 844518 · **Email** hardcastlecrags@ntrust.org.uk

A beautiful wooded valley with deep rocky ravines, tumbling streams and woodland rich in natural history, famous as the home of the hairy wood ant, which lives here in huge anthills. Waymarked walks lead through the valley and link with footpaths and the Pennine Way

- All year. **Events**: programme of events and guided walks; send s.a.e. for details
- Car park charge: midweek £1.50; weekend £2; motorcycle 60p; minibus £5 (NT members free; members' season ticket available from property to display in car). No coaches
- Guided walks for booked parties; contact Warden

HAZEL NUTS

- Limited access by arrangement only; accessible picnic tables near car park
- Braille guide; sensory trail
- School visits by arrangement. Regret no coaches
- Racks
- Under control at all times
- (5:E6) At end of Midgehole Road, 1½ml NW of Hebden Bridge off the A6033 Keighley road. Access on foot via riverside walk from Hebden Bridge [103:SD988291] **Bus**: First Calderline H8 from Hebden Bridge (passing close ≥ Hebden Bridge) **Station**: Hebden Bridge 2ml

**NT properties nearby** East Riddlesden Hall

## MAISTER HOUSE
East Yorkshire

160 High Street, Hull HU1 1NL · **Tel** 01482 324114 · **Fax** 01482 227003

Rebuilt in 1743 during Hull's heyday as an affluent trading centre, this house is a typical but rare survivor of a contemporary merchant's residence. The restrained exterior belies the spectacular plasterwork staircase inside. The house is now let as offices

- Daily except Sat & Sun (closed Good Fri & all BHols) 10–4. **Note**: Staircase and entrance hall only
- 80p, inc. guidebook. Unsuitable for parties. No parking. No WC
- (5:J6) Hull city centre [107:TA102287] **Bus**: Local services to within 100m; also services from surrounding areas **Station**: Hull ¾ml **Cycle**: NCN 65

**NT properties nearby** Nostell Priory, Treasurer's House

**Unless indicated, last admission is always 30 mins before closing time**

## MALHAM TARN ESTATE  North Yorkshire

Estate Office, Waterhouses, Settle BD24 9PT · **Tel/Fax** 01729 830416
**Email** malhamtarn@ntrust.org.uk

An outstanding area of upland limestone country, consisting of six farms, some with flower-rich hay meadows, limestone pavements and a National Nature Reserve around Malham Tarn, where there is a bird hide. In Malham village visitors can see an exhibition of farming in the Dales

- **Estate**: all year. **Townhead Barn** (interpretive centre in Malham village): Jan to Easter, Oct to Dec: Sun; Easter to Sept: daily except Mon. *Times*: 10–4

- Pay-and-display car park (not NT) in Malham village

- Guided walks programme, inc. for groups; tel. for details

- Access to Townhead Barn and bird hide along Estate Road by arrangement

- (5:E4) The estate extends from Malham village, 19ml NW of Skipton, north past Malham Tarn [98: SD8966] **Bus**: Pennine 210 from Skipton (passes close ≋ Skipton); Arriva Yorkshire 804 from Leeds **Station**: Settle 7ml

**NT properties nearby** Brimham Rocks, East Riddlesden Hall, Fountains Abbey & Studley Royal, Upper Wharfedale

## MARSDEN MOOR ESTATE  West Yorkshire

Estate Office, The Old Goods Yard, Station Road, Marsden, Huddersfield HD7 6DH · **Tel** 01484 847016 · **Fax** 01484 847071
**Email** marsdenmoor@ntrust.org.uk

The estate covers nearly 2429ha (5685 acres) of unenclosed common moorland and almost surrounds the village of Marsden. Although this is wild and open country, taking in the northern part of the Peak District National Park, it has a surprising diversity of interest: valleys, reservoirs, peaks and crags, as well as archaeological remains dating from pre-Roman times to the great engineering structures of the canal and railway ages. This bleak, windswept landscape supports classic moorland birds such as the golden plover, red grouse, curlew and diminutive twite. These birds, and others. breed here in such numbers that the estate is a designated SSSI and forms part of an international Special Area of Conserevation. The Huddersfield Narrow Canal has just been restored and a new Visitor Centre (not NT) is open at Tunnel End, Marsden with car parking adjacent to the Estate Office. To complement this we have also developed an exhibition area in what was previously our workshop

- All year. **Events**: Send s.a.e. to Estate Office for events and guided walks leaflet and a pocket guide to Marsden including 6 self-guided walks

- Free parking areas around the estate, including in Marsden village (not NT) and at Buckstones and Wessenden Head (NT)

- Exceptional views from Buckstones and Wessenden car parks

- Racks at Marsden rail station and in Marsden village

**There are special events at most Trust properties; please telephone 0870 458 4000 for details**

## MOULTON HALL 🏠 👤 — North Yorkshire
Moulton, Richmond DL10 6QH · **Tel** 01325 377227

A compact stone manor house, dating from 1650 and with a very fine carved wood staircase

**O** By arrangement with tenant, Viscount Eccles

**£** 50p. Unsuitable for coaches

**♿** Ring in advance about access

**→** (5:F2) 5ml E of Richmond; turn off A1, ½ml S of Scotch Corner [99: NZ235035] **Bus**: Arriva North East 34 Darlington–Richmond (passing close ☒ Darlington), alight Moulton village, ½ml **Station**: Darlington 9½ml

**NT properties nearby** Fountains Abbey & Studley Royal

## MOUNT GRACE PRIORY ✝ 👤 ☻ — North Yorkshire
Osmotherley, Northallerton DL6 3JG · **Tel** 01609 883494

England's most important Carthusian ruin, the remains of a 14th-century priory. The individual cells reflect the hermit-like isolation of the Carthusian monks; a reconstruction enables visitors to see the austere and simple furnishings. There is a small herb garden, nature trail and picnic area

**Note**: The priory is financed, administered and maintained by English Heritage

**O** 1 April to 31 Oct: daily; 1 Nov to 31 March 2003: daily except Mon & Tues. *Times*: April to Sept 10–6; Oct 10–5; Nov to March 10–1, 2–4. **Events**: leaflet from shop or tel. 01609 883494

**£** £3; concessions £2.30; child (under 16) £1.50; family £7.50. Parties of 11+ 15% discount. NT members free, except on certain special event days, when full admission is charged. Bulky bags and pushchairs must be left in reception

**🛍** Herbs for sale May to Aug

**♿** Close parking. Ground floor of reconstructed cell, shop & herb garden: accessible

**🌿** Wild flowers and herbs; birdsong and animal sounds

**🍴** Canned drinks, biscuits from shop (EH). Picnics welcome

**👶** Free children's activity sheet

**302 · YORKSHIRE**

🏫 School visits free Mon to Fri; must be booked in advance through EH (tel. 01904 601901)

➔ (5:G3) 6ml NE of Northallerton, ½ml E of A19 and ½ml S of its junction with A172 [99: SE449985] **Bus**: Arriva North East 80, 89 ≡ Northallerton–Stokesley, alight Priory Road End, ½ml **Station**: Northallerton 6ml **Cycle**: NCN 65 2½ml

**NT properties nearby** Nunnington Hall, Ormesby Hall, Rievaulx Terrace & Temples

## NOSTELL PRIORY 🏠 ✿ 🚶 ♥   West Yorkshire
Doncaster Road, Nostell, nr Wakefield WF4 1QE · **Tel** 01924 863892
**Fax** 01924 865282 · **Email** nostellpriory@ntrust.org.uk

---

Nostell Priory, one of Yorkshire's finest jewels, is an 18th-century architectural masterpiece by James Paine built on the site of a medieval priory for Sir Rowland Winn, 4th baronet in 1733. Later Robert Adam was commissioned to complete the state rooms which are among the finest examples of his interiors. The Priory houses one of England's finest collections of Chippendale furniture, designed specially for the house by the great cabinetmaker who was once an apprentice on the estate. Nostell Priory's other treasures include an oustanding art collection with works by Pieter Breughel the younger and Angelica Kaufmann and the remarkable 18th-century doll's house, complete with its original fittings and Chippendale furniture. Another rare treasure is the John Harrison long case clock with its extremely rare movement made of wood. In the grounds are delightful lakeside walks with a stunning collection of rhododendrons and azaleas in late spring

**What's new in 2002**: Restored Adam library and opening of the domestic areas of the house including the Servants' Hall and unrestored Great Kitchen which houses an exhibition of the recent works. Object of the week (weekdays in July & Aug): a chance to look more closely at an object from the house's important collection

🅾 **House**: 23 March to 3 Nov: daily except Mon & Tues (but open BHols inc. 3 & 4 June): 1–5.30. **Grounds**: 2 to 17 March: Sat & Sun 11–4 (house closed); 23 March to 3 Nov: daily except Mon & Tues (but open BHols inc. 3 & 4 June) 11–6; 9 Nov to 15 Dec: Sat & Sun 12–4. **Events**: send s.a.e for details of full programme, inc. craft and country fairs, open-air theatre and jazz and other musical spectaculars

£ House & gardens: £4.50; child £2.20; family £11. Grounds only: £2.50; child £1.20 (no family ticket)

🚶 Guided tours for booked parties outside normal hours

🛍 2 to 17 March: Sat & Sun 11–4; 23 March to 3 Nov: daily except Mon & Tues (but open BHols inc. 3 & 4 June): 11–5.30; 9 Nov to 15 Dec: Sat & Sun 11–4.30

♿ Visitors with disabilities may be set down by the house by arrangement. Lift to first-floor state rooms, domestic areas, shop and Stables tea-room accessible. Paths to Rose Garden and West Lawn; steep path to Lakeside Walk and Menagerie Pleasure Gardens. Batricar and wheelchairs available

☕ Stables tea-room serving light lunches and refreshments open as shop`. Party

---

**Please remember – your membership card is always needed for free admission**

bookings by written application with s.a.e. Picnics welcome in car park and vista parkland in front of house

🚼 Parent and baby facilities in the house and stable blocks. High-chairs, Trusty the Hedgehog lunch boxes, scribble and activity sheets

🏫 School parties to house weekday mornings, pre-booking essential. Schoolroom

🐕 Walks around vista, not in garden. Must be on leads

➡ (5:G6) On the A638 5ml SE of Wakefield towards Doncaster [111: SE407172] **Bus**: Arriva Yorkshire 485, 496/8 Wakefield–Doncaster; Yorkshire Traction 244/5 Barnsley–Pontefract **Station**: Fitzwilliam 1½ml **Cycle**: NCN 67 3 ml

**NT properties nearby** Clumber Park, Marsden Moor Estate, Mr Straw's House

# NUNNINGTON HALL 🏠✤🛡 North Yorkshire

Nunnington, York YO62 5UY · **Tel** 01439 748283 · **Fax** 01439 748284
**Email** nunningtonhall@ntrust.org.uk

The sheltered walled garden on the bank of the River Rye with its delightful mixed borders, orchards of traditional fruit varieties and spring-flowering meadows, complements this mellow 17th-century manor house. From the magnificent oak-panelled hall, follow three staircases to discover family rooms, the nursery, the haunted room and the attics, with their fascinating Carlisle collection of miniature rooms fully furnished to reflect different periods

🕐 23 March to 3 Nov: March, April, May, Sept Oct & Nov: daily except Mon & Tues (open BH Mons) 1.30–4.30 (but May & Sept last admission 5). June, July, Aug: daily except Mon (but open BH Mons inc. 3 June) 1.30–5

💷 £4.50; child £2; family £11. Garden only £2; child free. Party rates £4. Car parking 50m; unsuitable for trailer caravans

🛍 As house

♿ Close parking for disabled drivers; drop-off facility, enquire at reception. House: ground floor accessible. Garden: ramp to main garden; loose gravel paths. Tea-room: accessible; garden tables by river. Wheelchairs available

**For general enquiries, please telephone 0870 458 4000**

## 304 · YORKSHIRE

- Braille guide. Garden scents; river, peacock and duck sounds
- Tea-room and tea-garden: 12.30 until house closes
- Baby-changing facilities. Children's menu and highchairs. Children's guide. Sorry, no pushchairs, prams or baby back-carriers in house
- Contact Property Manager for details
- On leads and only in car park; shaded parking
- (5:H3/H4) In Ryedale, 4½ml SE of Helmsley (A170) Helmsley–Pickering road; 1½ml N of B1257 Malton–Helmsley road; 21ml N of York, B1363. Nunnington Hall is 7½ml SE of the NT Rievaulx Terrace and Temples [100: SE670795] **Bus**: Lawns 94 ⇌ Malton–Helmsley; otherwise Scarborough & District 128 Scarborough–Helmsley (passing close ⇌ Scarborough & Seamer), alight Wombleton, 3ml; Moorsbus from Helmsley

**NT properties nearby** Bridestones, Ormesby Hall, Rievaulx Terrace & Temples

## RIEVAULX TERRACE & TEMPLES   North Yorkshire

Rievaulx, Helmsley, York YO62 5LJ · **Tel** 01439 798340/01439 748283
**Fax** 01439 748284

A ½ml long grass terrace and adjoining woodland, with vistas over Rievaulx Abbey (English Heritage) to Ryedale and the Hambleton Hills. There is an abundance of spring flowers and two mid-18th-century temples. The Ionic Temple, intended as a banqueting house, has elaborate ceiling paintings and fine 18th-century furniture

**Note**: No access to Rievaulx Abbey from Terrace

- 23 March to 3 Nov: daily 10.30–6 (5 in Oct/Nov). Last admission 1 hr before closing. **Note**: Ionic Temple closed 1–2. **Events**: for details contact Property Secretary at Nunnington Hall, tel. 01439 748283
- £3.30; child £1.50; family £8. Party rates: £2.80. Parking at reception, but coach park 200m; unsuitable for trailer caravans
- Shop and visitor centre as property
- Level gravel path through woods to mown grass Terrace. Steps to Ionic Temple. Powered self-drive vehicle and manual wheelchair available. To pre-book tel. 01439 798340. Shop & reception: ramped access. WC facilities: please tel. for details

**Please see the area introductions for details of coast & countryside properties**

YORKSHIRE · 305

- Braille guide
- Ice creams only. Teas at Nunnington Hall, 7ml
- Baby-changing facilities. Children's quizzes
- Contact Property Manager at Nunnington Hall for information
- On leads only
- (5:H3) 2½ml NW of Helmsley on B1257 [100: SE579848] **Bus**: Moorsbus from Helmsley (connections from ⇌ Scarborough) Sun, June–Sept plus daily in Aug; York Country C12 from York (Suns June–Sept only); otherwise Scarborough & District 128 from Scarborough or Stephensons 57 from ⇌ York, alight Helmsley, thence 2½ml

**NT properties nearby** Bridestones, Nunnington Hall, Ormesby Hall

## ROSEBERRY TOPPING                                   North Yorkshire
c/o Peakside, Ravenscar, Scarborough YO13 0NE · **Tel** 01723 870423
**Email** roseberrytopping@ntrust.org.uk

The peculiar shape of this hill is due to a geological fault and a mining collapse earlier this century. From the summit at 320m there is a magnificent 360-degree view, which on a clear day allows the visitor to see as far as Teesside in one direction and the Yorkshire Dales in another. Newton and Cliff Ridge Woods skirt the northern edge of the property and Cliff Rigg quarry still retains evidence of the extraction of 'whinstone', once used for road-building. The area is rich in wildlife, particularly moorland birds. A spur of the Cleveland Way National Trail runs up to the summit

- All year. **Events**: guided walks and other events; tel. for details
- Free car park at Newton-under-Roseberry (not NT)
- (5:G2) [93: NZ575126] **Bus**: Arriva North East 81, 781 Redcar–Stokesley, alight Newton-under-Roseberry, thence ½ml **Station**: Great Ayton 1½ml

**NT properties nearby** Bridestones, Nunnington Hall, Ormesby Hall, Rievaulx Terrace & Temples, Yorkshire Coast

## TREASURER'S HOUSE                                           Yorkshire
Minster Yard, York YO1 7JL · **Tel** 01904 624247 · **Fax** 01904 647372
**Email** treasurershouse@ntrust.org.uk

Named after the Treasurer of York Minster and built over a Roman road, the house is not all that it seems. Nestled behind the Minster, the size, splendour and contents of this elegant house are a constant surprise to visitors – as are the famous ghost stories. Carefully restored and presented with 16th- and 20th-century decoration, furniture, china and glass by wealthy local Victorian industrialist Frank Green

- 23 March to 3 Nov: daily 11–4.30, **closed Fri**. **Events**: tel. for details of function hire and all special events. Licensed for wedding ceremonies

*Unless indicated, last admission is always 30 mins before closing time*

- £3.80; child £2; family (2 adults, 3 children) £9.50. For party rates tel. Property Manager. No parking facilities, but car park nearby in Lord Mayor's Walk

- At 32 Goodramgate. Mon to Fri 9.30–5.30; Sat 9–5.30; Sun 11–5 April to end Dec. Open BHols

- Disabled visitors may be set down at house. House: ground floor accessible with help. Tea-room: access via steep stairs, but refreshments can be brought to gallery on ground floor or into garden. Introductory video on ground floor on request. Garden: accessible and level

- Braille guide; tactile pictures in exhibition. Short 'scented' path in garden

- Licensed tea-room open as house. All food freshly prepared and baked on premises including traditional Yorkshire recipes. Available for booked parties and private functions (tel. 01904 624247)

- No pushchairs in house. Facilities for babies and nursing mothers. Children's guidebook, activity sheets. Children's menu and highchairs. Recipient of City of York Council's Child-Friendly Award 2000

- Booked school parties welcome; tel. for details

- Close to city cycle routes

- On leads and only in garden

- (5:H5) In Minster Yard, on N side of Minster [105: SE604523]
  **Bus**: From surrounding areas. Park-and-ride scheme from outskirts of city
  **Station**: York ½ml **Cycle**: NCN 65 ½ml

**NT properties nearby** Beningbrough Hall & Gardens

## UPPER WHARFEDALE                                North Yorkshire

Estate Office, Waterhouses, Settle BD24 9PT · **Tel/Fax** 01729 830416
**Email** upperwharfedale@ntrust.org.uk

2470ha (6100 acres) of the Upper Wharfe valley north of Kettlewell. The Trust owns nine farms here, including the hamlets of Yockenthwaite and Cray. This is classic Yorkshire Dales country, with drystone walls and barns, important flower-rich hay meadows, valleyside woodland and blanket bog

- **Estate**: all year. **Townhead Barn** (interpretive centre in Buckden): Jan to Easter, Oct to Dec: Sun; Easter to Sept: daily except Fri. *Times*: 10–4

**There are special events at most Trust properties; please telephone 0870 458 4000 for details**

## YORKSHIRE · 307

£ Pay-and-display car parks (not NT) in Kettlewell and Buckden

🚶 Guided walks programme; tel. for details

→ (5:E4) Upper Wharfedale extends from Kettlewell village (12ml N of Skipton) N to Beckermonds and Cray [98: SD935765] **Bus**: Pride of the Dales 74 Ilkley–Skipton–Grassington–Buckden; Arriva Yorkshire/Keighley & District 800/5/6 from Leeds and ⇌ Ilkley (Tues, Sat & Sun June–Sept only)

**NT properties nearby** Brimham Rocks, East Riddlesden Hall, Fountains Abbey & Studley Royal, Malham Tarn Estate

---

# YORKSHIRE COAST   North Yorkshire

Old Coastguard Station, The Dock, Robin Hood's Bay, Whitby YO22 4SJ
**Tel** 01947 885900
Ravenscar Coastal Centre, Peakside, Ravenscar, Scarborough YO13 0NE
**Tel/Fax** 01723 870423 · **Email** yorkshirecoast@ntrust.org.uk

---

A group of coastal properties extending for 40ml from Saltburn in the north to Filey in the south, and centred around Robin Hood's Bay. The Cleveland Way long-distance footpath follows the clifftop and gives splendid views. A wide range of habitats – meadow, woodland, coastal heath and cliff grassland – provide sanctuary to many species of wildlife, from orchids to nesting birds. The area is rich in industrial archaeology and the remains of the alum industry and jet and ironstone mining can be seen

**What's new in 2002**: The Old Coastguard Station in Robin Hood's Bay, an exciting exhibition and education centre, in partnership with the North York Moors National Park Authority. It shows how the elements have shaped this part of the coastline. Free admission

O All year. **Old Coastguard Station**: Provisional opening hours, tel. to confirm: April to May & Oct: Sat & Sun 10–5; Whitsun to end Sept: daily 10–5; Nov to March: Sat & Sun 11–4. Extended opening times during school hols, tel. for details. **Ravenscar Coastal Centre**: 31 March to 30 Sept: daily 10.30–5. Two holiday cottages at Ravenscar and one at the Old Coastguard Station (tel. 01225 791133 for brochure)

🚶 Tel. Old Coastguard Station and Ravenscar Coastal Centre for details of guided walks

🛍 Shops in Old Coastguard Station and Ravenscar Coastal Centre

🍴 Refreshments (not NT) in Robin Hood's Bay and Ravenscar

→ (5:I2) Coastal Centre in Ravenscar village, signposted off A171 Scarborough–Whitby. Old Coastguard Station in Robin Hood's Bay [94: NZ980025] **Bus**: Arriva North East 93/A Scarborough–Whitby to within 3ml **Station**: Scarborough 10ml

**NT properties nearby** Bridestones, Nunnington Hall, Ormesby Hall, Rievaulx Terrace & Temples

---

**For all your information needs check our website www.nationaltrust.org.uk**

# Introduction to the North East

England's far north-eastern counties of Northumberland, Durham and Tyne and Wear offer magnificent scenery, with wide open stretches of unspoilt moorland and upland pasture, and a long and dramatic coastline, arguably one of the finest in Britain.

In the south of the area, near Horden in Co Durham, lie two denes, **Warren House Gill** and **Foxholes Dene**. Connected by a narrow coastal strip, this piece of coast marks the 500th mile acquired through the Trust's coastal appeal Enterprise Neptune, now the Neptune Coastline Campaign. Just north of Easington is **Beacon Hill**, the highest point on the Durham coast and famed for its spectacular views; access is via **Hawthorn Dene**. Inland in Durham are beautiful woodland walks along the River Wear at **Moorhouse Woods**, just north of Durham City, and along the banks of the Derwent at the village of **Ebchester**. **Penshaw Monument**, an unroofed Doric temple, was built in 1844 to commemorate the 1st Earl of Durham, and is visible for miles around.

Meanwhile, the spectacular coastline continues north to the dramatic **Souter Lighthouse**, the famous bird colony on **Marsden Rock** and thence to **Druridge Bay**, where the Trust owns a mile of coast backed by golden sand dunes and grassland. From **Craster**, Trust ownership runs for 5 miles and includes the brooding ruins of **Dunstanburgh Castle**, as well as **Embleton Links** and **Low Newton-by-Sea**, where **Newton Pool** provides a superb habitat for many water birds. There are interesting 18th-century lime kilns at **Beadnell Harbour**, from where the road hugs the coast north to Bamburgh, passing **St Aidan's Dunes**, rich in dune grassland plants. There is a Trust information centre and shop at **Seahouses**, from where boats cross to the **Farne Islands** (all visitors pay the crossing fees). Just to the north is the dramatic **Lindisfarne Castle**, perched atop Holy Island.

Northumberland's hinterland is as stunning as its coastline. There are magnificent walks around **Allen Banks** and **Staward Gorge**, along the River Allen, and both **Ros Castle** and the **Hadrian's Wall Estate** offer breathtaking views. Circular walks are possible in the beautiful countryside around **Wallington** and at **Cragside** near Rothbury there are 40 miles of paths and the fascinating Power Circuit, designed to show visitors the industrial archaeology of the property. Ancient history abounds in this part of England – some of England's best preserved Roman remains can be seen at **Housesteads Fort,** and in the Kyloe Hills is **St Cuthbert's Cave**, in which the saint's body is said to have rested on its way from Lindisfarne to

---

**OS grid references for main properties with no individual entry (OS map series numbers given in brackets)**

| | |
|---|---|
| Allen Banks & Staward Gorge | [87] NY799630 |
| Beacon Hill & Hawthorn Dene | [88] NZ254460 |
| Beadnell Lime Kilns | [75] NU237286 |
| Druridge Bay | [81] NZ276961 |
| Ebchester | [88] NZ100551 |
| Embleton Links | [75] NU243235 |
| Lady's Well | [81] NT953029 |
| Marsden Rock | [88] NZ388665 |
| Moorhouse Woods | [88] NZ305460 |
| Newton Pool | [75] NU243240 |
| Penshaw Monument | [88] NZ333544 |
| Ros Castle | [75] NU081253 |
| St Aidan's Dunes | [75] NU211327 |
| St Cuthbert's Cave | [75] NU059352 |
| Warren House Gill & Foxholes Dene | [88] NZ444427 |

---

**Please remember – your membership card is always needed for free admission**

Durham. Also closely associated with Northumberland is St Ninian, who is linked with **Lady's Well** on the edge of the Cheviots.

### Highlights for Visitors with Disabilities ...
**Newton Pool** has a boarded walkway and adapted bird hide. **Cragside** has a lift to the first floor for visitors in wheelchairs. **Wallington** offers a leaflet showing the gradients of all its paths. **Souter Lighthouse** has a closed-circuit television and remote camera so that people unable to climb the lighthouse stairs can still enjoy the view from the top.

### ... and for Families
**Wallington** has much to offer the younger visitor, with its dolls' house collection, children's room and adventure playground in the West Woods. **Cragside** too has an adventure playground (new for 2001) and Nelly's labyrinth, a wild maze to explore. At **Souter Lighthouse** children can handle flags, have a go at morse code and use the CCTV remote camera.

### Further Information
Please contact the Membership Department, PO Box 39, Bromley BR1 3XL. Tel. 0870 458 4000. Email: enquiries@thenationaltrust.org.uk

PUFFINS

---

## ALLEN BANKS & STAWARD GORGE   Northumberland
Bardon Mill, Hexham NE47 7BU · **Tel** 01434 344218
**Email** allenbanks@ntrust.org.uk

---

Extensive area of hill and river scenery with waymarked walks through ornamental and ancient woodland. Picnic site accessible to wheelchairs at car park. Remains of medieval pele tower spectacularly sited within Staward Wood

- Daily all year, dawn to dusk
- £1; children free
- Car park & picnic area: accessible. Adapted WC with RADAR lock
- (6:F5) 3ml W of Haydon Bridge, ½ml S of A69, near the meeting point of the Tyne and Allen rivers [86:NY798640] **Bus**: Arriva Northumbria/Stagecoach in Cumbria 85, 685 Carlisle–Newcastle, to within ½ml **Cycle**: NCN 72 2½ml

**NT properties nearby** Hadrian's Wall, Housesteads Roman Fort

## CHERRYBURN   Northumberland
Station Bank, Mickley, nr Stocksfield NE43 7DD · **Tel** 01661 843276

The birthplace of Thomas Bewick (1753–1828), Northumberland's greatest artist, wood-engraver and naturalist. Bewick's birthplace cottage; with farmyard, garden and play lawn. Also 19th-century farmhouse, the latter home of the Bewick family, houses an exhibition on Bewick's life and work and small shop selling prints from his original wood engravings, books and gifts. Wood engraving, printing and bookbinding demonstrations in adjoining barn. Splendid views over the Tyne valley. The south bank of the River Tyne, where Bewick spent much of his childhood, is a short walk from the property

**What's new in 2002**: Changes to exhibition rooms. Traditional music, song, dance and storytelling workshops for pre-booked school or group visits (Mon, Thur, Fri mornings only)

- 29 March to end Oct: daily except Tues and Wed 1–5.30. **Events**: First BH Mon in May, May Day celebration (annual event) with traditional Northumbrian music and clog dancing and the Bewick whistling competition (trophy awarded, s.a.e. for entry form and details); maypole dancing for all and May King and Queen competition (prize awarded). Bring instruments and join in traditional music sessions. Admission May Day celebration: NT members £2 and £1; non members £5 and £2.50 (inc. property admission £3/£1.50). Traditional music, song or dance every Sun afternoon throughout the season. S.a.e. for programme. Usual admission charge (£3/£1.50)

- £3; child £1.50. Booked coaches welcome; exclusive use of property Mon, Thur & Fri mornings. Group bookings for printing/engraving or bookbinding demonstrations and/or traditional music/dance performances/workshops. S.a.e. to property for booking leaflet

- Situated in farmhouse at Cherryburn and open as house. Prints from Bewick's original wood engravings, specialist books and greetings cards, traditional music

**Please see the area introductions for details of coast & countryside properties**

and gifts. Send s.a.e. for mail order Bewick print price list or National Trust website link (mail orders April–Oct only)

- Car park 100m from house by sloping ramped path. House: level entrance; then 3 steps inside and 2 steps at rear exit. Grounds: some gravel paths; cobbled farmyard; companion necessary. Please tel. in advance

- Braille booklet; smooth and engraved woodblocks may be touched; garden and farmyard aromas!

- Coffee and biscuits. Picnic tables in grounds

- Farmyard animals usually include donkeys, pigs, poultry, lambs. Play lawn. Annual art competition. Join in maypole dancing and whistling competition on first BH Mon in May (prize for best-dressed May King/Queen) annual event: please note there is a charge for this event

- Pre-booked coach parties Mon, Thur & Fri mornings only. Wood-engraving, printing or bookbinding demonstrations. Art, artists, countryside, local history and country life in 18th and 19th centuries. Farmyard animals. Traditional music, song, dance and storytelling workshops for pre-booked school or group visits. Send s.a.e. for booking form

- (6:G5) 11ml W of Newcastle, 11ml E of Hexham; ¼ml N of Mickley Square (leave A695 at Mickley Square onto Riding Terrace leading to Station Bank). Cherryburn situated close to S bank of River Tyne. Free car park at property [88: NZ075627] **Bus**: Arriva Northumbria 602 Newcastle–Hexham (passes ≠ Newcastle) **Station**: Stocksfield (U) 1½ml or Prudhoe (U) 1½ml

**NT properties nearby** George Stephenson's Birthplace, Gibside

---

## CRAGSIDE HOUSE, GARDEN AND ESTATE

Northumberland

Rothbury, Morpeth NE65 7PX · **Tel** 01669 620333/620150 · **Fax** 01669 620066
**Email** cragside@ntrust.org.uk

---

Built on a bare and rugged hillside above Rothbury by the 1st Lord Armstrong, Cragside became one of the most modern and surprising houses for its time in the country. In the 1880s the house had hot and cold running water, central heating, fire alarms, telephones, a Turkish bath suite and a passenger lift, but most remarkable of all it was the first house in the world to be lit by hydroelectricity. No wonder it was described as 'the Palace of a Modern Magician'. Around and below the house is one of Europe's largest rock gardens; across the valley lies the terraced garden. Here exotic fruits were nurtured throughout the year in glasshouses, and still are today in the Orchard House. Seven million trees and bushes were planted to cover the bare hillside and create the 404ha (1000-acre) forest garden you can explore today

- **House**: 23 March to 3 Nov: daily except Mon (but open BH Mons). *Times*: 23 March to 30 Sept: 1–5.30, last admission 4.30; 1 Oct to 3 Nov, 1–4.30, last admission 3.30. **Estate & formal garden**: as house 10.30–7; last admission 5. Also 6 Nov to 15 Dec: daily except Mon & Tues 11–4. **Events**: send s.a.e. for details. House available for wedding ceremonies

**Unless indicated, last admission is always 30 mins before closing time**

£ £6.90; family £17.30; booked parties £5.90. Estate and formal garden only £4.40; family £11; booked parties £3.80. Car park 100m from house (9 car parks in grounds). Coach park 350m (advance booking essential). **Note**: Coaches cannot tour grounds as drive is too narrow in places

🛍 23 March to 3 Nov: as house 10.30–5.30. Nov & Dec: possible closure due to refurbishment. Tel. in advance, 01669 620448

♿ Parking area for disabled drivers in main car park. Elderly and disabled visitors may be set down outside the Stable Block and at the house. House: partially accessible, lift to first floor. Shop & restaurant in Stable Block: accessible. Estate: wheelchair path around Nelly's Moss North Lake; adapted picnic tables; parking at Nelly's Moss North Lake

Braille guides at the house

☕ Restaurant in Stable Block, as shop, 10.30–5.30, last serving 5 (tel. 01669 620134). Picnicking in all car parks and around Nelly's Moss Lakes

🚸 New adventure play area. Front sling baby carriers at house; children's guide at house

Education room/school party base. School parties may visit all attractions with a guide. Resource book for teachers. Visits must be booked with Education Officer (tel. 01669 621445 x 103)

🐕 On leads and only on estate

➔ (6:G3) 13ml SW of Alnwick (B6341) and 15ml NW of Morpeth on Wooler road (A697), turn left on to B6341 at Moorhouse Crossroads, entrance 1ml N of Rothbury; public transport passengers enter by Reivers Well Gate from Morpeth Road (B6344) [81: NU073022] **Bus**: Arriva Northumbria 416 Morpeth–Throplon, Postbus (both passing ≷ Morpeth) with connections from Newcastle (passing Tyne & Wear Metro Haymarket), alight Reivers Well Gate, ¾ml to house

**NT properties nearby** Wallington

---

## DUNSTANBURGH CASTLE           Northumberland
Craster, Alnwick · **Tel** 01665 576231

---

A magnificent ruin, dominating a lonely stretch of Northumberland's beautiful coastline. Originally built in 1316, the castle was later enlarged by John of Gaunt and then severely damaged during the Wars of the Roses, since when it has been derelict

**Note**: Dunstanburgh Castle is in the guardianship of English Heritage

🕐 1 April to 1 Nov: daily 10–6 or dusk if earlier; 2 Nov to 31 March 2003: daily except Mon & Tues 10–4 (closed 24–26 Dec & 1 Jan)

£ £1.70; £1.30 concession; 90p child. Car parks at Craster and Embleton, 1½ml (no coaches at Embleton)

🛍 Small shop for postcards and souvenirs

Free school visits; book through EH (tel. 0191 261 1585)

---

**There are special events at most Trust properties; please telephone 0870 458 4000 for details**

🐕 On leads only

➡ (6:H3) 9ml NE of Alnwick, approached from Craster on S and Embleton on N (pedestrians only) [75: NU258220] **Bus**: Arriva Northumbria 401, 501 Alnwick–Belford with connections from ➤ Berwick-upon-Tweed & Newcastle (passing Tyne & Wear Metro Haymarket), alight Craster, 1½ml **Station**: Chathill (U), not Sun, 5ml from Embleton, 7ml from Castle; Alnmouth, 7ml from Craster, 8¾ml from Castle **Cycle**: NCN 1 ¾ml

**NT properties nearby** Farne Islands, Lindisfarne Castle, Northumberland Coast

## FARNE ISLANDS ✝ 🚗 🐕 👤  Northumberland
**Tel** 01665 720651 (Property Manager) · **Infoline** 01665 721099

One of Britain's most important seabird sanctuaries, home to many different species, including puffins, eider ducks and four species of tern. Many of the birds are extremely confiding and visitors can enjoy close views. There is also a large colony of seals. St Cuthbert died on Inner Farne in 687 and the chapel built in his memory can be visited

🅾 **Note**: Only Inner Farne and Staple Islands can be visited. 29 March, April & 1 Aug to 30 Sept: daily 10.30–6. 1 May to 31 July (the breeding season): daily, Staple Island 10.30–1.30, Inner Farne 1.30–5. Visitors to Inner Farne should wear hats!

LITTLE TERN

£ May to end July £4.40; booked school parties £2.20 (per island). At other times £3.40; pre-booked school parties £1.90 (per island). Public car park in Seahouses opposite harbour. Admission fees do not include boatmen's charges. Tickets may be bought from Warden on landing and boat tickets from boatmen in Seahouses Harbour. No landing in bad weather. To enquire about landing contact the Property Manager: The Sheiling, 8 St Aidan's, Seahouses, Northumberland NE68 7SR (tel. 01665 720651). WC on Inner Farne

📷 Information centre & shop at 16 Main Street, Seahouses (tel. 01665 721099) 24 March to end Oct: daily; Nov to 24 Dec: daily except Mon & Tues. *Times*: March to end June, Sept & half-terms 10–5; July & Aug 10–6; Oct 11–4.30; Nov to 24 Dec 11–4

♿ Inner Farne: some wheelchair access; tel. Property Manager in advance

📕 Teachers' resource book. Guided walks

➡ (6:H2) 2–5ml off the Northumberland coast, opposite Bamburgh: trips every day from Seahouses Harbour, weather permitting [75: NU2337] **Bus**: As for Dunstanburgh Castle, but alight Seahouses **Station**: Chathill (U), not Sun, 4ml **Cycle**: NCN 1 ¾ml (from Seahouses harbour)

**NT properties nearby** Dunstanburgh Castle, Lindisfarne, Northumberland Coast

**For all your information needs check our website www.nationaltrust.org.uk**

## GEORGE STEPHENSON'S BIRTHPLACE

Northumberland

Wylam NE41 8BP · **Tel** 01661 853457 · **Fax** 01670 774317

A small stone tenement, built c.1760 to accommodate mining families. The furnishings reflect the year of Stephenson's birth here (1781), his whole family living in the one room

- **O** 23 March to 3 Nov: Thur, Sat, Sun, BH Mons & Good Fri 1–5.30
- **£** 80p. No parties. No WC. Parking by War Memorial in Wylam village, ½ml
- **→** (6:G5) 8ml W of Newcastle, 1½ml S of A69 at Wylam. Access on foot and bicycle through Country Park, ½ml E of Wylam [88: NZ126650] **Bus**: Go-Northern 684 Newcastle–Ovington, alight Wylam, 1ml **Station**: Wylam (U) ½ml **Cycle**: NCN 72

**NT properties nearby** Cherryburn, Gibside

## GIBSIDE

Tyne & Wear

nr Rowlands Gill, Burnopfield, Newcastle upon Tyne NE16 6BG
**Tel/Fax** 01207 542255 · **Email** gibside@ntrust.org.uk

One of the North's finest landscapes, much of which is SSSI, a 'forest garden' currently under restoration and embracing many miles of riverside and forest walks. There are several outstanding buildings, including a Palladian chapel, Column of Liberty, and others awaiting or undergoing restoration. The estate is the former home of the Queen Mother's family, the Bowes-Lyons

- **O** **Grounds**: 23 March to 3 Nov: daily except Mon (but open BH Mons) 10–6; last admission 4.30. 4 Nov to end March 2003: daily except Mon 10–4, last admission 1 hr before sunset. **Chapel**: 23 March to 3 Nov, daily except Mon 11–4.30. Winter by appointment only.
  **Events**: For list of events write to the above address or tel. 01207 542255. Services: evensong 1st Sun of each month 3pm. Weddings (civil and C of E ceremonies)
- **£** £3; family £8 (2 adults + 4 children) or £5 (1 adult + 3 children). Booked parties £2.60.
- Evening guided tours to be booked in advance, 15 or more, tour and light refreshments, £100 per party. For more information tel. 01207 542 255
- As grounds, 10–5 summer, 10–4 winter. Christmas shopping week & other events, send for list (tel. 01207 545801)

**Please remember – your membership card is always needed for free admission**

## NORTH EAST · 315

[♿] Some areas easier than others. The Grand Walk from the Chapel is quite flat and gives dramatic views. Tea-room, shop and WC all accessible and adjacent to car park. Wheelchairs. For information tel. Visitor Services Manager, 01207 542255

[👁] Braille guide; wooden pews and pulpit in Chapel may be touched; guided 'touch and smell' nature tours arranged

[🍴] Tea-room as shop. Light lunches, sandwiches, ice cream, afternoon teas. Groups welcome, advance booking essential (50 covers) (tel. 01207 545801). Children's facilities

[🏫] Much of Gibside is within the National Curriculum. Send for information

[🐕] On leads and only in the grounds. Owners must clean up after their dogs – bins provided

[→] (6:G5) 6ml SW of Gateshead, 20ml W of Durham; entrance on B6314 between Burnopfield and Rowlands Gill; from A1 take exit north of Metro Centre and follow brown property signs. [88: NZ172583] **Bus**: Go-Ahead Gateshead 611, Go-Northern 45 or 46 from Newcastle. On all, alight Rowlands Gill, ½ml **Station**: Blaydon (U) 5ml **Cycle**: NCN 14 ½ml

**NT properties nearby** Cherryburn, George Stephenson's Birthplace, Souter Lighthouse, Washington Old Hall

---

## HADRIAN'S WALL & HOUSESTEADS FORT
[🏛][⚐]                                                             Northumberland
Bardon Mill, Hexham NE47 6NN · **Tel** 01434 344363 (EH Custodian)

One of Rome's most northerly outposts, the Wall was built when the Roman Empire was at its height. Snaking across dramatic countryside, it remains one of Britain's most impressive ruins. Housesteads Fort, one of thirteen permanent bases along the Wall, is one of the best-preserved and conjures an evocative picture of Roman military life

**Note**: The Trust owns approx. 5ml of the Wall, running west from Housesteads Fort (inc. the Fort itself) to Cawfields Quarry, and over 1,000ha (2,471 acres) of farmland. Access to the Wall and the public rights of way is from car parks operated by Northumberland National Park Authority at Housesteads and Cawfields. Housesteads Fort is owned by the National Trust, and maintained and managed by English Heritage

[O] **Housesteads Fort & Museum**: Daily (closed 24–26 Dec & 1 Jan). *Times*: 1 April to 30 Sept 10–6, 1 Oct to 31 March 2003 10–4

[£] Hadrian's Wall, NT information centre and shop free. Housesteads Museum & Fort: £2.70; concessions £2; child £1.40. Free to NT and EH members. Car and coach parks (operated by National Park Authority) at Housesteads, ½ml walk to the Fort, and at the western end at Cawfields Quarry (charge for both, inc. NT members)

**For general enquiries, please telephone 0870 458 4000**

## 316 · NORTH EAST

[🛈] Shop & information centre at Housesteads car park (times subject to revision), March to May & Sept to Oct 10–5, June to Aug 10–6, Nov to Feb 2003 10–4 (tel. 01434 344525)

[♿] Parking near Housesteads Fort; ask at information centre for details. Information centre & shop: accessible

[👐] Braille guides

[🍴] Kiosk for hot and cold drinks, sandwiches and ice creams. Picnic tables outside information centre and seating inside

[👶] Children's guide

[🐕] On leads only (sheep and ground nesting birds)

[➜] (6:F5) 6ml NE of Haltwhistle, 3ml N of Bardon Mill rly station; ½ml N of B6318; best access from car parks at Housesteads and Cawfields [87: NY790688]
**Bus**: Stagecoach in Cumbria AD122 Hadrian's Wall service, June–Sept only, ☒ Hexham–Carlisle (passing ☒ Haltwhistle **Station**: Bardon Mill (U) 3ml

**NT properties nearby** Allen Banks

---

## LINDISFARNE CASTLE      Northumberland
Holy Island, Berwick-upon-Tweed TD15 2SH · **Tel** 01289 389244
**Fax** 01289 389349

Perched atop a rocky crag and accessible over a causeway at low tide only, the castle presents an exciting and alluring aspect. Originally a Tudor fort, it was converted into a private house in 1903 by the young Edwin Lutyens. The small rooms are full of intimate decoration and design, the windows looking down upon the charming walled garden planned by Gertrude Jekyll

**Note**: It is impossible to cross to the island between the 2hrs before high tide and the 3½hrs after. Tide tables are printed in local newspapers, and displayed at the causeway. To avoid disappointment check safe crossing times before making a long/special journey

[O] 16 March to 3 Nov: daily except Fri (but open Good Fri). As Lindisfarne is a tidal island times vary so that visitors may reach the castle at low tide. On open days the castle will open for 4¼hrs, which will always include 12–3 (last admission always 30 mins before closing). It will either open earlier or later, depending on the tide; for a copy of tide tables and detailed opening times, send s.a.e. to NT Northumbria office (see p.362), stating which month you wish to visit. Garden open only when gardener is present, but key provided upon request at castle.

[£] £4.20; family (2 adults, 2 children under 17) £10.50. No party rate. Parties of 15+ must book. Main public car park approx. 1ml away; parking off approach road to castle for disabled orange badge holders only, car-parking charges (inc. NT members). No large camera cases, boxes or rucksacks. No WC

[🛈] In Main Street, Holy Island Village (tel. 01289 389253)

---

**Please see the area introductions for details of coast & countryside properties**

NORTH EAST · 317

- ♿ Access very limited; steep, cobbled access ramp, many steps and stairs within castle
- Braille guide
- No back carriers in castle (including baby carriers); front sling baby carriers available. Baby-changing facility
- On leads and only as far as Lower Battery (first level after castle ramp)
- → (6:G1) On Holy Island, 6ml E of A1 across causeway [75: NU136417]
  **Bus**: Travelsure 477 from ≋ Berwick-upon-Tweed. Times vary with tides
  **Station**: Berwick-upon-Tweed 10ml from causeway

**NT properties nearby** Farne Islands

---

## ORMESBY HALL   Middlesbrough
Ormesby, Middlesbrough TS7 9AS · **Tel** 01642 324188 · **Fax** 01642 300937
**Email** ormesbyhall@ntrust.org.uk

---

A mid-18th-century Palladian mansion, notable for its fine plasterwork and carved wood decoration. The Victorian laundry and kitchen with scullery and game larder are especially interesting, and there is a particularly beautiful stable block (let to the Cleveland Mounted Police). A large model railway exhibition is on show. There is also an attractive garden and holly walk

- ⊙ 24 March to 3 Nov: daily except Mon, Fri & Sat (but open Good Fri and BH Mons) 2–5. **Events**: contact the Hall. The Hall is licensed for civil wedding ceremonies and receptions
- £ £3.70; child £1.80; family (2 adults, 3 children) £9. Garden, railway & exhibitions only: £2.50; child £1. Tel. for party rates. Parking 100m
- As house

**Unless indicated, last admission is always 30 mins before closing time**

## 318 · NORTH EAST

- ♿ Close parking for disabled drivers. Disabled passengers may be set down at front door. House: shallow step at entrance gives access to ground floor, shop, tea-room and garden
- Braille guide. Specialist group tours by arrangement; touch opportunities
- Tea-room as house
- Baby-changing facilities; children's menu, highchairs
- School groups on Mon & Tues, tel. for details
- In park only, on leads
- (6:I7) 3ml SE of Middlesbrough, W of A171. From the A19 take the A174 to the A172. Follow signs for Ormesby Hall. Car entrance on Ladgate Lane (B1380) [93: NZ530167] **Bus**: From Middlesbrough (passing close ≋ Middlesbrough) **Station**: Marton (U) 1½ml; Middlesbrough 3ml **Cycle**: NCN 65 2¼ml

**NT properties nearby** Mount Grace Priory, Nunnington Hall, Rievaulx Terrace & Temples, Roseberry Topping

---

## SOUTER LIGHTHOUSE                                          Tyne & Wear

Coast Road, Whitburn, Sunderland SR6 7NH · **Tel 0191 529 3161**
**Infoline** 01670 773966 · **Email** souter@ntrust.org.uk

Boldly painted in red and white hoops, this rocket-like lighthouse opened in 1871 and was the first to use alternating electric current, the most advanced lighthouse technology in its day. The engine room, light tower and keeper's living quarters are all on view, and there is a video, model and information display. A ground-floor closed circuit TV shows views from the top for those unable to climb. The Compass Room contains hands-on exhibits for all visitors, covering storms at sea, communication from ship to shore, pirates and smugglers, lighthouse life, lighting the seas and shipwreck. Immediately to the north is **The Leas**, 2½ml of beach, cliff and grassland with spectacular views, flora and fauna

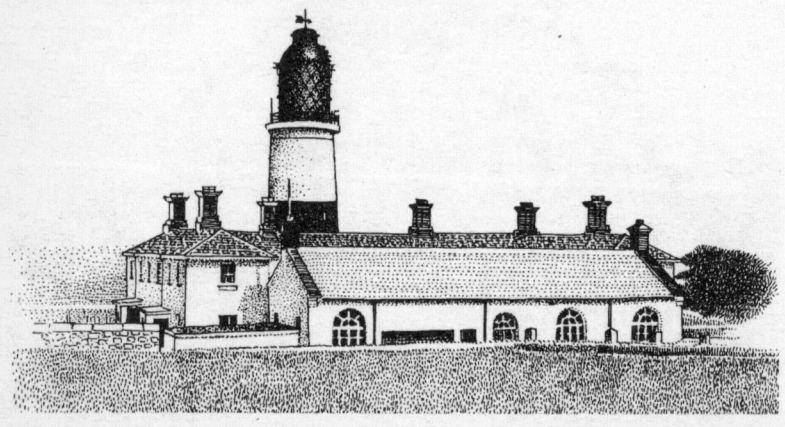

---

**There are special events at most Trust properties; please telephone 0870 458 4000 for details**

**O** 23 March to 3 Nov: daily except Fri (but open Good Fri) 11–5. Also opening 9 to 17 Feb 2003 (except Fri 15 Feb) for half-term. After 3 Nov property open other days by arrangement. Contact property for details. **Events**: Spring Plant Fair, Family Countryside Festival, Rockpool Rambles, Victorian evenings, Storytelling sessions for schools, Christmas lunches and talks; send s.a.e. for details

**£** £3; child £1.50; family £7.50. Booked parties £2.50. Car and coach park 100m

For booked parties

As lighthouse, entry free

Lighthouse: ground floor accessible; closed circuit TV gives view from the top. Shop: accessible. Restaurant: limited access. Adapted WC

Braille guide; items to touch, including engines and Morse code signaller

Induction loop at shop reception desk and in video room where property video shown

Tea-room as lighthouse. Access is free. Children's pirate parties, meetings and other functions by arrangement; tel. for details. Picnicking in grounds

Families welcome but for safety reasons back-packs are not permitted inside property. At busy times height restrictions for tower visit may apply

Education room; school base for single class groups only. Schools can visit on open days before property opens to public and must be booked; details from Education Officer

On leads and only in grounds

→ (6:I5) 2½ml S of South Shields on A183, 5ml N of Sunderland on A183 [88: NZ641408] **Bus**: Stagecoach in Sunderland E1 ⇌ Sunderland–South Shields (passes ⇌ Sunderland & Tyne & Wear Metro South Shields) **Station**: East Boldon (U) 3ml **Cycle**: NCN 1

**NT properties nearby** Gibside, Washington Old Hall

---

## WALLINGTON    Northumberland

Cambo, Morpeth NE61 4AR · **Tel** 01670 773600 · **Infoline** 01670 773967 · **Fax** 01670 774420 · **Email** wallington@ntrust.org.uk

---

Dating from 1688, Wallington House was home to many generations of the Blackett and Trevelyan families who have all left their mark over the centuries. The restrained Palladian exterior gives way to the magnificent rococo plasterwork of the interior which houses collections of ceramics, 19th-century painting and wallpapers and an early 20th-century dolls' house. The house is set in delightful grounds comprising lawns, lakes and woodland, as well as a beautiful walled garden containing many species of unusual plants and shrubs and a conservatory housing a wide variety of fuchsia

**Note**: Wallington House will be closed 1 Oct 2002 to 28 March 2004 for major repairs. The walled garden, grounds and all other facilities will remain open

**What's new in 2002**: Walled garden and grounds open throughout the year. Farm shop

- **House**: 23 March to 30 Sept: daily except Tues 1–5.30. **Walled garden**: daily. *Times*: April to end Sept 10–7, Oct 10–6, Nov to March 2003 10–4 or dusk if earlier. **Grounds**: daily in daylight. **Events**: varied programme, send s.a.e. for details or phone our info line, tel. 01670 773967. Wallington is available for weddings, corporate bookings and special events

- £5.70; child £2.85; family £14.25. Booked parties £5.20. Walled garden & grounds only £4.10; booked parties £3.60. £1 parking charge when ticket office closed (NT members free)

- Guided tours available outside normal opening hours; contact Events & Education Coordinator for details, tel. 01670 773602

- 1 Jan to 8 Feb: Sat & Sun only. 9 Feb to 22 March: daily except Mon & Tues. 23 March to 24 May: daily except Tues. 25 May to 8 Sept: daily. 9 Sept to 3 Nov: daily except Tue. 4 Nov to 22 Dec: daily except Mon & Tues. *Times*: 1 Jan to 22 March: 10.30–4. 23 March to 30 Sept: 10.30–5.30. 1 Oct to 22 Dec: 10.30–4 (tel. 01670 773611). Plant Centre (adjacent to shop) 23 March to 30 Sept

- Reserved parking for drivers with disabilities adjacent to ticket office and at Walled Garden (obtain pass from ticket office). House: ramped access; ground floor accessible. Conservatory, walled garden & grounds: largely accessible, access map available from ticket office. Wheelchairs and self-drive powered vehicle (book in advance, tel. 01670 773600). Level access to downstairs self-service restaurant and shop

- Braille guides to house, garden, park and estate. Scented roses

- Self-service restaurant (tel. 01670 773610) open as shop. Kiosk open during busy periods. Picnics in grassed courtyard and grounds

- Front sling baby carriers to be used in house, on loan from front desk; ask about other facilities for parents and babies. Adventure playground in West Woods. Dolls' houses and toy soldier collections. Children's guide. 'Spot the odd thing out' competition in summer holidays

**Please remember – your membership card is always needed for free admission**

NORTH EAST · 321

- 🎒 School visits welcome, book in advance with Events and Education Co-ordinator, tel. 01670 773602
- 🐕 On leads in grounds and walled garden
- ➡️ (6:G4) 12ml W of Morpeth (B6343), 6ml NW of Belsay (A696), take B6342 to Cambo [81: NZ030843] **Bus**: Arriva Northumbria 419, from Morpeth (Wed, Fri, Sat only) (passing close ≋ Morpeth); 508 from ≋ Newcastle, Sun, May to Aug only; otherwise National Express from Newcastle (passing close ≋ Newcastle), alight Capheaton Road End, 2ml

**NT properties nearby** Cragside

---

## WASHINGTON OLD HALL    Tyne & Wear
The Avenue, District 4, Washington Village NE38 7LE · **Tel** 0191 416 6879
**Fax** 0191 419 2065

---

A modest and unpretentious 17th-century manor house, incorporating the 12th-century remains of the home of George Washington's ancestors, and from where the family drew its name. Exhibition on tenement period of the house from 1860–1936. Display of memorabilia celebrating George Washington. Recreated Jacobean garden

- 🅾️ 24 March to 30 Oct: Sun to Wed and Good Fri 11–5. **Events**: 4 July, Independence Day celebrations. The Old Hall and garden are available for wedding ceremonies, suppers and other functions; tel. for further information
- 💷 £3; child £1.50. Parties by arrangement £2.50. Coaches must park on The Avenue
- 🛈 Introductory talks for booked group visits
- 🛍️ Souvenir desk in entrance hall open as house
- ♿ House: ground floor accessible. Garden: partly accessible; changes of level; some steps. Tel. for access arrangements
- 👁️ Braille guide; tactile opportunities in house and garden
- ☕ Small tea-room for light refreshments run by Friends of Washington Old Hall (closes at 4)
- 🎒 Teachers' notes; send s.a.e.
- 🐕 On leads and in garden only
- ➡️ (6:H5) 5ml W of Sunderland, 2ml E of A1, S of Tyne tunnel, follow signs to Washington, District 4, then Washington village; situated on E side of Avenue (adj. to church on the hill) Signposted from A1231 [88: NZ312566] **Bus**: Go-Wear Buses 194, 291–4 from Tyne & Wear Metro Heworth; also other services from surrounding areas **Station**: Heworth (Tyne & Wear Metro) 4ml; E Boldon (U) 6ml; Newcastle 7ml **Cycle**: NCN 7 1ml

**NT properties nearby** Gibside, Souter Lighthouse

**For general enquiries, please telephone 0870 458 4000**

# Introduction to Wales

Mae'r wybodaeth sydd yn y llawlyfr hwn am feddiannau'r Ymddiriedolaeth Genedlaethol yng Nghymru ar gael yn Gymraeg o Swyddfa'r Ymddiriedolaeth Genedlaethol, Sgwâr y Drindod, Llandudno LL30 2DE, ffôn 01492 860123.

Wales is famous for its spectacular coastline, rugged mountain scenery and lush green valleys. With three national parks and thousands of hectares designated as Areas of Outstanding Natural Beauty, visitors do not have to travel far to reach beautiful open countryside offering many recreational opportunities. The National Trust plays an active role in protecting and managing this countryside and owns 133 miles of the Welsh coastline. In fact, the first property ever given to the Trust was in Wales, at **Dinas Oleu** above Barmouth on the Cardigan Bay coast, given in 1895.

The **Gower Peninsula**, near Swansea, was the first place in Britain to be given AONB status and offers a diversity of habitats, including stunning beaches and walks with breathtaking views.

In Pembrokeshire, the 186-mile Coastal Path starts at Amroth and runs through several areas owned by the Trust, including the **Colby Estate & Woodland Garden**, from where there are dramatic views of Devon and Carmarthen Bay. To the west lies the fascinating **Stackpole Estate**, which includes **Barafundle Bay** and the delightful freshwater lily ponds at **Bosherston**. At Stackpole Quay itself there is a tea-room and several holiday cottages. An exhibition on Stackpole Court, demolished in 1963, is located in the former game larder overlooking the lake. There are NT car parks at the Quay and at **Broadhaven South**, an excellent bathing beach.

Further west, the Trust owns 15½ miles of the coastline of **St Bride's Bay**, including the former **Deer Park** at Marloes and the tiny harbour of **Martin's Haven**, where there is a NT car park. Nearby **Marloes Sands** offer wonderful walks. This part of the coast is excellent for wildlife, with ravens, choughs and grey seals to be seen, as well as a wide variety of interesting plants and insects.

The city of **St David's**, dedicated to the patron saint of Wales, is located in an area of spectacular geology, with rocky outcrops and coastal plateau, much of which is Trust-owned. There is an NT shop and visitor centre in St David's. The spectacular coastline and wonderful views continue northwards to Ceredigion, where the

| OS grid references for main properties with no individual entry (OS map series numbers given in brackets) | |
|---|---|
| Abergwesyn Common | [147] SN841551 |
| The Begwns | [148] SO163442 |
| Broadhaven | [151] SR976937 |
| Carneddau | [115] SH649604 |
| Cemlyn | [114] SH336932 |
| Cregennan | [124] SH660140 |
| Dinas Oleu | [124] SH615158 |
| Dolmelynllyn Estate | [124] SH728243 |
| Gower | [159] SS420900 |
| Hafod y Llan | [115] SH627507 |
| Henrhyd Falls | [160] SN855121 |
| Marloes Deer Park | [157] SM758091 |
| Marloes Sands | [157] SM770085 |
| Martin's Haven | [157] SM758091 |
| Mwnt | [145] SN190520 |
| Paxton's Tower | [159] SN541191 |
| Pen-y-Fan | [160] SO013215 |
| Penbryn | [145] SN295519 |
| Porth Dafarch | [114] SH234200 |
| Porthdinllaen | [123] SH278415 |
| Porthor | [123] SH166298 |
| Skirrid Fawr | [161] SO330180 |
| Stackpole Quay | [158] SR992958 |
| Sugar Loaf | [161] SO268167 |
| Swton | [114] SH301892 |
| Ysbyty Estate | [115] SH842488 |

**Please see the area introductions for details of coast & countryside properties**

beaches at **Mwnt** and **Penbryn** are especially popular and offer a range of facilities for visitors two miles inland from the Ceredigion coast. At Llanerchaeron the Trust has embarked on an ambitious project to revitalise a unique Welsh gentry estate by reintroducing many of its traditional activities.

Behind the coast lies a fascinating hinterland of green meadows, rivers and rolling hills. Much of this countryside is unspoilt and ideal for a relaxing holiday. At the heart of it lies **Dinefwr Park** near Llandeilo, the historic seat of the former Welsh princes of South Wales and an ancient deer park of much wildlife interest. The recently refurbished **Newton House** is now open to visitors and nearby is **Paxton's Tower**, an early 19th-century folly dedicated to Lord Nelson, and from which there are fine views of the Towy Valley. To the north is the **Dolaucothi Estate**, over 1000 ha (2500 acres) of delightful countryside with woodland walks and a visitor centre in the village of Pumsaint. The unique Roman gold mines here are also open to visitors.

The industrial heritage of Wales has left its scars on some of the southern valleys, but **Aberdulais Falls** near Neath provides a fascinating insight into how natural energy was harnessed to power the Industrial Revolution. Just north of the valleys, there is some of the country's most spectacular scenery in the Brecon Beacons, where the Trust owns over 3500ha (9000 acres) of the main range, including **Pen-y-Fan**, the highest point in southern Britain and **Henrhyd Falls**, the highest single drop waterfall in South Wales. Other notable vantage points are the **Sugar Loaf** and **Skirrid Fawr**. Near the border town of Monmouth is **The Kymin**, a hill upon which is an enigmatic tower known as the Round House, built by a dining club in 1794.

The turbulent history of the Welsh Marches is reflected in the local style of architecture, from the Norman castle at **Skenfrith** in the south to the rather more comfortable **Chirk Castle** near Wrexham. But Wales also has its fair share of classic country houses, including **Powis Castle** with its stunning gardens, the brooding **Penrhyn Castle**, **Erddig**, with its fascinating social history, and Anglesey's **Plas Newydd**, which commands some of the finest views in Europe. The spectacular gardens at **Bodnant** are equally celebrated.

Snowdonia is justly famous for its epic upland landscapes, including **Hafod y Llan** on the southern flank of Snowdon, acquired following a successful public appeal in 1998. The Watkin Path, one of the main routes up Snowdon, runs the length of the entire estate. The Trust owns eleven of the main mountain peaks, including **Tryfan** (part of the Carneddau property), where the first successful Everest climbers trained. The **Carneddau** and **Ysbyty Estate**, together covering over 15,000ha (37,000 acres), contain some of the most exciting scenery of all and include **Cwm Idwal**, a nature reserve famous for its flora since the 17th century. South-west of Betws-y-Coed is **Tŷ Mawr** in the charming little valley of Wybrnant, which offers many delightful walks.

In the south of the Snowdonia National Park at **Cregennan**, there are splendid walks amidst hill farms and upland lakes, with fine views towards Cadair Idris and over Cardigan Bay. The **Dolmelynllyn Estate** near Dolgellau contains one of Wales's most impressive waterfalls, **Rhaeadr Ddu**, which can be reached by footpath from Ganllwyd, as well as sheepwalks on **Y Llethr**, the highest peak in the Rhinog Mountains. This whole area is full of wildlife interest and is particularly noted for its late summer and autumn colours.

The north arm of Wales – the beautiful Llŷn Peninsula – is noted for its spectacular coastal scenery and since the delightful manor house of **Plas yn Rhiw** was given in 1952 by the three Misses Keating, the Trust has worked to consolidate its ownership

**Unless indicated, last admission is always 30 mins before closing time**

in this unspoilt and tranquil corner. Through successful coastline campaigns, it has been possible to acquire and protect such wonderful places as **Porthdinllaen**, a charming fishing village, and the famous 'whistling sands' of **Porthor**.

The National Trust owns large sections of the rugged and remote coast of Anglesey, including **Porth Dafarch**, a beach and headland near Holyhead. Also on Anglesey is the restored thatched cottage of **Swtan** which is managed by the local community for the Trust. Another Anglesey highlight is the lagoon at **Cemlyn**, internationally famous for its colonies of breeding terns, and managed as a nature reserve in conjunction with the North Wales Wildlife Trust.

### Highlights for Visitors with Disabilities ...
There is a wheelchair-accessible footpath to the legendary site of Gelert's Grave, and many excellent paths on the **Stackpole Estate**, including a lakeside route with two accessible bird hides and a level woodland route suitable for unaccompanied wheelchair users (tel. 01646 661359 for leaflet). **Erddig Country Park** at Felin Puleston now offers improved access pathways, suitable for unaccompanied wheelchair users and leading through woodland and along the River Clywedog; tel. 01978 355314 for details. At **Dinefwr**, Carmarthenshire, there is a boardwalk suitable for wheelchair users, through Bog Wood to the lake. On the Gower peninsula at **Rhossili** there is an accessible path leading to the old coastguard lookout. Picnic sites accessible to wheelchairs are located on the **Dolmelynllyn Estate** at Ganllwyd, at **Glan Faenol** on the Menai Strait and at **Porthdinllaen** on Llŷn. There is a path accessible to wheelchairs leading to a viewing terrace and beach cafe at Porthor (Whistling Sands) on Llŷn.

### ... and for Families
Particularly recommended are the beaches at **Broadhaven**, **Porthdinllaen** and **Porthor**, as well as **Rhossili**, where shipwrecks become visible at low tide, and **Mwnt**, from where dolphins can often be seen.

### Further Information
NT Office for Wales in Llandudno, tel.0870 609 5393

Please contact the above office for a free copy of the *NT Countryside Guide to Wales*, sponsored by Barclays, which gives full details of a range of Trust coast and countryside properties.

---

## ABERCONWY HOUSE   Conwy
Castle Street, Conwy LL32 8AY · **Tel** 01492 592246 · **Fax** 01492 585153

---

Dating from the 14th century, this is the only medieval merchant's house in Conwy to have survived the turbulent history of this walled town for nearly six centuries. Furnished rooms and an audiovisual presentation show daily life from different periods in its history

**Note**: The house has limited electric lighting and therefore is dark on dull days

**O** 23 March to 3 Nov: daily except Tues 11–5 (open BHols throughout the season incl. 3 & 4 June)

---

**There are special events at most Trust properties; please telephone 0870 458 4000 for details**

- £ £2; child £1; family £5. Booked groups £1.60; NT members free
- 🕐 Daily 9.30–5.30 (closed 25, 26 Dec)
- ♿ House: steps at entrance
- 🎒 Educational visits welcome; booked groups only
- ➡ (4:F2) At junction of Castle Street and High Street [115: SH781777]
  **Bus**: From surrounding areas
  **Station**: Conwy 300m
  **Cycle**: NCN 5

**NT properties nearby** Bodnant Garden, Conwy Suspension Bridge

## ABERDEUNANT                                    Carmarthenshire
Taliaris, Llandeilo SA19 6DL · **Tel** 01558 825912 · **Fax** 01558 822036

A traditional Carmarthenshire farmhouse in an unspoilt setting and providing a rare insight into an aspect of agricultural life that has all but disappeared

**Note**: As the property is extremely small, visitor access is limited to no more than 6 people at a time. Car parking is restricted and there is no access for coaches. The property is administered and maintained on the Trust's behalf by a resident tenant – the gegin fawr (farm kitchen) and one bedroom are open to the public by arrangement

- 🅾 Public footpaths give access to the surrounding land, but entry to the farmhouse is by guided tour only, which must be booked in advance. Tours take place as follows: April to Sept: first Sat & Sun of each month 12–5; Oct to March 2003: first Sat of each month 12–4. Places can be booked, tel. 01558 825912. The property is not suitable for coach groups
- £ £1.50; child 80p. No WC
- ➡ (4:E8) Full details are sent on booking [146:SN672308]

## ABERDULAIS FALLS                               Neath & Port Talbot
Aberdulais, nr Neath SA10 8EU · **Tel** 01639 636674 · **Fax** 01639 645069
**Email** aberdulais@ntrust.org.uk

For over 300 years this famous waterfall provided the energy to drive the wheels of industry, from the manufacture of copper in 1584 to the nearby tinplate works. It has also been visited by famous artists, such as Turner in 1796. The site today houses a unique hydroelectric scheme which has been developed to harness the waters of the River Dulais. The Turbine House provides access to an interactive computer, fish pass, observation window and display panels. Special lifts have been installed to allow disabled visitors access to the upper levels, which afford excellent views of the

**For all your information needs check our website www.nationaltrust.org.uk**

Falls. The waterwheel is the largest currently used in Europe to generate electricity, which makes Aberdulais Falls self-sufficient in environmentally friendly energy

**Note**: The operation of the fish pass, waterwheel and turbine is subject to water levels and maintenance

**O** 1 to 22 March: Fri, Sat & Sun, 11–4. 23 March to 3 Nov: daily, Mon–Fri 10–5, Sat, Sun & BHols 11–6. **Events**: held throughout the year, contact Property Warden for details. **Winter opening**: property and Christmas shop open 8 Nov to 22 Dec, Fri, Sat & Sun & Mon 23 Dec 11–4

**£** £3; child £1.50; family £7.50. Parties (min. 15) by arrangement with Property Warden £2.40; child £1.20. Children must be accompanied by an adult. Car park signposted to the rear of Dulais Rock Inn, 2min walk. Also, on-road parking on A4109 outside the property entrance; coaches must check beforehand as parking is limited

Guided tours in July and Aug, at other times by arrangement for pre-booked parties. Audio tours all year

Located near the entrance and open as property inc. Christmas

Limited car parking, tel. in advance. Site: largely accessible. In the Turbine House a special lift capable of carrying two wheelchair users and their helpers provides access to the roof level, with excellent views of the Falls, gorge and waterwheel; scissor lifts give access to further views of the Falls and River Dulais. Winner of British Gas ADAPT Commendation for access

Braille guide; tape guide with information for sighted companions

The Friends of Aberdulais Falls serve light refreshments in the Old Works Library and Victorian schoolroom at summer weekends and public holidays; other times by arrangement. Lunches and snacks available at Dulais Rock Inn (not NT)

Education facilities provided for pre-booked groups by arrangement with the Property Warden. In Victorian schoolroom: tours and talks on hydroelectric scheme, industrial archaeology, history for educational and other groups. Teachers' resource pack

On leads only

→ (4:F9) On A4109, 3ml NE of Neath. 4ml from M4 exit 43 at Llandarcy, take A465 signposted Vale of Neath [170: SS772995] **Bus**: First Cymru 158 Swansea–Banwen, 154/8, 161 from Neath; Stagecoach in South Wales X75 Swansea–Merthyr Tydfil. All pass close ⊠ Neath **Station**: Neath 3ml **Cycle**: NCN Cycle route 47. Access via BQ Neath, Neath Canal and Aberdulais Canal Basin

**Please remember – your membership card is always needed for free admission**

# BODNANT GARDEN 🏠❋☺ — Conwy

Tal-y-Cafn, Colwyn Bay LL28 5RE · **Tel** 01492 650460 · **Fax** 01492 650448
**Web** www.oxalis.co.uk/bodnant.htm

One of the world's most spectacular gardens, situated above the River Conwy with stunning views across Snowdonia. Begun in 1875, Bodnant is the creation of four generations of Aberconways and features huge Italianate terraces and formal lawns on its upper level, with a wooded valley, stream and wild garden below. There are dramatic colours throughout the season, with notable collections of rhododendrons, magnolias and camellias and the spectacular laburnum arch, a 55m tunnel of golden blooms, in mid May-early June

**Note**: The garden and refreshment pavilion are managed on behalf of the Trust by Lord Aberconway, VMH

- 🅾 16 March to 3 Nov: daily 10–5
- 💷 £5.20; child £2.60. Parties of 20+ £4.70; NT members free. Car park 50m from garden entrance
- 🛍 Plant centre & gift shop (not NT) open as garden
- ♿ Garden: steep in places, with many steps. Wheelchairs; not bookable. WC (RADAR lock). Refreshment pavilion & plant centre: accessible
- 👁 Braille guide. Scented roses and other plants
- 🍴 Refreshment pavilion 11–5. Picnicking in car park area only
- 👶 Baby-changing facilities; baby slings. Highchairs
- 🐕 On lead in car park only
- ➡ (4:F2) 8ml S of Llandudno and Colwyn Bay off A470, entrance ½ml along the Eglwysbach road. Signposted from A55 [115/116: SH801723] **Bus**: Arriva Cymru 25, Alpine 84 from Llandudno (passing ⊠ Llandudno Junction) **Station**: Tal-y-Cafn (U) 2ml

## CHIRK CASTLE & GARDEN  Wrexham

Chirk, Wrexham LL14 5AF · **Tel** 01691 777701 · **Fax** 01691 774706
**Email** chirkcastle@ntrust.org.uk

A magnificent Marcher fortress, completed in 1310. The rather austere exterior belies the comfortable and elegant state rooms inside, with elaborate plasterwork, superb Adam-style furniture, tapestries and portraits. In the formal gardens there are clipped yews, roses and a variety of flowering shrubs. The beautiful 18th-century parkland contains many mature trees as well as elaborate gates, made in 1719 by the Davies brothers. After 400 years of occupation, the Myddelton family still live here

- **Castle**: 23 March to 3 Nov: daily except Mon & Tues (open BHols inc. 4 June) 12–5 (closes 4 in Oct & Nov). **Garden**: as castle 11–6 (closes 5 in Oct & Nov); last admission 1hr before closing. **Events**: send s.a.e. for details of programme, which includes family fun days and snowdrop walks
- £5.60; child £2.80; family £14. Booked parties of 15+ £4.50. Garden only: £3.40; child £1.70. Parking 200m
- Connoisseurs' tour by arrangement (min. 15), Wed am only
- As castle
- Castle: stairclimber to state rooms may be available, tel. to check. Garden: mostly accessible; gravel paths. Tea-room: accessible. Room for CAPD. Courtesy coach from car park
- Braille guide; many touchable items
- Licensed tea-room as castle 11–5 (closes 4 in Oct & Nov). Picnics in car park and picnic area only
- Parent and baby room. Baby carriers; highchairs
- Educational visits particularly welcome. 'Hands-on' facilities. Education Officer and room. School parties must book
- On leads and only in car park
- (4:G3) Entrance 1ml off A5, 2ml W of Chirk village; 7ml S of Wrexham, signposted off A483 [126:SJ275388] **Bus**: Arriva North Midlands 2/A Wrexham–Oswestry **Station**: Chirk (U) $\frac{1}{4}$ml to gates, 1$\frac{1}{2}$ml to castle

**NT properties nearby** Erddig, Powis Castle

---

**Please see the area introductions for details of coast & countryside properties**

WALES · 329

## CILGERRAN CASTLE 🏛                           Pembrokeshire
nr Cardigan SA43 2SF · **Tel** 01239 615007

This 13th-century ruin is perched overlooking the spectacular Teifi gorge and has inspired many artists, including Turner

**Note**: Cilgerran Castle is in the guardianship of Cadw: Welsh Historic Monuments

🅾 Daily. *Times*: summer 9.30–6.30; winter: 9.30–4

💷 £2; children, students & senior citizens £1.50; family £5.50 (please tel. for prices for April 2002 onwards)

🛍 Daily except Sat, hours as castle

♿ Inner bailey & grounds: accessible

➡ (4:C7) On rock above left bank of the Teifi, 3ml SE of Cardigan, 1½ml E of A478 [145: SN195431] **Bus**: Midway 430 from Cardigan; otherwise Davies Bros 460/1 from 🚂 Carmarthen–Cardigan, alight Llechryd, 1¼ml by footpath

## COLBY WOODLAND GARDEN
🌺 🍎 🧺 🏞 🚶 ♿                                            Pembrokeshire
Amroth, Narberth SA67 8PP · **Tel** 01834 811885 · **Fax** 01834 831766

Attractive woodland garden with a fine collection of rhododendrons and azaleas. There are beautiful walks through secluded valleys along open and wooded pathways

**Note**: The early 19th-century house is not open; Mr & Mrs A Scourfield Lewis kindly allow access to the walled garden during visiting hours

🅾 **Woodland garden**: 23 March to 3 Nov: daily 10–5. **Walled garden**: 1 April to 31 Oct: 11–5. **Events**: regular guided walks with Gardener-in-charge in the season; evening entertainment; family fun days; tel. for details

💷 £2.80; child £1.40; family £7. Groups £2.30; child £1.15. Coaches welcome. Open evenings by arrangement

🛍 Shop, gallery & plant sales as property

♿ Close parking on request. Woodland garden: limited access; parts very steep. Garden video, tea-room & shop: accessible. Wheelchair and walking stick

👁 Braille guide

☕ Tea-room (not NT) as property. Picnicking in car park

👶 Baby-changing facilities. Children's quiz and safari fun packs

🐕 On leads, but not in walled garden

➡ (4:C9) 1½ml inland from Amroth beside Carmarthen Bay. Follow brown signs from A477 Tenby–Carmarthen road or off coast road at Amroth Castle [158: SN155080] **Bus**: Silcox 350, Arriva Cymru 351 from Tenby (passing 🚂 Kilgetty) **Station**: Kilgetty (U) 2½ml

**Unless indicated, last admission is always 30 mins before closing time**

## CONWY SUSPENSION BRIDGE 🛈

Conwy

Conwy LL32 8LD · **Tel** 01492 573282

Designed and built by Thomas Telford, this elegant suspension bridge was completed in 1826. It replaced the ferry, which was previously the only means of crossing the river. The toll-keeper's house has recently been restored and furnished as it would have been a century ago

- 23 March to 30 June, 1 Sept to 3 Nov: daily except Tues July & Aug: daily; open all BHols inc. 4 June). *Times*: 10–5
- £1; child 50p
- Educational visits welcome; booked groups only
- (4:F2) 100m from Conwy town centre, adjacent to Conwy Castle [115: SH785775] **Bus**: From surrounding areas **Station**: Conwy ½ml; Llandudno Junction ½ml **Cycle**: NCN 5

**NT properties nearby** Aberconwy House, Bodnant Garden

---

## DINEFWR 

Carmarthenshire

Llandeilo SA19 6RT · **Tel** 01558 825912 · **Fax** 01558 822036
**Email** dinefwr@ntrust.org.uk

An 18th-century landscape park which includes Newton House, built in 1660 but now with a Victorian Gothic façade. An exhibition explains the importance of Dinefwr in Welsh history. The medieval deer park, overlooked by the fountain garden, has restricted public access. It is home to around 100 fallow deer and the famous Dinefwr White Park Cattle. There are fine views over the Towy Valley with an ice house and boardwalk suitable for families and wheelchair users. There is also access to Dinefwr Castle, owned by the Wildlife Trust West Wales

- **House**: 23 March to 3 Nov: daily except Tues & Wed (open all BHols inc. 4 June). 11–5. (On Tues & Wed the library and old drawing room are available for hire.) **Parkland, deer park & boardwalk**: as house (last admission 4.15). **Events**: send s.a.e. marked 'Events' for details

**There are special events at most Trust properties; please telephone 0870 458 4000 for details**

[£] House & park £3.20; child £1.60; family £8. Parties(15+) £3. Park only £2.20; child £1.10; family £5.50. Coaches by appointment only

[i] Guided tours of Newton House and the deer park by arrangement in advance at a small additional charge

[♿] House: ramped access to ground floor and Fountain Garden. Tea-room: ramped access. Grounds: boardwalk through Bog Wood to Mill Pond dam

[👁] Braille guide; touch tour of house

[☕] Tea-room (not NT): as house

[👶] Baby-changing facilities, highchairs, children's menu. Quizzes and active events programme, safari sacks

[🐕] On leads and only in outer park

[→] (4:E8) On W outskirts of Llandeilo A40(T); from Swansea take M4 to Pont Abraham, thence A48(T) to Cross Hands and A476 to Llandeilo; entrance by police station [159: SN625225] **Bus**: From surrounding areas to Llandeilo, thence 1ml **Station**: Llandeilo ½ml

**NT properties nearby** Dolaucothi Gold Mines

## DOLAUCOTHI GOLD MINES                 Carmarthenshire
Pumsaint, Llanwrda SA19 8RR · **Tel** 01558 650177 · **Infoline** 01558 825146
**Fax** 01558 650707 · **Email** dolaucothi@ntrust.org.uk

These unique gold mines are set amid wooded hillsides overlooking the beautiful Cothi Valley. The Romans who exploited the site almost 2000 years ago left behind a complex of pits, channels, adits and tanks. Mining resumed in the 19th century and continued through to the 20th century, reaching a peak in 1938. Guided tours take visitors through the Roman and the more recent underground workings. The main mine yard contains a collection of 1930s mining machinery and an exhibition explaining the history of the site, video and interpretation. Gold-panning gives visitors the opportunity to experience the frustrations of the search for gold. Other attractions include waymarked walks and cycle hire, the ruins of a Roman settlement and Red Kite Information Centre in Pumsaint. Fishing and accommodation on the Estate, including a 45-pitch touring caravan site

[O] 22 March to 22 Sept: daily. *Times*: 10–5. Groups can be booked at other times. Last underground tour leaves at 4.30. Pumsaint Information Centre and Estate walks all year. **Note**: Underground tours last about 1hr and involve hillside walking, so stout footwear is recommended; helmets with lights are provided. These tours are unsuitable for visitors with poor mobility and children under 5 are not allowed on the guided underground tour of recent workings. There is a self-guided tour of a Roman mine tunnel for accompanied under 5s

[£] Site: £2.80; child £1.40; family £7 (price inc. gold-panning). Combined site & underground tour: £6.50; child £3.20; family £16, NT members £3; child £1.50; family £7.50. Groups by arrangement

**For all your information needs check our website www.nationaltrust.org.uk**

## 332 · WALES

- 🚶 Stout footwear recommended
- 🛍 As property
- ♿ Reception, exhibition centre and mineyard: accessible (ramps)
- ☕ As property
- 👶 Baby-changing facilities and highchairs. Quizzes and events programme. Children's parties (booking essential). Activity room
- 🏫 Room for school groups and children
- 🐕 On leads only, but not on tours
- ➜ (4:E7) Between Lampeter and Llanwrda on A482 [146: SN6640] **Bus**: Castle Garage 289 from Lampeter **Station**: Llanwrda (U), not Sun, except June to Sept, 8ml

---

## ERDDIG                                                                 Wrexham
nr Wrexham LL13 0YT · **Tel** 01978 355314 · **Infoline** 01978 315151
**Fax** 01978 313333 · **Email** erddig@ntrust.org.uk

---

One of the most fascinating houses in Britain, not least because of the unusually close relationship that existed between the family of the house and their servants. The beautiful and evocative range of outbuildings includes kitchen, laundry, bakehouse, stables, sawmill, smithy and joiner's shop, while the stunning state rooms display most of their original 18th- and 19th-century furniture and furnishings, including some exquisite Chinese wallpaper. The large walled garden has been restored to its 18th-century formal design and has a Victorian parterre and yew walk. It also contains the National Collection of Ivies. There is an extensive park with woodland walks

**Note: Due to the extreme fragility of their contents, the Tapestry and Small Chinese Rooms are open on Wed & Sat only. Most rooms have no electric light; visitors wishing to make a close study of pictures and textiles should avoid dull days**

- 🕐 **House**: 23 March to 3 Nov: daily except Thur & Fri (but open Good Fri). *Times*: March to Sept 12–5, Oct 12–4; last admission 1hr before closing. **Garden**: as house. *Times*: March to end June, Sept 11–6, July & Aug 10–6, Oct 11–5. **Events**: varied programme; send s.a.e. to Visitor Services Supervisor for details

- £ £6.60; child £3.30; family £16.50. Parties of 15+ £5.30. Garden & outbuildings only: £3.40; child £1.70; family £8.50. Parties of 15+ £2.70; NT members free. Parking 200m

- 🚶 Garden tours (groups 15+) by arrangement with Head Gardener

---

**Please remember – your membership card is always needed for free admission**

- Shop & plant sales as property 11–5.30. 3 Nov to 17 Dec: Christmas opening 3 Nov to 17 Dec: Fri, Sat & Sun 11–4. Shop Manager tel. 01978 315183

- House: access to ground floor across rough gravel; tel. general office in advance to discuss visit. Outbuildings: accessible. Garden: across yard to ramped access. Upstairs restaurant: access difficult. Downstairs refreshment area: accessible. Wheelchairs. Country park: fully accessible sensory meadow at Felin Puleston, with tactile information board and over 2200m of 'Access for All' footpath through woodland. WCs (RADAR lock)

- Braille guide; furniture, panelling, pewter and other items may be touched (prior notice appreciated). Audio induction loop system and audiovisual presentation

- Licensed restaurant as property 11–5.15. Also open for booked functions. Christmas opening 3 Nov to 17 Dec: Fri, Sat & Sun 11–4. Catering Manager (tel. 01978 315184). Picnicking in car park area only

- Feeding and baby-changing facilities. Children's guide. Baby carriers; highchairs

- School and youth groups Mon, Tues & Wed am by arrangement; send s.a.e. to Education Officer for details of education programme at the house and on the estate, or tel. 01978 315156

- On leads and only in car park and country park

- (4:H3) 2ml S of Wrexham, signposted A525 Whitchurch road, or A483/A5152 Oswestry road [117: SJ326482] **Station**: Wrexham Central (U) 1ml, Wrexham General 1½ml via Erddig Rd & footpath

**NT properties nearby** Chirk Castle

---

## LLANERCHAERON

Ceredigion

nr Aberaeron SA48 8DG · **Tel** 01545 570200 · **Infoline** 01558 825147
**Fax** 01545 571759
**Email** llanerchaeron@ntrust.org.uk

Llanerchaeron is a small 18th-century Welsh gentry estate, set in the beautiful Dyffryn Aeron. The estate survived virtually unaltered into the 20th century and was bequeathed to the National Trust by J. P. Ponsonby Lewes in 1989. The house was designed and built by John Nash in 1794–96 and is the most complete example of his early work. Llanerchaeron was a self-sufficient estate – evident in the dairy, laundry, brewery and salting house of the service courtyard, as well as the home farm buildings from the stables to the threshing barn. Llanerchaeron today is a working organic farm and the two restored walled gardens also produce home grown fruit and herbs. There are extensive walks around the estate and parkland

**What's new in 2002**: The house and servant quarters will open to visitors for the first time in June 2002 following extensive restoration

- **House and service courtyard**: 5 June to 3 Nov daily except Mon & Tues (but open BHols) 11.30–5. **Home farm, gardens & grounds**: 23 March to 3 Nov: daily except Mon & Tues (but open BHols) 11–5. **Parkland**: All year, dawn to dusk; access via gate by church. **Events**: send s.a.e. for details

**For general enquiries, please telephone 0870 458 4000**

**334** · WALES

- £ £4; child £2; family £10 (adult by bike or on foot £3.60, child by bike or on foot £1.80). Group (15+) adult £3.20; child £1.60
- Guided tours of the garden and Home Farm start 2 every Thur in July, Aug & Sept, additional £1 inc. NT members (groups of 10+ by arrangement)
- Easy access to whole site. Wheelchair
- Braille guide
- Cycle track from Aberaeron to the property along old railway track (2ml). Discount to people arriving by bike or on foot
- On leads and only in parkland
- (4:E6) 2½ml east of Aberaeron off A482 [146: SN480 602] **Bus**: Davies Bros 202 ≋ Carmarthen–Aberaeron (with connections from ≋ Aberystwyth)

**NT properties nearby** Dinefwr Park, Dolaucothi Gold Mines, Mwnt, Penbryn

## LLYWELYN COTTAGE/BWTHYN LLYWELYN

Gwynedd

Beddgelert LL55 4YA · **Tel** 01766 890293 · **Fax** 01766 890545

A shop and exhibtion are housed in this 17th-century cottage, situated in the picturesque village of Beddgelert, near the Aberglaslyn Pass and within the Snowdonia National Park. There are superb walks in the area, including a stroll to the legendary Gelert's grave

- **O** 23 March to 3 Nov: daily 11–5
- £ Free
- As Cottage
- Accessible
- (4:E3) At junction of A498 and A4085. Beddgelert is well signposted from A5 and A487 [115: SH590481] **Bus**: KMP 95 from Caernarfon (with connections from ≋ Bangor), Express 97/A from Porthmadog (passes close ≋ Porthmadog) **Station**: Penrhyndeudraeth (U) or Porthmadog (U) both 6ml

**NT properties nearby** Craflwyn, Hafod y Llan (Snowdon)

## THE NAVAL TEMPLE AND ROUND HOUSE

Monmouthshire

The Kymin, Monmouth · **Tel** 01874 625515

Once visited by Nelson and set in 4ha (9 acres) of woods and pleasure grounds, this is a small two-storey circular Georgian banqueting house and naval temple, a monument dedicated to the glories of the British Navy. The hilltop grounds near Monmouth in the Wye valley afford spectacular views of the surrounding countryside. After substantial renovations in 2001 the banqueting house will be opened to the public for the first time in spring 2002

**Please see the area introductions for details of coast & countryside properties**

WALES · 335

- **Roundhouse**: 31 March to 30 Sept: Sun & Mon 11–4, last entry 3.45. **Naval Temple & grounds**: open daily all year
- £2; child £1; family (2+3) £5. Group £1.60. Parking free, grounds free
- Parking available. Access to ground floor only
- (4:I9) 1 mile east of Monmouth between A466 and A4136 [[162] SO528125] **Bus**: Stagecoach in South Wales 60 from Newport (passing close ⮕ Newport), 69 from Chepstow (passing close ⮕ Chepstow), 83 from Abergavenny (passing close ⮕ Abergavenny), Duke's 416 from ⮕ Hereford. On all, alight Monmouth, thence 1½ml (steep)

## PENRHYN CASTLE
Gwynedd

Bangor LL57 4HN · **Tel** 01248 353084 · **Infoline** 01248 371337
**Fax** 01248 371281 · **Email** penrhyncastle@ntrust.org.uk

This dramatic neo-Norman fantasy castle sits between Snowdonia and the Menai Strait. Built by Thomas Hopper between 1820 and 1845 for the wealthy Pennant family, who made their fortune from Jamaican sugar and Welsh slate, the castle is crammed with fascinating things such as a one-ton slate bed made for Queen Victoria. Hopper also designed its interior with elaborate carvings, plasterwork and mock-Norman furniture. The castle contains an outstanding collection of paintings. The stable block houses an industrial railway museum, a countryside exhibition, a railway model museum and a superb dolls museum displaying a large collection of 19th- and 20th-century dolls. The 18.2ha (45 acres) of grounds include parkland, an extensive exotic tree and shrub collection and a Victorian walled garden

**What's new in 2002**: Victorian kitchen and other servants' rooms including scullery, larders and chef's sitting room restored to reveal the preparations for the banquet for the Prince of Wales' visit in 1894

- **Castle**: 23 March to 3 Nov: daily except Tues (but open 4 June). *Times*: March to June, Sept to 3 Nov 12–5, July & Aug 11–5 (last audio tour 4). **Victorian Kitchen**: as castle but last admission 4.45. **Grounds & stable block exhibitions**: days as castle. *Times*: March to June, Sept to 3 Nov 11–5, July & Aug 10–5.30; last admission to house & grounds 4.30. **Events**: send s.a.e. for details or tel. Infoline
- £6; child £3; family £15. Booked parties of 15+ £5. Garden and stable block exhibitions only £4; child £2. Audio tour (£1) for adults and children in Welsh and English. School and youth groups by arrangement. Parking 200m
- Specialist guided tours by arrangement
- As castle 11–5, now in stable block and with disabled access
- Castle: ground floor accessible (ramps and handrail). Wheelchair. Park: firm paths. Three-seater staff-driven buggy for garden and park, must be pre-booked
- Braille guides to castle and garden; audio tour; induction loop audio tour
- Sympathetic Hearing Scheme

**Unless indicated, last admission is always 30 mins before closing time**

- Licensed tea-room as grounds and stable block. Picnicking in grounds only
- Baby-changing facilities; baby carriers on loan but no baby back-carriers or pushchairs in castle. Highchairs. Activity sheets. Industrial railway museum and dolls museum. Adventure playground. Permanent orienteering course in grounds; maps and instructions from shop
- Booked educational visits welcome. Hands-on educational facilities; Education Officer on site. Permanent orienteering course. Send s.a.e. for education programme
- On leads and only in grounds
- (4:E2) 1ml E of Bangor, at Llandygai on A5122. Signposted from junction of A55 and A5 [115: SH602720]] **Bus**: Arriva Cymru 5/X Caernarfon–Llandudno; 6/7 Bangor–Bethesda; 66 Bangor–Gerlan. All pass close Bangor and end of drive to Castle **Station**: Bangor 3ml **Cycle**: NCN 5 1¼ml

**NT properties nearby** Plas Newydd

## PLAS NEWYDD

Anglesey

Llanfairpwll, Anglesey LL61 6DQ · **Tel** 01248 714795 · **Fax** 01248 713673
**Email** plasnewydd@ntrust.org.uk

Set amidst breathtakingly beautiful scenery and with spectacular views of Snowdonia, this elegant 18th-century house was built by James Wyatt and is an interesting mixture of Classical and Gothic. The comfortable interior, restyled in the 1930s, is famous for its association with Rex Whistler, whose largest painting is here. There is also an exhibition about his work. A military museum contains campaign relics of the 1st Marquess of Anglesey, who commanded the cavalry at the Battle of Waterloo. There is a fine spring garden and Australasian arboretum with an understorey of shrubs and wild flowers, as well as a summer terrace and, later, massed hydrangeas and autumn colour. A woodland walk gives access to a marine walk on the Menai Strait

**Note**: Historical cruises – boat trips on the Menai Strait – operate from the property, weather and demand permitting. Tel. for details

- **House**: 23 March to 3 Nov: daily except Thur & Fri (open Good Fri) 12–5. **Garden**: as house 11–5.30; rhododendron garden 31 March to early June only; woodland walk and marine walk open as house and garden. **Events**: 17 Aug open-air jazz concert with firework finale, tel. to join mailing list
- £4.60; child £2.30; family £11.50. Booked parties of 15+ £3.70. Garden only £2.60; child £1.30. Parking 400m
- Connoisseurs' and garden tours by arrangement
- 23 March to 31 Oct: daily 11–5. 1 Nov to 15 Dec: Christmas shop Fri, Sat & Sun 11–4
- Minibus between car park & house, ask at reception desk. House: ground floor accessible via ramps; garden shuttle service. Wheelchairs. Garden: all main paths accessible. Tea-room & shop: accessible

**There are special events at most Trust properties; please telephone 0870 458 4000 for details**

WALES · 337

- Braille guide. Aromatic shrubs; fragrant azaleas in spring
- As shop. Winner of Best Welsh Flavour award in the *Red Book, Eat Well in Wales*. Restaurant licence, home-cooked food with a regional and historical theme using local produce whenever possible. Member of the Taste of Wales scheme. Seasonal menu in Nov & Dec, when Christmas lunches can be booked. Picnicking in car park and playground area
- Parent and baby facilities. Baby carriers and reins; no baby back-carriers or pushchairs in house. Highchairs. Children's quiz and adventure playground. Tree house in garden
- Booked school groups welcome
- (4:E2) 2ml SW of Llanfairpwll and A5 on A4080 to Brynsiencyn; turn off A5 at W end of Britannia Bridge [114/115: SH521696] **Bus**: Arriva Cymru 42 from Bangor (passing ≋ Bangor & Llanfairpwll) **Station**: Llanfairpwll (U), no practical Sun service, 1¾ml **Cycle**: NCN 8 ¼ml

---

# PLAS YN RHIW

Gwynedd

Rhiw, Pwllheli LL53 8AB · **Tel/Fax** 01758 780219

---

A small manor house, rescued from neglect and lovingly restored by the three Keating sisters, who bought it in 1938. The views from the delightful grounds and gardens across Cardigan Bay are among the most spectacular in Britain. The house is 16th century with Georgian additions, and the ornamental gardens contain many interesting flowering trees and shrubs, with beds framed by box hedges and grass paths. Brilliant displays of snowdrops and bluebells can be found in the wood above at the appropriate season

- 23 March to 13 May: daily except Tues & Wed; 15 May to 30 Sept: daily except Tues. Oct: Sat & Sun only, but open daily 21 to 25 Oct (open all BHols inc. 4 June). *Times*: 12–5. Garden and snowdrop wood open occasionally at weekends in Jan & Feb; tel. or see local press for details
- £3.20; child £1.60; family £8. Garden only £2; child £1; family £5. Garden & snowdrop wood (Jan & Feb only) £2.50. Parking 80m. No coaches
- Advance notice is required; booked groups £1.40 per person extra (inc. NT members)
- As house
- House: ground floor accessible. Garden: very difficult; on steep hillside; narrow paths; steps
- Braille guides for house and estate. Scented plants

**For all your information needs check our website www.nationaltrust.org.uk**

- Picnic site in garden meadow
- School visits are welcomed, but Custodian must be informed 2 weeks in advance
- On leads and only on the woodland walk
- (4:D4) 16 ml from Pwllheli. Approach route changed due to landslip. Follow A499 and B4413 from Pwllheli. At Botwnnog, follow signs to Plas yn Rhiw along narrow lanes past Rhiw village. Entrance at bottom of steep hill. [123: SH237282] **Bus**: Arriva Cymru 17B, Nefyn 10 from Pwllheli (passing ≋ Pwllheli)

## POWIS CASTLE & GARDEN

Powys

Welshpool SY21 8RF · **Tel** 01938 551920 · **Infoline** 01938 551944
**Fax** 01938 554336
**Email** powiscastle@ntrust.org.uk

The world-famous garden, overhung with enormous clipped yews, shelters rare and tender plants. Laid out under the influence of Italian and French styles, the garden retains its original lead statues, an orangery and an aviary on the terraces. In the 18th century an informal woodland wilderness was created on the opposing ridge. Perched on a rock above the garden terraces, the medieval castle contains one of the finest collections in Wales. It was originally built c.1200 by Welsh princes and was subsequently adapted and embellished by generations of Herberts and Clives, who furnished the castle with a wealth of fine paintings and furniture. A beautiful collection of treasures from India is displayed in the Clive Museum

**Note**: All visitors (inc. NT members) need to obtain a ticket from Visitor Reception in the main car park on arrival. A timed ticket system for the Castle may be in operation at busy periods

- **Castle & museum**: 23 March to 30 June, 1 Sept to 3 Nov: daily except Mon & Tues; July & Aug: daily except Mon; (open all BHols inc. 4 June). *Times*: Castle & museum 1–5. **Garden**: as castle & museum 11–6. **Events**: varied programme, tel. for details
- £7.50; child £3.75; family £18.75. Parties £6.50 (NT members free). Garden only £5; child £2.50; family £12.50. Parties £4 (NT members free). All groups by written appointment only and coaches limited to four per day. No group rates Sun & BH Mons
- Pre-booked guided tours of the castle and/or garden by prior arrangement (additional charge), tel. for details
- As castle & garden 11–5. 8 Nov to 15 Dec: Christmas shop Fri, Sat & Sun 11–4
- Tel. in advance for information; due to layout of garden and design of castle, access is very limited and it is not possible to use wheelchairs inside castle. Photo album of castle interior available from restaurant for people unable to climb stairs. Garden is very steep and not recommended for disabled walkers or wheelchair users. Good access to restaurant, shop and plant shop. Wheelchair. WC. Elderly and disabled visitors may be set down at castle. Reserved parking for disabled drivers

**Please remember – your membership card is always needed for free admission**

WALES · 339

- Braille guide; scented flowers. 'Touch tour' guide of house, must be pre-booked
- Licensed restaurant open as castle 11–5. 8 Nov to 15 Dec: as shop
- Baby-feeding and changing facilities. Front baby carriers on loan. Castle unsuitable for baby back-carriers and pushchairs. Highchairs. Children's guides and questionnaires. Family quiz trails and activities in garden during school holidays
- School groups by written appointment only
- Lockable posts by cabin in car park
- Guide dogs only in castle and garden. Dogs cannot be walked in the park as it does not belong to the Trust and no dog-walking is allowed there
- (4:G5) 1ml S of Welshpool; pedestrian access from High Street (A490); cars turn right 1ml along main road to Newtown (A483); enter by first drive gate on right [126: SJ216064] **Bus**: Arriva North Midlands D71 Oswestry–Welshpool; D75 Shrewsbury–Llanidloes, alight High Street, 1ml **Station**: Welshpool 1¾ml via footpath from town

**NT properties nearby** Attingham, Chirk Castle, Erddig

## RHOSSILI VISITOR CENTRE　Swansea

Coastguard Cottages, Rhossili, Gower SA3 1PR · **Tel** 01792 390707
**Email** rhossili@ntrust.org.uk

The Trust owns and protects much land on the beautiful Gower peninsula. The Visitor Centre is situated adjacent to the Warren, the Down, Worm's Head, beach and coastal cliffs, and provides information about the area. There is also an exhibition and shop

- 2 Jan to 23 March: Sat & Sun; 24 March to 5 Nov: daily; 6 Nov to 19 Dec: daily except Mon & Tues. *Times*: Jan to 23 March & 6 Nov to 19 Dec 11–4; 24 March to 5 Nov 10.30–5.30
- Free. Car park and WC nearby (not NT); charge for parking
- As Visitor Centre
- Rough surface in car park (not NT). Disabled visitors may be set down at Visitor Centre. Shop & ground floor of Visitor Centre: accessible. Excellent viewpoint outside Visitor Centre. Path towards Worm's Head level and accessible

**For general enquiries, please telephone 0870 458 4000**

- Not in Visitor Centre; must be under control and on leads at lambing time
- (4:D9) SW tip of Gower Peninsula, approached from Swansea via A4118 and then B4247 [159:SS418883] **Bus**: First Cymru 18/A/C from Swansea (passing close ⇌ Swansea)

**NT properties nearby** Coastline around Gower peninsula, NT holdings on Gower total 2225ha (5500 acres)

## ST DAVID'S VISITOR CENTRE AND SHOP    Pembrokeshire

Captains House, High Street, St David's Haverfordwest SA62 6SD
**Tel/Fax** 01437 720385

The National Trust owns and protects much of the picturesque and historic St David's Head and surrounding coastline. The Visitor Centre is conveniently situated in the centre of the city of St David's opposite The Cross (owned by the National Trust). Recently refurbished, the Visitor Centre offers a complete guide to The National Trust in Pembrokeshire, its properties, beaches and walks

- 12 Jan to 28 Feb: closed for refurbishment. March: daily except Sun & Mon 10–4. April to Oct: daily 10–5.30. Nov & Dec: daily except Sun & Mon 10–4
- Open as visitor centre
- (4:B8) [115:SM753253]

## SEGONTIUM    Gwynedd

Caernarfon LL55 2LN · **Tel** 01286 675625

The remains of a Roman fort, built to defend the Roman Empire against rebellious tribes and later plundered to provide stone for Edward I's castle at Caernarfon. There is a museum containing relics found on-site

**Note**: Segontium is in the guardianship of Cadw: Welsh Historic Monuments and managed by the National Museums and Galleries of Wales

- Daily (closed 24–26 Dec & 1 Jan). *Times*: 1 April to 31 Oct: Mon to Sat 10–5, Sun 2–5; 1 Nov to 31 March 2003: Mon to Sat 10–4, Sun 2–4 (opening times may vary – tel. to check)
- Free entry to all National Museums and Galleries of Wales sites
- Site largely accessible
- (4:E2) On Llanbeblig road, A4085, on SE outskirts of Caernarfon [115: SH485624] **Bus**: From surrounding areas to Caernarfon (KMP 95 from Beddgelert and Arvonia 93, pass museum, on others ½ml walk to fort) **Station**: Bangor 9ml **Cycle**: NCN 8½ml

**NT properties nearby** Glan Faenol, Penrhyn Castle, Plas Newydd, Plas yn Rhiw

**Please see the area introductions for details of coast & countryside properties**

WALES · 341

## SKENFRITH CASTLE                                                                 Monmouthshire
Skenfrith, nr Abergavenny · **Tel** 01874 625515

A Norman castle, built to command one of the main routes between England and Wales. A keep stands on the remains of the motte, and the 13th-century curtain wall with towers has also survived

**Note**: Skenfrith Castle is in the guardianship of Cadw: Welsh Historic Monuments

- Daily
- Free
- Racks. Local 'Four Castles' cycle trail starts at nearby Abergavenny castle
- (4:H8) 6ml NW of Monmouth, 12ml NE of Abergavenny, on N side of the Ross road (B4521) [161: SO456203]

**NT properties nearby** Sugar Loaf Mountain, Westbury Court Garden

## TUDOR MERCHANT'S HOUSE                                                         Pembrokeshire
Quay Hill, Tenby SA70 7BX · **Tel/Fax** 01834 842279

A late 15th-century town house, characteristic of the area and of the time when Tenby was a thriving trading port. The ground-floor chimney at the rear of the house is a fine vernacular example, and the original scarfed roof-trusses survive. The remains of early frescos can be seen on three interior walls and the house is furnished to recreate family life from the Tudor period onwards. There is access to the small herb garden, weather permitting

- 23 March to 30 Sept: daily except Wed; 1 Oct to 3 Nov: daily except Wed & Sat. *Times*: March to Sept 10–5, Sun 1–5; Oct & Nov 10–3, Sun 12–3
- £2; child £1; family £5. Groups £1.60, child 80p. No WC. Car-parking in town
- (4:C9) [158: SN135004] **Bus**: From surrounding areas **Station**: Tenby 700m

**NT properties nearby** Colby Woodland Garden

## TŶ MAWR WYBRNANT                                                                      Conwy
Penmachno, Betws-y-Coed LL25 0HJ · **Tel** 01690 760213

Situated in the beautiful and secluded Wybrnant Valley, Tŷ Mawr was the birthplace of Bishop William Morgan, first translator of the entire Bible into Welsh. The house has been restored to its probable 16th–17th-century appearance and houses a display of

**Unless indicated, last admission is always 30 mins before closing time**

Welsh Bibles. A footpath leads from the house through woodland and the surrounding fields, which are traditionally managed

**Note**: No access for coaches

- [O] 23 March to 3 Nov: daily except Mon, Tues & Wed (but open all BHols inc. 4 June). *Times*: March to Sept 12–5; Oct to 3 Nov 12–4
- [£] £2; child £1; family £5. Booked parties of 15+ £1.60 (NT members free)
- [♿] House: ground floor accessible
- [▮] Educational groups particularly welcome for house and nature trail tours; booked school parties only
- [🐕] Under close control and only in countryside
- [→] (4:F3) At the head of the Wybrnant Valley. From A5 3ml S of Betws-y-Coed, take B4406 to Penmachno. House is 2½ml NW of Penmachno by forest road [115: SH770524] **Bus**: Arriva Cymru 64 Llanrwst–Cwm Penmachno (passing ≋ Betws-y-Coed), alight Penmachno, thence 2ml **Station**: Pont-y-pant (U) 1½ml

**NT properties nearby** Ty'n-y-Coed Uchaf

---

## TY'N-Y-COED UCHAF [🏠][📷][♿][🐕] Conwy

Penmachno, Betws-y-Coed LL24 0PS · **Tel** 01690 760229

---

A traditional smallholding with 19th-century farmhouse and outbuildings, providing a fascinating record of an almost-vanished way of life. The house is approached by an interesting walk along the River Machno through fields of nature and conservation interest (there is a ¾ml walk to get to the property)

**Note**: As the property is extremely small, visitors may occasionally have to wait for entry

- [O] 24 March to 3 Nov: Thur, Fri & Sun (but open BHols inc. 4 June). *Times*: March to Sept 12–5; Oct to 3 Nov 12–4. **Note**: Ty'n-y-Coed Uchaf is occupied by a tenant, so it is important to observe the opening times. Car park can be approached through the car park for Penmachno Woollen Mill
- [£] £2; child £1; family £5. Booked parties of 15+ £1.60. Parking at Penmachno Woollen Mill ¾ml
- [♿] Wheelchair-accessible path from Penmachno Woollen Mill car park through first 3 fields
- [▮] Educational groups are especially welcome; booked only
- [→] (4:F3) 1½ml S of Betws-y-Coed on the A5. Turn right at the sign for Penmachno Woollen Mill, then follow B4406 for ½ml [116: SH803521] **Bus**: Arriva Cymru 64 Llanrwst–Cwm Penmachno (passes ≋ Betws-y-Coed) **Station**: Betws-y-Coed (U) 3ml

**NT properties nearby** Tŷ Mawr Wybrnant

---

**There are special events at most Trust properties; please telephone 0870 458 4000 for details**

# Introduction to Northern Ireland

Northern Ireland is famed worldwide for its beauty. The spectacular and varied coastline, rolling green scenery and evocative mountains, interspersed with areas of wetland and open water, combine to produce a singularly attractive landscape.

Many of the properties owned by the National Trust in Northern Ireland are important for their wildlife interest, offering a wide range of opportunities to enjoy unspoilt habitats and fascinating flora and fauna. **Murlough National Nature Reserve** facilities open daily May to Sept 10–6; car £3, minibus £5; (tel 028 4375 1467), near Newcastle, was Ireland's first nature reserve. The oldest sand dunes here are at least 5,000 years old and the soil ranges from lime-rich to acid, supporting a wide variety of plants which in turn provide nesting sites for birds in spring. Nearby are the beautiful Mourne Mountains, where the Trust owns **Slieve Donard**, the highest peak and from the foot of which there is a footpath connecting with the **Mourne Coastal Path**. Further south, at the mouth of Carlingford Lough, are **Blockhouse** and **Green Islands**, important breeding locations for terns and leased to the RSPB.

**Strangford Lough** is one of Europe's most important wildlife sites. In order to protect this habitat and the interesting birds and animals it supports, the Trust operates a Wildlife Scheme embracing the entire foreshore of the Lough and some fifty islands. Depending on the season, visitors may see vast flocks of wintering wildfowl and nesting birds. Seals, otters and other marine animals can also be seen, as well as interesting flowers. The Strangford Lough Wildlife Centre (tel 028 4488 1411) is located in the grounds of the **Castle Ward Estate** and has exhibitions, leaflets and other information. Also on the shores of the Lough is **Mount Stewart**, with its magnificent garden and splendid views over the surrounding countryside.

The County Down coastline has much to offer the walker and naturalist, with rocky shore and heathland at **Ballymacormick Point** and wildfowl, wading birds and gulls

| OS grid references for properties with no individual entry | |
|---|---|
| Ballymacormick Point | J525837 |
| Ballyconagan | D146520 |
| Bar Mouth & Grangemore Dunes | C782365 |
| Blockhouse & Green Islands | J254097 |
| Carrick-a-Rede/Larrybane | D062450 |
| Cushendun | D248327 |
| Cushleake Mountain | D228364 |
| Dunseverick Castle | C987445 |
| Fair Head/Murlough Bay | D185430 |
| Kearney & Knockinelder | J650517 |
| Lighthouse Island | J596858 |
| Murlough Nature Reserve | J410350 |
| Orlock Point | J539838 |
| Portstewart Strand | C720360 |
| Slieve Donard/Mourne Coastal Path | J389269 |
| Strangford Lough | J574498 |
| Whitepark Bay | D023440 |

to be seen at **Orlock Point**. Offshore is **Lighthouse Island**, which has a bird observatory and can be visited by arrangement with Mr Neville NcKee, 67 Temple Rise, Templepatrick, Co. Down (tel. 028 9443 3068). On the outer arm of the Ards Peninsula is the picturesque former fishing village of **Kearney**, (Information Centre open daily April to Sept: 10–6) where the Trust owns thirteen houses and from where there are attractive walks to the beach at **Knockinelder**.

The north coast of Counties Londonderry and Antrim is even more dramatic than that of Co. Down, and much of this coastline is also under Trust ownership. In the far

**For all your information needs check our website www.nationaltrust.org.uk**

west is the landscaped estate of **Downhill**, where the **Mussenden Temple** perches on the cliff-edge. East of Downhill is **Portstewart Strand**, a 2 mile-long stretch of dunes and sandy beach. (Visitor facilities are open here from May to the end of Aug, daily 10–6, car-parking £2.50, dogs must be kept on leads during summer months, tel 028 7083 6396). Nearby at the mouth of the River Bann are the **Bar Mouth** and **Grangemore Dunes**, a wildlife sanctuary with observation hide.

Further east still, the **Giant's Causeway** needs no introduction, but it is only one part of the beautiful 14-mile **North Antrim Cliff Path**. The path runs from the Causeway, pst the ruins of **Dunseverick Castle**, through the majestic sweep of **Whitepark Bay** (car park charge £2.50 June to Aug), with its sandy beach and backdrop of white chalk cliffs to the tiny stack of basalt rock, **Carrick-a-Rede** (the 'rock on the road'), which is connected to the mainland in summer by a swinging rope bridge. There is a car park at **Larrybane**, from where there is access to the bridge and good views of seabird colonies, Rathlin Island and, in good weather, the west coast of Scotland.

The distinctive headland of **Fair Head** rises 190m and gives dramatic views of nearby **Murlough Bay** and the Western Isles of Scotland. This is fine walking country and full of wildlife, but much of the land is grazed by livestock and so dogs must be on leads at all times. To the south-east is **Cushleake Mountain**, an exceptional example of raised blanket peat bog and home to rare plants and birds, and the delightful coastal village of **Cushendun**, where there are cottages designed by Clough Williams-Ellis, architect of Portmeirion in Wales. On the peaceful island of Rathlin the Trust recently opened new waymarked paths at **Ballyconagan**, a traditional farm which has remained unchanged for centuries. And at the Trust's **Manor House** visitors can enjoy comfortable bed and breakfast accommodation (tel. 028 2076 3964 to book).

The interior of Northern Ireland is full of interest and beauty. Here can be found the delightful country houses of **Springhill**, **The Argory** and **Ardress House**, as well as fascinating reminders of Ulster's industrial heritage, such as **Gray's Printing Press** in Strabane, **Wellbrook Beetling Mill** near Cookstown and **Patterson's Spade Mill** near Belfast, where the Trust also owns the magnificent **Crown Liquor Saloon**. In the west, the lush valleys and pastures of County Fermanagh provide a splendid setting for **Florence Court** and **Castle Coole**, as well as for the spectacular woodland and wetlands of the **Crom Estate** around Lough Erne.

GIANT'S CAUSEWAY

**Please remember – your membership card is always needed for free admission**

# NORTHERN IRELAND · 345

Under the National Trust Garden Scheme a number of private gardens are generously opened to the public in order to generate income for Trust gardens in Northern Ireland. For the 2002 programme please tel 028 9751 0721.

## Highlights for Visitors with Disabilities ...
**Murlough Nature Reserve** offers a boarded walkway to the dunes and beach (strong pusher needed), with wheelchair and adapted WC available in summer; at the **Giant's Causeway** a bus service to the Causeway stones is available and is equipped with a hoist for wheelchairs; there is also easy access to the shop and tea-room; at **Carrick-a-Rede** there is a special viewing platform for disabled visitors; a 1400m walk around **Florence Court** has recently been upgraded to allow wheelchair access. Many of our holiday cottages are suitable for visitors with disabilities.

## ... and for Families
A hands-on demonstration of 19th-century linen production at **Wellbrook Beetling Mill** is very popular with all ages. The beach at **Portstewart Strand** is an ideal place for a family day out – there is a wardening service and areas where vehicles are not permitted; **Strangford Lough Wildlife Centre** at Castle Ward has a theatre with wildlife films and information, and around the Lough there are many observation points where wildlife can be seen. Several properties have children's play areas and activities, including **Florence Court**, **Castle Ward** and **The Argory**. Most properties run a programme of family events: please telephone for details.

## Further Information
NT Office for Northern Ireland, tel. 028 9751 0721; please contact for copies of free leaflets or details about hiring Trust venues for private functions.

---

## ARDRESS HOUSE                                          Co. Armagh
64 Ardress Road, Portadown BT62 1SQ · **Tel/Fax** 028 3885 1236
**Email** ardress@ntrust.org.uk

House tours of this elegant 17th-century farmhouse include the Adam-style drawing-room, fine furniture and paintings. The farmyard, with traditional farm implements, is very popular with children. The attractive garden has woodland and riverside walks and there is a programme of family events such as Apple Blossom Day and Hallowe'en

- 16 March to May: Sat, Sun & BHols; June to Aug: daily (except Tues unless BHols); Sept: Sat & Sun. *Times*: 2–6.
- £2.70; child £1.35; family £6.75. Parties £2.20
- Access to house by guided tour only
- As house
- House: 3 ground-floor rooms accessible via 3 steps or side door from farmyard. Information room: ground-floor farm exhibition accessible. Garden: gravel paths
- Touch tours by arrangement

**For general enquiries, please telephone 0870 458 4000**

**346** · NORTHERN IRELAND

- 🦻 Sympathetic Hearing Scheme
- 🧒 Children's play area
- 🏫 Booked school groups welcome, especially those in the Schools Community Relations Programme
- 🐕 On leads and only in garden
- ➡️ (7:D7) [H914559] **Bus**: Ulsterbus 67 Portadown–Kesquin Bridge (passing close NIR Portadown Stn) to within ½ml (tel. 028 3834 2511) **Station**: Portadown 7ml

**NT properties nearby** The Argory, Derrymore House

---

# THE ARGORY   Co. Armagh

Moy, Dungannon BT71 6NA · **Tel** 028 8778 4753 · **Fax** 028 8778 9598
**Email** argory@ntrust.org.uk

---

This handsome 1820 house is unchanged since 1900. The cluttered interiors evoke the Bond family's Edwardian taste and interests, and include a barrel organ that is played once a month for musical house tours. Horse carriages, a harness room, the acetylene gas plant and a laundry are in the imposing stable yard. The beautiful estate offers garden, woodland and riverside walks for all ages, with superb spring bulbs. There is a year-round programme of craft fairs, walks, musical tours and family days. The Octagon Room is available for private hire

**Note**: The house has no electric light. Visitors wishing to make a close study of the interior and paintings should avoid dull days early and late in the season

- 🅾️ **Grounds**: Oct to April: daily 10–4; May to Sept: daily 10–8. **House**: 16 March to May, weekends & BHols; June, July & Aug: daily (June weekdays opens 1pm), Sept weekends 12–6
- £ House: £4; child £2; family £10. Group £3.25. Child group £1.65. Grounds: cars £2 (refunded if visit house). Parking 100m. Coaches must book with Property Manager
- 🚶 Access to house by guided tour only
- 📷 April, May, June & Sept: Sat, Sun & BH Mons; July & Aug: daily. *Times*: April, May, June & Sept 2–6; July & Aug: Mon to Fri 2.30–4.30, Sat & Sun 2–6. All BHols 1–6
- ♿ Disabled drivers may park near east door of house. House: ramp at east door by arrangement at reception; ground floor accessible; illustrated booklet for those unable to tour upstairs. Garden & pleasure grounds: accessible (some deep gravel round house). Tea-room & reception area: accessible
- 👁️ Tours for visually impaired visitors by arrangement
- 🦻 Sympathetic Hearing Scheme
- ☕ Tea-room as shop. Picnics welcome
- 🧒 Adventure playground

---

**Please see the area introductions for details of coast & countryside properties**

# NORTHERN IRELAND · 347

- 📚 Booked school groups welcome, especially those in the Schools Community Relations Programme. Education centre, Teachers' resource book and pupil worksheets. Key Stages 1, 2 & 3 programmes. Tel. 028 8778 9484
- 🐕 On leads and only in grounds and garden
- ➡️ (7:C7) 4ml from Moy, 3ml from M1, exit 13 or 14 (signposted). NB coaches must use exit 13; weight restrictions at Bond's Bridge [H872580]
  **Bus**: Ulsterbus 67 Portadown–Dungannon (both pass close NIR Portadown Stn), alight Charlemont, 2½ml walk (tel. 028 3834 2511) **Cycle**: NCN 95 (7ml)

**NT properties nearby** Ardress House

## CARRICK-A-REDE                                                    Co. Antrim

**Tel** 028 2073 1159/1582 · **Fax** 028 2073 2963 · **Email** carrickarede@ntrust.org.uk

On the North Antrim Coastal Path, just east of Ballintoy, is one of Northern Ireland's best-loved attractions: the Carrick-a-Rede rope bridge. Salmon fishermen sling this precarious bridge to the island over a 24m-deep chasm. Those bold enough to cross are rewarded with fantastic views and wildlife

- 🕓 Rope bridge: 17 March to Sept (weather permitting) daily 10–6; July & Aug 10–8. Access to North Antrim Coastal Path all year round
- 💷 Larrybane car park: car £3, minibus £6, coach £10, motorbike £1.50
- ♿ No access to bridge due to steps; viewing platform for wheelchairs; ramped access to tea-room and toilet; adapted WC
- ☕ Tea-room: May weekends 1–5; June to August daily 12–6
- 📚 Booked school groups welcome, tel. 028 2073 1582, especially those in the Schools Community Relations Programme. Key Stage 2 programme
- 🐕 On leads. We do not recommend that dogs cross the rope bridge
- ➡️ (7:D4) On B15, 7ml E of Bushmills, 5ml W of Ballycastle [D062450]
  **Bus**: Ulsterbus 172, 177, 252, 376 (tel. 028 7034 3334) **Cycle**: NCN 93 (5ml)

**NT properties nearby** Giant's Causeway, The Manor House on Rathlin Island

**Unless indicated, last admission is always 30 mins before closing time**

# CASTLE COOLE

Co. Fermanagh

Enniskillen BT74 6JY · **Tel** 028 6632 2690 · **Fax** 028 6632 5665
**Email** castlecoole@ntrust.org.uk

Castle Coole is one of the finest neo-classical houses in Ireland, built by James Wyatt in the late 18th century. The guided tour shows the opulent Regency interior decoration, furnishings and furniture, the state bedroom prepared for George IV in 1821 and the elegant hall where evening concerts are often held. The nearby servants' tunnel, stable yard and ice house are set within a stunning landscape park ideal for long walks. Programme of fine musical evenings and family days. The Hall is available for private hire

- **House**: 16 March to May: Sat, Sun & BH Mon (inc. 29 March); June: daily except Tues (unless BHol); July & Aug: daily; Sept: Sat & Sun. *Times*: 12–6, last house tour 5.15. **Parkland**: May to Sept: daily 10–8; Oct to April: daily 10–4

- House: £3.50; child £1.75; family £8.50. Parties £3. Grounds: £2 per car (refunded if also visiting the house)

- Access to house by guided tour only

- In Tallow House, April, May & Sept: Sat, Sun & BH Mons; June, July & Aug: daily. *Times*: 1–5

- Disabled visitors may be set down at house; ask at reception on arrival. House: ramped access to ground floor. Reception area: ramped access. Wheelchair available

- Sympathetic Hearing Scheme

- Tea-room in Tallow House open as shop (shop and tea-room opening times may vary according to demand). Groups welcome

- Baby-changing facilities

- Booked school groups welcome, especially those involved in the Schools Community Relations Programme; a teachers' resource book is available

**There are special events at most Trust properties; please telephone 0870 458 4000 for details**

NORTHERN IRELAND · **349**

🚲 Racks in car park

🐕 On leads and only in grounds

➡ (7:A7) 1½ml SE of Enniskillen on main Belfast–Enniskillen road (A4) [H260430]
**Bus**: Request stop only for Ulsterbuses 95, 193, 261, 295 (tel. 028 6632 2633)
**Cycle**: NCN 91

**NT properties nearby** Crom Estate, Florence Court

---

## CASTLE WARD                      Co. Down

Strangford, Downpatrick BT30 7LS · **Tel** 028 4488 1204 · **Fax** 028 4488 1729
**Email** castleward@ntrust.org.uk

---

A beautiful 300-ha (750-acre) walled estate in a stunning location overlooking Strangford Lough. The mid-Georgian mansion is an architectural curiosity of its time, built inside and out in two distinct architectural styles: Classical and Gothic. The Victorian laundry, playroom, cornmill, leadmine and sawmill give the full flavour of how the estate worked. There are woodland and lough-side paths and horse trails, formal gardens, Old Castle Ward, Temple Water and the Strangford Lough Wildlife Centre. There are many spaces available for private hire, a caravan site and holiday cottages

**What's new in 2002**: An exciting events programme

🅾 **House & Strangford Wildlife Centre**: 16–18, 23–24, 29 March; April, Sept & Oct: Sat, Sun & BHols; May: daily except Tues; June, July & Aug: daily. *Times*: 12–6 (May & June: weekdays 1–6). **Grounds**: daily. May to Sept 10–8; Oct to April 10–4

💷 House: £4.50; child £1.75; family £9.50; groups £3.50; groups outside normal hours £4.50. Grounds: car £3 (refunded if visiting house), coach £15, horsebox £5

🎭 Access to house by guided tour only

🛍 April, May, Sept & Oct: Sat, Sun & BH Mons; June to end Aug: daily. *Times*: 1–5, Sat, Sun & BHols 1–6

♿ Car park for disabled drivers behind stables; limited spaces. Disabled visitors may be set down at house. House: access via 6 steps. Formal garden: accessible. Restaurant & interpretation centre: accessible. Wheelchairs. Wheelchair access to shore of Strangford Lough

For all your information needs check our website www.nationaltrust.org.uk

## 350 · NORTHERN IRELAND

- 👁 Braille guide. Scented plants
- 👂 Sympathetic Hearing Scheme
- ☕ Tea-room as shop. Party organisers should tel. receptionist in advance to book visits and arrange teas. Picnics welcome
- 🚼 Changing facilities in WC. Adventure playground. Victorian pastime centre; toys & dressing up
- 🏫 Booked school groups welcome (tel. 028 4488 1543) especially those involved in the Schools Community Relations Programme. Education Centre. A resource book for teachers and pupil worksheets. Key Stages 1 & 2 programmes
- 🐕 On leads and only in grounds
- ➡ (7:F7) 7ml NE of Downpatrick, 1½ml W of Strangford village on A25, on S shore of Strangford Lough, entrance by Ballyculter Lodge [J752494] **Bus**: Ulsterbus 16E Downpatrick–Strangford, with connections from Belfast (passing close NIR Belfast Great Victoria Street Stn); bus stop at gates (tel. 028 4461 2384)

**NT properties nearby** Mount Stewart, Murlough National Nature Reserve, Rowallane Garden

---

## CROM ESTATE　　　　　　　　　　　　Co. Fermanagh

Newtownbutler BT92 8AP · **Tel** 028 6773 8118
(Visitor Centre) · 028 6773 8174 · **Fax** 028 6773 8118
**Email** crom@ntrust.org.uk

---

Set in a romantic and tranquil landscape of islands, woodland and historical ruins on the shores of Upper Lough Erne, Crom is one of Ireland's most important nature conservation areas with many rare species. There are nature trails, a programme of guided walks, boats for hire, a jetty for overnight boats, coarse angling, comfortable holiday cottages, a wildlife exhibition and rooms for private hire. There is a programme of guided walks and family days

**Note**: The 19th-century castle is private and not open to the public

- ⭕ 17 March to end Sept: daily. *Times*: 17 March to end June & Sept 10–6 (Sun 12–6); July & Aug 10–8 (Sun 12–8)
- 💷 £4 per car or boat, £12 minibus, £25 coach
- 🚶 Guided walks programme or by special arrangement
- 🛍 In visitor centre, April, May, June & Sept: Sat, Sun & BHols; July & Aug: daily. *Times*: 1–5
- ♿ Designated parking in car park. Tea-room, shop & exhibition: accessible. Wheelchair and self-drive vehicle. Estate: gravel paths
- 👂 Sympathetic Hearing Scheme in visitor centre
- ☕ Tea-room as shop; also by arrangement
- 🚼 Baby-changing facilities. Children's area in information centre

---

**Please remember – your membership card is always needed for free admission**

- Booked school groups welcome, especially those involved in the Schools Community Relations Programme
- On leads only
- (7:A8) 3ml W of Newtownbutler, on Newtownbutler–Crom road, or follow signs from Lisnaskea [J363245] **Bus**: Ulsterbus 95 Enniskillen–Clones (with connections from Belfast), alight Newtownbutler, 3ml (tel. 028 6632 2633) **Cycle**: NCN 91 (NB Ferry from Derrymore Church must be booked 24 hrs in advance)

**NT properties nearby** Castle Coole, Florence Court

## CROWN LIQUOR SALOON                                Co. Antrim
46 Great Victoria Street, Belfast BT2 7BA · **Tel** 028 9024 9476
**Web** www.belfasttelegraph.co.uk/crown

The most famous pub in Belfast and one of the finest examples of a High Victorian public house in existence, with rich ornamentation and snugs still intact

- Daily. Mon to Sat 11.30am–12 midnight, Sun 12.30–10pm
- Full bar facilities, snack lunches
- (7:E6) [J738332] **Bus**: Opposite Europa Buscentre (tel. 028 9024 6485 [Citybus] or 028 9033 3000 [Ulsterbus]) **Station**: Opposite Belfast Great Victoria Street **Cycle**: NCN 9 ½ml

**NT properties nearby** Mount Stewart, Patterson's Spade Mill

## DERRYMORE HOUSE                                    Co. Armagh
Bessbrook, Newry BT35 7EF · **Tel** 028 3083 8361

An elegant late 18th-century thatched cottage, built by Isaac Corry, who represented Newry in the Irish House of Commons for thirty years from 1776. Set amidst a picturesque estate, it is typical of the informal thatched retreats boasted by many estates in the 18th century

- **House**: 30 March, 1, 2 April & May to end Aug: Thur, Fri & Sat 2–5.30. **Grounds**: May to Sept 10–8; Oct to April 10–4
- £2.25; child £1; family £4.50. Parties £1.30
- Access to house by guided tour only
- Ground floor: one room accessible. Grounds: accessible
- On leads and only in grounds
- (7:D8) Off the Newry–Camlough road at Bessbrook, 1½ml from Newry [J056279] **Bus**: Ulsterbus 42, 44, 341C from Newry (passing close NIR Newry) (tel. 028 3026 3531) **Station**: Newry 2ml **Cycle**: NCN 9

**NT properties nearby** Ardress House

## DOWNHILL CASTLE, MUSSENDEN TEMPLE, BISHOP'S GATE & BLACK GLEN

Co. Londonderry

**Tel/Fax** 028 7084 8728 · **Email** downhillcastle@ntrust.org.uk

Set on a stunning and wild headland with fabulous clifftop walks and views over Ireland's north coast is the landscaped estate of Downhill, laid out in the late 18th century by the eccentric Earl and Bishop, Frederick Hervey. Estate includes ruins, mausoleum, beautiful gardens and the renowned Mussenden Temple perched on the cliff edge which is available for private hire

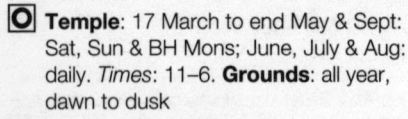

- **Temple**: 17 March to end May & Sept: Sat, Sun & BH Mons; June, July & Aug: daily. *Times*: 11–6. **Grounds**: all year, dawn to dusk
- Car £3; minibus £8; coach £15; motorbike £1.50
- Disabled drivers may park at Bishop's Gate. Garden: wheelchair paths. Glen Walk: partly accessible
- Picnics welcome
- Booked school groups welcome, tel. 028 2073 1582, especially those in the Schools Community Relations Programme. Key Stage 2 programme
- Racks at all entrances
- On leads only
- (7:C4) 1ml W of Castlerock and 5ml W of Coleraine on the Coleraine–Downhill coast road (A2) [J757357] **Bus**: Ulsterbus 134 Coleraine–Limavady (tel. 028 7034 3334) **Station**: Castlerock ½ml **Cycle**: NCN 93

**NT properties nearby** Giant's Causeway, Hezlett House, Portstewart Strand

---

## FLORENCE COURT

Co. Fermanagh

Enniskillen BT92 1DB · **Tel** 028 6634 8249 · **Fax** 028 6634 8873
**Email** florencecourt@ntrust.org.uk

Florence Court is a fine 18th-century house and estate set against the stunning backdrop of the Cuilcagh Mountains. It was the home of the Earls of Enniskillen and is one of the most important houses in Ulster. Now, with many original contents back in the house, it is a popular attraction for all ages. The house tour includes the exquisite rococo decoration, fine Irish furniture and service quarters. Some fine rooms are available for private hire. There are extensive walks in the grounds, also a sawmill, holiday cottage, walled garden and programme of concerts, family days, guided walks and country fairs

---

**Please see the area introductions for details of coast & countryside properties**

NORTHERN IRELAND · 353

- **House**: 17, 24, 29 to 31 March: April, May & Sept: Sat, Sun & BH Mons; June to Aug: daily. *Times*: 12–6 (1–6 Mon to Fri in June). **Grounds**: daily. *Times*: May to end Sept 10–8; Oct to end April 10–4

- £3.50; child £1.75; family £8.50. Group £3. Grounds only: March to Sept: £2.50 per car (refunded if visiting house)

- Access to house by guided tour only

- As house, but weekends only in June (some weekday opening according to demand; tel. 028 6634 8788)

- House: ground floor accessible. Garden: accessible. Restaurant: accessible. 2 wheelchairs and self-drive vehicle. Grounds: wheelchair path

- Sympathetic Hearing Scheme

- Stables Restaurant as house

- Parent and baby room, baby slings; highchair. Play area

- Booked school groups welcome, tel. 028 6634 8873, especially those in the Schools Community Relations Programme; Education Centre; Key Stages 1 & 2 programmes; teachers' resource book and pupil worksheets

- Covered cycle parking

- On leads and only in garden and grounds

- (7:A7) 8ml SW of Enniskillen via A4 Sligo road and A32 Swanlinbar road, 4ml from Marble Arch Caves [H175344] **Bus**: Ulsterbus 192 Enniskillen–Swanlinbar alight Creamery Cross, 2ml walk (tel. 028 6632 2633) **Cycle**: NCN 91

**NT properties nearby** Castle Coole, Crom Estate

## GIANT'S CAUSEWAY                                                Co. Antrim

44a Causeway Road, Bushmills BT57 8SU · **Tel** 028 2073 1159/1582
**Fax** 028 2073 2963
**Email** giantscauseway@ntrust.org.uk

This famous geological phenomenon renowned for its polygonal columns of layered basalt is the only World Heritage Site in Ireland. Resulting from a volcanic eruption 60 million years ago, the Causeway is a designated Area of Outstanding Natural Beauty and has attracted visitors for centuries. It harbours a wealth of local and natural history that can be enjoyed from the North Antrim Coastal Path. **Events**: Programme of family days all year round

**Note**: The car park and tourist information office are owned and run by Moyle District Council

- **Stones & North Antrim Coastal Path**: all year

- Council car park charge (inc. NT members). Causeway Coaster to stones £1 return; members free, Stones tour: age 12+ tba; under 12s & NT members free

- Guided tours of the stones June to Aug, NT members & children under 12 free

**Unless indicated, last admission is always 30 mins before closing time**

## 354 · NORTHERN IRELAND

- As tea-room
- Close parking; minibus with hoist for transport to Causeway during season. Shop, tea-room & visitor centre: ramped access. Wheelchair-accessible paths
- Braille guide
- Sympathetic Hearing Scheme
- Daily: March, April, May, Sept & Oct: 10–5; June: 10–6; July & Aug: 10–7
- Booked school visits welcome, tel. 028 2073 1582, especially those in the Schools Community Relations Programme. Education Centre; a teachers' resource book and pupil worksheets; Key Stages 1, 2, 3 & 4 programmes
- On leads and only outside the stones
- (7:D4) On B146 Causeway–Dunseverick road [C945438] **Bus**: Ulsterbus 172, 177, 252 or 376 (tel. 028 7034 3334) **Station**: Coleraine or Portrush 8ml **Cycle**: NCN 93

**NT properties nearby** Carrick-a-Rede, Hezlett House, Portstewart Strand

---

## GRAY'S PRINTING PRESS    Co. Tyrone
49 Main Street, Strabane BT82 8AU · **Tel 028 7188 4094**

---

An 18th-century printing press, where John Dunlap, the printer of the American Declaration of Independence, and James Wilson, grandfather of President Woodrow Wilson, learnt their trade. There is a collection of 19th-century hand-printing machines, as well as an audiovisual display. The former stationer's shop is now a local museum run by Strabane District Council

- April to end Sept: daily except Mon, Sun & BHols 2–5; other times by arrangement
- £2.50; child £1.50; family £5.50. Parties £1.75
- Guided tours by arrangement
- Audiovisual display accessible
- Booked school visits welcome, especially those involved in the Schools Community Relations Programme. A teachers' resource book is available
- (7:B5) [H345977] **Bus**: Ulsterbus Express 273 Belfast–Derry City, alight Strabane centre; few mins walk (tel. 028 9033 3000) **Cycle**: NCN 92

**NT properties nearby**
Wellbrook Beetling Mill

---

**There are special events at most Trust properties; please telephone 0870 458 4000 for details**

## HEZLETT HOUSE 🏠 Co. Londonderry
107 Sea Road, Castlerock, Coleraine BT51 4TW · **Tel/Fax** 028 7084 8567
**Email** hezletthouse@ntrust.org.uk

One of the few buildings in Ireland surviving from before the 18th century, this 17th-century thatched house has an interesting cruck-truss roof construction and is simply furnished in late Victorian style. There is a small museum of farm implements

- 🅾 16 March to end May & Sept: Sat, Sun & BHols; June to Aug: daily except Tues (unless BHols). *Times*: 12–5.
- 💷 £2.50; child £1.25; family £6. Parties £2; parties outside normal hours £3
- 🧍 Guided tours. Parties must book in advance (max.15 in house at any one time)
- ♿ House: ground floor accessible
- 🏫 Booked school groups welcome, especially those in the Schools Community Relations Programme
- 🅿 Parking space at side of house
- 🐕 On leads and only in gardens
- ➡ (7:C4) 5ml W of Coleraine on Coleraine–Downhill coast road, A2 [C772349] **Bus**: Ulsterbus 134 Coleraine–Limavady, alight crossroads, few mins walk (tel. 028 7034 3334) **Station**: Castlerock ¾ml **Cycle**: NCN 93

**NT properties nearby** Downhill, Giant's Causeway, Portstewart Strand

## MOUNT STEWART HOUSE, GARDEN & TEMPLE OF THE WINDS 🏠 🏛 ❀ 🧍 🛡 Co. Down
Newtownards BT22 2AD · **Tel** 028 4278 8387/8487 · **Fax** 028 4278 8569
**Email** mountstewart@ntrust.org.uk

The famous gardens at Mount Stewart were planted in the 1920s and have recently been nominated a World Heritage Site. The magnificent series of outdoor 'rooms' and vibrant parterres contain many rare plants that thrive in the mild climate of the Ards. There are dramatic views over Strangford Lough from the Temple of the Winds. The house tour includes world-famous paintings and stories about the prominent political figures to whom the Londonderry family played host. Some rooms are available for private hire. **Events**: a full programme of garden walks and events, jazz afternoons

- 🅾 **House**: 16–18, 23–24, 29–31 March, April & Oct: Sat, Sun & BH Mon (inc. 3–5 April); May & Sept: daily except Tues; June, July & Aug: daily. *Times*: 12–6. **Formal garden**: March: as house; April to end Sept: daily; Oct to Dec: Sat & Sun. *Times*: March to end Sept 11–6; Oct to Dec: 11–5. **Lakeside gardens and walks**: May to end Sept 10–8; Oct to end April 10–4
- 💷 House, gardens & Temple of the Winds: £4.75; child £2.25; family £9.75. Parties £4; child £2. Gardens only £3.75; child £2; family £8.50. Parties £3.50; child £1.75

## 356 · NORTHERN IRELAND

🚶 Access to house by guided tour only

🏠 March: Sun & St Patrick's Day; April & Oct: Sat, Sun & BH Mon; May to end Sept: daily. *Times*: March 2–5; April to end Sept 12.30–5.30 (but Sun & BH Mons 12.30–6) tel. 028 4278 8878

♿ House: access to ground floor. Gardens: accessible, free route-map; path around lake largely level. Restaurant & shop: accessible. Wheelchairs and 2 self-drive buggies

🌼 Scented plants

🔊 Sympathetic Hearing Scheme

☕ The Bay Restaurant as shop, tel. 028 4278 8801

👶 Baby-changing facilities

🏫 Booked school groups welcome, especially those involved in the Schools Community Relations Programme. Education Centre; Key Stages 1 & 2 programmes; teachers' resource book and pupils' worksheets. Tel. 028 4278 8830

🚲 Racks

🐕 On leads only

➡️ (7:F7) 15ml SE of Belfast on Newtownards–Portaferry road, A20, 5ml SE of Newtownards [J553695] **Bus**: Ulsterbus 10 Belfast–Portaferry bus stop at gates (tel. 028 9033 3000) **Station**: Bangor 10ml

**NT properties nearby** Castle Ward, Patterson's Spade Mill, Rowallane Garden

---

## PATTERSON'S SPADE MILL    Co. Antrim
Antrim Road, Templepatrick BT39 0AP · **Tel/Fax** 028 9443 3619

The last surviving water-driven spade mill in Ireland and popular with all ages. Hear and smell the grit on a guided tour of traditional spade-making, including history and culture of the humble turf and garden spade. You can purchase one of only 200 tailormade spades handmade every year. Picnics welcome. **Events**: tel. for details

---

**Please remember – your membership card is always needed for free admission**

- **O** 17–18, 23–24, 29 March; April, May & Sept: Sat, Sun & BH Mon; June to end Aug: daily. *Times*: 2–6
- **£** £3.25; child £1.50; family £8.50. Parties £2; parties outside normal opening hours £4
- Access to mill by guided tour only
- Viewing platform: ramped access. Wheelchair
- Machinery sounds; some items and raw materials may be touched
- Booked school groups welcome, especially those in the Schools Community Relations Programme. Teachers' resource book and Key Stage 2 pupils' worksheets
- → (7:E6) 2ml NE of Templepatrick on Antrim–Belfast road, A6; exit 4 of M2 [J263/856] **Bus**: Ulsterbus 110 & 120, bus stop at gates (tel. 028 9033 3000) **Station**: Antrim 8ml

**NT properties nearby** Mount Stewart, Rowallane Garden, Springhill

## ROWALLANE GARDEN                                                             Co. Down
Saintfield, Ballynahinch BT24 7LH · **Tel** 028 9751 0131 · **Fax** 028 9751 1242
**Email** rowallane@ntrust.org.uk

A unique and natural landscaped garden of trees and shrubs, containing many exotic species from around the world. There are spectacular displays of azaleas and rhododendrons and a notable rock garden with primulas, alpines and heathers. The walled garden has mixed borders which include the National Collection of Penstemon; there are also several areas managed as wildflower meadows.
**Events**: year-round programme of garden workshops, fairs and musical events

- **O** Daily May to end Sept 10–8; Oct to end April 10–4 (closed 24 Dec to 1 Jan)
- **£** £3; child £1.25; family £7. Parties £2, parties outside opening hours: £3
- Close parking by arrangement. Garden: largely accessible; wheelchair. Tea-room: accessible
- Scented plants. Tours with Head Gardener, tel. for details
- Sympathetic Hearing Scheme
- Tea-room April & Sept: Sat & Sun; May to end Aug: daily. *Times*: April & Sept 2–6; May & June 12.30–5; July & Aug: 1–5
- Booked school groups welcome, especially those in the Schools Community Relations Programme

**For general enquiries, please telephone 0870 458 4000**

## 358 · NORTHERN IRELAND

- Cycle shed; ask at reception
- On leads only
- (7:E7) 11ml SE of Belfast, 1ml S of Saintfield, W of the Downpatrick road (A7) [J412581] **Bus**: Ulsterbus 15 Belfast–Downpatrick (passing NIR Belfast Great Victoria Street Stn) (tel. 028 9033 3000)

**NT properties nearby** Castle Ward, Mount Stewart, Patterson's Spade Mill

---

# SPRINGHILL                                                      Co. Londonderry

20 Springhill Road, Moneymore, Magherafelt BT45 7NQ
**Tel/Fax** 028 8674 8210 · **Email** springhill@ntrust.org.uk

---

An atmospheric 17th-century 'plantation' house, and one of the prettiest houses in Ulster. The house tour takes in the exceptional library, Conyngham family furniture, gun room, nursery, resident ghost and the unusual and colourful costume exhibition which has some fine 17th-century Irish pieces. There are waymarked paths in the estate, walled gardens, a caravan site and beautiful barn for hire. **Events**: programme of special tours and family days

- 16 March to end June & Sept: Sat, Sun & BH Mon; July & Aug: daily. *Times*: 12–6
- £3.50; child £1.75; family £7.25. Parties £2.75; parties outside normal opening £4 per person
- Access to house by guided tour only
- As house
- Close parking. House: ground floor accessible. Garden: gravel paths. Small sales area accessible by arrangement. Picnic area: accessible
- Herb garden
- Sympathetic Hearing Scheme
- Light refreshments in servants' hall, as house. Picnic areas in garden and woodland
- Baby-changing facilities. Toy collection; children's costumes and activities. Play area

**Please see the area introductions for details of coast & countryside properties**

- Booked school groups welcome, tel. 028 8674 8215, especially those in the Schools Community Relations Programme; Education Centre; Key Stages 1, 2 & 3 programmes; teachers' resource book and pupil worksheets
- On leads and only in grounds
- (7:C6) 1ml from Moneymore on Moneymore–Coagh road, B18 [H866828] **Bus**: Ulsterbus 210 & 110 Belfast–Cookstown, alight Moneymore village, ¾ml (tel. 028 9033 3000)

**NT properties nearby** Wellbrook Beetling Mill

## WELLBROOK BEETLING MILL    Co. Tyrone

20 Wellbrook Road, Corkhill, Cookstown BT80 9RY
**Tel** 028 8674 8210/8675 1735 · **Email** wellbrook@ntrust.org.uk

Linen manufacture was of major importance in 18th-century Ireland, and beetling was the final stage in the production process. This water-powered hammer mill has its original machinery, still in working order, and there is a 'hands-on' demonstration of how linen was manufactured in the 19th century, which is popular with children. The mill is situated in an attractive glen through which there are many good walks.
**Events**: Tel. for details of flax sowing and pulling days

- 16 March to end June & Sept: Sat, Sun & BH Mon; July & Aug: daily. *Times*: 12–6
- £2.50; child £1.25; family £5.50. Parties £2; booked parties outside normal hours £3
- Access to mill by guided tour only
- As mill
- Access leaflet. Close parking. Mill: access to ground level only. Shop & picnic area: accessible
- 'Touch and Sound' tours by arrangement
- Booked school visits welcome, especially those in the Schools Community Relations Programme; Key Stage 2 programme and teachers' resource book
- On leads and in grounds only
- (7:C6) 4ml W of Cookstown, ½ml off Cookstown–Omagh road (A505): from Cookstown turn right at Kildress Parish Church, or follow Orritor Road (A53) to avoid town centre [H750792] **Bus**: Ulsterbus 90 from Cookstown, with connections from Belfast (tel. 028 7963 2218) **Cycle**: NCN 95

**NT properties nearby** Springhill

## National Trust Books

The National Trust publishes a wide range of books that promote its work and the great variety of properties in its care. These superbly illustrated books make excellent presents, as well as memorable souvenirs of visits. We have over 70 exciting titles which you can buy at National Trust shops, at good bookshops worldwide, through our website: **www.nationaltrust.org.uk/bookshop** or by mail order from: Antique Collectors' Club, Sandy Lane, Old Martlesham, Woodbridge, Suffolk IP12 4SD, tel. 01394 389950, fax 01394 389999.

Tempting dishes from this year's selection of cookery books include Orange-flower Cheese Tart as featured in *Traditional Puddings* and Spiced Bean Pottage, a great Tudor favourite from *Vegetarian Recipes*. A new *Living Landscapes* series looks at the natural and social history of different types of habitat: *Hedges and Walls* and *Parkland*. Illustrated with stunning pictures, *Living in Style* explores the fascinating world of historical styles and ornament.

If you would like a catalogue which contains details of all our books, please write to: Publications, The National Trust, 36 Queen Anne's Gate, London SW1H 9AS, enclosing a stamped, self-addressed envelope. Copies of guidebooks to National Trust properties can be obtained from Reception at the same address or via the National Trust website.

---

### How you can support the National Trust
# WORKING AS A VOLUNTEER

The National Trust welcomes the active involvement of members in its work through its volunteer programme. Some 38,000 volunteers, members and non-members of all ages and backgrounds, currently support staff at Trust properties, offices and in the community. Volunteers are involved in over 150 ways, from tasks requiring professional skills or experience to those for which only enthusiasm and energy are required.

For more information about the opportunities open to volunteers, including local volunteer groups, please send a first-class stamp to the **National Trust Membership Department, PO Box 39, Bromley, Kent BR1 3XL**, or look at our website **www.nationaltrust.org.uk/volunteers**

# Holidays with The National Trust

**Holiday cottages.** The Trust owns and manages over 290 holiday cottages set in some of the most outstanding locations across England, Wales and Northern Ireland. The portfolio includes a 15th-century converted stable block looking out over lawns to Ightham Mote in Kent, a former lighthouse keeper's cottage on the Northumberland coast, a glorious manor house in Cornwall and an erstwhile gamekeeper's cottage in Norfolk. For a brochure please call our 24-hour brochure line 0870 458 4411, or see our website at **www.nationaltrustcottages.co.uk**

**Holidays on National Trust farms.** Many Trust farmers and tenants are diversifying into a wide range of services and products. Whether you are looking for somewhere to stay in a beautiful area of the country or something special to buy, we hope that you will support local people by purchasing local products and services. For details of Bed and Breakfast addresses, Camping and Caravan Sites and Farm Food and Crafts please send a first class stamp to our Membership Department (see p.362).

**Working holidays.** The Trust hosts some 400 Working Holidays on coast and countryside properties throughout England, Wales and Northern Ireland. The opportunities range from repairing hurdle fences at a Welsh castle to footpath improvements on Lundy Island and drystone walling in the Peak District. Each holiday is run by Trust staff and trained leaders, so experience is not necessary – just plenty of energy and enthusiasm! There is a wide variety of holidays for all ages from 16 to 70. For a brochure please call 0870 429 2428.

**National Trust Short Break Collection.** The National Trust Short Break Collection, operated by leading short break operator Superbreak, offers over 850 great value hotels throughout Britain for year-round short breaks. There is a broad choice of locations, many close to National Trust properties, making them an ideal base from which to visit that Trust house or garden you've always wanted to see. For every short break booked, a financial contribution is made to the Trust's conservation work. For a brochure please call 0870 600 1818 quoting ref NT HBK.

**National Trust Travel Collection.** The National Trust Travel Collection is a programme of tours and cruises managed by leading tour operator Page & Moy. Whether you are fascinated by historic houses, like to marvel at spectacular scenery, explore great cities or simply enjoy travelling to distant corners of the world to experience the sights and sounds of different cultures, the National Trust Travel Collection has a holiday that is perfect for you. And for those who enjoy life on board a cruise ship, there is a choice of exclusive National Trust cruises. Page & Moy makes a financial contribution to the work of the Trust for each holiday booked, and so far over £1 million has been raised in this way. For a brochure please call 0870 010 6434 quoting ref N00040.

For more information on any of the above, please consult our website **www.nationaltrust.org.uk** and click on **Holidays and Travel**.

# Making contact

The National Trust adheres to the English Tourism Council's Visitors' Charter for Visitor Attractions.

We are very willing to answer questions and receive comments from members and visitors. Many properties provide their own comment cards and boxes which visitors are encouraged to use. All comments will be noted, and action taken where necessary, but it is not possible to answer every comment or suggestion individually.

Enquiries by telephone, email or in writing should be made to the Trust's Membership Department (see 1 below), open seven days a week (9.30–5.30 weekdays, 9–4 weekends and Bank Holidays). Detailed property enquiries eg accessibility for wheelchairs, should be made to the individual property. Business callers should contact the appropriate Regional Office by telephone (0870 numbers are national rates), listed below. Please note that some office addresses are subject to change during 2002/3. You can obtain details from our website, **www.nationaltrust.org.uk** or by calling the Membership Department.

1. **National Trust Membership Department**, PO Box 39, Bromley, Kent BR1 3XL (tel. 0870 458 4000; fax. 020 8466 6824; email enquiries@thenationaltrust.org.uk) for all general enquiries, including membership and requests for information

2. **London Central Office**, 36 Queen Anne's Gate, London SW1H 9AS tel. 0870 609 5380; fax. 020 7222 5097. National Trust guidebooks can be purchased from the reception desk

3. **National Trust Regional Offices in England**

    **Devon & Cornwall:** tel. 01392 881691 (Devon); 01208 74281 (Cornwall)

    **Wessex** (*Bristol/Bath, Dorset, Gloucestershire, Somerset & Wiltshire*): tel: 01985 843600

    **Thames & Solent** (*Berkshire, Buckinghamshire, Hampshire, Isle of Wight, Greater London & Oxfordshire*) tel. 01494 528051

    **South East** (*East Sussex, Kent, Surrey, West Sussex*): tel. 01372 453401

    **East Anglia** (*Bedfordshire, Cambridgeshire, Essex, Hertfordshire, Norfolk, Suffolk*): tel. 0870 609 5388

    **East Midlands** (*Derbyshire, Leicestershire, Lincolnshire, Northamptonshire, Nottinghamshire & Rutland*) tel. 01909 486411

    **West Midlands** (*Birmingham, Herefordshire, Shropshire, Staffordshire, Warwickshire & Worcestershire*) tel. 01743 708100

    **North West** (*Cheshire, Cumbria, Greater Manchester & Lancashire, Merseyside*): tel. 0870 609 5391

**Yorkshire & North East** (*Co. Durham, N. Lincolnshire, Northumberland, Newcastle & Tyneside, Yorkshire [including Teesside]*):
tel. 01904 702021 (Yorkshire); 01670 774691 (North East)

4. **National Trust Office for Wales,** Trinity Square, Llandudno, LL30 2DE
tel. 01492 860123; fax. 01492 860233

5. **National Trust Office for Northern Ireland,** Rowallane House, Saintfield, Ballynahinch, Co. Down BT24 7LH tel. 028 9751 0721; fax. 028 9751 1242)

6. **Volunteering & Community Involvement Office**, 33 Sheep St, Cirencester, Glos GL7 1RQ (tel. 0870 609 5383), or contact the Regional Volunteers Coordinator in each region (see list of Regional Offices above) for details of volunteer opportunities

7. **National Trust Enterprises**, The Stable Block, Heywood House, Westbury, Wilts BA13 4NA (tel. 0870 609 5381) for matters relating to shops, restaurants, holidays and the gift catalogue. For **Holiday Cottage** information,
tel. 0870 458 4411 for a brochure

8. **National Trust Estates Dept**, 33 Sheep Street, Cirencester, Glos GL7 1RQ
tel. 0870 609 5382

9. **National Trust for Scotland**, Wemyss House, 28 Charlotte Square, Edinburgh EH2 4ET tel. 0131 243 9300

10. **National Trust Theatre Projects**, The National Trust, Sutton House, 2 & 4 Homerton High Street, Hackney, London E9 6JQ
tel. 020 8986 0242

## The National Trust Online

If you have not yet discovered the National Trust's website then do take a look! It can be found at **www.nationaltrust.org.uk** and is full of information designed to keep you up to date with the Trust. A searchable directory gives you access to property opening times and facilities, and you can also read about current news and forthcoming events. There is also educational information and an online bookshop through which you can order a comprehensive range of National Trust titles, plus links to other organisations and much more. We are continuing to develop our website, so do check back from time to time to see what is happening. In addition, this year's Handbook contains details of those properties which can be contacted direct by email – see individual entries for more information. General email enquiries should be sent to **enquiries@thenationaltrust.org.uk**

# About the National Trust

The National Trust

- is a registered charity
- is independent of Government
- was founded in 1895 to preserve places of historic interest or natural beauty permanently for the nation to enjoy
- relies on the generosity of its supporters, through membership subscriptions, gifts, legacies and the contribution of many thousands of volunteers
- now protects and opens to the public over 200 historic houses and gardens and 49 industrial monuments and mills
- owns more than 248,000 hectares (612,000 acres) of the most beautiful countryside and almost 600 miles of outstanding coast for people to enjoy
- looks after forests, woods, fens, farmland, downs, moorland, islands, archaeological remains, nature reserves, villages – for ever, for everyone
- has the unique statutory power to declare land inalienable – such land cannot be voluntarily sold, mortgaged or compulsorily purchased against the Trust's wishes without special parliamentary procedure. This special power means that protection by the Trust is for ever
- spends all its income on the care and maintenance of the land and buildings in its protection, but cannot meet the cost of all its obligations – four in every five of its historic houses run at a loss – and is always in need of financial support.

# Data Protection Charter

There are many ways in which we would like to make your membership of the National Trust more enjoyable, and many ways in which you can support our work.

We write to our members from time to time about different aspects of our work, but we are conscious of the need to avoid waste. We try to ensure that we send each letter only to those to whom it will be most relevant. If at any time you believe that we have contacted you unnecessarily please let us know.

To comply with the Data Protection Act we need to advise you that we sometimes wish to share the names and addresses of selected members with our local members' centres and associations, and also with National Trust Enterprises, our wholly-owned trading company. National Trust Enterprises runs our retail operations and restaurants, and our holiday cottages. All of its profits are ploughed back into the National Trust.

We also occasionally write to our members about special products developed to support the National Trust, such as the National Trust Travel Collection. We do not divulge our members' personal details to any charities or companies that are not connected with the National Trust.

If you would rather we did not use your personal details for any of these purposes, please advise us, quoting your membership number. Any enquiries concerning these or other data protection issues should be directed to our Membership Department, which can be contacted on tel. 0870 458 4000, or by email via our website **www.nationaltrust.org.uk**

## How you can help the National Trust

We rely greatly upon additional support, beyond membership fees, to help us to protect and manage the coastline, countryside, historic buildings and gardens in our care. You can help us in several ways, such as making a donation or considering a gift to the National Trust in your Will.

### ● Donations

The Trust has several special programmes to give donors the opportunity to see at first hand the work that they support. If you would like to make a donation or to receive information about the Guardian, Benefactor or Patron programmes which include special 'behind-the-scenes' events, please write to the Development Team at our London Central Office or call 020 7222 9251.

### ● Legacies

Any legacy, no matter what the size, helps to provide a vital source of income for the Trust. It is our second largest income source after membership subscription fees and without it we could not survive. Also, legacies are NOT spent on administrative costs but go directly to help fund major restoration works, to acquire new properties or to benefit any other area of the Trust's work which a legator may wish to specify.

If you would like further information about legacies and the National Trust or to request our new free booklet, please contact the Head of Legacies at our London Central Office or call 020 7447 6739.

# Index of properties by county

*Properties with no individual entry are shown in italics*

## ENGLAND

### Bedfordshire
Dunstable Downs 194
Whipsnade Estate 194
Whipsnade Tree
  Cathedral 211
Willington Dovecote &
  Stables 213

### Berkshire
*Ankerwycke 155*
Basildon Park 118
*Finchampstead Ridges 114*
*Pinkney's Green 115*

### Bristol
Blaise Hamlet 47
Westbury College
  Gatehouse 110

### Buckinghamshire
Ascott 116
Boarstall Duck Decoy 120
Boarstall Tower 121
Bradenham Village 123
Buckingham Chantry
  Chapel 124
Claydon House 130
Cliveden 131
*Coombe Hill 114*
Dorneywood Garden 133
Hughenden Manor 138
King's Head 140
Long Crendon
  Courthouse 143
Pitstone Windmill 151
Princes Risborough
  Manor House 152
Stowe Gardens 163

Waddesdon Manor 167
West Wycombe Park 170
West Wycombe Village 171

### Cambridgeshire
Anglesey Abbey 188
Houghton Mill 200
Peckover House 206
Ramsey Abbey
  Gatehouse 207
Wicken Fen 212
Wimpole Hall 213
Wimpole Home Farm 215

### Cheshire
*Alderley Edge 264*
*Bickerton Hill 264*
*Caldy Hill 264*
Hare Hill 275
*Helsby Hill 264*
Little Moreton Hall 278
Lyme Park 279
Nether Alderley Mill 281
Quarry Bank Mill 281
Styal Country Park 281
Tatton Park 287
*Thurstaston Common 264*

### Cornwall
Antony 42
Bedruthan Steps 52
Boscastle 48
Carnewas 52
Cornish Engines 59
Cotehele 60
Cotehele Mill 62
Glendurgan Garden 68
Godolphin Estate 68
Kynance Cove 85
Lanhydrock 82
Lawrence House 83

Levant Steam Engine 84
The Lizard 85
St Anthony Head 96
St Michael's Mount 97
Tintagel Old Post Office 105
Trelissick Garden 106
Trengwainton Garden 107
Trerice 108

### Cumbria
Acorn Bank Garden & Mill 265
*Arnside Knott 264*
Beatrix Potter Gallery 266
Borrowdale 266
*Brandelhow Park 263*
Buttermere 267
Cartmel Priory Gatehouse 268
Claife 276
Coniston 268
Dalton Castle 269
Derwent Island House 269
Duddon 290
Ennerdale 267
Eskdale 290
Fell Foot Park 271
Gondola 274
Grasmere 275
Great Langdale 275
Hawkshead 276
Hill Top 277
*Keld Chapel 263*
Little Langdale 268
*Sandscale Haws 264*
Sizergh Castle 284
*Skelghyll Woods 286*
Stagshaw Garden 286
*Tarn Hows 264*
Townend 288
Troutbeck 290

Ullswater  289
Wasdale  290
*Wetheral Woods  264*
Windermere  290
Wordsworth House  291

## Derbyshire

Calke Abbey  218
*Dovedale  216*
*Edale  216*
Hardwick Hall  224
High Peak Estate  225
*Hope Woodlands  216*
Kedleston Hall  226
*Kinder Scout  216*
*Leek & Manifold Light Railway  216*
Longshaw Estate  227
*Mam Tor  216*
*Milldale  216*
Museum Of Childhood  232
The Old Manor  228
*South Peak  216*
Stainsby Mill  229
Sudbury Hall  231
*Winnats Pass  216*
Winster Market House  234

## Devon

A La Ronde  41
*Abbotsham  38*
Arlington Court  42
*Baggy Point  38*
*Bolt Tail  38*
Bradley  48
Branscombe  49
Buckland Abbey  50
*Bucks Mills  38*
Castle Drogo  53
The Church House  54
Clyston Mill  76
Coleton Fishacre House & Garden  56
Compton Castle  57
*Countisbury  38*
*East Titchberry  38*
Finch Foundry  66
*Fingle Bridge  38*
*Foreland Point  38*
*Gammon Head  38*
Greenway  70
Heddon Valley  72
*Hembury Woods  38*
*Hentor  38*
*Holne Woods  38*
Killerton  75
*Kingswear  38*
Knightshayes Court  79
*Little Dartmouth  38*
Loughwood Meeting House  87
Lundy  87
Lydford Gorge  88
Marker's Cottage  77
*Morte Point  38*
Newhall Equestrian Centre  77
The Old Mill  93
Overbecks  93
*Parke Estate  38*
*Plym Bridge Woods  38*
*Portledge  38*
*Portlemouth Down  38*
*Prawle Point  38*
*Salcombe Hill  38*
Saltram  98
*Sand Point  40*
*Selworthy see* Somerset: Holnicote
Shute Barton  99
*Soar Mill Cove  88*
*South Hole  38*
*Starehole Bay  38*
*Steps Bridge  38*
*Trowlesworthy Warren  38*
Watersmeet House  109
*Whiddon Deer Park  38*
*Willings Walls  38*
*Woody Bay  38*

## Dorset

*Badbury Rings see* Kingston Lacy  78
Brownsea Island  49
*Burton Bradstock  40*
*Cerne Giant  39*
Clouds Hill  56
*Cogden Beach  38*
*Coney's Castle  39*
Corfe Castle  58
*Golden Cap  38*
Hardy Monument  71
Hardy's Cottage  72
*Hartland Moor  38*
*Hod Hill  39*
Kingston Lacy  78
*Lamberts Castle  39*
*Langdon Hill Wood  40*
Max Gate  89
*Melbury Down  39*
*Pilsdon Pen  39*
*Spyway Farm  38*
*Stonebarrow Hill  40*
Studland  104
*Turnworth Down  39*
White Mill  111

## Durham

*Beacon Hill  308*
Ebchester  308
Foxholes Dene  308
Hawthorn Dene  308
Moorhouse Woods  308
Warren House Gill  308

## East Sussex: see Sussex

## East Yorkshire: see Yorkshire

## Essex

*Blake's Wood  186*
Bourne Mill  193
Coggeshall Grange Barn  194
*Copt Hall Marshes  186*
*Danbury Common  186*
*Dedham Vale  186*
Hatfield Forest  199
*Lingwood Common  186*
*Northey Island  186*
Paycocke's  206
Rayleigh Mount  207

## Gloucestershire
Ashleworth Tithe Barn 44
Chedworth Roman Villa 54
*Dover's Hill 39*
Dyrham Park 65
*Ebworth Estate 39*
Hailes Abbey 70
*Haresfield Beacon 39*
Hidcote Manor Garden 73
Horton Court 74
Little Fleece Bookshop 85
Lodge Park 86
*Minchinhampton Common 39*
Newark Park 92
*Rodborough Common 39*
Sherborne Park Estate 86
Snowshill Manor 99
Westbury Court Garden 110
Woodchester Park 112

## Hampshire
*Bramshaw Commons 114*
*Hale Purlieu 114*
*Harting Down 114*
Hinton Ampner Garden 137
Mottisfont Abbey 144
Sandham Memorial Chapel 156
The Vyne 166
West Green House Garden 170
Winchester City Mill 172

## Herefordshire
Berrington Hall 240
Brockhampton Estate 243
Croft Castle 246
The Weir 260

## Hertfordshire
Ashridge Estate 189
Shaw's Corner 208

## Isle of Wight
Bembridge Windmill 120
Brighstone Shop 123
Mottistone Manor Garden 145
The Needles Old Battery 146
Old Town Hall, Newtown 149
*Tennyson Down 114*

## Kent
Chartwell 125
*Chiddingstone 113*
*Coldrum Long Barrow 113*
Emmetts Garden 134
Ightham Mote 139
Knole 141
Old Soar Manor 148
Quebec House 153
*Royal Military Canal 113*
St John's Jerusalem 156
Scotney Castle Garden 157
Sissinghurst Castle Garden 159
Smallhythe Place 160
South Foreland Lighthouse 161
Sprivers Garden 161
Stoneacre 163
*Toys Hill 113*
The White Cliffs of Dover 171

## Lancashire
*Eaves & Waterslack Woods 264*
Gawthorpe Hall 273
*Heysham 264*
*Holcombe Moor 264*
Rufford Old Hall 283
*Stubbins Estate 264*

## Leicestershire
Staunton Harold Church 230
Ulverscroft Reserve 234

## Lincolnshire
Belton House 217
Grantham House 222
Gunby Hall 222
Monksthorpe Chapel 223
Tattershall Castle 233
Whitegates Cottage 223
Woolsthorpe Manor 235

## London
Blewcoat School Shop 176
Carlyle's House 176
*Chislehurst Common 175*
*East Sheen Common 175*
Eastbury Manor House 177
Fenton House 177
George Inn 178
Ham House 179
*Hawkwood 175*
Lindsey House 180
Morden Hall Park 180
Osterley Park 181
*Petts Wood 175*
Rainham Hall 183
'Roman' Bath 183
*Selsdon Wood 175*
Sutton House 184
*Watermeads 175*
2 Willow Road 185

## Greater Manchester
Dunham Massey 270
White Cottage 271

## Merseyside
Formby 272
20 Forthlin Road 273
Speke Hall 285
*Stocktons Wood 264*

## Norfolk

*Beeston Regis Heath 186*
Blakeney Point 190
Blickling Hall 191
Brancaster 193
*Darrow Wood 187*
Elizabethan House Museum 196
Felbrigg Hall 196
*Horsey Mere 186*
Horsey Windpump 199
*Incleborough Hill 186*
*Morston Marshes 186*
Oxburgh Hall 205
St George's Guildhall 208
Sheringham Park 209
*Stiffkey Marshes 186*
*West Runton 186*

## Northamptonshire

Canons Ashby House 220
Lyveden New Bield 228
Priest's House 229

## Northumberland

Allen Banks 309
*Beadnell Lime Kilns 308*
Cherryburn 310
Cragside 311
*Druridge Bay 308*
Dunstanburgh Castle 312
*Embleton Links 308*
Farne Islands 313
George Stephenson's Birthplace 314
Hadrian's Wall & Housesteads Fort 315
*Lady's Well 309*
Lindisfarne Castle 316
*Newton Pool 308*
*Ros Castle 308*
*St Aidan's Dunes 308*
*St Cuthbert's Cave 308*
Staward Gorge 309
Wallington 319

## North Yorkshire: see Yorkshire

## Nottinghamshire

Clumber Park 221
Mr Straw's House 230
The Workhouse, Southwell 236

## Oxfordshire

*Alfred's Castle 117*
Ashdown House 117
*Badbury Hill 114*
Buscot Old Parsonage 124
Buscot Park 125
Chastleton House 127
*Coleshill Estate 114*
*Dragon Hill 115*
Great Coxwell Barn 135
Greys Court 135
Priory Cottages 153
*Uffington Castle 115*
*Watlington Hill 114*
*White Horse Hill 114*

## Shropshire

Attingham Park 238
Benthall Hall 240
Carding Mill Valley 244
Dudmaston 248
Long Mynd 244
Morville Hall 254
Sunnycroft 257
Town Walls Tower 258
*Wenlock Edge 237*
Wilderhope Manor 262

## Somerset (inc. Bath)

Barrington Court 46
Bath Assembly Rooms 47
*Beacon Hill 40*
*Bicknoller Hill 40*
*Brean Down 40*
Clevedon Court 55
Coleridge Cottage 56
*Collard Hill 40*
*Crook Peak 40*
Dunster Castle 63
Dunster Watermill 64
Fyne Court 67
Glastonbury Tor 67
Holnicote Estate 74
King John's Hunting Lodge 78
*Leigh Woods 40*
Lytes Cary Manor 89
*Middle Hope 40*
Montacute House 91
Priest's House 95
Prior Park 95
*Sand Point 40*
*Shute Shelve Hill 40*
Stembridge Tower Mill 100
Stoke-Sub-Hamdon Priory 101
Tintinhull Garden 105
Treasurer's House 106
*Walton Hill 40*
*Wavering Down 40*
West Pennard Court Barn 110

## Staffordshire

Biddulph Grange 242
Ilam Park 252
Kinver Edge 252
Moseley Old Hall 254
Shugborough Estate 256
Wall Roman Site 259

## Suffolk

Angel Corner 188
Dunwich Heath 195
Flatford: Bridge Cottage 198
Ickworth 201
*Kyson Hill 186*
Lavenham Guildhall 202
Melford Hall 203
*Minsmere Beach 186*
Orford Ness 204
*Pin Mill 186*
Sutton Hoo 210
Theatre Royal 211
Thorington Hall 211

## Surrey
Box Hill 122
Clandon Park 128
Claremont 129
Dapdune Wharf 154
Devil's Punchbowl 133
*Frensham Common 114*
Hatchlands Park 136
*Hindhead 114*
Leith Hill 142
Oakhurst Cottage 148
Polesden Lacey 151
River Wey & Godalming Navigations 154
Runnymede 155
Shalford Mill 158
Winkworth Arboretum 173
Witley Centre 174

## Sussex
Alfriston Clergy House 116
Bateman's 119
*Birling Gap 113*
Bodiam Castle 121
*Chyngton Farm 114*
*Crowlink 113*
*Devil's Dyke 114*
*Frog Firle Farm 114*
Lamb House 142
Monk's House 144
Nymans Garden 147
Petworth House 149
Sheffield Park Garden 158
Standen 162
Uppark 165
Wakehurst Place 169

## Tyne & Wear
Gibside 314
Marsden Rock 308
Souter Lighthouse 318
Washington Old Hall 321

## Warwickshire
Baddesley Clinton 239
Charlecote Park 244
Coughton Court 245
Farnborough Hall 249
Kinwarton Dovecote 253
Packwood House 255
Upton House 258

## West Midlands
Wightwick Manor 261

## West Sussex: see Sussex

## West Yorkshire: see Yorkshire

## Wiltshire
Avebury 44
Avebury Manor 45
*Cley Hill 39*
The Courts Garden 62
Dinton Park 94
*Figsbury Ring 39*
Fox Talbot Museum 81
Great Chalfield Manor 69
Lacock Abbey & Village 81
Little Clarendon 84
Mompesson House 90
*Pepperbox Hill 39*
Philipps House 94
Stonehenge Down 101
Stourhead 102
Westwood Manor 111
*Win Green Hill 39*

## Worcestershire
Bredon Barn 242
*Clent Hills 237*
Croome Park 247
The Fleece Inn 250
The Greyfriars 250
Hanbury Hall 250
Hawford Dovecote 251
Middle Littleton Tithe Barn 253
Wichenford Dovecote 260

## Yorkshire (East Yorkshire, North Yorkshire inc. Middlesbrough, and West Yorkshire)
Beningbrough Hall 293
Blakey Topping 294
Braithwaite Hall 294
Bridestones Moor 294
Brimham Rocks 295
*Cayton Bay 292*
Crosscliff Moor 294
East Riddlesden Hall 296
*Farndale 292*
Fountains Abbey 297
Hardcastle Crags 299
*Hayburn Wyke 292*
*Hudswell Woods 292*
Maister House 299
Malham Tarn Estate 300
Marsden Moor Estate 300
Moulton Hall 301
Mount Grace Priory 301
*Newbiggin Cliffs 292*
Nostell Priory 302
Nunnington Hall 303
Ormesby Hall 317
*Peak Alum Works 292*
*Port Mulgrave 292*
Ravenscar 307
Rievaulx Terrace 304
Roseberry Topping 305
*Runswick 292*
*Scarthwood Moor 292*
Studley Royal 297
Treasurer's House 305
Upper Wharfedale 306
Yorkshire Coast 307

# WALES

## Anglesey
Plas Newydd 336

## Carmarthenshire
Aberdeunant 325

Dinefwr Park 330
Dolaucothi Gold Mines 331

## Ceredigion
Llanerchaeron 333
*Mwnt 323*
*Penbryn 323*

## Conwy
Aberconwy House 324
Bodnant Garden 327
Conwy Bridge 330
Tŷ Mawr Wybrnant 341
Ty'n-y-Coed Uchaf 342

## Gwynedd
*Carneddau Estate 323*
*Cregennan 323*
*Cwm Idwal 323*
*Dinas Oleu 322*
*Dolmelynllyn Estate 323*
Glan Faenol 324
Llywelyn Cottage 334
Penrhyn Castle 335
Plas yn Rhiw 337
*Porthdinllaen 324*
*Porthor 324*
*Rhaeadr Ddu 323*
Segontium 340
*Tryfan 323*
*Y Llethr 323*
*Ysbyty Estate 323*

## Monmouthshire
The Naval Temple & Round House 334
Skenfrith Castle 341
*Skirrid Fawr 323*
*Sugar Loaf 323*

## Neath & Port Talbot
Aberdulais Falls 325

## Pembrokeshire
*Broadhaven 322, 324*
Cilgerran Castle 329
Colby Woodland Garden 329
*Marloes Deer Park & Sands 322*
*Martin's Haven 322*
St David's 340
*Stackpole Estate 322*
Tudor Merchant's House 341

## Powys
*Brecon Beacons 323*
*Henrhyd Falls 323*
*Pen-y-Fan 323*
Powis Castle 338

## Swansea
Rhossili Visitor Centre 339

## Wrexham
Chirk Castle 328
Erddig 332

---

# N. IRELAND

## Antrim
*Ballyconagan 344*
Carrick-a-Rede 347
Crown Liquor Saloon 351
*Cushendun 344*
*Cushleake Mountain 344*
*Dunseverick Castle 344*
*Fair Head 344*
Giant's Causeway 353
*Larrybane 344*
Patterson's Spade Mill 356
*Whitepark Bay 344*

## Armagh
Ardress House 345
The Argory 346
Derrymore House 351

## Down
*Ballymacormick Point 343*
*Blockhouse Island 343*
Castle Ward 349
*Green Island 343*
*Kearney 343*
*Knockinelder 343*
*Lighthouse Island 343*
Mount Stewart 355
*Mourne Coastal Path 343*
*Murlough Reserve 343*
*Orlock Point 343*
Rowallane Garden 357
*Slieve Donard 343*
*Strangford Lough 343*

## Fermanagh
Castle Coole 348
Crom Estate 350
Florence Court 352

## Londonderry
*Bar Mouth 344*
Bishop's Gate 352
Black Glen 352
Downhill Castle 352
*Grangemore Dunes 344*
Hezlett House 355
Mussenden Temple 352
*Portstewart Strand 344*
Springhill 358

## Tyrone
Gray's Printing Press 354
Wellbrook Beetling Mill 359

# Index by property name
*Properties with no individual entry are shown in italics*

A La Ronde  41
*Abbotsham  38*
Aberconwy House  324
Aberdeunant  325
Aberdulais Falls  325
Acorn Bank Garden & Mill  265
*Alderley Edge  264*
*Alfred's Castle  117*
Alfriston Clergy House  116
Allen Banks  309
Angel Corner  188
Anglesey Abbey  188
*Ankerwycke  155*
Antony  42
Ardress House  345
The Argory  346
Arlington Court  42
*Arnside Knott  264*
Ascott  116
Ashdown House  117
Ashleworth Tithe Barn  44
Ashridge Estate  189
Attingham Park  238
Avebury  44
Avebury Manor  45
*Badbury Hill  114*
*Badbury Rings  78*
Baddesley Clinton  239
*Baggy Point  38*
*Ballyconagan  344*
*Ballymacormick Point  343*
*Bar Mouth  344*
Barrington Court  46
Basildon Park  118
Bateman's  119
Bath Assembly Rooms  47
*Beacon Hill (Durham)  308*
*Beacon Hill (Somerset)  40*
*Beadnell Lime Kilns  308*
Beatrix Potter Gallery  266
Bedruthan Steps  52
*Beeston Regis Heath  186*
Belton House  217

Bembridge Windmill  120
Beningbrough Hall  293
Benthall Hall  240
Berrington Hall  240
*Bickerton Hill  264*
*Bicknoller Hill  40*
Biddulph Grange  242
*Birling Gap  113*
Bishop's Gate  352
Black Glen  352
Blaise Hamlet  47
*Blake's Wood  186*
Blakeney Point  190
Blakey Topping  294
Blewcoat School Shop  176
Blickling Hall  191
*Blockhouse Island  343*
Boarstall Duck Decoy  120
Boarstall Tower  121
Bodiam Castle  121
Bodnant Garden  327
*Bolt Tail  38*
Borrowdale  266
Boscastle  48
Bourne Mill  193
Box Hill  122
Bradenham Village  123
Bradley  48
Braithwaite Hall  294
*Bramshaw Commons  114*
Brancaster  193
*Brandelhow Park  263*
Branscombe  49
*Brean Down  40*
Brecon Beacons  323
Bredon Barn  242
Bridestones Moor  294
Bridge Cottage, Flatford  198
Brighstone Shop  123
Brimham Rocks  295
*Broadhaven  322*

Brockhampton Estate  243
Brownsea Island  49
Buckingham Chantry Chapel  124
Buckland Abbey  50
*Bucks Mills  38*
*Burton Bradstock  40*
Buscot Old Parsonage  124
Buscot Park  125
Buttermere  267
*Caldy Hill  264*
Calke Abbey  218
Canons Ashby House  220
Carding Mill Valley  244
Carlyle's House  176
*Carneddau Estate  323*
Carnewas  52
Carrick-a-Rede  347
Cartmel Priory Gatehouse  268
Castle Coole  348
Castle Drogo  53
Castle Ward  349
*Cayton Bay  292*
*Cerne Giant  39*
Charlecote Park  244
Chartwell  125
Chastleton House  127
Chedworth Roman Villa  54
Cherryburn  310
*Chiddingstone  113*
Chirk Castle  328
*Chislehurst Common  175*
The Church House  54
*Chyngton Farm  114*
Cilgerran Castle  329
Claife  276
Clandon Park  128
Claremont  129
Claydon House  130
*Clent Hills  237*

Clevedon Court 55
*Cley Hill 39*
Cliveden 131
Clyston Mill 76
Clouds Hill 56
Clumber Park 221
*Cogden Beach 38*
Coggeshall Grange Barn 194
Colby Woodland Garden 329
*Coldrum Long Barrow 113*
Coleridge Cottage 56
*Coleshill Estate 114*
Coleton Fishacre 56
*Collard Hill 40*
Compton Castle 57
*Coney's Castle 39*
Coniston 268
Conwy Bridge 330
*Coombe Hill 114*
Copt Hall Marshes 186
Corfe Castle 58
Cornish Engines 59
Cotehele 60
Cotehele Mill 62
Coughton Court 245
*Countisbury 38*
The Courts Garden 62
Cragside 311
*Cregennan 323*
Croft Castle 246
Crom Estate 350
*Crook Peak 40*
Croome Park 247
Crosscliff Moor 294
*Crowlink 113*
Crown Liquor Saloon 351
*Cushendun 344*
*Cushleake Mountain 344*
*Cwm Idwal 323*
Dalton Castle 269
*Danbury Common 186*
Dapdune Wharf 154
*Darrow Wood 187*
*Dedham Vale 186*
Derrymore House 351

Derwent Island House 269
*Devil's Dyke 114*
Devil's Punchbowl 133
*Dinas Oleu 322*
Dinefwr Park 330
Dinton Park 94
Dolaucothi Gold Mines 331
*Dolmelynllyn Estate 323*
Dorneywood Garden 133
Dovedale 216
*Dover's Hill 39*
Downhill Castle 352
*Dragon Hill 115*
Druridge Bay 308
Duddon 290
Dudmaston 248
Dunham Massey 270
*Dunseverick Castle 344*
Dunstable Downs 194
Dunstanburgh Castle 312
Dunster Castle 63
Dunster Watermill 64
Dunwich Heath 195
Dyrham Park 65
East Riddlesden Hall 296
*East Sheen Common 175*
*East Titchberry 38*
Eastbury Manor House 177
*Eaves & Waterslack Woods 264*
*Ebchester 308*
*Ebworth Estate 39*
Edale 216
Elizabethan House Museum 196
*Embleton Links 308*
Emmetts Garden 134
Ennerdale 267
Erddig 332
Eskdale 290
*Fair Head 344*
Farnborough Hall 249
*Farndale 292*
Farne Islands 313
Felbrigg Hall 196
Fell Foot Park 271

Fenton House 177
*Figsbury Ring 39*
Finch Foundry 66
*Finchampstead Ridges 114*
*Fingle Bridge 38*
Flatford (Bridge Cottage) 198
The Fleece Inn 250
Florence Court 352
*Foreland Point 38*
Formby 272
20 Forthlin Road 273
Fountains Abbey 297
Fox Talbot Museum 81
*Foxholes Dene 308*
*Frensham Common 114*
*Frog Firle Farm 114*
Fyne Court 67
*Gammon Head 38*
Gawthorpe Hall 273
George Inn 178
George Stephenson's Birthplace 314
Giant's Causeway 353
Gibside 314
*Glan Faenol 324*
Glastonbury Tor 67
Glendurgan Garden 68
Godolphin Estate 68
*Golden Cap 38*
Gondola 274
*Grangemore Dunes 344*
Grantham House 222
Grasmere 275
Gray's Printing Press 354
Great Chalfield Manor 69
Great Coxwell Barn 135
Great Langdale 275
*Green Island 343*
Greenway 70
The Greyfriars 250
Greys Court 135
Gunby Hall 222
Hadrian's Wall 315
Hailes Abbey 70
*Hale Purlieu 114*
Ham House 179

Hanbury Hall  250
Hardcastle Crags  299
Hardwick Hall  224
Hardy Monument  71
Hardy's Cottage  72
Hare Hill  275
*Haresfield Beacon*  39
*Harting Down*  114
Hartland Moor  38
Hatchlands Park  136
Hatfield Forest  199
Hawford Dovecote  251
Hawkshead  276
*Hawkwood*  175
*Hawthorne Dene*  308
*Hayburn Wyke*  292
Heddon Valley  72
*Helsby Hill*  264
*Hembury Woods*  38
*Henrhyd Falls*  323
*Hentor*  38
*Heysham*  264
Hezlett House  355
Hidcote Manor Garden  73
High Peak Estate  225
Hill Top  277
*Hindhead*  114
Hinton Ampner Garden  137
*Hod Hill*  39
Holcombe Moor  264
*The Holies*  118
*Holne Woods*  38
Holnicote Estate  74
*Hope Woodlands*  216
*Horsey Mere*  186
Horsey Windpump  199
Horton Court  74
Houghton Mill  200
Housesteads Fort  315
*Hudswell Woods*  292
Hughenden Manor  138
Ickworth  201
Ightham Mote  139
Ilam Park  252
*Incleborough Hill*  186
*Kearney*  343
Kedleston Hall  226

*Keld Chapel*  263
Killerton  75
*Kinder Scout*  216
King John's Hunting Lodge  78
King's Head  140
Kingston Lacy  78
*Kingswear*  38
Kinver Edge  252
Kinwarton Dovecote  253
Knightshayes Court  79
*Knockinelder*  343
Knole  141
Kynance Cove  85
*Kyson Hill*  186
Lacock Abbey & Village  81
*Lady's Well*  309
Lamb House  142
*Lamberts Castle*  39
*Langdon Hill Wood*  40
Lanhydrock  82
*Lardon Chase*  118
*Larrybane*  344
Lavenham Guildhall  202
Lawrence House  83
*Leek & Manifold Light Railway*  216
*Leigh Woods*  40
Leith Hill  142
Letocetum  259
Levant Steam Engine  84
*Lighthouse Island*  343
Lindisfarne Castle  316
Lindsey House  180
*Lingwood Common*  186
Little Clarendon  84
*Little Dartmouth*  38
Little Fleece Bookshop  85
Little Langdale  268
Little Moreton Hall  278
The Lizard  85
Llanerchaeron  333
Llywelyn Cottage  334
Lodge Park  86
Long Crendon Courthouse  143
Long Mynd  244
Longshaw Estate  227

Loughwood Meeting House  87
Lundy  87
Lydford Gorge  88
Lyme Park  279
Lytes Cary Manor  89
Lyveden New Bield  228
Maister House  299
Malham Tarn Estate  300
*Mam Tor*  216
Marker's Cottage  77
*Marloes Deer Park & Sands*  322
Marsden Moor Estate  300
*Marsden Rock*  308
*Martin's Haven*  322
Max Gate  89
*Melbury Down*  39
Melford Hall  203
*Middle Hope*  40
Middle Littleton Tithe Barn  253
*Milldale*  216
*Minchinhampton Common*  39
Minsmere Beach  195
Mompesson House  90
Monk's House  144
Monksthorpe Chapel  223
Montacute House  91
*Moorhouse Woods*  308
Morden Hall Park  180
*Morston Marshes*  186
Morte Point  38
Morville Hall  254
Moseley Old Hall  254
Mottisfont Abbey  145
Mottistone Manor Garden  144
Moulton Hall  301
Mount Grace Priory  301
Mount Stewart  355
*Mourne Coastal Path*  343
*Murlough Reserve*  343
Museum Of Childhood  232

Mussenden Temple 352
*Mwnt 323*
The Naval Temple and Round House 334
The Needles Old Battery 146
Nether Alderley Mill 281
Newark Park 92
*Newbiggin Cliffs 292*
Newhall Equestrian Centre 77
*Newton Pool 308*
*Northey Island 186*
Nostell Priory 302
Nunnington Hall 303
Nymans Garden 147
Oakhurst Cottage 148
The Old Manor 228
The Old Mill 93
Old Soar Manor 148
Old Town Hall, Newtown 149
Orford Ness 204
*Orlock Point 343*
Ormesby Hall 317
Osterley Park 181
Overbecks 93
Oxburgh Hall 205
Packwood House 255
*Parke Estate 38*
Patterson's Spade Mill 356
Paycocke's 206
*Paxton's Tower 323*
*Peak Alum Works 292*
Peckover House 206
*Pen-y-Fan 323*
*Penbryn 323*
Penrhyn Castle 335
*Pepperbox Hill 39*
*Petts Wood 175*
Petworth House 149
Philipps House 94
*Pilsdon Pen 39*
*Pin Mill 186*
*Pinkney's Green 115*
Pitstone Windmill 151
Plas Newydd 336

Plas yn Rhiw 337
*Plym Bridge Woods 38*
Polesden Lacey 151
*Port Mulgrave 292*
Porthdinllaen 324
Porthor 324
*Portledge 38*
*Portlemouth Down 38*
*Portstewart Strand 344*
Powis Castle 338
*Prawle Point 38*
Priest's House (Easton) 229
Priest's House (Muchelney) 95
Princes Risborough Manor House 152
Prior Park 95
Priory Cottages 153
Quarry Bank Mill 281
Quebec House 153
Rainham Hall 183
Ramsey Abbey Gatehouse 207
Ravenscar 307
Rayleigh Mount 207
*Rhaeadr Ddu 323*
Rhossili Visitor Centre 339
Rievaulx Terrace 304
River Wey & Godalming Navigations 154
*Rodborough Common 39*
'Roman' Bath 183
*Ros Castle 308*
Roseberry Topping 305
Rowallane Garden 357
*Royal Military Canal 113*
Rufford Old Hall 283
Runnymede 155
*Runswick 292*
*St Aidan's Dunes 308*
St Anthony Head 96
*St Cuthbert's Cave 308*
St David's 340
St George's Guildhall 208
St John's Jerusalem 156

St Michael's Mount 97
*Salcombe Hill 38*
Saltram 98
*Sand Point 40*
Sandham Memorial Chapel 156
*Sandscale Haws 264*
*Scarthwood Moor 292*
Scotney Castle Garden 157
Segontium 340
*Selsdon Wood 175*
*Selworthy 74*
*Seven Sisters 113*
Shalford Mill 158
Shaw's Corner 208
Sheffield Park Garden 158
Sherborne Estate 86
Sheringham Park 209
Shugborough Estate 256
Shute Barton 99
*Shute Shelve Hill 40*
Sissinghurst Castle Garden 159
Sizergh Castle 284
*Skelghyll Woods 286*
Skenfrith Castle 341
*Skirrid Fawr 323*
*Slieve Donard 343*
Smallhythe Place 160
Snowshill Manor 99
*Soar Mill Cove 38*
Souter Lighthouse 318
South Foreland Lighthouse 161
*South Hole 38*
*South Peak 216*
Speke Hall 285
Springhill 358
Sprivers Garden 161
*Spyway Farm 38*
Stackpole Estate 322
Stagshaw Garden 286
Stainsby Mill 229
Standen 162
*Starehole Bay 38*
Staunton Harold Church 230

INDEX· 375

# 376 · INDEX

Staward Gorge 309
Stembridge Tower Mill 100
*Steps Bridge 38*
*Stiffkey Marshes 186*
*Stocktons Wood 264*
Stoke-Sub-Hamdon Priory 101
Stoneacre 163
*Stonebarrow Hill 40*
Stonehenge Down 101
Stourhead 102
Stowe Gardens 163
*Strangford Lough 343*
Mr Straw's House 230
*Stubbins Estate 264*
Studland 104
Studley Royal 297
Styal Country Park 281
Sudbury Hall 231
*Sugar Loaf 323*
Sunnycroft 257
Sutton Hoo 210
Sutton House 184
*Tarn Hows 264*
Tattershall Castle 233
Tatton Park 287
*Tennyson Down 114*
Theatre Royal 211
Thorington Hall 211
*Thurstaston Common 264*
Tintagel Old Post Office 105
Tintinhull Garden 105
Town Walls Tower 258
Townend 290
*Toys Hill 113*
Treasurer's House (Martock) 106
Treasurer's House (York) 305
Trelissick Garden 106
Trengwainton Garden 107

Trerice 108
Troutbeck 290
*Trowlesworthy Warren 38*
*Tryfan 323*
Tudor Merchant's House 341
*Turnworth Down 39*
Tŷ Mawr Wybrnant 341
Ty'n-y-Coed Uchaf 342
*Uffington Castle 115*
Ullswater 289
Ulverscroft Reserve 234
Uppark 165
Upper Wharfedale 306
Upton House 258
The Vyne 166
Waddesdon Manor 167
Wakehurst Place 169
Wall Roman Site 259
Wallington 319
*Walton Hill 40*
*Warren House Gill 308*
Wasdale 290
Washington Old Hall 321
*Watermeads 175*
Watersmeet House 109
*Watlington Hill 114*
*Wavering Down 40*
*Weathercock Hill 117*
The Weir 260
Wellbrook Beetling Mill 359
*Wenlock Edge 237*
West Green House Garden 170
West Pennard Court Barn 110
*West Runton 186*
West Wycombe Park 170
West Wycombe Village 171
Westbury College Gatehouse 110

Westbury Court Garden 110
Westwood Manor 111
*Wetheral Woods 264*
*Whiddon Deer Park 38*
Whipsnade Estate 194
Whipsnade Tree Cathedral 211
The White Cliffs of Dover 171
White Cottage 271
*White Horse Hill 114*
White Mill 111
Whitegates Cottage 223
*Whitepark Bay 344*
Wichenford Dovecote 260
Wicken Fen 212
Wightwick Manor 261
Wilderhope Manor 262
*Willings Walls 38*
Willington Dovecote & Stables 213
2 Willow Road 185
Wimpole Hall 213
Wimpole Home Farm 215
*Win Green Hill 39*
Winchester City Mill 172
Windermere 290
Winkworth Arboretum 173
*Winnats Pass 216*
Winster Market House 234
Witley Common 174
Woodchester Park 112
*Woody Bay 38*
Woolsthorpe Manor 235
Wordsworth House 291
The Workhouse, Southwell 236
*Y Llethr 323*
Yorkshire Coast 307
*Ysbyty Estate 323*